005.8 SMI

Microsoft®

SOFTWARE
ITEM ....1 x CD-Rom

This book is due for return on or before the last date shown below.

Microsoft Windows
Security Resource Kit,
Second Edition

Brian Komar
Security Team

PUBLISHED BY
Microsoft Press
A Division of Microsoft Corporation
One Microsoft Way
Redmond, Washington 98052-6399

Library of Congress Control Number 2005920874

Printed and bound in the United States of America.

1 2 3 4 5 6 7 8 9   QWT   9 8 7 6 5

Distributed in Canada by H.B. Fenn and Company Ltd.

A CIP catalogue record for this book is available from the British Library.

Microsoft Press books are available through booksellers and distributors worldwide. For further information about international editions, contact your local Microsoft Corporation office or contact Microsoft Press International directly at fax (425) 936-7329. Visit our Web site at www.microsoft.com/learning/. Send comments to *rkinput@microsoft.com*.

Microsoft, Active Directory, ActiveSync, ActiveX, Authenticode, BackOffice, BizTalk, DirectX, FrontPage, IntelliSense, MapPoint, Microsoft Press, MSDN, NetMeeting, Outlook, PowerPoint, SharePoint, Visual Basic, Visual SourceSafe, Visual Studio, Win32, Windows, Windows Media, Windows Mobile, Windows NT, Windows Server, and Windows Server System are either registered trademarks or trademarks of Microsoft Corporation in the United States and/or other countries.

The example companies, organizations, products, domain names, e-mail addresses, logos, people, places, and events depicted herein are fictitious. No association with any real company, organization, product, domain name, e-mail address, logo, person, place, or event is intended or should be inferred.

Acquisitions Editor: Martin DelRe
Project Editor: Karen Szall
Technical Editor: Ronald Beekelaar
Copy Editor: Christina Palaia
Production: Elizabeth Hansford
Indexer: Seth Maislin

Body Part No. X11-11859

Contents at a Glance

Contents

Part II   Securing Active Directory

3   Configuring Security for User Accounts and Passwords 31

4   Configuring Authentication for Microsoft Windows. 69

Part IV Securing Common Services

Foreword

Security is not binary. It is not a switch or even a series of switches. It cannot be expressed in absolute terms. Do not believe anyone who tries to convince you otherwise. Security is relative—there is only more secure and less secure. Furthermore, security is dynamic—people, process, and technology all change. The bottom line is that all these factors make managing security difficult.

This book has been designed and written to help you increase, assess, and maintain the security of computers running Microsoft Windows 2003, Windows 2000, and Windows XP. It will also help you better understand how people and process are integral parts of security. By applying the principles, practices, and recommendations detailed in this book, we hope that you are not only better equipped to manage security but also better equipped to think about security!

Good luck!

Ben Smith and Brian Komar
March 2005

Acknowledgments

The names of the authors on the front cover are the 10 percent of the iceberg that you see above the water. Behind every good book, there are legions of dedicated and highly skilled people—this book epitomizes this basic truth. Through both versions of this volume, we have been fortunate and honored to be surrounded by the very best people in the industry—this book is their creation also.

From the outset, we wanted to create a book that would be readable and useful. Readers who know the two of us will realize that Michelle Goodman and Christina Palaia, the copy editors from the first and second editions, respectively, had one of the most daunting tasks: taming our verbosity! Their attention to detail, memories, and remarkable ability to minimize the number of adverbs used per sentence proved invaluable. Elizabeth Hansford, Joel Panchot, and William Teel did an amazing job of creating a great-looking book—a truly gargantuan task. Seth Maislin created the index. Thank you!

Although it is grammatically correct to say that books are written, in reality they are built. Karen Szall did a fantastic job of assembling this book, and we are indebted to her for it. We also would like to thank the first person who worked on this book in 2001—Martin DelRe, the acquisitions editor. Thanks for sticking with it again, Martin!

We are particularly grateful to our close friend Ronald Beekelaar, who read every single word of this version and nearly all of the first version. His impact on the quality of this book cannot be overstated. There is no better technical reviewer or editor out there. This edition was also reviewed by many of our colleagues at Microsoft, including Andreas Luther, Ayman AlRashed, Allen Stewart, Bill Sisk, Chase Carpenter, Chris Reinhold, Claudio Vacalebre, Dallas Davis, Didier Vandenbroeck, Eric Fitzgerald, George Spanakis, Joel Schaeffer, Jose Luis Auricchio, Joe Davies, Kai Axford, Ken Anderson, Mark Kradel, Mark Pustilnik, Matt Clapham, Matt Kestian, Mike Greer, Ryan Vatne, Shain Wray, and Shawn Rabourn. In particular, we would like to acknowledge and thank Ayman, whose careful reading and advice really helped make this a better book, and Michael Glass, for organizing and facilitating the review. In the end, however, all errors and omissions are ours alone.

Most important, we would like to thank our wives: Beth Boatright and Krista Kunz. Their support and tolerance are remarkable and much appreciated—more so than we can ever express in words. Thank you.

Ben Smith and Brian Komar
February 2005

Introduction

Welcome to the *Microsoft Windows Security Resource Kit*, Second Edition. This book provides detailed information about security features in Microsoft Windows Server 2003, Windows 2000, and Windows XP, and explains how to better secure computers running these operating systems.

About This Resource Kit

Although you are welcome to read the book from cover to cover, it is divided into six parts for your convenience. Each part covers a different aspect of Windows Server 2003, Windows 2000, and Windows XP security that you can read in advance of implementing security on computers running these operating systems or as a reference on the job.

The six parts of this book are as follows:

- **Part 1, "Applying Key Principles of Security"** provides an overview for thinking about security on a daily basis. Part 1 also introduces some of the fundamental challenges of managing security and provides guidance on how to overcome them.

- **Part 2, "Securing Active Directory"** provides information on the security of the Active Directory directory service—from handling design issues associated with forests and domains to controlling access to objects and attributes. Part 2 has detailed information on how to secure accounts and authentication—the two central components of security in Windows Server 2003, Windows 2000, and Windows XP. Part 2 also describes how you can use Group Policy to increase the security of networks that use Active Directory.

- **Part 3, "Securing the Core Operating System"** provides detailed information on how to increase the security of Windows Server 2003, Windows 2000, and Windows XP. Part 3 also discusses how to better secure applications, such as Microsoft Office System 2003, Microsoft Office XP, and Microsoft Internet Explorer, as well as mobile devices.

- **Part 4, "Securing Common Services"**   describes how to secure common services that run on Windows Server 2003 and Microsoft Windows 2000 Server, including Domain Name System (DNS), Dynamic Host Configuration Protocol (DHCP), Windows Internet Name Service (WINS), Terminal Services, Certificate Services, Routing and Remote Access Service (RRAS), and Microsoft Internet Information Services 6.0.

- **Part 5, "Managing Security Updates"**   includes detailed information on the process of managing security updates, including service packs, software updates, and hotfixes, and discusses strategies for deploying security updates. Part 5 also describes techniques for assessing the security of computers running Windows Server 2003, Windows 2000, and Windows XP.

- **Part 6, "Planning and Performing Security Assessments and Incident Responses"**   provides detailed explanations of security assessments, including vulnerability scanning, IT audits, and penetration testing, and discusses how each can be used to assess the security of your network. Part 6 also provides information on how to design an incident response procedure and introduces methods for investigating security incidents.

Resource Kit Companion CD

The *Microsoft Windows Security Resource Kit*, Second Edition, companion CD includes a variety of tools and scripts to help you work more efficiently when implementing and managing security on computers running Windows Server 2003, Windows 2000, and Windows XP. Several of these tools are discussed in the book; however, many are not. You can find documentation for each tool in the folder in which the tool is contained. Many of these tools are from the *Microsoft Windows Server 2003 Resource Kit*, so they are designed to be implemented with Windows Server 2003 operating systems. Specifically, these are the tools and scripts found in the root of the SecurityRKTools folder. The companion CD also includes a fully searchable electronic version (eBook) of this book.

> **Note**   Third-party software and links to third-party sites are not under the control of Microsoft Corporation, and Microsoft is therefore not responsible for their content, nor should their inclusion on this CD be construed as an endorsement of the product or the site.

Resource Kit Support Policy

Microsoft Corporation does not support the tools and scripts supplied on the *Microsoft Windows Security Resource Kit*, Second Edition, companion CD. Microsoft does not guarantee the performance of the tools or scripting examples or of any bug fixes for these tools and scripts. However, Microsoft Press provides a way for customers who purchase the *Microsoft Windows Security Resource Kit*, Second Edition, to report any problems with the software and receive feedback for such issues. To report any issues or problems, send e-mail to rkinput@microsoft.com. This e-mail address is only for issues related to the *Microsoft Windows Security Resource Kit*, Second Edition. Microsoft Press also provides corrections for books and companion CDs through the World Wide Web at *http://www.microsoft.com/learning/support/*. To connect directly to the Microsoft Knowledge Base and enter a query regarding a question or issue that you have, go to *http://support.microsoft.com*. For issues related to the Windows operating system, please refer to the support information included with your product.

System Requirements

System Requirements for Tools and Scripts

To use the tools included on the companion CD, you'll need to have installed Microsfot Windows Server 2003, Windows 2000, or Windows XP.

 Note   The *Microsoft Windows Security Resource Kit*, Second Edition, companion CD includes a variety of tools and scripts. Many of these tools are from the *Microsoft Windows 2003 Server Resource Kit*. For any additional information on tool requirements, consult the documentation included with each tool.

Recommended System Requirements for the eBook

The following system configuration is recommended for the best viewing experience with Microsoft Press eBooks:

- Microsoft Windows 2003, Windows 2000, or Windows XP
- Pentium II (or similar) with 266-megahertz (MHz) or higher processor
- 64 megabytes (MB) of RAM
- 8× or faster CD-ROM drive
- 800×600 display settings with high-color (16-bit)
- Microsoft Internet Explorer 5.5 or later

Part I
Applying Key Principles of Security

Chapter 1
Key Principles of Security

Managing information security is difficult. To do it well requires a combination of technical, business, and people skills, many of which are not intuitive. The foundation of information security is risk management. Without a good understanding of risk management, it is impossible to secure any large modern network. More often than not, the failure of network administrators and managers to build a secure network results in the organization's most closely held information being as secure as the lunch menu. Thus, either the lunch menu will be very secure, or the security of important information will be very weak. Neither situation is workable in the long run.

Not every network administrator is a security expert, and most need not be. However, all network administrators must understand the basics of security. Classically, information security is dominated by confidentiality, integrity, and availability, usually referred to by the mnemonic *C-I-A triad*. This view relates to the historically strong ties between information security and cryptography for which the security concepts of confidentiality and integrity refer to the cryptography concepts of encryption and hashing. The modern security professional needs to keep more in mind conceptually than just the insular C-I-A triad—for example, attacks used to inflict monetary damages or carried out in the furtherance of a greater exploit extend the protection that networks provide. You can follow several key principles to secure your networks and applications. By acting on these key principles when completing your day-to-day tasks, you can secure your network—even without being a security expert. And if you are a security specialist or want to become one, you must master these key principles.

Understanding Risk Management

The first key principle of security is that no network is completely secure—information security is really about risk management. In the most basic of terms, the more important the asset is and the more it is exposed to security threats, the more resources you should put into securing it. Thus, it is imperative that you understand how to evaluate an asset's value, the threats to an asset, and the appropriate security measures. In general, without training, administrators respond to a security threat in one of three ways:

- Ignore the threat, or acknowledge it but do nothing to prevent it from occurring.
- Address the threat in an ad hoc fashion.
- Attempt to completely secure all assets to the utmost degree, without regard for usability or manageability.

None of these strategies takes into account what the actual risk is, and all of them will almost certainly lead to long-term failure.

Learning to Manage Risk

Managing security risks can be an incredibly daunting task, especially if you fail to do so in a well-organized and well-planned manner. Risk management often requires experience with financial accounting and budgeting as well as the input of business analysts. Building a risk assessment of an organization's security can take months and generally involves many people from many parts of the company. You can follow this simple process for assessing and managing risk:

- **Set a scope.** If you try to assess and manage all security risks in your organization, you are likely to be overwhelmed and certain to miss critical details. Before starting the risk assessment, set the scope of the risk assessment project. This will enable you to better estimate the time and cost required to assess the security risks in the project and to document and track the results more easily.

- **Identify assets and determine their value.** The first step in assessing risk is to identify assets and determine their value. When determining an asset's value, take these three factors into account:
  - ❏ The financial impact of the asset's compromise or loss
  - ❏ The nonfinancial impact of the asset's compromise or loss
  - ❏ The value of the asset to your competitors

  The financial impact of an asset's compromise or loss includes revenue and productivity lost because of downtime, costs associated with recovering services, and direct equipment losses. The nonfinancial impact of an asset's compromise or loss includes resources used to shape public perception of a security incident, such as advertising campaigns, and loss of public trust or confidence, known as *goodwill in accounting*. The value of the asset to your organization should be the main factor in determining how you secure the resource. If you do not adequately understand your assets and their value, you might end up securing the lunch menu in the cafeteria as stringently as you secure your trade secrets.

- **Predict threats and vulnerabilities to assets.**   The process of predicting threats and vulnerabilities to assets is known as *threat modeling*. Through the exercise of modeling threats, you will likely discover threats and vulnerabilities that you did not know about or had overlooked, and you will document the more well-known threats and vulnerabilities. You can then proactively mitigate risk rather than having to react to it after a security incident.

> **More Info**   See *Threat Modeling* (Microsoft Press, 2004) by Frank Swiderski and Window Snyder for in-depth information on threat modeling.

- **Document the security risks.**   After completing the threat model, it is essential that you document the security risks so that they can be reviewed by all relevant people and addressed systematically. When documenting the risks, you might want to rank them. You can rank risks either *quantitatively* or *qualitatively*. Quantitative rankings will use actual and estimated financial data about the assets to assess the severity of the risks. For example, you might determine that a single incident of a security risk will cost your organization $20,000 in financial losses, whereas another will cost the organization only $5,000. Qualitative rankings use a system to assess the relative impact of the risks. For example, a common qualitative system is to rank the product of the probability of the risk occurring and the value of the asset on a 10-point scale. Neither quantitative nor qualitative risk assessment is superior to the other; rather, they complement each other, each with its own best use. Quantitative ranking often requires acute accounting skills, whereas qualitative ranking often requires acute technical skills.

- **Determine a risk management strategy.**   After completing the risk assessment, you must determine what general risk management strategy to pursue and what security measures you will implement in support of the risk management strategy. The result from this step is a risk management plan. The risk management plan should clearly state the risk, threat, impact on the organization, risk management strategy, and security measures that will be taken. As a security administrator, you will likely be responsible for or involved in implementing the security measures in the risk management plan.

- **Monitor the assets.**   Once the actions defined in the risk management plan have been implemented, you will need to monitor the assets for realization of the security risks. As we've mentioned, realization of a security risk is called a *security incident*. You will need to trigger actions defined in contingency plans and start investigating the security incident as soon as possible to limit the damage to your organization.

- **Track changes to risks.**   As time progresses, changes to your organization's hardware, software, personnel, and business processes will add and obsolete security risks. Similarly, threats to assets and vulnerabilities will evolve and increase in sophistication. You will need to track these changes and update the risk management plan and the associated security measures regularly.

Risk Management Strategies

Once you have identified an asset and the threats to it, you can begin determining which security measures to implement. The first step is to decide on the appropriate risk management strategy. The rest of this section examines the four general categories of risk management that you can pursue:

- Acceptance
- Mitigation
- Transference
- Avoidance

Accepting Risk

By taking no proactive measures, you accept the full exposure and consequences of the security threats to an asset. Accepting risk is an extreme reaction to a threat. You should accept risk only as a last resort when no other reasonable alternatives exist, or when the costs associated with mitigating or transferring the risk are prohibitive or unreasonable. When accepting risk, it is always a good idea to create a contingency plan. A contingency plan details a set of actions that will be taken after the risk is realized and will lessen the impact of the compromise or loss of the asset.

Mitigating Risk

The most common method of securing computers and networks is to mitigate security risks. By taking proactive measures either to reduce an asset's exposure to threats or reduce the organization's dependency on the asset, you are mitigating the security risk. Generally, reducing an organization's dependency on an asset is beyond the scope of a security administrator's control; however, mitigating risk is the primary job function of a security administrator. One of the simplest examples of mitigating a security risk is installing antivirus software. By installing and maintaining antivirus software, you greatly reduce a computer's exposure to computer viruses, worms, and Trojan horses. Installing and maintaining antivirus software does not eliminate the possibility of a computer being infected with a virus because there will inevitably be new viruses that the antivirus software cannot yet protect the computer against. Thus, when a risk is mitigated, you still should create a contingency plan to follow if the risk is realized.

When deciding to mitigate risk, one of the key financial metrics to consider is how much your organization will save because of mitigating the risk, less the cost of implementing the security measure. If the result is a positive number and no other prohibitive factors exist, such as major conflicts with business operations, implementing the security measure is generally a good idea. On occasion, the cost of implementing the security measure will exceed the amount of money saved but will still be worthwhile—for example, when human life is at risk.

Transferring Risk

An increasingly common and important method of addressing security risks is to transfer some of the risk to a third party. You can transfer a security risk to another party to take advantage of economies of scale, such as insurance, or to take advantage of another organization's expertise and services, such as a Web hosting service. With insurance, you are paying a relatively small fee to recuperate or lessen financial losses if the security risk should occur. This is especially important when the financial consequences of your security risk are abnormally large, such as making your organization vulnerable to class action lawsuits. When contracting a company to host your organization's Web site, you stand to gain sophisticated Web security services and a highly trained, Web-savvy staff that your organization might not have afforded otherwise. When you engage in this type of risk transference, the details of the arrangement should be clearly stated in a contract known as a *service level agreement (SLA)*. Always have your organization's legal staff thoroughly investigate all third parties and contracts when transferring risk.

Avoiding Risk

The opposite of accepting risk is to avoid the risk entirely. To avoid risk, you must remove the source of the threat, exposure to the threat, or your organization's reliance on the asset. Generally, you avoid risk when there are little to no possibilities for mitigating or transferring the risk, or when the consequences of realizing the risk far outweigh the benefits gained from undertaking the risk. For example, a law enforcement agency might want to create a database of known informants that officers can access through the Internet. A successful compromise of the database could result in lives being lost. Thus, even though many ways to secure access to the database exist, there is zero tolerance of a security compromise. Therefore, risk must be avoided by not placing the database on the Internet, or perhaps not storing the information electronically at all.

Understanding Security

The most fundamental skill in securing computers and networks is understanding the big picture of security. By understanding the big picture of how to secure computers and networks as well as the limitations of security, you can avoid spending time, money, and energy attempting impossible or impractical security measures. You can also spend less time resecuring assets that have been jeopardized by poorly conceived or ineffective security measures.

Granting the Least Privilege Required

Always think of security in terms of granting the least amount of privileges required to carry out the task. If an application that has too many privileges should be compromised, the attacker might be able to expand the attack beyond what it would if the application had been under the least amount of privileges possible. For example, examine the consequences of a network administrator unwittingly opening an e-mail attachment that launches a virus. If the administrator is logged on using the domain Administrator account, the virus will have Administrator privileges on all computers in the domain and thus unrestricted access to nearly all data on the network. If the administrator is logged on using a local Administrator account, the virus will have Administrator privileges on the local computer and thus would be able to access any data on the computer and install malicious software such as key-stroke logging software on the computer. If the administrator is logged on using a normal user account, the virus will have access only to the administrator's data and will not be able to install malicious software. By using the least privileges necessary to read e-mail, in this example, the potential scope of the compromise is greatly reduced.

Defending in Depth

Imagine the security of your network as an onion. Each layer you pull away gets you closer to the center, where the critical asset exists. On your network, defend each layer as though the next outer layer is ineffective or nonexistent. The aggregate security of your network will dramatically increase if you defend vigilantly at all levels and increase the fault tolerance of security. For example, to protect users from launching an e-mail-borne virus, in addition to antivirus software on the users' computers, you could use e-mail client software that blocks potentially dangerous file types from being executed, block certain potentially dangerous attachments according to their file type, and ensure that the user is running under a limited user account rather than an administrator account on the local computer. Although any one of these measures could stop a given attack, together they will stop a much greater range of attacks and layer the defenses.

Reducing the Attack Surface

Attackers are functionally unlimited and thus possess unlimited time, whereas you have limited time and resources. (The concept of being functionally unlimited is detailed in Chapter 2, "Understanding Your Enemy.") An attacker needs to know of only one vulnerability to attack your network successfully, whereas you must pinpoint all your vulnerabilities to defend your network. The smaller your attack surface, the better chance you have of accounting for all assets and their protection. Attackers will have fewer targets, and you will have less to monitor and maintain. For example, to lower the attack surface of individual computers on your network, you can disable services that are not used and remove (or better yet, never install) software that is not necessary.

Avoiding Assumptions

Making assumptions will generally result in you overlooking, prematurely dismissing, or incorrectly assessing critical details. Often these details are not obvious or are buried deep within a process or technology. That is why you must test, test, test! You might also want to hire a third party to assess the security of your network or applications. Some organizations might even have legal or regulatory compliance statutes that require them to undergo this type of evaluation.

Protecting, Detecting, and Responding

Because at some point in time it is given that some portion of security will fail, when you think about securing a computer or a network, think about how you can protect the asset proactively, detect attempted security incidents, and respond to security incidents. This is a simple security life cycle. By looking at security from this perspective, you will be better prepared to handle unpredictable events.

Securing by Design, Default, and Deployment

When you design networks, ensure that the following criteria are met:

- Your design is completed with security as an integral component.
- Your design is secure by default.
- The deployment and ongoing management of the implementation maintains the security of the network.

By accomplishing these three goals, you can address security proactively and natively rather than reactively and artificially. Adding on security at the end is a very good way to ensure that you have plenty of vulnerabilities for attackers. For example, if at the end of the development of a line-of-business application you attempt to add security to the database where the information is stored, what will happen if the application no longer connects to the database after the security measures? The safe money is that the security measure will be trumped and the database will remain vulnerable. The proper place to address security is in the design phase.

The 10 Immutable Laws of Security

In 2000, Scott Culp of the Microsoft Security Response Center published the article "10 Immutable Laws of Security" on the Microsoft Web site, which you can read at *http://www.microsoft.com/technet/archive/community/columns/security/essays /10imlaws.mspx*. Despite the fact that Internet and computer security are changing at a staggering rate, these laws remain true. These 10 laws do an excellent job of describing some of the intractable limitations of security currently:

- **If a bad guy can persuade you to run his program on your computer, it's not your computer anymore.**   Often attackers attempt to encourage the user to install software on the attacker's behalf. Many viruses and Trojan horse applications operate this way. For example, the ILOVEYOU virus succeeded only because unwitting users ran the script when it arrived in an e-mail message. Another class of applications that attackers prompt a user to install are spyware applications. Once installed, spyware monitors a user's activities on her computer and reports the results to the attacker.

- **If a bad guy can alter the operating system on your computer, it's not your computer anymore.**   A securely installed operating system and the securely procured hardware that it is installed on is referred to as a *Trusted Computing Base (TCB)*. If an attacker can replace or modify any of the operating system files or certain components of the system's hardware, the TCB can no longer be trusted. For example, an attacker might replace the file Passfilt.dll, which is used to enforce password complexity, with a version of the file that also records all passwords used on the system. If an operating system has been compromised or you cannot prove that it has not been compromised, you should no longer trust the operating system.

- **If a bad guy has unrestricted physical access to your computer, it's not your computer anymore.**   Once an attacker possesses physical access to a computer, you can do little to prevent the attacker from gaining Administrator privileges on the operating system. With Administrator privilege compromised, nearly all persistently stored data is at risk of being exposed. Similarly, an attacker with physical access could install hardware or software to monitor and record keystrokes that is completely transparent to the user. If a computer has been physically compromised or you cannot prove otherwise, you should not trust the computer.

- **If you allow a bad guy to upload programs to your Web site, it's not your Web site anymore.**   An attacker who can execute applications or modify code on your Web site can take full control of the Web site. The most obvious symptom of this is an attacker defacing an organization's Web site. A corollary to this law is that if a Web site requests input from the user, attackers will use bad input. For example, you might have a form that asks for a number between 1 and 100. Whereas normal users will enter numbers within the specified data range, an attacker will try to use any data input he feels will break the back-end application.

- **Weak passwords trump strong security.**   Even if a network design is thoroughly secure, if users and administrators use blank, default, or otherwise simple passwords, the security will be rendered ineffective once an attacker cracks the password.

- **A machine is only as secure as the administrator is trustworthy.**   One constant on all networks is that you must trust the network administrators. The more administrative privileges an administrator account has, the more the administrator must be trusted. In other words, if you do not trust someone, do not give her Administrator privileges.

- **Encrypted data is only as secure as the decryption key.**   No encryption algorithm will protect the ciphertext from an attacker if she possesses or can gain possession of the decryption key. Encryption alone is not a solution to a business problem unless there is a strong component of key management and unless users and administrators are vigilant in protecting their keys or key material.

- **An out-of-date virus scanner is only marginally better than no virus scanner at all.**   New computer viruses, worms, and Trojan horses are always emerging and existing ones evolving. Consequently, antivirus software can become outdated quickly. As new or modified viruses are released, antivirus software is updated. Antivirus software that is not updated to recognize a given virus will not be able to prevent it.

- **Absolute anonymity isn't practical, in real life or on the Web.**   Two issues related to security that are often confused are *privacy* and *anonymity*. Anonymity means that your identity and details about your identity are completely unknown and untraceable, whereas privacy means that your identity and details about your identity are not disclosed. Privacy is essential, and technology and laws make achieving it possible. On the other hand, anonymity is not possible or practical when on the Internet or when using computers in general.

- **Technology is not a panacea.**   Although technology can secure computers and computer networks, it is not—and will never be—a solution in and of itself. You must combine technology with people and processes to create a secure computing environment.

The 10 Immutable Laws of Security Administration

As a follow-up to his article on security, Microsoft's Scott Culp wrote "10 Immutable Laws of Security Administration," which you can find at *http://www.microsoft.com /technet/archive/community/columns/security/essays/10salaws.mspx*. These 10 laws address the security issues that network administrators must contend with, issues entirely separate from the day-to-day security concerns of users:

- **Nobody believes anything bad can happen to them, until it does.**   Because attacks on computer networks often cannot be seen, felt, or heard, it is easy for users and administrators to place concern about attacks out of their minds. With attacks far from your mind, it is difficult to see the need for security. Unfortunately, after a security incident takes place, the need for security is frequently still dismissed and the breach regarded as a one-time incident. Attackers *will* attempt to compromise the security of your network. It is not a question of if or when—it is a question of how frequently. You must protect your networks against attackers, detect their attempts to compromise your network, and respond when security incidents do occur.

- **Security only works if the secure way also happens to be the easy way.**   For most users and administrators, the more difficult or invasive a security measure is, the more likely they are to ignore it, forget it, or subvert it. Ideally, security should be transparent to users and administrators. When the security measure requires a user or an administrator to change his behavior, you should create clear and easy-to-follow procedures for completing the task in question and explain your rationale for implementing the security measure.

- **If you don't keep up with security fixes, your network won't be yours for long.**   After a security update is announced and the vulnerability is explained, a race begins between attackers attempting to exploit the vulnerability and administrators attempting to apply the security update. If you do not keep up with applying security updates, an attacker will exploit one of the known vulnerabilities on your network.

- **It doesn't do much good to install security fixes on a computer that was never secure to begin with.**   Although installing security updates will prevent exposure to newly discovered vulnerabilities, installing security updates in and of itself will not result in a secure computer. For a computer to be secure, it is essential that the base operating system be securely configured.

- **Eternal vigilance is the price of security.**   Security is an ongoing effort. The security administrator must remain vigilant to attacks and attackers who constantly strive to increase the level of sophistication of their attacks. An infinite number of potential attackers exist, and they have infinite time on their hands to crack your network. Attackers have little to lose and need to know only one exploit. Security administrators, on the other hand, have a finite amount of time and resources to defend their organization's network. A security administrator is defeated when a single attack is successful against the network.

- **There really is someone out there trying to guess your passwords.**   Because of the mythic qualities surrounding attackers—much like the monster under the bed—it is easy to push the possibility of attackers out of your mind. Unlike the monster under the bed, attackers do exist and they do attack networks. In movies, attackers break powerful encryption algorithms; in real life, they guess simple passwords and exploit mundane, known vulnerabilities.

- **The most secure network is a well-administered one.**   Although a security expert can secure a network, it will not remain secure if it is not well managed—from the Chief Information Officer (CIO), to the security administrator, to the end user.

- **The difficulty of defending a network is directly proportional to its complexity.**   The more complex a network is, the greater the chance for administrators to misconfigure computers, lose track of the configuration of computers, and fail to understand how the network really works. When in doubt, keep it simple.

- **Security isn't about risk avoidance; it's about risk management.**   You will never avoid all security risks. It would be too costly and impractical. Claims of unbreakable security stem from ignorance or arrogance and are always wrong.

- **Technology is not a panacea.**   Although it is essential to ensure the bits and bytes on your network are configured securely, doing so will not prevent rogue administrators, poor processes, careless users, or apathetic managers. No technology will prevent poor judgment.

Chapter 2
Understanding Your Enemy

If you know the enemy and know yourself, you need not fear the result of a hundred battles. If you know yourself but not the enemy, for every victory gained you will also suffer a defeat. If you know neither the enemy nor yourself, you will succumb in every battle.

— The Art of War, *Sun Tzu*

Although Sun Tzu's classic military-strategy text, *The Art of War*, was written more than 2000 years before computers were invented, many of the statements it contains are relevant to computer security. Figure 2-1 expresses the principle of battle in a binary decision table.

	Know your enemy	Do not know your enemy
You know yourself	You will generally succeed	You will succeed sometimes
Do not know yourself	You will succeed sometimes	You will never succeed

Figure 2-1 Decision table of knowing your enemy and yourself

Knowing Yourself

In respect to information security, knowing yourself and your enemy is not necessarily a straightforward endeavor—if it were, networks would be much more secure than they are today. To know yourself, you must do the following:

- Accurately assess your own skills.
- Possess detailed documentation of your network.
- Understand the level of organizational support you receive.

Accurately Assessing Your Own Skills

The skill set of a network administrator should include formal training on operating systems and applications; experience designing, installing, and configuring networks and network services; and the ability to predict problems before they occur and solve them when they do. To prevent design and configuration mistakes that can lead to security breaches, you must be able to assess your network management skill set accurately. Overestimating your knowledge of a network, operating system, or application can easily lead to vulnerabilities that attackers can exploit. Accurately assessing your skill set enables you to be proactive in obtaining training and acquiring the services of experienced consultants if the situation requires it.

For example, you might be asked to install and configure an Internet Web server for customers to access their order history on a Web application that your organization is deploying. Although you might be an experienced MCSE who has installed and configured intranet Web servers, you might not have any knowledge or experience with Internet Web applications or configuring servers that have direct Internet connectivity. By not accurately assessing your skills, you could easily and unwittingly expose customer information to attackers and not realize it until the information has already been compromised.

Possessing Detailed Documentation on Your Network

A key requirement of securing your organization's network is maintaining detailed documentation about the physical infrastructure of your network, complete and up-to-date network diagrams, and documentation of the configuration of computers, applications, and the Audit log. Without this documentation, network administrators might overlook resources that must be secured, and the network will almost certainly be inconsistent in its level of security. Without baseline performance and security information, it is difficult to detect attacks, regardless of whether they are successful. For example, your network might have a direct connection to the Internet that is no longer used but is still connected to a router. Over time, a router's access control list (ACL) can become outdated and can present a significant security risk. This is because the outdated ACL can enable an attacker to compromise your organization's network by using tactics that did not exist when the router was secure and was monitored. Although such situations might seem obscure, they are quite common for organizations that have grown by being acquired by another organization. When consolidating IT resources, you can easily overlook these types of details. Similarly, it often takes such organizations a long time to create detailed documentation on their newly formed networks.

Understanding the Level of Organizational Support You Receive

The level of support that you receive from your organization—from management to your end users—greatly determines how you will secure network resources. This is often called your organization's *security position* or *security posture*. The security position of your organization includes the level of executive sponsorship for security policies and procedures, security requirements mandated by industry or government regulations, end user compliance with security policies and procedures, and training for end users and administrators. Your organization's security policies and procedures are central to the level of organizational support that you have.

In general, the completeness and clarity of an organization's security policies and procedures can indicate the support network administrators will receive for securing a network. Failing to understand your organization's security position can result in you oversecuring network resources to the point that end users will work around security measures and cause security vulnerabilities. For example, your organization might create policies that greatly restrict the types of Web applications that can be installed on a Web server, causing departments to purchase and deploy their own Web servers. Because the IT department does not know of the rogue Web servers, it cannot manage the application of security updates and service packs to those servers.

Identifying Your Attacker

Knowing your enemy is as complicated as knowing yourself—maybe even more so. Too often, network administrators know their enemies only through stereotypes of attackers, and like most stereotypes, these are generally not accurate and rely on fear. For example, when you see movies that portray computer crime, more often than not, the penetration of the computer systems involves breaking an encryption key. The movie attacker fiercely pounds at his keyboard to break the encryption key by guessing it, which usually happens within a matter of seconds. Or he quickly writes a program with a well-designed user interface featuring big numbers that crack each character in the encryption key one by one. Although both attacks add drama to these movies, they are not only mathematically absurd and impossible, they also are not an accurate depiction of how networks are attacked. If this is all you know about the people who will attack your network, your network will be compromised.

In reality, breaking an industry-standard encryption key such as the 30-year-old Data Encryption Standard (DES) algorithm takes special hardware, significant computer programming skills, and plenty of time. To prove the insecurity of the DES algorithm, the Electronic Frontier Foundation (EFF) spent more than a year building a computer, using custom-built hardware and software, that could crack a 56-bit DES key. It took three days to crack the key.

You could design and build a network more secure than a government currency vault, but it would take only one computer that does not have the latest service pack installed for an attacker to compromise the network. A computer network looks very different from the attacker's point of view than from your viewpoint, as the defender. For example, you might think applying a security update for a known vulnerability to all but one computer on your network is a successful security deployment. To the attacker, this lone computer without the security update is the key to compromising the network.

By understanding (or "knowing") the attacker, you can think like an attacker when designing security for your network. For example, many organizations complete vulnerability assessments on their networks. But you might want to consider training members of your organization's IT staff or hiring external experts to attempt to break into the network from the outside. We describe this process in detail in Chapter 28, "Assessing the Security of a Network." In fact, there are those in the field of computer security who boldly assert that you cannot secure a computer network without being able to attack one.

When most people think about attackers, or hackers, they generally think of a know-it-all 14-year-old boy who wears a black T-shirt every day and is pale as a vampire as a result of all the hours he spends in front of his computer or video game console. Although this stereotypical attacker certainly exists, he represents only a small portion of the attacker population. For convenience, we'll group attackers into two general categories: external attackers (those outside your organization) and internal attackers (those within it).

Understanding External Attackers

The majority of attackers that you hear about in the media work outside the organizations they attack. These attackers include everyone from teenagers to professional hackers employed by governments and rogue nations. In addition to the attackers who are outright malicious, there exist groups of self-styled "white hat," or nonmalicious, attackers. Although these attackers might not have malicious intentions, they present significant dangers to networks, too. For example, a "harmless" attacker might break into a network for the challenge, but while attempting to compromise a server, might render it inoperable, resulting in a denial-of-service condition. When examining attackers, it can be helpful to think about the dangers they present in terms of their skill level—be it novice, intermediate, or advanced.

Novice Attackers

Novice attackers generally possess only rudimentary programming skills and basic knowledge of the inner workings of operating systems and applications. These attackers represent the majority of attackers. Although this group of attackers might not possess significant skills, they are a threat to networks primarily because of the number of them out there and the knowledge they lack. For example, a novice attacker is much more apt to destroy information (either intentionally or accidentally) even though it will reveal her compromise of the network and quite possibly result in her apprehension. Although secure networks will rarely be compromised by novice attackers, networks that are not vigilantly secured are extremely vulnerable to this type of attacker because of the sheer number of them.

Novice attackers exploit known vulnerabilities with tools created by more experienced attackers, and thus are often called *script kiddies*. They also present a serious threat to obvious security vulnerabilities, such as weak passwords. Novice attackers who are also employees (making them internal attackers) often present the same level of danger as external attackers because they already possess valid network credentials with which they can launch attacks and they have access to network documentation.

Intermediate Attackers

Attackers with intermediate skills are less numerous than novice attackers but generally possess programming skills that enable them to automate attacks and better exploit known vulnerabilities in operating systems and applications. This group of attackers is capable of penetrating most networks if given enough time, but they might not be able to do so without being detected. These attackers frequently port attacks from other operating systems and conduct more sophisticated attacks than novice attackers. Attackers with an intermediate skill level often launch such attacks as an attempt to increase their notoriety or boost their skill level by creating tools to attack networks and publishing information that helps other attackers break into networks.

Advanced Attackers

Attackers with advanced skills usually are not only accomplished programmers but also have experience breaking into networks and applications. These attackers discover vulnerabilities in operating systems and applications and create tools to exploit previously unknown vulnerabilities. Advanced attackers are generally capable of compromising most networks without being detected, unless those networks are extremely secure and have well-established incident response procedures.

Understanding Internal Attackers

Contrary to what you might hear in the media, the majority of attacks on networks are conducted by attackers who have company badges—in other words, your fellow employees. Attackers who are employees of the organization they're attacking present a unique danger to networks for several reasons. Such attackers have the following in their favor:

- Higher levels of trust
- Physical access to network resources
- Human resources protections

Higher Levels of Trust

Almost all networks place a much higher level of trust in users and computers accessing resources on the local area network (LAN) than on publicly available network resources, such as servers connected to the Internet. Many networks allow authentication methods and unencrypted data transmissions on LANs that they would never consider using on the Internet. It is also much easier for attackers to enumerate information about the configuration of computers and applications when they have valid credentials on the network. Employees have valid credentials on the network, which also gives them greater initial access to network resources than external attackers might initially have. It can be very difficult to discern whether an employee is using her credentials legitimately or illegitimately—especially when she is a network administrator.

Physical Access to Network Resources

Employees have much greater physical access to network resources—namely, the computers of their coworkers. In general, when an attacker has physical control of a computer, that computer can no longer be protected from the attacker; rather, it is only a matter of time and computing power before the attacker can recover all data on the computer. Similarly, employees have much greater access to documentation on the network, which can be a critical resource for attacking it.

Human Resources Protections

Employees, even those who attack network resources, are often protected by employment laws and HR policies that can greatly hinder their employer from detecting them or preventing them from doing further damage once detected. For example, local laws might prohibit an organization from inspecting the Internet usage of its employees without a court order. An employee could take advantage of this by attacking internal Web resources.

What Motivates Attackers

Attackers attempt to break into computer networks for many reasons. Although all attackers present a clear and present danger to networks, the motivation of the attacker will greatly determine the actual threat posed. By understanding what might motivate potential attackers to attempt to compromise your organization's network, you can predict what type of threats the network faces. Armed with this knowledge, once you detect an attack, you might be more able to prevent further damage or better equipped to identify who the attacker is.

Many attackers are motivated by more than one factor. Here are the reasons that attackers attempt to break into computer networks, in ascending order of the danger they present:

- Notoriety, acceptance, and ego
- Financial gain
- Challenge
- Activism
- Revenge
- Espionage
- Information warfare

Notoriety, Acceptance, and Ego

An attacker's quest for notoriety, desire for acceptance, and ego comprise one of the most common motivations for attempts to break into computer networks and applications. Attackers motivated by notoriety often are naturally introverted and seeking a way to gain acceptance in the electronic hacker community; thus, their exploits are very public. Examples of such attacks include defacing Web sites and creating computer viruses and worms.

By breaking into a network of a major company or government agency and defacing its Web site, an attacker is virtually guaranteed national and international publicity and enshrined in the electronic hacker community. For example, Attrition.org runs a Web site that catalogs nearly all Web site defacements in recent years. Querying any major search engine for the phrase *Web site defacement* invariably returns thousands of accounts of an organization's Web site being defaced, including those of most major corporations and government agencies.

Although not normally regarded as attackers, people who create and release computer viruses and worms cause billions of dollars of damage each year. In 1991, the Michelangelo virus opened a Pandora's box of sorts for computer viruses. Although the Michelangelo virus did little actual damage, the coverage that it received in the mainstream media, including newspapers, magazines, and television news, brought computer viruses into the popular consciousness and opened the door for other malicious publicity seekers. Since then, many other computer viruses have created similar media frenzies, such as Fun Love, ILOVEYOU, Melissa, and most recently, Code Red, Nimda, Slammer, and Blaster, each of which to some extent improved on the previous one.

Popular media and antiauthoritarian romanticism transformed outlaws of the U.S. western frontier—such as Jesse James and Billy the Kid—from common criminals who robbed banks and murdered people into cult heroes. Similarly, several attackers have gained cult hero status in the hearts and minds of computer geeks. Two recent examples include Kevin Mitnick and Adrian Lamo. Other attackers and prospective attackers seek the attention of the media and hacker communities that Mitnick and Lamo received and are envious, if not worshipful. The cult following of these two hacker legends is particularly strong with impressionable teenagers who have not fully developed their own sense of morality and rarely understand the true consequences their actions have on business continuity and information technology.

In all these examples and in many similar incidents, the exploits of the attackers received international publicity. Attackers motivated by notoriety, acceptance, and ego look at these incidents as proof that they too can become famous. You can probably imagine the sense of accomplishment an attacker might feel, seeing his handiwork in the headlines of major newspapers and discussed on television news programs by political pundits. Often attackers know that their actions are illegal but consider their behavior harmless because there is no clear victim, no one physically harmed, and no tangible goods stolen or destroyed. Thus, in the minds of many attackers, they are not doing anything discernibly wrong. Certainly this is not the case. For example, although the direct financial consequences of Web site defacements are often low, the loss of public confidence in how well the organization can ensure the confidentiality and privacy of their employee, business partner, and customer information can be severe. On the other hand, when these types of attacks are successfully carried out against companies that you or your organization do business with, they are almost always indications of greater security issues inside the company. This can result in indirect financial losses from customer distrust and defection.

Financial Gain

We can separate attackers motivated by monetary gain into two categories: those motivated by direct financial gain, and those motivated by indirect financial gain.

Attackers motivated by direct financial gain are little more than common criminals, akin to bank robbers with computer skills. These attackers break into computer networks or applications to steal money or information. In the past few years, several high-profile thefts of credit card information from the databases of companies that conduct online commerce have been perpetrated. These attackers did one of three things with the credit card information that they stole: they used the credit cards to purchase products or make cash withdrawals, sold the credit card numbers to other criminals, or attempted to extort money from the companies from which they stole the credit cards. In nearly every case, the attacker was apprehended, but not before causing significant damage. For example, in 1994, a Russian attacker broke into Citibank and transferred roughly $10 million to accounts in several countries. He was captured, and all but $400,000 was recovered. But the real damage to Citibank was in its customers' loss of trust because of Citibank's inability to secure customers' bank accounts. The attacker was sentenced to three years in prison and fined $240,000, whereas U.S. Federal Sentencing Guidelines call for a minimum 6- to 10-year sentence for someone with no prior criminal record who robs a bank in person.

Another way that attackers seek financial gain from attacking networks and applications is to break into an organization's network successfully and then offer to help the organization secure the network. Although many of these attackers maintain the position that they are "good guys" wanting only to help the target organization, in reality, they are little more than extortionists demanding protection money, like a 1920s gangster in cyberspace.

Some attackers are motivated by financial gain but in an indirect manner. A researcher or computer security company might make a large effort to discover vulnerabilities in commercial software applications and operating systems, and then use its discovery and the publication of such previously unknown vulnerabilities as a marketing tool for its own security assessment services. The publicity that a company or individual receives from unearthing a serious vulnerability in a commercial software application, especially a widely used application, can be priceless. For example, most significant vulnerabilities discovered in a widely used software application will be reported on the front page of major news and computer industry Web sites and in the technology or business sections of major newspapers. The discoverer of such a vulnerability might even receive airtime on the cable news television networks. For most small computer consulting companies, obtaining this type of publicity normally would be out of the question.

There is a critical point in the process of discovering commercial software vulnerabilities at which one leaves the realm of ethical behavior and becomes an attacker: the reporting of that vulnerability to the general public without the software company's knowledge or consent. Most commercial software companies are more than willing to work with researchers who have discovered security vulnerabilities to ensure that a software patch is available before the vulnerability is announced. Many software companies will also give credit to the person and company that discover the vulnerability, thus balancing the interests of their software users with the public recognition earned by the person and company reporting the vulnerability. However, many researchers not only publish the vulnerability without notifying the software vendor, they also create code to exploit the vulnerability. Further complicating this issue are laws such as the 1998 Digital Millennium Copyright Act (DMCA), which prohibits individuals from exposing vulnerabilities in certain software and hardware encryption techniques used for digital rights management. The bottom line is this: although discovering vulnerabilities for indirect financial gain can be done illegitimately by extortion, it can also be done legitimately to advance the mutual business goal of software vendors and researchers—protecting consumers.

Challenge

Many attackers initially attempt to break into networks for the mere challenge. In many ways, attackers view networks as a game of chess—a battle of minds that combines strategic and tactical thinking, patience, and mental strength. However, chess has precisely defined rules, and attackers clearly operate outside the rules. Attackers motivated by the challenge of breaking into networks often do not even comprehend their actions as criminal or wrong. Attackers motivated by the challenge are often indifferent to which network they attack; thus, they will attack everything from military installations to home networks. These attackers are unpredictable, both in their skill level and dedication.

Activism

Generally, two types of attackers fall into the activism class. The first type, self-dubbed "hacktivists," have been known to create secure communication software for people living under repressive regimes. For most organizations, this group of activist-attackers is relatively harmless.

The other type of activist-attacker, however, is a legitimate threat. This type breaks into networks as part of a political movement or cause. For example, such an attacker might break into a Web site and change the content to voice his own message. The "Free Kevin Mitnick" hacktivists frequently did this in an attempt to get Mitnick released from U.S. federal custody after he was arrested on multiple counts of computer crime. Attackers motivated by a specific cause might also publish intellectual property that does not belong to them, such as pirated software or music. They might carry out sophisticated denial-of-service attacks, called *virtual sit-ins*, on major Web sites to call attention to a particular cause.

Revenge

Attackers motivated by revenge are often former employees who feel they were wrongfully terminated or who hold ill will toward their former employers. These attackers can be particularly dangerous because they focus on a single target and—being former employees—often have intricate knowledge of the security of the networks. For example, on July 30, 1996, employees of Omega Engineering arrived at work to discover that they could no longer log on to their computers. Later they discovered that nearly all their mission-critical software had been deleted. The attack was linked to a logic bomb planted by an administrator who had been fired three weeks earlier. The attack resulted in more than $10 million in losses, prompting the layoff of 80 employees. In early 2002, the former administrator was sentenced to 41 months in prison, which pales in comparison to the financial and human damages that he caused.

Espionage

Some attackers break into networks to steal secret information for a third party. Attackers who engage in espionage are generally very skilled and can be well funded. Two types of espionage exist: industrial and international. A company might pay its own employees to break into the networks of its competitors or business partners, or the company might hire someone else to do this. Because of the negative publicity associated with such attacks, successful acts of industrial espionage are underreported by the victimized companies and law enforcement agencies. A widely publicized industrial espionage incident using computers took place in Japan. In December 2001, an engineer at Japan's NEC Toshiba Space Systems broke into the network of the National Space Development Agency of Japan. This engineer illegally accessed the antenna designs for a high-speed Internet satellite made by Mitsubishi in an attempt to help NEC gain business from the space agency. As a result, the Japan Space Agency prohibited NEC from bidding on new contracts for two months, but no criminal charges were filed.

Attackers who engage in international espionage attempt to break into computer networks run by governments, or they work for governments and rogue nations to steal secret information from other governments or corporations. The most famous case of computer-related international espionage is documented in Cliff Stoll's book *The Cuckoo's Egg: Tracking a Spy Through the Maze of Computer Espionage* (Pocket Books, 2000). In 1986, Stoll, an astronomer by trade, was working as a computer operator at Lawrence Berkeley Lab when he discovered a 75-cent discrepancy in an accounting log from the mainframe computer. One thing led to another, and eventually Stoll discovered that German attackers being paid by the KGB were breaking into both military and nonmilitary computers to steal secret information.

Information Warfare

Information warfare is another motivation for attacking computer networks that is becoming increasingly dangerous as people around the world rely on networks for mission-critical services. Major wars have been marked by the evolution of weapons systems—the machine gun changed the nature of combat in World War I, the tank changed the nature of combat in World War II, and airpower changed the nature of combat in Vietnam. Behind the scenes, each war also marked the evolution of electronic combat. From intercepted telegrams broken by hand, to radar jamming, to satellite transmissions that could be broken only by stealing the encryption keys (despite the power of many supercomputers)—electronic combat and intelligence have become deciding factors in modern warfare. Although no widely reported incidents of cyber-terrorism exist, you can be certain that these attempts have been made. There is evidence of information warfare in China, Israel, Pakistan, India, and the United States. The U.S. president's Critical Infrastructure Protection Board was formed in 2001 specifically to address countering the threat of cyber-terrorism and information warfare against the United States.

Why Defending Networks Is Difficult

In traditional combat, defenders enjoy a distinct advantage over their attackers. However, in information technology, several factors give attackers the advantage:

- Attackers have unlimited resources.
- Attackers need to master only one attack.
- Defenders cannot take the offensive.
- Defenders must serve business goals.
- Defenders must win all the time.

Attackers Have Unlimited Resources

At any given time, defenders must protect their network against both attackers around the globe and their own employees. This accumulation of attackers, as a group, limits a defender's resources. Many attackers can spend all day systematically attempting to break into your network. Attackers can collaborate to develop new and more sophisticated attacks. As a network administrator, you have other duties besides defending the network, and unlike attackers, you go home at night, take sick days, and go on vacations. Over time, some attackers will cease attempting to break into your network, but new ones will take their place. Defending networks against unrelenting hordes of attackers with much more time than you gives attackers an advantage.

Attackers Need to Master Only One Attack

As a network administrator, you have to secure many servers and applications. You must learn how all your operating systems, applications, and network devices work, as well as how to secure and manage them. You must determine the threats to each component of your network and keep current with newly reported vulnerabilities. Attackers, on the other hand, need to master attacking only a single application or operating system feature to compromise it and break into your network.

Defenders Cannot Take the Offensive

Although attackers can attack networks with a certain amount of impunity, defenders can retaliate only through litigation, which is expensive and time-consuming. Attacking an attacker is not only illegal in most countries, it is impractical. This is because attackers often use previously compromised third-party computers, called *zombie systems*, or many zombie systems acting in unison to attack networks. By using zombie systems to carry out or amplify an attack, an attacker can protect her identity. Frequently attackers use the networks of colleges and universities as attack vectors because of their openness, computing power, and bandwidth. An attack can also originate from another legitimate organization whose employee has attacked your network or whose network has already been compromised by an intruder. In any of these cases, retaliating against an intruder can result in your organization illegally attacking an unwitting individual, company, or organization. Thus, legally and practically, you cannot retaliate against attackers.

Defenders Must Serve Business Goals

Although network administrators are responsible for securing their organizations' networks, they also must install and configure operating systems and applications that help employees meet the goals of the business. In some situations the pursuit of company business goals conflicts with maintaining the security of the network.

For example, company executives might travel with laptops that contain sensitive information about the company. The executives might be unwilling to comply with security policies that require long and complex passwords. Knowing this, a network administrator might supply the executives with smart cards that they must use to access their laptops. This security measure will better protect the information on the laptop, but it also introduces other potential problems, such as the loss or misplacement of smart cards. To mitigate this situation, a network administrator might decide to create a second account for local computer users that could be used without the protection of a smart card, granting certain trusted employees the new account password, which could result in a serious security vulnerability.

Another situation in which the pursuit of business goals can interfere with the protection of the network occurs when your organization has a business rule that conflicts with the security of the network. For example, your organization might have a business rule that requires network traffic to the payroll server to be encrypted. This security measure will make data transmission of employee compensation secure, but makes it impossible for you to monitor network traffic to determine whether traffic is legitimate or illegitimate. It also prevents you from using any type of network intrusion detection software. In both scenarios, having to serve business goals jeopardizes your ability to protect the network.

Defenders Must Win All the Time

An attacker needs only one successful attack to compromise a network, whereas a network administrator must prevent *all* attacks to succeed in his role. These are ominous odds for ill-equipped or under-resourced network administrators. Given all the other problems defenders of networks face, it is inevitable that the security of your network will be compromised at some point. As a network administrator, you must ensure that these compromises are detected early and happen infrequently.

Is defending a network impossible? Not at all. But one thing is certain: it is impossible to defend a network without trained, skilled, and knowledgeable network administrators. By applying the key principles of security outlined in Chapter 1, "Key Principles of Security," to the information this book presents on securing computers running Microsoft Windows Server 2003, Windows 2000, and Windows XP, you can build a strong foundation for defending your networks.

Part II
Securing Active Directory

Chapter 3

Configuring Security for User Accounts and Passwords

The account is the central unit of security on computers running Microsoft Windows Server 2003, Windows 2000, Windows XP, and the applications that run on them. Rights and permissions are assigned to accounts and checked by a resource such as a file or a folder at the time of access. It is important to understand that a user and a user account are different entities. Anyone who possesses the credentials associated with a user account can use that account, despite the name on it—a computer can control and audit access to resources based on the user account token, not on the physical identity of the person using the account.

For example, you might be asked to restrict access to a certain file to allow only your organization's payroll managers access, whereas in reality you are restricting access to the file to allow access by the user account that the payroll managers use. Thus, you must protect the credentials used to validate that the person attempting to use the account is the person to whom the account was issued. By default, the credentials needed to use an account are the account name and password.

Securing Accounts

Each user, computer, or group account is a security principal on systems running Windows Server 2003, Windows 2000, and Windows XP. Security principals receive permissions to access resources such as files and folders. User rights, such as interactive logons, are granted or denied to accounts directly or by membership in a group. The accumulation of these permissions and rights define what security principals can and cannot do when working on the network.

User accounts are either domain or local in scope. In Windows Server 2003 and Windows 2000, domain accounts are stored in the Active Directory directory database (Ntds.dit) on domain controllers, whereas local accounts are stored in individual Security Accounts Manager (SAM) databases on the hard drives of workstations and member servers whether domain joined or not. Domain accounts can be used to authenticate to any machine in the forest and any domains that trust logons performed by the domain where the account exists, whereas local accounts are used to authenticate access to resources on the local computer only.

Understanding Security Identifiers

Although users reference their accounts by the user name or universal principal name (UPN), the operating system internally references accounts by their security identifiers (SIDs). For domain accounts, the SID of a security principal is created by concatenating the SID of the domain with a relative identifier (RID) for the account. SIDs are unique within their scope (domain or local) and are never reused. This is an example of a SID:

```
S-1-5-21-833815213-1531848612-156796815-1105
```

A SID is composed of several components:

S-*<revision>-<identifier authority>-<subauthorities>-<relative identifier>*

- **Revision**   This value indicates the version of the SID structure used in a particular SID. The revision value is 1 in Windows Server 2003, Windows 2000, and Windows XP. Although there might be another revision in the future, right now there is only 1.

- **Identifier authority**   This value identifies the authority that can issue SIDs for this particular type of security principal. The identifier authority value in the SID for an account or group in Windows Server 2003, Windows 2000, and Windows XP is 5 for the NT Authority.

- **Subauthorities**   The most important information in a SID is contained in a series of one or more subauthority values. All values up to but not including the last value in the series collectively identify a domain in an enterprise. This part of the series is known as the *domain identifier*. The last value in the series identifies a particular account or group relative to a domain. This value is the RID. In the example just given, this value is 1105.

By default, several security principals are created during installation of the operating system or domain; the SIDs for these accounts are called *well-known SIDs*. Table 3-1 lists the well-known SIDs for Windows Server 2003, Windows 2000, and Windows XP.

Table 3-1   **Well-Known SIDs**

SID	Security Principal	Notes
S-1-0	Null Authority	The authority for the Nobody SID.
S-1-0-0	Nobody	Nobody is a null SID and is used when there is no SID. Practically, this SID is not used in any version of Windows. This should not be confused with null credentials, which uses the Everyone SID.
S-1-1	World Authority	The authority for the Everyone SID.
S-1-1-0	Everyone	A group that includes all users, even anonymous users and guests in Windows 2000. In Windows XP and Windows Server 2003, the Everyone group does not contain the Anonymous SID. Users or services that attempt to access an object anonymously are not granted access if the access control list (ACL) on the object includes the Everyone group. Anonymous access is granted only for objects whose ACL explicitly contains the Anonymous SID. This behavior can be changed so that the Everyone group does contain Anonymous by changing the registry value for "EveryoneIncludesAnonymous." For more information on anonymous users, see the sidebar titled "Sorting Out Anonymous Access" in Chapter 11, "Creating and Configuring Security Templates."
S-1-2	Local Authority	The authority for the Local SID.
S-1-2-0	Local	This SID is added to the access token for the logged-on account that did not log on over the network. If the account logged on through the network, it will have the Network SID added to the access token.
S-1-3	Creator Authority	The authority for the Creator Owner SIDs, which are used to facilitate access control entry (ACE) inheritance.
S-1-3-0	Creator Owner	This SID is used in inheritable ACE. It is replaced by the SID of the account who is the creator when the ACE is inherited.
S-1-3-1	Creator Group	This SID is used in inheritable ACE. It is replaced by the SID of the primary group for the account that is the creator when the ACE is inherited. The primary group is used by the POSIX subsystem and Apple Macintosh clients.
S-1-5	NT Authority	The NT Authority is the authority for objects in the Windows security subsystem.
S-1-5-1	Dialup	This SID is added to the access token of accounts connecting to the computer directly through locally attached modems.

Table 3-1   **Well-Known SIDs**

SID	Security Principal	Notes
S-1-5-2	Network	This SID is added to the account's token when it is accessing the system through the network
S-1-5-3	Batch	This SID is added to the account's token when it is accessing the system through the batch queuing facility by launching a process as a batch job.
S-1-5-4	Interactive	This SID is added to the account's token during an interactive logon session, which includes console, Terminal Services, and Microsoft Internet Information Services (IIS) logons.
S-1-5-5-*X-Y*	Logon Session	This SID is used to control access to window-stations from processes launched by the user during a given logon session.
S-1-5-6	Service	This SID is added to the access token of an account that was logged on as a system service.
S-1-5-7	Anonymous	The Anonymous SID is used when no credentials are presented. When a computer receives a request such as net use \\server\ipc$ /user:"" "" Windows will assign the session the Anonymous SID when connecting to the interprocess communication share.
S-1-5-9	Enterprise Controllers	This SID is held by all domain controllers and used in Active Directory to control replication and other forest-wide functions.
S-1-5-10	Principal Self (or Self)	Self is a placeholder in an ACE on a user, group, or computer object in Active Directory. When you grant permissions to Self, you grant these permissions to the security principal represented by the object. During an access check, the operating system replaces the SID for Self with the SID for the security principal represented by the object.
S-1-5-11	Authenticated Users	After accounts successfully authenticate, this SID is added to their access token. It is important to note that despite the name of this SID, computers are members of this group as well. In Windows 2000, Authenticated Users includes the same accounts as the Everyone group with the exception of Anonymous and Guest accounts. In Windows XP and Windows Server 2003, because Anonymous has been removed from the Everyone group by default, the only difference between Authenticated Users and Everyone is that the Everyone group also includes Guests.

Table 3-1   Well-Known SIDs

SID	Security Principal	Notes
S-1-5-12	Restricted Code	This SID is added to the user's access token when using the Protect My Computer option in RunAs in Windows 2000 and Windows XP. In Windows Server 2003, this option is labeled "Run this program with restricted access" because of the restricted token that is used. This SID is not in Windows 2000. For more information on restricted tokens, see the sidebar "Using the RunAs Service" later in this chapter.
S-1-5-13	Terminal Server User	The Terminal Server User SID is added to the access token of all users who logged on through Terminal Services. This SID is added to the access token only if the terminal server is configured for "Terminal Server 4.0 compatibility mode" in Windows 2000 or "Relaxed Security" in Windows Server 2003.
S-1-5-14	Remote Interactive Logon	This SID is added to the access token of accounts that log on using a Remote Desktop Connection.
S-1-5-18	Local System	The Local System SID is the security context in which core components of the operating system run. In Windows 2000, Local System is the only built-in account with which to run system services.
S-1-5-19	Local Service	Local Service, available in Windows Server 2003 and Windows XP only, is used to run system services that do not require operating system–wide permissions to operate and do not require access to network resources. Security for system services is covered in Chapter 9, "Managing Security for System Services."
S-1-5-20	Network Service	Network Service, available in Windows Server 2003 and Windows XP only, is used to run system services that do not require operating system–wide permissions to operate, but do need access to resources on other computers. Security for system services is covered in Chapter 9, "Managing Security for System Services."
S-1-5- <domain SID>-500	Administrator	This is the default Administrator account for all installations of the Windows operating system. Although you can rename the account, the RID for this account will always be 500.
S-1-5- <domain SID>-501	Guest	This is the default Guest account for all installations of the Windows operating system. Although you can rename the account, the RID for this account will always be 501.

Table 3-1   **Well-Known SIDs**

SID	Security Principal	Notes
S-1-5- *<domain SID>*-502	KRBTGT	This is the account used by the Kerberos Key Distribution Center (KDC) in Windows Server 2003 and Windows 2000.
S-1-5- *<domain SID>*-512	Domain Admins	Members of the Domain Admins group have complete control over all objects in the domain. The Domain Admins group is also a member of the local Administrators group on all computers in the domain. Membership in this group should be kept to a minimum.
S-1-5- *<domain SID>*-513	Domain Users	By default all user accounts are automatically granted membership in the Domain Users group.
S-1-5- *<domain SID>*-514	Domain Guests	By default the Guest account is automatically granted membership in the Domain Guests group.
S-1-5- *<domain SID>*-515	Domain Computers	By default all computer accounts are automatically granted membership in the Domain Computers group.
S-1-5- *<domain-SID>*-516	Domain Controllers	By default all domain controller computer accounts are automatically granted membership in the Domain Controllers group.
S-1-5- *<domain SID>*-517	Cert Publishers	This is a group that includes all computers that host an enterprise Certification Authority (CA). Cert Publishers are authorized to publish certificates for User objects in Active Directory.
S-1-5- *<root domain SID>*-518	Schema Admins	Members of the Schema Admins group can create classes and attributes in the schema as well as manage the schema master flexible single-master operation (FSMO). By default, the Schema Admins group contains only the Administrator account from the first in the forest domain. Only members of the Enterprise Admins group can add to and remove accounts from the Schema Admins group. The Schema Admins group is changed from a global group to a universal group when the forest root domain is converted to native mode.

Table 3-1   **Well-Known SIDs**

SID	Security Principal	Notes
S-1-5- *<root do- main SID>*- 519	Enterprise Admins	Members of the Enterprise Admins group have complete control of all objects in the forest. Enterprise Admins are members of all the built-in domain local Administrators groups in each domain in the forest. Enterprise Admins can also manage all objects not associated with any single domain, such as the objects in the Configuration container. The Enterprise Admins group is changed from a global group to a universal group when the forest root domain is converted to native mode.
S-1-5- *<domain SID>*-520	Group Policy Creator Owners	Members of the Group Policy Creator Owners group can fully manage all Group Policy in the domain. Because this group can control security policies by deploying or removing Group Policy objects (GPOs), membership should be minimal to nonexistent. By default, this group contains the Administrator account from the first in the forest domain.
S-1-5- *<domain SID>*-553	RAS and IAS Servers	Computers that are running the Routing and Remote Access service or Internet Authentication Service (IAS) are added to the group automatically. Members of this group have access to certain properties of User objects, such as Read Account Restrictions, Read Logon Information, and Read Remote Access Information. By default, this group contains no members.
S-1-5-32- 544	Administrators	The built-in Administrator account is the only default member of this group. If the computer is added to a domain, the Domain Admins group is added to the local Administrators group, making all members of the Domain Admins group local administrators on all computers in the domain. Local administrators have complete control over all local resources, including accounts and files. Membership in the local Administrators group should be limited to only those accounts that require this level of access.

Table 3-1   **Well-Known SIDs**

SID	Security Principal	Notes
S-1-5-32-545	Users	Members of the Users group have limited access on the system. By default, members of the Users group have Read/Write permissions only to their own profiles. User security settings are designed to prohibit members of the Users group from compromising the security and integrity of the operating system and installed applications. Users cannot modify computerwide registry settings, operating system files, or program files, and they cannot install applications that can be run by other users. As a result, the Users group is secure to the extent that members cannot run viruses or Trojan horse applications that affect the operating system or other users of the operating system absent some other way to elevate privileges.
S-1-5-32-546	Guests	By default, members of the Guests group are denied access to the Application and System Event logs and are not given the Authenticated Users SID in their access token. By default, the only member of this group is the built-in Guest account, which is disabled by default.
S-1-5-32-547	Power Users	Although members of the Power Users group have less system access than administrators but more than users, they should be considered administrators for security purposes because they can generally elevate their privileges to become administrators without much effort, for instance, by replacing files in %systemroot%\system32 with a version that will elevate the Power User's security context to administer or system.
S-1-5-32-548	Account Operators	Members of the Account Operators group can manage user accounts and groups but cannot manage accounts that are members of Administrators, Domain Admins, Server Operators, Backup Operators, Print Operators, and Account Operators groups. Nor can they change the membership of these groups. Account Operators can also log on locally, including domain controllers.

Table 3-1   **Well-Known SIDs**

SID	Security Principal	Notes
S-1-5-32-549	Server Operators	Members of the Server Operators group can manage resources on the local server, and they have the ability to perform the following tasks: ■ Log on locally and lock, unlock, and shut down the server ■ Create, manage, and delete shared folders ■ Create, manage, and delete printers ■ Back up and restore files and folders
S-1-5-32-550	Print Operators	Members of the Print Operators group can manage printers and print jobs. Print Operators can also log on locally and shut down servers, including domain controllers.
S-1-5-32-551	Backup Operators	Members of the Backup Operators group can back up and restore files on the local computer, regardless of the permissions that protect those files, including files and folders encrypted using the encrypting file system (EFS). Members of this group can also log on to the computer interactively and shut it down. However, Backup Operators cannot change security settings. By default, the Backup Operators group has no members.
S-1-5-32-552	Replicator	The Replicator group is used for file replication in Windows NT. It is not used natively by Windows 2000 and later operating systems.
S-1-5-32-544	Pre–Windows 2000 Compatible Access	The Pre–Windows 2000 Compatible Access group is granted permissions in ACLs on objects in Active Directory. When the first domain controller for each domain is promoted, the DCPROMO Wizard asks whether you want to use this group. If you enable pre–Windows 2000 compatibility, the Everyone group will be made a member of the Pre–Windows 2000 Compatible group. In Windows Server 2003, the Anonymous account is also added to this group because it is no longer included in Everyone by default. This setting is particularly relevant to a domain operating in mixed mode with Windows NT 4.0 backup domain controllers (BDCs) that are also Remote Access Service (RAS) servers. You should not place any members in this group unless you have a clear business or technical requirement to do so.

Table 3-1   **Well-Known SIDs**

SID	Security Principal	Notes
S-1-5-32-555	Remote Desktop Users	The Remote Desktop Users group enables members to log on remotely by using Remote Desktop Services. By default, this group contains no members.
S-1-5-32-556	Network Configuration Operators	Members of the Network Configuration Operators group have limited administrative privileges that allow them to configure networking features, such as IP address configuration of the machine's network adapters for computers running Windows XP. By default, this group contains no members.
S-1-5-32-557	Incoming Forest Trust Builders	A new group in Windows Server 2003, members of this group can create incoming, one-way trusts to the forest.
S-1-5-32-558	Performance Monitor Users	Members of the Performance Monitor Users group, added in Windows Server 2003, can use the Performance Monitor on computers without Administrator privileges.
S-1-5-32-559	Performance Log Users	Members of the Performance Log Users group, added in Windows Server 2003, can remotely access and schedule logging of performance counters.
S-1-5-32-560	Windows Authorization Access Group	Members of this group have access to the computed tokenGroupsGlobalAndUniversal attribute on User objects. For more information on this group, see Microsoft Knowledge Base article 331951, "Some Applications and APIs Require Access to Authorization Information on Account Objects," at *http://support.microsoft.com/kb/331951*.
S-1-5-32-561	Terminal Server License Servers	This SID is held by all terminal server license servers.
S-1-5--<domain SID>-???	HelpServices-Group	This is the group for the Help and Support Center. Support_388945a0 is a member of this group by default.

Understanding Access Tokens

When a user successfully logs on to the network, an access token is created. A copy of the access token is attached to every process and thread that executes on the user's behalf. The access token is used by the computer to determine whether the user has the appropriate authority to access information or to perform an action or operation. The contents of an access token include the following:

- **Account SID**   The SID for the account.

- **Group SIDs**   A list of SIDs for security groups that include the account. In a native mode domain, this list also includes the SID that is stored in the account's SID-History attribute.

- **Rights**   A list of rights and logon privileges that the account possesses directly or through security group membership.

- **Owner**   The SID for the user or security group who, by default, becomes the owner of any object that the user either creates or takes ownership of.

- **Primary group**   The SID for the user's primary security group. This information is used by the POSIX subsystem when using the File Server for Macintosh or Print Server for Macintosh services to provide file and print services from servers running Windows NT 4.0 or later to Macintosh clients. (For information on File Server for Macintosh and Print Server for Macintosh, see Chapter 9, "Managing Security for System Services.")

- **Source**   The process that caused the access token to be created, such as the Session Manager, LAN Manager, or Remote Procedure Call (RPC) Server process.

- **Type**   A value indicating whether the access token is a primary token or an impersonation token. A primary token is an access token that represents the security context of a process. An impersonation token is an access token that a thread within a service process can use to adopt a different security context temporarily, such as the security context for a client of the service.

- **Impersonation level**   A value that indicates to what extent a service can adopt the security context of a client represented by this access token.

- **Statistics**   Information about the access token itself. The operating system uses this information internally.

- **Restricted SIDs**   An optional list of SIDs added to an access token by a process with authority to create a restricted token. Restricting SIDs can limit a thread's access to a level lower than that allowed to the user.

- **Session ID**   A value that indicates whether the access token is associated with the client's logon session.

You can see the details of your access token by using the Whoami.exe utility. Figure 3-1 shows the contents of an access token using Whoami.exe.

```
C:\Program Files\Resource Kit>whoami /all
[User]     = "FINANCE\twalters"   S-1-5-21-833815213-1531848612-1567696815-1105

[Group  1] = "FINANCE\Domain Users"  S-1-5-21-833815213-1531848612-1567696815-513
[Group  2] = "Everyone"  S-1-1-0
[Group  3] = "BUILTIN\Users"  S-1-5-32-545
[Group  4] = "FINANCE\Group Policy Creator Owners"  S-1-5-21-833815213-1531848612-15676968
15-520
[Group  5] = "LOCAL"  S-1-2-0
[Group  6] = "NT AUTHORITY\INTERACTIVE"  S-1-5-4
[Group  7] = "NT AUTHORITY\Authenticated Users"  S-1-5-11

(X) SeChangeNotifyPrivilege        = Bypass traverse checking
(X) SeUndockPrivilege              = Remove computer from docking station

C:\Program Files\Resource Kit>_
```

Figure 3-1   Viewing the contents of an access token using Whoami.exe

On the CD   Whoami.exe is located on the CD included with this book for Windows 2000 and Windows XP. Whoami.exe is in the default installation of Windows Server 2003 and the output is much easier to read.

Configuring Account Security Options

User accounts are a core unit of network security. Consequently, you might want to secure user accounts to a greater degree than the default settings provide. Active Directory enables you to secure individual user accounts in several ways, including these options:

- **Logon Hours**   Determines the days and times of the week, in one-hour periods, when a user can log on to the network. Group Policy provides a setting to log a user off the network forcibly when the allowed logon hours have expired.

- **Logon To (Logon Workstation in Windows 2000)**   Restricts accounts to interactively logging on to only certain computers on the network, specified by the computers' NetBIOS name(s).

- **User Must Change Password At Next Logon**   Forces the user to change his password at the next interactive logon. This is a useful option for new accounts and for facilitating random force password changes.

- **User Cannot Change Password**   This setting prevents users from changing their own passwords. This option is commonly used with shared accounts, such as those used on a kiosk PC.

- **Password Never Expires**   Exempts the password from domain password expiration policy restrictions. You should use this option only when you have a clear business reason, such as for accounts that are not used interactively and thus would not receive a password expiration notification, including service accounts that must run in the domain context.

- **Store Password Using Reversible Encryption**   Stores the password in such a way that it can be decrypted by the operating system to be compared with a plaintext password. This option is required when using legacy protocols such as Challenge Handshake Authentication Protocol (CHAP) or Shiva Password Authentication Protocol (SPAP) for authentication. When this option is selected, the next time the user changes her password, the new password will be stored using a reversibly encrypted form of the password that will be created. This hash is sent across the network for authentication purposes, then is decrypted and matched to the plaintext copy of the password. You should set this option only for accounts that require the plaintext of the password to be known by the domain controller, such as those used in IIS digest authentication and authentication from Macintosh computers.

> **Important**   You cannot set the following account options on the built-in Administrator account in Windows 2000, although they can be set in Windows Server 2003:
>
> - Password Never Expires
> - Store Password Using Reversible Encryption
> - Account Is Disabled (except in Windows XP and Windows Server 2003)
> - Smart Card Is Required For Interactive Logon
> - Account Is Trusted For Delegation
> - Account Is Sensitive And Cannot Be Delegated
> - Use DES Encryption Types For This Account
> - Do Not Require Kerberos Preauthentication

- **Account Is Disabled**   Prevents the account from being used, but does not delete the account. You commonly set this option when a user has been terminated, but items associated with the user account might still be required, such as private keys or mailbox access.

- **Smart Card Is Required For Interactive Logon**   Requires that a smart card be used for interactive logons, which include Terminal Services logons and service logons, but not network logons. Users with this option set on their accounts will not be allowed to log on interactively by using their user names and passwords. In Windows 2000, the password that was previously used for the account before setting this option is preserved. If you enable this setting, you should set the password to a random value to prevent the account from being used for other types of logons, such as network logons. In Windows XP and Windows Server 2003, the password will be automatically reset.

- **Account Is Trusted For Delegation**   Enables services running under this account to perform operations on behalf of other user or computer accounts. This option is available on both computer and user accounts and is commonly used with applications that run on Web servers, as well as on COM servers and servers running Microsoft SQL Server. You should set this option only if you know that it is required for proper functionality of a distributed application, such as on Web server accounts running applications that use Kerberos and Windows Integrated Security with IIS 5.0/6.0. Additionally, for users to use EFS to encrypt files on remote servers, the server's account must be trusted for delegation so that the server can generate a profile locally for the account and user of the user's keys. All domain controllers in Active Directory are implicitly trusted for delegation. In Windows Server 2003, this feature is configured on the Delegation tab of the Properties of an account.

> **Caution**   If an attacker should compromise a computer that is trusted for delegation, he would be able to use the credentials of any user or computer that authenticates to the compromised computer to access other network resources. All computers that have this option set should be protected, physically and logically, in the same manner as your domain controllers because the potential consequences of a compromise are very similar.

- **Account Is Sensitive And Cannot Be Delegated**   Prevents an account from being delegated.

- **Use DES Encryption Types For This Account**   Enables the account to use Data Encryption Standard (DES) encryption, which supports multiple levels of encryption, for interoperability with Unix-based Kerberos realms, rather than the RC4 algorithm used by default in Windows 2000 and Windows Server 2003.

- **Do Not Require Kerberos Preauthentication**   Disables Kerberos preauthentication, which is employed by default, for interoperability with MIT Kerberos v4 realms.

- **Account Expiration**   Automatically disables an account on a specified date in the future. Often organizations will synchronize this setting with the employment duration of temporary, vendor, or intern employees to ensure that such users do not have continued access to the network after their employment ends.

You can control Remote Access permissions for each user account by allowing or denying Remote Access privileges, as well as setting caller ID, callback, static IP addresses, and routes. Once you have converted your domain to native mode, you can configure Remote Access policies to control Remote Access permissions. Remote Access policies allow for much greater granular control of Remote Access permissions and are discussed in depth in Chapter 22, "Implementing Security for Routing and Remote Access." You can also determine whether a user can use Terminal Services and how the terminal server session can be used by configuring Environment, Sessions, Remote Control, and Terminal Services Profile settings on a user account in Active Directory.

Securing Administrative Accounts

Regardless of the security deployed on a network, you will always have one collection of user accounts that are inherently trusted administrators. Administrators are granted rights and permissions that enable them to subvert nearly any security mechanism through their innate rights, by elevation of privileges, or through physical compromise of the hardware. Although you might have thoroughly vetted administrators during the hiring process, the administrator account on most networks is only an ill-protected or ill-created password away. Once compromised, an administrator account is a passport to the entire network and all the data on it. Therefore, it is paramount to secure administrator accounts. In addition to applying account security options, consider the following best practices for administrator accounts:

- **Minimize the number of accounts that are granted Administrator access.**   Windows Server 2003 and Windows 2000 enable you to delegate authority over nearly every object in Active Directory and the file system. Additionally, most services install special management groups. For example, when you install the Domain Name System (DNS) or Dynamic Host Configuration Protocol (DHCP) in Windows Server 2003 or Windows 2000, a domain local group is automatically created with permissions to manage the respective services.

- **Use Restricted Groups to control membership in administrative groups.**   Restricted Groups in Group Policy enable you to control group membership automatically. Domain controllers refresh Group Policy every 5 minutes by default; thus, every 5 minutes, accounts that are not defined in the Restricted Groups policy settings are removed from the security group. If you audit account management events, enforcement of this policy will log an event to the Security Event log under the event ID 637. The Caller field in the error message will list the computer name of the domain controller computer on which the change was made instead of the user account name.

- **Require multiple-factor authentication.**   You can require smart card or other multiple-factor authentications for accounts with administrative access, especially members of the Enterprise Admins group or the Domain Admins group. By doing this, you can avoid the risks associated with passwords and add an element of physical security to using administrator accounts. You can also require smart cards for Terminal Services logons from Windows XP.   /

■ **Restrict the use of administrator accounts to specific computers.**   Because an attacker can easily hijack an administrator's credentials by having previously compromised a computer that an administrator later logs on to, administrator accounts should only be used on computers that can be trusted from logical or physical compromise, such as a server console. Doing this can create management inconveniences. However, for high security requirements, you can use the Logon Workstation account option to restrict the interactive logon to certain computers for administrator accounts. By combining this setting with good physical security of the computers to which the account is restricted, you greatly increase the security of the Administrator account.

■ **Do not use administrative accounts for routine activities.**   By not using administrative accounts for routine activities such as browsing the Internet, you can limit the damage that a virus or Trojan horse could do to a computer if compromised. Instead, use the Secondary Logon (RunAs) service. See the following sidebar for details of this service.

■ **Do not allow users to be local administrators.**   Unless you have a clear business or technical reason for doing so, you should prohibit users from having local administrative privileges. Users who have local administrative privileges can reconfigure the computer and have unrestricted access to the operating system and registry. Not only could this lead to information disclosure if a user shares confidential data without proper security, but many viruses and Trojan horses rely on this level of access to infect computers and spread to other machines. Additionally, users with local administrative access can exempt their machines from Group Policy and otherwise manipulate their computers to render security measures ineffective.

■ **Vet employees before granting them administrative access.**   You should work with your organization's Human Resources department to evaluate network administrators during the hiring process to prevent granting access to potentially malicious or overly careless administrators.

■ **Lock servers and workstations.**   Locking unattended servers and workstations is especially important when using accounts with administrative access. An attacker might need only a few seconds at a computer that is logged on with administrative privileges to compromise the system. You can require smart cards for interactive logons, implement Group Policy to set the smart card removal behavior to lock the workstation when the smart card is removed, and require your administrators to carry their smart cards with them at all times.

Using the RunAs Service

Windows 2000 introduced the RunAs service, although in Windows XP it is sometimes called the Secondary Logon service. This service enables an interactive user to use a different security context to run applications and utilities. You can use the RunAs service at the command line or by pressing the SHIFT key while right-clicking an application, or by creating a shortcut to an application and selecting the option to invoke RunAs automatically. In Windows XP and in Windows Server 2003, you can also use the RunAs service with smart cards. RunAs is not scriptable by any method other than keystroke-passing utilities because the service requires that the password be typed interactively.

If you are logging on to the RunAs service in Windows Server 2003 or Windows XP by using a privileged security context such as an Administrator account, you can create a restricted token for the secondary logon session. An access token will be created for the logged-on user that eliminates all users rights held by the user except Bypass Traverse Checking, including inherent rights received by having membership in the local Administrators group. It also prevents the application from accessing the user's profile and only allows Read access to the registry hives HKEY_LOCAL_MACHINE and HKEY_CURRENT_USER. Because Whoami.exe does not display deny DACLs, you will not see the Administrators group membership denied when inspecting a restricted token except in Windows Server 2003 where Whoami.exe will report "Group used for Deny only."

Implementing Account Password Security

By default, the only protection that accounts are given is user-chosen passwords. Users—and for that matter, administrators—historically have been poor generators of random passwords and even worse at keeping passwords secret. Your organization might have near-perfect security, but one weak password can cause the exposure of company secrets, can be used to launch a successful denial-of-service attack, or can sabotage the network. Unless you employ multifactor authentication methods for all users on your network, you should implement password security settings.

In Windows Server 2003 and Windows 2000, you can create password policies at the domain level for all domain accounts though Group Policy, or at the OU level for local accounts on systems running Windows 2000 and later operating systems that are members of the domain. Table 3-2 lists password policies in Active Directory that you can set for all accounts in the domain. As you might notice, the default settings were made much more secure in Windows Server 2003 in an effort to be more secure out of the box.

Table 3-2   Default Password Policy Settings in Windows Server 2003, Windows 2000, and Windows XP

Setting	Default Value in Windows 2000 and Windows XP	Default Value in Windows Server 2003	Range
Enforce Password History	One password remembered	24 passwords remembered	0 to 24
Maximum Password Age	42 days	42 days	0 to 999
Minimum Password Age	0 days	1 day	0 to 999
Minimum Password Length	0 characters	7 characters	0 to 14
Password Must Meet Complexity Requirements	Disabled	Enabled	Enabled or disabled
Store Password Using Reversible Encryption For All Users In The Domain	Disabled	Disabled	Enabled or disabled

Enforce Password History

You can force users to vary their passwords by setting the Enforce Password History option. When configuring this setting, you must define how many passwords will be retained in history. If you do not configure this setting, the user can reuse a password, even if it has expired, simply by changing the password to the previous password. Set this value to 24, the maximum.

Maximum Password Age

You can also configure how long users can use a password by configuring the Maximum Password Age setting. Users are forced to change their password when the password expires. By enabling this setting, you can avoid a situation in which a user or administrator uses the same password indefinitely. However, configuring passwords to expire too frequently can result in users incrementing passwords in an unsophisticated manner, such as changing WeakPass1 to WeakPass2, or writing the password in an obvious place, such as on a sticky note attached to their monitor.

Tip   The maximum length of time that a user can use a password should be in accordance with the time it would take to successfully issue a brute force attack against the password offline. Unfortunately, no magic calculation exists for this, given the continuing improvements in the hardware and software used to carry out these attacks. The general recommendation from Microsoft absent of any business requirements is to set this to 42 days.

Password Never Expires

The Maximum Password Age setting can be overridden on individual domain and local user accounts by setting the Password Never Expires option on the account. This is commonly used for service accounts, for which no interactive logon exists. Thus, no notification that the password is about to expire is needed.

Minimum Password Age

The Minimum Password Age setting prevents users from circumventing the enforcement of password history and password expiration. For example, if a minimum password age is not configured, at the expiration date of a password, a user could simply change her password to dummy values a sufficient number of times to reuse her previous password. For example, if you keep a password history of 24 previous passwords, the default minimum password age in Windows Server 2003 will prevent users from reusing their existing password for 24 days because they are allowed to change their password only once per day. Microsoft recommends setting this value to 2 days to prevent users from using this technique. The certified Common Criteria configuration of Windows 2000 also recommends setting this value to 2.

> **More Info**   For more information on the Common Criteria evaluation of Windows 2000, see the Microsoft Web site at *http://www.microsoft.com/technet/security /prodtech/win2000/secureev.mspx*.

Minimum Password Length

The Minimum Password Length setting determines the minimum number of characters a user must use in his password. The longer a password is, the more difficult it is to compromise, generally. However, one of the side effects of requiring long passwords is that users will choose passwords that are easy to guess or they will write them down. Part of the problem with users' conception of passwords is the very word *password*, which implies that the secret information should be a single word. When implementing a long minimum password length (10 characters or more), it is essential to educate users on how to create good passwords. For networks with high security requirements, the minimum password length should be set to 12 to 14.

> **Tip**   A password of 20 or more characters can actually be set so that it is easier for a user to remember than an 8-character password. The following is a 39-character password: *The last good book I bought cost $59.99*, for example. It might be simpler for a user to remember a phrase such as this than to remember a shorter password such as A@^Sw23d. To this end, it is helpful to teach users about pass phrases rather than passwords.

Password Complexity Issues

Windows 2000 and later provides a built-in filter, Passfilt.dll, that requires passwords to contain characters of different types. By enabling this filter, you will increase the total keyspace for passwords. For example, without creating a password filter, a user could use only lowercase Roman letters in her password.

The *character set*, or pool of available characters, for lowercase Roman letters is 26. Thus, a password of 8 characters would have 26^8 or 208,827,064,576 (2.089 × 10^11) possible combinations. On the surface, this might seem a mind-boggling number. However, at 1,000,000 attempts per second—a capability of many password-cracking utilities—it would take less than 60 hours to try all possible passwords. If the character set included lowercase Roman letters, uppercase Roman letters, and numbers, it would contain 62 characters. An 8-character password would now have 218,340,105,584,896 (2.18 × 10^14) possible combinations. At 1,000,000 attempts per second, it would take 6.9 years to cycle through all possible permutations. In 2003, however, password brute force guessing tools, such as Rainbow Crack, have evolved to compute all possible hashes in advance. Consequently, passwords with small characters sets, such as LAN Manager authentication uses, are vulnerable if an attacker can acquire the password hash. See Chapter 4, "Configuring Authentication for Microsoft Windows," for detailed information on LAN Manager authentication and password cracking.

In practice, password keyspaces do not completely apply because humans rarely create passwords with a random distribution of characters. Brute force attacks and modified dictionary attacks often employ sophisticated logic to exploit known characteristics of human-created passwords, such as using the number *1* much more frequently than any other number or appending a number to a dictionary word. Although these calculations are important, you must use them carefully and underestimate the time that you think it will take to successfully perform a brute force attack on a password.

The built-in password complexity filter requires all passwords to be at least eight characters in length and include characters from three of these five categories:

- English uppercase letters (A, B, C,...Z)
- English lowercase letters (a, b, c,...z)
- Westernized Arabic numerals (0, 1, 2,...9)
- Nonalphanumeric characters (`~!@#$%^&*_-+=|\{}[]:;"'<>,.?/)
- Unicode characters such as the Euro symbol (€)

Additionally, neither the user name of the user nor any part of the user's name (first, middle, or last) that is longer than 3 characters can be used in the password. You also can use other ASCII characters in passwords, such as é and ½ (Alt+0233 and Alt+0189). Additionally, if your organization has its own password security requirements, you can create a custom password filter and install it on each domain controller. Creating your own password filter requires programming in C++ and familiarity writing programs using Windows APIs. The main difficulty in custom password filters is managing them over time across your organization. Currently, there is no way to centrally manage custom password filters. Each time a new computer is added to the network or a domain controller is promoted you will need to install the custom password filter. Similarly, if the password filter changes, you will need to replace it on all computers on your network.

Creating stringent requirements for password length and complexity does not necessarily translate into users and administrators using strong passwords. For example, IceCream! meets the technical complexity requirements for a password defined by the system, but anyone who looks at the password can see that there is nothing complex about it. By knowing the person who created this password, you might be able to guess his password based on his favorite food. One strategy for educating users on choosing strong passwords is to create a poster describing poor passwords and display it in common areas, such as near the water fountain or copy machine.

Note   Computer accounts have passwords, too. When computers join the domain, they generate a password with which to authenticate. This password is the encryption key for setting secure channels between the computer and domain controllers. For computers running Windows 2000 and later, the computer password is generated using CryptoGenRand and is changed every 30 days by default. Remember, once authenticated, computer accounts are part of the Authenticated Users group; consequently, if an attacker can physically compromise the computer, she can use the computer account to access resources secured with this group. The computer account password is secured on the local computer by the System Key.

Guidelines for creating strong passwords include the following:

- Avoid using words, common or clever misspellings of words, and foreign words.
- Avoid incrementing passwords with a digit.
- Avoid using passwords that others can easily guess by looking at your desk (such as names of pets, sports teams, and family members).

- Avoid using words or phrases from popular culture.

- Avoid thinking of passwords as *words* per se—think secret codes.

- Use passwords that require you to type with both hands on the keyboard.

- Use uppercase and lowercase letters, numbers, and symbols in all passwords.

- Use pass phrases, such as "How did I ever manage to drop the ball?"

- Absent of system restrictions, always go for length.

- Pad passwords with strings of characters. For example, pad your existing password with a repeating string such as BENBENBENBENBEN, which adds 15 characters to the password.

- Use the space character within the password.

> **Warning**   In general, it is good practice to audit passwords regularly to ensure users and administrators are creating strong passwords. Before performing any type of audit on user passwords, you must get formal approval from your company's human resources and legal departments. Privacy laws vary greatly from country to country—and many countries and states specifically prohibit accessing this type of information. Also, if you do perform password audits, make sure you secure the account database on the system where the audit will be performed.

Store Passwords Using the Reversible Encryption For All Users In The Domain Setting

The setting to store passwords using reversible encryption for all users in the domain is required if the domain controller needs the ability to decrypt the password to a plaintext form for use with certain authentication methods, including CHAP, and for use with some Macintosh computers. Setting this option greatly weakens the security of passwords and should be done only if required for the entire domain. This option can be set on individual user accounts rather than at the domain level if only some passwords need to be stored reversibly.

Although you will need to adjust the settings in Table 3-3 for your own organization, at a minimum, you should configure the password policy detailed in the table.

Table 3-3   Recommended Minimum Password Policy Settings

Setting	Value
Enforce Password History	24 passwords remembered
Maximum Password Age	42 days
Minimum Password Age	2 days
Minimum Password Length	8 characters (12 to 14 for networks with high security needs)

Table 3-3   Recommended Minimum Password Policy Settings

Setting	Value
Password Must Meet Complexity Requirements	Enabled
Store Password Using Reversible Encryption For All Users In The Domain	Disabled

> **Tip**   As a best practice, accounts with high levels of access, such as enterprise or domain administrators, should use passwords with at least 15 characters. This will prevent a LAN Manager password hash from being created. LAN Manager password hashes are explained in Chapter 4, "Configuring Authentication for Microsoft Windows."

Account Lockout Settings

You can also set account lockout policies for the entire domain or for local accounts on individual computers by using security policies. You must configure three settings when implementing an account lockout policy, as Table 3-4 shows.

Table 3-4   Default Account Lockout Settings in Windows Server 2003, Windows 2000, and Windows XP

Setting	Default Value	Range
Account Lockout Threshold	Not applicable	1–99,999 minutes (A value of 0 will never reset the number of failed attempts tracked in a given attempt to log on.)
Account Lockout Duration	0 attempts (disabled)	1–999 attempts
Reset Account Lockout Counter After	Not applicable	1–99,999 minutes (A value of 0 will require an administrator to unlock the account.)

Although account lockout settings are common, often they are the cause of numerous support calls to the help desk; in fact, I like to call account lockout the "increase your support costs" feature of Windows account policies. If passwords are appropriate in length and complexity, these settings provide little additional security. On a similar—albeit much more sinister—note, an attacker could easily exploit an account lockout policy to carry out a denial-of-service attack by locking out all user accounts, including service accounts, by running a simple Active Directory Services Interface (ADSI) VBScript.

A better security approach is to educate users and administrators on how to create strong passwords, enable auditing of account logon events, and actively review Audit log files for excessive failed logon attempts that might indicate a brute force or dictionary attack on an account. Doing this can not only greatly improve your security, it can also decrease your organization's support costs. Unfortunately, because of historical reasons, many IT auditors will still cite lack of account lockout policy as a security risk. Weak passwords are the security risk; account lockout does not at all mitigate that risk in a reasonable, effective manner.

 Note   In Windows 2000 and later, members of the Administrator account are not affected by account lockout settings.

Granting Rights and Permissions Using Groups

In Windows Server 2003, Windows 2000, and Windows XP, the capabilities granted to accounts comprise two areas: *rights* and *permissions*. Rights are actions or operations that an account can or cannot perform. Permissions define which resources accounts can access and the level of access they have. Resources include Active Directory objects, file system objects, and registry keys. Although accounts are the central unit of security in the Windows operating system, assigning rights and permissions directly to accounts is difficult to manage and troubleshoot and frequently leads to misapplication of rights and permissions. Consequently, rights and permissions should not be assigned directly to accounts; rather, they should be assigned to groups, and accounts should be placed into groups. Creating a structure of groups to assign rights and permissions is an essential part of securing the Windows operating system.

User Rights and Permissions

The actions an account can perform and the degree to which a user can access information are primarily determined by user rights and permissions. Accounts receive rights and permissions either by having the right or permission assigned directly to the account, or through membership in a group that has been granted the right or permission. The following section provides an overview of user rights. For implementation information on user rights, see Chapter 11, "Creating and Configuring Security Templates."

User Rights

Administrators can assign specific rights to group accounts or to individual user accounts. These rights authorize users to perform specific actions, such as logging on to a system or backing up files and directories. User rights are different from permissions: user rights apply to accounts, and permissions are attached to objects (such as printers or folders). Two types of user rights exist:

- **Privileges**   A right assigned to an account and specifying allowable actions on the network. An example of a privilege is the right to back up files and directories.

- **Logon rights**   A right assigned to an account and specifying the ways in which the account can log on to a system. An example of a logon right is the right to log on to a system locally.

Privileges   Some privileges can override permissions set on an object. For example, a user logged on to a domain account as a member of the Backup Operators group has the right to perform backup operations for all domain servers. However, this requires the ability to read all files on those servers, even files whose owners have set permissions that explicitly deny access to all users, including members of the Backup Operators group. A user right—in this case, the right to perform a backup—takes precedence over all file and directory permissions. The following list shows the privileges that can be granted to an account by assigning user rights. These privileges can be managed with the user rights policy settings in Group Policy.

- **Act As Part Of The Operating System (SeTcbPrivilege)**   Having this privilege literally allows the account or applications running under the account to be part of the trusted computing base. It allows a process to authenticate as any user, and therefore gain access to resources under any user identity. Only low-level authentication services that are highly trusted should require this privilege. The user or process that is granted this privilege might create security tokens that grant more rights than their normal security contexts provide. Do not grant this privilege unless you are certain it is needed.

- **Add Workstations To Domain (SeMachineAccountPrivilege)**   Allows the user to add computers to a specific domain. Users can add only up to 10 computers to the domain by default. To increase the number of computers a user can add to the domain, set the ms-DS-MachineAccountQuota property of the domain naming context to the appropriate value. See the Knowledge Base article 251335, "Domain Users Cannot Join Workstation or Server to a Domain," at *http://support.microsoft.com/kb/251335* for precise steps on how to do this. You can also delegate the user the ability to create computer accounts in an OU.

- **Back Up Files And Directories (SeBackupPrivilege)**   Allows the user to circumvent file and directory permissions to back up the data stored on the system. Specifically, this privilege is similar to granting the following permissions on all files and folders on the local computer: Traverse Folder/ Execute File, List Folder/Read Data, Read Attributes, Read Extended Attributes, and Read Permissions.

- **Bypass Traverse Checking (SeChangeNotifyPrivilege)**   Allows the user to pass through directories to which she otherwise has no access while navigating an object path in any Windows file system or in the registry. This privilege does not allow the user to list the contents of a directory, only to traverse directories, which is often needed to successfully browse Web sites or file shares. Without this right, the operating system will check the ACL of the directory to ensure the user has the Traverse Folder/Execute File ACE.

- **Change The System Time (SeSystemTimePrivilege)**   Allows the user to set the time in the internal clock of the computer. In Windows 2000 and later, by default domain users do not possess this privilege to prevent them from changing their system clock and thereby interfering with Kerberos authentication.

- **Create A Pagefile (SeCreatePagefilePrivilege)**   Allows the user to create and change the size of a pagefile. This is done by specifying a paging file size for a given drive in the Performance Options dialog box, which is accessible through the System Properties dialog box.

- **Create A Token Object (SeCreateTokenPrivilege)**   Allows a process to create a token that it can then use to gain access to local resources when the process uses *NtCreateToken()* or other token-creation APIs. By default, only the Local Security Authority (LSA) can create access tokens.

- **Create Global Objects (SeCreateGlobalPrivilege)**   This privilege was added to Windows 2000 in Service Pack 4 and is included by default in Windows Server 2003. This privilege controls the creation of global system objects by applications, including operations such as file mapping in Terminal Server sessions. This privilege also applies when creating symbolic links in the Object Manager.

- **Create Permanent Shared Objects (SeCreatePermanentPrivilege)**   Allows a process to create a directory object in the Object Manager. This privilege is useful to kernel-mode components that plan to extend the object namespace. Because components running in kernel mode already have this privilege assigned to them, it is not necessary to assign this privilege specifically.

- **Debug Programs (SeDebugPrivilege)**   Allows the user to attach a debugger to any process. Without this privilege, you can still debug programs that you own. This privilege provides powerful access to sensitive and critical system operating components—you should not grant this permission to anyone unless you have clear business reasons to do so, and even then, you should analyze whether alternatives are possible.

- **Enable Computer And User Accounts To Be Trusted For Delegation (SeEnableDelegationPrivilege)**   Allows the user to select the Trusted For Delegation setting on a user or computer object. The user or object that is granted this privilege must have Write access to the account control flags on the user or computer object. A server process either running on a computer that is trusted for delegation or being run by a user who is trusted for delegation can access resources on another computer. The process uses a client's delegated credentials, as long as the client account does not have the Account Cannot Be Delegated account control flag set. Misuse of this privilege or of the Trusted For Delegation settings might make the network vulnerable to sophisticated attacks using Trojan horse programs that impersonate incoming clients and use their credentials to gain access to network resources.

- **Force Shutdown Of A Remote System (SeRemoteShutdownPrivilege)**   Allows a user to shut down a computer from a remote location on the network.

- **Generate Security Audits (SeAuditPrivilege)**   Allows a process to generate entries in the Security log for auditing of object access. The process can also generate other security audits. The Security log is used to trace unauthorized system access.

- **Impersonate Client After Authentication (SeImpersonatePrivilege)**   Allows processes to impersonate users. This privilege was added to Windows 2000 in Service Pack 4. In Windows Server 2003, impersonation is granted only to Administrators, LocalSystem, Network Service, Local Service, and COM+ processes running as specific identities. If your application calls any impersonation function, including SetThreadToken, it might fail unless it has the SeImpersonatePrivilege privilege. For more information on impersonation, see Michael Howard's article "Impersonation Issues" on the MSDN Web site at *http:// msdn.microsoft.com/library/en-us/dncode/html/secure03132003.asp.*

- **Increase Quotas (SeIncreaseQuotaPrivilege)**   This privilege determines who can change the maximum memory that can be consumed by a process This privilege is useful for system tuning but can be abused in a denial-of-service attack. This privilege is named "Adjust memory quotes for a process."

- **Increase Scheduling Priority (SeIncreaseBasePriorityPrivilege)**   Allows a process with Write access to another process to increase the execution priority of that other process. A user with this privilege can change the scheduling priority of a process through the Task Manager.

- **Load And Unload Device Drivers (SeLoadDriverPrivilege)**   Allows a user to install and uninstall device drivers that are not installed by the Plug and Play manager and to control (stop and start) devices. Because device drivers run as trusted (highly privileged) programs, this privilege can be misused to install hostile programs, including rootkits, and give these programs destructive access to resources. This privilege should not be granted widely.

- **Lock Pages In Memory (SeLockMemoryPrivilege)** Allows a process to keep data in physical memory, preventing the system from paging the data to virtual memory on disk. Exercising this privilege might significantly affect system performance. This privilege is obsolete and is therefore never used by default.

- **Manage Auditing And Security Log (SeSecurityPrivilege)** Allows a user to specify object access auditing options for individual resources such as files, Active Directory objects, and registry keys. Object access auditing is not performed unless you have enabled the audit policy settings that enable object auditing. A user with this privilege can also view and clear the security log from the Event Viewer.

- **Modify Firmware Environment Values (SeSystemEnvironmentPrivilege)** Allows modification of the system environment variables, either by a process or by a user through the System Properties dialog box.

- **Perform Volume Maintenance Tasks (SeManageVolumePrivilege)** Allows a user to manage volumes or disks.

- **Profile Single Process (SeProfileSingleProcessPrivilege)** Allows a user to use performance-monitoring tools to monitor nonsystem processes. This privilege is required by the Performance Microsoft Management Console (MMC) snap-in only if it is configured to collect data through Windows Management Instrumentation (WMI).

- **Profile System Performance (SeSystemProfilePrivilege)** Allows a user to use performance-monitoring tools to monitor system processes. This privilege is required by the Performance MMC snap-in only if it is configured to collect data through WMI.

- **Remove Computer From Docking Station (SeUndockPrivilege)** Allows a user to undock a portable computer through the user interface. Of course, even users without this right can use manual overrides or small hammers to remove laptops from docking stations.

- **Replace A Process Level Token (SeAssignPrimaryTokenPrivilege)** Allows a process to replace the default token associated with a subprocess that has been started. This privilege should be held only by the LocalSystem account. It is used, among other things, to create restricted tokens.

- **Restore Files And Directories (SeRestorePrivilege)** Allows a user to circumvent file and directory permissions when restoring backed-up files and directories and to set any security principal as the owner of an object.

- **Shut Down The System (SeShutdownPrivilege)** Allows a user to shut down the local computer. Removing this right for users of terminal server application servers will prevent users from accidentally or intentionally shutting down the server, thereby preventing other users from accessing the system.

- **Synchronize Directory Service Data (SeSyncAgentPrivilege)** Allows a process to read all objects and properties in the directory, regardless of the protection on the objects and properties. This privilege is required to use Lightweight Directory Access Protocol (LDAP) directory synchronization (Dirsync) services.

- **Take Ownership Of Files Or Other Objects (SeTakeOwnershipPrivilege)** Allows a user to take ownership of any securable object in the system, including Active Directory objects, files and folders, printers, registry keys, processes, and threads.

Logon Rights Logon rights are assigned to users and specify the ways in which a user can log on to a system. The following list describes the various logon rights:

- **Access This Computer From A Network (SeNetworkLogonRight)** Allows a user to connect to the computer over the network.

- **Deny Access To This Computer From the Network (SeDenyNetworkLogonRight)** Denies a user the ability to connect to the computer over the network. By default, this privilege is not granted to anyone except the built-in Support account. Use caution when setting this privilege because it is possible to lock yourself out of the system.

- **Log On As A Batch Job (SeBatchLogonRight)** Allows a user to log on using a batch-queue facility. By default, this privilege is granted only to administrators. When an administrator uses the Add Scheduled Task Wizard to schedule a task to run under a particular user name and password, that user is automatically assigned the Log On As A Batch Job right. When the scheduled time arrives, the Task Scheduler service logs the user on as a batch job rather than as an interactive user, and the task runs in the user's security context.

- **Deny Logon As A Batch Job (SeDenyBatchLogonRight)** Denies a user the ability to log on using a batch-queue facility. By default, this privilege is granted to no one.

- **Log On As A Service (SeServiceLogonRight)** Allows a security principal to log on as a service to establish a security context. The LocalSystem, Network Server, and Local Service accounts always retain the right to log on as a service. Any service that runs under a separate account must be granted this right.

- **Deny Logon As A Service (SeDenyServiceLogonRight)**   Denies a security principal the ability to log on as a service to establish a security context.

- **Log On Locally (Allow Log on Locally in Windows Server 2003) (SeInteractive-LogonRight)**   Allows a user to log on at the computer's console and using a Terminal Services session and through IIS. Use caution when setting this privilege because it is possible to lock yourself out of the system by removing this right from your account. In Windows Server 2003, it is possible for a user to establish a Terminal Services session to a particular server without this right because of the addition of the Allow Logon To Terminal Server logon right.

- **Deny Logon Locally (SeDenyInteractiveLogonRight)**   Denies a user the ability to log on at the computer's console. By default, this right is granted to no one. Use caution when setting this privilege because it is possible to lock yourself out of the system.

- **Allow Logon to Terminal Server (SeRemoteInteractiveLogonRight)**   Allows user the right to log on using Terminal Services in Windows XP and Windows Server 2003. When you grant this user right, you no longer have to grant the user the Log On Locally right in addition to this right as was required in Windows 2000 for terminal server access.

- **Deny Logon to Terminal Server**   Denies user the ability to log on using Terminal Services. If the user possesses the Log On Locally right, he will be able to log on at the server console.

You can view the privileges and logon rights assigned to users and computers by using the Showprivs.exe tool, which you can find on the CD included with this book. This command-line tool enables you to enter the name of a privilege or right, and it will return all the accounts and groups that have been assigned that privilege or right. This tool does not list services that have inherent rights or privileges as LocalSystem does for nearly all privileges. Although the Showprivs.exe list is not complete, it certainly is useful.

In Windows 2000 and Windows XP, you can view the privileges that the logged-on user holds by using the Whoami.exe tool, which you can find on the CD included with this book. (Whoami.exe is included as a system file in default installations of Windows Server 2003.) Type **whoami /all** at the command prompt.

Active Directory, File, and Registry Permissions

Active Directory, file, and registry permissions are granted by using DACLs. You grant permissions to objects by creating an ACE for the account or for a group of which the account is a member. File and registry permissions are discussed in depth in Chapter 8, "Controlling Access to Data."

Group Types and Scope

Windows Server 2003, Windows 2000, and Windows XP enable you to organize users and other domain objects into groups to manage rights and permissions. Defining security groups is a major requirement for securing a distributed network.

You can assign the same security permissions to large numbers of accounts in one operation by using security groups. This ensures consistent rights and permissions for all members of a group. Using security groups to assign rights and permissions also means that the ACLs on resources remain fairly static and are much easier to control and audit. User accounts that require access to a specific resource are added to or removed from the appropriate security groups as needed so that the ACLs change infrequently, are smaller, and are easier to interpret.

Special Groups

There are some groups whose membership even administrators cannot manage— these groups are called *special groups*. Membership in a special group is granted to accounts automatically as a result of their activity on the machine or network. It is essential that you understand how these groups function because they are often misused and can seriously impact your network's security if not properly implemented. See Table 3-1 for a listing of the special groups, their SIDs, and a description of each.

Computer Local Groups

Computer local groups are security groups that are specific to a computer and are not recognized elsewhere in the domain or on other computers. These groups are a primary means of managing rights and permissions to resources on a local computer. Several types of built-in local groups exist by default on computers that run Windows Server 2003, Windows 2000, or Windows XP. Figure 3-2 shows local accounts in the Computer Management MMC in Windows 2000 Server.

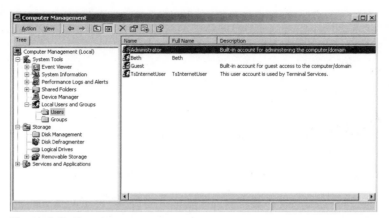

Figure 3-2   Local accounts

> **Tip**   No local accounts on domain controllers exist in Windows Server 2003 and Windows 2000. Domain controllers have a special local Administrator account called the Directory Services Restore Administrator. This account is stored in a normally inaccessible local SAM and can be used only when the computer is interactively booted into Directory Services Restore Mode. You must be at the console to use this account.

The computer local groups follow:

- Administrators
- Backup Operators
- Guests
- Power Users
- Replicator
- Users
- HelpServicesGroup
- Network Configuration Operators
- Remote Desktop Users

Understanding Power Users

The default Windows 2000 and later security settings for Power Users are backward compatible with the default security settings for Users in the Windows NT 4.0 operating system. This allows Power Users to run legacy applications that are not certified for Windows Server 2003, Windows 2000, and Windows XP Professional and therefore cannot be run under the more secure Users context. In a secure environment, you should investigate how to run applications under the Users context, rather than making all users members of the Power Users group. Power Users can perform many systemwide operations, such as changing system time and display settings and creating user accounts and shares. Power Users also have Modify access to the following:

- HKEY_LOCAL_MACHINE\Software
- Program files
- %windir%
- %windir%\system32

If nonadministrators gain permissions to modify files in the %windir%\system32 folder, they can take control of the operating system by replacing the operating system files with malicious files. This is one reason members of the Power Users group must be considered local administrators for all intents and purposes.

In addition to the built-in groups, you can create additional computer local groups that fit the security needs of your organization. You can add global groups from any trusted domain to local groups to grant rights and permissions to local resources. You cannot add computer local groups from one computer to computer local groups on another computer.

More Info   See *Writing Secure Code, Second Edition,* by Michael Howard and David LeBlanc (Microsoft Press, 2003) for more information on determining the rights and permissions required to run applications.

Built-In Domain Groups

Just as built-in computer local groups exist on all computers, built-in groups also exist in Active Directory domains. These built-in groups have predelegated rights and permissions. These are the built-in domain groups:

- Administrators
- Backup Operators
- Server Operators
- Account Operators
- Print Operators
- Pre–Windows 2000 Compatible Group

The domain built-in groups Replicator, Guests, and Users also exist in Active Directory domains and function as though they are computer local built-in groups, but with a scope that includes all computers in the domain.

Domain Local Groups

Domain local groups exist in Windows 2000 or Windows Server 2003 domains after the domains have been converted to native mode. These groups can contain members from anywhere in the forest, trusted forests, or a trusted pre–Windows 2000 domain. Domain local groups can be used only to grant permissions to resources on machines that are members of the domain in which they exist.

Global Groups

Global groups in Windows 2000 and Windows Server 2003 domains can contain accounts from their own domain and can be used to populate ACLs in all trusted domains. Once a domain is converted to native mode, global groups can be nested—that is, they can contain other global groups from the same domain. Global groups never contain accounts or global groups from other domains, regardless of whether the domain is in mixed mode or native mode. Active Directory domains contain several built-in global groups:

- Domain Admins
- Enterprise Admins (Windows Server 2003 and Windows 2000 only)
- Schema Admins (Windows Server 2003 and Windows 2000 only)
- RAS and IAS Servers (Windows Server 2003 and Windows 2000 only)
- Group Policy Creator Owners

Universal Groups

Once you convert an Active Directory domain to native mode, you can use universal security groups. As with global groups, you can use universal groups in any trusted domain. However, universal groups can have members from any domain in the forest. Because of this forestwide scope, membership in universal groups is stored in the global catalog. The global catalog is fully replicated throughout the forest, which means that universal group membership should be kept fairly static, especially in forests where convergence does not occur quickly.

Implementing Role-Based Security

All rights and permissions in Windows Server 2003, Windows 2000, and Windows XP are granted on a discretionary basis—meaning that any account with Full Control, Change Permissions, or Take Ownership permissions can grant or deny permissions on the object to other security principals. To create a secure network, you should create a structure for granting rights and permissions that is scalable, flexible, manageable, and above all else, secure. By using a role-based structure for granting rights and permissions, you can control access to information in this manner. In a role-based structure, rights and permissions are never granted or denied to specific accounts, but instead to groups based on job roles or functions.

To implement role-based security for access control, each type of group is used for a specific purpose to create a discrete separation of the account and the assignment of permissions based on the job function or role of the user. Create domain local groups or local groups, and assign them permissions to resources. Create global groups based on job function or role. Place the global groups in the appropriate domain local groups or local groups, and place users in the appropriate global groups. This process is shown in Figure 3-3. A convenient way to remember this process is by using the mnemonic A-G-DL-P. Accounts are placed into global groups, global groups are placed into domain local groups, and permissions are assigned to domain local groups.

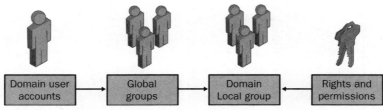

| Domain user accounts | → | Global groups | → | Domain Local group | ← | Rights and permissions |

Figure 3-3   Implementing role-based security

Domain local groups and local groups are assigned permissions to resources based on the permission needed on the resource. For example, a payroll server can use the following local groups:

- Payroll_data_Read
- Payroll_data_Modify
- Payroll_data_FC

> **Tip** Because the icon for domain local, local, and global groups is the same in the user interface, you need to use a meaningful naming convention for group names. Often, lowercase letters are used for domain local group names and local group names, and uppercase letters are used for global group names. Another strategy is to preface each group name with its type, such as DL_*groupname* and GG_*groupname*. Doing this arranges the groups by type when they are alphabetized in the user interface.

Global groups are created based on job functions or roles. For example, a payroll department could contain the following global groups:

- PAYROLL_MGRS
- PAYROLL_ADMINS
- PAYROLL_USERS

After converting to native mode, global groups can be placed in other global groups to further stratify the A-G-DL-P model into A-G-G-DL-P.

Now suppose all payroll managers require Modify rights on the payroll data. After ensuring that payroll managers are members of the PAYROLL_MGRS group, place the group in the Payroll_data_Modify domain local group. All payroll managers will have Modify access on the payroll information.

Universal Groups vs. Global Groups

Once in native mode, Active Directory adds the ability to use universal groups. When should you use universal groups for security purposes?

First, you can use universal groups when more than one resource with the same security needs exists in many domains in the forest and users for these resources exist in many domains in the forest. You cannot gracefully achieve this many-to-many mapping without using universal groups. For example, suppose a forest has an empty root domain and four child domains. Each of these domains has a payroll server for the payroll department that uses domain local groups to assign permission to payroll data. Each domain has a global group for payroll managers containing all the payroll managers from the domain. Instead of adding all four payroll manager groups to servers in all four domains, you create a universal group called All_Payroll_Managers and add the payroll managers global group from each domain into it. Place this group in the appropriate domain local groups on the payroll servers. By doing this, you will have significantly fewer groups to manage and simpler ACLs on resources. When using universal groups, the role-based security structure is A-G-U-DL-P.

Second, you can use universal groups when assigning permissions to Active Directory objects in a multiple-domain forest. The role-based security structure to use in this scenario is A-G-U-P. You will need to do this because objects either will need to move between domains or will not be owned by any specific domain, such as objects in the Configuration container.

The benefits of using a role-based security structure include the following:

- Groups are segmented in discrete areas. Only domain local groups or local groups have permissions assigned to them and contain only global groups or universal groups. Moreover, global groups contain only accounts or other groups.

- Permissions are close to the resources, not the account. This enables resource administrators to be able to control security over the resource, without significant access to accounts.

- When users transfer jobs or are terminated, permissions are not tied to their user accounts, making permission reassignment or removal simpler.

- Permissions can be mapped and traced easily.

- Permissions are controlled by group management, not by changing permissions on resources, making audit logs much easier to read and manage.

- Permissions scale as the number of users increases and the frequency of changes to user accounts increases.

- Authorization can be implemented by assigning the resource owners the sole management of domain local groups or local groups with permission to the resources that they manage.

Best Practices

- **Protect administrative accounts.**   Avoid using administrative accounts for routine computing needs, minimize the number of administrators, and avoid giving users administrative access.

- **Use security groups.**   By properly nesting security groups, you can implement a role-based security model for granting permissions.

- **Apply least privilege.**   Assign users and administrators the least privilege they need to complete their job tasks; this includes delegating privileges and rights appropriately.

- **Create password policies that reflect organizational culture.**   Create policies to enforce the use of passwords that balance complexity, randomness, and length.

- **Educate users and other administrators on how to create strong passwords.**   Despite enabling password policies that enforce the use of technically strong passwords, users make many common mistakes when creating passwords, mistakes that can undermine a well-planned policy.

Additional Information

- Knowledge Base article 315276: "How to Set Logon User Rights by Using the NTRights Utility" (*http://support.microsoft.com/kb/315276*)

- Knowledge Base article 822703: "How to Determine Whether Users Changed Their Passwords Before an Account Lockout" (*http://support.microsoft.com/kb/822703*)

- Account Lockout and Management Tools on the Microsoft Web site: *http://www.microsoft.com/downloads/details.aspx?displaylang=en&familyid=7af2e69c-91f3-4e63-8629-b999adde0b9e* and *http://www.microsoft.com/technet/prodtechnol/windowsserver2003/technologies/security/bpactlck.mspx*

- "The Great Debates: Pass Phrases vs. Passwords" on the Microsoft Web site: *http://www.microsoft.com/technet/community/columns/secmgmt/smarch.mspx*

- "The Great Debates: Pass Phrases vs. Passwords. Part 2 of 3" on the Microsoft Web site: *http://www.microsoft.com/technet/security/secnews/articles/itproviewpoint100504.mspx*

- For developers, see Authorization in the MSDN Platform Library for information on SIDs, privileges, and rights: *http://msdn.microsoft.com/library/en-us/secauthz/security/access_control.asp*

Chapter 4

Configuring Authentication for Microsoft Windows

Authentication attempts to answer the question, "User: How do I know that it is really you?" Ideally, the authenticating database would be able to identify the actual person attempting to access a given account, but this problem has proved frustratingly complex to solve when cost is a consideration, even with the most sophisticated biometrics. Until the technical and economic barriers, not to mention serious privacy issues, can be resolved, authentication revolves around identifying a user by that user's knowledge of a shared secret (for example, a password or PIN) and possibly of something that only that user would possess (for example, a smart card or ID token). This chapter details how network authentication works in Microsoft Windows Server 2003, Windows 2000, and Windows XP.

Storing and Transmitting Credentials

The operating system is responsible for securely storing and transmitting credentials (user names and passwords) for accounts. Windows 2000 and Windows XP support a variety of protocols to transmit credentials across the network to authenticate accounts, including user accounts, computer accounts, and service accounts. The operating system also stores credentials in a variety of formats.

When a user logs on to Windows Server 2003, Windows 2000, or Windows XP by using the Windows Logon dialog box, several components work together to authenticate her credentials securely. Figure 4-1 shows the information flow of authentication.

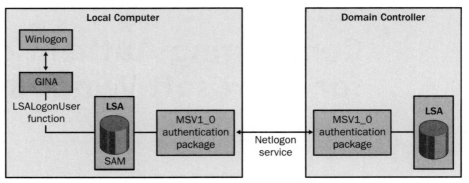

Figure 4-1   Authentication in Windows Server 2003, Windows 2000, and Windows XP

Windows Server 2003, Windows 2000, and Windows XP use Kerberos v5 as the default authentication protocol for domain authentication and also support authentication using the LAN Manager (LM), NT LAN Manager (NTLM), and NT LAN Manager version 2 (NTLMv2) protocols. Because few networks use a single operating system version or applications that use the same authentication methods, Windows Server 2003, Windows 2000, and Windows XP support current and legacy authentication methods to preserve compatibility with downlevel operating systems and applications. As a network administrator, you can, however, tune authentication in the Windows operating system based on your technical requirements.

LAN Manager

LAN Manager authentication is supported in Windows Server 2003, Windows 2000, and Windows XP to support legacy applications as well as some very specific implementations, such as internode authentication within a cluster. LM passwords are limited to 14 characters. For LM authentication, passwords are not stored by the operating system. Instead, passwords are encrypted with the LAN Manager one-way function (OWF), which is formed by converting the password to uppercase characters, adding padding for passwords with fewer than 14 characters, dividing the 14-character password into 7-character halves, and encrypting a constant value with the 7-character halves by using the Data Encryption Standard (DES) encryption algorithm. This process is illustrated in Figure 4-2.

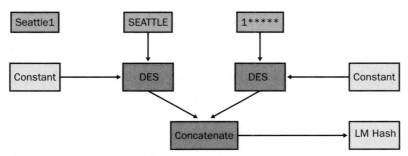

Figure 4-2   LM password storage

When a user authenticates a password by using the LM authentication protocol, the authentication is done with a simple challenge/response interaction from the authenticating domain controller or computer. Figure 4-3 shows the process of authenticating an account by using LM.

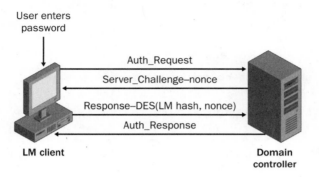

Figure 4-3 LM authentication

In Figure 4-3, the client sends an authentication request to the logon server. The server returns a challenge, which comprises a random number, or nonce. The client then uses the LM password hash to encrypt the nonce by using the DES encryption algorithm. Next, the server decrypts the encrypted nonce from the client by using the LM password it has stored in the accounts database. If the nonce matches the nonce sent to the client, the client's credentials are validated. The NTLM authentication sequence works the same way, albeit with larger nonces. If an attacker is able to capture all packets in a challenge/response authentication sequence, he could attempt brute force attacks on the packets to determine the password; this requires multiple cryptographic operations that, although time-consuming, can reveal weak passwords. Challenge/response sequences are not vulnerable to precomputation attacks because the nonces are random.

By reducing the character set for letters to include only uppercase letters, limiting passwords to 14 characters, and separating passwords into 7-character pieces, LM password hashes are especially vulnerable to brute force and dictionary attacks. Many tools available on the Internet can easily crack most LM password hashes given enough computer power and time. Although the idea had been around for some time, Project Rainbow Crack, made public in 2003, enables individuals to precalculate LM password hashes and store them in a series of tables. The tables need to be generated only once; thus, once an attacker or administrator has obtained the password hash, all that is left is a simple lookup in the table to reveal the plaintext password. All password hashes are vulnerable to precomputation attacks, just as all are vulnerable to brute force attacks within the limits of time and computational power. The precomputation attack on LM authentication works because of the confluence of two important factors:

- **Passwords are not salted.**   A salt value, which is a pseudorandom string, is appended to passwords before they are stored. The value is different on a different system. For example, the plaintext password "Swordfish123" would have different password hashes stored on different systems even though the password is the same. Because LM authentication does not use a salt, the password hash for "Swordfish123" is the same on all systems running the Windows operating system worldwide. This is the primary reason that the Rainbow tables need be generated only one time.

- **A small total number of passwords are available.**   The keyspace for LM authentication is very, very limited. In fact, all LM password hashes, stored in Rainbow tables, can be stored on as few as two DVDs.

> **More Info**   See the Project Rainbow Crack Web site for detailed information on precomputing password hashes at *http://www.antsight.com/zsl/rainbowcrack/*.

Windows Server 2003, Windows 2000, and Windows XP, like Windows NT 4.0, store the LM hash for local accounts in the Security Accounts Manager (SAM) database, which is stored persistently in encrypted partitions of the registry. Windows Server 2003 and Windows 2000 store the LM hash for domain accounts in the Active Directory directory service. You can, however, prevent the Windows operating system from generating and storing LM hashes. Of course, this will also prevent LM authentication from working, but many, if not most, networks running operating systems earlier than Windows 2000 do not rely on LM authentication. Before preventing LM authentication on your network globally, be sure to test critical resources fully for compatibility. The easiest way to do this is to create passwords longer than 14 characters for test accounts and use those accounts to test services and applications. The Windows operating system will not create LM hashes when passwords longer than 14 characters are created. Windows 2000 Service Pack 2 adds functionality that enables you to remove LM password hashes from Active Directory or the local computer SAM databases. Windows Server 2003 and Windows XP also support this. The following table shows the registry key and value to add to the registry to remove LM password hashes. You can also add a custom registry modification to Windows 2000 security templates and deploy the change by using Group Policy.

Location	HKLM\SYSTEM\CurrentControlSet\Control\Lsa
Type	DWORD
Key	NoLMHash

Windows XP and Windows Server 2003 both have a setting in the Security Options section of security templates to do this: "Network Security: Do Not Store LAN Manager Hash Value On Next Password Change." To confuse the matter, Windows XP and Windows Server 2003 look for a registry value, not a key as Windows 2000 does.

The following table shows the key in Windows 2000.

Location	HKLM\SYSTEM\CurrentControlSet\Control\Lsa
Type	Key
Name	NoLMHash

The following table shows the value in Windows XP and Windows Server 2003.

Location	HKLM\SYSTEM\CurrentControlSet\Control\Lsa
Type	DWORD
Value	NoLMHash
Set to	1

You must implement this registry change on all domain controllers in the domain to fully prevent the creation of LM password hashes for domain accounts. Additionally, this change will not take place until users change their passwords the first time after the registry has been changed. You can also prevent the LM authentication protocol from being used by computers running Windows Server 2003, Windows 2000, or Windows XP by setting the LM compatibility to a level greater than 0. We discuss LM compatibility levels in further detail momentarily when we examine NTLMv2.

> **Tip**   Although removing LM hash values is a good step to take to reduce the risk of passwords being revealed, the real issue here is preventing the attacker from accessing the password hashes to begin with. Anyone with physical access to a computer, including the administrators of the system, can extract the password hashes. An attacker with physical access to the network (either wired or wireless) can also sniff entire challenge/response sequences to obtain material to attack through brute force if network communication is not protected.

NTLM

NT LAN Manager, also known as NTLM, first was included in Microsoft Windows NT and is an improvement over the LM authentication protocol. Unlike LM passwords, which use an ASCII character set, NTLM passwords are based on the Unicode character set, are case-sensitive, and can be up to 128 characters long. As with LM, the operating system does not actually store the password; rather, it stores a representation of the password by using the NTLM OWF. The NTLM OWF is computed by using the MD4 hash function, which computes a 16-byte hash, or *digest*, of a variable-length string of text, which in this case is the user's password.

> **Note**   A hash function takes a variable-length binary input and produces a fixed-length binary output that is irreversible. Because the binary output has a relatively short fixed length, theoretically many binary inputs produce the same binary output. However, it is nearly impossible practically to find two different inputs that result in the same hash. This is called a collision. Hash functions that produce predictable collisions, as is the case with SHA0, should not be used. At the time of the writing of this book, research is showing that both MD5 and SHA1 might be vulnerable to predictable collisions, similar to SHA0. Common hash functions include MD4, MD5, and SHA1.

Another difference between NTLM and LM is that NTLM passwords are not broken into smaller pieces before having their hash algorithm computed. NTLM uses the same challenge/response process for authentication as LM does. NTLM is the default authentication provider in Windows NT and Windows 2000 and later when not a member of an Active Directory domain, and even then is still used for many functions. To preserve backward compatibility, the LM hash is always sent with the NT hash. If you have removed LM hashes from the account database by creating a password greater than 14 characters or configuring the NoLMHash registry option, the Windows operating system will create a null value for the LM hash. Although this value cannot be used to authenticate the user, the null value will still be transmitted with the NLTM authentication sequence.

NTLMv2

NTLMv2, the second version of the NTLM protocol, was first available in Windows NT 4.0 Service Pack 4 and is included in Windows 2000 and later. NTLMv2 passwords follow the same rules as NTLM passwords; however, NTLMv2 uses a slightly different process for authentication. NTLMv2 also requires that the clocks of clients and servers be within 30 minutes of each other.

If both the client and the server support NTLMv2, enhanced session security is negotiated. This enhanced security provides separate keys for message integrity and confidentiality, provides client input into the challenge to prevent chosen plaintext attacks, and uses the Hash-Based Message Authentication Code (HMAC)-MD5 algorithm for message integrity checking. Because the datagram variant of NTLM does not have a negotiation step, use of otherwise-negotiated options (such as NTLMv2 session security and 128-bit encryption for message confidentiality) must be configured. Table 4-1 lists the registry key for setting NTLM negotiation options.

Table 4-1   Setting NTLM Negotiation Options

Location	HKLM\SYSTEM\CurrentControlSet\Control\Lsa\MSV1_0\
Type	DWORD
Value	NtlmMinServerSec
Default value	0x00000000

Table 4-2 lists the registry key for configuring the levels of NTLMv2 support.

Table 4-2   Configuring the Levels of NTLMv2 Support

Location	HKLM\SYSTEM\CurrentControlSet\Control\Lsa\MSV1_0\
Type	DWORD
Value	NtlmMinClientSec
Default value	0x00000000

Table 4-3 lists the values for the client negotiation options just described.

Table 4-3   Values for Setting NTLMv2 Client Negotiation Options

Value	Description
0x00000010	Message integrity
0x00000020	Message confidentiality
0x00080000	NTLMv2 session security
0x20000000	128-bit encryption

Tip   You can combine multiple NTLMv2 options by performing a logical OR on the settings in Table 4-3.

Enable NTLMv2 by setting the LM compatibility level using Group Policy. The six LM compatibility settings are described in Tables 4-4 and 4-5. Table 4-4 describes the impact on the authenticating client. Table 4-5 describes the impact on the authenticating server. As you can see, levels 0 through 3 have no impact on which authentication protocols are accepted by the computer, whereas levels 4 and 5 do not impact which protocols are sent.

Table 4-4   Authenticating Client Impact of LAN Manager Compatibility Levels

Level	Sends	Accepts	Prohibits Sending
0	LM, NTLM,	LM, NTLM, NTLMv2	NTLMv2, Session security
1	LM, NTLM, Session security	LM, NTLM, NTLMv2	NTLMv2
2	NTLM, Session security	LM, NTLM, NTLMv2	LM and NTLMv2
3	NTLMv2, Session security	LM, NTLM, NTLMv2	LM and NTLM

Table 4-5   Authenticating Server Impact of LAN Manager Compatibility Levels

Level	Sends	Accepts	Prohibits Accepting
4	NTLMv2, Session security	NTLM, NTLMv2	LM
5	NTLMv2, Session security	NTLMv2	LM and NTLM

Setting LM compatibility to value 2 on all of your Windows-based computers will prevent LM authentication from being sent, but will allow all computers to accept it. Setting all client computers to value 2 and all server computers to value 4 will ensure than no computer sends LM and only client computers accept it. As you can see, setting LM compatibility is not exactly straightforward. Rather than making a global change in LM compatibility, you should consider rolling out the change in stages to simplify troubleshooting if you should run into application compatibility problems. You can do this both by slowly increasing the LM compatibility on computers and by deploying higher compatibility levels only to certain machines by using Group Policy. Windows-based computers do not negotiate LM protocols; if the authentication protocol the client uses to start the sequence is not supported by the server, the authentication fails. The client computer will not attempt to fall back on another authentication protocol. The registry key for setting LM compatibility levels is shown in Table 4-6. You can also set this option using Group Policy in the Security Options portion of the Security Templates.

Table 4-6   Setting LM Compatibility Levels

Location	HKLM\SYSTEM\CurrentControlSet\Control\Lsa
Type	DWORD
Key	LMCompatibilityLevel
Default value	0 in Windows 2000 and Windows XP, 2 in Windows Server 2003

Kerberos

Kerberos v5 is the default authentication protocol for computers running Windows Server 2003, Windows 2000, and Windows XP that are members of Active Directory. Windows operating systems earlier than Windows 2000 do not support the use of Kerberos and will use one of the LM authentication methods. The implementation of Kerberos in the Windows operating system is compliant with RFC 1510 and is interoperable with other Kerberos v5 realms that are RFC 1510 compliant with some minor configuration. Kerberos provides the following benefits:

- **Mutual authentication**   Kerberos enables the client to verify a server's identity, one server to verify the identity of another, and the client to verify its identity to the server.

- **Secure transmission over the wire**   Kerberos messages are encrypted with a variety of encryption keys to ensure no one can tamper with the data in a Kerberos message. Furthermore, the actual password is not sent across the network when using Kerberos. This does not mean, however, that an attacker cannot carry out a brute force attack against an intercepted authentication sequence—in fact, RFC 1510 specifically mentions this limitation: "The Kerberos protocols generally assume that the encryption used is secure from cryptanalysis; however, in some cases, the order of fields in the encrypted portions of messages are arranged to minimize the effects of poorly chosen keys. It is still important to choose good keys. If keys are derived from user-typed passwords, those passwords need to be well chosen to make brute force attacks more difficult. Poorly chosen keys still make easy targets for intruders." Because passwords are used as the base key material, users still must choose strong passwords.

- **Prevention of replay of authentication packets**   Kerberos minimizes the possibility of someone obtaining and reusing a Kerberos authentication packet by using timestamps as an authenticator. By default in Windows 2000 and later, all system clocks are synchronized with the domain controller that authenticated them through the Network Time Protocol (NTP). For Kerberos tickets to remain valid, the system clocks must be synchronized to within 5 minutes of each other.

- **Delegated authentication**   Windows services impersonate clients when accessing resources on clients' behalf. Kerberos includes a proxy mechanism that enables a service to impersonate its client when connecting to other services. Among other things, this allows for n-tier applications to use user credentials on back-end systems without relying on duplicated accounts or passthrough authentication as would be required with LM authentication protocols. Windows Server 2003 provides a safer mechanism to use delegation through constrained delegation and supports other authentication protocols through protocol translation.

The following four components allow Kerberos v5 authentication between client computers and users that use Kerberos to domain controllers that run Windows Server 2003 or Windows 2000:

- **Key distribution center (KDC)**   The network service that supplies both ticket-granting tickets (TGTs) and service tickets to users and computers on the network. The KDC manages the exchange of shared secrets between a user and a server when they authenticate with each other. The KDC contains two services: the Authentication Service and the Ticket Granting Service. The Authentication Service provides the initial authentication of the user on the network and provides the user with a TGT. Whenever users request access to a network service, they supply their TGT to the Ticket Granting Service. The Ticket Granting Service then provides the user with a service ticket for authentication with the target network service. In an Active Directory network, the KDC service runs on all domain controllers.

- **Ticket-granting ticket (TGT)**   Provided to users the first time they authenticate with the KDC. The TGT is a service ticket for the KDC. Whenever the user needs to request a service ticket for a network service, she presents the TGT to the KDC to validate that she has already authenticated with the network. For additional security, the Windows operating system verifies, by default, that the user account is still active every time a TGT is presented to the KDC. In other words, the KDC verifies that the account has not been disabled. If the account has been disabled, the KDC will not issue any new service tickets to the user. In Windows 2000 when the user's TGT is received, the server that has been trusted for delegation can request service tickets for the user to any other service on the network. In Windows Server 2003, the server can directly request a session ticket through protocol translation. Also different in Windows Server 2003, by using their Service Principal Name (SPN) you can determine which services the computer can delegate to. This is a huge security improvement over delegation in Windows 2000. Figure 4-4 shows the Delegation tab of a computer account in Windows Server 2003.

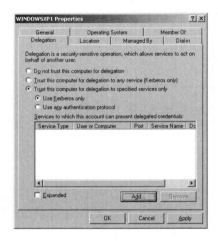

Figure 4-4   Delegation options in Windows Server 2003

- **Service ticket**   Provided by a user whenever he connects to a service on the network. The user acquires the service ticket by presenting the TGT to the KDC and requesting a service ticket for the target network service. The service ticket contains the target server's copy of a session key and contains information about the user who is connecting. This information is used to verify that the user is authorized to access the desired network service by comparing the authentication information—namely, the user's security identifier (SID) and his group SIDs—against the discretionary access control list (DACL) for the object that he is attempting to access. The service ticket is encrypted using the key that is shared between the KDC and the target server. This ensures that the target server is authenticated because only the target server can decrypt the session key.

- **Referral ticket**   Issued any time a user attempts to connect to a target server that is a member of a different domain. The referral ticket is actually a TGT to the domain where the resource is located. The referral ticket is encrypted using an interdomain key between the initial domain and the target domain that is exchanged as part of the establishment of transitive trust relationships.

All Kerberos authentication transactions will be composed of some combination of these three message exchanges:

- **Authentication Service Exchange**   Used by the KDC to provide a user with a logon session key and a TGT for future service ticket requests. The Authentication Service Exchange comprises a Kerberos Authentication Service Request (*KRB_AS_REQ*) sent from the user to the KDC and a Kerberos Authentication Service Reply (*KRB_AS_REP*) returned by the KDC to the user.

- **Ticket-Granting Service Exchange**   Used by the KDC to distribute service session keys and service tickets. The service ticket that is returned is encrypted using the master key shared by the KDC and the target server so that only the target server can decrypt the service ticket. A Ticket-Granting Service Exchange comprises a Kerberos Ticket-Granting Service Request (*KRB_TGS_REQ*) sent from the user to the KDC and a Kerberos Ticket-Granting Service Reply (*KRB_TGS_REP*) returned by the KDC to the user.

- **Client/Server Authentication Exchange**   Used by a user when presenting a service ticket to a target service on the network. The message exchange comprises a Kerberos Application Request (*KRB_AP_REQ*) sent from the user to the server and a Kerberos Application Response (*KRB_AP_REP*) returned by the target server to the user.

To use the Client/Server Authentication Exchange, the user enters her login name, password, and domain in the Windows Logon dialog box. The client computer then locates a KDC by querying the Domain Name System (DNS) server. Next, the user's computer sends a Kerberos Authentication Service Request (*KRB_AS_REQ*) to the domain controller. The user's account information and the current computer time are encoded by using the long-term key shared between the user's account and the KDC. Finally, the authentication service at the KDC authenticates the user, generates a TGT for her, and sends the TGT to her in a Kerberos Authentication Service Response (*KRB_AS_REP*) message.

When a user authenticates herself by using Kerberos, a series of packets is exchanged to complete the validation of her credentials. Figure 4-5 illustrates this process. The user sends a Ticket-Granting Service Exchange Request (*KRB_TGS_REQ*) to the KDC to acquire a service ticket for her computer. The *KRB_TGS_REQ* contains an authenticator and the TGT that was issued to the user. The Ticket Granting Service of the KDC checks the TGT and the authenticator. If both are valid, the Ticket Granting Service generates a service ticket and sends it back to the user as a Ticket-Granting Service Response (*KRB_TGS_REP*). At the client computer, the service ticket is presented to the Local Security Authority, which will create an access token for the user. (We discuss the Local Security Authority in a moment.) From then on, any process acting on behalf of the user can access the local machine's resources.

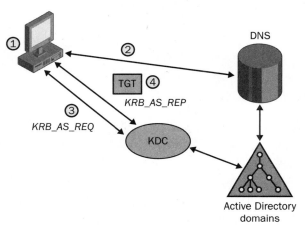

Figure 4-5   Initial Kerberos authentication

This sequence provides the user with the proper TGT. Now the user must acquire a service ticket for that computer. The following steps and Figure 4-6 explain how the service ticket for the computer is acquired.

1. The user sends a Ticket-Granting Service Request (*KRB_TGS_REQ*) to the KDC to acquire a service ticket for the target computer. The *KRB_TGS_REQ* includes the TGT and an authenticator.

2. The Ticket Granting Service of the KDC checks the authenticator and the TGT, generates a new service ticket, and sends it back to the user as a Kerberos Ticket-Granting Service Response (*KRB_TGS_REP*). The service ticket is encrypted by using the target service's long-term key, which is known only by the KDC and the target service.

3. The user sends the service ticket and an authenticator to the target server by using a Kerberos Application Request (*KRB_AP_REQ*).

4. The target server verifies the ticket with the authenticator, decrypts the session key by using the master key that is shared with the KDC, and sends back an authenticator to the user in a Kerberos Application Response (*KRB_AP_REP*). This provides mutual authentication of the user and server.

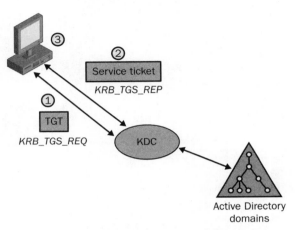

Figure 4-6   Obtaining a Kerberos session ticket

You can view the Kerberos tickets that have been issued to your user and computer accounts by using either Klist.exe, a command-line tool, or Kerbtray.exe, a GUI tool. Both of these utilities not only display the tickets, but also all their properties and expiration dates.

After initially authenticating with the network, the user must authenticate with other computers as she accesses resources on them. Every time the user connects to a resource or service on a remote computer, she has to perform a network authentication. Figure 4-7 shows how Kerberos clients, KDCs, and services communicate.

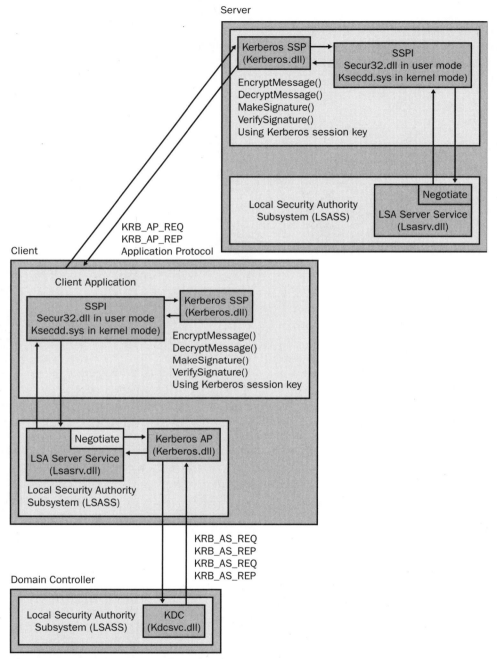

Figure 4-7   Communication flow of Kerberos in Windows 2000 and Windows Server 2003

Storing Secrets in Windows

In addition to storing passwords in Active Directory or SAM databases, Windows Server 2003, Windows 2000, and Windows XP store passwords and other secrets in other locations for a variety of purposes.

LSA Secrets

The Local Security Authority (LSA) maintains information about all aspects of local operating system security. The LSA performs the following tasks:

- Authenticates users
- Manages local security policy
- Manages audit policy and settings
- Generates access tokens

In addition, the LSA stores information used by the operating system, known as *LSA secrets*. LSA secrets include items such as persistently stored Remote Access Service (RAS) information; trust relationship passwords; and user names, passwords, and account names. Perhaps most important, account names and passwords for services that run under a user account context are stored as LSA secrets. LSA secrets can be revealed locally by accounts with the Debug Programs user right. Consequently, you should be careful about the information applications have stored in LSA secrets. Attackers who physically compromise the computer or become system administrators can easily gain access to the information stored as LSA secrets if no other precautions are taken, such as using the System Key (Syskey.exe).

 More Info   *Writing Secure Code, Second Edition,* by Michael Howard and David LeBlanc (Microsoft Press, 2003) contains detailed information and code samples of how to retrieve LSA secrets. Additionally, you can view most LSA secrets by using LSADUMP2.exe from BindView. The tool is available at *http://razor.bindview.com /tools/.*

Using System Key (Syskey.exe)

The System Key utility was first available in Windows NT 4.0 Service Pack 2 and is enabled by default in Windows Server 2003, Windows 2000, and Windows XP. You can configure the System Key by typing **syskey** at the command prompt if you are an administrator on the computer. The System Key is the master key used to protect the password encryption key and the computer account password; therefore, protection of the System Key is a critical system security operation. You have three options for managing the System Key:

- **Level 1**   Uses a machine-generated random key as the System Key and stores the key on the local system. Because the key is stored on the operating system, it allows for unattended system restart. By default, System Key Level 1 is enabled on all computers running Windows 2000 and later operating systems.

- **Level 2**   Uses a machine-generated random key and stores the key on a floppy disk. The floppy disk with the System Key is required for the system to start before the system is available for users to log on. Because the System Key is stored on the floppy disk, the operating system is vulnerable to destruction of the floppy disk, which would render the operating system unable to boot.

- **Level 3**   Uses a password chosen by the administrator to derive the System Key. The operating system prompts for the System Key password when the system begins the initial startup sequence, before the system is available for users to log on. The System Key password is not stored anywhere on the system; instead, an MD5 hash of the password is used as the master key to protect the password encryption key. If the password is forgotten, the operating system will be rendered unable to boot.

Setting the System Key to Level 2 or Level 3 greatly increases the security of the operating system and the secrets it contains (such as contents of the SAM database and LSA secrets) in the event an attacker physically compromises the computer. However, the Level 2 and Level 3 settings can be difficult to manage because you cannot recover forgotten or lost keys. If a key is lost, the computer will not be able to boot. You should develop a secure method of archiving System Keys if you decide to implement System Key Level 2 or Level 3 on your network. In most corporate environments, using Syskey in mode 2 and 3 is not feasible because of the potential loss of data or availability interruption. The bottom line is that you must provide risk-adequate physical security for computers that store critical information, including credentials for other accounts.

Data Protection API

The Data Protection API (DPAPI) enables secrets to be stored securely by applications by using a key derived from the user's password. The encryption of secrets can only be done locally, unless roaming profiles are used. If the user's password is reset, the key used for DPAPI will be lost unless it has been previously archived. DPAPI is available only in Windows Server 2003, Windows 2000, and Windows XP. By using DPAPI, applications can store the encrypted information in any manner, for example, in the registry or a database. DPAPI is used by Windows XP and Windows Server 2003 to protect encrypting file system (EFS) keys in Workgroup scenarios.

Cached Credentials

By default, Windows Server 2003, Windows 2000, and Windows XP cache the credentials of domain accounts used to log on to the network at the local computer. The credentials include the user's user name, password, and domain. Rather than storing the actual credential information, the information is stored in an irreversibly encrypted form and on the local computer. After a user has successfully logged on to the network from the computer once, he can use his domain credentials, even if the computer is not attached to the network or if no domain controllers are available. This functionality is critical to laptop users and users in branch offices without local domain controllers. You can control the number of credentials stored on a computer at any time by setting the registry key shown in Table 4-7.

Table 4-7   Controlling the Number of Stored Credentials on a Computer

Location	HKEY_LOCAL_MACHINE\Software\Microsoft\Windows NT \Current Version\Winlogon\
Type	REG_SZ
Key	CachedLogonsCount
Default value	10
Recommended value	0–50, depending on your security needs

In high-security networks, you might want to set the number of cached credentials to 0. This setting requires all users of the computer to have their domain account credentials validated by a domain controller. This prevents a user who has been terminated from disconnecting her computer from the network, logging on by using cached credentials, and destroying information. When you implement this setting, laptop users can log on only when connected to the network, greatly limiting their mobility. Although the cached credential verifier is irreversibly encrypted, it is not invulnerable to brute force attack; hence, the cached credential is resistant to brute force attacks as much as the user has chosen a strong password.

Credential Manager

Windows XP introduces a new method of managing credentials as well as the credentials of a user who is logged on that is also implemented in Windows Server 2003. This functionality is provided by the Credential Manager, labeled Stored User Names And Passwords in Control Panel. The Credential Manager dynamically and manually creates credential sets (a user name and password) for resources that are available in the user interface and from the command line. You can manage the following types of credentials with the Credential Manager:

- User names and passwords

- X.509 certificates, including smart cards

- Passport accounts

> **Note**   The Credential Manager and DPAPI are long-term replacements for the Protected Storage service, which is no longer considered a secure method of storing secrets. The most significant Windows application that still uses the P-store is Microsoft Internet Explorer, which stores Auto-Complete information, including names and passwords used for forms-based authentication. See Chapter 12, "Managing Microsoft Internet Explorer Security and Privacy," for more information on the Protected Storage service.

Best Practices

- **Remove LM hashes.**   If LAN Manager authentication is not used on your network, remove the LM password hashes from all domain controllers and local computers.

- **Configure LM compatibility.**   Set the LM compatibility to the highest level that applications on your network will support.

- **Upgrade to Windows Server 2003 if you are using delegation.**   Because a computer that is trusted for delegation can use the credentials of any user who authenticates to it on any computer on the network, in Windows 2000 a security compromise of that computer could cause the compromise of the entire domain or forest. Constrained delegation greatly helps limit the potential damage if a computer that is trusted for delegation is compromised.

Additional Information

- The following Knowledge Base articles:
  - ❑ 147706: "How to Disable LM Authentication on Windows NT" (*http://support.microsoft.com/kb/147706*)
  - ❑ 299656: "How to prevent Windows from storing a LAN Manager hash of your password in Active Directory and local SAM databases" (*http://support.microsoft.com/kb/299656*)
  - ❑ 239869: "How to Enable NTLM 2 Authentication" (*http://support.microsoft.com/kb/239869*)
  - ❑ 102716: "User Authentication with Windows NT" (*http://support.microsoft.com/kb/102716*)
  - ❑ 175641: "LMCompatibilityLevel and Its Effects" (*http://support.microsoft.com/kb/175641*)
  - ❑ 266280: "Changing User Rights from a Batch File or Command Line" (*http://support.microsoft.com/kb/266280*)
- RFC 1510: "The Kerberos Network Authentication Service (v5)"
- RFC 3244: "Microsoft Windows 2000 Kerberos Change Password and Set Password Protocols"

> **Note** The two articles above can be accessed through the Request for Comments repository. Go to *http://ietf.org/rfc.html* and enter the RFC number in the RFC Number text box.

- "Windows 2000 Kerberos Authentication" white paper (*http://www.microsoft.com/windows2000/techinfo/howitworks/security/kerberos.asp*)
- "Data Protection and Recovery in Windows XP" white paper (*http://www.microsoft.com/technet/prodtechnol/winxppro/support/DataProt.asp*)
- "Troubleshooting Kerberos Delegation" white paper (*http://www.microsoft.com/technet/prodtechnol/windowsserver2003/technologies/security/tkerbdel.mspx*)
- "Kerberos Authentication in Windows Server 2003" white paper (*http://www.microsoft.com/windowsserver2003/technologies/security/kerberos/default.mspx*)
- "Microsoft Windows Server 2003: Kerberos Protocol Transition and Constrained Delegation" white paper (*http://www.microsoft.com/technet/prodtechnol/windowsserver2003/technologies/security/constdel.mspx*)

Chapter 5

Configuring Security on Active Directory Objects and Attributes

All objects and attributes in the Active Directory directory service are individually secured through the use of discretionary access control lists. Although the default security on Active Directory might be suitable for your organization, you might need to adjust the security of objects or attributes to increase the overall security of Active Directory. You also might need to delegate authority over objects or attributes, or create custom objects and attributes that need to have security defined for them. For each of these situations, you must know how Active Directory objects are secured by default and how you can configure permissions.

Understanding the Active Directory Schema

All the objects that you can create in Active Directory and all their properties are defined in the Active Directory Schema. In Microsoft Windows Server 2003 and Windows 2000, the only copy of the schema is hosted by the domain controller that holds the schema flexible single-master operation (FSMO) role, which by default is the first domain controller in the forest. The schema is replicated from the schema master to all domain controllers in the forest through normal Active Directory replication. In the schema, objects and properties are defined as object classes and attributes. Once an object class has been defined and attributes assigned to it, you can instantiate, or create, objects of that class.

Attributes

The attributes defined in the schema represent the possible properties that can be used in object classes. Attributes are defined in the schema only one time and are reused for each object class with which they are associated. For example, nearly every object class includes the attribute *cn*, which will be populated with the common name of the object in the Lightweight Directory Access Protocol (LDAP) naming convention. Table 5-1 lists the contents of an attribute.

Table 5-1   Contents of an Attribute

Contents	Description
Common name	LDAP display name of the attribute.
Description	Description of the attribute.
X.500 object ID (OID)	Object identifier for the attribute.
Globally unique identifier (GUID)	128-bit randomly generated number that uniquely identifies the attribute.
Syntax	Data type of the attribute.
Range	Range of values for the attribute. For integers, range defines the minimum and maximum value; for strings, range defines the minimum and maximum length.
Multi-/single value	Defines whether the attribute will contain one value or more than one value.
Index	Determines whether the attribute is indexed.
Global Catalog	Determines whether the attribute is replicated to the Global Catalog for all objects that use it.
Security descriptor	Defines the base security for the attribute.
Metadata	Represents data used by Active Directory for internal processing, such as replication metadata.

Members of the Schema Admins group can add attributes to the schema of a forest. Attributes can be deleted in Windows Server 2003, but they cannot be deleted in Windows 2000; however, they can de deactivated, which prohibits them from being used in object classes.

Classes

Object classes are collections of attributes that can be instantiated to create objects. Active Directory is based on the X.500 1993 specification for directory services that defines the hierarchal structure of classes. X.500 requires that object classes be assigned to one of three categories:

- **Structural classes** Structural classes are the only kind of class from which you can create objects in Active Directory. A structural class can be used in defining the structure of the directory and is derived from either an abstract class or another structural class. A structural class can include any number of auxiliary classes in its definition. For example, *user* and *organizationalUnit* are structural object classes.

- **Abstract classes** Abstract classes are templates that are used only to derive new structural classes. Abstract classes cannot be instantiated in the directory. This means that no object can belong to an abstract class only; each object of an abstract class must also belong to some structural subclass. A new abstract class can be derived from an existing abstract class. Classes of the abstract category exist for the sole purpose of providing attributes for subordinate classes, referred to as *subclasses*. A subclass contains all mandatory and optional attributes of the class from which it is derived, known as its *superclass*, in addition to those attributes specific to the class itself. Likewise, a subclass of a subclass contains all attributes of both its superclasses, and so forth.

- **Auxiliary classes** Auxiliary classes are similar to include files in the C programming language; they contain a list of attributes. Adding the auxiliary class to the definition of a structural or abstract class adds the auxiliary class's attributes to the definition. An auxiliary class cannot be instantiated in the directory, but new auxiliary classes can be derived from existing auxiliary classes. For example, the *securityPrincipal* class is an auxiliary class, and it derives its attributes from the parent abstract class named *top*. Although you cannot create a security principal object in the directory (because auxiliary classes cannot have instances), you can create an object of the structural class *user*, which has the *securityPrincipal* class as an auxiliary. The attributes of the *securityPrincipal* class contribute to making the *user* object recognizable to the system as a security account. Similarly, the *group* class has *securityPrincipal* as an auxiliary class.

An object class is defined by the attributes that are tagged as either mandatory or optional. Mandatory attributes must be populated with values when an object is created, whereas optional attributes can have null values.

Security on the Active Directory Schema

Before viewing the Active Directory Schema, you must register the schema management .dll file. You can do this by typing **regsvr32 schmmgmt.dll** at the command prompt or in the Run command and then adding the Active Directory Schema Microsoft Management Console (MMC) snap-in to a blank MMC. You can also automatically register the schema management .dll file and all other management .dll files by installing the Windows Server 2003 and Windows 2000 Administrator's Pack. You do this by running Adminpak.msi from any server that runs Windows Server 2003 or Windows 2000 or from the installation CD.

The schema FSMO is read-only by default. Only members of the Schema Admins group can mark the schema as writeable. Once the changes to the schema have been made, the schema must replicate to all domain controllers in the forest.

Because modifications to the schema are difficult to irreversible, you should exercise caution when making modifications or extensions to the schema. You should also ensure that the Schema Admins group has no members unless the schema is in the process of being modified or extended. Only members of the Enterprise Admins group and the Domain Admins from the forest root domain can manage membership in the Schema Admins group.

Configuring DACLs to Secure Active Directory Objects

All objects and their properties in Active Directory have security descriptors to control access to the object and the values of the object's attributes. As with NTFS file system objects, the Active Directory object's security descriptor includes a discretionary access control list (DACL) and a system access control list (SACL) in addition to the object's ownership data. Figure 5-1 shows a security descriptor.

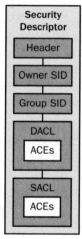

Figure 5-1   Contents of a security descriptor for Active Directory objects and attributes

What Are DACLs?

DACLs can be configured at the discretion of any account that possesses the appropriate permissions to modify the configuration, including Take Ownership, Change Permissions, or Full Control permissions. A security descriptor consists of several elements, as described in this list:

- **Header**   Metadata pertaining to the access control entries (ACEs) associated with the DACL.

- **SID (user)**   The security identifier (SID) of the owner of the object.

- **SID (group)**   The security identifier of the built-in Administrators or Domain Admins group if the account that owns the object is a member of either of these groups.

- **Generic deny ACEs**   Access control entries that deny access to an account or security group based on their SIDs. These ACEs can be inherited from the object's parent or assigned directly to the object, and they are specific to the object and child objects based on the security settings defined in the object class in the schema.

- **Generic allow ACEs**   Access control entries that allow access to objects to an account or security group based on their SIDs. These ACEs can be inherited from the object's parent or assigned directly to the object, and they are specific to the object and child objects.

- **Object-specific deny ACEs**   Access control entries that deny access to child objects to an account or security group based on their SIDs. These ACEs can be inherited from the object's parent or assigned directly to the object, and they apply to specific classes of child objects.

- **Object-specific ACEs**   Access control entries that deny access to an account or security group based on their SIDs. These ACEs can be inherited from the object's parent or assigned directly to the object, and they apply to specific classes of child objects.

Table 5-2 shows the settings of an example DACL an OU might have.

Table 5-2   Example of a DACL

Group	Permissions	Apply to
Enterprise Admins	Allow Full Control	This object and all child objects (Generic ACE)
Authenticated Users	Allow Read	This object (Generic ACE)
Security Managers	Allow Reset Password	User objects (Object-specific ACE)

Figure 5-2 displays the user interface for this DACL.

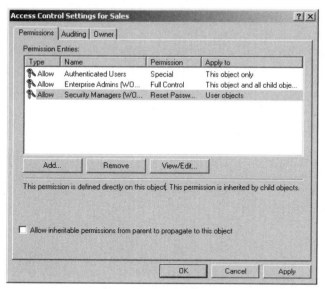

Figure 5-2   User interface view of DACL example shown in Table 5-2

Generic ACEs offer limited control over the kinds of child objects that can inherit them. Generic ACEs distinguish between objects that can contain other objects, such as OU objects, and objects that cannot contain other objects, such as user objects. Windows Server 2003 reports where permissions were inherited from in the user interface. For example, the DACL on an OU object can include a generic ACE that allows a member of a group object the permission to delete members of other group objects in the OU. Because this ACE can be performed on container objects and child objects, it will be inherited by other container objects, such as user objects.

Object-specific ACEs offer greater granularity of control over the types of child objects that can inherit them. For example, an OU object's DACL can have an object-specific ACE that is marked for inheritance only by user objects. Other types of objects, such as computer objects, will not inherit the ACE. This capability is the crux of object-specific ACEs: their inheritance can be limited to specific object classes of child objects.

These two categories of ACEs control access to objects in a somewhat similar fashion. Generic ACEs apply to an entire object. If a generic ACE gives a particular user Read access, the user can read all information associated with the object—including all of the properties of the object and their values.

Object-specific ACEs can apply to any individual property of an object or to a set of properties. These ACE types are used only in access control lists (ACLs) for Active Directory objects, which, unlike other object types, store most of their information in properties. It is often desirable to place independent controls on each property of an Active Directory object, and object-specific ACEs make that possible. For example, when you define permissions for a user object, you can use one object-specific ACE to allow Principal Self (the user) Write access to the Phone-Home-Primary property (*homePhone*). You also can use other object-specific ACEs to deny Principal Self access to the Logon-Hours property (*logonHours*) and other properties that set restrictions on the user account.

How DACLs Work

When access to an Active Directory object is requested, the Local Security Authority (LSA) compares the access token of the user or process requesting access to the object to the DACL. The security subsystem checks the object's DACL, looking for ACEs that apply to the user and group SIDs referenced in the thread's access token. The security subsystem then steps through the DACL until it finds any ACEs that either allow or deny access to the user or one of the user's groups. The subsystem does this by first examining ACEs that have been explicitly assigned to the object and then examining ones that have been inherited by the object.

If an explicit deny is found, access is denied. Explicit deny ACE entries are always applied, even if conflicting explicit allow ACEs exist. Explicit allow ACEs are examined, as are inherited deny and allow ACEs. The ACEs that apply to the user are accumulated. Inherited deny ACEs overrule inherited allow ACEs, but are overruled themselves by explicit allow permissions. If none of the user or group SIDs in the access token match the DACL, the user is denied access implicitly. Figure 5-3 shows the process of evaluating access token contents against a DACL.

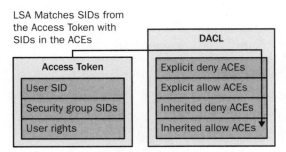

Figure 5-3   Access control in Active Directory

Tip   Accounts with Full Control, Modify Permissions, or Modify Owner permissions can change the DACL and SACL on the object.

Securing Active Directory Objects and Attributes

In Active Directory, all attributes of all objects and the objects themselves have permissions that can be defined when the object is created or after it has been created. You must be able to examine these permissions and secure them according to your organization's security policy. This is especially true if your organization is planning on extending the Active Directory Schema to include additional attributes or objects.

You can secure Active Directory objects at their creation globally for all newly created objects of a given object class by modifying the default security descriptor for the object class in the schema. You can also secure objects after their creation by creating an object-specific ACE on the parent container in which the object will be created or by configuring the DACL on the object directly.

The method used to build a DACL for a new Active Directory object differs slightly from the method used to build DACLs for other object types. Two key differences exist. First, when building a DACL for a new Active Directory object, each object class defined in the schema has a default DACL that is applied to all objects when they are created. Second, the rules for creating a DACL distinguish between generic inheritable ACEs and object-specific inheritable ACEs in the parent object's security descriptor. Generic inheritable ACEs can be inherited by all types of child objects. Object-specific inheritable ACEs can be inherited only by the type of child object to which they apply. Other objects that have DACLs, such as files, do not have object-specific ACEs.

Configuring Default DACLs on Objects and Attributes

You can configure the default DACL on object classes by modifying the schema. To modify the schema, you must be a member of the Schema Admins security group and the schema FSMO must be marked as writeable. To configure a default DACL on an object class, perform the following steps:

1. Open a blank MMC from the command prompt by typing **MMC**.
2. Add the Active Directory Schema MMC snap-in to the blank MMC.
3. Right-click the object class that you want to modify. Then select Properties and click the Security tab of the object class.
4. Configure the default DACL and close the open windows.

Important   The schema partition of Active Directory must replicate fully throughout the forest before all new objects receive the new default security as defined on the default DACL.

Figure 5-4 shows a custom security group named Security Managers being granted Full Control permissions over all new user objects in the forest. Because a single schema exists for the entire forest, the DACL that you modify will be applied to all new objects of that object class created in any domain in the forest. Consequently, if you are assigning permissions to a new security group rather than modifying the existing permissions, you should use universal groups to ensure that the permissions are applicable throughout the Active Directory forest. You can then make the appropriate global groups members of the universal group.

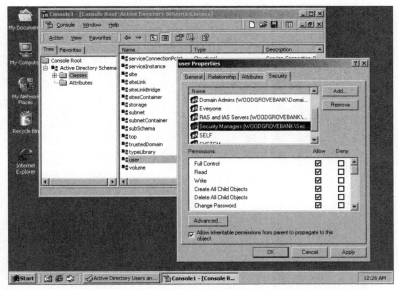

Figure 5-4   Adding a security group to an object class default DACL

The new default DACL applies only to new objects. Existing objects of the object class of which you have modified the default DACL are not affected. The change affects only objects created after the schema has replicated to the domain controller where the new object is created. Settings in the default DACL remain with the object even if they are moved to a different container.

Securing Objects After Creation

Setting the default DACL on an object class is an effective way to configure the security of Active Directory objects during their creation because the change is forestwide in scope and affects only newly created objects. However, you might want to configure an object-specific ACE on the parent object, such as an OU. The object-specific ACE is applied to the object when the object is created or when objects are moved into the parent object. For example, rather than assigning the Security Managers security group Full Control of all newly created user objects in the forest, you might want to grant them Full Control only over all user objects in an OU. You can do this by editing the DACL for the OU. The following steps explain how to do this:

1. Open Active Directory Users and Computers.

2. Right-click the OU, click Properties, and select the Security tab.

3. Click the Advanced button.

4. Click Add and add the appropriate security groups to the DACL. Then click OK.

5. In the Apply Onto drop-down menu, ensure that the correct object class is chosen.

6. Configure the new access that you are granting or denying.

7. Close all windows.

Tip   You must enable the Advanced Features view in Active Directory Users and Computers to expose the Security tab on objects.

Figure 5-5 shows the creation of an object-specific ACE for granting Full Control over user objects to the Security Managers custom security group.

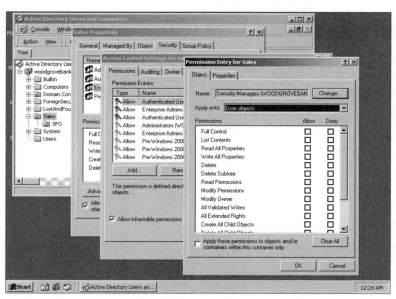

Figure 5-5   Adding an object-specific ACE to an OU

When adding an object-specific ACE to an OU, the OU (or any other type of parent object) immediately propagates the inheritance of the permissions to all objects of that object class in the OU and in all child OUs. Similarly, when objects of that object class are moved into the OU, the permissions are inherited by the object. If the object-specific ACEs are removed from the OU, the permissions are immediately removed from the objects of that object class in the OU and all child OUs. If an object of that object class is moved to a new parent container, the ACE is removed from the object.

Active Directory not only enables you to configure security on objects but also to configure security on individual properties. Setting security on properties entails the same process as setting permissions on objects.

Configuring DACLs from the Command Line

Although configuring DACLs by using the MMC is convenient, you might want to set permissions from the command line. You can do this in one of two ways: through Active Directory Services Interface (ADSI) scripts, or by using the Support Tools utility Dsacls.exe. You can install Support Tools from the Windows Server 2003 or Windows 2000 Server installation CD, from the Support\Tools directory.

> **More Info**   Writing custom ADSI programs is beyond the scope of this book. The Microsoft® Windows® 2000 Scripting Guide provides detailed information on controlling access to objects in Active Directory using ADSI at *http://www.microsoft.com /resources/documentation/windows/2000/server/scriptguide/en-us/default.mspx.*

Dsacls.exe is the command-line equivalent of the Security tab in the Properties dialog box for an Active Directory object in Active Directory tools, such as Active Directory Users and Computers. You can display all permissions on a given object in Active Directory by typing **dsacls "ou=sales.dc=woodgrovebank,dc=com"**. Another convenient feature of Dsacls.exe is its ability to reset the security on an object or set of objects to the default DACL of the object's object class in the schema. To reset the security on an object, type **dsacls "ou=sales,dc=woodgrovebank,dc=com" /S**. This is a common use of Dsacls.exe in a test environment when you are evaluating changing permissions on Active Directory objects. The complete syntax of Dsacls.exe can be referenced in the Support Tools Help file. In Windows Server 2003, this feature was added to the user interface in the Advanced area of the Security tab.

Another important tool for managing DACLs on Active Directory objects is Acldiag.exe, which you can also obtain from Support Tools. Acldiag.exe enables you to do the following:

- Compare the current DACL on the object against the default DACL on the object's class. For example, typing **acldiag "cn=alisonbrown,ou=sales,dc=woodgrovebank,dc=com" /schema** would compare the DACL of the user object *Alison Brown* to the default DACL on the object class user.

- Determine the effective permissions that a user or group has to an object. Typing **acldiag "cn=alisonbrown,ou=sales,dc=woodgrovebank,dc=com" /geteffective:*** would retrieve the effective permissions for the user object *Alison Brown* and all the properties of the object and then print them to the console.

- Export the permissions to a comma-delimited or tab-delimited file. By using the switches /cdo or /tdo at the end of an Acldiag command, you can format the output in comma-delimited or tab-delimited format. This is especially useful if you want to import the permissions into a spreadsheet or database.

> **Tip**   You can direct the output of any command-line program to a text file or local printer by using the standard redirector in the operating system. To direct the output to a file, append the command string with >filename. To direct the output to a local printer, append the command string with **>lpt1**. For example, **acldiag "cn=alisonbrown,ou=sales,dc=woodgrovebank,dc=com" /geteffective:* /cdo > alisonDACL.csv** will compile the effective permissions for all users on the user object *Alison Brown* on a comma-separated file named AlisonDACL.csv.

Best Practices

- **Always apply the theory of least privilege.**   Whenever you are configuring security on an Active Directory object, assign only the least permissions needed by the users to complete their job functions and always test the changes in a test environment before making changes on your production Active Directory to prevent disrupting service by changes that overly restrict access.

- **Use a consistent model for assigning permissions.**   Do not assign permissions to individual users; rather, use a well-defined model for assigning permissions to security groups and placing user accounts into the security groups.

- **Avoid assigning permissions to domain local groups.**   Domain local security groups are valid only in the domain; thus, permissions replication to the Global Catalog will not be applied as expected. Assign forestwide permissions by using universal groups. (For more on this model, see the "Implementing Role-Based Security" section in Chapter 3, "Configuring Security for User Accounts and Passwords.")

- **Document changes made to DACLs.**   Be certain to record changes that you make to Active Directory object DACLs. This will simplify troubleshooting in the event of an error arising from the new permissions.

- **Remove users from the Schema Admins security group.**   When the schema is not in the process of being extended or altered, remove users from the Schema Admins security group to ensure that the schema is not unintentionally altered.

- **Make the Schema Master read-only.**   When you are not making changes to the schema, ensure that the schema is not write-enabled.

- **Use Restricted Groups.**   Use Restricted Groups in Group Policy to limit membership in the Schema Admins security group.

Additional Information

- Knowledge Base article 218596: "How to Assign Access Control Permissions on the Properties of an Active Directory Object" (*http://support.microsoft.com/kb /218596*)

- Knowledge Base article 292304: "How to Prevent Windows 2000 Users from Changing Personal Detail Information" (*http://support.microsoft.com/kb /292304*)

- MSDN Library, "Active Directory Programmer's Guide" (*http:// msdn.microsoft.com/library/en-us/ad/ad/active_directory.asp*)

- "Microsoft Windows 2000 Scripting Guide" section on ADSI (*http:// www.microsoft.com/resources/documentation/windows/2000/server/scriptguide /en-us/default.mspx*)

- MSDN Library, "Access Control," from the Platform SDK (http:// msdn.microsoft.com/library/default.asp?url=/library/en-us/secauthz/security /order_of_aces_in_a_dacl.asp)

Chapter 6
Implementing Group Policy for Security

One of the most powerful and useful security features in Microsoft Windows Server 2003 and Windows 2000 is Group Policy. Group Policy enables administrators to manage large numbers of users and computers running Windows Server 2003, Windows 2000, and Microsoft Windows XP Professional centrally in the Active Directory directory service. The biggest security benefit of Group Policy is that you can use it to deploy and maintain a consistent security baseline configuration on computers that are members of a domain.

Understanding Group Policy

Group policies have two types of application: those that apply to the computer, and those that apply to the user. Computer-related group policies are always applied, regardless of which user account is used to log on to the computer. The user-related group policies apply specifically to the user account that is used to log on to a computer. Security policies are applied to the computer and thus will apply to all users of the computer, including members of the Administrators group. By default, a local security policy, Setup security, captures the security settings applied to each computer running Windows 2000 and later at installation. You can implement Group Policy settings on a local computer, although local group policies are not stored in and enforced by Active Directory. Group policies deployed through Active Directory are associated with site, domain, and OU containers in the form of Group Policy objects (GPOs).

A GPO can be associated with any site, domain, or OU, and the GPO can be linked to multiple sites, domains, or OUs. Conversely, a given site, domain, or OU can have multiple GPOs linked to it. In the event that multiple GPOs are linked to a particular site, domain, or OU, you can prioritize the order in which these GPOs are applied.

By linking GPOs to Active Directory sites, domains, and OUs, you can implement Group Policy settings for as broad or narrow a portion of the organization as you require, including the following:

- A GPO linked to a site applies to all computers in the site.
- A GPO applied to a domain applies to all users and computers in the domain, even if the users and computers are located within OUs in the domain. GPOs associated with parent domains are not inherited by child domains.
- A GPO applied to an OU applies to all users and computers located directly in the OU and, by inheritance, to all users and computers in child OUs.

The accumulation of GPO settings from a site, a domain, and all nested OUs is applied. GPOs are stored on a per-domain basis. Because domains are autonomous units, child domains do not inherit Group Policy from parent domains. You can link a GPO to a site, domain, or OU in another trusted domain, but this is not generally recommended for performance reasons. GPOs associated only with a site are stored in the forest root domain, and those policies are retrieved from a domain controller in the forest root domain. GPOs are applied in a hierarchical arrangement. If there are conflicts, the latest setting processed will be the one that is applied. By default, GPOs are cumulative and processed in the following order:

1. The local Group Policy object (LGPO) is applied.
2. GPOs linked to sites are processed.
3. GPOs linked to domains are processed.
4. GPOs linked to OUs are processed. In the case of nested OUs, GPOs associated with parent OUs are processed prior to GPOs associated with child OUs.

Computer-Related Group Policies

Computer-related group policies are specific to the computer and apply to all users of the computer. Computer-related group policies are applied during the startup phase of the operating system and are fully applied by default before the Windows Logon dialog box appears. Table 6-1 lists the types of computer-related Group Policy settings.

Table 6-1   Computer-Related Group Policy Settings

Group	Description
Software Settings	Enables software to be installed on computers.
Windows Settings	Enables security templates to be deployed and computer startup and shutdown scripts to be executed.
Administrative Templates	Enables computer-related registry changes to be made. These built-in settings, unlike Microsoft Windows NT 4.0 System Policies, do not make permanent changes, sometimes called "tattooing," to the registry.

By using Software Installation policies, you can ensure that security-related software is installed on all computers on the network. For example, you might want to use a GPO to assign antivirus software to all desktop and laptop computers in your organization.

You can import security templates into the computer configuration portion of Group Policy to deploy uniform security to computers on your organization's network. Table 6-2 describes the security settings in Group Policy.

Table 6-2   Security Settings in Group Policy

Area	Description
Account Policies	Password policies, account lockout policies, and Kerberos policies
Local Policies	Audit policy, user rights assignment, security options
Event Log	Application, system, and Security Event log settings
Restricted Groups	Membership of security-sensitive groups
System Services	Startup parameters and permissions for system services
Registry	Permissions for registry keys
File System	Permissions for folders and files
Wireless Network (IEEE 802.11) Policies	Basic 802.11 wireless network connectivity settings for computers running Windows Server 2003 and Windows XP
Public Key Policies	Controls a collection of Public Key Infrastructure (PKI)–related settings, including encrypting file system (EFS) recovery agents and automatic certificate enrollment
Software Restriction Policies	Policy settings for controlling software execution for computers running Windows Server 2003 and Windows XP
IP Security Policies	Central management console for IP Security (IPSec) policies

You can use Windows Settings to run scripts at the startup or shutdown of a computer. Startup scripts execute before the Security dialog box appears, and shutdown scripts run after the user has logged off but before services cease.

Administrative Templates are settings that configure the Windows Server 2003, Windows 2000, and Windows XP registries. In addition to the administrative templates included by default, you can import custom settings by creating and importing .adm files. In contrast with using Windows NT System Policies, when you use Group Policy, policy settings made through Administrative Templates do not tattoo the registry and are applied immediately, rather than after one or more reboots.

> **More Info**   Security templates are discussed in detail in Chapter 11, "Creating and Configuring Security Templates."

Preferences vs. Policies

Registry policy or .adm templates take the form of *policies* (registry entries under specific registry keys) or *preferences* (registry keys anywhere else). The .adm files are used to define policies or preferences. We recommend you use policies rather than preferences. Policies do not tattoo the registry. If you use a GPO to deploy policies and preferences, when the GPO is removed, the policies will be removed. However, the preferences will remain. Preferences are not refreshed unless the GPO changes. Users can change their preferences, and these preferences will not be restored until Group Policy changes and the GPOs are reapplied. Policies, on the other hand, are given an access control list (ACL) in the registry so that users cannot change them. If you must use preferences, you need to add them using the .adm file.

Computer-related policy settings are stored in the registry hive HKEY_LOCAL_MACHINE (HKLM), and user-related policy settings are stored in the registry hive HKEY_CURRENT_USER (HKCU). In each of these registry hives, Group Policy settings are stored in these two registry keys:

- \Software\Policies
- \Software\Microsoft\Windows\CurrentVersion\Policies

User-Related Group Policies

In addition to the computer-related group policies applied to the computer a user logs on to, user-related group polices are applied to specific users. By default, user-related group policies are applied immediately after the user's credentials are successfully authenticated but before the user gains control of the Windows Explorer shell. Table 6-3 describes the various types of user-related group policies.

Table 6-3   User-Related Group Policy Settings

Group	Description
Software Settings	Enables software to be assigned or published to a user
Windows Settings	Enables security templates to be deployed and user logon and logoff scripts to be executed
Administrative Templates	Enables registry changes to be made for the user

Software can be deployed to users in two ways: it can be *assigned*, or it can be *published*. The only difference between assigning and publishing applications to users is whether the application shows up in the Start menu, which it does with Assigned applications. Software packages also will be installed on the computer when the user invokes the application by attempting to open a file with the default file type that the application uses (if this option is enabled in the policy). The application will appear in Control Panel under Add/Remove Programs.

Important   Applications installed by using Group Policy Software Installation policies will install only the application's core files once per computer if multiple users of the computer have the same application assigned or published to them. The application information unique to each user will be written to the Application Data folder in the user profile or the HKEY_USERS (HKU) registry hive for the user. For each user, upon logon, the information associated with that user's account in HKU is used to populate the dynamic registry hive HKEY_CURRENT_USER (HKCU) for the logon session.

The Windows Settings for users contain options for configuring logon and logoff scripts, folder redirection behavior, Microsoft Internet Explorer settings, PKI enterprise trusts, and Remote Installation Services (RIS) settings.

The Administrative Templates settings for users function similarly to the settings for computers.

Important   Before deploying GPOs, you should test the settings in a test environment to ensure that the GPOs do not prevent users from completing tasks required by their job function. If possible, you should also conduct a pilot deployment in the production environment.

Using Group Policy Objects

All computers running Windows Server 2003, Windows 2000, and Windows XP have a local GPO that defines their default configuration. The local GPO applies to all users of a computer. In addition, if the computers are members of an Active Directory domain, you can deploy GPOs to all computers in a site, domain, or OU.

The Local Group Policy Object

You can configure a local Group Policy for any computer, regardless of whether the computer is a member of Active Directory. To configure the LGPO, use the Group Policy Microsoft Management Console (MMC) snap-in and select to focus on the local computer. The local Group Policy Editor is shown in Figure 6-1.

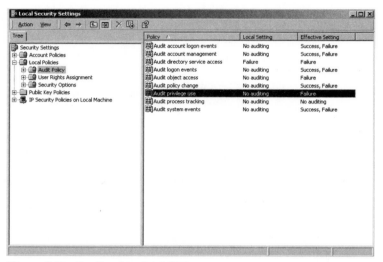

Figure 6-1   Configuring the LGPO

Group Policy is processed in this order:

1. LGPO
2. Site GPOs
3. Domain GPOs
4. Organizational unit GPOs
5. Nested organizational unit GPOs

The LGPO cannot be filtered by a user account. Unlike GPOs in Active Directory, there is no discretionary access control list (DACL) permission named Apply Group Policy; there is only the Read permission. User accounts need the Read permission to either read the GPO settings or have them apply to the logon session. The Apply Group Policy permission is checked during Group Policy processing. If the user has this permission on the GPO, it will be processed.

Site Group Policy Objects

GPOs that are linked to site containers affect all computers or users in a forest of domains that have membership in the site. Computers running Windows Server 2003, Windows 2000, and Windows XP are automatically members of the Default-First-Site-Name site unless other sites and subnet objects have been defined. Site information replicates to all domain controllers in the forest. Therefore, any GPO that is linked to a site container is applied to all computers in that site, regardless of the domain. This enables a single GPO to span multiple domains but also results in cross-domain authentication because domain controllers must retrieve the policy from the domain in which it is stored.

Site GPOs are effective for managing settings that apply to a group of computers that exist on the same high-speed communications channel. For example, you might want to assign proxy server settings in Internet Explorer by site or install antivirus software from a server on the same high-speed network as the computer.

Domain Group Policy Objects

GPOs that are linked to a domain affect all computers or users in the domain. By default, two GPOs exist in each Active Directory domain:

- Default Domain Policy
- Default Domain Controllers Policy

The Default Domain Policy contains the default security policy for all computers in the domain and the account policies for domain accounts. The Default Domain Controllers Policy contains the default security policy for domain controllers and augments the security policy of the Default Domain Policy. For example, the Default Domain Controllers Policy prohibits nonadministrators from logging on interactively. Domain controllers should never be removed from the Default Domain Controllers Policy because of inherent functionality in Active Directory.

OU Group Policy Objects

One of the primary purposes of OU containers is to facilitate the deployment of GPOs to users and computers. Unlike domains, OUs are flexible: objects, including security principals, can easily be moved between OUs, and OUs can be created and deleted without much consequence. You can create OUs that facilitate the application of GPOs based on the security needs of the users or computers. The domain controller's OU is the only OU created by default in each domain. Its purpose is to facilitate the deployment of the Default Domain Controllers GPO.

Processing Group Policy Objects

Group policies are processed and applied initially when the computer starts up and when the user logs on. After the initial application, group policies are processed and applied at regular intervals. By default, during the refresh interval, the client computer retrieves the GPOs only if the GPO version stored in Active Directory is incremented. You can change this behavior in the Group Policy settings that affect group policies. In addition, you can manually refresh Group Policy settings.

Initial Group Policy Application

GPOs are processed when the computer is started and when the user logs on using the Security dialog box. When a computer boots up, settings from the LGPO are applied. Then, the computer retrieves all the settings from the site, if present. All Group Policy processing takes place on the client; therefore, a previously compromised computer cannot be trusted to process and implement Group Policy correctly. If two or more GPOs are linked to a container, they are processed starting with those of the lowest precedence, which appear lower in the user interface. Domain GPOs are then retrieved and processed, as are OU Group Policy objects (if present), beginning with the root OU and continuing to the computer's parent object.

Settings in GPOs are cumulative; however, if the settings conflict with each other, the policy processed later overrides the previous setting. For example, suppose that at the domain level, a software package is assigned and the number of previously cached logons is set to five. Now suppose that a policy at the OU level defines a startup script and sets the number of cached logons to two. The resultant settings will include installation of the software package, application of the startup script, and caching of two logons.

When the user logs on, the GPOs are processed in the same order that the computer-related group policies are applied. If a setting creates a conflict between the computer-related Group Policy applied and the user-related group policies applied (such as conflicting Task Scheduler Administrative Templates settings), the computer-related Group Policy setting will generally apply.

Group Policy Refresh

Group Policy is processed periodically, according to a defined interval. By default, for nondomain controllers, this occurs every 90 minutes with a randomized offset of up to 30 minutes. For domain controllers, Group Policy is refreshed every 5 minutes. You can change these default values by using a Group Policy setting in Administrative Templates. Setting the value to 0 minutes causes the refresh rate to be set to 7 seconds.

Although most changes made to GPOs or settings in new GPOs are enforced during the refresh cycles, the following settings are not enforced:

- Computer-related group policies for Software Installation
- User-related group policies for Software Installation
- User-related group policies for folder redirection
- Some settings in the Security Settings

These settings are refreshed the next time that the computer is restarted or the user interactively logs on.

> **Note** Security Settings in a computer-related Group Policy are refreshed every 16 hours, regardless of whether a change in Group Policy is detected by the client. This will provide assurance that security settings are enforced every 16 hours, even if they are changed locally.

On-Demand Processing

You can also trigger a background refresh of Group Policy on demand from the client. However, the application of Group Policy cannot be pushed to clients on demand from the server. To refresh Group Policy manually on computers running Windows 2000, use the Secedit command as follows:

Computer-related group policies	Type **secedit /refreshpolicy machine_policy /enforce** at the command prompt.
User-related group policies	Type **secedit /refreshpolicy user_policy /enforce** at the command prompt.

To refresh Group Policy manually on computers running Windows Server 2003 and Windows XP, use the Gpupdate command as follows:

Computer-related group policies	Type **gpupdate /target:computer /force** at the command prompt.
User-related group policies	Type **gpupdate /target:user /force** at the command prompt.
Both computer-related and user-related group policies	Type **gpupdate /force** at the command prompt.

Altering Group Policy Application

When you create Group Policy structure in your organization, you might need to alter the default processing of GPOs. Group Policy provides four options for doing this:

- Block Inheritance
- No Override
- Group Policy object filtering
- Loopback mode processing

> **Note**   You can also filter Group Policy on Windows Server 2003 and Windows XP by using Windows Management Instrumentation (WMI) filters if the computers have accounts in a Windows Server 2003–based Active Directory.

Block Inheritance

You might have a situation in which a subcontainer such as an OU should not receive GPOs from parent objects. For example, suppose you have configured a GPO and linked it to the domain container, thus applying it to all computers. But what if you want to ensure that computers in a specific OU containing computers do not inherit the domain Group Policy settings? In this case, you can implement Block Inheritance on the OU container, which will prevent all GPOs from the parent container from being processed and, therefore, from being applied to the computer or user. Note that you cannot block the inheritance of individual GPOs with this setting. Blocking inheritance blocks all GPOs from a higher level in the processing hierarchy.

No Override

You might be the administrator of GPOs linked to the domain and need to ensure that certain policies are applied, even if an OU has the Block Inheritance option configured or a GPO configured with an opposite or conflicting setting. In this case, you can mark the individual GPO as No Override. A GPO with the No Override option set on a parent object will be applied even if the Block Inheritance option is configured on the child object. Unlike Block Inheritance, No Override is specified on individual GPOs.

> **Note**   If you have the Group Policy Management Console (GPMC) installed, this setting is called Enforced rather than No Override.

Group Policy Object Filtering

When a GPO is applied to a container, it applies to all computer and user objects in the container and all subcontainers. You might need to have some computers or users exempted by the GPO. Rather than create a special container and use a series of No Override and Block Inheritance restrictions, you can filter Group Policy by using the DACLs on the GPO.

You can view and modify the security settings in the Security tab on the Properties page of the specific GPO. The Security tab for a GPO is accessible by right-clicking the root node in the Group Policy snap-in, clicking Properties, and then clicking Security. Alternately, on the Properties page of a given site, domain, or OU, you can select the Group Policy tab, right-click the appropriate GPO in the Group Policy Object list, select Properties, and then click Security.

For the GPO to be applied to a computer or user, the computer and user objects in Active Directory must have both Read and Apply Group Policy permissions on the GPO. By default, members of the Authenticated Users group are granted both Apply Group Policy and Read permissions. Computer and user accounts automatically receive membership in the Authenticated Users group after the successful validation of their credentials, which occurs before Group Policy is processed. Therefore, the default behavior is for every GPO to apply to all users and computers. By default, the groups Domain Admins, Enterprise Admins, and Local System have Full Control permissions, without the Apply Group Policy access control entry (ACE). However, administrators are members of Authenticated Users, which means that they will receive the settings in the GPO by default.

Preventing Group Policy from applying to a specified group requires removal of the Apply Group Policy ACE from that group. If you remove the Apply Group Policy ACE (clear the Allow check box) for Authenticated Users, you can explicitly grant this permission to individual security groups that should receive the policy settings. Alternatively, you could set Apply Group Policy to Deny for certain security groups that should not have the policy applied. Because an explicit deny permission always overrides an allow permission, the computer or user accounts in the security group will not process the GPO.

Note   Group Policy administrators also need the Read and Write permissions to manage the GPO. Use caution when altering the default assignment of Read for the Authenticated Users group.

Loopback Mode Processing

Another scenario in which you might need to alter the default processing of Group Policy is when you have computer and user objects in different containers in Active Directory. The OU that holds the user object has restrictive GPO settings activated, such as preventing users from altering network settings, removing Control Panel items, and preventing certain applications from running. When a user logs on to her workstation, the GPO policies act to protect the network and standardize the desktop configuration; however, the user can also manage a Windows 2000 file and print server. When the user logs on to the server, the Group Policy settings prevent her from completing the management task she is required to do. Rather than create a separate account for the user to use when managing the server, you can implement Group Policy loopback mode.

Group Policy loopback mode is itself a Group Policy setting that you can enable in the Computer Configuration section of Group Policy. Group Policy loopback mode has two settings:

- **Replace**   When you enable Group Policy loopback mode using this setting, the GPO that applies to the user object will not be processed, rather the user-related Group Policy settings from the location of the computer account will be applied in addition to the computer-related Group Policy settings. This setting is commonly used to resolve the scenario just described.

- **Merge**   When you use this setting, user configuration settings from the computer object location will be applied after the user configuration settings from the location of the user object. This results in the computer location's user settings combining with the user location's user settings and overriding them in the event of conflicts.

You can set the Group Policy loopback mode by enabling User Group Policy Loopback Processing Mode policy in the Computer Configuration section of Group Policy\Administrative Templates\System\Group Policy.

Managing Group Policy

One GPO can be used to configure the security on all computers in a site, domain, or OU. This makes securing the management of Group Policy very important. For example, an administrator of an OU could exempt computers and users in the OU from receiving Group Policy settings configured at the domain level if that administrator has the ability to manage Group Policy. When implementing security in your forest, you must consider the management of Group Policy.

Default Group Policy Permissions

By default, several groups have administrative authority over Group Policy. These settings might or might not be appropriate for your organization. Table 6-4 describes the permissions for managing Group Policy.

Table 6-4   Group Policy Permissions

Permission	Object	Description
Full Control	GPO	Gives full control over the GPO to the user account or security group
Write	GPO	Enables the user account or security group to modify the settings in the GPO
Read	GPO	Enables the user account or security group to read the setting in the GPO
Apply Group Policy	GPO	Enables the user account or security group to have the GPO processed during the initial logon or refresh cycle
Read/Write gPLink	Container	Enables the user account or security group to link GPOs to the container
Read/Write gPOptions	Container	Enables the user account or security group to block the inheritance of GPOs to the container

By default, the groups Domain Admins, Enterprise Admins, Creator Owner, and Local System have full control over all GPOs linked to domains and OUs. The Authenticated Users group has Read and Apply Group Policy permissions.

Delegating Group Policy Management

In Active Directory, you can delegate the permissions to manage Group Policy either by using the Delegation of Control Wizard or by using the Security tab of the Properties dialog box of a GPO or container object. Delegation of control in Active Directory is flexible enough to allow you to grant administrative control over GPOs according to the security requirements of your organization.

Adding Users to the Group Policy Creator Owners Group

By default, members of the Domain Admins and Group Policy Creator Owners security groups can create new GPOs in their home domain. Although members of the Group Policy Creator Owners security group can create new GPOs, they do not have the permission to link the GPO to a container. After a member of the Group Policy Creator Owners security group has created a GPO and it has been linked to a container, that user account retains the explicit permissions to modify the GPO. Other members of the Group Policy Creator Owners security group do not have any permissions on GPOs created by other members of the group.

gPLink Permission

User accounts that have the Read/Write gPLink permission can link existing GPOs to the container for which they possess this permission. User accounts that have been granted Write or Full Control permissions over a domain or OU container possess this permission by default. This permission does not allow the user account to create new GPOs.

gPOptions Permission

User accounts that have the Read/Write gPOptions permission can enable the Block Inheritance option of a domain or OU container. User accounts that have been granted Write or Full Control permissions over a domain or OU container possess this permission by default. Possessing this permission does not grant the user account any additional permissions on GPOs.

Best Practices

- **Use Group Policy to deploy a security baseline.**   Use Group Policy to deploy security settings on computers running Windows Server 2003, Windows 2000, and Windows XP. Because GPOs can easily be refreshed and are always applied by clients, they are an excellent method of ensuring a consistent security baseline and additional level of security for computers based on their role.

- **Use caution when delegating authority over Group Policy.**   Administrators who manage Group Policy can easily compromise the security of your network by maliciously or accidentally deploying security templates or security-related settings that weaken or remove the base security of computers that run Windows Server 2003, Windows 2000, and Windows XP.

- **Minimize the use of Block Inheritance, No Override, and Group Policy object filtering.**   Use these methods of altering the default behavior of Group Policy only when required and when no reasonable design workarounds exist. Using these options will greatly increase the difficulty of troubleshooting Group Policy, and the resulting confusion could lead to the misapplication of Group Policy.

- **Use the Group Policy Management Console (GPMC) for troubleshooting.**   A vast improvement over the default Group Policy Object Editor in the operating system, the GPMC is especially useful for troubleshooting when Group Policy does not apply in the expected manner.

Additional Information

- Windows Server 2003 Group Policy Technology Center (*http:// www.microsoft.com/windowsserver2003/technologies/management/grouppolicy /default.mspx*)

- Group Policy Management Console (GPMC) tool (*http://www.microsoft.com /windowsserver2003/gpmc/default.mspx*)

- "Best Practices for Delegating Active Directory Administration" white paper (*http://www.microsoft.com/technet/prodtechnol/windowsserver2003/technologies /directory/activedirectory/actdid1.mspx*)

- "Windows 2000 Group Policy" white paper (*http://www.microsoft.com /windows2000/techinfo/howitworks/management/grouppolwp.asp*)

- "Step-by-Step Guide to Understanding the Group Policy Feature Set" (*http:// www.microsoft.com/technet/prodtechnol/windows2000serv/howto/grpolwt.mspx* and *http://www.microsoft.com/technet/prodtechnol/windowsserver2003 /technologies/directory/activedirectory/stepbystep/gpfeat.mspx*)

- Microsoft Windows 2000 Resource Kit, "Group Policy" section (*http:// www.microsoft.com/resources/documentation/windows/2000/server/reskit/en-us /distrib/dsec_pol_zbgy.asp*)

- "Implementing Registry-Based Group Policy" white paper (*http:// www.microsoft.com/WINDOWS2000/techinfo/howitworks/management /rbppaper.asp*)

- "Implementing Common Desktop Management Scenarios" white paper (*http:// www.microsoft.com/technet/prodtechnol/windowsserver2003/technologies /management/csws2003.mspx*)

- "Microsoft Platform SDK Documentation: Group Policy" (*http:// msdn.microsoft.com/library/en-us/policy/policy/group_policy_start_page.asp*)

- "Group Policy Registry Table" (*http://www.microsoft.com/resources /documentation/Windows/2000/server/reskit/en-us/regentry/GPRef.asp*)

- The following Knowledge Base articles:

    - Knowledge Base article 221577: "How to Delegate Authority for Editing a Group Policy Object (GPO)" (*http://support.microsoft.com/kb/221577*)

    - Knowledge Base article 294777: "How to Delegate Group Policy Control to Users in Trusted Domain" (*http://support.microsoft.com/kb/294777*)

    - Knowledge Base article 315676: "How to Delegate Administrative Authority in Windows 2000" (*http://support.microsoft.com/kb/315676*)

    - Knowledge Base article 321476: "How to Change the Default Permissions on GPOs in Windows 2000" (*http://support.microsoft.com/kb/321476*)

Chapter 7

Designing Domains and Forests for Security

The security of your network depends on the design of the Active Directory directory service—it is the heart of your network security. Although no one "right" way of designing Active Directory exists, many ways of designing Active Directory will put your organization at serious risk. The technology is flexible enough to be deployed according to the business requirements of any organization. However, an Active Directory implementation has several important security considerations. This chapter is by no means an exhaustive text on how to design Active Directory. But it will provide guidance on designing Active Directory forests and domains with security in mind.

Autonomy and Isolation in Active Directory

In Microsoft Windows NT, members of the Domain Admins group have complete control over all objects in their own domain but no inherent control over any objects in a trusting domain. Similarly, changes made to one domain do not affect trusting or trusted domains. Furthermore, within the domain, the primary domain controller (PDC) owns the only writeable copy of the Security Accounts Manager (SAM). For these reasons, domains are considered discrete security boundaries in Windows NT.

Unlike Windows NT, Active Directory domains are *not* security boundaries because they are not fully isolated from each other. Understanding how autonomy and isolation operate in Active Directory is critical when designing and deploying a secure

Active Directory. When discussing autonomy and isolation, we need to separate the rights and permissions of two types of administrative capabilities: Active Directory service administrators and Active Directory data administrators.

Active Directory service administrators are responsible for the configuration and management of the directory service itself. This includes tasks such as maintaining domain controller servers and managing directory-wide configuration settings. Active Directory service administrators also must be considered data administrators because of the rights and permissions required to allow them to be Active Directory data administrators at will. Because all domain controllers are trusted equally in the forest, anyone who is an Active Directory service administrator, such as a member of the Domain Admins group, or someone who has compromised a domain controller, can potentially compromise other domains in the forest. All Active Directory service administrators in the forest must be trusted equally.

Active Directory data administrators are responsible for managing data stored in Active Directory objects or on computers joined to Active Directory, but they have no authority over the configuration or management of the directory service itself. In this respect, Active Directory data administrators have autonomy over the systems and objects they manage, but do not enjoy isolation from Active Directory service administrators. Active Directory data administrator roles include the following functions:

- The management of a subset of objects in Active Directory, such as user accounts in a specific OU
- The management of data that is stored on computers joined to the domain

When designing Active Directory, you must consider your organization's security requirements for autonomy and isolation of authority in relation to Active Directory services and Active Directory data management. Your security requirements will have a significant effect on how you design Active Directory to facilitate delegation of authority and administrative responsibility.

Autonomy of authority means that Active Directory services and data administrators can independently manage all or part of the resources over which they have authority. Isolation of authority means that accounts and people not authorized for Active Directory services and Active Directory data management are prevented from controlling or interfering with service management (services management isolation) or from controlling or viewing a subset of data in the directory or on member computers joined to the directory (data management isolation).

Designing Forests for Active Directory Security

The forest is the largest management unit of Active Directory as well as the ultimate unit of autonomy and isolation of authority. Active Directory design begins with answering the question, "How many forests will my organization require?" The answer to this question is based on security considerations for autonomy and isolation of authority. Characteristics of forests and security considerations that can affect your design include the following:

- Enterprise administration boundaries and isolation of authority
- Default permissions and schema control
- Global Catalog boundaries
- Domain trust requirements
- Domain controller isolation

Enterprise Administration Boundaries and Isolation of Authority

The forest is the boundary of enterprise administration. The built-in Administrator account in the forest root domain is the forest owner because this account, along with members of the Enterprise Admins and the forest root Domain Admins security groups, has ultimate authority over all objects in all domains in the forest. Collectively, members of the Enterprise Admins and forest root Domain Admins groups are known as *enterprise administrators*. In reality, all domain administrators should be considered enterprise administrators when it comes to security. Reasons for this are explained later in this chapter. Enterprise administrators control the Active Directory objects in the configuration container that do not belong to any one domain, including Enterprise Certification Authority objects and other configuration data that affects all domains in the forest. Needless to say, these accounts have high security requirements.

Because enterprise administrators have authority over all domains in the forest, the domain administrators in each domain must trust the enterprise administrators. You cannot truly restrict enterprise administrators from managing objects in any domain in the forest. Enterprise administrators can always regain control over objects. Some organizations with political challenges, such as those frequently encountered in mergers and acquisitions, might find the scope of this enterprise authority too great and require more than one forest. If your organization requires strict isolation of authority between domains, you will need to deploy multiple forests with manually created trusts between domains in the different forests. These are similar to the structures commonly used in Windows NT domains and are greatly improved in Microsoft Windows Server 2003.

Default Permissions and Schema Control

Each Active Directory forest has one collection of object classes and attributes defined in the Active Directory Schema container and used as templates for objects created in the directory. Object classes in the schema can be instantiated in any domain in the forest. The default permissions on all objects created in the forest are derived from the schema. Thus, alterations or extensions to the schema affect the security of the entire forest, and permissions to make changes to the schema must be restricted. The only user accounts that can make changes to the schema of a forest are members of the Schema Admins security group, which is created by default in the forest root domain and contains only the built-in Administrator account for the forest root domain. Only enterprise administrators (members of the forest root domain Administrators, Domain Admins, and Enterprise Admins groups) can modify membership in the Schema Admins group. If your organization employs multiple groups that require autonomy and isolation of object classes or default security on objects, you will need to create multiple forests.

Global Catalog Boundaries

The Global Catalog contains a read-only listing of all objects and a subset of attributes from every object in every domain in the forest. The Global Catalog is used by applications to locate objects and look up attributes of objects. The Global Catalog also provides a boundary of searchable objects that can be accessed by all security principals in the forest. Therefore, if objects that should not be universally searchable exist, your organization will require multiple forests. Similarly, Microsoft Exchange 2000 Server and Exchange Server 2003 use the Global Catalog to populate the global address list (GAL) for internal e-mail recipients, with a single Exchange organization mapping to a single forest. Thus, creating multiple forests impacts your organization's Exchange design as well. If your organization requires multiple forests, you can still have a single address book by using Microsoft Identity Integration Server 2003 to integrate Global Catalogs.

Domain Trust Requirements

Within an Active Directory forest, all domains are connected by Kerberos trusts. Kerberos trusts are two-way and transitive in nature. This differs from Windows NT–style trusts, which are one-way and nontransitive. Each child domain trusts its parent domain, and each tree root trusts the forest root domain. Thus, the forest root domain is the key to transitive trust in the forest. Removal of the Kerberos trusts between domains in the forest will destroy Active Directory functionality. In Windows NT, it was common to create a domain that trusted logons from another domain that itself did not trust logons from the trusted domain—in other words, implementing one-way trust relationships was common.

In Active Directory, however, all Kerberos key distribution centers (KDCs) in the forest are trusted equally and implicitly. Therefore, credentials from a compromised KDC and a legitimate KDC are indistinguishable by other KDCs and will be implicitly accepted. If your organization's security requirements dictate that domains must have only one-way trusts with other domains in your organization or isolation of Kerberos KDCs, the domains must be created in separate forests. The only external Kerberos trust relationships that can be created in Microsoft Windows 2000 are trusts between a Windows 2000 domain and an MIT Kerberos realm. You can create Windows NT–style trusts between Active Directory domains in a different forest, but those trusts cannot be used by other domains in either forest. If you require trusts between multiple domains in different Windows 2000 forests, each trust must be created manually between each of the domain pairs.

Windows Server 2003 adds the capability to create cross-forest trusts. Because cross-forest trusts offer full Kerberos integration between forests (two-way and transitive), you can use them to create federated trusts. Although the functionality gained by creating cross-forest trusts is outside the scope of this book, one important addition to Windows Server 2003 security in cross-forest trusts is selective authentication. For more information on selective authentication, see the following sidebar titled "Understanding SIDHistory and Selective Authentication."

Understanding SIDHistory and Selective Authentication

Each security principal has a unique security identifier (SID) assigned to it at creation. SIDs uniquely identify accounts—in fact, they are the only thing that the security manager uses to distinguish accounts from one another. During domain consolidation or migrations, you might need to move an account from one domain to another. In native mode, moving objects between domains is possible but SIDs are all relative to the domain in which they are created. To preserve the account's access to resources after a new account has been created in the target domain, an attribute called SIDHistory is added to the object and populated with the account's SID from the original domain.

Domain controllers will not only populate the access token with the account's SID and the SID of groups the user belongs to in the domain, they will also add the SIDs in the SIDHistory attribute. Although this is a major convenience for domain consolidation and migration, it also can be a security risk. For example, while this type of an attack is non-trivial, a user who could edit her account's SIDHistory attribute could add the SID of a domain administrator from another domain. Because SIDs are not secret information, learning the SID is a trivial operation. The user is now a service administrator and, hence, can potentially control any object in the forest. This is not good. You can prevent this by enabling SID filtering, which prevents SIDHistory information from appearing in the access token of a user from another forest. In fact, after you apply Service Pack 4 for Windows 2000 on your domain controllers running Windows 2000, SID filtering is enabled for external trusts. It is also enabled by default in Windows Server 2003 for external trusts. You can disable SID filtering in Windows 2000 during times that it is required. (For information about SID filtering limitations, see Knowledge Base article 289243.)

Windows Server 2003 adds the capability to authenticate accounts selectively across domain trusts. After enabling selective authentication, domain controllers will verify that the individual account has been permitted to access resources in the domain, rather than using the all-or-nothing approach employed by SID filtering. When creating a forest trust using the New Trust Wizard in the Active Directory Domains and Trusts Microsoft Management Console (MMC), you are prompted to select whether you would like to enable domainwide authentication or selective authentication for each of the forest domains. You can change your choice later by looking at the properties of the trust and going to the Authentication tab. After creating the cross-forest trust, you can grant selected accounts from the other forest the Allowed To Authenticate permission on computer accounts in this forest. Accounts that do not have this permission will not be able to connect and authenticate to those computers. Both domains must be in full Windows Server 2003 functional level, and the Domain Name System (DNS) must be resolving properly across domains.

Domain Controller Isolation

In Active Directory, each domain controller holds replicas of at least three logical partitions in the Active Directory database: the schema container, the configuration container, and the domain naming context for the domain controller's domain. The first two containers are replicated among all domain controllers in the forest, and the latter is replicated among all domain controllers for the same domain. Because all domain controllers' replicas of the Active Directory database are writeable and can replicate shared information to domain controllers in other domains, compromise of a single domain controller can affect the entire forest.

For example, it is possible for an attacker who has physical access to any domain controller to view or manipulate data stored anywhere in the forest or on any computer in the forest. That attacker can even make offline changes to forestwide partitions in the directory database, thus compromising the entire implementation. Consequently, physical access to all domain controllers must be restricted to trusted personnel. Similarly, any account with Active Directory service administrator privileges in a domain can potentially hijack a domain controller under its control to compromise the entire forest, either by data manipulation or denial-of-service attack. If your organization requires complete isolation of domains, even from other domain administrators—as is commonly the case in large holding corporations or hosting solutions—you must deploy multiple forests.

Protection of the Forest Root Domain

Regardless of how many forests your organization implements, you must protect the forest root domain. This is because compromise of this domain could have catastrophic effects on your network. You must protect the following two main components of a forest root domain:

- Enterprise administrator accounts
- Physical security of forest root domain controllers

Enterprise Administrator Accounts

The forest root domain contains the built-in Administrator account for the root, which by default is the only member of the Enterprise Admins, Schema Admins, and Administrators security groups. If an attacker compromises this account or any accounts placed into these groups, the attacker can gain complete control over the entire forest. You can build several safeguards into your Active Directory design to protect these accounts and security groups. The following list describes these safeguards:

- **Limit the number of enterprise and domain administrators.**   Make only the accounts that require enterprise authority members of the Enterprise Admins, Domain Admins, and Schema Admins security groups. In most organizations, this will likely be very few accounts. Also, because domain administrators can impact operations and security of the entire forest, you should restrict membership to only trusted employees who should use these accounts only when absolutely necessary. Because delegation in Active Directory is so powerful and granular, the biggest battle in reducing the number of enterprise administrators will be political.

- **Use Restricted Groups.**   You can use Restricted Groups in the Group Policy security settings to limit membership in built-in Administrators, Enterprise Admins, Domain Admins, and Schema Admins security groups. Restricted Groups, by default, are enforced every 16 hours on each domain controller.

- **Perform all administration locally.**   Restrict the enterprise administrator accounts to logging on interactively to forest root domain controllers. This will prevent enterprise administrator accounts from being attacked on nondomain controllers by keystroke loggers or weekly secure remote administration communication channels.

- **Use smart cards.**   For accounts that require enterprise administrator rights or permissions, require the use of smart cards for interactive logon and enable the smart card removal behavior to lock the computer if the smart card is removed from the reader. Before enabling the option to require a smart card for interactive logon, be sure to change the password on the account to a strong password. Ideally, this password should be random and longer than 50 characters to prevent brute force attacks. In Windows Server 2003, a random password of 127 characters is automatically created when you select the option to require the use of smart cards for logon.

- **Use strong passwords.**   For the built-in Administrator account create a password with a minimum of 15 characters. This will prevent a LAN Manager (LM) password hash from being created. Ideally, use a longer password or pass phrase.

- **Provide physical security over the forest root domain controllers.**   If the physical security of a forest root domain controller is compromised, all accounts in the forest root domain are vulnerable, including enterprise administrative accounts. Remember, even if strong passwords are employed, any password can be broken, given adequate hardware resources and time.

Physical Security of Forest Root Domain Controllers

In a multiple-domain forest, the forest cannot function without the presence of the forest root domain. For example, suppose your organization houses all the domain controllers from the forest root domain in a single facility and that facility is destroyed by a natural disaster such as a tornado or hurricane or human-caused event such as arson. If the forest root domain cannot be recovered by using backup media, your organization's Active Directory must be completely rebuilt. Similarly, the physical compromise of a domain controller can lead to the exposure of Active Directory account password hashes. The password hashes can then be attacked offline.

As previously discussed, the physical compromise of a domain controller can compromise the entire forest if an attacker exploits a domain controller's ability to write data to other domain controllers in the forest, or if the attacker utilizes implicit and equal trust given to all KDCs by other KDCs to attack other domains. You must design Active Directory with the location and physical security of domain controllers in mind, and you might need to implement multiple forests to isolate sensitive accounts or operations.

Designing Domains for Active Directory Security

After your organization decides whether to require more than one forest, you should design the domain structure for your organization. The forest is the ultimate security boundary in Active Directory. Domains, on the other hand, are limited security boundaries with respect to the autonomy of domain accounts and administration, although the forest root domain is a special case in domain security. As previously mentioned, the forest root domain is central to the forestwide Kerberos trusts and houses the enterprise administrative groups and accounts.

With the exception of the forest root domain, the Domain Admins security group has autonomous authority over all objects in the domain but has only user access outside its own domain. Members of the Domain Admins security group in the forest root domain can manipulate the membership of the Enterprise Admins and Schema Admins security groups and thus can control all objects in the forest. You might have trusted administrators who require domainwide administrative privileges for some part of their duties but not forestwide administrative capabilities. By creating a separate domain, you avoid having to place these administrators into the Domain Admins group of the forest root domain.

All Active Directory service administrators in domains—including Domain Admins, Server Operators, and the other built-in domain administrator security groups—must be highly trusted because they have the ability to jeopardize forest security by domain controller compromise. If your organization's administrators do not meet this isolation criterion, you must decide on one of the following:

- Accepting the risk and using a single forest
- Mitigating the risk by not granting administrators who are not as trusted as other administrators membership in Active Directory service administrator groups
- Avoiding the risk by creating separate forests

If you build two domains in your forest, each containing resources and accounts, you need to consider that the domain administrators in the forest root domain will also be domain administrators in the other domain. This is because all members of the Administrators group in the root domain have enterprise administration rights. In this situation, which is generally true for multiple-domain scenarios, you might consider deploying an empty root forest design. In this design, the forest root is used to contain only the enterprise administrative accounts; all production resources and user accounts reside in child domains. By employing an empty root design, you can preserve the ability to manage the forest centrally and use a single Global Catalog, while enabling autonomy and limited isolation between domains.

Although enterprise administrators can create Group Policy objects (GPOs) at the site level, the domain is also the unit of isolation for domain account policies. These settings apply to all computer and user accounts in the domain and cannot be applied on a more granular level, such as an OU or individual account. Account policies include the following:

- **Password policy**   Determine the password composition and validating rules that must be met, such as password length and complexity requirements

- **Account lockout policy**   Define thresholds for the automatic locking of accounts

- **Kerberos ticket policy**   Determine the lifetime of Kerberos tickets, as well as parameters relating to renewal of existing Kerberos tickets

> **More Info**   Account policies are discussed in depth in Chapter 3, "Configuring Security for User Accounts and Passwords."

The account policy for the domain is configured, by default, in the default domain policy GPO. Although you can configure account policies on GPOs linked to OUs, those settings affect only local computer SAM databases, not domain accounts. If your organization consists of business units that require different account policies, you must create multiple domains.

Because domain administrators can create data administrators by delegating control over all domain resources to other user accounts, including Group Policy, you should limit the number of domain administrators in your organization. The Domain Admins security group is automatically added to the local Administrators security group on all computers that are members of the domain. Because this gives domain administrators full control over all computers in the domain, including servers, domain administrators are also data administrators for all computers, accounts, and information in the domain. If possible, you should apply the same security thresholds for domain administrators as enterprise administrators because these accounts are inherently powerful in a manner similar to enterprise administrative accounts.

Designing DNS for Active Directory Security

The successful operation of Active Directory depends on the successful operation of DNS. After your organization has designed its forest and domain plan, you must design the DNS infrastructure to support Active Directory. DNS provides three crucial functions for Active Directory in Windows Server 2003 and Windows 2000:

- **Name resolution** DNS resolves host names to IP addresses and vice versa. DNS is the default location mechanism in Windows Server 2003 and Windows 2000.

- **Service locator** Computers that run Windows 2000 and later use DNS to locate services (represented by Service resource records, also known as SRV records) such as the Global Catalog and Kerberos KDCs, as well as domain controllers, domains, and site information.

- **Namespace definition** DNS establishes the namespace used to define Active Directory.

> **Tip** You do not have to use a Windows-based DNS server to support an Active Directory implementation. At minimum, the DNS server that you use must support the use of SRV records. Microsoft also strongly recommends that your DNS server support incremental zone transfers (IXFRs) and dynamic updates. Windows Server 2003 and Windows 2000 DNS provide all these features.

Several common designs for DNS support Active Directory. Each of these models has security benefits and drawbacks, and other valid designs are possible. These are the common designs:

- Single namespace
- Delegated namespace
- Internal namespace
- Segmented namespace

Regardless of which DNS model you adopt for Active Directory, you must ensure the security of the DNS server and services because the compromise of DNS services can lead to a denial-of-service attack or the disclosure of information. An attacker or rogue administrator could compromise your DNS server and erase Service resource records (SRV records), causing Active Directory replication to fail and client logons to be rejected or Group Policy to not be applied. An attacker or rogue administrator could also change SRV record information to redirect replication and logon traffic to illegitimate servers to retrieve information from the packets. This process is known as *DNS poisoning*.

> **More Info** See Chapter 18, "Implementing Security for DNS Servers," for in-depth information on how to secure DNS.

Single Namespace

In a single-namespace Active Directory, SRV records are intermingled with all the other resource records for your organization. Although this is the simplest design, you risk the external exposure of your namespace and SRV records, which could prove useful to an attacker. Also, a single namespace requires a potentially complex set of permissions to update and manage the DNS zone information.

Delegated Namespace

In a delegated namespace, a subzone of your public namespace is delegated to support Active Directory. This enables you to segregate your Active Directory SRV records from your publicly available records, such as your Web presence. This design also enables your Active Directory administrators to manage a specific portion of DNS, while the current DNS administrators can continue to maintain their portion of DNS.

Internal Namespace

You might want to use an internal namespace for Active Directory. For example, a company whose external Web presence is woodgrovebank.com might create a DNS namespace for Active Directory named *woodgrovebank.corp*. Although using a nonpublic domain can add security to your Active Directory installation and alleviates any concerns over who would manage the portion of DNS that supports Active Directory, this DNS design can limit the scalability of Active Directory. Alternatively, you might want to register a public DNS namespace and only use it internally for Active Directory.

Segmented Namespace

You might want to use the same namespace for Active Directory as you use for your public presence but not use the same DNS infrastructure. For example, your organization's ISP could host your public DNS namespace, but you could host a parallel namespace internally to support Active Directory. If you choose this configuration, you can isolate your Active Directory DNS infrastructure, while preserving the possibility of public scalability for later. If you select this DNS design, you more than likely will have to replicate some entries from your public DNS infrastructure to your internal DNS infrastructure manually.

Active Directory–Integrated Zones and Security

In addition to standard primary and secondary zones, Windows Server 2003 and Windows 2000 support Active Directory–integrated zones. Active Directory–integrated zones improve the security of standard zones by doing the following:

- **Allowing DNS records to be dynamically updated securely**   Primary zones have a binary dynamic update permission—the zone either accepts or denies dynamic updates. Active Directory–integrated zones add a third option: to allow only secure dynamic updates. If you choose this option, when a computer attempts to update or create a resource record in DNS, the DNS server will forward the attempt to Active Directory. There, the change will be compared to the discretionary access control list (DACL) on the zone object and to the resource record, if it exists. The change will occur only if the computer has the necessary permissions.

- **Enabling DNS records to be secured as Active Directory objects**   Because resource records are stored as objects in Active Directory objects, security on those objects can be configured as your organization requires.

- **Securing the DNS records during zone transfer**   In a default standard zone transfer, records are sent as clear text, which means that securing the connection between DNS servers for zone transfers requires additional configuration. However, when DNS zones are stored as Active Directory–integrated objects, Active Directory replication is used to facilitate the transfer of zone updates. This replication is automatically encrypted by using remote procedure call (RPC) encryption without additional configuration.

Active Directory–integrated zones can be hosted only on DNS servers that are also domain controllers. Thus, Active Directory–integrated zones are appropriate only for internal use or for use in an isolated forest with exposure to public networks, as is common with perimeter network (also known as DMZ, demilitarized zone, and screened subnet) Active Directory installations.

Designing the Delegation of Authority

Rather than granting all administrators the rights and permissions of Active Directory service administrators by making them members of the Domain Admins or other Active Directory service administrator security groups, as was commonly done in Windows NT domains, Active Directory enables you to place accounts and resources into OUs and delegate an appropriate level of authority over those objects to administrative staff. By doing this, you can create data management administrators who have autonomous or semiautonomous authority over Active Directory objects, domain member computers, and data. The simplest way to do this in Active Directory is to create OUs based on management requirements and to delegate authority over the OU (or objects in the OU) to specific data administrator security groups. Consequently, OUs are the primary management unit in Active Directory. By delegating limited control over objects in a domain, you can minimize the number of Active Directory service administrators while ensuring that data administrators have only the rights and permissions they require to complete their job tasks.

Delegation of administration enables you to create custom administrative security groups that administer the users, computers, or other objects in an OU, OU tree, or domain. To accomplish this, you must first design an effective OU structure. When designing an OU structure, consider three things: Group Policy, delegation of authority, and your organization's management model. Place all objects with similar administrative and security requirements in an OU or OU tree. Then create the custom security groups, and delegate administration of the OUs (or objects in OUs) to the appropriate groups. Windows Server 2003 and Windows 2000 offer granular control over the administrative tasks that can be delegated. On an OU, you can delegate authority over the following:

- The OU
- The OU and all child OUs
- Specific types of objects in the OU
- Specific attributes of specific objects in an OU
- Tasks that affect specific types of objects in an OU

You can delegate authority either by setting the permissions on the container by using the object's Security tab, by using command-line utilities such as Dsacls.exe, or by using the Delegation of Control Wizard in the MMC. The Delegation of Control Wizard might not expose all the permissions you want to modify on an object, so you might need to use the Security tab or even ADSIEdit from the Windows Server 2003 or Windows 2000 Support Tools to edit the DACL of the object directly. In some cases, you will need to make further modifications to delegate the necessary authority—for example, when delegating the ability to unlock accounts. For more information, see Microsoft Knowledge Base article 279723, "How to Grant Help Desk Personnel the Specific Right to Unlock Locked User Accounts" (*http://support.microsoft.com/kb/279723*).

> **Tip** A new command-line tool called Dsrevoke enables you to view and remove permissions on the domain and OU containers in Active Directory. You can download Dsrevoke from the Microsoft Web site at *http://www.microsoft.com/downloads /details.aspx?familyid=77744807-c403-4bda-b0e4-c2093b8d6383&displaylang=en*. Dsrevoke will work on domain controllers running either Windows 2000 or Windows Server 2003.

When delegating authority to objects in Active Directory, you must consider how the administrators will manage the objects over which you have given them authority. Several administrative interfaces are available:

- **Server Console** Performing domain administration of a Windows environment while physically seated at a user's workstation can be a significant security risk and should be avoided whenever possible. This can be mitigated by logging on at the server console.

- **Terminal Services** Consider using Terminal Services in remote administration mode for administrative tasks, which requires that you delegate to the user performing the administration the right to connect to the server using a remote administration terminal session, as described in Knowledge Base article 253831, "Remote Administration of Terminal Services by Non-Administrators Accounts" (*http://support.microsoft.com/kb/253831*). In Windows 2000, Terminal Services is considered by the system to be an interactive logon, so its users will need the right to log on locally to the server. Because the system does not differentiate between a Terminal Services "local" logon and a physical "local" logon, you must ensure that your servers are secured against physical access by users who have been granted the right to log on locally to facilitate terminal session management. In Windows Server 2003, an additional logon right was added for logons through Terminal Services, so you no longer have to grant interactive logon rights to users who will only be using the computer through a Terminal Services session.

- **MMC** You can install Windows Server 2003 or Windows 2000 Administrative Tools by installing Adminpak.msi from the CD or from the System32 directory on any server installation. By installing these tools on the workstations of administrative staff, you provide them with the interfaces needed to manage servers remotely without granting them local logon rights on those servers. You can limit which MMC snap-ins the administrator can use by implementing the appropriate settings in Group Policy.

Best Practices

- **Use multiple forests if you require discrete isolation.**   If your security policy calls for discrete isolation of control between domains, use separate forests.

- **Physically secure domain controllers.**   If an attacker or rogue administrator can physically compromise domain controllers, he not only can gain access to the information stored on the domain controller, but he can potentially compromise information on the domain controller to jeopardize the entire forest.

- **Train administrators.**   Once you have delegated authority to a user over a set of objects, you have created an administrator of some degree. You should, at a minimum, provide training to make the administrator aware of the capabilities and limits of her account, the ways she can protect her account, and the techniques she can use to complete the tasks for which you have given her responsibility.

- **Perform audits.**   You should always audit delegated objects to ensure that the administrator is completing the tasks he has been assigned and to provide an audit trail to detect misuse of administrative authority.

- **Complete background checks.**   Work with your organization's HR department to complete background checks on all enterprise and domain administrators. Also, carefully consider the employees to whom you delegate authority and the level of responsibility and accountability you require of them.

- **Minimize the number of Active Directory service administrators.**   The fewer accounts with Active Directory service administration rights and permissions— especially membership in the Enterprise Admins or Domain Admins security group—the more secure they generally will be.

- **Control membership in security groups with high security requirements.**   Use Restricted Groups in Group Policy to control membership in security groups such as Active Directory service administrators and other custom security groups that have high security requirements. Allow only other service administrator groups to modify the membership of service administrator groups. Do not include users or groups from external trusted forests in Active Directory service administrator groups in your forest, unless the Active Directory service administrators from the external forest are as trusted as your forest's Active Directory service administrators.

- **Isolate the management of computers on which Active Directory service accounts are used.**   Allow only Active Directory service administrator groups to manage workstations used by Active Directory service administrators. For example, a rogue administrator or attacker could install Trojan horse software such as keystroke-logging applications to retrieve passwords. After an administrator logs on to the computer using an enterprise administrator account or a domain administrator account, the rogue administrator could retrieve her password.

- **Use smart cards.** Require the use of smart cards for accounts with high security requirements—preferably all administrative accounts in the forest.

- **Delegate control over OUs or objects within OUs.** Use OUs as your primary unit of management. Delegate authority over OU containers or objects within an OU to administrators.

- **Use Active Directory–integrated DNS.** Use Active Directory–integrated zones to take advantage of security enhancements offered by Active Directory over standard zone files.

- **Document delegated permissions.** When delegating authority, be sure to document the permissions you grant to users. Active Directory does not differentiate between permissions that have been delegated and those that are default permissions.

Additional Information

- "Best Practice Guide for Securing Active Directory Installations and Day-to-Day Operations, Parts 1 and 2" white paper (*http://www.microsoft.com/technet /prodtechnol/windows2000serv/technologies/activedirectory/maintain/bpguide /default.mspx*)

- "Multiple Forest Considerations in Windows 2000 and Windows Server 2003" white paper (*http://www.microsoft.com/technet/prodtechnol /windowsserver2003/technologies/directory/activedirectory/mtfstwp.mspx*)

- "How Domains and Forest Trusts Work" (*http://www.microsoft.com/Resources /Documentation/windowsserv/2003/all/techref/en-us/W2K3TR_trust_how.asp*)

- "Best Practice Active Directory Design for Managing Windows Networks" (*http://www.microsoft.com/technet/prodtechnol/windows2000serv/technologies /activedirectory/plan/bpaddsgn.mspx*)

- "Windows 2000 Domain Architecture: Design Alternatives" (*http:// www.microsoft.com/technet/prodtechnol/windows2000serv/technologies /activedirectory/plan/w2kdomar.mspx*)

- "Design Considerations for Delegation of Administration in Active Directory" (*http://www.microsoft.com/technet/prodtechnol/windows2000serv/technologies /activedirectory/plan/addeladm.mspx*)

■ The following Knowledge Base articles:

❑ 315676: "How to Delegate Administrative Authority in Windows 2000" (*http://support.microsoft.com/kb/315676*)

❑ 221577: "How to Delegate Authority for Editing a Group Policy Object (GPO)" (*http://support.microsoft.com/kb/221577*)

❑ 235531: "Default Security Concerns in Active Directory Delegation" (*http://support.microsoft.com/kb/235531*)

❑ 279723: "How to Grant Help Desk Personnel the Specific Right to Unlock Locked User Accounts" (*http://support.microsoft.com/kb/279723*)

❑ 301191: "How to Integrate DNS with Existing DNS Infrastructure if Active Directory Is Enabled in Windows 2000" (*http://support.microsoft.com /kb/301191*)

❑ 323418: "How to Integrate DNS with an Existing DNS Infrastructure if Active Directory Is Enabled in Windows Server 2003" (*http://support.microsoft.com/kb/323418*)

❑ 253831: "Remote Administration of Terminal Services by Non-Administrators Accounts" (*http://support.microsoft.com/kb/253831*)

❑ 289243: "MS02-001: Forged SID Could Result in Elevated Privileges in Windows 2000" (*http://support.microsoft.com/kb/289243*)

Part III
Securing the Core Operating System

Chapter 8

Controlling Access to Data

In Microsoft Windows Server 2003, Windows 2000, and Windows XP, a security principal's level of access to files and folders is determined by NTFS file system and share permissions. These permissions are discretionary: anyone with ownership of a file or folder, Change Permissions, or Full Control permissions can assign access control at his discretion. When freshly installed, Windows Server 2003, Windows 2000, and Windows XP assign default permission structures to the file system; however, you will need to alter these permissions to ensure that only the appropriate users have access to files stored on the computer.

Securing File and Folder Permissions

All file and folder objects stored on an NTFS volume have security descriptors to control access to the object. The security descriptor includes a discretionary access control list (DACL) and a system access control list (SACL), in addition to information that identifies the object's owner. Figure 8-1 shows the contents of a security descriptor.

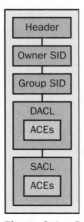

Figure 8-1   Contents of a security descriptor

DACLs owe their name to the fact that they can be configured at the discretion of any account that possesses Take Ownership, Change Permissions, or Full Control permissions to the file system object. DACLs are defined by security descriptors, which consist of several elements as described in Table 8-1.

Table 8-1   Elements of a Security Descriptor

Element	Description
Header	Metadata pertaining to the access control entries (ACEs) associated with the DACL.
SID (user)	The security identifier (SID) of the owner of the object.
SID (group)	The SID of the primary group of the object's owner.
Generic deny ACEs	ACEs that deny access to an account or security group based on that group's SIDs. These ACEs can be inherited from the object's parent or assigned directly to the object.
Generic allow ACEs	ACEs that allow access to child objects to an account or security group based on that group's SIDs. These ACEs can be inherited from the object's parent or assigned directly to the object.

What Does Owning a Resource Mean?

The owner of a resource, such as a file or folder, is the account that ultimately determines the access control over that resource. The owner has complete control over the resource, including the ability to assign permissions to other accounts. Even if the owner is explicitly denied access to a resource, the owner can still change the permissions on the resource to restore her access. File ownership is also used by the quota system in Windows Server 2003, Windows 2000, and Windows XP to calculate the amount of disk space used by each tracked account, if disk quotas are enabled. The default owner of files and folders in Windows Server 2003, Windows 2000, and Windows XP installations is the built-in Administrators group, although a user who creates a file or folder is the owner of anything she creates.

Members of the Administrators group can always take ownership of files and folders on the local computer—even if NTFS permissions prohibit administrators from accessing the resource. This ensures that files can be recovered by an administrator in the event that a user leaves the company or permissions are incorrectly configured and must be corrected. When a member of the Administrators group takes ownership of a resource, the ownership is granted to the Administrators group. However, the SID of the individual administrator is also recorded and stored in the DACL for accountability reasons. When a user who is not a member of the Administrators group takes ownership of a resource, ownership is associated with her account's SID.

Windows Server 2003 enables Administrators to replace the owner of a file or folder in the graphical user interface. Although the user interface prevents you from assigning ownership of an object to any user account in Windows 2000 and Windows Server 2003, you can complete this action from the command line if you are a member of the Administrators group or have the privilege to Restore files and directories on the computer using the command-line tool Subinacl.exe. The syntax for replacing the owner of a file using Subinacl.exe follows:

```
Subinacl /file filename.ext /setowner=domain\newowner
```

You can use Subinacl.exe to configure permissions on the following items:

- Files
- Folders
- Registry keys
- Services
- Printers
- Kernel objects
- Shares
- Metabases

Subinacl.exe is a low-level utility and should be used with caution. For routine permission changes on files and folders, other tools such as Xcacls.exe and Cacls.exe are easier to use but do not offer nearly the number of options that Subinacl.exe does.

You can define NTFS permissions at either the folder or file level. For folders, you can assign the following standard permissions in the Security tab of the folder's properties page:

- Full Control
- Modify
- Read & Execute
- List Folder Contents
- Read
- Write

For individual files, these are the standard permissions:

- Full Control
- Modify
- Read & Execute
- Read
- Write

Standard NTFS permissions are compilations of several special permissions, including these:

- **Traverse Folder/Execute File**   Traverse Folder allows or denies navigating through folders, even though the user does not have permissions to access files or folders within that folder. This permission applies to folders only. Execute File allows or denies running program files and applies to files only. Setting the Traverse Folder permission will not automatically set the Execute File permission on the files in the folder. Additionally, by default the Everyone group is assigned the Bypass Traverse Checking user right, which prevents the Traverse Folder permissions from being assessed when a resource is accessed.

- **List Folder/Read Data**   List Folder allows or denies viewing file names and subfolder names within the folder and applies to folders only. Read Data allows or denies viewing data in files and applies to files only.

- **Read Attributes**   Allows or denies viewing the attributes of a file or folder, such as Read-Only and Hidden attributes.

- **Read Extended Attributes**   Allows or denies viewing the extended attributes of a file or folder. Specific programs define the extended attributes.

- **Create Files/Write Data**   Create Files allows or denies creating files within a folder. Write Data allows or denies making changes to a file and overwriting existing content.

- **Create Folders/Append Data**   Create Folders allows or denies creating folders within a folder. Append Data allows or denies making changes to the end of the file but not changing, deleting, or overwriting any existing data in the file.

- **Write Attributes**   Allows or denies changing the attributes of a file or folder, such as Read-Only and Hidden attributes.

- **Write Extended Attributes**   Allows or denies changing the extended attributes of a file or folder. The extended attributes are defined by specific programs.

- **Delete Subfolders and Files**   Allows or denies deleting subfolders and files when applied at a parent folder, even if the Delete permission has not been granted on the specific subfolder or file.

- **Delete**   Allows or denies the deletion of a file or folder.

- **Read Permissions**   Allows or denies reading permissions assigned to a file or folder.

- **Change Permissions**   Allows or denies modification of the permissions assigned to a file or folder.

- **Take Ownership**   Allows or denies taking ownership of the file or folder.

Table 8-2 displays how, in Windows Server 2003, Windows 2000, and Windows XP, the special permissions map to the basic permissions.

Table 8-2   File and Folder Permissions Mapping in Windows Server 2003, Windows 2000, and Windows XP

	Basic Permissions					
Special Permissions	**Full Control**	**Modify**	**Read & Execute**	**List Folder Contents***	**Read**	**Write**
Traverse Folder /Execute File	X	X	X	X		
List Folder/Read Data	X	X	X	X	X	
Read Attributes	X	X	X	X	X	
Read Extended Attributes	X	X	X	X	X	
Create Files/Write Data	X	X				X
Create Folders /Append Data	X	X				X
Write Attributes	X	X				X
Write Extended Attributes	X	X				X
Delete Subfolders and Files	X					
Delete	X	X				
Read Permissions	X	X	X	X	X	X
Change Permissions	X					
Take Ownership	X					

* Permissions apply to folder objects only.

How DACLs Work

When a user attempts to access a file or folder on an NTFS partition, the user's access token is compared with the DACL of the file or folder. If no ACEs correspond to a SID in the user's access token, the user is implicitly denied access to the resource. If ACEs correspond to the user's access token, the ACEs are applied in the following order:

- **Explicit deny**   An ACE applied directly to the resource that denies access. An explicit deny always overrides all other permissions.

- **Explicit allow**   An ACE applied directly to the resource that grants access. An explicit allow always overrides an inherited deny but is always overridden by explicit deny ACEs.

- **Inherited deny**   An ACE inherited from the resource's parent object. An inherited deny ACE overrides an inherited allow permission but is overridden by an explicit allow.

- **Inherited allow**   An ACE inherited from the resource's parent object.

ACEs that apply to the user are cumulative, meaning that the user receives the sum of the ACEs that apply to his user account and groups of which he is a member. For example, if an access control list (ACL) contains two allow ACEs that apply to the user, one for Read access and the other for Write access, the user will receive Read and Write access.

> **Caution**   Because explicit allow ACEs override inherited deny ACEs, you should assign explicit permissions with caution. For example, if the Sales_Managers group has been denied the Write permission on all files and folders in the d:\finance_audit folder but a user named Tom is granted Write permissions to the d:\finance_audit\review\TPS.xls file, Tom will be able to modify the TPS.xls file—even if he is a member of the Sales_Managers group, which is denied Write permissions by inheritance.

Assigning DACLs at Creation

When a file or folder is created, it inherits from its parent object the permissions that are applicable to its type of object. This includes both permissions that are inherited by the parent object and permissions that are explicitly assigned to the parent object. Once created, you can augment the inherited permissions by adding ACEs to the newly created resource.

In Windows Server 2003, Windows 2000, and Windows XP, each file and folder has the Allow Inheritable Permissions From The Parent Object To Propagate To This Object property enabled by default. If you alter the permissions on the parent object, the permission change will automatically flow to the child object. If you want to modify this behavior, you need to decide whether you want to remove the inherited permissions or copy them to the object. If you choose to remove the inherited permissions, the only permissions that will remain are those explicitly granted to the object. If you choose to copy the permissions, the object will have the same permissions as it had previously, but the formerly inherited permissions will instead be explicitly assigned to the object.

Note In the user interface of Windows Server 2003, Windows 2000, and Windows XP, explicit permissions are displayed with a check in a white check box and inherited permissions are displayed with a check in a gray check box. Gray check boxes cannot be directly modified unless the permissions are made explicit, which changes the check boxes to white to indicate explicit assignment.

How DACLs Are Handled When Files and Folders Are Copied or Moved

The way DACLs are handled for files and folders that are moved and copied into other locations can be confusing. If you are responsible for securing files and folders, you must understand several intricacies of copying and moving files and folders, or you might unwittingly create a security risk.

The first thing you need to know is that creating a copy of a file on the same partition actually creates a new file in the destination container. Thus, all permissions are inherited from the new parent object. The original object's permissions are unchanged. This action creates a potential security risk because two copies of the same file that have different security settings can exist.

Second, when a file is moved on the same partition, it is not physically relocated to a different address on the disk—instead, the reference to the object in the file system hierarchy is updated. When the ACL on a parent object or an object itself is changed, the permissions structures are updated, but moving an object on the same partition does not trigger a refresh of ACLs. Therefore, all previously inherited and explicit permissions on the moved object *initially* remain unchanged. The Security tab for the object will indicate that the permissions are inherited from its parent object, but until the ACL is refreshed, the Security tab shows inherited permissions from the object's previous parent, along with any permissions assigned directly to the object. The next time that the ACLs for the object itself or for any parent object in the inheritance hierarchy are changed, the inherited permissions on the object will be received from the object's new location in the file system hierarchy. However, the moved object will retain any explicitly assigned permission.

This behavior is a departure from the way that permissions on moved file system objects functioned in Microsoft Windows NT, where objects that were moved within the same partition retained all permissions. If you want to achieve Windows NT–style retention of all permissions on an object you move within the same partition, before moving the object, you must deselect the inheritance attribute on the object and copy the existing inherited permissions so that they become explicit permissions. Or you must remove existing inherited permissions altogether and assign any desired explicit permissions. You can then move the object and re-enable permissions inheritance, which will refresh the ACL on the object. When the ACL is refreshed in this manner, the moved object retains its explicit permissions but receives new inherited permissions from its new parent.

Finally, when you move a file or folder to a different partition or computer, the operation is actually a copy-and-delete process. The file is copied in the new location, thus creating a new file system object, and upon successful creation of the new object, the original is deleted. Creating a copy of a file system object—regardless of whether the copy is created on the same partition or on a different partition or computer—always creates a new instance of the object in the destination location. Therefore, all permissions on the object are inherited from the new parent. Original copies of the object are either deleted (in a move operation across partitions or computers) or unaffected (in a copy operation). Therefore, you should exercise caution when moving or copying files and folders to different partitions or computers because the permissions on the newly created object might not be consistent with the permissions on the original object.

In Windows Server 2003, Windows 2000, and Windows XP, file and folder permissions are automatically inherited from parent objects. Therefore, understanding the default permission on files and folders is important in planning directory structures. You might need to change the default permissions to meet your organization's security policy. Table 8-3 provides a legend of permission inheritance in Windows Server 2003, Windows 2000, and Windows XP.

Table 8-3   Permissions Inheritance Legend

Abbreviation	Description
CI (Container Inherit)	The ACE will be applied to the current directory and inherited by subdirectories.
OI (Object Inherit)	The ACE will be applied to files in the directory and inherited by files in subdirectories.
IO (Inherit Only)	The ACE will not be applied to the current folder or file but will be inherited by child folders.
NI (Not Inherited)	The ACE is not propagated to any child objects.

More Info   The default file and registry permissions can be found in the following white papers:

- "Windows Server 2003" (*http://www.microsoft.com/windowsserver2003 /techinfo/overview/secdef.mspx*)

- "Windows XP" (*http://www.microsoft.com/downloads/details.aspx? FamilyID=60ce1ef5-8d6d-49a0-8eb5-4e362cde75e7&displaylang=en*)

- "Windows 2000" (*http://www.microsoft.com/windows2000/techinfo/planning /security/secdefs.asp*)

Command-Line Tools

In Windows Server 2003, Windows 2000, and Windows XP, the Xcopy.exe utility can be used to preserve the permissions and ownership of files and folders when they are copied. Additionally, you can use several command-line tools to control the file and folder permissions:

- Cacls.exe

- Xcacls.exe

- Subinacl.exe

- Robocopy.exe

On the CD   Robocopy.exe, Xcacls.exe, and Subinacl.exe are located on the CD included with this book. Cacls.exe is included in the default installation of Windows Server 2003, Windows 2000, and Windows XP.

Cacls.exe

Cacls.exe is a command-line utility that enables basic management of file and folder permissions. The usage for Cacls.exe follows:

```
CACLS filename [/T] [/E] [/C] [/G user:perm] [/R user [...]] [/P user:perm [...]]
[/D user [...]]
```

Table 8-4 shows the command-line options for Cacls.exe. You can also use wildcard characters to specify more than one file in a command.

Table 8-4   Command-Line Options for Cacls.exe

Option	Description
filename	Placeholder for the name of the file. Running Cacls.exe with just the file name displays the DACL of the file or folder.
/T	Changes DACLs of specified files in the current directory and all subdirectories.
/E	Edits the existing DACL instead of replacing it.
/C	Continues processing even if an access denied error occurs.
/G *user:perm*	Grants the specified user access rights to the file or folder using explicit permissions.
user	Specifies the domain and user name for which you are modifying permissions. You can specify more than one user in a command.
perm	Specifies the permissions as follows: R for Read, W for Write, C for Change (Write), F for Full Control, N for None.
/R *user*	Revokes all the specified user's access rights (valid only with /E).
/P *user:perm*	Replaces the specified user's access rights.
/D *user*	Denies the specified user access to the file or folder.

Tip   You can redirect console output from the command line by using a standard redirection character. For example, to redirect output from the Cacls.exe tool to a file, type **Cacls.exe** filename.ext>**output.txt**. The results of running the command will be written to the Output.txt file rather than to the console.

Xcacls.exe

Xcacls.exe is a more robust version of Cacls.exe. Not only does Xcacls.exe give you greater control over the special permissions, it is scriptable: unlike Cacls.exe, Xcacls.exe allows you to suppress message prompts. The usage for Xcacls.exe follows:

```
xcacls filename [/T] [/E] [/C] [/G user:perm;spec] [/R user]
[/P user:perm;spec [...]] [/D user [...]] [/Y]
```

Table 8-5 shows the command-line options for Xcacls.exe.

Table 8-5   Command-Line Options for Xcacls.exe

Option	Description
filename	Placeholder for the name of the file. Running Xcacls.exe with just the file name displays the DACL of the file or folder.
/T	Recursively walks through the current directory and all its subdirectories applying the chosen access rights to the matching files or directories.
/E	Edits the existing DACL instead of replacing it.
/C	Causes Xcacls.exe to continue if an access denied error occurs.

Table 8-5   Command-Line Options for Xcacls.exe

Option	Description
/G user:perm;spec	Grants access to the user to the matching file or directory. The *perm* variable applies the specified access right to files.
perm	Specifies the permissions as follows: R for Read, C for Change (Write), F for Full Control, P for Change Permissions, O for Take Ownership, X for Execute, E for Read, W for Write, D for Delete.
/R user	Revokes all access rights for the specified user.
/P user:perm;spec	Replaces access rights for the user.
/D user	Denies the user access to the file or directory.
/Y	Disables confirmation when replacing user access rights. By default, Xcacls.exe prompts for confirmation and, when used in a batch routine, causes the routine to stop responding until the confirmation is entered. The /Y option was introduced to avoid this confirmation so that Xcacls.exe can be used in batch mode.

On the CD   Xcacls.exe is located of the CD that is included with this book. Xcacls.vbs, a Microsoft Visual Basic script, is also included on the CD. You can use Xcacls.vbs to assign permissions in a similar way that you do with Xcacls.exe, albeit from a script. Xcacls.exe is designed to be used at the command line or in batch files; Xcacls.vbs is designed to be used in a scripting environment, where better automation and error handling are required. In addition, you can edit Xcacls.vbs by using any text editor to add custom functionality, such as logging permission changes to a file.

Subinacl.exe

Subinacl.exe is a low-level utility for managing DACLs on many types of objects, including files and folders. The syntax for using Subinacl.exe follows:

```
subinacl [view_mode] [/
test_mode] object_type object_name [action[=parameter]] [action[=parameter]] ...
[/playfile file_name] [/help [/full] [keyword]]
```

The options you can use with Subinacl.exe are explained in Table 8-6.

Table 8-6   Command-Line Options for Subinacl.exe

Option	Description
view_mode	Defines the level of detail in the output of Subinacl.exe. You can use the following switches with this option: ■ /noverbose ■ /verbose
/test_mode	When this option is specified, changes are not actually made to the object's security descriptor. This option enables you to view what the results of the command would be without actually making the changes.

Table 8-6   **Command-Line Options for Subinacl.exe**

Option	Description
object_type	Specifies the type of object on which you are modifying the permissions. You can use these types of objects: ■ /file ■ /subdirectories ■ /onlyfile ■ /share ■ /clustershare ■ /keyreg ■ /subkeyreg ■ /service ■ /printer ■ /kernelobject
object_name	Defines the name of an object on which you are viewing or modifying the permissions.
action	Sets the action that you are attempting to carry out on the object. The action switches include the following: ■ /display (default) ■ /setowner=*owner* ■ /replace=[*DomainName*]*OldAccount*=[*DomainName*]*NewAccount* ■ /changedomain=*OldDomainName*=*NewDomainName* ■ /migratetodomain=*SourceDomain*=*DestDomain* ■ /findsid=[DomainName\]*Account*[=stop] ■ /suppresssid=[*DomainName*]*Account* ■ /confirm ■ /perm ■ /audit ■ /ifchangecontinue ■ /cleandeletedsidsfrom=*DomainName* ■ /accesscheck=[*DomainName*]*UserName* ■ /setprimarygroup=[*DomainName*]*Group* ■ /grant=[*DomainName*]*UserName*[=*Access*] ■ /deny=[*DomainName*]*UserName*[=*Access*] ■ /revoke=[*DomainName*]*UserName* ■ /playfile *filename*

Robocopy.exe

Robocopy.exe is a 32-bit Windows command-line application that simplifies the task of maintaining an identical copy of a folder tree in multiple locations, either on the same computer or in separate network locations. Robocopy is robust—it retries operations after network errors and efficiently copies only changed files. Robocopy is flexible—you can copy a single folder or walk a directory tree, specifying multiple file names and wildcard characters for source files.

 On the CD   For detailed information on using Robocopy, see the Robocopy.doc file on the CD included with this book.

Securing File and Folder Access by Using Share Permissions

NTFS permissions always apply to files and folders, regardless of whether they are accessed locally or over the network through a file share. When you share a folder, the share and its contents are accessed by the server service running on the machine on which the share is created. Share permissions differ from NTFS permissions in that they apply only when the share is accessed over the network and they do not offer the level of granularity provided by NTFS permissions. Table 8-7 explains the permissions that you can assign to a share.

Table 8-7   Share Permissions

Permission	Description
Full Control	Full control over all folders and files in the share
Change	Read and Write permissions to files and folders
Read	Read permission for files and folders

By default in Windows 2000 and Windows XP, when a share is created, the share permissions are set to Everyone Full Control. In Windows Server 2003, share permissions are set to Everyone Read. Like NTFS permissions, share permissions are cumulative. Furthermore, deny permissions override allow permissions.

When a user attempts to access a file or folder on a share, cumulative share permissions as well as the cumulative NTFS permissions are calculated. The user accessing the share receives the more restrictive set of these two sets of permissions. For example, if the share permissions are left to the default setting of Everyone Full Control and the user has only Read and Execute permissions on the files and folders in the share, the user will have only Read and Execute access.

Although share permissions are not nearly as granular as NTFS permissions, they are still useful if implemented correctly. For example, you can achieve a higher degree of security on a share's contents by removing the default share permissions and granting members of the Everyone group Change permissions. This will prevent the changing of permissions on the files and folders in the share remotely through the network redirector. When you remove the Everyone Full Control share permission, the owner of a file can modify permissions only through an interactive logon session, either at the server console or through Terminal Services.

Using the Encrypting File System

Although properly configured DACLs will protect data, sometimes you need a greater degree of protection. Your organization might have some data that must be kept confidential from administrators, even those who have Full Control permissions on the files. Also, your organization might have data that is stored temporarily on laptops issued to employees that must remain confidential even if the physical security of the laptop is compromised. The encrypting file system (EFS) enables users and administrators to encrypt files and folders to extend file and folder security beyond NTFS permissions.

EFS combines asymmetric and symmetric encryption to encrypt files and manage the encryption keys. EFS uses symmetric encryption—either the DES-X algorithm or the 3DES algorithm (Windows Server 2003 and Windows XP only)—to encrypt the data and asymmetric encryption to manage the symmetric encryption keys. The default configuration of EFS allows users to encrypt files without any configuration by an administrator. When a user encrypts a file, EFS automatically generates a public-key pair for the user and either obtains a digital certificate by requesting one from a Certification Authority (CA) or self-creates a certificate if no CA is available to issue certificates.

File encryption and decryption is supported on a per-file or entire-directory basis. Directory encryption is transparently enforced. All files (and subdirectories) created in a directory marked for encryption are automatically encrypted. If you move a file from an encrypted directory to an unencrypted directory on the same volume, the file remains encrypted, whereas moving or copying it to another volume on the computer causes the file to be transparently decrypted as long as you are the user who encrypted the file. Encryption and decryption can be set using the properties of the file or folder in Windows Explorer. Additionally, command-line tools and administrative interfaces are provided for advanced users and recovery agents to ease management of encrypted files.

A file need not be decrypted before use; encryption and decryption are done transparently when bytes travel to and from the disk. EFS automatically detects an encrypted file and locates the user's certificate and associated private key to decrypt the file.

How EFS Works

EFS works differently depending on whether a computer is a member of a domain or it is a stand-alone computer. The following description explains how EFS works in a domain environment.

When a user chooses to encrypt a file, the file is loaded into protected memory and the user's computer generates a random encryption key known as a file encryption key (FEK). The computer uses a symmetric encryption algorithm—either DES-X or, if configured, 3DES in Windows Server 2003 and Windows XP—to encrypt the file using the FEK as the key, as Figure 8-2 shows.

Figure 8-2   Encrypting the contents of a file using EFS

Next, the computer retrieves the user's EFS certificate from the user's profile and extracts the user's public key. If the user does not have an EFS certificate, the computer generates an EFS certificate based on the user's account information, including the user's password. The FEK is encrypted using the RSA algorithm with the public key from the user's EFS certificate and is added to the header of the file in the data decryption field (DDF). This process is shown in Figure 8-3.

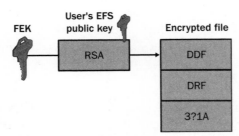

Figure 8-3   Encrypting the FEK of a file using the EFS public key of the user account

The final step in encrypting the file is accomplished by the computer retrieving the certificate for each EFS recovery agent. For each EFS recovery agent certificate, the computer extracts the public key and encrypts the FEK by using the RSA encryption algorithm and stores the encrypted FEK in the data recovery field (DRF) located in the file's header. This process is shown in Figure 8-4.

Figure 8-4   Encrypting the FEK of a file using the EFS recovery agent's public key

The only users who can view the information in the file are those who encrypted the file and anyone who possesses a recovery agent's private key, unless additional users are added after the file is encrypted. Even another user with Full Control permissions on the file will not be able to read it. When a user attempts to open the file, the user's private key is retrieved and used to decrypt the FEK. The decrypted FEK is then used to decrypt the file. Files secured with EFS are not paged out of volatile memory when decrypted, preventing data from the file from being stored in the page file. When the user saves the file, a new FEK is generated and the process of creating the EFS header is repeated.

If the user opens the file and moves it to a non-NTFS partition or to a remote server, the file will be transparently decrypted. Users with Back Up Files And Folders user rights on a computer containing encrypted files will be able to back up the files. However, if the backup is restored to a non-NTFS partition, the contents of the files will be unintelligible.

EFS Command-Line Tools

In addition to configuring EFS in Windows Explorer, you can use two command-line tools to get information about EFS encrypted files or manipulate EFS encryption: Efsinfo.exe and Cipher.exe.

On the CD   Efsinfo.exe is located on the CD included with this book. Cipher.exe is available in Windows Server 2003, Windows XP Professional, and Windows 2000 Service Pack 3 or later.

Efsinfo.exe

Efsinfo.exe is a command-line tool that enables you to retrieve information from the EFS header of a file encrypted with EFS. You must have the permission to read the attributes of the file to retrieve the information from the file you specify. The syntax for using Efsinfo.exe follows:

```
EFSINFO [/U] [/R] [/C] [/I] [/Y] [/S:dir] [pathname [...]]
```

The options for using Efsinfo.exe are described in Table 8-8.

Table 8-8   Efsinfo.exe Options

Option	Description
/U	Displays user information from the DDF.
/R	Displays recovery agent information from the DRF.
/C	Displays certificate thumbprint information for the user account that encrypted the file. You access the properties of a certificate by double-clicking an issued certificate in the certificate's Microsoft Management Console (MMC).
/I	Forces the utility to continue the specified operation even after errors have occurred. By default, Efsinfo.exe stops when an error is encountered.
/Y	Displays your current EFS certificate thumbprint on the local PC.
/S:dir	Performs the specified operation on directories in the given directory and all subdirectories.

Cipher.exe

Cipher.exe enables you to manipulate EFS-encrypted files from the command prompt. The version of Cipher.exe in Windows 2000 is different from that in Windows Server 2003 and Windows XP and the two cannot be interchanged. In Windows 2000, the syntax of the Cipher.exe command is this:

```
CIPHER [/E | /D] [/S:dir] [/P:keyfile] [/K:keyfile] [/L:keyfile] [/I] [/F] [/Q]
[filename [...]]
```

Table 8-9 describes the options available when using Cipher.exe in Windows 2000.

Table 8-9   Cipher.exe Options in Windows 2000

Option	Description
/E	Encrypts the specified files. Directories are marked so that files added afterward will be encrypted.
/D	Decrypts the specified files. Directories are marked so that files added afterward will no longer be encrypted.
/S	Performs the specified operation on files in the given directory and all subdirectories.
/A	Encrypts files and the folders in which they are stored.
/I	Forces the computer to continue performing the specified operation even after errors have occurred. By default, Cipher.exe stops when an error is encountered.
/F	Forces the encryption operation on all specified files, even those already encrypted. For files that have already been encrypted, a new FEK is generated and the EFS header re-created. Files already encrypted are skipped by default when using the /F option.
/K	Forces the computer to generate and use a new FEK for all files. When this option is specified, the computer attempts to update the user's EFS certificate. This option is useful after deploying EFS certificates from your Public Key Infrastructure (PKI).
/Q	Reports only the most essential information.

Used without parameters, Cipher.exe displays the encryption state of the current directory and any files it contains. You can use multiple file names and wildcards. You must put spaces between multiple parameters.

Important   The Cipher.exe tool was replaced in Windows 2000 Service Pack 3 with a version that adds the /W option. The /W option permanently deletes, or wipes, all deleted data from a directory. This removes all artifacts of files that have been deleted but not necessarily removed from the hard disk. If the directory specified is a mount point to another volume, the data on that volume will be removed.

The Windows Server 2003 and Windows XP version of Cipher.exe includes all the options that the Windows 2000 version does as well as the options described in Table 8-10.

Table 8-10   Additional Cipher.exe Options in Windows Server 2003 and Windows XP

Option	Description
/R	Generates a .pfx file and a .cer file. You can use the certificate in the .cer file as the recovery agent and export the .pfx file (which contains the private key and the certificate) for archival. You can store these files in a secure offline location until they are needed to recover encrypted files. By removing the EFS recovery agent (RA) from the local computer, you prevent an attacker from using the RA account to gain access to encrypted files and folders.
/U	Updates the FEK and recovery agent on all encrypted files. The only other option that works with /U is /N.
/N	Works only in combination with /U. When used with /U, /N suppresses the updating of the FEK and recovery agent. This option is used to locate encrypted files on a hard disk.

Differences in Using EFS with Local Accounts

When EFS is used with local accounts, the EFS certificate used by default is self-generated based on the user's logon credentials on the local computer. In Windows 2000, if the physical security of the computer is compromised, encrypted files are left vulnerable because a number of tools enable an attacker to reset the password on local accounts. After the password is reset, the attacker can log on to the computer as the user and decrypt the files because the attacker has access to the EFS private key stored in the user profile. If you are using Windows 2000 and EFS with local accounts, you can increase the protection of the local account database by enabling the System Key (Syskey.exe) in either mode 2 or mode 3. By default, if the Administrator account is used to encrypt files and folders, the encryption FEK and RA FEK are the same.

In Windows Server 2003 and Windows XP, the EFS private key is stored by using the Data Protection API (DPAPI), which encrypts secrets by using an encryption key based on the user's password. If the password is reset administratively, the DPAPI encryption key no longer is valid. Thus, resetting the password causes the derived EFS private key to be inaccessible. Furthermore, the encrypted files would remain confidential. Windows Server 2003 and Windows XP issue a warning when an administrator attempts to reset the password of a local user. To prevent losing data with encrypted files, always ensure that you have an exported data recovery agent stored in a secure location.

Additional EFS Features in Windows Server 2003 and Windows XP

Several enhancements to EFS were made in Windows Server 2003 and Windows XP. These features are built on the features of EFS in Windows 2000 but add support for additional functionality and security. The main improvements include these:

- Encryption of offline files
- Remote encryption of files using WebDAV
- Sharing of encrypted files

Encryption of Offline Files

Windows Server 2003 and Windows XP enable offline files and folders to be encrypted using EFS. Offline folders use a common database on the local computer to store all offline files, and they limit access to those files through explicit DACLs. The database displays the files to the user in a manner that hides the database structure and format so that it appears to the user as a normal folder. Other users' files and folders are not displayed and are not available. Because the offline folders directory is stored in a folder common to all users of a system (\%systemroot%\CSC), no individual user can encrypt its contents. Thus, the entire database is encrypted by the System account.

One limitation of encrypting the offline files database is that files and folders are not displayed in an alternate color when the user is working offline. The remote server can contain copies of the files that have been individually encrypted on the server, and when the user is online and working with server-based copies of those files, the files can be displayed in an alternate color. Although the files are encrypted, this might seem to be an inconsistency to the user.

> **Important**   The offline folders feature, also known as the *client-side caching (CSC)* feature, runs as a System process and therefore can be accessed by any user or process that can run as System, including administrators on the local machine. Therefore, when sensitive data is stored in offline folders, administrative access should be restricted to users and the System Key should be used in mode 2 or mode 3.

Remote Encryption of Files Using WebDAV

Windows Server 2003 and Windows XP support a new method for encrypting files on remote servers using a protocol known as Web-Based Distributed Authoring and Versioning (WebDAV). When the client running Windows Server 2003 or Windows XP maps a drive to a WebDAV access point on a remote server, files can be encrypted locally on the client and then transmitted as raw encrypted files to the WebDAV server by using an HTTP PUT command. Similarly, encrypted files downloaded to a client running Windows Server 2003 and Windows XP are transmitted as raw encrypted files and are decrypted locally on the client by using an HTTP GET command. The Temporary Internet Files directory is used for intermediate transfer of the files by using HTTP where the WebDAV detects and sets the encrypted file attribute for Windows Server 2003 and Windows XP. Therefore, only public-key pairs and private-key pairs on the client are used to encrypt files, even though the files are stored on a remote server.

The WebDAV redirector is a new mini-redirector that supports the WebDAV protocol for remote document sharing by using HTTP. The WebDAV redirector supports the use of existing applications, and it allows file sharing across the Internet (through firewalls, routers, and so on) to HTTP servers. Microsoft Internet Information Services 6.0 (Windows Server 2003), 5.0 (Windows 2000), and 5.1 (Windows XP) support WebDAV folders, known as *Web folders*. The WebDAV redirector does have some limitations on the files that can be transmitted using the WebDAV protocol. The actual limitation varies depending on the amount of virtual memory available, but in general, only files of less than 400 megabytes can be transferred in Windows Server 2003 and Windows XP with EFS over WebDAV. Files and folders, when encrypted using a WebDAV share, appear as unencrypted if a user or administrator logs on to the server locally. Once a file has been encrypted using WebDAV, that file should be accessed and decrypted only by using WebDAV. This unique behavior does not affect the ability to back up and restore the server by using Ntbackup.exe or the Windows NT backup API set.

Administrators and users should not encrypt files locally on a volume that hosts a WebDAV share. All administration should be done through the WebDAV share only. You can create a WebDAV folder in Windows Server 2003, Windows 2000, and Windows XP by enabling Web Sharing on the properties of any folder. Note that if a user does not have a key to decrypt the file on a WebDAV share, she will receive an access denied error if she attempts to modify the advanced EFS attributes of the file.

Sharing of Encrypted Files

In Windows Server 2003 and Windows XP, EFS supports the sharing of files between multiple users on a per-file basis. However, users must be specified individually instead of by security group, and multiple encryption accounts are not supported on folders. Once a file has been encrypted, you can add users to the list of those who can decrypt the encrypted file by selecting the Advanced Properties dialog box of an encrypted file and clicking the Details button. Individual users can add other users (but not groups) from the local machine or from the Active Directory directory service, provided the user has a valid EFS certificate and keys. Figure 8-5 shows this process.

Figure 8-5   Sharing files encrypted with EFS in Windows Server 2003 and Windows XP

Introduction to Designing a Data Recovery Agent Policy

When utilizing EFS, you must ensure that files can be recovered if a user's EFS private key is lost or the files need to be retrieved for legal reasons. The data recovery agent (DRA) private key can decrypt files and remove the encryption attribute on them.

> **More Info**   Establishing a data recovery policy requires in-depth knowledge of PKI and thus is outside the scope of this book. For more information on designing a data recovery policy, see the "Data Protection and Recovery in Windows XP" white paper at *http://www.microsoft.com/technet/prodtechnol/winxppro/support/dataprot.asp*.

EFS automatically enforces a recovery policy that requires a recovery agent be available for files to be encrypted. The recovery policy is a type of public-key policy that provides user accounts to be designated as DRAs. A default recovery policy is automatically established when the Administrator account logs on to the system for the first time, making the administrator the recovery agent.

The default recovery policy is configured locally for workgroup computers. For computers that are part of an Active Directory–based domain, the recovery policy is configured in a domain OU Group Policy object (GPO). If no recovery agent policy is created, the computer's local recovery agent policy is used. Recovery certificates are issued by a CA and are managed by using the Certificates MMC snap-in or by using the Cipher.exe /r command in Windows Server 2003 and Windows XP.

In a network environment, the domain administrator controls how EFS is implemented in the recovery policy for all users and computers in the scope of influence. In a default Windows Server 2003, Windows 2000, or Windows XP installation, when the first domain controller is set up, the domain administrator is the specified recovery agent for the domain. The way the domain administrator configures the recovery policy determines how EFS is implemented for users on their local machines. You can choose to have recovery agents configured or an empty recovery agent:

- **Recovery agent scenario**   When an administrator adds one or more recovery agents, a recovery agent policy is in effect. These agents are responsible for recovering any encrypted data within their scope of administration. This is the most common type of recovery policy. You can ensure all recovery agents are available to all computers running Windows Server 2003, Windows 2000, or Windows XP by using Group Policy.

- **Empty recovery scenario**   When an administrator deletes all recovery agents and their public-key certificates, an empty recovery policy is in effect. An empty recovery policy means that no recovery agent exists, and if the client operating system is Windows 2000, EFS is disabled altogether. Windows Server 2003 and Windows XP support EFS with an empty DRA policy.

In a Windows 2000 environment, if an administrator attempts to configure an EFS recovery policy with no recovery agent certificates, EFS is automatically disabled. In a Windows Server 2003 or Windows XP Professional environment, the same action enables users to encrypt files without a DRA. Windows Server 2003 enables you to disable EFS for computers in the domain by completing the following steps:

1. Open Active Directory Users and Computers, right-click the domain that has the recovery policy you want to change, and then click Properties.

2. Click the Group Policy tab, right-click the recovery policy you want to change, and then click Edit. The path is Computer Configuration, Windows Settings, Security Settings, Public Key Policies, Encrypting File System.

3. Clear the Allow Users To Encrypt Files Using Encrypting File System (EFS) check box.

You can also disable EFS on individual computers running Windows Server 2003 or Windows XP by adding the EfsConfiguration (DWORD) registry value to HKEY_LOCAL_MACHINE\SOFTWARE\Microsoft\Windows NT\CurrentVersion\EFS. When this value is set to 1, it disables EFS; when it is set to 0, it enables EFS.

When a domain user logs on at a domain computer that is within the scope of the EFS recovery policy, all DRA certificates are cached in the computer's certificate store. This means that EFS on every domain computer can easily access and use the DRA's public key (or multiple public keys, if multiple DRAs are designated). On computers where an EFS recovery policy is in effect, every encrypted file contains at least one data recovery field in which the file's FEK is encrypted by using the DRA's public key and stored. By using the associated private key, any designated DRA can decrypt any encrypted file within the scope of the EFS recovery policy.

Securing Registry Permissions

The registry is a dynamic, hierarchical database that contains values of variables for the operating system and applications. The operating system and other programs also store data about users and the current configuration of the system and its components in the registry. Because the registry is available whenever the system is running, programs that start and stop can keep persistent data in the registry and the settings are saved when the system shuts down. The registry is constructed of six hives that are used for different purposes, as described in Table 8-11.

Table 8-11   Default Registry Hives

Hive	Abbreviation	Description
HKEY_CURRENT_USER	HKCU	Stores information about the profile of the currently logged-on user that is persistently stored in HKU
HKEY_USERS	HKU	Contains subkeys for all local user profiles
HKEY_CLASSES_ROOT	HKCR	Contains file association and COM registration information
HKEY_LOCAL_MACHINE	HKLM	Contains entries for the configuration of the operating system and applications
HKEY_CURRENT_CONFIG	HKCC	Contains the current hardware profile that is persistently stored in HKLM\SYSTEM\CurrentControlSet\Hardware Profiles\Current
HKEY_PERFORMANCE_DATA	HKPD	Contains information about performance counters

When the computer is running, the registry is loaded in memory and active. When the computer is powered down, the persistent information stored in the registry is written to the hard disk. Table 8-12 lists the storage location for some common registry hives.

Table 8-12   Default Storage Locations of Common Hives

Hive	Storage Location
HKEY_LOCAL_MACHINE\SYSTEM	%systemroot%\system32\Config\System
HKEY_LOCAL_MACHINE\SAM	%systemroot%\system32\Config\Sam
HKEY_LOCAL_MACHINE\SECURITY	%systemroot%\system32\Config\Security
HKEY_LOCAL_MACHINE\SOFTWARE	%systemroot%\system32\Config\Software
HKEY_CURRENT_USER	%systemdrive%\Documents and Settings\<*username*>\Ntuser.dat
HKEY_USERS	%systemdrive%\Documents and Settings\<*username*>\Local Settings\Application Data\Microsoft\Windows\Usrclass.dat
HKEY_USERS\DEFAULT	%systemroot%\system32\Config\Default

When you use an administrative tool to change the configuration of a system feature or service, the change usually takes effect immediately or soon thereafter. However, if you make the same change by editing the registry, you might need to log off and log on again, restart the service, or restart. In general, if you change the value of any entry in HKLM\Services\System\CurrentControlSet001, you must restart the computer for the changes to take effect. Also, if you use a registry editor to change values for most entries in HKEY_CURRENT_USER, you must log off and log on again for the changes to take effect.

> **More Info**   For detailed information on the structure of the registry and the specifics of the data stored in the registry, see the Technical Reference to the Registry eBook (Regentry.chm) in the *Microsoft Windows 2000 Server Resource Kit*, Supplement One (Microsoft Press, 2000).

Configuring Registry Permissions

As with files and folders stored on NTFS partitions, the registry is secured by using DACLs. Unlike NTFS permissions, registry permissions are assigned to container objects only. An individual registry value inherits its security from its parent object. A registry key has two basic permissions: Full Control and Read. The Full Control permission includes all of the special permissions in Table 8-12. The Read permission is composed of the following special permissions: Read Control, Query Value, Notify, and Enumerate Subkeys. Table 8-13 lists the special permissions on registry keys.

Table 8-13   **Special Registry Permissions**

Permission	Description
Query Value	Allows the value of the registry key to be read
Set Value	Allows the value of an existing key to be written
Create Subkey	Allows the creation of subkeys
Enumerate Subkeys	Allows the enumeration of subkeys
Notify	Required to request change notifications for a registry key or for subkeys of a registry key
Create Link	Reserved for use by the operating system
Delete	Allows the key to be deleted
Write DACL	Allows the modification of the DACL
Write Owner	Allows the modification of the owner
Read Control	Allows the SACL to be read

In Windows Server 2003, Windows 2000, and Windows XP, you can use Regedt32.exe to alter registry permissions from the user interface or you can use the Subinacl.exe command-line tool. Changing permissions on registry values requires the same techniques as modifying NTFS permissions does.

Best Practices

- **Use least privilege.**   Whenever assigning permissions, assign the least privilege the user needs to complete her job function.

- **Assign permissions at the highest possible point in a hierarchy.**   Always assign permissions at the highest point in the container hierarchy and allow them to be inherited by child objects to simplify their application.

- **Assign permissions to security groups, not users.**   Assigning permission to security groups by using a structured model makes assigning permissions scalable and flexible. This is helpful when users and files change.

- **Use caution when encrypting files.**   Always archive the DRA when encrypting files with EFS to prevent files from being irreversibly encrypted.

Additional Information

- "Data Protection and Recovery in Windows XP" (*http://www.microsoft.com /technet/prodtechnol/winxppro/support/dataprot.mspx*)

- "New Security Tool for Encrypting File System" (*http://www.microsoft.com /technet/security/tools/cipher.mspx*)

- "Access Control Lists" (*http://msdn.microsoft.com/library/en-us/secauthz /security/access_control_lists.asp*)

- The following Knowledge Base articles:

  - 243756: "How to Use Encrypting File System (EFS) with Internet Information Services" (*http://support.microsoft.com/kb/243756*)

  - 223338: "Using a Certificate Authority for the Encrypting File Service" (*http://support.microsoft.com/kb/223338*)

  - 241201: "How to Back Up Your Encrypting File System Private Key" (*http://support.microsoft.com/kb/241201*)

  - 242296: "How to Restore an Encrypting File System Private Key for Encrypted Data Recovery in Windows 2000" (*http://support.microsoft.com /kb/242296*)

  - 243026: "Using Efsinfo.exe to Determine Information About Encrypted Files" (*http://support.microsoft.com/kb/243026*)

  - 255742: "Methods for Recovering Encrypted Data Files" (*http://support.microsoft.com/kb/255742*)

  - 273856: "Third-Party Certificate Authority Support for Encrypting File System" (*http://support.microsoft.com/kb/273856*)

  - 230520: "How to Encrypt Data Using EFS in Windows 2000" (*http://support.microsoft.com/kb/230520*)

  - 329741: "EFS Files Appear Corrupted When You Open Them" (*http://support.microsoft.com/kb/329741*)

  - 221997: "Cannot Gain Access to Previously Encrypted Files on Windows 2000" (*http://support.microsoft.com/kb/221997*)

  - 227825: "Backup Tool Backs Up Files to Which You Do Not Have Read Access" (*http://support.microsoft.com/kb/227825*)

❑ 230490: "The Encrypted Data Recovery Policy for Encrypting File System" (*http://support.microsoft.com/kb/230490*)

❑ 223178: "Transferring Encrypted Files That Need to Be Recovered" (*http://support.microsoft.com/kb/223178*)

❑ 223316: "Best Practices for Encrypting File System" (*http://support.microsoft.com/kb/223316*)

❑ 223448: "Cannot Use Shared Encrypted Files in Windows 2000" (*http://support.microsoft.com/kb/223448*)

❑ 254156: "Encrypted Files Made Available Offline Not Encrypted on the Client" (*http://support.microsoft.com/kb/254156*)

❑ 272279: "How to Troubleshoot the File Replication Service and the Distributed File System" (*http://support.microsoft.com/kb/272279*)

❑ 283223: "Recovery of Encrypted Files on a Server" (*http://support.microsoft.com/kb/283223*)

❑ 290260: "EFS, Credentials, and Private Keys from Certificates Are Unavailable After a Password Is Reset" (*http://support.microsoft.com/kb/290260*)

❑ 248723: "Info: Understanding Encrypted Directories" (*http://support.microsoft.com/kb/248723*)

Chapter 9
Managing Security for System Services

In Microsoft Windows Server 2003, Windows 2000, and Windows XP, many applications run independent of any user account and regardless of whether a user is logged on to the computer. These applications are registered as *services,* or more specifically, *Service Control Programs (SCPs).* Services are controlled by the Service Control Manager (SCM), which runs as Services.exe. The configuration of services is stored in the registry, under the key HKLM\SYSTEM\CurrentControlSet\Services. You can use the Srvany.exe utility to cause an executable to run as a service.

 On the CD   Srvany.exe is located on the CD included with this book.

Managing Service Permissions

To view or manipulate services, you must have appropriate access to the SCM. Permissions to the SCM cannot be altered, although permissions over specific services can be modified. Tables 9-1 and 9-2 list the default permissions for the SCM in Windows 2000, Windows Server 2003, and Windows XP, respectively. These services are not exposed in a human-readable format in the registry.

Table 9-1   SCM Permissions in Windows 2000

Group	Permissions Granted
Everyone	■ Connect to the SCM ■ Enumerate services ■ Query the status of services ■ Read the permissions on services
Administrators Local System	■ Full Control

Table 9-2   SCM Permissions in Windows Server 2003 and Windows XP

Group	Permissions Granted
Authenticated Users remotely logged on to the computer	■ Connect to the SCM ■ Enumerate services ■ Query the status of services ■ Read the permissions on services
Authenticated Users locally logged on, in-cluding Local Service, Network Service	■ Connect to the SCM ■ Enumerate services ■ Query the status of services ■ Read the permissions on services
Administrators and LocalSystem	■ Full Control

To view or manage the permissions on services, you must use either the Subinacl.exe tool or the Security Templates Microsoft Management Console (MMC) snap-in. You can control services by using the Services MMC snap-in under Administrative Tools by typing **services.msc** at the command prompt or Run command or by editing the registry directly. Security configuration of services includes the ability to do the following:

■ Configure the startup value for each service

■ Stop, start, pause, and resume services

■ Configure the security context under which the service runs

■ Configure the discretionary access control list (DACL) for the service

Configuring the Startup Value for a Service

When the computer starts, the SCM retrieves service startup and dependency information from the registry and starts SCPs accordingly. Table 9-3 lists the startup values that can be assigned to services.

Table 9-3   Startup Values for Services

Startup Value	Registry Value	Description
Boot Start	0x0	Ntldr or Osloader preloads the driver so that it is in memory during system boot. This value is used only for kernel-mode drivers, which are generally not manageable by administrators. This value can be set only in the registry.
System Start	0x1	The driver loads and initializes after Boot Start drivers have initialized. The Boot Start drivers are loaded before the Starting Windows screen appears. This value can be set only in the registry.
Automatic	0x2	The SCM starts services with an Automatic startup value during the boot process when the Starting Windows screen appears. The progress bar indicates the loading and starting of services. Some services are not loaded until after the network devices have been initialized.
Manual	0x3	The SCM starts the service when prompted by another application or a user with the necessary permissions. Often services will start dependent services only when they are needed.
Disabled	0x4	The SCM will not permit the service to be started.

When a service is started, it runs in the Services.exe process, the Lsass.exe process, its own instance, or an instance of Svchost.exe. To view the process in which a service is running, you can use the Tlist.exe command from Windows 2000 Support Tools. Type **tlist–s** at the command prompt. Figure 9-1 shows the output of running Tlist /s on Windows 2000. Both Windows Server 2003 and Windows XP include the Tasklist tool in the default installation. Type **tasklist /svc** at the command prompt.

You should configure services to start up automatically or manually only if they are necessary for the operation of the computer or applications that run on the computer. By setting unused services to Disabled, you can decrease the potential attack surface of the computer. You can set a service startup value to Disabled in the Services MMC snap-in, through Security Templates, or by manually setting the registry startup value to 4.

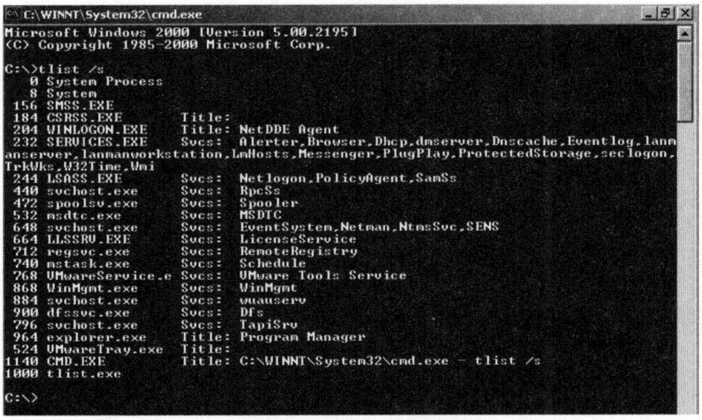

Figure 9-1   Using the Tlist command to map services to processes

Stopping, Starting, Pausing, and Resuming Services

You can control the operating status of services by using the Services MMC snap-in. You can also do so from the command line by using the Net command if you have permissions to do so. In Windows Server 2003, Windows 2000, and Windows XP, you generally must have local administrative privileges to stop or pause services, unless you have been granted appropriate permissions for those services. You can use the following commands from the command line or in a batch file to control services:

- Net start *servicename* starts a stopped service.
- Net stop *servicename* stops a started service.
- Net pause *servicename* pauses a started service.
- Net continue *servicename* continues a paused service.

> **Note**   You can use either a service's name or its display name with the Net command. If the display name of the service has a space embedded in it, place the service name within quotes. You can also suppress the prompt by appending /Y to the Net command. This is useful when configuring batch files.

When a service is stopped, it will no longer respond to or initiate requests. Each service responds differently to being paused; you should research how a service will respond to being paused before pausing it. As mentioned, you must have the appropriate permissions to stop and start a service.

Obtaining Information on Services

Although you can use the Services MMC snap-in to retrieve information on services, such as startup mode, security context, and application path, you cannot view information from many services quickly. In Windows Server 2003 and Windows XP, you can also use Windows Management Instrumentation (WMI) to obtain the critical security information for services running on the computer either programmatically or from the command line. To view or configure services from the command line, launch the WMI console by typing **WMIC** at the command prompt. The computer will take a minute or two to load the WMI Command line (WMIC) shell for the first time. At the *wmic:root\cli>* prompt, type **service**. WMI will retrieve information from all services configured to run on the computer and display it to the console. WMI will display the following security-related information for each service:

- **Start Mode** Whether the service is set to start up automatically or manually or is disabled
- **Desktop Interaction** Whether the service can interact with the desktop (Windows Station 0)
- **Path Name** The full path of the service's executable file
- **Process ID** The process ID (PID) the service is using
- **Service Type** Whether the service will run in a shared process (Svchost.exe) or its own unique process
- **Started** Whether the service is currently running (true) or not (false)
- **Start Name** The security context the service runs in
- **State** Whether the service is running, stopped, or paused

You can also create programs, either Windows Script Host (WSH) scripts or console applications, that retrieve information on services through WMI.

Configuring the Security Context of Services

Each service runs under a security context. The security context in which a service runs determines its rights and permissions. In Windows 2000, most services run under the LocalSystem account. This account has full control over all resources on the computer. Services that run in the LocalSystem account security context not only have membership in the local Administrators group, but they also have rights not normally assigned to any user account, such as process manipulation rights. More directly, LocalSystem is the trusted computing base of the operating system. Thus, you do not want to run a service under the LocalSystem account unless it is absolutely required. In Windows Server 2003 and Windows XP, services can run under the LocalSystem account or under either the Local Service account or the Network Service account—both of which have limited rights and permissions on the local computer roughly equivalent to those possessed by Authenticated Users. Additionally, Local Service is unable to authenticate to other computers and thus can be used only with console-bound services. When a service running under Network Service needs to interact with another computer, it will authenticate using the computer's account. In Windows Server 2003, 21 services were moved from running under LocalSystem to running under Local Service or Network Service to be more secure by default.

In Windows Server 2003, Windows 2000, and Windows XP, you can also run a service in the security context of a user account. If you run a service under the security context of a user account, the password for the account will be stored as a Local Security Authority (LSA) secret. If a computer is compromised and the attacker gains Administrator or System access, the attacker can retrieve LSA secrets, including the user names and passwords of service accounts. Therefore, if you run services under the security context of a user account, always use a local user account. If the computer should be compromised and the LSA secrets exposed, the attacker will not gain domain credentials—this will significantly minimize the impact of the security incident. This is especially true of service accounts that require elevated privileges. In addition, do not use the same password for all service accounts because the compromise of one of the accounts could lead to a greater network compromise.

Warning   Microsoft strongly recommends that services that run in an elevated security context, such as LocalSystem, not be allowed to interact with the desktop. The desktop that runs in Windows Station 0 is the security boundary of any computer running the Windows operating system. Any application running on the interactive desktop can interact with any window on the interactive desktop, even if that window is not displayed on the desktop. This is true for every application, regardless of the security context of the application that creates the window and the security context of the application running on the desktop.

The Windows message system does not allow an application to determine the source of a window message. Because of this, any service that opens a window on the interactive desktop exposes itself to applications that are executed by the logged-on user. If the service tries to use window messages to control its functionality, the logged-on user can disrupt that functionality by using malicious messages. This class of attack is commonly known as Shatter attacks. An example of a vulnerability in an application that interacts with the desktop is given in the Microsoft Security Bulletin MS04-019, which resolved a vulnerability in the Utility Manager in Microsoft Windows NT 4.0 and later. Prior to when this patch was installed, an attacker could escalate his privilege on a computer to LocalSystem by exploiting the vulnerability discussed in the security bulletin.

Configuring the DACL for the Service

Each service has a DACL that determines the permissions that users have over the service. The DACL for services is not exposed in the Services MMC console. You can view the DACL on a service by using Subinacl.exe or by reading the security configuration of a computer into a security template and viewing the service's DACL by using the Security Templates MMC snap-in. The basic permissions for services are listed in Table 9-4.

Table 9-4   Service Permissions

Permission	Full Name	Description
Full Control	*SERVICE_ALL_ACCESS*	Grants full control over the service
Query Template	*SERVICE_QUERY_CONFIG*	Allows the service configuration to be viewed
Change Template	*SERVICE_CHANGE_CONFIG*	Allows the service configuration to be modified
Query Status	*SERVICE_QUERY_STATUS*	Allows the SCM to be queried for the status of a service
Enumerate Dependents	*SERVICE_ENUMERATE_DEPENDENTS*	Allows the dependent services to be displayed
Start	*SERVICE_START*	Allows the service to be started
Stop	*SERVICE_STOP*	Allows the service to be stopped
Pause And Continue	*SERVICE_PAUSE_CONTINUE*	Allows the service to be paused and resumed
Interrogate	*SERVICE_INTERROGATE*	Allows the service to respond to status queries
User Defined Control	*SERVICE_USER_DEFINED_CONTROL*	Allows for special instructions to be given to the service
Delete	*DELETE*	Allows the service to be deleted
Read Permissions	*READ_CONTROL*	Allows the DACL of the service to be viewed
Change Permissions	*WRITE_DAC*	Allows the DACL of the service to be modified
Take Ownership	*WRITE_OWNER*	Allows the owner of the service to be modified

You must know the full name of the service to read the permissions for it when using the Subinacl.exe utility. The following listing shows how to use Subinacl.exe to read permissions on a service in Windows XP:

```
===================
+Service netlogon
===================
/owner              =system
/primary group      =system
/audit ace count    =1
/apace =everyone                 SYSTEM_AUDIT_ACE_TYPE-0x2
    FAILED_ACCESS_ACE_FLAG-0x80      FAILED_ACCESS_ACE_FLAG-0x0x80
    SERVICE_ALL_ACCESS
/perm. ace count    =4
/pace =authenticated users    ACCESS_ALLOWED_ACE_TYPE-0x0
    SERVICE_QUERY_CONFIG-0x1     SERVICE_QUERY_STATUS-
    0x4SERVICE_ENUMERATE_DEPEND-0x8   SERVICE_INTERROGATE-
    0x80READ_CONTROL-0x20000          SERVICE_USER_DEFINED_CONTROL-0x0100
/pace =builtin\power users    ACCESS_ALLOWED_ACE_TYPE-0x0
    SERVICE_QUERY_CONFIG-0x1      SERVICE_QUERY_STATUS-0x4
    SERVICE_ENUMERATE_DEPEND-0x8   SERVICE_START-0x10
    SERVICE_INTERROGATE-0x80      READ_CONTROL-0x20000
    SERVICE_USER_DEFINED_CONTROL-0x0100
/pace =builtin\administrators     ACCESS_ALLOWED_ACE_TYPE-0x0
    SERVICE_ALL_ACCESS
/pace =system                 ACCESS_ALLOWED_ACE_TYPE-0x0
    SERVICE_QUERY_CONFIG-0x1      SERVICE_QUERY_STATUS-0x4
    SERVICE_ENUMERATE_DEPEND-0x8        SERVICE_START-0x10
    SERVICE_STOP-0x20SERVICE_PAUSE_CONTINUE-0x40
    SERVICE_INTERROGATE-0x80
READ_CONTROL-0x20000          SERVICE_USER_DEFINED_CONTROL-0x0100
```

Figure 9-2 shows the default permissions for the Net Logon service in Windows XP using the Security Templates MMC snap-in.

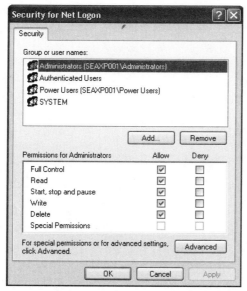

Figure 9-2   Managing service permissions with the Security Templates MMC snap-in

Default Services in Windows Server 2003, Windows 2000, and Windows XP

In Windows Server 2003, Windows 2000, and Windows XP, many services are installed by default with the operating system. Each service is configured according to different security needs. You should evaluate each service to determine whether the service is required by computers on your network and whether you need to change the permissions on the startup value, change the startup value itself, or change the permissions for the service. The following list describes each of these default services.

> **Note**   Unless otherwise noted, all services are installed by default in Windows Server 2003, Windows 2000, and Windows XP.

- **Alerter**   Notifies selected users and computers of administrative alerts. If this service is turned off, the computer will not be able to receive administrative alerts, such as those from the Messenger service or Performance Monitor. This service should be disabled unless you use administrative alerts. It is disabled by default in Windows Server 2003 and Windows XP.

- **Application Layer Gateway Service**   Provides support for third-party plug-ins to Windows Server 2003 and Windows XP Windows Firewall/Internet Connection Sharing (ICS). Stopping or disabling this service prevents Windows Firewall or ICS from working. You should set this service to start manually.

- **Application Management**   Provides software installation services, such as Assign, Publish, and Remove. This service processes requests to enumerate, install, and remove applications deployed over a corporate network. This service is called when you use Add or Remove Programs in Control Panel to install or remove an application when you are deploying software by Group Policy. If the service is disabled, users will be unable to install, remove, or enumerate applications deployed by using Group Policy. This service should be set to Disabled unless you are installing applications through Group Policy. The service is started by the first call made to it—it does not terminate until you stop it manually or restart the computer.

- **ASP.NET State Service**   Part of Microsoft .NET Framework 1.1, which is installed by default in Windows Server 2003, this service provides support for out-of-process session states for ASP.NET applications running in Microsoft Internet Information Services (IIS) 6.0. If this service is stopped, out-of-process requests will not be processed. If you are not running ASP.NET applications on your server, this service can be disabled; by default it is set to start manually.

- **Automatic Updates**   Enables the download and installation of critical Windows updates. If the service is disabled, the operating system can be manually updated at the Windows Update Web site (*http://windowsupdate.microsoft.com*). Automatic Updates is a default service in Windows Server 2003 and Windows XP and is added to Windows 2000 computers during the application of Windows 2000 Service Pack 3. You should enable this service to start automatically unless you have your own security update management solution. You can configure Automatic Updates by using System in Control Panel or by using Group Policy.

- **Background Intelligent Transfer Service**   Uses idle network bandwidth to transfer data to avoid interfering with other network connections. This service is available only in Windows Server 2003 and Windows XP and should be set to Manual because it is used by the Automatic Updates service to download security updates.

- **Certificate Services**   Creates, manages, and revokes X.509 certificates when Certificate Services is installed in Windows Server 2003 or Windows 2000 Server. This service should be set to start automatically if Certificate Services is being run on the server.

- **ClipBook**   Enables the ClipBook Viewer to create and share "pages" of data to be viewed by a remote computer using Network DDE (NetDDE), which is described later in this chapter. This service is turned off by default, and it is started only when a user starts the ClipBook Viewer application. If you disable this service, the local ClipBook will not be able to send or receive ClipBook data from remote computers, but the ClipBook will still function properly on the local computer. You should disable this service.

- **Cluster Service**   Operates the server cluster solutions in the Windows platform. This service is available only in Windows Server 2003, Enterprise Edition, and Windows 2000 Advanced Server and Datacenter Server with clustering or Network Load Balancing (NLB) installed. You can remove this service by removing clustering using Add or Remove Programs in Control Panel in Windows 2000.

- **COM+ Event System**   Provides automatic distribution of events to subscribing COM components. If the service is turned off, the System Event Notification System (SENS) stops working—COM+ login and logoff notifications will not occur. Other COM+ Inbox applications, such as the Volume Snapshot service, will not work correctly. You should set this service to Manual, unless your COM+ components are installed on the computer.

- **COM+ System Application**   Manages the configuration and tracking of COM+-based components. If the service is stopped, most COM+-based components will not function properly. If this service is disabled, a COM+ application installed on the computer will not start. This service is available only in Windows Server 2003 and Windows XP and should be set to start manually, unless you install COM+ applications on computers on your organization's network.

- **Computer Browser**   Maintains an up-to-date list of computers on your network and supplies the list to programs that request it. The Computer Browser service is used by Windows-based computers that need to view network domains and resources. If you disable this service, the computer will no longer participate in browser elections and will not maintain a server list. You can safely disable this service on most clients and servers on networks that use computers that run only Windows 2000 and later versions of the operating system.

- **Cryptographic Services**   Provides three management services: Catalog Database Service, which confirms the signatures of Windows files and Microsoft ActiveX components; Protected Root Service, which adds and removes trusted root Certification Authority certificates from the computer; and Key Service, which helps enroll the computer for certificates. If Cryptographic Services is stopped, the three management services will not function properly. You should set this service to start automatically. This service is available only in Windows Server 2003 and Windows XP.

- **DHCP Client**   Manages network configuration by registering and updating IP addresses if the computer has network adapters configured to use the Dynamic Host Configuration Protocol (DHCP) to obtain TCP/IP information. It is also responsible for updating dynamic Domain Name System (DNS) servers. You should set this service to start automatically, unless you have statically configured IP addresses and information and do not require the automatic updating of DNS.

- **DHCP Server**   Uses DHCP to allocate IP addresses to and allow the advanced configuration of network settings—such as DNS servers and Windows Internet Name Service (WINS) servers—on DHCP clients automatically. If the DHCP Server service is turned off, DHCP clients will not receive IP addresses or network settings automatically. This service is available only in Windows Server 2003 and Windows 2000 Server when the DHCP service is installed. You can remove this service by using Add or Remove Programs in Control Panel.

- **Distributed File System (DFS)**   Manages logical volumes distributed across a local area network (LAN) or wide area network (WAN). DFS is a distributed service that integrates disparate file shares into a single logical namespace. This service is available only in Windows Server 2003 and Windows 2000 Server when DFS is installed. It must be running on domain controllers.

- **Distributed Link Tracking (DLT) Client**   Maintains links between the NTFS file system files within a computer or across computers in a domain. The DLT Client service ensures that shortcuts and object linking and embedding (OLE) links continue to work after the target file is renamed or moved. If the DLT Client service is disabled, you will not be able to track links. Likewise, users on other computers will not be able to track links for documents on your computer. In a workgroup, you should disable this service because it is not used frequently. In a domain environment, you should use this service only if you frequently move files and folders on NTFS volumes.

- **Distributed Link Tracking (DLT) Server**   Stores information so that files moved between volumes can be tracked for each volume in the domain. The DLT Server service runs on each domain controller in a domain. This service enables the DLT Client service to track linked documents that have been moved to a location in another NTFS v5 (the version of NTFS used in Windows 2000 and later) volume in the same domain. If the DLT Server service is disabled, links maintained by the DLT Client service might be less reliable. You should disable this service unless you are using link tracking on your network.

- **Distributed Transaction Coordinator**   Coordinates transactions that are distributed across multiple computer systems and/or resource managers, such as databases, message queues, file systems, or other transaction-protected resource managers. The Distributed Transaction Coordinator is necessary if transactional components will be configured through COM+. This service is also required for transactional queues in Microsoft Message Queuing (MSMQ) and Microsoft SQL Server operations that span multiple systems. Disabling this service prevents these transactions from occurring. You should set this service to Disabled on all computers where it is not being used.

- **DNS Client**   Resolves and caches DNS names. The DNS Client service must be running on every computer that will perform DNS name resolution. The capability to resolve DNS names is crucial for locating domain controllers in Active Directory domains. Running the DNS Client service is also critical for enabling location of the devices identified by using DNS names. If the DNS Client service is disabled, your computers might not be able to locate the domain controllers of the Active Directory domains and Internet connections. You should set this service to start automatically unless you are certain that the computer will not require any host name resolution services.

- **DNS Server**   Enables DNS name resolution by answering queries and update requests for DNS names. This service is available only in Windows Server 2003 and Windows 2000 Server when DNS is installed. You can remove this service by using Add or Remove Programs in Control Panel.

- **Error Reporting Service**   In Windows Server 2003 and Windows XP, by default, when an application crashes, the user is prompted to report the incident, along with the crash-dump information. This information is sent to Microsoft for analysis. You can configure this service by using System in Control Panel. For example, you can define which applications should and should not send crash-dump information. To prevent this service from running, you must set it to Disabled. You should always set this service to Disabled unless you would like to report the information to Microsoft.

- **Event Log**   Logs event messages issued by programs and the Windows operating system. Event Log reports contain information that can be useful in diagnosing problems. Reports are viewed in Event Viewer. The Event Log service writes to log files the events sent by applications, services, and the operating system. If the Event Log service is disabled, you will not be able to track events, which reduces your ability to diagnose problems with your system quickly. In addition, you will not be able to audit security events. You cannot disable this service.

- **Fast User Switching Compatibility**   Enables computers running Windows XP in a workgroup to use fast-user switching to switch quickly between multiple active logon sessions. This feature was designed for home users and does not work when the computer is a member of a domain. You should disable this service.

- **Fax Service**   Enables you to send and receive faxes. This service is not installed by default and can be added and removed by using Add or Remove Programs in Control Panel.

- **File Replication**   Maintains file synchronization of file directory contents among multiple servers. File Replication is the automatic file replication service in Windows Server 2003 and Windows 2000. It is used to copy and maintain files on multiple servers simultaneously and to replicate the Windows 2000 system volume (SYSVOL) on all domain controllers. In addition, this service can be configured to replicate files among alternate targets associated with the fault-tolerant DFS. If this service is disabled, file replication will not occur and server data will not be synchronized. Stopping the File Replication service can seriously impair a domain controller's ability to function.

- **File Server for Macintosh**   Enables Macintosh-based computers to store and access files on a Windows-based server machine. If this service is turned off, Macintosh-based clients will not be able to view any NTFS shares. This service is not installed by default and can be removed by using Add or Remove Programs in Control Panel. You should remove this service if you are not sharing files with Macintosh-based clients.

- **FTP Publishing Service**   Provides FTP connectivity and administration through the IIS console. Features include bandwidth throttling, use of security accounts, and extensible logging. You should remove this service if you are not running an FTP site. You can do so by using Add or Remove Programs in Control Panel.

- **Help and Support**   Enables the Help and Support application in Windows Server 2003 and Windows XP to provide dynamic help to users. If disabled, the Help and Support service application will not function.

- **HTTP SSL Service**   In Windows Server 2003, IIS uses this service to facilitate the creation and management of Secure Sockets Layer (SSL) sessions. Unless you have installed IIS and are running a Web site that requires SSL, you should disable this service.

- **Human Interface Devices**   Enables generic input access to the Human Interface Devices (HID), which activates and maintains the use of predefined hot buttons on keyboards, remote controls, and other multimedia devices. If this service is stopped, the hot buttons it controls will no longer function. You should set this service to Disabled unless you use a custom keyboard or other input device for hotkey mappings. This service exists only in Windows Server 2003 and Windows XP.

- **IIS Admin Service**   Allows administration of IIS. If this service is not running, you will not be able to run Web, FTP, Network News Transfer Protocol (NNTP), or Simple Mail Transfer Protocol (SMTP) sites, and you will not be able to configure IIS. You should remove or disable this service if you will not be using the IIS Admin Web site to manage the Web components, such as IIS or FTP, on the computer. You can remove this service by using Add or Remove Programs in Control Panel.

- **IMAPI CD-Burning COM Service**   Enables computers running Windows Server 2003 and Windows XP that are equipped with a CD-ROM drive to create CDs. You should disable this service on computers that do not have a CD-R or CD-RW drive and set the service to start manually on computers that do and that require burning CDs using this service. This service will start when you send files to a CD-R or CD-RW drive. This service is disabled in Windows Server 2003.

- **Indexing Service**   Indexes contents and properties of files on local and remote computers and provides rapid access to files through a querying language. The Indexing Service also enables quick searching of documents on local and remote computers as well as a search index for content shared on the Web. If this service is either stopped or disabled, all search functionality will be provided by traversing the folder hierarchy and scanning each file for the requested string. When the service is turned off, search response is typically much slower. You should disable this service on servers and set it to start automatically on workstations.

- **Internet Authentication Service (IAS)**   Performs centralized authentication, authorization, auditing, and accounting of users who are connecting to a network (LAN or remote) by using virtual private network (VPN) equipment, Remote Access Service (RAS), or 802.1x wireless and Ethernet/switch access points. IAS implements the Internet Engineering Task Force (IETF) standard Remote Authentication Dial-In User Service (RADIUS) protocol. If IAS is disabled or stopped, authentication requests will fail over to a backup IAS server, if one is available. If none of the other backup IAS servers are available, users will not be able to connect. This service only appears in the Services list in Windows Server 2003 and Windows 2000 Server when IAS is installed. You should remove this service on computers that are not RADIUS servers, proxies, or clients by using Add or Remove Programs in Control Panel.

- **Internet Connection Sharing**   Provides network address translation (NAT), addressing, and name resolution services for all computers on your home or small-office network through a dial-up or broadband connection in Windows 2000. This service is available only in Windows 2000 and should be disabled unless the computer will be used as a gateway to another network.

- **Intersite Messaging**   Allows the sending and receiving of messages between Windows server sites. This service is used for mail-based replication between sites. The Active Directory directory service includes support for replication between sites by using SMTP over IP transport. If you are not using the SMTP service in IIS, you should remove this service by using Add or Remove Programs in Control Panel, unless the computer is a domain controller that uses SMTP for intersite replication.

- **IPSec Services (IPSec Policy Agent in Windows 2000)**   Manages IP Security (IPSec) policy, including the Internet Key Exchange (IKE) protocol, and coordinates IPSec policy settings with the IP security driver. If you know you will not be using IPSec, you should set this service to manual startup. Otherwise, you should set this service to start automatically.

- **Kerberos Key Distribution Center**   Enables users to log on to the network using the Kerberos v5 authentication protocol. If this service is stopped on a domain controller, users will be unable to log on to the domain and access services when using that domain controller for authentication. This service exists only on Windows Server 2003 and Windows 2000 Active Directory domain controllers.

- **License Logging**   Tracks Client Access License usage for server products, such as IIS, Terminal Services, and File and Print Services, as well as products such as SQL Server and Microsoft Exchange Server. If this service is disabled, licensing for these programs will work properly, but usage will no longer be tracked. This service is available only in Windows Server 2003 and Windows 2000 Server and should be disabled unless you are tracking license usage.

- **Logical Disk Manager**   Watches Plug and Play events for new drives to be detected and passes volume and/or disk information to the Logical Disk Manager Administrative Service to be configured. If disabled, the Disk Management MMC snap-in display will not change when disks are added or removed. This service should not be disabled if dynamic disks are in the system. You should set this service to start manually.

- **Logical Disk Manager Administrative Service**   Performs administrative services for disk management requests. This service is started only when you configure a drive or partition or when a new drive is detected. This service does not run by default, but it is activated whenever dynamic disk configuration changes occur or when the Disk Management MMC snap-in is open. The service starts, completes the configuration operation, and then exits. You should set this service to start manually.

- **Message Queuing**   Provides a messaging infrastructure and development tool for creating distributed messaging applications for the Windows operating system. Microsoft Message Queuing (MSMQ) provides guaranteed message delivery, efficient routing, security, support for sending messages within transactions, and priority-based messaging. Disabling MSMQ affects a number of other services, including COM+ Queued Component (QC) functionality, some parts of Windows Management Instrumentation (WMI), and the MSMQ Triggers service. If you are not using a message queue on the computer, you should remove the Message Queuing service by using Add or Remove Programs in Control Panel.

- **Messenger**   Sends messages to or receives them from users and computers. This service also sends and receives messages transmitted by administrators or the Alerter service. If disabled, Messenger notifications cannot be sent to or received from the computer or from users currently logged on, and the NET SEND and NET NAME commands will no longer function. You should disable this service unless you have applications that send administrative alerts, such as uninterruptible power supply (UPS) software or print notifications. The Messenger service is disabled by default in Windows Server 2003 Service Pack 1 and Windows XP Service Pack 2.

- **Microsoft Software Shadow Copy Provider**   Manages software-based volume shadow copies taken by the Volume Shadow Copy service in Windows Server 2003 and Windows XP. If this service is stopped, software-based volume shadow copies cannot be managed. You should disable this service unless you are using volume shadow copies to archive data, in which case the service should be set to manual.

- **Net Logon**   Supports pass-through authentication of account logon events for computers in a domain. This service is started automatically when the computer is a member of a domain. It is used to maintain a secure channel to a domain controller for use by the computer in the authentication of users and services running on the computer. In the case of a domain controller, the Net Logon service handles the registration of the computer's DNS names specific to domain controller locator discoveries. On domain controllers, the service enables pass-through authentication for other domain controllers by forwarding pass-through authentication requests to the destination domain controller, where the logon credentials are validated. If this service is turned off, the computer will not operate properly in a domain. Specifically, it can deny NT LAN Manager (NTLM) authentication requests and, in the case of a domain controller, will not be discoverable by client machines. You should set this service to start automatically for all domain members and manually for nondomain members. You will need to start this service before joining the domain on non-domain-joined computers if you set it to start manually.

- **NetMeeting Remote Desktop Sharing**   Allows authorized users to access your Windows desktop remotely from another PC over a corporate intranet by using Microsoft NetMeeting. The service must be explicitly enabled by NetMeeting and can be disabled in NetMeeting or shut down by using the notification area icon. Disabling the service unloads the NetMeeting display driver used for application sharing. You should disable this service unless you are using NetMeeting for business needs.

- **Network Connections**   Manages objects in the Network and Dial-Up Connections folder, in which you can view both network and remote connections. This service takes care of network configuration (client side) and displays the status in the notification area on the desktop (the area on the taskbar to the right of the taskbar buttons). You can also access configuration parameters through this service. Disabling this service will prevent you from configuring your LAN settings and domain members from receiving group policies. You should set this service to start manually.

- **Network DDE**   Provides network transport and security for dynamic data exchange (DDE) by applications running on the same computer or on different computers. This service is not started by default, and it is started only when invoked by an application that uses Network DDE (NetDDE), such as Clipbrd.exe or DDEshare.exe. If you disable the service, any application that depends on NetDDE will time out when it tries to start the service. You should disable this service unless you use NetDDE-enabled applications.

- **Network DDE DSDM**   Manages shared dynamic data exchange and is used only by Network DDE to manage shared DDE conversations. You should disable this service unless you use NetDDE-enabled applications.

- **Network Location Awareness (NLA)**   Collects and stores network configuration and location information and notifies applications when this information changes. Disabling this service will prevent Windows Firewall from working. You should set this service to start manually.

- **Network News Transfer Protocol (NNTP)**   Creates an NNTP-enabled news server. If the service is off, client computers will not be able to connect and read or retrieve posts. You should remove this service by using Add or Remove Programs in Control Panel if you are not running an NNTP server.

- **NT LM Security Support Provider**   Enables applications to log on to validate authentication credentials by calling through the NLTM Security Support Provider (SSP). If this service is stopped, users will not be able to log on to applications that call the NTLM SSP. Most applications do not call this SSP directly. You should set this service to start manually.

- **Performance Logs and Alerts**   Configures performance logs and alerts. This service is used to collect performance data automatically from local or remote computers that have been configured by using the Performance Logs and Alerts snap-in. If the service is stopped by a user, all currently running data collections will terminate and no scheduled collections will occur. You should set this service to Disabled unless you are monitoring the performance of a server by using the Performance Logs and Alerts MMC snap-in.

- **Plug and Play**   Enables a computer to recognize and adapt to hardware changes with little or no user input. With Plug and Play, a user can add or remove devices without any intricate knowledge of computer hardware and without being forced to manually configure hardware or the operating system. Disabling this service will prevent the computer from starting. You should set this service to start automatically.

- **Portable Music Serial Number Service**   Enables a computer running Windows Server 2003 or Windows XP to retrieve information about portable music players attached to the computer as part of the Digital Rights Management (DRM) features. You should disable this service on computers that will not be used with portable music devices, such as MP3 players.

- **Print Server for Macintosh**   Enables Macintosh clients to route printing to a print spooler located on a computer running Windows Server 2003 or Windows 2000 Server. If this service is stopped, printing will be unavailable to Macintosh clients. If the computer does not have a printer used by Macintosh-based clients, you should remove this service by using Add or Remove Programs in Control Panel.

- **Print Spooler**   Queues and manages print jobs locally and remotely. The print spooler is the heart of the Windows printing subsystem and controls all printing jobs. This service manages the print queues on the system and communicates with printer drivers and I/O components. If the Print Spooler service is disabled, you will not be able to print and other users will not be able to print to a printing device attached to your computer. You should set this service to Automatic, unless you are certain that no one will be printing to or from the computer. If users will not be printing to or from the computer, you should set this service to Disabled.

- **Protected Storage**   Provides protected storage for sensitive data, such as private keys, to prevent access by unauthorized services, processes, or users. Protected Storage (P-Store) is a set of software libraries that allows applications to fetch and retrieve security and other information from a personal storage location, hiding the implementation and details of the storage itself. The storage location provided by this service is not secure or protected from modification. P-Store uses the Hash-Based Message Authentication Code (HMAC) and the SHA1 cryptographic hash function to encrypt the user's master key. This component requires no configuration. Disabling it will make information protected with this service inaccessible to you. P-Store is an earlier service that has been supplanted by the Data Protection API (DPAPI), which is currently the preferred service for protected storage. You should set this service to start automatically. Microsoft Internet Explorer stores Autocomplete forms, user names, passwords, and URL histories in P-Store.

- **QoS Admission Control (RSVP)**   Provides network signaling and local traffic-control setup functionality for Quality of Service–aware programs and control applets. You should set this service to start manually.

- **QoS RSVP**   Invoked when an application uses the Generic Quality of Service (GQoS) API to request a specific quality of service on the end-to-end connection it uses. If disabled, QoS is not guaranteed to the application. The application must then decide whether to accept best-effort data transmission or refuse to run. You should set this service to start manually.

- **Remote Access Auto Connection Manager**   Creates a connection to a remote network whenever a program references a remote DNS or NetBIOS name or address. This service detects an attempt to resolve the name of a remote computer or share or an unsuccessful attempt to send packets to a remote computer or share. The service brings up a dialog box that offers to make a dial-up or VPN connection to the remote computer. Disabling the service has no effect on the rest of the operating system. You should disable this service unless you have a specific reason to use it.

- **Remote Access Connection Manager**   Creates a network connection. This service manages the actual work of connecting, maintaining, and disconnecting dial-up and VPN connections from your computer to the Internet or other remote networks. Double-clicking a connection in the Network and Dial-Up Connections folder and selecting the Dial button generates a work request for this service that is queued with other requests for creating or destroying connections. This service will unload itself when no requests are pending. But in practice, the Network and Dial-Up Connections folder calls on this service to enumerate the set of connections and to display the status of each one. So, unless the Network and Dial-Up Connections folder contains no connections, the service will always be running. The service cannot be disabled without breaking other portions of the operating system, such as the Network and Dial-Up Connections folder. You should set this service to Manual, unless you are certain that you will not be using remote access connections, in which case you should disable the service.

- **Remote Desktop Help Session Manager**   Manages and controls the Remote Assistance feature in Windows Server 2003 and Windows XP. If this service is stopped or disabled, Remote Assistance will be unavailable. You should disable this service unless your organization uses the Remote Assistance feature, in which case you should set the service to start manually.

- **Remote Installation (Boot Information Negotiation Layer (BINL) in Windows 2000)**   Enables you to install Windows Server 2003, Windows 2000, and Windows XP on computers equipped with pre-execution-compatible network interface cards. The BINL service is the primary component of Remote Installation Services (RIS). If BINL is no longer needed on the system, you can discontinue its use by using the Add/Remove Windows Components option in Control Panel to remove the RIS component. If turned off, RIS will not allow client machines to install the operating system remotely. This service is available in Windows Server 2003 and Windows 2000 Server only when RIS is installed.

- **Remote Procedure Call (RPC)**   Provides the RPC endpoint mapper and other miscellaneous RPC services. If this service is turned off, the computer will not boot. You should set this service to start automatically.

- **Remote Procedure Call (RPC) Locator**   Provides the name services for RPC clients. This service helps locate RPC servers that support a given interface (also known as an *RPC named service*) within an enterprise. This service is turned off by default. Note that no operating system component uses this service, although some applications might. You should set this service to start manually.

- **Remote Registry**   Allows remote registry manipulation. This service lets users connect to a remote registry and read and/or write keys to it—provided they have the required permissions. This service is usually used by remote administrators and performance monitor counters. If disabled, the service doesn't affect registry operations on the computer on which it runs; therefore, the local system will run in the same manner. Other computers or devices will no longer be able to connect to this computer's registry. You must be running this service to use some patch management tools, such as Microsoft Baseline Security Analyzer (MBSA). You should set this service to start automatically.

- **Remote Storage Engine**   Migrates infrequently used data to tape. This service leaves a marker on disk, allowing the data to be recalled automatically from tape if you attempt to access the file. If you are not using remote storage, you should remove or disable this service. Otherwise, you should set it to start manually.

- **Remote Storage File**   Manages operations on remotely stored files. If you are not using the remote storage feature of Windows Server 2003 or Windows 2000, you should remove or disable this service.

- **Remote Storage Media**   Controls the media used to store data remotely. If you are not using the remote storage feature of Windows Server 2003 or Windows 2000, you should remove or disable this service.

- **Remote Storage Notification**   Enables Remote Storage to notify you when you have accessed an offline file. Because it takes longer to access a file that has been moved to tape, Remote Storage will notify you if you are attempting to read a file that has been migrated and will allow you to cancel the request. If this service is turned off, you will not receive any additional notification when you try to open offline files. Nor will you be able to cancel an operation that involves an offline file. If you are not using the remote storage feature of Windows Server 2003 or Windows 2000, you should remove or disable this service.

- **Removable Storage**   Manages removable media drives and libraries. This service maintains a catalog of identifying information for removable media used by a system, including tapes, CDs, and so on. This service is used by features such as Backup and Remote Storage to handle media cataloging and automation. This service stops itself when there is no work to do. If you are not using the remote storage feature of Windows Server 2003 or Windows 2000, you should disable this service.

- **Resultant Set of Policy Provider**   This service enables you to connect to a Windows Server 2003 domain controller, access the WMI database for that computer, and simulate Resultant Set of Policy (RSoP) for Group Policy settings that would be applied to a user or computer located in Active Directory in a Windows 2000 or later domain. You should set this service to Disabled and enable it only when using RSoP.

- **Routing and Remote Access**   Offers routing services in LAN and WAN environments, including VPN services. If this service is turned off, incoming remote access and VPN connections, dial-on-demand connections, and routing protocols will not be available. In a routing context, Routing and Remote Access Service (RRAS) drives the TCP/IP stack-forwarding engine. The forwarding code can be enabled outside the service for various reasons, most notably Internet Connection Sharing (ICS). You should set this service to Disabled.

- **Secondary Logon (RunAs Service in Windows 2000)**   Allows you to run specific tools and programs with different permissions than your current logon provides. You should set this service to start automatically.

- **Security Accounts Manager**   Startup of this service signals to other services that the Security Accounts Manager (SAM) subsystem is ready to accept requests. This service should not be disabled. Doing so will prevent other services in the system from being notified when the SAM is ready, which can in turn cause those services to not start correctly.

- **Server**   Provides RPC support, file print sharing, and named pipe sharing over the network. The Server service allows the sharing of your local resources (such as disks and printers) so that other users on the network can access them. It also allows named pipe communication between applications running on other computers and your computer, which is used for RPC. You should set this service to start automatically.

■ **Shell Hardware Detection**   Monitors and provides notification for AutoPlay hardware events, such as the insertion of CD-ROM disks or USB storage devices. You should disable this service on servers and set it to start automatically on workstations. This service to not available in Windows 2000.

■ **Simple Mail Transfer Protocol (SMTP)**   Transports e-mail across the network. The SMTP service is used as an e-mail submission and relay agent. It can accept and queue e-mail for remote destinations and retry at specified intervals. The Collaboration Data Objects (CDO) for Windows Server 2003 or Windows 2000 COM components can use the SMTP service to submit and queue outbound e-mail. If you are not using this service, you should remove it by using Add or Remove Programs in Control Panel.

■ **Single Instance Storage Groveler**   Is an integral component of Remote Installation Services (RIS). The Single Instance Storage Groveler is installed only when you add the RIS component from Add or Remove Windows Components in Control Panel or select it when initially installing the operating system. If the service is turned off, RIS installation images will expand to their full image size and you will not be able to conserve space on the hard drive. You should remove the RIS service by using Add or Remove Programs in Control Panel if the computer is not a RIS server.

■ **Site Server ILS Service**   As part of IIS, this service scans TCP/IP stacks and updates directories with the most current user information. Windows 2000 is the last version of the operating system to support the Site Server Internet Locator Service (ILS). You should remove this service by using Add/Remove Programs in Control Panel if you are not using it on your Web server.

■ **Smart Card**   Manages and controls access to a smart card inserted into a smart card reader attached to the computer. The Smart Card service is based on Personal computer/Smart Card (PC/SC) consortium standards for accessing information on smart card devices. Disabling the Smart Card service will result in a loss of smart card support in the system. You should set this service to Disabled unless the computer uses smart cards for authentication, in which case, you should set the service to start manually.

■ **Smart Card Helper**   Provides support for earlier smart card readers attached to the computer. This component is designed to provide enumeration services for the Smart Card service so that earlier non–Plug and Play smart card reader devices can be supported. Turning off this service will remove support for non–Plug and Play readers. You should set this service to Disabled unless the computer uses smart cards for authentication, in which case, you should set the service to start manually.

- **SNMP Service**   Allows incoming Simple Network Management Protocol (SNMP) requests to be serviced by the local computer. SNMP includes agents that monitor activity in network devices and report to the network console workstation. If the service is turned off, the computer no longer responds to SNMP requests. If the computer is being monitored by network management tools, the tools will not be able to collect data from the computer or control its functionality using SNMP. If you are not monitoring the computer with SNMP, you should remove this service by using Add or Remove Programs in Control Panel.

- **SNMP Trap Service**   Receives SNMP trap messages generated by local or remote SNMP agents and forwards the messages to SNMP management programs running on the computer. If the service is turned off, SNMP applications will not receive SNMP traps that they are registered to receive. If you are using a computer to monitor network devices or server applications through SNMP traps, you might miss significant system occurrences. If you are not monitoring the computer with SNMP, you should remove this service by using Add or Remove Programs in Control Panel.

- **SSPD Discovery Services**   Enables the discovery of Universal Plug and Play (UPnP) devices in Windows XP. You should set this service to Disabled, unless you actively use UPnP devices on your network.

- **Still Image Service**   Loads necessary drivers for imaging devices (such as scanners and digital still-image cameras), manages events for those devices and associated applications, and maintains device state. The service is needed to capture events generated by imaging devices (such as button presses and connections). If the service is not running, events from the imaging devices connected to the computer will not be captured and processed. This service should be disabled unless digital images are downloaded on the computer from digital imaging devices.

- **System Event Notification**   Tracks system events, such as Windows logon network events and power events, and notifies COM+ Event System subscribers of these events. System Event Notification System (SENS) is started automatically and depends on the COM+ Event System service. Disabling this service has the following effects:

  - The Win32 APIs *IsNetworkAlive()* and *IsDestinationReachable()* will not work well. These APIs are mostly used by mobile applications and portable computers.

  - SENS interfaces do not work properly. In particular, SENS Logon/Logoff notifications will not work.

❑ The Work Offline notification will not work. Internet Explorer 5.0 or later uses SENS on portable computers to trigger when the user goes offline or online (by triggering the Work Offline prompt).

❑ SyncMgr (Mobsync.exe) will not work properly. SyncMgr depends on connectivity information and Network Connect/Disconnect and Logon/Logoff notifications from SENS.

❑ COM+ Event System will try to notify SENS of some events but will not be able to.

■ **System Restore Service**   Performs the automated backup and restore of a core set of specified system and application file types (for example, .exe, .dll) that cannot be changed in Windows XP. System Restore Service does not back up any user data. You can configure System Restore Service by using System in Control Panel. You should set this service to start automatically, unless you are certain that you will not be using it.

■ **Task Scheduler**   Enables a program to run at a designated time. This service allows you to perform automated tasks on a chosen computer. Task Scheduler is started each time the operating system is started. If Task Scheduler is disabled, jobs that are scheduled to run will not run at their designated time or interval. You should set this service to start manually.

■ **TCP/IP NetBIOS Helper**   Enables support for the NetBIOS over TCP/IP (NetBT) service and NetBIOS name resolution. This service is an extension of the kernel mode NetBT. It should be considered an integral part of NetBT, rather than a normal service. This service does two things for NetBT, which you cannot do in kernel mode:

❑ Performs DNS name resolution

❑ Pings a set of IP addresses and returns a list of reachable IP addresses

If this service is disabled, NetBT's clients—including the Workstation, Server, Netlogon, and Messenger services—could stop responding. As a result, you might not be able to share files and printers, you might not be able to log on, and Group Policy will no longer be applied. You should set this service to start automatically.

■ **Telephony**   Provides Telephony API (TAPI) support for programs that control telephony devices and IP-based voice connections on the local computer and through the LAN on servers that are running the service. If no other dependent service is running and you stop the Telephony service, it will be restarted when any application makes an initialization call to the TAPI interface. If the service is disabled, any device that depends upon it will not be able to run. You should set this service to start manually.

- **Telnet**   Allows a remote user to log on to the system and run console programs by using the command line. A computer running the Telnet service can support connections from various TCP/IP telnet clients. You should disable this service unless you use the Telnet service to manage your computer.

- **Terminal Services**   Provides a multisession environment that allows client devices to access a virtual interactive logon to a computer running Windows Server 2003, Windows XP, or Windows 2000 Server. Terminal Services allows multiple users to be connected interactively to the computer in their own isolated session. You should set this service to start automatically unless you are certain that you will not be using Windows Terminal Services, Remote Desktop, Fast-User Switching, or Remote Assistance, in which case you can disable this service.

- **Terminal Services Licensing**   Installs a license server and provides registered client licenses when connecting to a Windows Server 2003 or Windows 2000 terminal server. If this service is turned off, the server will be unavailable to issue terminal server licenses to clients when they are requested. If another license server is discoverable on a domain controller in the forest, the requesting terminal server will attempt to use it. You should remove this service by using Add or Remove Programs in Control Panel.

- **Terminal Services Session Directory**   Provides services for clustered Terminal Services to allow client devices to access and reconnect to virtual Windows desktop sessions in Windows Server 2003. This service is disabled by default and should be enabled only if the server is participating in a cluster to application terminal servers.

- **Themes**   Provides management themes in the Windows XP user interface. You should set this service to start automatically. It is disabled by default in Windows Server 2003.

- **Trivial FTP Daemon**   Trivial File Transfer Protocol (TFTP) is an integral part of Remote Installation Services. To disable this service, uninstall RIS. Disabling the Trivial FTP Daemon service directly will cause RIS to malfunction. You should remove RIS by using Add or Remove Programs in Control Panel if the computer is not a RIS server.

- **Uninterruptible Power Supply**   Manages communications with an uninterruptible power supply (UPS) connected to the computer by a serial port. If this service is turned off, communications with the UPS will be lost. You should disable this service unless you have a UPS device connection to the computer.

- **Universal Plug and Play Device Host**   Manages the operation of UPnP devices on the local computer. Disabling this service will prevent the use of UPnP devices; however, regular Plug and Play devices will continue to function normally. You should disable this service unless your network actively uses UPnP devices.

- **Upload Manager**   Manages synchronous and asynchronous file transfers on computers running Windows Server 2003 or Windows XP between clients and servers on the network. If this service is stopped, synchronous and asynchronous file transfers between clients and servers on the network will not occur. Driver data is anonymously uploaded from customer computers to Microsoft and then used to help users find the drivers required for their systems. If users do not need to use Windows Update to locate updates to drivers, this service should be disabled.

- **Utility Manager**   Starts and configures accessibility tools from one window. Utility Manager allows faster access to some accessibility tools and displays the status of the tools or devices that it controls. This service saves users time because an administrator can designate that certain features start when the Windows operating system starts. Utility Manager includes three built-in accessibility tools: Magnifier, Narrator, and On-Screen Keyboard. You should disable this service if you are not going to use it.

- **Virtual Disk Service**   Provides a single interface for managing block storage virtualization whether done in operating system software, redundant array of independent disks (RAID) storage hardware subsystems, or other virtualization engines. You should disable this service unless you require its features.

- **Volume Shadow Copy**   Manages and implements Volume Shadow copies used for backup and other purposes. This service is set to start manually and you should disable it only if you would like to disable Volume Shadow Copy functionality in Windows XP and Windows Server 2003.

- **WebClient**   Enables computers running Windows Server 2003 or Windows XP to modify Internet-based or intranet-based files, including Web-Based Distributed Authoring and Versioning (WebDAV) extensions for HTTP. You should set this service to start manually except on servers where it should be disabled. It is disabled by default in Windows Server 2003.

- **Windows Audio**   Enables Windows Server 2003 or Windows XP to manage audio devices. In Windows Server 2003, it is disabled by default, and in Windows XP it starts automatically.

- **Windows Firewall/Internet Connection Sharing (ICS)**   Provides personal firewall and Internet connection sharing in Windows Server 2003 and Windows XP. You should configure this service to start automatically on computers that will be using Windows Firewall or ICS.

- **Windows Image Acquisition (WIA)**   Manages the retrieval of images from digital cameras and scanners from devices attached to computers that run Windows Server 2003 or Windows XP. You should set this service to Disabled unless you use these devices on computers. It is disabled by default in Windows Server 2003.

- **Windows Installer**   Installs, repairs, or removes software according to instructions contained in .msi files provided with the applications. If disabled, the installation, removal, repair, and modification of applications that make use of the Windows Installer will fail. You should set this service to start manually.

- **Windows Internet Name Service (WINS)**   Enables NetBIOS name resolution. Presence of the WINS server(s) is crucial for locating the network resources identified by using NetBIOS names. WINS servers are required unless all domains have been upgraded to Active Directory, all computers on the network are running Windows 2000, and you no longer have applications that rely on NetBIOS to locate other computers or users. If you are not running a WINS server on the computer, you should remove this service by using Add or Remove Programs in Control Panel.

- **Windows Management Instrumentation (WMI)**   Provides system management information. WMI is an infrastructure for building management applications and instrumentation. WMI provides access to the management data through a number of interfaces, including COM API, scripts, and command-line interfaces. If this service is turned off, WMI information will be unavailable and Group Policy might not be applied correctly. You should leave this service to start automatically.

- **Windows Management Instrumentation Driver Extensions**   Tracks all the drivers that have registered WMI information to publish. If the service is turned off, clients cannot access the WMI information published by drivers. However, if the WMI APIs detect that the service is not running, the APIs will attempt to restart the service.

- **Windows Time**   Sets the computer clock. Windows Time (W32Time) maintains date and time synchronization on all computers running on a Windows network. It uses the Network Time Protocol (NTP) to synchronize computer clocks so that an accurate clock value, or timestamp, can be assigned to network validation and resource access requests. The implementation of NTP and the integration of time providers make W32Time a reliable and scalable time service for enterprise administrators. For computers not joined to a domain, W32Time can be configured to synchronize time with an external time source. If this service is turned off, the time setting for local computers will not be synchronized with any time service in the Windows domain or with an externally configured time service. You should set this service to start automatically.

- **WinHTTP Web Proxy Auto-Discovery Service**   Implements the Web Proxy Auto-Discovery (WPAD) protocol for Windows HTTP Services (WinHTTP). WPAD is a protocol that enables an HTTP client to discover a proxy configuration automatically. This service, available only in Windows Server 2003, should be disabled unless its functionality is specifically required.

■ **Wireless Configuration**   Provides the automatic configuration of supported 802.11 wireless network adapters in Windows Server 2003 and Windows XP. You should set this service to start automatically unless you will not be using wireless network adapters on the computer, in which case, you should disable the service.

■ **WMI Performance Adapter**   Provides performance library information from WMI HiPerf providers. The service, available only in Windows Server 2003, is a manual service and is not running by default. You should allow this service to start manually.

■ **Workstation**   Provides network connections and communications. The Workstation service is a user-mode wrapper for the Microsoft Networks redirector. The service loads and performs configuration functions for the redirector, provides support for making network connections to remote servers, provides support for the Windows Network (WNet) APIs, and furnishes redirector statistics. If this service is turned off, no network connections can be made to remote computers using Microsoft Networks.

■ **World Wide Web Publishing Service**   Provides HTTP services for applications on the Windows platform. The service depends on the IIS administration service and kernel TCP/IP support. If this service is turned off, the operating system will no longer be able to act as a Web server. See also the IIS Admin Service entry in this list.

Best Practices

■ **Disable unused services.**   For computers running Windows Server 2003, Windows 2000, and Windows XP, carefully evaluate which services are required to support your organization's software applications. Disable any services you are certain you will not need to minimize the potential attack surface of the computer.

These are the recommended minimum services to run:

Service	Setting
COM+ Event System	Manual
DHCP Client	Automatic (if needed)
DNS Client	Automatic
Event Log	Automatic
Logical Disk Manager	Automatic
Logical Disk Manager Administrative Service	Manual
Net Logon	Automatic
Network Connections	Manual

Service	Setting
Performance Logs and Alerts	Manual
Plug and Play	Automatic
Protected Storage	Automatic
Remote Procedure Call (RPC)	Automatic
Remote Registry	Automatic (required for Microsoft Base-line Security Analyzer)
Security Accounts Manager	Automatic
Server	Automatic
System Event Notification	Automatic
TCP/IP NetBIOS Helper	Automatic
Window Management Instrumenta-tion (WMI)	Automatic
Windows Management Instrumenta-tion Driver Extensions	Manual
Windows Time (W32Time)	Automatic
Workstation	Automatic

Domain controllers require these additional services:

Service	Setting
Distributed File System (DFS)	Automatic
DNS Server	Automatic
File Replication	Automatic
Intersite Messaging	Automatic
Kerberos Key Distribution Center	Automatic
NT LM Security Support Provider	Automatic

Additional Information

- *Microsoft Windows Internals*, Fourth Edition (Microsoft Press, 2005)

- Services on MSDN (*http://msdn.microsoft.com/library/en-us/dllproc/base/services.asp*)

- Knowledge Base article 288129: "How to Grant Users Rights to Manage Services in Windows 2000" (*http://support.microsoft.com/kb/288129*)

- Knowledge Base article 325349: "How to Grant Users Rights to Manage Services in Windows Server 2003" (*http://support.microsoft.com/kb/325349*)

- Knowledge Base article 327618: "Security, Services, and the Interactive Desktop" (*http://support.microsoft.com/kb/327618*)

Chapter 10

Implementing TCP/IP Security

TCP/IP is an industry-standard suite of protocols designed to facilitate communication between computers on large networks. TCP/IP was developed in 1969 by the U.S. Department of Defense Advanced Research Projects Agency (DARPA) as the result of a resource-sharing experiment called ARPANET (Advanced Research Projects Agency Network). Since 1969, ARPANET has grown into a worldwide community of networks known as the Internet, and TCP/IP has become the primary protocol used on all networks. Unfortunately, TCP/IP was not designed with security in mind and thus has very few security components by default. Consequently, it is often a source of network vulnerabilities. The Microsoft Windows operating system provides several methods that you can use to add security to TCP/IP, including securing the TCP/IP stack and using IP Security (IPSec). We will examine both techniques in this chapter.

Securing TCP/IP

You cannot successfully secure computer networks without knowing how TCP/IP works. Nearly all computers today use TCP/IP as their primary network communication protocol. Thus, without physical access to a computer, an attacker must use TCP/IP to attack it. Consequently, TCP/IP security is often your first line of defense against attackers attempting to compromise your organization's network and therefore should be part of any defense-in-depth strategy for securing networks. You can configure additional security for the TCP/IP protocol stack in Microsoft Windows Server 2003, Windows 2000, and Windows XP to protect a computer against common attacks, such as denial-of-service attacks, and to help prevent attacks on applications that use the TCP/IP protocol.

Understanding Internet Layer Protocols

TCP/IP primarily operates at two levels in the OSI model: the Internet layer and the transport layer. The Internet layer is responsible for addressing, packaging, and routing functions. The core protocols of the Internet layer include the Internet Protocol (IP), Address Resolution Protocol (ARP), and Internet Control Message Protocol (ICMP):

- **IP**   A routable protocol responsible for logical addressing, routing, and the fragmentation and reassembly of packets
- **ARP**   Resolves IP addresses to Media Access Control (MAC) addresses and vice versa
- **ICMP**   Provides diagnostic functions and reporting errors for unsuccessful delivery of IP packets

The TCP/IP protocol suite includes a series of interconnected protocols called the *core protocols*. All other applications and protocols in the TCP/IP protocol suite rely on the basic services provided by several protocols, including IP, ARP, and ICMP.

IP

IP is a connectionless, unreliable datagram protocol primarily responsible for addressing and routing packets between hosts. *Connectionless* means that a session is not established to manage the exchange of data. *Unreliable* means that delivery is not guaranteed. IP always makes a best-effort attempt to deliver a packet. An IP packet might be lost, delivered out of sequence, duplicated, or delayed. IP does not attempt to recover from these types of errors. The acknowledgment of packets delivered and the recovery of lost packets is the responsibility of a higher-layer protocol, such as Transmission Control Protocol (TCP). IP is defined in RFC 791.

An IP packet consists of an IP header and an IP payload. The IP header contains information about the IP packet, and the IP payload is the data being encapsulated by the IP protocol to be transmitted to the receiving host. The following list describes the key fields in the IP header:

- **Source IP Address**   The IP address of the source of the IP datagram.
- **Destination IP Address**   The IP address of the destination of the IP datagram.
- **Identification**   Used to identify a specific IP datagram and all fragments of a specific IP datagram if fragmentation occurs.
- **Protocol**   Informs IP at the destination host whether to pass the packet up to TCP, User Datagram Protocol (UDP), ICMP, or other protocols.

■ **Checksum**   A simple mathematical computation used to verify the integrity of the IP header. If the IP header does not match the checksum, the receiving host will disregard the packet. This checksum does not include any information outside the IP header.

■ **Time To Live (TTL)**   Designates the number of networks on which the datagram is allowed to travel before being discarded by a router. The TTL is set by the sending host and is used to prevent packets from endlessly circulating on an IP network. When forwarding an IP packet, routers decrease the TTL by at least one.

■ **Fragmentation And Reassembly**   If a router receives an IP packet that is too large for the network to which the packet is being forwarded, IP fragments the original packet into smaller packets that fit on the downstream network. When the packets arrive at their final destination, IP on the destination host reassembles the fragments into the original payload. This process is referred to as fragmentation and reassembly. Fragmentation can occur in environments that have a mix of networking technologies, such as Ethernet and Token Ring. The fragmentation and reassembly process works as follows:

1. When an IP packet is sent, the sending host places a unique value in the Identification field.

2. The IP packet is received at the router. If the router determines that the Maximum Transmission Unit (MTU) of the network onto which the packet is to be forwarded is smaller than the size of the IP packet, the router fragments the original IP payload into multiple packets, each of which is smaller than the receiving network's MTU size. Each fragment is sent with its own IP header that contains the following:

   ❑ The original Identification field, which identifies all fragments that belong together.

   ❑ The More Fragments flag, which indicates that other fragments follow. The More Fragments flag is not set on the last fragment because no other fragments follow it.

   ❑ The Fragment Offset field, which indicates the position of the fragment relative to the original IP payload.

3. When the fragments are received by the destination host, they are identified by the Identification field as belonging together. The Fragment Offset field is then used to reassemble the fragments into the original IP payload.

ARP

Address Resolution Protocol performs IP address–to–MAC address resolution for outgoing packets. As each outgoing addressed IP datagram is encapsulated in a frame, source and destination MAC addresses must be added. Determining the destination MAC address for each frame is the responsibility of ARP. ARP is defined in RFC 826.

ICMP

Internet Control Message Protocol provides troubleshooting facilities and error reporting for packets that are undeliverable. For example, if IP is unable to deliver a packet to the destination host, ICMP sends a Destination Unreachable message to the source host. Table 10-1 shows the most common ICMP messages.

Table 10-1   Common ICMP Messages

Message	Description
Echo Request	Troubleshooting message used to check IP connectivity to a desired host. The Ping utility sends ICMP Echo Request messages.
Echo Reply	Response to an ICMP Echo Request.
Redirect	Sent by a router to inform a sending host of a better route to a destination IP address.
Source Quench	Sent by a router to inform a sending host that its IP datagrams are being dropped because of congestion at the router. The sending host then lowers its transmission rate.
Destination Unreachable	Sent by a router or the destination host to inform the sending host that the datagram cannot be delivered.

When the result of an ICMP request is a Destination Unreachable message, a specific message is returned to the requestor detailing why the Destination Unreachable ICMP message was sent. Table 10-2 describes the most common of these messages.

Table 10-2   Common ICMP Destination Unreachable Messages

Unreachable Message	Description
Host Unreachable	Sent by an IP router when a route to the destination IP address cannot be found
Protocol Unreachable	Sent by the destination IP node when the Protocol field in the IP header cannot be matched with an IP client protocol currently loaded
Port Unreachable	Sent by the destination IP node when the destination port in the UDP header cannot be matched with a process using that port
Fragmentation Needed and DF Set	Sent by an IP router when fragmentation must occur but is not allowed because of the source node setting the Don't Fragment (DF) flag in the IP header

ICMP does not make IP a reliable protocol. ICMP attempts to report errors and provide feedback on specific conditions. ICMP messages are carried as unacknowledged IP datagrams and are themselves unreliable. ICMP is defined in RFC 792.

Understanding Transport Layer Protocols

The transport layer is responsible for providing session and datagram communication services over the IP protocol. The two core protocols of the transport layer are the Transmission Control Protocol (TCP) and User Datagram Protocol (UDP):

- **TCP**   Provides a one-to-one, connection-oriented, reliable communications service. TCP is responsible for the establishment of a TCP connection, the sequencing and acknowledgment of packets sent, and the recovery of packets lost during transmission.

- **UDP**   Provides a one-to-one or one-to-many, connectionless, unreliable communications service. UDP is used when the amount of data to be transferred is small (such as data that fits into a single packet), when the overhead of establishing a TCP connection is not desired, or when the applications or upper-layer protocols provide reliable delivery.

How TCP Communication Works

When two computers communicate using TCP, the computer that initiates the communication is known as the client, regardless of whether it is running a client or server operating system, and the responding computer is known as the host. If the client and host are on the same network segment, the client computer first uses ARP to resolve the host's MAC address by sending a broadcast for the IP address of the host. Once the client has the MAC address of the host, it can commence communication to the port on the host by using the transport layer protocol specified by the application. There are 65,535 TCP and UDP ports, beginning with 0. Ports 1023 and below are regarded as well-known ports for legacy reasons, and ports above 1023 are known as high ports. Functionally, no difference exists between the well-known ports and the high ports. On the host, an application is bound to a certain port it specifies and is initialized in a listening state, where it waits for requests from a client. When the client initiates a connection to a TCP port, a defined series of packets, known as a three-way handshake and illustrated in Figure 10-1, constructs a session for reliable packet transmission. The steps for establishing connections follow:

1. The client sends the host a synchronization (SYN) message that contains the host's port and the client's Initial Sequence Number (ISN). TCP sequence numbers are 32 bits in length and are used to ensure session reliability by facilitating out-of-order packet reconstruction.

2. The host receives the message and sends back its own SYN message and an acknowledgment (ACK) message, which includes the host's ISN and the client's ISN incremented by 1.

3. The client receives the host's response and sends an ACK, which includes the ISN from the host incremented by 1. After the host receives the packet, the TCP session is established.

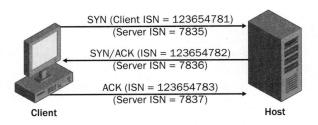

Figure 10-1   Three-way TCP handshake

When the communication between the client and host is complete, the session is closed once the following steps occur:

1. The client sends a finalization (FIN) message to the host. The session is now *half closed*. The client no longer sends data but can still receive data from the host. Upon receiving this FIN message, the host enters a passive closed state.

2. The host sends an ACK message, which includes the client's sequence number augmented by 1.

3. The host ends its own FIN message. The client receives the FIN message and returns an ACK message that includes the host's sequence number augmented by 1.

4. Upon receiving this ACK message, the host closes the connection and releases the memory the connection was using.

The Netstat.exe Command

To see port activity on your computers that run Windows Server 2003, Windows 2000, or Windows XP, you can use the Netstat.exe command. Netstat.exe will also show the status of TCP ports. The syntax for using Netstat.exe follows, and Table 10-3 describes the options available when using this command.

```
NETSTAT [-a] [-e] [-n] [-o] [-s] [-p proto] [-r] [interval]
```

Table 10-3   Netstat.exe Options

Option	Description
-a	Displays all connections and listening ports.
-e	Displays Ethernet statistics. This can be combined with the -s option.
-n	Displays addresses and port numbers in numerical form.
-o	Displays the owning process ID (PID) associated with each connection. This option does not exist in Windows 2000.
-p *protocol*	Shows connections for the protocol specified by *protocol*, which can be TCP, UDP, TCPv6, or UDPv6. If used with the -s option to display per-protocol statistics, the value for *protocol* can be IP, ICMP, TCP, or UDP.
-r	Displays the routing table.
-s	Displays per-protocol statistics. By default, statistics are shown for IP, ICMP, TCP, and UDP.
interval	Determines the refresh interval for the data displayed by Netstat.

Tip   To find the process associated with a given active port in Windows Server 2003 and Windows XP, you can locate the PID associated with the port by typing **netstat–ano**. You can then find the process associated with the PID by typing **tasklist /FI "PID eq XX"**, where *XX* is the PID of the process.

As mentioned in Table 10-3, the -o option of Netstat.exe is not available in Windows 2000; however, you can download utilities from the Internet that have similar functionality that run in Windows 2000.

Common Threats to TCP/IP

Several types of threats to TCP/IP can either compromise network security or lead to information disclosure. Although these attacks are more prevalent on the Internet, you should be concerned about them on internal computers as well. These common threats include the following:

■ Port scanning

■ Spoofing and hijacking

■ Denial of service

Port Scanning

To communicate with TCP/IP, applications running on host computers must listen for incoming TCP or UDP connections, and host operating systems must listen for broadcast and other network maintenance traffic. By scanning a computer to see which ports a host is listening for and which protocols it uses, an attacker might be able to locate weaknesses in the host that he can later use to attack the computer. Attackers often perform port scans to reveal this information. Several types of port scans exist:

- **Ping sweeps**   An attacker might use an automated tool to send ICMP Echo Request packets to entire networks or subnets. By default, all active hosts will respond unless they have firewalls enabled that filter ICMP traffic. This lets the attacker know that the host exists and is active. An attacker can also analyze the structure of the ICMP packet to determine the operating system running on the host.

- **Port enumeration**   An attacker might want to enumerate all the services running on a host computer. Because hosts must respond to client computers to carry out legitimate operations, attackers can exploit this behavior to obtain critical information.

> **Tip**   You can download a command-line port-scanning tool from Microsoft called Port Query (Portqry.exe). This tool, found at *http://support.microsoft.com /kb/832919*, tests the security of hosts and performs network diagnostics. Port Query 2.0 also includes enhancements that enable it to retrieve basic information from services that communicate through session and application layer protocols, such as Lightweight Directory Access Protocol (LDAP) and remote procedure call (RPC). In addition, many free utilities that can perform port scans are available on the Internet.
>
> Additionally, you can download a tool from Microsoft called Port Reporter (PortRptr.exe). Port Reporter runs as a system service that logs packets that are sent and received and the processes that sent or received them. You can download Port Reporter from the Microsoft Web site at *http://support.microsoft.com/kb /837243*. Conveniently, Port Reporter also has a companion parsing utility that you can download to help analyze the log files generated by Port Reporter.

- **Banner grabbing**   Many common services respond with banners when sessions are initiated or requested. These banners contain basic information on the service or server. For example, by using Telnet to connect to port 25 of a Windows 2000 server running the default Simple Mail Transfer Protocol (SMTP) service, you can retrieve this banner:

```
220 SFOFS001.finance.woodgrovebank.com Microsoft ESMTP MAIL Service, Version: 5
.0 .2195.5329 ready at Sat, 12 Oct 2002 16:18:44 -0800
```

From interpreting this banner, you can determine that the target server is named SFOFS001. Given the version number, 5.0.2195.5329, the server SFOFS001 is probably a file server running Windows 2000 with Service Pack 3 installed and is physically located in the Pacific Time zone—most likely in San Francisco. The server is running a built-in instance of the SMTP service, which is installed as part of Microsoft Internet Information Services (IIS) 5.0. Knowing that IIS is installed by default in Windows 2000 and that this server does not appear to be a Web server, it is likely that the server has a default installation of Windows 2000.

> **Important**   Changing service banners can also break applications that rely on them for information about the server they are communicating with. Furthermore, changing banners can break an application running on the computer that uses the information from service banners from other services running on the computer.

- **Half scan**   This type of port scanning does not follow the precise TCP three-way handshake protocol and leaves TCP connections half open. Because most host System logs do not log packets until the host receives the final ACK, half scans can enable an attacker to gain information about a host without being detected.

Spoofing and Hijacking

Attackers might want to spoof or mimic legitimate TCP/IP packets to attack a computer or network. Usually, spoofing a packet requires that the attacker handcraft a TCP/IP packet and send it to either the host she wants to attack or a third-party host that she has previously compromised to attack the targeted host or network. Many types of spoofing attacks exist. The following three are among the most well known:

- **Land attack**   Takes advantage of security flaws in the many implementations of TCP/IP. To carry out a land attack, an attacker opens a legitimate TCP session by sending a SYN packet but spoofs the packet so that the source address and port and the destination address and port match the host IP address and the port to which the packet is being sent.

  For example, to carry out a land attack on an e-mail server with the IP address 192.168.183.200, an attacker can create a packet with the source address of 192.168.183.200 and the source port of 25, rather than using the source address and port of his own computer. Now the source and destination addresses will be the same, as will the source and destination ports. If not patched to protect against the land attack, the packet will continually attempt to make a connection with itself on its own port 25, resulting in a denial-of-service situation.

- **Smurf attack**   Uses a third-party network to carry out a denial-of-service attack on a host system by spoofing an ICMP Echo Request packet. The attacker obtains the host IP address and creates a forged ICMP Echo Request packet that looks like it came from the host IP address. The attacker sends thousands of copies of the spoofed packet to the broadcast address on an improperly secured third-party network. This results in every computer in the third-party network responding to each spoofed packet by sending an ICMP Echo Reply packet to the host system. The amount of ICMP traffic that is generated by this attack will deny legitimate traffic from reaching the target host.

- **Session hijacking**   Takes advantage of flaws in many implementations of the TCP/IP protocol by anticipating TCP sequence numbers to hijack a session with a host. To hijack a TCP/IP session, the attacker creates a legitimate TCP session to the targeted host, records the TCP sequence numbers used by the host, and then computes the round-trip time (RTT). This step often takes many exchanges in sequence. Using the stored sequence numbers and the RTT, the attacker can potentially predict future TCP sequence numbers. The attacker can then send a spoofed packet to another host, using the targeted host IP address as the source address and the next sequence number. If successful, the second host system will believe the packet originated from the targeted system and accept packets from the attacker. This type of attack is particularly effective when the second host trusts the targeted host.

> **More Info**   IP spoofing by predicting TCP/IP sequence numbers was the basis for the famous Christmas 1994 attack on Tsutomu Shimomura by Kevin Mitnick. The attack is chronicled in the book *Takedown: The Pursuit and Capture of Kevin Mitnick, America's Most Wanted Computer Outlaw—By the Man Who Did It* (Hyperion, 1996).

Denial of Service

Denial-of-service attackers attempt to exploit the way the TCP/IP protocol works to prevent legitimate traffic from reaching the host system. One of the most common types of denial-of-service attacks is a SYN flood. A SYN flood attempts to create a situation in which the host system's maximum TCP connection pool is locked in a half-open state, thus denying legitimate traffic to and from the host. To carry out a SYN flood, the attacker creates a spoofed IP packet with an unreachable IP address for a source address, or she clips the receive wire on the Ethernet cable she is using. When the host receives the packet, it responds by sending a SYN/ACK response and waits for the final ACK in the TCP three-way handshake, which never comes. The session will remain in the half-open state until the predefined time-out is reached. This process is repeated until no more TCP sessions are allowed by the host system, which then cannot create any new sessions.

> **More Info**   See *Assessing Network Security* (Microsoft Press, 2004) by Kevin Lam, David LeBlanc, and Ben Smith for more information on common attacks on TCP/IP.

Configuring TCP/IP Security in Windows

The remainder of this section presents several ways you can secure your computers that run Windows Server 2003, Windows 2000, and Windows XP against attacks on TCP/IP, including basic TCP/IP binding configurations, custom registry settings, and TCP/IP filtering.

Implementing Basic TCP/IP Security

Three basic settings, outlined in the following list, will increase the security of TCP/IP for each network adapter in Windows Server 2003, Windows 2000, and Windows XP. You will need to ensure that each of these settings is compatible with your network and the applications that either run on the computer or must be accessible from the computer.

- **File And Printer Sharing For Microsoft Networks**   By default, File And Printer Sharing For Microsoft Networks is bound on all network interfaces. The File And Printer Sharing For Microsoft Networks component enables other computers on a network to access resources on your computer. By removing the binding to File And Printer Sharing For Microsoft Networks from a network interface, you can prevent other computers from enumerating or connecting to files and printers that have been shared through that network interface. Stopping the Server service will also prevent a computer from hosting file or print shares. After removing this binding from a network interface, the File and Print Services computer will no longer listen for Server Message Block (SMB) connections on TCP port 139 of that interface but will still listen on port 445 for other SMB packets. Direct hosted "NetBIOS-less" SMB traffic uses port 445 (TCP and UDP). If NetBIOS is still used for other services on the computer, port 139 will still be listening, just not for File and Print Services. Removing this setting will not interfere with the computer's ability to connect to other shared files or printers. You can unbind File And Printer Sharing For Microsoft Networks in the Network And Dial-Up Connections Control Panel or on the Properties page of the network interface. You can prevent the Windows operating system from listening for direct SMB traffic by deleting the default value from the registry entry HKLM\SYSTEM\CurrentControlSet\Services\NetBT\Parameters\TransportBindName. A host-based firewall, such as Windows Firewall in Windows XP and Windows Server 2003, is also an effective option for preventing other computers from connecting to SMB ports.

- **NetBIOS Over TCP/IP** Windows Server 2003, Windows 2000, and Windows XP support file and printer sharing traffic by using the SMB protocol directly hosted on TCP. This differs from earlier operating systems in which SMB traffic requires the NetBIOS over TCP/IP (NetBT) protocol to work on a TCP/IP transport. If both the direct-hosted and NetBT interfaces are enabled, both methods are tried at the same time and the first to respond is used. This enables the Windows operating system to function properly with operating systems that do not support direct hosting of SMB traffic. NetBIOS over TCP/IP traditionally uses the following ports:

NetBIOS name	137/UDP
NetBIOS name	137/TCP
NetBIOS datagram	138/UDP
NetBIOS session	139/TCP

> **Note** Direct-hosted "NetBIOS-less" SMB traffic uses port 445 (TCP and UDP). If you disable NetBIOS over TCP/IP (NetBT) and unbind File And Printer Sharing For Microsoft Networks, the computer will no longer respond to any NetBIOS requests. Applications and services that depend on NetBT will no longer function once NetBT is disabled. Therefore, verify that your clients and applications no longer need NetBT support before you disable it.

- **DNS Registration** By default, computers running Windows Server 2003, Windows 2000, and Windows XP attempt to register their host names and IP address mappings automatically in the Domain Name System (DNS) for each adapter. If your computer is using a public DNS server or cannot reach the DNS server, as is often the case when the computer resides in a perimeter network, you should remove this behavior on each adapter.

Configuring Registry Settings

Denial-of-service attacks are network attacks aimed at making a computer or a particular service on a computer unavailable to network users. Denial-of-service attacks can be difficult to defend against. To help prevent denial-of-service attacks, you can harden the TCP/IP protocol stack on computers that run Windows Server 2003, Windows 2000, and Windows XP. You should harden the TCP/IP stack against denial-of-service attacks, even on internal networks, to prevent denial-of-service attacks that originate from inside the network as well as on computers attached to public networks. You can harden the TCP/IP stack by customizing these registry values, which are stored in the registry key HKLM\SYSTEM\CurrentControlSet\Services\Tcpip\Parameters\:

- **EnableICMPRedirect** When ICMP redirects are disabled (by setting the value to 0), attackers cannot carry out attacks that require a host to redirect the ICMP-based attack to a third party.

- **SynAttackProtect** Enables SYN flood protection in Windows Server 2003, Windows 2000, and Windows XP. You can set this value to 0, 1, or 2. The default setting, 0, provides no protection. Setting the value to 1 will activate SYN/ACK protection contained in the TCPMaxPortsExhausted, TCPMaxHalfOpen, and TCPMaxHalfOpenRetried values. Setting the value to 2 will protect against SYN/ACK attacks by more aggressively timing out open and half-open connections and preventing scalable windows. In Windows Server 2003, you can set this to be either on (1) or off (0). Turning it on is effectively the same as setting it to 2 in Windows 2000 and Windows XP. Windows Server 2003 Service Pack 1 enables SynAttackProtect.

- **TCPMaxConnectResponseRetransmissions** Determines how many times TCP retransmits an unanswered SYN/ACK message. TCP retransmits acknowledgments until the number of retransmissions specified by this value is reached.

- **TCPMaxHalfOpen** Determines how many connections the server can maintain in the half-open state before TCP/IP initiates SYN flooding attack protection. This entry is used only when SYN flooding attack protection is enabled on this server—that is, when the value of the SynAttackProtect entry is 1 or 2 and the value of the TCPMaxConnectResponseRetransmissions entry is at least 2.

- **TCPMaxHalfOpenRetired** Determines how many connections the server can maintain in the half-open state even after a connection request has been retransmitted. If the number of connections exceeds the value of this entry, TCP/IP initiates SYN flooding attack protection. This entry is used only when SYN flooding attack protection is enabled on this server—that is, when the value of the SynAttackProtect entry is 1 and the value of the TCPMaxConnectResponseRetransmissions entry is at least 2.

- **TCPMaxPortsExhausted** Determines how many connection requests the system can refuse before TCP/IP initiates SYN flooding attack protection. The system must refuse all connection requests when its reserve of open connection ports runs out. This entry is used only when SYN flooding attack protection is enabled on this server—that is, when the value of the SynAttackProtect entry is 1, and the value of the TCPMaxConnectResponseRetransmissions entry is at least 2.

- **TCPMaxDataRetransmissions** Determines how many times TCP retransmits an unacknowledged data segment on an existing connection. TCP retransmits data segments until they are acknowledged or until the number of retransmissions specified by this value is reached.

- **EnableDeadGWDetect**   Determines whether the computer will attempt to detect dead gateways. When dead gateway detection is enabled (by setting this value to 1), TCP might ask IP to change to a backup gateway if a number of connections are experiencing difficulty. Backup gateways are defined in the TCP/IP Configuration dialog box in Network Control Panel for each adapter. When you leave this setting enabled, it is possible for an attacker to redirect the server to a gateway of his choosing.

- **EnablePMTUDiscovery**   Determines whether path MTU discovery is enabled (1), for which TCP attempts to discover the largest packet size over the path to a remote host. When path MTU discovery is disabled (0), the path MTU for all TCP connections is fixed at 576 bytes.

- **DisableIPSourceRouting**   Determines whether a computer allows clients to predetermine the route that packets take to their destination. When this value is set to 2, the computer will disable source routing for IP packets.

- **KeepAliveTime**   Determines how often TCP attempts to verify that an idle connection is still intact by sending a keep-alive packet. If the remote computer is still active, it will respond and the session will remain open. Keep-alive packets are not automatically sent by the TCP/IP stack in the Windows operating system. The default value is set to 2 hours (7,200,000) when keep-alive transmissions are enabled.

- **NoNameReleaseOnDemand**   Determines whether the computer will release its NetBIOS name if requested by another computer or a malicious packet attempting to hijack the computer's NetBIOS name.

- **PerformRouterDiscovery**   Determines whether the computer performs router discovery on this interface. Router discovery solicits router information from the network and adds the information retrieved to the route table. Setting this value to 0 prevents the interface from performing router discovery.

Table 10-4 lists the registry entries that you can make to harden the TCP/IP stack on your computers that run Windows Server 2003, Windows 2000, and Windows XP. These settings must be added to the registry and configured appropriately.

Table 10-4   Registry Settings to Harden TCP/IP

Value	Data (DWORD)
EnableSecurityFilters	0
SynAttackProtect	2 (1 in Windows Server 2003)
TCPMaxConnectResponseRetransmissions	2
TCPMaxHalfOpen	500
TCPMaxHalfOpenRetired	400
TCPMaxPortsExhausted	5
TCPMaxDataRetransmissions	3

Table 10-4   Registry Settings to Harden TCP/IP

Value	Data (DWORD)
EnableDeadGWDetect	0
EnablePMTUDiscovery	0
DisableIPSourceRouting	2
KeepAliveTime	300,000
NoNameReleaseOnDemand	1
PerformRouterDiscovery	0

Additionally, you can secure the TCP/IP stack for Windows Sockets (Winsock) applications such as FTP servers and Web servers. The driver Afd.sys is responsible for connection attempts to Winsock applications. Afd.sys in Windows Server 2003, Windows 2000, and Windows XP supports large numbers of connections in the half-open state without denying access to legitimate clients. Afd.sys can use a dynamic backlog, which is configurable, rather than a static backlog. You can configure four parameters for the dynamic backlog:

- **EnableDynamicBacklog**   Switches between using a static backlog and a dynamic backlog. By default, this parameter is set to 0, which enables the static backlog. You should enable the dynamic backlog for better security on Winsock.

- **MinimumDynamicBacklog**   Controls the minimum number of free connections allowed on a listening Winsock endpoint. If the number of free connections drops below this value, a thread is queued to create additional free connections. Making this value too large (setting it to a number greater than 100) will degrade the performance of the computer.

- **MaximumDynamicBacklog**   Controls the maximum number of half-open and free connections to Winsock endpoints. If this value is reached, no additional free connections will be made.

- **DynamicBacklogGrowthDelta**   Controls the number of Winsock endpoints in each allocation pool requested by the computer. Setting this value too high can cause system resources to be occupied unnecessarily.

Each of these values must be added to the registry key HKLM\SYSTEM\CurrentControlSet\Services\AFD\Parameters. Table 10-5 lists the parameters and the recommended levels of protection.

Table 10-5   Registry Settings to Harden Winsock

Value	Data (DWORD)
EnableDynamicBacklog	1
MinimumDynamicBacklog	20
MaximumDynamicBacklog	20,000
DynamicBacklogGrowthDelta	10

Using TCP/IP Filtering

Windows Server 2003, Windows 2000, and Windows XP include support for TCP/IP filtering, a feature known as TCP/IP Security in Microsoft Windows NT 4.0. TCP/IP filtering enables you to specify which types of inbound local host IP traffic are processed for all interfaces. This feature prevents traffic from being processed by the computer in the absence of other TCP/IP filtering, such as that provided by Routing and Remote Access Service (RRAS), Windows Firewall (in Windows XP and Windows Server 2003 SP1), and other TCP/IP applications or services. TCP/IP filtering is disabled by default.

When configuring TCP/IP filtering, you can permit either all or only specific ports or protocols listed for TCP ports, UDP ports, or IP protocols. Packets destined for the host are accepted for processing if they meet one of the following criteria:

- The destination TCP port matches the list of TCP ports.

- The destination UDP port matches the list of UDP ports.

- The IP protocol matches the list of IP protocols.

- The packet is an ICMP packet.

> **Note**   TCP/IP port filtering applies to all interfaces on the computer and cannot be applied on a per-adapter basis. However, you can configure allowed ports and protocols on a per-adapter basis.

In addition to being able to configure TCP/IP filtering in the Options tab of the TCP/IP advanced properties in the user interface, you can apply the settings directly to the registry. Table 10-6 lists the registry values to configure TCP/IP filtering. TCP/IP filtering is set in the key HKLM\SYSTEM\CurrentControlSet\Services\Tcpip\Parameters, whereas the specific settings for each interface are configured in the key HKLM\SYSTEM\CurrentControlSet\Services\Tcpip\Parameters\Interfaces*Interface_GUID*.

Table 10-6   Registry Values for TCP/IP Filtering

Setting	Type	Description
EnableSecurityFilters	DWORD	1 enables TCP/IP filtering; 0 disables TCP/IP filtering.
UdpAllowedPorts	MULTI_SZ	0 allows all UDP ports; an empty (null) value blocks all UDP ports; otherwise, the specific allowed UDP ports are listed.
TCPAllowedPorts	MULTI_SZ	0 allows all TCP ports; an empty (null) value blocks all TCP ports; otherwise, the specific allowed TCP ports are listed.

Table 10-6   Registry Values for TCP/IP Filtering

Setting	Type	Description
RawIpAllowedProtocols	MULTI_SZ	0 allows all IP protocols; an empty (null) value blocks all IP protocols; otherwise, the specific allowed IP protocols are listed.

Using Windows Firewall in Windows Server 2003 and Windows XP

Windows Server 2003 and Windows XP both include a personal firewall called Internet Connection Firewall (ICF) in their initial release. Its much improved successor, called Windows Firewall, was released in Windows Server 2003 Service Pack 1 and Windows XP Service Pack 2. Windows Firewall is a stateful firewall—it monitors incoming traffic received by the network adapter configured to use Windows Firewall and it inspects the source and destination addresses of each message that it handles. To prevent unsolicited traffic from the public side of the connection from entering the private side, Windows Firewall keeps a table of all communications that have originated from the Windows Firewall computer. When used in conjunction with Internet Connection Sharing (ICS), Windows Firewall creates a table for tracking all traffic originated from the Windows Firewall/ICS computer and all traffic originated from private network computers. Inbound Internet traffic is allowed to reach the computers in your network only when a matching entry in the table shows that the communication exchange originated within your computer or private network or is permitted by rule to an application or port.

Windows Firewall improves on ICF, which operated on a binary basis, either off or on, by adding an option to enable the firewall but not allow exemptions to the packet filtering. This mode blocks all unsolicited inbound traffic. As an administrator, you can determine whether users, even if they are not local administrators, can enable Windows Firewall through the Group Policy option Prohibit Use Of Internet Connection Firewall On Your DNS Domain Network, which is listed in the computer portion of Group Policy under Administrative Templates, Network, Network Connections.

Additionally, through the use of profiles, network administrators can configure Windows Firewall settings to be different (presumably more relaxed) when connected to the corporate network. The two profiles that are added to Group Policy in Windows XP SP2 and Windows Server 2003 SP1 are the Domain profile and the Standard profile. The client computer determines whether it is connected to the corporate network by using the Network Location Awareness (NLA) system service. When the network adapter is initialized when connecting to a network, the NLA service compares the connection-specific DNS suffix of the connection it received from Group Policy to the domain suffix of the domain to which the computer belongs. If the two match, NLA judges that the computer is connected to the corporate network, and the domain profile is applied. Because the DNS suffix is generally provided by the Dynamic Host Configuration Protocol (DHCP) server from which the computer gets its IP address, the use of profiles should not be used on networks that require a great degree of security. An attacker with ample resources could potentially force a client computer into the domain profile if she has sufficient knowledge of the target's network. Although this scenario is remote at best, it is worth considering the security conditions under which your network operates.

Using Windows Firewall, you can create exceptions by defining which programs and services are allowed to receive unsolicited traffic from other computers. Exceptions configured through Programs and Services are global on the system, whereas exceptions configured through Services are interface specific. For programs and services, which can be configured locally or through Group Policy, Windows Firewall enables you to create an exception when traffic originates on the local subnet or from within a predefined range of IP addresses, but it blocks the traffic when the traffic originates from remote networks. Figures 10-2 and 10-3 show the configuration of the predefined File And Printer Sharing exception, which restricts the scope of the exception to the local subnet.

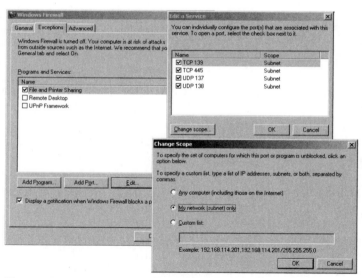

Figure 10-2   Restricting a service to accept packets from only the local subnet

If an application needs to receive unsolicited traffic when Windows Firewall is enabled and is blocked by Windows Firewall, for administrators, the operating system will prompt the user to grant the application executable a specific exception to the rule while non-administrators will receive an error message. You can also add applications to the Programs and Services list by the name of the executable rather than having to create a static, always-open port such as was required in the Internet Connection Firewall.

You can configure services to allow unsolicited traffic from the Internet to be forwarded by the Windows Firewall computer to the private network. For example, if you are hosting an HTTP Web server service and have enabled the HTTP service on your Windows Firewall computer, unsolicited HTTP traffic will be forwarded by the Windows Firewall computer to the HTTP Web server. A set of operational information, known as a *service definition*, is required by Windows Firewall to allow the unsolicited Internet traffic to be forwarded to the Web server on your private network. The Services tab of Windows Firewall Advanced Settings dialog box is shown in Figure 10-3.

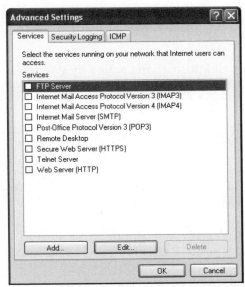

Figure 10-3   Services tab of Windows Firewall Advanced Settings dialog box

If there is no service definition for the service that you would like to allow to be connected, you can add custom services in the Services tab of the Advanced Settings dialog box. Windows Firewall can also perform port translation for incoming connections. When you create a custom service, you will need to specify the following:

- **Description of service**   Determines how the service is displayed in the Services tab

- **Name or IP address**   Determines the host name or IP address of the computer offering the service if the service is not hosted on the local computer

- **External port**   Defines the TCP or UDP port on the Windows Firewall computer that will listen to inbound traffic to the service

- **Internal port**   Defines the TCP or UDP port to which the Windows Firewall computer will forward the inbound traffic to the computer defined in the Name Or IP Address field

Communications that originate from a source outside the Windows Firewall computer, such as the Internet, are dropped by the firewall unless an entry in the Services tab is made to allow passage. Windows Firewall silently discards unsolicited communications, preventing common attacks, such as port scanning and NetBIOS enumeration. Windows Firewall does not block outgoing network traffic because this provides little extra protection and is completely unusable by average users.

Windows Firewall can create a Security log so you can view the activity that is tracked by the firewall. You can choose whether to log dropped, successful, or dropped and successful packets. By default, packets are logged to %systemroot%\pfirewall.log. The log file has a default maximum size of 4098 KB. Table 10-7 describes the fields in the packet log file.

Table 10-7   Description of Information Logged by Windows Firewall

Field	Description
Date	Specifies the date that the recorded transaction occurred in the format *YY-MM-DD*.
Time	Specifies the time that the recorded transaction occurred in the format *HH:MM:SS*.
Action	Specifies which operation was observed by the firewall. The options available to the firewall are OPEN, CLOSE, DROP, and INFO-EVENTS-LOST. An INFO-EVENTS-LOST action indicates the number of events that happened but were not placed in the log.
Protocol	Specifies which IP protocol was used for the communication.
Src-ip	Specifies the source IP address of the computer attempting to establish communications.
Dst-ip	Specifies the destination IP address of the communication attempt.
Src-port	Specifies the source port number of the sending computer. Only TCP and UDP will return a valid src-port entry.
Dst-port	Specifies the port of the destination computer. Only TCP and UDP will return a valid dst-port entry.
Size	Specifies the packet size in bytes.
Tcpflags	Specifies the TCP control flags found in the TCP header of an IP packet: ■ **ACK** Acknowledgment field significant ■ **FIN** No more data from sender ■ **PSH** Push function ■ **RST** Reset the connection ■ **SYN** Synchronize sequence numbers ■ **URG** Urgent Pointer field
Tcpsyn	Specifies the TCP synchronization number in the packet.
Tcpack	Specifies the TCP acknowledgment number in the packet.
Tcpwin	Specifies the TCP window size in bytes in the packet.

Table 10-7   Description of Information Logged by Windows Firewall

Field	Description
Icmptype	Specifies a number that represents the Type field of the ICMP message.
Icmpcode	Specifies a number that represents the Code field of the ICMP message.
Info	Specifies an information entry that depends on the type of action that oc-curred. For example, an INFO-EVENTS-LOST action will create an entry of the number of events that happened but were not placed in the log since the last occurrence of this event type.

In addition to the Group Policy objects that were added to manage Windows Firewall configuration, Windows Server 2003 SP1 and Windows XP SP2 add the ability to configure the firewall during scripted installations and from the command line.

For scripted installations, you can create a configuration file called Netfw.inf to replace the version on the installation media for Windows XP SP2:

1. Extract Netfw.inf from the installation media for Windows XP SP2, or copy it from an unaltered installation.

2. Make the desired changes to the configuration by editing the INF file.

3. Save the modified INF file as Netfw.inf.

4. Replace the default Netfw.inf with the modified Netfw.inf on the installation share for Windows XP SP2 or run the command Netsh firewall reset on the computer running Windows XP with SP2 for computers that have already had the operating system installed. If you are completing scripted installs from CD-based media, you can copy the modified Netfw.inf to the computer during installation and run the Netsh firewall reset command from a script called in the run-once registry key.

5. For information on customizing the Netfw.inf file, see the white paper: "Using the Windows Firewall INF File in Microsoft Windows XP Service Pack 2" on the Microsoft Web site at

    http://www.microsoft.com/downloads/details.aspx?FamilyID=cb307a1d-2 f97-4e63-a581-bf25685b4c43&displaylang=en

6. From the command line or programmatically from batch file or scripts, you can use Netsh to manage the Windows Firewall configuration. For example, to see the current settings of Windows Firewall, you can type "**netsh firewall show config**" at the command prompt. You can also add and delete settings as well as revert to the settings in the Netfw.inf file. Because the network shell uses IntelliSense context-specific technology, you only need type the first couple unique letters from each string, for example, "netsh fi sh co" is the same as "netsh firewall show config." This is nice for those of us who are constantly challenged by typing skills (or patience) that leave something to be desired.

Using IPSec

By its design, TCP/IP is an open protocol created to connect heterogeneous computing environments with the least amount of overhead possible. As is often the case, interoperability and performance design goals do not generally result in security—and TCP/IP is no exception to this. TCP/IP provides no native mechanism for the confidentiality or integrity of packets. To secure TCP/IP, you can implement IP Security. IPSec implements encryption and authenticity at a lower level in the TCP/IP stack than application-layer protocols such as Secure Sockets Layer (SSL) and Transport Layer Security (TLS). Because the protection process takes place lower in the TCP/IP stack, IPSec protection is transparent to applications. IPSec is a well-defined, standards-driven technology.

The IPSec process encrypts the payload after it leaves the application at the client and then decrypts the payload before it reaches the application at the server. An application does not have to be IPSec aware because the data transferred between the client and the server is normally transmitted in plaintext.

IPSec is composed of two protocols that operate in two modes with three different authentication methods. IPSec is policy driven and can be deployed centrally by using Group Policy. To deploy IPSec, you must determine the following:

- Protocol
- Mode
- Authentication methods
- Policies

Securing Data Transmission with IPSec Protocols

As mentioned, IPSec is composed of two protocols: IPSec Authentication Header (AH) and IPSec Encapsulating Security Payload (ESP). Each protocol provides different services; AH primarily provides packet integrity services, whereas ESP provides packet confidentiality services. IPSec provides mutual authentication services between clients and hosts, regardless of whether AH or ESP is being used.

Using AH

IPSec AH provides authentication, integrity, and anti-replay protection for the entire packet, including the IP header and the payload. AH does not provide confidentiality. When packets are secured with AH, the IPSec driver computes an Integrity Check Value (ICV) after the packet has been constructed but before it is sent to the computer. In the Windows operating system, you can use either the Hash-Based Message Authentication Code (HMAC) SHA1 or HMAC MD5 algorithm to compute the ICV. Figure 10-4 shows how AH modifies an IP packet.

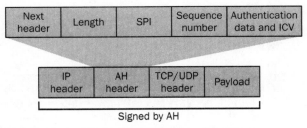

Figure 10-4   AH modifications to an IP packet

The fields in an AH packet include these:

- **Next Header**   Indicates the protocol ID for the header that follows the AH header. For example, if the encrypted data is transmitted using TCP, the next header value would be 6, which is the protocol ID for TCP.

- **Length**   Contains the total length of the AH.

- **Security Parameters Index (SPI)**   Identifies the security association (the IPSec agreement between two computers) that was negotiated in the Internet Key Exchange (IKE) protocol exchange between the source computer and the destination computer.

- **Sequence Number**   Protects the AH-protected packet from replay attacks in which an attacker attempts to resend a packet that he has previously intercepted, such as an authentication packet, to another computer. For each packet issued for a specific security association (SA), the sequence number is incremented by 1 to ensure that each packet is assigned a unique sequence number. The recipient computer verifies each packet to ensure that a sequence number has not been reused. The sequence number prevents an attacker from capturing packets, modifying them, and then retransmitting them later.

- **Authentication Data**   Contains the ICV created against the signed portion of the AH packet by using either HMAC SHA1 or HMAC MD5. The recipient performs the same integrity algorithm and compares the result of the hash algorithm with the result stored within the Authentication Data field to ensure that the signed portion of the AH packet has not been altered in transit. Because the TTL, Type of Service (TOS), Flags, Fragment Offset, and Header Checksum fields are not used in the ICV, packets secured with IPSec AH can cross routers, which can change these fields.

Using ESP

ESP packets are used to provide encryption services to transmitted data. In addition, ESP provides authentication, integrity, and anti-replay services. When packets are sent using ESP, the payload of the packet is encrypted and authenticated. The encryption is done with either Data Encryption Standard (DES) or 3DES, and the ICV calculation is done with either HMAC SHA1 or HMAC MD5.

> **Tip**   When designing an IPSec solution, you can combine AH and ESP protocols in a single IPSec SA. Although both AH and ESP provide integrity protection for transmitted data, AH protects the entire packet from modification, whereas ESP protects only the IP payload from modification.

ESP encrypts the TCP or UDP header and the application data included within an IP packet. It does not include the original IP header unless IPSec tunnel mode is used. Figure 10-5 shows how ESP modifies an IP packet.

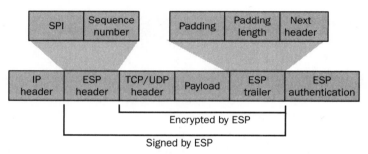

Figure 10-5   ESP modifications to an IP packet

The ESP header has two fields that are inserted between the original IP header and the TCP or UDP header from the original packet:

- **Security Parameters Index (SPI)**   Identifies the SA that was negotiated between the source computer and the destination computer for IPSec communication. The combination of the SPI, the IPSec protocol (AH or ESP), and the source and destination IP addresses identifies the SA used for the IPSec transmission within the ESP packet.

- **Sequence Number**   Protects the ESP-protected packet from replay attacks. This field is incremented by 1 to ensure that packets are never received more than once. If a packet is received with a sequence number that's already been used, that packet is dropped.

The ESP trailer is inserted after the application data from the original packet and includes the following fields:

- **Padding**   A variable length from 0 to 255 bytes that brings the length of the application data and ESP trailer to a length divisible by 32 bits so that they match the required size for the cipher algorithm.

- **Padding Length**   Indicates the length of the Padding field. After the packet is decrypted, this field is used to determine the length of the Padding field.

- **Next Header**   Identifies the protocol used for the transmission of the data, such as TCP or UDP.

Following the ESP trailer, the ESP protocol adds an ESP authentication trailer to the end of the packet. The ESP authentication trailer contains a single field:

- **Authentication Data**   Contains the ICV, which verifies the originating host that sent the message and ensures that the packet was not modified in transit. The ICV uses the defined integrity algorithm to calculate the ICV. The integrity algorithm is applied to the ESP header, the TCP/UDP header, the application data, and the ESP trailer. Because the ICV does not include the IP header, ESP packets can cross routers.

ESP provides integrity protection for the ESP header, the TCP/UDP header, the application data, and the ESP trailer. ESP also provides inspection protection by encrypting the TCP/UDP header, the application data, and the ESP trailer.

Choosing Between IPSec Modes

IPSec operates in two modes: transport mode and tunnel mode. IPSec transport mode is used for host-to-host connections, and IPSec tunnel mode is used for network-to-network or host-to-network connections.

Using IPSec Transport Mode

IPSec transport mode is fully routable, as long as the connection does not cross a network address translation (NAT) interface, which would invalidate the ICV. Used this way, IPSec must be supported on both hosts, and each host must support the same authentication protocols and have compatible IPSec filters configured and assigned. IPSec transport mode is used to secure traffic from clients to hosts for connections where sensitive data is passed.

Using IPSec Tunnel Mode

IPSec tunnel mode is used for network-to-network connections (IPSec tunnels between routers) or host-to-network connections (IPSec tunnels between a host and a router). Used this way, IPSec must be supported on both endpoints, and each endpoint must support the same authentication protocols and have compatible IPSec filters configured and assigned. IPSec tunnel mode is commonly used for site-to-site connections that cross public networks, such as the Internet.

Selecting an IPSec Authentication Method

During the initial construction of the IPSec session—also known as the Internet Key Exchange, or IKE—each host or endpoint authenticates the other host or endpoint. When configuring IPSec, you must ensure that each host or endpoint supports the same authentication methods. IPSec supports three authentication methods:

- Kerberos
- X.509 certificates
- Preshared key

> **Tip** Because IPSec requires mutual authentication, it also can be used to control network access to computers on your network that store high-value assets. For more information on how you can use IPSec this way, see the white paper "Using Microsoft Windows IPSec to Help Secure an Internal Corporate Network Server" on the Microsoft Web Site at *http://www.microsoft.com/downloads/details.aspx? FamilyID=a774012a-ac25-4a1d-8851-b7a09e3f1dc9&displaylang=en.*

Authenticating with Kerberos

Kerberos is used for IPSec mutual authentication by default. For Kerberos to be used as the authentication protocol, both hosts in transport mode or both endpoints in tunnel mode must receive Kerberos tickets from the same Active Directory forest. Thus, you should choose Kerberos for IPSec authentication only when both hosts in transport mode or both endpoints in tunnel mode are within your own organization. Kerberos is an excellent authentication method for IPSec because it requires no additional configuration or network infrastructure.

> **Important** Some types of traffic are exempted by default from being secured by IPSec, even when the IPSec policy specifies that all IP traffic should be secured. The IPSec exemptions apply to Broadcast, Multicast, Resource Reservation Setup Protocol (RSVP), IKE, and Kerberos traffic. Kerberos, a security protocol itself, can be used by IPSec for IKE authentication.

> **Important**   To remove the exemption for Kerberos and RSVP, set the value
> *NoDefaultExempt* to 1 in the registry key HKEY_LOCAL_MACHINE\SYSTEM
> \CurrentControlSet\Services\IPSEC.

Authenticating with X.509 Certificates

You can use X.509 certificates for IPSec mutual authentication of hosts or endpoints. Certificates enable you to create IPSec-secured sessions with hosts or endpoints outside your Active Directory forests, such as with business partners in extranet scenarios. You also must use certificates when using IPSec to secure virtual private network (VPN) connections made by using Layer Two Tunneling Protocol (L2TP). To use certificates, the hosts must be able to check that the other's certificate is valid.

Authenticating with Preshared Key

You can use a preshared key, which is a simple, case-sensitive text string, to authenticate hosts or endpoints. Preshared key authentication should be used only when testing or troubleshooting IPSec connectivity because the preshared key is not stored in a secure fashion by hosts or endpoints.

Creating IPSec Policies

IPSec is a policy-driven technology. In Windows Server 2003, Windows 2000, and Windows XP, you can have only one IPSec policy assigned at a time. IPSec policies are dynamic, meaning you do not have to stop and start the IPSec service or restart the computer when assigning or unassigning IPSec policies. You can also use Group Policy to deploy IPSec policies to clients running Windows Server 2003, Windows 2000, and Windows XP. The Windows operating system includes three precreated IPSec policies:

- **Client (Respond Only)**   A computer configured with the Client policy will use IPSec if the host it is communicating with requests using IPSec and supports Kerberos authentication.

- **Server (Request Security)**   A computer configured with the Server policy will always attempt to negotiate IPSec but will permit unsecured communication with hosts that do not support IPSec. The Server policy permits unsecured ICMP traffic.

- **Secure Server (Require Security)**   A computer configured with the Secure Server policy will request that IPSec be used for all inbound and outbound connections. The computer will accept unencrypted packets but will always respond by using IPSec-secured packets. The Secure Server policy permits unsecured ICMP traffic.

In addition to the precreated policies, you can create custom IPSec policies. When creating your own IPSec policies, you must configure rules that include the following settings:

- IP filter list
- Tunnel settings
- Filter actions
- Authentication methods
- Connection types

IPSec rules determine which types of network traffic will initiate IPSec between the computer and the host or endpoint it is communicating with. A computer can have any number of IPSec rules. You should ensure that only one rule is created for each type of traffic. If multiple rules apply to a given type of traffic, the most specific rule will be processed first.

IP Filter List

The IP filter list defines the types of network traffic to which the IPSec rule applies. You must define the following details for each entry in the filter list:

- **Source address**   Can be a specific IP address, a specific IP subnet address, or any address. Windows Server 2003 adds the ability to use logical addresses in filters for greater flexibility.

- **Destination address**   Can be a specific IP address, a specific IP subnet address, or any address.

- **Protocol**   The protocol ID or transport protocol used by the protocol. For example, Point-to-Point Tunneling Protocol (PPTP) uses Generic Routing Encapsulation (GRE) packets. GRE packets are identified by their protocol ID, which is protocol ID 47. Telnet, on the other hand, uses TCP as its transport protocol, so an IPSec filter for Telnet would define the protocol type only as TCP.

- **Source port**   If the protocol were to use TCP or UDP, the source port could be defined for the protected connection. The source port is set to a specific port or to a random port, depending on the protocol being defined. Most protocols use a random port for the source port.

- **Destination port**   If the protocol uses TCP or UDP, the protocol uses a specific port at the server to accept transmissions. For example, Telnet configures the server to listen for connections on TCP port 23.

When configuring IP filter lists for transport mode connections, you should always choose to have the IPSec rule mirrored to secure the return communication defined in the rule. For tunnel mode connections, you must manually specify both the inbound and outbound filter list.

Tunnel Settings

The tunnel setting determines whether IPSec operates in transport or tunnel mode. If you want IPSec to operate in transport mode, select This Rule Does Not Specify A Tunnel when creating an IPSec rule using the Security Rule Wizard. If you want the filter to operate in tunnel mode, you must specify the IP address of the endpoint of the tunnel.

Filter Actions

For each filter rule, you must choose a filter action. The filter action defines how the traffic defined in the IP filter will be handled by the filter rule. The three filter actions are listed here and are shown in Figure 10-6.

- **Permit** Allows packets to be transmitted without IPSec protection. For example, Simple Network Management Protocol (SNMP) includes support for devices that might not be IPSec aware. Enabling IPSec for SNMP would cause a loss of network management capabilities for these devices. In a highly secure network, you could create an IPSec filter for SNMP and set the IPSec action to Permit to allow SNMP packets to be transmitted without IPSec protection. Packets that are permitted are not subject to IPSec authentication.

- **Block** Discards packets. If the associated IPSec filter is matched, all packets with the block action defined are discarded. Packets that are blocked are not subject to IPSec authentication.

- **Negotiate Security** Allows an administrator to define the desired encryption and integrity algorithms to secure data transmissions if an IPSec filter is matched.

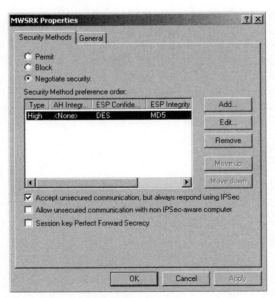

Figure 10-6 IPSec filter actions

In addition to these three basic actions, you can define settings that indicate how the computer will react if non-IPSec-protected data is received and how frequently new session keys are defined to protect the IPSec data. Options include the following:

- **Accept Unsecured Communication, But Always Respond Using IPSec**   You use this option when the IPSec protection is enforced only at the servers, not at the clients. In a typical IPSec deployment, clients are configured to use IPSec if requested by the server but to never initiate an IPSec SA. This setting allows the initial packet to be received by the server, which then starts the IKE process to negotiate an SA between the client and the server. Although it is riskier to have the initial packet of a data transmission accepted by using plaintext, the response packet sent from the server will not be transmitted until an SA is established.

- **Allow Unsecured Communication With Non IPSec-Aware Computers**   In a mixed network, this option allows non-IPSec-aware clients to connect to the server. Clients running Windows Server 2003, Windows 2000, and Windows XP, if configured to do so, will connect to the server and negotiate IPSec protection. Non-IPSec-aware clients will still be allowed to connect by using unprotected data streams.

- **Session Key Perfect Forward Secrecy**   Using Perfect Forward Secrecy ensures that an existing key is never used as the foundation of a new key. When you use Perfect Forward Secrecy, all keys are generated without using existing keys. This reduces the risk of continual data exposure should a key be compromised because previous keys cannot be used to determine future keys.

Authentication Methods

For each filter rule, you must choose an authentication method. You can enable multiple authentication methods for each rule and determine their order of precedence by editing the filter rule after it has been created.

Connection Types

You must specify to which type of interfaces each filter rule applies. In Windows 2000 and Windows XP, you can choose to have the rule apply to the following:

- All network connections
- Local area network (LAN) connections
- Remote access connections

> **Note**   You can create IPSec policies by using the command line or from batch files and scripts in addition to using the user interface. Each operating system has introduced a new tool for doing this: for Windows 2000 you can use IPSecpol.exe, for Windows XP you can use IPSeccmd.exe, and for Windows Server 2003 you can use IPSeccmd.exe or Netsh.

How IPSec Works

IPSec can be initiated by either the sending host or the receiving host. The two hosts or endpoints enter into a negotiation that will determine how the communication will be protected. The negotiation is completed in the IKE, and the resulting agreement is a set of security associations, or SAs.

IKE has two modes of operation, main mode and quick mode. We will examine each mode momentarily. IKE also serves two functions:

- Centralizes SA management, reducing connection time
- Generates and manages the authenticated keys used to secure the information

The SA is used until the two hosts or endpoints cease communication, even though the keys used might change. A computer can have many SAs. The SA for each packet is tracked using the Security Parameters Index (SPI).

Main Mode

During the main mode negotiation, the two computers establish a secure, authenticated channel—the main mode SA. IKE automatically provides the necessary identity protection during this exchange. This ensures no identity information is sent without encryption between the communicating computers, thus enabling total privacy. Following are the steps in a main mode negotiation:

1. **Policy negotiation**   These four mandatory parameters are negotiated as part of the main mode SA:

   - The encryption algorithm (DES or 3DES)
   - The hash algorithm (MD5 or SHA1)
   - The authentication method (certificate, preshared key, or Kerberos v5 authentication)
   - The Diffie-Hellman (DH) group to be used for the base keying material

   If certificates or preshared keys are used for authentication, the computer identity is protected. However, if Kerberos v5 authentication is used, the computer identity is unencrypted until encryption of the entire identity payload takes place during authentication.

2. **DH exchange (of public values)**   At no time are actual keys exchanged; only the base information needed by DH to generate the shared, secret key is exchanged. After this exchange, the IKE service on each computer generates the master key used to protect the final step: authentication.

3. **Authentication**   The computers attempt to authenticate the DH exchange. Without successful authentication, communication cannot proceed. The master key is used, in conjunction with the negotiation algorithms and methods, to authenticate identities. The entire identity payload—including the identity type, port, and protocol—is hashed and encrypted by using the keys generated from the DH exchange in the second step. The identity payload, regardless of which authentication method is used, is protected from both modification and interpretation.

    After the hosts have mutually authenticated each other, the host that initiated the negotiation presents an offer for a potential SA to the receiving host. The responder cannot modify the offer. Should the offer be modified, the initiator rejects the responder's message. The responder sends either a reply accepting the offer or a reply with alternatives. After the hosts agree on an SA, quick mode negotiation begins.

Quick Mode

In this mode, SAs are negotiated on behalf of the IPSec service. The following are the steps in quick mode negotiation:

1. **Policy negotiation**   The IPSec computers exchange their requirements for securing the data transfer:

    ❑   The hash algorithm for integrity and authentication (MD5 or SHA1)

    ❑   The algorithm for encryption, if requested (3DES or DES)

    ❑   A description of the traffic to protect

2. **Session key material refresh or exchange**   IKE refreshes the keying material, and new, shared, or secret keys are generated for authentication and encryption (if negotiated) of the packets. If a rekey is required, a second DH exchange takes place or a refresh of the original DH exchange occurs.

3. **SA exchange**   The SAs and keys are passed to the IPSec driver, along with the SPI.

    A common agreement is reached, and two SAs are established: one for inbound communication, and one for outbound communication.

During the quick mode negotiation of shared policy and keying material, the information is protected by the SA negotiated during main mode. As mentioned in step 3, quick mode results in a pair of SAs: one for inbound communication and one for outbound communication, each having its own SPI and key. Figure 10-7 shows a summary of what is negotiated during main mode and quick mode.

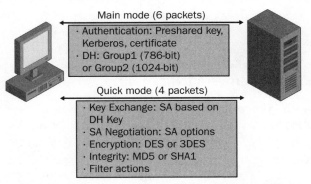

Main mode (6 packets)

· Authentication: Preshared key, Kerberos, certificate
· DH: Group1 (786-bit) or Group2 (1024-bit)

Quick mode (4 packets)

· Key Exchange: SA based on DH Key
· SA Negotiation: SA options
· Encryption: DES or 3DES
· Integrity: MD5 or SHA1
· Filter actions

Figure 10-7   Main mode and quick mode negotiation

IPSec, Routers, and NAT

IPSec creates a new IP header for a packet that can be routed as normal IP traffic. Routers and switches in the data path between the communicating hosts simply forward the packets to their destination. However, when a firewall or gateway lies in the data path, you must create firewall rules that allow traffic on the following IP protocols and UDP ports:

- **IP protocol ID 50**   Create inbound and outbound filters to allow ESP traffic to be forwarded.

- **IP protocol ID 51**   Create inbound and outbound filters to allow AH traffic to be forwarded.

- **UDP port 500**   Create inbound and outbound filters to allow IKE traffic to be forwarded.

Because of the nature of the NAT and port address translation (PAT) technologies, which require that packets be altered to change IP address and port information, IPSec is not compatible with NAT. IPSec does not allow manipulation of packets during transfer. The IPSec endpoint will discard packets that have been altered by NAT because the ICVs will not match. Windows Server 2003 does allow IPSec ESP to pass NAT routers but encapsulates the IPSec-protected packet inside a UDP packet through a technology called NAT-T. NAT-T was added to Windows XP in Service Pack 2. Additionally, an L2TP/IPSec client that supports NAT-T for Windows 2000 can be downloaded from the Microsoft Web site at *http://support.microsoft.com/kb/818043*.

Monitoring IPSec

You can monitor IPSec in Windows 2000 with IPSecmon.exe and in Windows Server 2003 and Windows XP using the IP Security Monitor Microsoft Management Console (MMC) snap-in. In addition, you can create log files in Windows Server 2003, Windows 2000, and Windows XP to view IPSec negotiations.

Using IPSecmon in Windows 2000

In Windows 2000, you can view the status of IPSec SAs and basic information on IPSec sessions by running IPSecmon from the Run prompt. IPSecmon displays information about each SA and the overall statistics of IPSec and IKE sessions. Figure 10-8 shows IPSecmon in Windows 2000. The built-in Server IPSec policy is applied to the computer running Windows 2000 named SFOFS001. The SFOFS001 computer has attempted to negotiate IPSec with three other computers: SEADC001, SFODC001, and SFOXP001. However, SFOFS001 has successfully negotiated an SA with SFOXP001 only. The IPSec session with SFPXP001 uses the IPSec protocol ESP with 3DES as the encrypting algorithm and HMAC SHA1 as the authentication algorithm.

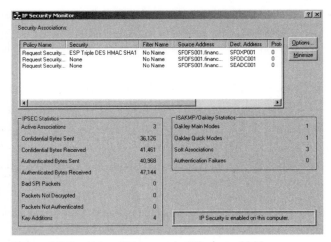

Figure 10-8   Using IPSecmon in Windows 2000

Using the IP Security Monitor MMC Snap-In

In Windows Server 2003 and Windows XP, IPSecmon has been replaced with an MMC snap-in that provides all the information that IPSecmon did in Windows 2000, only in much greater detail. You can use the IP Security Monitor MMC snap-in to view details of each SA, whereas in Windows 2000 you could view only the basic details of an SA. Figure 10-9 shows the IP Security Monitor MMC snap-in in Windows XP, which enables you to view the exact SA details negotiated during both main mode and quick mode.

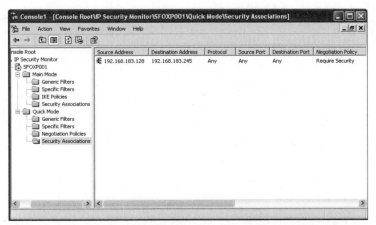

Figure 10-9   Using the IP Security Monitor MMC snap-in in Windows XP

Using IPSec Logs

You can have IPSec log the IKE exchanges to a log file on the hard drive for trouble-shooting or monitoring needs. To have your computer log IKE exchanges, you must create a registry value named *EnableLogging* in the registry key HKLM\SYSTEM \CurrentControlSet\Services\PolicyAgent\Oakley. To enable logging, set the value to 1 and restart the IPSec services. The log file will be written to the file %systemroot% \debug\oakley.log. If you use preshared keys for authentication, the key will appear in the log file in plaintext.

Note   Although the IPSec log file will contain more detailed information than a net-work capture made with Network Monitor, you can also use Network Monitor to determine how IPSec SA negotiations function in relation to the other traffic on the network.

Additional Changes to IPSec in Windows Server 2003

Several important changes were made to IPSec in Windows Server 2003. The changes can be grouped into three categories: management, security, and interoperability.

For improved management, the IP Security Monitor MMC snap-in that was first shipped with Windows XP has been added to the server platform to replace the IPSecmon.exe tool in Windows 2000. Windows Server 2003 also adds the ability to use logical addresses in addition to IP addresses. This can be useful when the IP addresses for computers change somewhat frequently, as can happen if computers get their addresses from a DHCP server. The most important manageability change to IPSec in Windows Server 2003 is the ability to configure IPSec through the network shell, Netsh. You can enter the network shell by typing **netsh** at the command line and can execute Netsh commands by placing them in batch files. In fact, several setting for IPSec can be set only through Netsh:

- Default exemption handling
- Strong certificate revocation list (CRL) checking
- IKE logging
- IPSec driver logging
- Persistent policies
- Startup exemptions

For example, you can set the default exemption level to allow multicast and broadcast traffic by typing the following string at the command prompt:

Netsh ipsec dynamic set config ipsecexempt value=2

You can set it back to its default value by typing:

Netsh ipsec dynamic set config ipsecexempt value=3

To improve the security of IPSec, several enhancements were made. The DH key length was increased to 2048 bits to better protect the secret key. To prevent an attacker from exploiting a system between the time the system is powered on and when the IPSec driver is loaded and running, Windows Server 2003 adds a computer startup policy. The computer startup policy, which can be configured through Netsh, is by default configured to allow DHCP traffic and the return of initiated outbound sessions through stateful packet filtering. Another feature that is only manageable through Netsh is persistent policy. Persistent policy is always applied before and remains in effect regardless of whether IPSec policies are applied locally or by the Active Directory directory service. The other area that was greatly changed to improve security is the default exemption handling. In Windows 2000, five types of network traffic were exempted from IPSec. Table 10-8 contains the default exemptions in Windows 2000 and Windows Server 2003. By default, Windows Server 2003 IPSec default exemptions are set to 3. You can set default exemptions by setting the value for the registry key HKLM\SYSTEM\CurrentControlSet\Services\IPSec\NoDefautExempt.

Table 10-8   IPSec Default Exemptions in Windows Server 2003 and Windows 2000

Value	0	1	2	3
Windows Server 2003	RSVP IKE Kerberos Multicast Broadcast	IKE Multicast Broadcast	RSVP IKE Kerberos	IKE
Windows 2000 and Windows XP	RSVP IKE Kerberos Multicast Broadcast	IKE Multicast Broadcast	Not available	Not available

For interoperability, Windows Server 2003 improves integration between IPSec and Network Load Balancing (NLB) and allows IPSec to be used across NAT and PAT routers through NAT traversal.

Best Practices

- **Create a TCP/IP hardening policy.** Ensure that the TCP/IP stack on your computers that run Windows Server 2003, Windows 2000, and Windows XP is appropriately secure in regard to the threats to it. This is especially true of any computer directly connected to the Internet or in perimeter networks.

- **Use Windows Firewall for mobile and home computers running Windows XP.** Windows Firewall provides an excellent degree of protection for mobile clients and home computers. Be certain to provide training for users on how to enable and disable Windows Firewall.

■ **Use IPSec to secure communications on corporate networks.**   By using IPSec, you can increase the security for data transmission on your network as well as control network access to high-value servers.

■ **Use IPSec hardware accelerators when possible.**   By using IPSec hardware accelerators on computers that will have many IPSec sessions at a time, such as servers, you can prevent the computers' CPU performance from being overly taxed.

Additional Information

■ Internet Assigned Numbers Authority (IANA) TCP and UDP port number assignment list (*http://www.iana.org/assignments/port-numbers*)

■ IANA IP protocol ID number list (*http://www.iana.org/assignments /protocol-numbers*)

■ "5-Minute Security Advisor—Essential Security Tools for Home Office Users" (*http://www.microsoft.com/technet/columns/security/5min/5min-105.asp*)

■ "Deploying Windows Firewall Settings for Microsoft Windows XP with Service Pack 2" white paper (*http://www.microsoft.com/downloads/details.aspx? FamilyID=4454e0e1-61fa-447a-bdcd-499f73a637d1&displaylang=en*)

■ "IPSec Architecture" white paper (*http://www.microsoft.com/technet/itsolutions /network/security/ipsecarc.mspx*)

■ "IPSec Implementation" white paper (*http://www.microsoft.com/technet /itsolutions/network/security/ipsecimp.mspx*)

■ "Using Microsoft Windows IPSec to Help Secure an Internal Corporate Network Server" white paper (*http://www.microsoft.com/downloads/details.aspx? FamilyID=a774012a-ac25-4a1d-8851-b7a09e3f1dc9&displaylang=en*)

■ "Improving Security with Domain Isolation: Microsoft IT Implements IP Security (IPSec)" white paper (*http://www.microsoft.com/technet/itsolutions/msit /security/ipsecdomisolwp.mspx*)

■ "Security Considerations for Network Attacks" white paper (*http:// www.microsoft.com/technet/security/topics/network/secdeny.mspx*)

■ "Best Practices for Preventing DoS/Denial of Service Attacks" white paper (*http://www.microsoft.com/technet/security/bestprac/dosatack.asp*)

■ Knowledge Base article 309798: "How to Configure TCP/IP Filtering in Windows 2000" (*http://support.microsoft.com/kb/309798*)

■ Knowledge Base article 816792: "How to Configure TCP/IP Filtering in Windows Server 2003" (*http://support.microsoft.com/kb/816792*)

Chapter 11

Creating and Configuring Security Templates

Security templates are files that contain settings for securing your computers that run Microsoft Windows Server 2003, Windows 2000, and Windows XP. You can apply security templates to the local computer or import them into a Group Policy object (GPO) in the Active Directory directory service. When you import a security template into a GPO, Group Policy processes the template and makes the corresponding settings to the computers affected by the GPO. You can use security templates to apply consistent security settings to a large group of computers when you cannot use Group Policy. The Windows operating system provides a set of precreated security templates for you to use in specific scenarios but also gives you the ability to create custom security templates. Additionally, you can download security templates from the Security Guidance Center on the Microsoft Web site (*http://www.microsoft.com/security/guidance /default.mspx*) that contain security settings for networks of varying degrees of security.

Using Security Template Settings

Security templates offer seven categories of security settings. You use each category to apply specific computer-based security settings. The categories of security settings follow:

- **Account Policies** Define password policies, account lockout policies, and Kerberos policies

> **Important** Account policy settings applied at the OU level affect the local Security Accounts Manager (SAM) databases but not the user accounts in Active Directory. The account policies for domain accounts can be configured only at the domain-level Group Policy.

- **Local Policies**   Define audit policy, user rights assignment, and security option settings for computers

- **Event Log**   Defines the properties of the Application, Security, and System logs

- **Restricted Groups**   Define and enforce membership in security groups

- **System Services**   Define settings for services installed on a computer

- **Registry**   Defines security and auditing permissions for registry keys and their subtrees

- **File System**   Defines NTFS file system security and auditing settings for any files and folders included within this policy

Group Policy has several categories in addition to those in security templates. The following categories are maintained under the Security Settings portion of the computer-related GPO settings.

- **Wireless Network (IEEE 802.11) Policies**   Define settings to configure wireless network settings, including 802.1x authentication, in Windows XP and Windows Server 2003. This category is not available in Windows 2000.

- **Public Key Policies**   Define settings for enterprise Certification Authority (CA) trust lists, encrypting file system (EFS) data recovery agents, trusted root CAs, and automatic certificate renewal settings.

- **Software Restriction Policies**   Define policies for controlling applications that run on a computer running Windows XP or Windows Server 2003. Software restriction policies are not available in Windows 2000.

- **IP Security Policies**   Define the IP Security (IPSec) policy that is assigned to the computer.

Account Policies

Account policies define security on domain and local accounts. Account policy settings for domain accounts must be configured at the domain level. When you define individual account policy settings for a specific OU, the account policies apply to local accounts on the computers that are affected by the group policy. Account policies contain three subcategories of configuration:

- Password Policy

- Account Lockout Policy

- Kerberos Policy

Table 11-1 describes the policy settings for each category.

Table 11-1   Account Policy Settings

Setting	Subcategory	Description
Enforce Password History	Password Policy	Determines the number of unique new passwords that must be associated with a user account before an old password can be reused. The value must be set to a number of passwords between 0 and 24.
Maximum Password Age	Password Policy	Determines the number of days that a password can be used before the system requires the user to change it. You can set passwords to expire after a number of days between 1 and 999, or you can specify that passwords never expire by setting the number of days to 0.
Minimum Password Age	Password Policy	Determines the number of days that a password must be used before the user can change it. You can set values to a number of days between 1 and 999, or you can allow changes immediately by setting the number of days to 0.
Minimum Password Length	Password Policy	Determines the least number of characters a user account's password can contain. You can set values to a number of characters between 1 and 14. Setting this value to 0 will allow users to use a blank password.
Password Must Meet Complexity Requirements	Password Policy	Determines whether passwords must meet complexity requirements, which disallow passwords to contain any portion of the user account's Full Name for names that contain more than three characters, require passwords to have at least six characters and use at least one character from three of the following five categories: ■ English uppercase letters ■ English lowercase letters ■ Base-10 digits ■ Nonalphanumeric symbols, such as !, $, #, and % ■ Unicode characters, such as € or β
Store Password Using Reversible Encryption For All Users In The Domain	Password Policy	Determines whether passwords are encrypted such that the account database can decrypt the passwords when needed to verify an account password with a plaintext version.

Table 11-1   **Account Policy Settings**

Setting	Subcategory	Description
Account Lockout Threshold	Account Lockout Policy	Determines the number of failed logon attempts that will cause a user account to be locked out. You can set values to a number of failed logon attempts between 1 and 999, or you can specify that the account will never be locked out by setting the value to 0.
Account Lockout Duration	Account Lockout Policy	Determines the number of minutes a locked-out account remains locked out before automatically becoming unlocked. The range is 1–99,999 minutes. You can specify that the account will be locked out until an administrator explicitly unlocks it by setting the value to 0.
Reset Account Lockout After	Account Lockout Policy	Determines the number of minutes that must elapse after a failed logon attempt before the bad logon attempt counter is reset to 0. The range is 1–99,999 minutes.
Enforce User Logon Restrictions	Kerberos Policy	Determines whether the key distribution center (KDC) validates that the user possesses the Log On Locally or Access The Computer From The Network user rights for every session ticket request.
Maximum Lifetime For Service Ticket	Kerberos Policy	Determines the maximum number of minutes that a granted session ticket can be used. The setting must be greater than 10 minutes.
Maximum Lifetime For User Ticket	Kerberos Policy	Determines the maximum number of hours that a user's ticket-granting ticket (TGT) can be used before it is renewed or a new one is requested.
Maximum Lifetime For User Ticket Renewal	Kerberos Policy	Determines the number of days during which a user's TGT can be renewed.
Maximum Tolerance For Computer Clock Synchronization	Kerberos Policy	Determines the maximum number of minutes Kerberos will tolerate between the time set on a client's system clock and the time set on a server's system clock when issuing and using Kerberos tickets. This is to prevent replay attacks on authentication packets.

More Info   Account policies are discussed in depth in Chapter 3, "Configuring Security for User Accounts and Passwords."

Local Policies

Local policies determine security settings on the local computer. These policies are separated into three subcategories:

- Audit Policy
- User Rights Assignment
- Security Options

The following tables describe the policy settings for each category as well as important security considerations, where appropriate. Table 11-2 contains a description of each audit policy in Windows Server 2003, Windows XP, and Windows 2000. For detailed information on each audit policy, see Chapter 15, "Auditing Microsoft Windows Security Events."

Table 11-2   Audit Policy Settings

Setting	Description
Audit Account Logon Events	Determines whether to audit each instance of a user logging on or logging off of another computer used to validate the account
Audit Account Management Events	Determines whether to audit each event in which an account is created, modified, or deleted on a computer
Audit Directory Service Access	Determines whether to audit the event of a user accessing an Active Directory object that has its own system access control list (SACL) specified
Audit Logon Events	Determines whether to audit each instance of a user logging on, logging off, or making a network connection to this computer
Audit Object Access	Determines whether to audit the event of a user accessing a file, folder, registry key, or printer object that has its own SACL specified
Audit Policy Change	Determines whether to audit every instance of a change to user rights assignment policies, audit policies, or trust policies
Audit Privilege Use	Determines whether to audit each instance of a user exercising a user right with the exception of the Bypass Traverse Checking, Debug Programs, Create A Token Object, Replace Process Level Token, Generate Security Audits, Backup Files And Directories, and Restore Files And Directories user rights
Audit Process Tracking	Determines whether to audit detailed tracking information for events such as program activation, process exit, handle duplication, and indirect access of system objects
Audit System Events	Determines whether to audit when a user restarts or shuts down the computer or when an event occurs that affects either the system security or the Security log

Table 11-3 contains descriptions of the user right assignments portion of security templates. For more detailed information on user rights, see Chapter 3, "Configuring Security for User Accounts and Passwords."

Table 11-3   User Rights Assignment Policy Settings

Setting	Description
Access This Computer From The Network	Determines which users and groups are allowed to connect to the computer over the network. This right is required when accessing a computer using network protocols such as Server Message Block (SMB), NetBIOS, Common Internet File System (CIFS), HTTP, and COM+. By default, all members of the Everyone group possess this right. In Windows Server 2003, because the Everyone group no longer includes Anonymous, anonymous users cannot access from the network computers that run Windows Server 2003.
Act As Part Of The Operating System	Allows a process to authenticate as any user and therefore gain access to the same resources under the security context of that user. Only low-level authentication services should require this privilege. Services that require this permission should be properly evaluated for security and monitored for publicly reported vulnerabilities.
Add Workstations To Domain	Determines which groups or users can add workstations to a domain. This policy is valid only on domain controllers. By default, any authenticated user has this right and can create up to 10 computer accounts in the domain with this right.
Adjust Memory Quotas For A Process (Increase Quotas in Windows 2000)	Determines which accounts can change the maximum amount of memory that is dedicated to a process. This right should be granted only to accounts that specifically require this capability, such as some services that do not run under any of the built-in service accounts: Local System, Local Service, or Network Service.
Allow Log On Locally	Determines which users can log on at the computer interactively by using the Windows Logon dialog box, Terminal Services, or Microsoft Internet Information Services (IIS).
Allow Log On Through Terminal Services	Determines which groups or users can log on using Remote Desktop Services. Remote Desktop Users and Administrators have this right by default. This right applies only to computers running Windows Server 2003 and Windows XP.
Back Up Files And Directories	Determines which groups and users can run processes to back up files and folders without regard to NTFS permissions.
Bypass Traverse Checking	Determines which groups and users can traverse directory trees even though they might not have permissions on the traversed directory.
Change The System Time	Determines which groups and users can change the time and date on the system clock of the computer.
Create A Pagefile	Determines which users and groups can create and change the size of a pagefile.

Table 11-3 **User Rights Assignment Policy Settings**

Setting	Description
Create A Token Object	Determines which accounts can be used by processes to create a token that can then be used to gain access to any local resources when the process uses *NtCreateToken()* or other token-creation APIs.
Create Global Objects	Determines whether the account can create global system objects during Terminal Services sessions. You should grant this right only if you have applications using Terminal Services that create such objects.
Create Permanent Shared Objects	Determines which accounts can be used by processes to create a directory object in the Object Manager. By default, only kernel-mode components, which run under the security context of LocalSystem, possess this right. Only LocalSystem should possess this right.
Debug Programs	Determines which users can attach a debugger to any process. This privilege provides powerful access to sensitive and critical operating system components in the kernel. In Windows Server 2003, removing the Debug Programs right can result in an inability to use the Windows Update service. However, patches can still be manually downloaded and installed or applied through other means. This right does not impact a user's ability to use application debug software to analyze the failure of applications running on a computer.
Deny Access To This Computer From The Network	Determines which users are prevented from accessing a computer over the network. This policy setting supersedes the Access This Computer From The Network policy setting if a user account is subject to both policies.
Deny Log On As A Batch Job	Determines which accounts are prevented from logging on to the batch queuing facility of the Windows operating system to schedule tasks. This policy setting supersedes the Log On As A Batch Job policy setting if a user account is subject to both policies.
Deny Log On As A Service	Determines which service accounts are prevented from registering a process as a service. This policy setting supersedes the Log On As A Service policy setting if an account is subject to both policies.
Deny Log On Locally	Determines which users are prevented from logging on at the computer. This policy setting supersedes the Allow Log On Locally policy setting if an account is subject to both policies.
Deny Log On Through Terminal Services	Determines which groups or users are prevented from logging on using Remote Desktop Services. This right supersedes Allow Log On Through Terminal Services if an account possesses both rights. This right applies only to computers running Windows Server 2003 and Windows XP.

Table 11-3   User Rights Assignment Policy Settings

Setting	Description
Enable Computer And User Accounts To Be Trusted For Delegation	Determines which users can set the Trusted For Delegation setting on a user or computer object. See Chapter 7, "Designing Domains and Forests for Security," for more information on delegation of credentials.
Force Shutdown From A Remote System	Determines which users are allowed to shut down a computer from a remote location on the network. You should grant this right only to accounts that require the ability to shut down a computer remotely, such as systems management software services.
Generate Security Audits	Determines which accounts a process can use to add entries to the Security log. By default, only LocalSystem, Local Service, and Network Service have this right.
Impersonate A Client After Authentication	Determines whether the application running under an account with this privilege can impersonate the user's credentials to access other resources. This privilege is rarely required by accounts other than the built-service accounts.
Increase Scheduling Priority	Determines which accounts can use a process with Write permission to access to another process to increase the execution priority assigned to the other process. A user with this privilege can change the scheduling priority of a process by using the Task Manager.
Load And Unload Device Drivers	Determines which users can dynamically load and unload device drivers. This right is necessary for installing drivers that are not installed on the computer by default. Because this right gives the account the ability to install kernel-level components, you should only give this right to accounts that you trust as much as your system administrators.
Lock Pages In Memory	This right is obsolete and therefore is never checked.
Log On As A Batch Job	Determines which groups or users can log on using a batch-queue application such as the Task Scheduler.
Log On As A Service	Determines which service accounts can register a process as a service.
Manage Auditing And Security Log	Determines which users can specify object access auditing options for individual resources such as files, Active Directory objects, and registry keys. It also gives the account the ability to alter or erase the contents of the Security log. This privilege should only be granted to non-Administrator accounts that specifically require the ability to manage the security log because any user with this right can erase the security log. Administrators always posses this privilege.
Modify Firmware Environment Values	Determines which groups or users can modify systemwide environment variables.

Table 11-3   User Rights Assignment Policy Settings

Setting	Description
Perform Volume Maintenance Tasks	Determines which users and groups have the authority to run volume maintenance tools, such as Disk Cleanup and Disk Defragmenter. This right applies only to computers running Windows Server 2003 and Windows XP.
Profile Single Process	Determines which users can use performance monitoring tools to monitor the performance of nonsystem processes.
Profile System Performance	Determines which users can use performance monitoring tools to monitor the performance of system processes.
Remove Computer From Docking Station	Determines which users can undock a laptop computer from its docking station without using manual bypass controls in the docking station or more severe physical measures.
Replace A Process Level Token	Determines which user accounts can initiate a process to replace the default token associated with a launched subprocess. Only built-in system accounts possess this right.
Restore Files And Directories	Determines which groups and users can run processes to restore files and folders without regard to NTFS permissions. Users with this permission can also reassign ownership of files and folders.
Shut Down The System	Determines which users that are logged on locally to the computer can shut down the operating system.
Synchronize Directory Service Data	Determines which accounts can perform directory synchronization (dirsync) operations in Active Directory. This right is not used in Windows XP.
Take Ownership Of Files Or Other Objects	Determines which users can take ownership of system objects, including Active Directory objects, files and folders, printers, registry keys, processes, and threads.

Table 11-4 contains descriptions of each security option contained in security templates. The Description column notes in which version of the operating system the setting is available. The names of some services have been changed slightly between Windows 2000 and Windows Server 2003, and, unless otherwise indicated, the names of the security options are listed as they appear in Windows Server 2003.

Table 11-4   Security Options Policy Settings

Setting	Description
Accounts: Administrator Account Status	Determines whether the Administrator account is enabled or disabled. Absent the presence of other administrator accounts, disabling Administrator could prevent regular maintenance on the computer and increase the difficulty of disaster recovery scenarios. This option is not available in Windows 2000.
Accounts: Guest Account Status	Determines whether the Guest account is enabled or disabled. If the Guest account is disabled and the security option Network Access: Sharing And Security Model is configured to allow only Guests, network logons and file sharing will not work correctly.

Table 11-4   **Security Options Policy Settings**

Setting	Description
Accounts: Limit Local Account Use Of Blank Passwords To Console Logon Only	Determines whether the accounts with blank passwords are able to access network resources. By default, this setting is enabled. This option is not available in Windows 2000.
Accounts: Rename Administrator Account	Enables administrators to rename the Administrator account; however, because the relative identifier (RID) for the Administrator account is well known, renaming the Administrator account does not prevent moderately skilled attackers from determining the new account name. After changing the display name of the Administrator account, you can monitor audit logs to look for attackers attempting to use the new name for this account. If an attacker attempts to use the renamed account, you will know that he has some level of knowledge and skill in compromising networks and at least some access to your organization's network.
Accounts: Rename Guest Account	Enables administrators to rename the Guest account; however, because the RID for the Guest account is well known, renaming the Guest account does not prevent moderately skilled attackers from determining the new account name. After changing the display name of the Guest account, you can monitor audit logs to look for attackers attempting to use the new name for this account. If an attacker attempts to use the renamed account, you will know that she has some level of knowledge and skill in compromising networks and at least some access to your organization's network.
Audit: Audit The Access Of Global System Objects	Determines whether access of global system objects that have SACLs configured (for example, mutexes and semaphores) is audited. You should enable this option only if you are troubleshooting operating system internal operations.
Audit: Audit Use Of Backup And Restore Privilege	Determines whether the Audit Privileged Use audit policy should include use of the Backup/Restore privilege. If enabled, both of these settings ensure that all backup and restoration operations are logged to the Security log.
Audit: Shut Down System Immediately If Unable To Log Security Audits	Determines whether the system will stop if security events cannot be logged. If this setting is enabled and security events cannot be written to the Security log file, the computer will display stop error (commonly known as the blue screen of death) that reads 0xC00000244 {Audit Failed}. To recover the system, an administrator must log on to reset the HKEY_LOCAL_MACHINE\SYSTEM\CurrentControlSet\Control\Lsa\CrashOnAuditFail registry value to 1.

Table 11-4   Security Options Policy Settings

Setting	Description
DCOM: Machine Access Restrictions In Security Descriptor Definition Language (SDDL) Syntax	Determines the access permissions to Distributed Component Object Model (DCOM) applications for users of the computer running Windows XP. By default, with Windows XP Service Pack 2, anonymous users cannot call DCOM applications on remote computers, whereas all other users can call local and remote DCOM applications as long as they have launch permissions. You should change this option only if you have DCOM applications that no longer work as a result of Windows XP Service Pack 2 or Windows Server 2003 Service Pack 1.
DCOM: Machine Launch Restrictions In Security Descriptor Definition Language (SDDL) Syntax	Determines which accounts can instantiate a DCOM application locally or remotely for users of computers running Windows XP. By default, with Windows XP Service Pack 2, anonymous users cannot launch or activate DCOM applications, whereas all other users can. You should change this option only if you have DCOM applications that no longer work as a result of Windows XP Service Pack 2 or Windows Server 2003 Service Pack 1.
Devices: Allow Undock Without Having To Log On	Determines whether a laptop computer can be removed from the docking station that has a mechanical release by a Windows XP user who has not logged on. This setting does not preclude the possibility that crowbars and hammers can be used to remove a laptop from a docking station when the user is not logged on.
Devices: Allowed To Format And Eject Removable Media	Determines whether a user can format or gracefully eject removable media, such as Zip disks. This setting is called Allowed To Eject Removable NTFS Media in Windows 2000.
Devices: Prevent Users From Installing Printer Drivers	Determines whether members of the Users group are prevented from installing print drivers that are not provided by default or installed from print servers. This setting is enabled by default. Because printer drivers can access kernel-level components, you should enable this option to help prevent the intentional or unintentional installation of malicious software that can subvert the trusted base of computing.
Devices: Restrict CD-ROM Access To Locally Logged-On User Only	Determines whether users not logged on interactively can access CD-ROM drives on the local computer when an interactive user is using the CD-ROM. This setting should be set to Disabled unless you have situations in which remote and local users must access a shared CD-ROM at the same time.
Devices: Restrict Floppy Access To Locally Logged-On User Only	Determines whether users not logged on interactively can access floppy disk drives on the local computer when an interactive user is using the floppy disk drive. This setting should be set to Disabled unless you have situations in which remote and local users must access a shared floppy disk drive at the same time.

Table 11-4   Security Options Policy Settings

Setting	Description
Devices: Unsigned Driver Installation Behavior	Determines what should happen when an attempt is made to install a device driver that has not been certified by the Windows Hardware Quality Lab (WHQL). You can set this to Silently Succeed, Warn But Allow Installation, or Do Not Allow Installation. You might need to change this setting to silently succeed before installation of drivers if you are performing scripted installations of drivers that have not been approved and signed.
Domain Controller: Allow Server Operators To Schedule Tasks	Determines whether Server Operators are allowed to submit jobs by means of the AT scheduling facility. This setting does not affect tasks submitted through Task Scheduler. Whereas Task Scheduler uses the credentials from the account that scheduled the task, the AT scheduling facility uses the LocalSystem credentials. By default, the AT scheduling facility can be used only by administrators. This setting is primarily intended for backward compatibility. You should consider migrating scheduled tasks to Task Scheduler rather than continuing to use the AT facility and enabling this option. This setting is available only in Windows Server 2003.
Domain Controller: LDAP Server Signing Requirements	Determines whether a domain controller will request or require Lightweight Directory Access Protocol (LDAP) packets to be digitally signed when not used in conjunction with Secure Sockets Layer (SSL) or Transport Layer Security (TLS). By default, domain controllers do not request LDAP signing, which is used to prevent some man-in-the-middle attacks, to ensure compatibility with downlevel domain controllers. If this setting is not enabled, domain controllers will sign LDAP communications if the client requests it, as will occur if Network Security: LDAP Client Signing Requirements is set to negotiate or require. If you enable this setting, computers that do not perform LDAP signing will not be able to communicate with domain controllers by using LDAP. Domain controllers running Windows 2000 must have at least Service Pack 3 installed to use LDAP signing. You do not need to enable this option if you are using IPSec Authentication Header (AH) on domain controllers.
Domain Controller: Refuse Machine Account Password Changes	Determines whether the computer account password will be changed according to the computer account expiration interval, which is 30 days by default. You might enable this setting if a computer will be disconnected from the network for more than 30 days and do not want to have to reset the computer account when the computer is reconnected. There are few organizations that require enabling this setting.

Table 11-4   **Security Options Policy Settings**

Setting	Description
Domain Member: Digitally Encrypt Or Sign Secure Channel Data (Always)	Determines whether secure channels require encryption or signing. Secure channels are used by the Netlogon service during authentication. To help protect authentication traffic from man-in-the-middle attacks, from replay attacks, and from other types of network attacks, Windows-based computers create a communication channel that is known as a secure channel through the Netlogon service to authenticate computer accounts. If enabled, the computer will be unable to establish a secure channel with any domain controller that cannot encrypt or sign secure channel data. For example, computers running Microsoft Windows NT 4.0 will not be able to join a domain when domain controllers have this setting enabled.
Domain Member: Digitally Encrypt Secure Channel Data (When Possible)	Determines whether secure channels will be encrypted if requested. Secure channels are used by the Netlogon service during authentication when possible. See Domain Member: Digitally Encrypt Or Sign Secure Channel Data (Always) in this table for more information.
Domain Member: Digitally Sign Secure Channel Data (When Possible)	Determines whether secure channels will be signed when requested. Secure channels are used by the Netlogon service during authentication when possible. See Domain Member: Digitally Encrypt Or Sign Secure Channel Data (Always) in this table for more information.
Domain Member: Maximum Machine Account Password Age	Determines the maximum interval between when computers that belong to a domain must change their password. By default, this interval is 30 days. Although this setting does not appear in security templates in Windows 2000, it applies to computers running Windows 2000 when configured.
Domain Member: Require Strong (Windows 2000 Or Later) Session Key	Determines whether a secure channel can be established with a domain controller that cannot encrypt secure channel traffic with a 128-bit session key. Enabling this setting prevents a secure channel from being established with any domain controller that cannot encrypt secure channel data with a strong key. Disabling this setting allows 64-bit session keys. A stronger session key will better protect secure channel communication. All domain controllers must be running Windows 2000 or Windows Server 2003 to use this setting.
Domain Member: Disable Machine Account Password Changes	Determines whether a domain member periodically changes its computer account password. If this setting is enabled, the domain member does not attempt to change its computer account password. If this setting is disabled, the domain member attempts to change its computer account password every 30 days by default.

Table 11-4   **Security Options Policy Settings**

Setting	Description
Interactive Logon: Do Not Display Last User Name In Logon Screen	Determines whether the user name of the last logged-on user appears in the Windows Logon dialog box when the next user attempts to log on. Consider enabling this setting on computers in public areas to prevent user account names and their home domain name from being disclosed. Although it provides little security benefit, this setting can be used to enhance the privacy of users on shared computers.
Interactive Logon: Disable Ctrl+Alt+Del Requirement For Logon	Determines whether a user must press Ctrl+Alt+Del to invoke the Windows Logon dialog box. You should enable this setting only if you have users with special accessibility requirements.
Interactive Logon: Message Text For Users Attempting To Log On	Determines the text in the message box that a user must agree to before the Windows Logon dialog box appears. You must also configure the message title for this option to take effect. You should consult your organization's legal department about what text should be used in this warning. This text is limited to 512 characters in length within a single paragraph in Windows 2000. Windows XP and Windows Server 2003 are not subject to these limits.
Interactive Logon: Message Title For Users Attempting To Log On	Determines the title of the message box containing the text that a user must agree to before the Windows Logon dialog box appears. You must also configure the message text for this option to take effect.
Interactive Logon: Number Of Previous Logons To Cache (In Case Domain Controller Is Not Available)	Determines the number of previous logon sessions to cache as cached credentials. Cached credentials can be used on the computer to log on when no domain controllers are reachable. You can set this to a value between 0 and 50. If you set this option to 0, users will not be able to log on unless a domain controller is available to validate their credentials. Setting the value to 10, which is the default, will cache the logon credentials from the last 10 users to log on to the computer.
Interactive Logon: Prompt User To Change Password Before Expiration	Determines how far in advance, between 0 and 999 days, to warn users that their password will expire. This setting is 14 days by default.
Interactive logon: Require Domain Controller Authentication To Unlock	Determines whether a domain controller must validate a user's credentials when unlocking a computer. By default, if present, cached credentials are used to validate a user's credentials when unlocking a computer. Enabling this setting, while increasing the level of security by ensuring the account has not been disabled since the previous logon, can cause mobile users difficulty when transitioning from being connected to the network to being away from the network when using hibernation.

Table 11-4   Security Options Policy Settings

Setting	Description
Interactive Logon: Require Smart Card	Determines whether users must perform interactive logons by using a smart card. When properly managed, the use of physical tokens, such as smart cards, greatly improves the integrity of logon sessions by providing greater assurance that the person logging on to the system is the rightful holder of the account.
Interactive Logon: Smart Card Removal Behavior	Determines what should happen when the smart card for a logged-on user is removed from the smart card reader. You can configure this setting to lock the workstation when the smart card is removed, to log off the current user, or to do nothing.
Microsoft Network Client: Digitally Sign Client Communications (Always)	Determines whether the computer will always digitally sign SMB communications by using SMB signing when connecting to SMB resources on other computers. Enabling this setting requires the corresponding server settings to be enabled on computers that host SMB resources. Enabling digital signing in high-security networks helps to prevent the impersonation of clients and servers. This type of impersonation is known as session hijacking. An attacker who has access to the same network as the client or the server uses session hijacking tools to interrupt, end, or steal a session in progress. An attacker could intercept and modify unsigned SMB packets, modify the traffic, and then forward it so that the server might perform unwanted actions. Alternatively, the attacker could pose as the server or as the client after a legitimate authentication and then gain unauthorized access to data.
Microsoft Network Client: Digitally Sign Client Communications (When Possible)	Determines whether the computer will, when requested, digitally sign SMB communications by using SMB signing. Otherwise, the computer will communicate normally when connecting to SMB resources. See Microsoft Network Client: Digitally Sign Client Communications (Always) in this table for more information.
Microsoft Network Client: Send Unencrypted Password To Connect To Third-Party SMB Servers	Determines whether the computer is allowed to send passwords in plaintext to SMB servers that do not support encryption.
Microsoft Network Server: Amount Of Idle Time Required Before Suspending Session	Determines the number of minutes that must pass in a SMB session before the session is disconnected because of inactivity. After an SMB connection is disconnected, the user or computer account must be authenticated again, which occurs transparently to the user. The default value for this setting is 15 minutes.

Table 11-4   **Security Options Policy Settings**

Setting	Description
Microsoft Network Server: Digitally Sign Server Communications (Always)	Determines whether the computer will require digital signing for connections to local SMB resources from remote computers. Computers that do not digitally sign client communications will not be able to connect to computers with this setting enabled. Enabling this setting on heavily used computers, such as domain controllers, file servers, or print servers, can cause CPU performance degradation. See Microsoft Network Client: Digitally Sign Client Communications (Always) in this table for more information.
Microsoft Network Server: Digitally Sign Server Communications (When Possible)	Determines whether the computer will require digital signing for connections to local SMB resources from remote computers when possible. Computers that do not digitally sign client communications will be able to connect to computers with this setting enabled and will be signed if the client digitally signs SMB communication. Enabling this setting on heavily used computers, such as domain controllers, file servers, or print servers, can cause CPU performance degradation. See Microsoft Network Client: Digitally Sign Client Communications (Always) in this table for more information.
Microsoft Network Server: Disconnect Users When Logon Time Expires	Determines whether to disconnect users from SMB resources that are connected to the local machine outside the user account's valid logon hours for all computers in the domain. You should enable this setting if you have users whose logon times are restricted. If you do not use logon restriction times, this setting is not applicable.
Network Access: Allow Anonymous SID/Name Translation	Determines whether an anonymous user can request security identifier (SID) attributes for another user. Disabling this setting can cause some compatibility issues with Windows NT 4.0— namely, users in Windows NT 4.0 resource domains will no be able to grant permissions to access files, shared folders, and registry objects to user accounts from account domains that contain Windows Server 2003 domain controllers.
Network Access: Do Not Allow Anonymous Enumeration Of SAM Accounts	Determines whether anonymous users can enumerate account information or share information. This setting, along with Network Access: Do Not Allow Anonymous Enumeration Of SAM Accounts And Shares, were added in Windows XP Service Pack 1 and Windows Server 2003 to replace the functionality of the Windows 2000 registry setting Restrict Anonymous. This option replaces the Everyone group with Authenticated Users for accessing information in the SAM database and in file shares. This setting does not impact domain controllers. When this setting is enabled, it is no longer possible to establish trust relationships with Windows NT 4.0 domains, and users will no longer be able to authenticate from computers running Windows 95, Windows 98, or Windows NT 4.0. This setting is not available in Windows 2000.

Table 11-4   **Security Options Policy Settings**

Setting	Description
Network Access: Do Not Allow Anonymous Enumeration Of SAM Accounts And Shares	Determines whether anonymous users can enumerate account information or share information. This setting has the same impact in Windows XP Service Pack 1 and Windows Server 2003 as did the Restrict Anonymous registry value set to 2 did in Windows 2000. When enabled, you cannot grant access to users of resource domains because administrators in the trusting domain will not be able to enumerate lists of accounts in the other domain. Adding printers becomes more difficult for users, the global address list might not appear in Outlook, and Systems Management Server (SMS) functionality will be greatly limited. You should enable this setting only after extensive compatibility testing.
Network Access: Do Not Allow Storage Of Credentials Or .NET Passports For Network Authentication	Determines whether the passwords or credentials are stored for later use in Windows XP or Windows Server 2003. Enabling this setting will prevent stored credentials to drive mappings and Passport credentials from being saved to the Credential Manager. This setting does not impact forms-based credentials stored using Autocomplete in Microsoft Internet Explorer, which are stored in Protected Storage.
Network Access: Let Everyone Permissions Apply To Anonymous Users	Determines which anonymous connections receive rights and permissions assigned to the Everyone group on the computer as they do in Windows 2000 and earlier. This setting is disabled by default on computers running Windows XP Service Pack 1 and Windows Server 2003. You should enable this setting only if you experience application incompatibility. This setting is not available in Windows 2000.
Network Access: Named Pipes That Can Be Accessed Anonymously	Determines which communication sessions (pipes) will have attributes and permissions that allow anonymous access. The following named pipes allow anonymous access: ■ **COMNAP** Systems Network Architecture (SNA) Base named pipe used for mainframe connectivity ■ **COMNODE** SNA Server named pipe used for mainframe connectivity ■ **SQL\Query** Default named pipe for Microsoft SQL Server ■ **SPOOLSS** Named pipe for the print spooler service ■ **EPMAPPER** Named pipe for the remote procedure call (RPC) endpoint mapper ■ **LOCATOR** Named pipe used by the RPC Locator service ■ **TrkWks** Named pipe used by the Distributed Link Tracking Client service ■ **TrkSvr** Named pipe used by the Distributed Link Tracking Server service You should remove anonymous access to these named pipes on computers that do not use these specific services.

Table 11-4   Security Options Policy Settings

Setting	Description
Network Access: Remotely Accessible Registry Paths	Determines which registry paths will be accessible remotely if the Remote Registry Service is enabled. Users must have the appropriate access control on the registry key or value to read or alter it.
Network Access: Restrict Anonymous Access To Named Pipes And Shares	Determines whether anonymous access is permitted to named pipes and shares except for those defined in the following security options: ■ Network Access: Named Pipes That Can Be Accessed Anonymously ■ Network Access: Shares That Can Be Accessed Anonymously
Network Access: Shares That Can Be Accessed Anonymously	Determines which network shares can be accessed by anonymous users. This setting should not be enabled unless there is a specific application compatibility reason to do so. All users should be authenticated before accessing network resources such as shares.
Network Access: Sharing And Security Model For Local Accounts	Determines how network logons that use local accounts are authenticated. If this option is set to Classic, network logons that use local account credentials authenticate by using those credentials. If this option is set to Guest Only, network logons that use local accounts are automatically mapped to the Guest account. The Classic model allows fine control over access to resources. By using the Classic model, you can grant different types of access to different users for the same resource. When you use the Guest Only model, all users will be treated equally. All users authenticate as Guest and receive the same level of access to a given resource, which can be either Read Only or Modify. By default, in a workgroup, this setting is set to Guest Only in Windows XP, but is set to Classic upon being added to the domain. This setting is not available in Windows 2000.
Network Security: Do Not Store LAN Manager Hash Values For Passwords	Determines whether LAN Manager (LM) password hashes are created for user accounts. This setting does not take effect until the next time the user changes her password. See Chapter 4, "Configuring Authentication for Microsoft Windows," for more information on the LM authentication protocol.
Network Security: Force Logoff When Logon Hours Expire	Determines whether to disconnect the SMB session for users who are connected to the local computer outside their user account's valid logon hours. This setting should be enabled.
Network Security: LAN Manager Authentication Level	Determines the value of the HKEY_LOCAL_MACHINE\SYSTEM\CurrentControlSet\Control\LSA\LMCompatibility registry key, which controls how LM, NT LAN Manager (NTLM), and NT LAN Manager version 2 (NTLMv2) authentication protocols are used. See Chapter 4, "Configuring Authentication for Microsoft Windows," for detailed information on LM compatibility levels.

Table 11-4   Security Options Policy Settings

Setting	Description
Network Security: LDAP Client Signing Requirements	Determines whether your computer's communications with an LDAP server must be digitally signed. This option can be configured to not require LDAP signing, negotiate signing if SSL or TLS is not being used to protect the session, or require that all LDAP communications are signed regardless pf whether SSL or TLS are being used to protect the session.
Network Security: Minimum Session Security For NTLM SSP Based (Including Secure RPC) Clients	Determines the minimum security standards for NTLMv2 session security of client connections. See Chapter 4, "Configuring Authentication for Microsoft Windows," for details on NTLMv2 session security.
Network Security: Minimum Session Security For NTLM SSP Based (Including Secure RPC) Servers	Determines the minimum security standards for NTLMv2 session security of client connections. See Chapter 4, "Configuring Authentication for Microsoft Windows," for details on NTLMv2 session security.
Recovery Console: Allow Automatic Administrative Logon	Determines whether the Recovery Console will require a password or whether it will log on automatically. You should enable this setting only on computers that have strong physical security.
Recovery Console: Allow Floppy Copy And Access To All Drives And All Folders	Determines the behavior of copying files when operating in the Recovery Console. Because physical access is required to use the Recovery Console, this setting does little to impact the overall security of computers running Windows Server 2003, Windows XP, or Windows 2000.
Shutdown: Allow System To Be Shut Down Without Having To Log On	Determines whether a computer can be shut down without the user having to log on to the operating system. Unless you have a specific reason for allowing anyone with physical access to the computer to shut down the computer, you should not enable this option. Of course, this setting will not prevent malicious users from removing the power cord or pressing the power button if they have physical access to the computer. This option is convenient to enable on kiosk computers that might accidentally have been locked by a user or that frequently need to be restarted without saving data.
Shutdown: Clear Virtual Memory Pagefile When System Shuts Down	Determines whether the virtual memory data stored in the pagefile should be cleared before the computer is shut down. On servers with large amounts of RAM, enabling this setting could result in lengthy shutdown and restart times. This setting will not affect computers that have been forcefully shut down, such as results when the power cord is removed.

Table 11-4   Security Options Policy Settings

Setting	Description
System Cryptography: Force Strong Key Protection For User Keys Stored On The Computer	Determines the behavior of asking for the user's password when attempting to access the user's private keys stored on the computer. You can select one of the following options: ■ User Input Is Not Required When New Keys Are Stored And Used ■ User Is Prompted When The Key Is First Used ■ User Must Enter A Password Each Time They Use A Key
System Cryptography: Use FIPS Compliant Algorithms For Encryption, Signing, And Hashing	Determines whether Federal Information Processing Standard (FIPS) algorithms are used for encryption and integrity in TLS/SSL, EFS, and Terminal Services: ■ **TLS/SSL** If enabled, determines whether TLS and SSL sessions will use the TLS_RSA_WITH_3DES_EDE_CBC_SHA cipher suite, which means that the computer will only be permitted to construct TLS or SSL sessions using RSA for key exchange, 3DES for encryption, and SHA-1 for integrity. ■ **EFS** If enabled, 3DES will be used for file encryption rather than AES-256 in Windows Server 2003 and DESX in Windows XP. ■ **Terminal Services** If enabled, 3DES will be used for encrypting all Terminal Services network communication. This setting is not available in Windows 2000 and should be enabled only on computers that explicitly require it.
System Objects: Default Owner For Objects Created By Members Of The Administrators Group	Determines whether the Administrators group or the object creator is the default owner of any system objects that are created.
System Objects: Require Case Insensitivity For Non-Windows Subsystems	Determines whether the POSIX and OS/2 subsystems require case insensitivity for file names. This setting has little impact on the security of computers running Windows Server 2003, Windows XP, or Windows 2000.
System Objects: Strengthen Default Permissions Of Global System Objects (e.g., Symbolic Links)	Determines the strength of the default discretionary access control lists (DACLs) on system objects such as mutexes and semaphores. If enabled, this setting allows nonadministrator users to read shared objects, but they cannot modify shared objects that they did not create. By default, this setting is enabled and should be disabled only if there is a specific application compatibility reason to do so.

Table 11-4   Security Options Policy Settings

Setting	Description
System Settings: Optional Subsystems	Determines which subsystems are supported on a computer running Windows Server 2003. By default, only the POSIX subsystem is installed and operational. The POSIX subsystem is not required by computers running Microsoft Services for UNIX 3.0, which installs its own subsystem rather than using the built-in POSIX subsystem. This setting is not available in Windows XP or Windows 2000.
System Settings: Use Certificate Rules On Windows Executables For Software Restriction Policies	Determines whether the certificate revocation list (CRL) is validated on EXE files or software restriction policies before the file is run. This option, only available in Windows Server 2003, can slow down the loading of applications.

Event Log

You can control the behavior of Windows Server 2003, Windows 2000, and Windows XP Event logs by using security templates. Table 11-5 describes the Event log policy settings. These options are discussed in detail in Chapter 15, "Auditing Microsoft Windows Security Events."

Table 11-5   Event Log Policy Settings

Setting	Description
Maximum Application Log Size	Determines maximum size of the Application log before the retention policy setting takes effect.
Maximum Security Log Size	Determines maximum size of the Security log before the retention policy setting takes effect.
Maximum System Log Size	Determines maximum size of the System log before the retention policy setting takes effect.
Prevent Local Guests Group From Accessing Application Log	Determines whether guests can read the Application log.
Prevent Local Guests Group From Accessing Security Log	Determines whether guests can read the Security log.
Prevent Local Guests Group From Accessing System Log	Determines whether guests can read the System log.
Retain Application Log	Determines the number of days' worth of events that should be retained for the Application log if this log is set to retain events by an age.
Retain Security Log	Determines the number of days' worth of events that should be retained for the Security log if this log is set to retain events by an age.

Table 11-5   Event Log Policy Settings

Setting	Description
Retain System Log	Determines the number of days' worth of events that should be retained for the System log if this log is set to retain events by an age.
Retention Method For Application Log	Determines the retention method for the Application log. You can set this to Overwrite Events As Needed, Overwrite Events By Days, or Do Not Overwrite Events. This option requires that the log be cleared manually. When the maximum log size is reached, new events will be discarded.
Retention Method For Security Log	Determines the retention method for the Security log. You can set this to Overwrite Events As Needed, Overwrite Events By Days, or Do Not Overwrite Events. This option requires that the log be cleared manually. When the maximum log size is reached, new events will be discarded.
Retention Method For System Log	Determines the retention method for the System log. You can set this to Overwrite Events As Needed, Overwrite Events By Days, or Do Not Overwrite Events. This option requires that the log be cleared manually. When the maximum log size is reached, new events will be discarded.

Restricted Groups

Restricted groups enable you to control the Members and Member Of properties security groups. You can control which accounts have membership in a group by defining the Members list. You can define which groups the restricted group is a member of by defining the Member Of list. When the security template is enforced by Group Policy, any current member of a restricted security group that is not on the Members list is removed from the security group. Any user on the Members list who is not currently a member of the restricted group is added to the security group.

System Services

You can use system services policies to configure the default startup behavior of services and the permissions to those services. By using system services policies, you can prevent users and power users from stopping or starting services to which they have default rights. You can also disable services that are not used on your network to keep them from starting. See Chapter 9, "Managing Security for System Services," for detailed information on configuring security for system services.

Registry

You can use registry policies to control the DACL and SACL of registry keys. By using registry policies, you can increase security on registry keys, or you can decrease the security, which is sometimes needed to run applications under user security contexts.

File System

You can use file system policies to control the DACL and SACL of NTFS files and folders. By using file system policies, you can increase the security of files and folders, or you can decrease their security, which is sometimes needed to run applications under user security contexts.

Wireless Network (IEEE 802.11) Policies

Windows Server 2003 adds the capability to manage wireless network settings, including 802.1x authentication, for computers running Windows XP and Windows Server 2003. You can configure a wireless policy that configures the following:

- How often the computer checks for new wireless policies (by default, every 3 hours)

- Whether the computer will connect to any available wireless network, only infrastructure networks, or only ad hoc computer-to-computer wireless networks using 802.11 protocols

- Whether the Wireless Zero Configuration service should manage connectivity to wireless networks

- Whether the computer should automatically connect to nonpreferred networks (wireless networks the computer has never connected to)

- The service set identifier (SSID), authentication, and encryption protocols for wireless networks to be added as preferred networks

- 802.1x authentication details for networks that use 802.1x for security

Public Key Policies

Public key policies are available only in the computer-related section of Group Policy. You can use public key policies to define settings for the following:

- **Automatic Enrollment For Computer Certificates**   You can specify automatic enrollment and renewal for computer certificates. When auto-enrollment is configured, the specified certificate types are issued automatically to all computers within the scope of the public-key Group Policy. Computer certificates that are issued by auto-enrollment are renewed automatically from the issuing CA. Auto-enrollment does not function unless at least one enterprise CA is online to process certificate requests.

- **Add Trusted Root Certificates For Groups Of Computers**   When you install an enterprise root CA or a stand-alone root CA, the certificate of the CA is added automatically to the Trusted Root Certification Authority Group Policy for the domain. You also can add certificates for other root CAs to Trusted Root Certification Authority Group Policy. The root CA certificates that you add become trusted root CAs for computers within the scope of the Group Policy. For example, if you want to use a third-party CA as a root CA in a certification hierarchy, you must add the certificate for the third-party CA to the Trusted Root Certification Authority Group Policy.

- **Create Certificate Trust Lists (CTLs) For Computers And Users**   You can create CTLs to trust specific CAs and to restrict the uses of certificates issued by the CAs. For example, you might use a CTL to trust certificates that are issued by a commercial CA and restrict the permitted uses for those certificates. You might also use CTLs to control trust on an extranet for certificates that are issued by CAs that are managed by your business partners. You can configure CTLs for computers and for users. Before you can create CTLs, you must have a valid trust list signing certificate, such as the Administrator certificate or the Trust List Signing certificate, that has been issued by an enterprise CA.

- **Designate EFS Recovery Agent Accounts**   You can use the Group Policy console to designate alternative EFS recovery agents by adding the EFS recovery agent certificates into public-key Group Policy, which means you must first issue EFS recovery agent certificates to designated recovery agent user accounts on local computers. When you are configuring the EFS recovery settings, you have two choices: You can add recovery agent certificates that are published in Active Directory, or you can add recovery agent certificates from a file located on a disk or in a shared folder that is available on the computer from which you are configuring public-key settings. If you add recovery agent certificates from files, you must first export the appropriate certificates to the disk or shared folder that will be used to add the files during the EFS recovery Group Policy configuration process.

Software Restriction Policies

Software Restriction Policies, sometimes known by their development name SAFER, enable administrators to have some degree of control over execution of programs on computers running Windows XP and Windows Server 2003. Although not explicitly a security feature because they can be subverted by individuals with physical access to the computer or advanced knowledge of the Win32 API system, they are an option for implementing system-level control over written security policies. For example, you might want to prohibit VBScript files from running on user workstations except for those written by your organization's IT staff. This is a task that Software Restriction Policies will perform very well.

Basic Operation of SRPs

Software Restriction Policies (SRPs) have two operational modes, called security levels, that determine how SRPs work:

- **Disallowed**   Under this security level, all executable content defined by file extension (38 types by default) is prohibited from running on a computer, except that content specifically allowed by SRP rules. It is very difficult to use the Disallowed security level without preventing the operating system or applications from running properly.

- **Unrestricted**   Under this security level, all executable content is allowed to run as it would if SRPs were not configured, except for that content specifically prevented from running by SRP rules. This is the default security level for SRP once enabled through Group Policy or locally.

SRPs define files with file extensions in the Designated File Types list as executable content. There are 38 file extensions originally included on the list—many of which are obviously executable file types, such as .exe and .vbs, but some of which are not-so-obviously executable files types, such as .url and .oxc. You can add additional files types to the Designated File Types list in Group Policy. By default, SRPs do not provide enforcement on software libraries (.dll) files that are called by executable content. When a program is disallowed because of a software restriction policy, the user receives and the following error: "Windows cannot open this program because it has been prevented by a software restriction policy. For more information, open Event Viewer or contact your system administrator," and an event is written to the Security log.

In the Enforcement properties of SRPs in Group Policy you can change this behavior to also restrict the execution of instructions in dynamic-link libraries (DLLs). Additionally, in the Enforcement properties you can determine whether the SRPs apply to all users of the computer to which they are assigned (the default setting) or to all users with the exception of local administrators.

Configuring SRP Rules

SRPs use rules to determine whether executable files are run when SRPs are enabled. By default, four rules grant access to registry keys that are used in the operation of SRPs. After creating the SRP, you must configure additional rules to control which files can be run on the target computer. Following are the four kinds of rules in order of precedence:

- **Hash rules**   A hash rule specifies the exact file that you wish to allow or disallow by its cryptographic hash. When you create a hash rule, the Windows operating system generates a hash of the file that you select using the MD5 hash algorithm or the SHA-1 algorithm if the registry option for enforcing FIPS compliance is enabled. Attributes of the file, such as its name, are not including in the creation of this hash to prevent simple manipulation of file-subverting SRPs. Because hash rules are the most specific type of rule, they take precedence over other rules if there is a conflict. Hash rules are useful to prevent specific files from being run in Windows XP and Windows Server 2003. For example, you can create a rule that prevents a file that is known to spread a virus from running. A hash rule is the most appropriate rule to create. Keep in mind, though, that only a single bit inside the file needs to change before the file will have a different hash result and the SRP rule is rendered ineffective.

- **Certificate rules**   Certificate rules allow or disallow files from running based on the certificate that was used to sign the file. Certificate rules are particularly useful when used to grant exceptions from path rules. For example, you can create a path rule that disallows all .vbs content to help prevent malicious script files from being run in Windows XP. Because your organization uses VBScript for logon scripts. This rule would also prevent the logon script from running. To avoid this, you could create a certificate rule that allows all files signed with the IT department's code-signing certificate. Because certificate rules take precedence over path rules, all .vbs files would not be prohibited from running, except those signed by the IT department.

- **Path rules**   Path rules allow or disallow files from running based on either file location on the computer hard disk or the file name and extension. For flexibility, path rules allow you to use the wildcard characters ? and * (asterisk). For example, you can specify that any executable in the Program Files folder be allowed to run by creating a path rule for c:\program files*. For most applications of SRPs, path rules are the most important and most-used rules. Path rules are superseded by both hash rules and certificate rules. When there are multiple matching path rules, the most specific matching rule takes precedence.

- **Internet Explorer Internet Zone rules**   Internet Zone rules have a very specific operation: they control whether or not MSI files will be run after being downloaded by Internet Explorer. You can configure Internet zone rules for each of the five Internet Explorer security zones. Because Internet zone rules are specific to MSI files, they are of limited usefulness.

Troubleshooting SRP Rules

SRPs were designed with troubleshooting in mind because they can very quickly become exceedingly complex. SRPs log attempts to open disallowed files and other operations to the System log. All SRP events are logged under event IDs 865, 866, and 867. You can retrieve these events from the System log by typing **EventQuery -l System -fi "ID ge 865" -fi "ID le 868" -v -fo list** at the command prompt. Appending the string with **> srp.txt** will write the events to a text file called Srp.txt in the current directory.

In addition to the Event log, you can also enable advanced logging, which will write every SRP action, including all rule evaluations, to a text file. To enable advanced logging, add the string value **LogFileName** with the path in the data field for the value, where *path* is the path to create the log file in to the following registry key:

HKEY_LOCAL_MACHINE\SOFTWARE\Policies\Microsoft\Windows\Safer \CodeIdentifiers

If you have many SRP rules, not only will advanced logging create large log files, it will also likely degrade the performance of the computer. You should enable advanced logging only when actively troubleshooting an issue.

In the process of troubleshooting, you might need to remove the SRP. If you cannot do this through the local Group Policy or from Active Directory Group Policy, you can restart the computer in safe mode and delete the registry key HKCU or HKLM\SOFT-WARE\Policies\Microsoft\Windows\Safer\CodeIdentifiers, depending on whether the SRP was deployed to the user or the computer. If the SRP is being deployed by Group Policy, disable the GPO. After restarting the computer, the SRP will no longer be applied.

IP Security Policies

You can assign IPSec policy to computers that are members of the domain by using the security settings. By assigning IPSec policies through Group Policy, you can ensure the integrity of the confidentiality of data transmission. See Chapter 10, "Implementing TCP/IP Security," for information on configuring IPSec policies.

How Security Templates Work

All computers that run Windows Server 2003, Windows 2000, or Windows XP have a local GPO that includes security settings and is applied when the computer starts up. You can also configure security templates by using Group Policy at the site, domain, and OU levels.

Applying Security Templates to a Local Computer

Security templates provide the base security for computers running Windows Server 2003, Windows 2000, or Windows XP and are applied when the computers are upgraded from Windows NT or during installation. Computers running Windows Server 2003, Windows 2000, or Windows XP include the Security Templates Microsoft Management Console (MMC) snap-in, which enables you to optimize the baseline security of a local computer and create security templates—text-based files that contain security settings—for all the security areas supported by the Security Configuration Toolset. The Security Configuration Toolset includes the following:

- Security Templates MMC snap-in
- Security Configuration and Analysis MMC snap-in
- Secedit.exe command-line utility

Security Templates MMC Snap-In

The Security Templates MMC snap-in enables you to create and modify security templates. By default, the Security Templates MMC snap-in lists all the templates in the %windir%\security\templates folder, which includes several security templates included with Windows Server 2003, Windows XP, and Windows 2000. Figure 11-1 shows the Security Templates MMC snap-in in Windows XP.

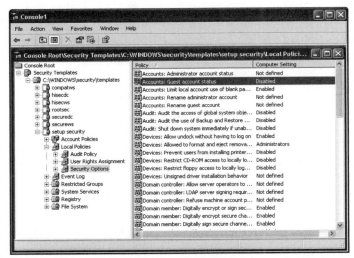

Figure 11-1 Security Templates MMC snap-in in Windows XP

You can create a blank security template by right-clicking the Security Template store and selecting New Template. You can then populate the settings. When a setting in the security template is marked as Not Configured, the computer's setting will not change.

Tip Read the wording of the security settings carefully. Many settings disable a certain behavior; configuring some settings as Disabled will enable the behavior.

Security Configuration and Analysis MMC Snap-In

You can use the Security Configuration and Analysis MMC snap-in to complete two different tasks: analyze the security settings of the local computer, and configure the security settings on the local computer by using security templates.

Because the security settings configured when the local computer security policy was applied can change because of security settings in Group Policy or by installing applications, you might want to review and verify the security settings periodically on computers running Windows Server 2003, Windows 2000, or Windows XP. The Security Configuration and Analysis MMC snap-in enables you to perform a security analysis quickly and review the differences between the current settings on a computer and the settings contained in a security template.

The Security Configuration and Analysis MMC snap-in performs security analysis by comparing the current state of system security against an analysis database. During creation, the analysis database uses at least one security template. If you choose to import more than one security template, the database will merge the various templates and create one composite template. The database resolves conflicts in order of import—the last template that is imported takes precedence.

To analyze the current security settings of a local computer by using the Security Configuration and Analysis MMC snap-in, follow these steps:

1. Open a blank MMC and add the Security Configuration and Analysis MMC snap-in to it.

2. In the console tree, right-click Security Configuration And Analysis and click Open Database.

3. In the Open Database dialog box, create a new database by entering a name for the database in the File Name box and click Open.

4. In the Import Template dialog box, select the Setup Security template and click Open.

5. In the details pane, right-click Security Configuration And Analysis and then click Analyze Computer Now.

6. In the Error Log file path, click OK to create a log file in the default location.

For example, you might want to analyze a computer running Windows XP to compare its security settings to the default policy that is applied during installation. Figure 11-2 shows the results of comparing the computer's security settings with the Setup Security template.

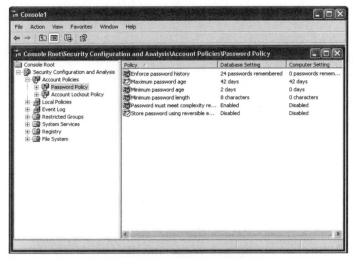

Figure 11-2   Output of using the Security Configuration and Analysis MMC snap-in in Windows XP

You can use the output of the analysis to perform a side-by-side comparison of the security settings. The Security Configuration and Analysis MMC snap-in displays the result of the analysis by using the icons described in Table 11-6.

Table 11-6   Using the Output of the Security Configuration and Analysis MMC Snap-In

Icon	Description
Red X	The entry is defined in the analysis database and on the system, but the security setting values do not match.
Green check	The entry is defined in the analysis database and on the system, and the setting values match.
Question mark	The entry is not defined in the analysis database and therefore was not analyzed. This occurs when a setting was not defined in the analysis database or when the user running the analysis did not have sufficient permissions.
Exclamation point	This item is defined in the analysis database but does not exist on the actual system.
No highlight	The item is not defined in the analysis database or on the system.

You can also use the Security Configuration and Analysis MMC snap-in to configure local system security directly. You can import security templates that have been created with the Security Templates MMC snap-in and apply these templates to the local computer. This immediately configures the system security with the levels specified in the template. To use the snap-in to configure the security settings on a local computer, follow the steps to analyze security outlined earlier—only instead of choosing to analyze the security of the computer, choose to configure security on the computer.

Secedit.exe Command-Line Utility

The Secedit.exe utility includes all the functionality of the Security Configuration and Analysis MMC snap-in and has the ability to force a refresh of Group Policy in Windows 2000. In Windows Server 2003 and Windows XP, you must use the Gpupdate.exe command-line utility to force a refresh of Group Policy. By calling the Secedit.exe command-line tool from a batch file or automatic task scheduler, you can use it to apply templates and analyze system security automatically. You can view the options for how to use Secedit.exe by typing **secedit** at the command prompt.

Applying Security Templates by Using Group Policy

In addition to the local security policy, you can use Group Policy to deploy the settings in security templates to provide incremental security. Security settings are deployed by the same rules that apply to other Group Policy settings, except that they are not as volatile as other Administrative Templates settings. You can place all client computers that have the same security requirements into an OU and create a GPO that contains security settings to deploy the new security settings to those computers.

You can import a previously created and tested security template into a GPO by right-clicking Security Settings in the computer-related configuration section of a GPO. When you do this, the settings from the template are applied in an incremental fashion. If you import more than one template and you have conflicting settings, the settings from the last imported security template take precedence. To completely clear the security settings in the GPO before importing the security template, ensure that you select the option to clear the database before importing when you select the security template that you want to import.

Default Security Templates

Windows Server 2003, Windows 2000, or Windows XP includes several built-in security templates that you can use as a baseline for creating your own templates or for resetting the security on a computer. The built-in templates include the following:

- **Basic**   The Basic security templates apply the default access control settings. The Basic templates can also be used to revert back to the defaults after making any undesirable changes. There are Basic templates for workstation and service computers.

- **Optional Component File Security**   The Optional Component File Security templates apply default security to optional component files that might be installed during or after Setup. The Optional Component File Security templates should be used in conjunction with the Basic templates to restore default security to system files that are installed as optional components.

- **Compatible**   To ensure that all users can run applications that are not compliant with the Windows 2000 and later application specification without changing file and registry permissions you can apply this template. Power Users have additional capabilities (such as the capability to create shares) that go beyond the more liberal access control settings necessary to run legacy applications. In this situation, the Compatible template opens up the default access control policy for the Users group in a manner that is consistent with the requirements of legacy applications such as Microsoft Office 97. A computer that is configured with the Compatible template is not as secure as it would be by default.

- **Secure**   The Secure template focuses on making operating system and network behavior more secure by making changes, such as removing all members of the Power Users group and requiring more secure passwords. The Secure template does not focus on securing application behavior. This template does not modify permissions, so users with the proper permissions can still use legacy applications, even though all members are removed from the Power Users group by defining the Power Users group as a restricted group.

- **High Secure**   The High Secure template increases the security defined by several of the parameters in the Secure template. For example, the Secure template might enable SMB packet signing, but the High Secure template requires SMB packet signing. Furthermore, the Secure template might warn about the installation of unsigned drivers, whereas the High Secure template blocks the installation of unsigned drivers. In short, the High Secure template configures many operational parameters to their extreme values without regard for performance, operational ease of use, or connectivity with clients using third-party or earlier versions of NTLM. The High Secure template also changes the default access permissions for Power Users to match those assigned to Users. This allows administrators to grant Users privileges reserved for Power Users, such as the ability to create shares, without having to give those users unnecessary access to the registry or file system. The High Secure template is primarily designed for use in an all Windows 2000 networks because the settings require Windows 2000 technology. Using High Secure templates in an environment with Microsoft Windows 98 or Windows NT can cause problems.

- **No Terminal Server User SID**   The default file system and registry access control lists that are on servers grant permissions to a terminal server SID. The terminal server SID is used only when the terminal server is running in application compatibility mode. If the terminal server is not being used, this template can be applied to remove the unnecessary terminal server SIDs from the file system and registry locations. However, removing the access control entry for the terminal server SID from these default file system and registry locations does not increase the security of the system. Instead of removing the terminal server SID, simply run the terminal server in full security mode. When the computer is running in full security mode, the terminal server SID is not used.

- **System Root Security**   Rootsec.inf specifies the root permissions introduced in Windows Server 2003 and Windows XP. By default, Rootsec.inf defines these permissions for the root of the system drive. This template can be used to reapply the root directory permissions if they are inadvertently changed, or the template can be modified to apply the same root permissions to other volumes. As specified within the template, it does not overwrite explicit permissions that are defined on child objects; it propagates only the permissions that are inherited by child objects.

- **Default Security**   Setup Security.inf is a computer-specific template that represents the default security settings that are applied during the installation of Windows Server 2003, Windows 2000, or Windows XP, including the file permissions for the root of the system drive. You can use this template or portions of it for disaster recovery purposes. Setup Security.inf should never be applied by using Group Policy.

- **Internet Explorer ACLS**   Windows Server 2003 includes a template called Iesacls.inf that contains the audit entries added in the Windows Server 2003 Internet Explorer Enhanced Security Configuration (ESC).

Creating Custom Security Templates

You might want to add more security settings to security templates to meet your organization's security requirements. Windows Server 2003, Windows 2000, and Windows XP enable you to add settings to a security template by directly editing the security template file or, in the case of system services, configuring the security template on a computer that has the desired services installed.

Adding Registry Entries to Security Options

You might want to add a security-related registry configuration to a security template that you will be deploying on many computers in your organization. By using security templates, the registry value will be dynamically applied and enforced by Group Policy each time the security settings are refreshed, by default every 16 hours.

You can customize the list of registry values exposed in the Security Options section of security templates by modifying and then registering the information in the Sceregvl.inf file located in the %windir%\inf folder. Although you must register the Sceregvl.inf file on the computers on which you will view and modify security templates, you do not have to register it on every computer to which the security template will be applied. Once the Sceregvl.inf file has been modified and registered, your custom registry values are exposed in the security templates on that computer. You can then create security templates or policies that define your new registry values and apply them to local computers or through Group Policy.

To add a registry value to a security template, follow these steps:

1. Open the Sceregv1.inf file from %windir%\inf by using Notepad.exe or another text editor.

2. Add the registry value and security template settings to the [Register Registry Values] section using the information shown in Table 11-7.

3. Add a display value for the value in the security template in the [Strings] section.

4. Save the Sceregvl.inf file

5. Reregister the Scecli.dll file by typing **regsvr32 scecli.dll** at the command prompt.

For example, you might want to add a policy that prevents CDs from playing automatically. The registry value for this setting is named Autorun and is written to the key HKEY_LOCAL_MACHINE\System\CurrentControlSet\Services\CDRom. To add this setting to security templates, you need to add the following section to the Sceregvl.inf file:

```
[Register Registry Values]
MACHINE\System\CurrentControlSet\Services\CDRom\Autorun,4,%Autorun%,0
[Strings]
Autorun = Prevents CD-ROMs from auto-playing CDs
```

This is the syntax for the registry value section:

RegistryPath,RegistryType,DisplayName,DisplayType,Options

Table 11-7 describes each of the fields.

Table 11-7   Syntax for the Registry Values in Sceregvl.inf

Field	Description
RegistryPath	Defines the full path of the registry key and value that you want to add to the security templates. Only values that exist in the HKEY_LOCAL_MACHINE hive can be configured, and this hive is referenced by the keyword MACHINE.
RegistryType	This is a number that defines the type of the registry value, as follows: ■ 1 REG_SZ ■ 2 REG_EXPAND_SZ ■ 3 REG_BINARY ■ 4 REG_DWORD ■ 7 REG_MULTI_SZ
DisplayName	Defines the variable for the string that is displayed in the security templates.

Table 11-7   Syntax for the Registry Values in Sceregvl.inf

Field	Description
DisplayType	Specifies the type of dialog box the security template will render to allow the user to define the setting for the registry value. Supported *Display-Types* include the following:
	■ **0; Boolean** Enables you to enable or disable the registry value. If Enabled is selected, the registry value is set to 1. If Disabled is selected, the registry value is set to 0.
	■ **1; numeric** Enables you to set the value to a numeric value ranging from 0 to 99,999. Numeric display types can specify "unit" strings such as "minutes" and "seconds" in the Options field.
	■ **2; string** Causes the UI to render a text box. The registry value is set to the string entered by the user.
	■ **3; list** Enables you to select one of several options from a list box. The registry value is set to the numeric value associated with the option. The options presented in the security template are defined in the Options field.
	■ **4; multivalued (not available in Windows 2000)** Enables you to enter multiple lines of text. This display type should be used to define values for MULTI_SZ types. The registry value is set to the strings entered by the user, where each line is separated by a null byte.
	■ **5; bitmask (not available in Windows 2000)** Enables you to select from a series of check boxes, where each check box corresponds to a numeric value defined in the Options field.
Options	Qualifies different *DisplayTypes*, as follows:
	■ If *DisplayType*=1 (numeric), the Options field might contain a string that defines the units for the numeric value. The "unit" string has no impact on the value set in the registry.
	■ If *DisplayType*=3 (list), the Options field defines the list options. Each option consists of a numeric value separated by the pipe character (|), followed by the text for the choice. The registry value is set to the numeric value associated with the choice made by the user. See the LMCompatibilityLevel entry in Sceregvl.inf for an example of a registry value that allows the user to select from one of five possible values.
	■ If *DisplayType*=5 (bitmask), the Options field defines the choices that are available. Each choice consists of a numeric value separated by the pipe character (|), followed by the text for the choice. The registry value is set to the bitwise OR of the choices selected by the user. See the NTLMMinClientSec entry in Sceregvl.inf for an example of a registry value of this type.

Adding Services, Registry Values, and Files to Security Templates

You can manage the security of services, registry values, and files by using security templates. By default, all the services, registry values, and files that are in the base installation of Windows Server 2003, Windows 2000, or Windows XP are manageable in security templates. You can manage the startup behavior and the permissions on the service by using security templates. For registry values and files, you can manage the DACL and SACL. If you have a service, registry value, or file that is not in the default installation, such as a service that is added by an application, you can edit the security template on a computer running Windows Server 2003, Windows 2000, or Windows XP that does have the service, registry value, or file that you want to manage. When you save this template, it will automatically update the newly added resource.

Best Practices

- **Use security templates properly.**   Never edit the built-in security templates, especially templates such as Setup Security.inf, which gives you the option to reapply the default security settings. Instead of just modifying a predefined template, customize the predefined template and then save the changes under a different template name.

- **Monitor the size of security templates when using Group Policy.**   Security templates can become very large if many settings are made, especially file and registry ACLs. For example, the Setup Security.inf template is 770 KB. Security templates this large could cause network performance degradation when applied by using Group Policy.

- **Create templates for specific computer roles.**   Because security templates are easy to create and customize, they can easily be created to fit the security requirements of computers in different roles. For example, your Web server might have different security requirements than a domain controller.

- **Test security templates.**   Always test security templates in a nonproduction environment to ensure that the settings do not prevent legitimate uses of the computer. Furthermore, it is possible to prevent all accounts from accessing a computer using settings in security templates.

Additional Information

- Security Configuration Guides for Windows Server 2003, Windows 2000, and Windows XP at the Microsoft Security Guidance Center Web site (*http://www.microsoft.com/security/guidance/default.mspx*)

- "Threats and Countermeasures: Security Settings in Windows Server 2003 and Windows XP" white paper (*http://www.microsoft.com/downloads/details.aspx?FamilyId=1B6ACF93-147A-4481-9346-F93A4081EEA8&display lang=en*)

- The following Knowledge Base articles:

  - 823659: "Client, Service, and Program Incompatibilities That May Occur When You Modify Security Settings and User Rights Assignments" (*http://support.microsoft.com/kb/823659*)

  - 816297: "How to Define Security Templates by Using the Security Templates Snap-In in Windows Server 2003" (*http://support.microsoft.com/kb/816297*)

  - 313434: "How to Define Security Templates in Security Templates Snap-In in Windows 2000" (*http://support.microsoft.com/kb/313434*)

  - 816585: "How to Apply Predefined Security Templates in Windows Server 2003" (*http://support.microsoft.com/kb/816585*)

  - 309689: "How to Apply Predefined Security Templates in Windows 2000" (*http://support.microsoft.com/kb/309689*)

  - 321679:"How to Manage Security Templates in Windows 2000 Server" (*http://support.microsoft.com/kb/321679*)

  - 214752: "How to Add Custom Registry Settings to Security Configuration Editor" (*http://support.microsoft.com/kb/214752*)

  - 238965: "Removing Additional Permissions Granted to Terminal Services Users" (*http://support.microsoft.com/kb/238965*)

  - 246261:"How to Use the RestrictAnonymous Registry Value in Windows 2000" (*http://support.microsoft.com/kb/246261*)

  - 321470: "Unexpected Results Occur If You Set File Security by Using Either Group Policy or Security Templates" (*http://support.microsoft.com/kb/321470*)

❑ 313222: "How to Reset Security Settings Back to the Defaults" (*http://support.microsoft.com/kb/313222*)

❑ 314834: "How to Clear the Windows Paging File at Shutdown" (*http://support.microsoft.com/kb/314834*)

❑ 237399: "The Default NTFS Permissions Are Not Applied to a Converted Boot Partition" (*http://support.microsoft.com/kb/237399*)

❑ 810076: "Updates to Restricted Groups ('Member of') Behavior of User-Defined Local Groups" (*http://support.microsoft.com/kb/810076*)

❑ 324036: "How To Use Software Restriction Policies in Windows Server 2003" (*http://support.microsoft.com/kb/324036*)

■ "Using Software Restriction Policies to Protect Against Unauthorized Software" white paper (*http://www.microsoft.com/technet/prodtechnol/winxppro/maintain/rstrplcy.mspx*)

Chapter 12

Managing Microsoft Internet Explorer Security and Privacy

Most organizations that use Microsoft operating systems also use Microsoft Internet Explorer. In fact, browsing the Internet has become a mission-critical business activity; however, it also can provide attackers a direct avenue into the corporate network, bypassing traditional perimeter security mechanisms, such as firewall rules. Consequently, when securing computers running Microsoft Windows Server 2003, Windows 2000, and Windows XP on your network, you should also consider how you will secure Internet Explorer. Even if your organization does not use Internet Explorer as its primary Web browser, you should take steps to secure it because it is a core component of the operating system.

Security Settings in Internet Explorer

The Web browser has become a mission-critical application for nearly all organizations. Unfortunately, browsing Web sites on the Internet also can be a major security risk because Web browsers provide attackers with direct access to an organization's local area network (LAN). Fortunately, Internet Explorer enables administrators to configure privacy and security settings easily and enables knowledgeable users to view privacy and security information to make decisions on whether to trust specific Web sites. Service Pack 2 for Windows XP and Service Pack 1 for Windows Server 2003 add major security enhancements for Internet Explorer to make Internet Explorer more secure by default, more manageable by administrators, and easier to use for end users.

Privacy Settings

In April 2002, the World Wide Web Consortium (W3C)—found at *http://www.w3c.org*—ratified the Platform for Privacy Preferences Project (P3P), an industry standard providing a simple, automated way for users to gain more control over the use of their personal information on Web sites they visit. Internet Explorer 6 fully supports P3P version 1.0. P3P helps protect the privacy of users' personal information on the Internet by making it easier for users to decide whether and under which circumstances personal information is disclosed to Web sites.

In Internet Explorer 6, users can define their privacy preferences for disclosing personal information. When users browse Web sites, Internet Explorer determines whether those sites abide by the P3P privacy standards. If the Web site does support P3P standards, Internet Explorer compares the user's privacy preferences to the Web site's privacy policy information. To be P3P compliant, a Web site must provide a clear definition of its privacy policies, including these:

- The organization that is collecting information about users
- The type of information that is being collected
- What the information will be used for
- Whether the information will be shared with other organizations
- Whether users can access the information about them and change how the organization will use that information
- The method for resolving disputes between users and the organization
- How the organization will retain the collected information
- Where the organization publicly maintains detailed information that users can read about their privacy policies

Internet Explorer 6 provides a way to view a Web site's P3P privacy information known as a *privacy report* on P3P-compliant Web sites by using the Privacy Report option on the View menu. For example, to view the privacy report for the Microsoft Web site, follow these steps:

1. Open Internet Explorer.
2. In the Address box, type **http://www.microsoft.com**.
3. Click View, and then click Privacy Report.
4. From the Web Sites With Content On The Current Page box, select *http://www.microsoft.com*, and then click Summary.

Figure 12-1 shows the privacy report for the Microsoft Web site.

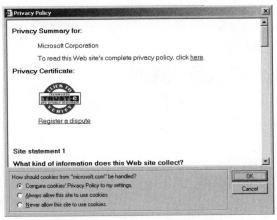

Figure 12-1   P3P privacy report for Microsoft.com

In addition to viewing P3P-compliant Web site privacy reports, Internet Explorer 6 enables P3P support for user cookie management. A *cookie* is a small file that an individual Web site stores on your computer. Web sites can use cookies to maintain information and settings, such as your customization preferences. Two types of cookies exist: *persistent cookies* and *session cookies*. Persistent cookies include an expiration date that identifies when the browser can delete them. Session cookies do not have an expiration date; they are deleted when the user closes the browser.

Internet Explorer 6 includes advanced cookie management capabilities that determine whether cookies can be stored on a user's computer. When you configure your privacy preferences, you can configure Internet Explorer to handle cookies in the following ways:

- **Prevent all cookies from being stored on your computer.**   This setting might prevent you from viewing certain Web sites, such as e-commerce Web sites that save shopping cart information in cookies.

- **Block or restrict first-party cookies.**   First-party cookies originate in the same domain as the Web site being visited. This setting blocks those cookies.

- **Block or restrict third-party cookies.**   Third-party cookies do not originate in the same domain as the Web site being visited and therefore are not covered by that Web site's privacy policy. For example, many Web sites contain advertising from third-party sites that use cookies. This setting blocks those cookies.

- **Use the Allow option.**   Enabling this option permits Web sites to place cookies on your computer without notifying you. Previous versions of Internet Explorer included a similar option.

- **Use the Prompt option.**   This option enables you to determine on a cookie-by-cookie basis whether to allow the cookie to be placed on your hard drive.

An additional option enables you to always allow session cookies. Figure 12-2 shows the Advanced Privacy Settings user interface in which you can configure cookie management in Internet Explorer 6.

Figure 12-2   Advanced Privacy Settings user interface in Internet Explorer

For convenience, Internet Explorer offers six predefined privacy configurations and an option to create a custom configuration. By default, Internet Explorer 6 Privacy configuration is set to Medium for sites in the Internet zone. In addition to the predefined configurations, you can override the settings for individual Web sites in the Privacy tab of the Internet Options dialog box (on the Tools menu). These are the predefined privacy configurations:

- **Block All Cookies**   Prevents all Web sites from storing cookies on your computer, and Web sites cannot read existing cookies on your computer. This setting can prevent some Web sites from being viewed or Web applications from working correctly. Per-site privacy actions do override this setting.

- **High**   Prevents Web sites from storing cookies that do not have a compact privacy policy—a condensed, computer-readable P3P privacy statement. The browser prevents Web sites from storing cookies that use personally identifiable information without your explicit consent. Per-site privacy actions override this setting.

- **Medium High**   Prevents Web sites from storing third-party cookies that do not have a compact privacy policy or that use personally identifiable information without your explicit consent. The browser prevents Web sites from storing first-party cookies that use personally identifiable information without your implicit consent. The browser also restricts access to first-party cookies that do not have a compact privacy policy so that they can be read only in the first-party context. Per-site privacy actions override this setting.

- **Medium (default)**   Prevents Web sites from storing third-party cookies that do not have a compact privacy policy or that use personally identifiable information without your implicit consent. The browser allows first-party cookies that use personally identifiable information without your implicit consent but deletes these cookies from your computer when you close the browser. The browser also restricts access to first-party cookies that do not have a compact privacy policy so that they can be read only in the first-party context. Per-site privacy actions override this setting.

- **Low**   Allows Web sites to store cookies on your computer, including third-party cookies that do not have a compact privacy policy or that use personally identifiable information without your implicit consent. However, closing the browser deletes these third-party cookies from your computer. The browser also restricts access to first-party cookies that do not have a compact privacy policy so that they can be read only in the first-party context. Per-site privacy actions override this setting.

- **Accept All Cookies**   Allows all Web sites to store cookies on your computer and allows Web sites that create cookies on your computer to read them. Per-site privacy actions do not override this setting.

Pop-Up Blocker

One of the security enhancements that was added to Internet Explorer in Service Pack 2 for Windows XP and Service Pack 1 for Windows Server 2003 is an integrated pop-up blocking feature. Enabled by default for Web sites in the Internet and Restricted Sites zones, the Pop-up Blocker blocks most pop-ups that are spawned automatically by Web sites. When pop-ups are blocked, a sound is played and the Information bar appears at the top of the browser window to tell the user that a pop-up was blocked, although you can disable either of these options if you like. You can also configure how aggressively Internet Explorer blocks pop-ups spawned by Web sites by using three levels: Low, Medium, and High.

- **Low**   Allows automatic pop-ups from sites that use Secure Sockets Layer (SSL) or Transport Layer Security (TLS), but blocks those spawned from other sites except for those launched from Microsoft ActiveX controls or dynamic HTML (DHTML) controls. Pop-up windows are launched when a user clicks a hyperlink that opens a pop-up window.

- **Medium**   Blocks most automatic pop-ups. This setting blocks pop-up windows that are automatically spawned by Web sites except for those launched from Microsoft ActiveX controls or dynamic HTML (DHTML) controls. Pop-up windows are launched when a user clicks a hyperlink that opens a pop-up window.

- **High** Blocks all pop-ups. This setting prevents all automatic and user-initiated pop-up windows from being launched except for those launched from Microsoft ActiveX controls or dynamic HTML (DHTML) controls. Pop-up windows are launched when a user clicks a hyperlink that opens a pop-up window. As an override, users can hold down the Ctrl key while clicking a hyperlink to launch the pop-up. Before you set Internet Explorer to prevent all pop-up windows from being launched in your organization, you should consider the potential usability problems and support costs that might be incurred from users who have difficulty using Web sites that require pop-up windows.

Security Zones

On most networks, the Web browser on a user's computer is an open communication channel from the Internet directly, or with minimal protection from firewalls, to the computer and the local network the computer is attached to. An attacker can embed scripts in a Web site that, when viewed, attack the computer or the local network of the user browsing that Web site. To prevent attacks delivered through Web sites, you can use Internet Explorer security settings, which are configured by using security zones. Security zones in Internet Explorer are customizable, enabling you to configure browser security for sites of different trust levels while maintaining Web site functionality.

These are the security zones in Internet Explorer:

- **Local Machine Zone (0)** The Local Machine Zone (LMZ) is an additional security zone in Internet Explorer that by default does not appear in the user interface. The LMZ contains security settings for content that is run from the local computer, for example, an .htm file on the desktop or a locally installed Web application. You can unhide the LMZ, and have it appear as the My Computer security zone in Internet Explorer by setting the registry value HKEY_CURRENT_USER\SOFTWARE\Microsoft\Windows\CurrentVersion\Internet Settings\Zones\0\Flags to 47 (hexadecimal). To hide it, set the registry value to 21 (hexadecimal).

  The security of the LMZ was greatly augmented in Windows XP SP2 and Windows Server 2003. The LMZ now has the highest level of security of any of the default levels, including High. Any content in the LMZ that uses active scripting or attempts to load an ActiveX control is prevented from running unless the user clicks the Information bar and explicitly allows the content to be run. Because this behavior could interfere with the operation of intranet-based Web applications that access local files, developers can add the Mark of the Web to files to make local files run in the Local Intranet zone rather than in the LMZ. For more information on adding the Mark of the Web to Web sites, see the MSDN Library at *http://msdn.microsoft.com*.

- **Local Intranet (1)**   The Local Intranet zone applies to all local intranet domains, Web sites that bypass the proxy server, dotless IP names, and all Universal Naming Convention (UNC) paths. Internet domains are considered local based on the domains listed in the Domain Name System (DNS) suffix search order in the TCP/IP properties. The Web sites that bypass the proxy server are defined as local in the Connections tab of Internet Options, which is often configured by the proxy server or firewall. By default, the security on this zone is set to Medium-Low. In addition, you can add sites to the Local Intranet zone this way:

  1.   Open Internet Explorer.

  2.   On the Tools menu, select Internet Options.

  3.   Click the Security tab in the Internet Options dialog box and then click the Local Intranet zone icon.

  4.   Click Sites, and then click Advanced.

  5.   Enter the name of the site to add to the Local Intranet zone in the Local Intranet dialog box. Click OK and close all open windows.

- **Trusted Sites (2)**   The Trusted Sites zone applies only to Web sites added to it. By default, all Web sites placed in this zone must use *https://*, meaning that they are protected by Secure Sockets Layer (SSL) or Transport Layer Security (TLS), to verify the confidentiality and integrity of the data coming from the Web site as well as to authenticate the Web site itself. You can remove this restriction but should do so only if absolutely required. The security on this zone is set to Low by default, and it contains no Web sites.

- **Internet (3)**   The Internet zone applies to all Web sites not defined in any other security zone. By default, the security on this zone is set to Medium—only a limited amount of trust is given to Web sites in this zone. You should configure the security on this zone to meet your organization's business and technical needs.

- **Restricted Sites (4)**   The Restricted Sites zone applies only to Web sites added to it. The security level on this zone is set to High by default. Sites in this zone are given little trust.

Security zones group Web sites into categories based on levels of trust. When using Internet Explorer to browse Web sites, the security zone of the Web site is displayed in the lower right-hand corner of the Internet Explorer status bar, as shown in Figure 12-3.

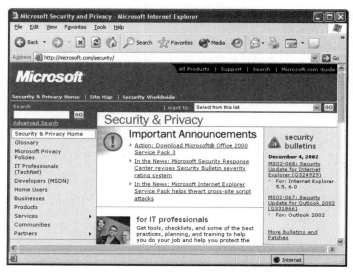

Figure 12-3   Viewing the current security zone in Internet Explorer

You can use four predefined levels of security with these security zones:

- **High**   Greatly restricts what you can do when browsing Web sites, including disabling all ActiveX and Java content. This security setting disables active scripting. (We discuss active scripting later in this section.)

- **Medium**   Provides a moderate level of protection, including preventing unsigned ActiveX controls from being downloaded and prompting users for confirmation when downloading any ActiveX content. Active scripting is enabled in this security setting. This level sets Java security to High.

- **Medium-Low**   Provides the same level of protection for non-Java content that the Medium security level does, without prompting the user for as many of the security options. This level sets Java security to Medium.

- **Low**   Provides little to no security control over Web site content. This level sets Java security to Low. You should not use this security level.

Table 12-1 shows the security configuration of the predefined security zone levels in Internet Explorer after the installation of Windows XP Service Pack 2 or Windows Server 2003 Service Pack 1. We discuss these security options, known as URLActions, in more detail momentarily. In addition to the predefined security levels, as mentioned earlier, you can create a custom level of security and assign it to a security zone.

Table 12-1   Default URLActions in Internet Explorer

	Security Level			
Security Option	Low	Medium-Low	Medium	High
Automatic Prompting For ActiveX Controls	Enable	Enable	Disable	Disable
Binary And Script Behaviors	Enable	Enable	Enable	Disable
Download Signed ActiveX Controls	Enable	Prompt	Prompt	Disable
Download Unsigned ActiveX Controls	Prompt	Disable	Disable	Disable
Initialize And Script ActiveX Controls Not Marked As Safe	Prompt	Disable	Disable	Disable
Run ActiveX Controls And Plug-Ins	Enable	Enable	Enable	Disable
Script ActiveX Controls Marked Safe For Scripting	Enable	Enable	Enable	Disable
Automatic Prompting For File Downloads	Enable	Enable	Disable	Disable
File Download	Enable	Enable	Enable	Disable
Font Download	Enable	Enable	Enable	Prompt
Access Data Sources Across Domains	Enable	Prompt	Disable	Disable
Allow META REFRESH	Enable	Enable	Enable	Disable
Allow Scripting Of Internet Explorer Webbrowser Control	Disable	Disable	Disable	Disable
Allow Script-Initiated Windows Without Size Or Position Constraints	Enable	Enable	Disable	Disable
Allow Web Pages To Use Restricted Protocols For Active Content	Prompt	Prompt	Prompt	Disable
Display Mixed Content	Prompt	Prompt	Prompt	Prompt
Don't Prompt For Client Certificate Selection When No Certificates Or Only One Certificate Exists	Enable	Enable	Disable	Disable
Drag And Drop Or Copy And Paste Files	Enable	Enable	Enable	Prompt
Installation Of Desktop Items	Enable	Prompt	Prompt	Disable
Launching Programs And Files In An IFRAME	Enable	Prompt	Prompt	Disable

Table 12-1   Default URLActions in Internet Explorer

| Security Option | Security Level | | | |
	Low	Medium-Low	Medium	High
Navigate Subframes Across Different Domains	Enable	Enable	Enable	Disable
Open Files Based On Content, Not File Extension	Enable	Enable	Enable	Disable
Software Channel Permissions	Low safety	Medium safety	Medium safety	High safety
Submit Nonencrypted Form Data	Enable	Enable	Prompt	Prompt
Use Pop-up Blocker	Disable	Disable	Enable	Enable
Userdata Persistence	Enable	Enable	Enable	Disable
Web Sites In Less Privileged Web Content Zone Can Navigate Into This Zone	Prompt	Enable	Enable	Disable
Active Scripting	Enable	Enable	Enable	Disable
Allow Paste Operations Via Script	Enable	Enable	Enable	Disable
Scripting Of Java Applets	Enable	Enable	Enable	Disable
User Authentication	Automatic logon with current user name and password	Automatic logon only in Intranet zone	Automatic logon only in Intranet zone	Prompt for user name and password

When configuring security zones, you must remember that although security zones are configured and maintained in Internet Explorer, they also apply to other applications, such as Microsoft Office XP, Microsoft Outlook Express, Microsoft Outlook Preview Pane and HTML messages, and HTML Help applications. When a Web-based application, file, or site is opened, the Windows operating system determines to which zone the application, file, or site belongs. The zone provides the base level of security for the application, file, or site. By default, security zone settings are loaded at logon from the user's registry key into HKEY_CURRENT_USER (HKCU). You can make security zone settings systemwide, overriding any user-specific security zone settings by enabling the Group Policy setting Security Zones: Use Only Machine Settings or by creating the registry key (DWORD = 1) Security_HKLM_only in HKEY_LOCAL_MACHINE\Software\Policies\Microsoft\Windows\CurrentVersion \Internet Settings\. Even when this policy is enabled, the user's security zone settings from the user's registry hive are displayed in the user interface, but Internet Explorer uses only the computer settings that are stored in the HKEY_LOCAL_MACHINE (HKLM) registry hive.

The security settings in Internet Explorer are divided into the following categories:

- ActiveX controls and plug-ins
- Download options
- Miscellaneous options
- Scripting options
- User authentication option

Unfortunately, no single correct implementation of these settings exists for all users or all organizations. You must analyze the business and technical requirements of your organization to configure these security settings in Internet Explorer.

ActiveX Controls and Plug-Ins

ActiveX controls enable Web sites to deliver interactive content to users through Internet Explorer. The ActiveX controls and plug-ins section of Internet Explorer security includes settings for how Internet Explorer approves, downloads, runs, and scripts ActiveX controls. If a user downloads an ActiveX control that is hosted on a Web site that belongs to a security zone different than the page on which it is used, Internet Explorer applies the more restrictive of the two sites' security zone settings. You must be an administrator on a computer to install ActiveX controls. Once an ActiveX control is installed, it is available for all users of the computer. You can view ActiveX controls, as well as browser helper objects (BHOs) and browser extensions, by clicking Manage Add-ons in the Programs tab of the Internet Options dialog box in Control Panel or in the Internet Options dialog box (on the Tools menu) in Internet Explorer. These are the ActiveX security settings:

- **Automatic Prompting For ActiveX Controls**   Determines whether users are always prompted before installing ActiveX controls with the Information bar, even if the ActiveX control is signed and from a trusted publisher. If they are not prevented from doing so by other URLActions for ActiveX controls, users with administration rights can choose to install the ActiveX control by clicking the Information bar and following the prompts. You can choose from the following settings:
    - **Disable**   Installs ActiveX controls as defined by the other URLActions settings for ActiveX controls for the security zone in which the content is running
    - **Enable**   Blocks the installation of all ActiveX controls and prompts users to install the control by using the Information bar

- **Binary And Script Behaviors**   Restricts binary and script behaviors in the Restricted Sites zone and Local Machine Zone. This option was added in Windows XP SP2 and Windows Server 2003 SP1. Binary and script behaviors are compiled HTML components (HTC), Windows Script Components (WSC), or COM components that are delivered from a Web server rather than code executed at run time on the client. You can choose from the following settings:

  - ❑ **Disable**   Prevents all binary and script behaviors for content in the security zone.

  - ❑ **Enable**   Allows all binary and script behaviors for content in the security zone.

  - ❑ **Administrator Approved**   Allows only specific behaviors configured by administrators through Group Policy or custom registry key changes. The LMZ Lockdown allows only Administrator Approved behaviors.

- **Download Signed ActiveX Controls**   Determines whether users can download signed ActiveX controls from a page in the specified security zone. You can choose from the following settings:

  - ❑ **Disable**   Prevents all signed controls from downloading. Although this setting greatly enhances the security of Internet Explorer, it can prevent users from accessing Internet resources they need to use to complete their job functions. You must be an administrator on a computer to install an ActiveX control.

  - ❑ **Enable**   Downloads valid signed controls without user intervention and prompts users to choose whether to download signed controls that have been revoked or have expired.

  - ❑ **Prompt**   Prompts users to choose whether to download controls signed by publishers that are not trusted. Controls signed by trusted publishers are silently downloaded even if this option is selected.

- **Download Unsigned ActiveX Controls**   Determines whether users can download unsigned ActiveX controls from the zone. Unsigned controls are potentially harmful, especially when they come from an untrusted Web site. You can choose from the following settings:

  - ❑ **Disable**   Prevents unsigned controls from running. You should always disable the downloading of unsigned ActiveX controls.

  - ❑ **Enable**   Runs unsigned controls without user intervention.

  - ❑ **Prompt**   Prompts users to choose whether to allow the unsigned control to run. You should enable this setting only for the Trusted Sites or My Computer zone when you have a specific reason, such as testing an ActiveX control in the development process.

- **Initialize And Script ActiveX Controls Not Marked As Safe**   ActiveX controls are classified as either *trusted* or *untrusted*. This option controls whether a script can interact with untrusted controls in the security zone. Untrusted controls are not meant for use on Internet pages, but some Web sites might require them. Object safety should be enforced unless you can trust all ActiveX controls and scripts on pages in the zone. You can set this option to one of the following:

    - ❑ **Disable**   Enforces object safety for untrusted data or scripts. ActiveX controls that cannot be trusted are not loaded with parameters or scripted.

    - ❑ **Enable**   Overrides object safety. ActiveX controls are run, loaded with parameters, and scripted without setting object safety for untrusted data or scripts. This setting is not recommended, except for secure and administered zones. This setting causes Internet Explorer to initialize and script both untrusted and trusted controls and to ignore the Script ActiveX Controls Marked Safe For Scripting option, thus removing all security for controls not marked as safe.

    - ❑ **Prompt**   Attempts to enforce object safety. However, if ActiveX controls cannot be made safe for untrusted data or scripts, users are given the option of allowing the control to be loaded with parameters or to be scripted.

- **Run ActiveX Controls And Plug-Ins**   Determines whether Internet Explorer can run ActiveX controls and plug-ins from pages in the security zone. You can set this option to one of the following:

    - ❑ **Administrator Approved**   Runs only those controls and plug-ins that you have approved for your users. To select the list of approved controls and plug-ins, use Internet Explorer System Policies And Restrictions. The Control Management category of policies enables you to manage these controls.

    - ❑ **Disable**   Prevents controls and plug-ins from running.

    - ❑ **Enable**   Runs controls and plug-ins without user intervention.

    - ❑ **Prompt**   Prompts users to choose whether to allow the controls or plug-ins to run.

- **Script ActiveX Controls Marked Safe For Scripting**   Determines whether an ActiveX control that is marked safe for scripting can interact with a script. This option affects only controls that are loaded with *<param>* tags. You can choose from the following settings:

    - ❑ **Disable**   Prevents script interaction.

    - ❑ **Enable**   Allows script interaction without user intervention.

    - ❑ **Prompt**   Prompts users to choose whether to allow script interaction.

Download Options

The Download options specify how Internet Explorer downloads files and fonts. These are the options:

- **Automatic Prompting For File Downloads**   Determines whether users are always prompted before downloading any type of file. You can choose from the following settings:

  - ❑ **Disable**   The Attachment Execution Service (AES) does not prompt users before downloading each file.

  - ❑ **Enable**   Users are always prompted before downloading a file. The Attachment Execution Service (AES) evaluates the danger associated with the file type and provides users with help determining whether they should download the file in addition to checking the signature of files signed with Authenticode. Additionally, because AES stores information on which security zone the file was downloaded from in an alternate data stream, users continue to be prompted before later running the file unless it has been signed by a trusted publisher. You can disable the retention of zone information in files downloaded by Internet Explorer by configuring the Group Policy option Do Not Preserve Zone Information In File Attachments.

- **File Download**   Controls whether file downloads are permitted based on the security zone of the Web page that contains the download link, not the zone from which the file originated. You can set this option to one of the following settings:

  - ❑ **Disable**   Prevents files from being downloaded from the zone
  - ❑ **Enable**   Allows files to be downloaded from the zone

- **Font Download**   Determines whether Web pages within the zone can download HTML fonts. You can set this option to one of the following settings:

  - ❑ **Disable**   Prevents HTML fonts from being downloaded
  - ❑ **Enable**   Downloads HTML fonts without user intervention
  - ❑ **Prompt**   Prompts users to choose whether to allow the download of HTML fonts

Miscellaneous Options

The Miscellaneous options control whether users can access data sources across domains, submit data by using nonencrypted forms, launch applications and files from *IFRAME* elements, install desktop items, drag and drop files, copy and paste files, and access software channel features from this zone. These are the options:

- **Access Data Sources Across Domains**   Specifies whether components that connect to data sources should be allowed to connect to a different server to obtain data. You can set this option to one of the following settings:
    - ❑ **Disable**   Allows database access only in the same domain as the Web page
    - ❑ **Enable**   Allows database access to any source, including other domains
    - ❑ **Prompt**   Prompts users before allowing database access to any source in other domains

- **Allow META REFRESH**   Specifies whether Web pages can use meta-refreshes to reload pages after a preset delay. You can set this option to one of the following settings:
    - ❑ **Disable**   Prevents Web pages from using meta-refreshes
    - ❑ **Enable**   Allows Web pages to use meta-refreshes

- **Allow Scripting Of Internet Explorer Webbrowser Control**   Determines whether Web pages can use scripts to access the Webbrowser control. The Webbrowser control is the control in Internet Explorer that renders the Internet Explorer user interface and content that appears in the interface. Developers can also use the Webbrowser control in custom applications that access Web sites when writing their own Web browser from scratch. To prevent malicious code running on a Web site from changing the Internet Explorer interface, this setting was added in Windows XP SP2 and Windows Server 2003 SP1. You can choose from the following settings:
    - ❑ **Disable**   Prevents Web pages from using scripts to access the Webbrowser control. All preconfigured zones are set to disabled.
    - ❑ **Enable**   Allows Web pages to access the Webbrowser control through scripting. You should enable this control only if you have a specific application that requires it.

- **Allow Script-Initiated Windows Without Size Or Position Constraints**   Determines whether scripts running on Web pages can create pop-up windows that exceed the viewable size of the display. If enabled, this option also allows windows that block out all toolbars, the Start button, and taskbar or pop-up windows that are positioned in specific places on the screen that cover error messages for toolbars. These techniques are often used to trick users into installing spyware. You can set this option to one of the following:

  - **Disable**   Prevents scripts running on Web pages from spawning pop-up windows that have the following characteristics:

    - Extend above the top or below the bottom of the parent window

    - Overlap the parent window horizontally

    - Stay with the parent window if the parent window moves

    - Appear above the parent windows so that other windows (such as dialog boxes) are hidden

  - **Enable**   Allows scripts running on Web pages from spawning pop-up windows unconstrained

- **Allow Web Pages To Use Restricted Protocols For Active Content**   Determines whether a Web page accessed through a protocol restricted in a particular security zone can run active content such as script, ActiveX, or binary behaviors. You can add additional protocols to the restricted list in Group Policy. You can set this option to one of the following settings:

  - **Disable**   Prevents prohibited protocols from being used by Web sites

  - **Enable**   Allows any protocol for active content

- **Display Mixed Content**   Specifies whether Web pages can display content from both secure and nonsecure servers in the same window. You can set this option to one of the following settings:

  - **Disable**   Prevents Web pages from displaying nonsecure content.

  - **Enable**   Allows Web pages to display both secure and nonsecure content.

  - **Prompt**   Prompts users before allowing Web pages to display both secure and nonsecure content. You should set this option to prompt you when not everything on the Web site you are viewing is secured by SSL or TLS.

- **Don't Prompt For Client Certificate Selection When No Certificates Or Only One Certificate Exists**   Specifies whether users are prompted to select a certificate when no trusted certificate or only one trusted certificate has been installed on the computer. You can choose from the following settings:

  - **Disable**   Allows users to be prompted for a certificate

  - **Enable**   Prevents users from being prompted for a certificate

- **Drag And Drop Or Copy And Paste Files**   Controls whether users can drag and drop files or copy and paste them from Web pages within the zone. You can set this option to one of these settings:

    - **Disable**   Prevents users from dragging and dropping files or copying and pasting them from the security zone

    - **Enable**   Enables users to drag and drop files or copy and paste them from the security zone without being prompted

    - **Prompt**   Prompts users to choose whether they can drag and drop files or copy and paste them from the security zone

- **Installation Of Desktop Items**   Controls whether users can install desktop items from Web pages within the zone. You can choose one of these settings:

    - **Disable**   Prevents users from installing desktop items from this zone

    - **Enable**   Enables users to install desktop items from this zone without being prompted

    - **Prompt**   Prompts users to choose whether they can install desktop items from this zone

- **Launching Programs And Files In An** *IFRAME*   Controls whether users can launch programs and files from an *IFRAME* element (containing a directory or folder reference) in Web pages within the zone. You can choose from these settings:

    - **Disable**   Prevents programs from running and files from downloading from *IFRAME* elements on Web pages in the zone

    - **Enable**   Runs programs and downloads files from *IFRAME* elements on Web pages in the zone without user intervention

    - **Prompt**   Prompts users to choose whether to run programs and download files from *IFRAME* elements on Web pages in the zone

- **Navigate Subframes Across Different Domains**   Controls whether readers of a Web page can navigate the subframe of a window with a top-level document that resides in a different domain. You can set this option to one of the following settings:

    - **Disable**   Allows users to navigate only among Web page subframes that reside in the same domain

    - **Enable**   Allows users to navigate among all Web page subframes, regardless of the domain, without being prompted

    - **Prompt**   Prompts users to choose whether to navigate among Web page subframes that reside in different domains

- **Open Files Based On Content, Not File Extension**   Determines whether Internet Explorer checks the Multipurpose Internet Mail Extensions (MIME) type associated with the file extension of a file being downloaded or run instead of simply trusting the file extension and opening the file with default application mapping in the registry. You can choose from the following settings:

  - ❑ **Disable**   Opens the file with the application specified in the file extension mapping in the registry.

  - ❑ **Enable**   Checks the MIME type of the file to determine which application to use when opening the file.

- **Software Channel Permissions**   Controls the permissions given to software distribution channels. You can set this option to any of the following:

  - ❑ **High Safety**   Prevents users from being notified about software updates by e-mail, prevents software packages from being automatically downloaded to users' computers, and prevents software packages from being automatically installed on users' computers.

  - ❑ **Low Safety**   Notifies users about software updates by e-mail, allows software packages to be automatically downloaded to users' computers, and allows software packages to be automatically installed on users' computers.

  - ❑ **Medium Safety**   Notifies users about software updates by e-mail and allows software packages to be automatically downloaded to (but not installed on) users' computers. The software packages must be validly signed; users are not prompted about the download.

- **Submit Nonencrypted Form Data**   Determines whether HTML pages in the zone can submit forms to or accept them from servers in the zone. Forms sent with SSL encryption are always allowed; this setting affects only data that is submitted by non-SSL forms. You can choose from the following settings:

  - ❑ **Disable**   Prevents information from forms on HTML pages in the zone from being submitted

  - ❑ **Enable**   Allows information from forms on HTML pages in the zone to be submitted without user intervention

  - ❑ **Prompt**   Prompts users to choose whether to allow information from forms on HTML pages in the zone to be submitted

- **Use Pop-up Blocker**   Determines whether the built-in Pop-up Blocker is enabled. You can choose from the following settings:

  - ❑ **Disable**   Disables the built-in Pop-up Blocker

  - ❑ **Enable**   Enables the built-in Pop-up Blocker

- **Userdata Persistence**   Determines whether a Web page can save on the computer a small file of personal information associated with the page. You can set this option to one of the following settings:
    - ❑ **Disable**   Prevents a Web page from saving a small file of personal information to the computer
    - ❑ **Enable**   Allows a Web page to save a small file of personal information to the computer
- **Web Sites In Less Privileged Web Content Zone Can Navigate Into This Zone**   Determines whether Web sties running in a security zone with higher security requirements can change the security zone to one with less security, for instance, running content from the Internet zone in the Local Intranet zone. You can choose from the following settings:
    - ❑ **Disable**   Allows a Web site to run context in a more permissive security context
    - ❑ **Enable**   Prevents a Web site from running in a more permissive security context

Scripting Options

The Scripting options specify how Internet Explorer handles scripts embedded in Web pages:

- **Active Scripting**   Determines whether Internet Explorer can run script code on Web pages in the zone. You can set this option to one of the following settings:
    - ❑ **Disable**   Prevents scripts from running
    - ❑ **Enable**   Runs scripts without user intervention
    - ❑ **Prompt**   Prompts users about whether to allow the scripts to run
- **Allow Paste Operations Via Script**   Determines whether a Web page can cut, copy, and paste information using the Clipboard. You can choose one of the following settings:
    - ❑ **Disable**   Prevents a Web page from cutting, copying, and pasting information using the Clipboard
    - ❑ **Enable**   Allows a Web page to cut, copy, and paste information using the Clipboard without user intervention
    - ❑ **Prompt**   Prompts users about whether to allow a Web page to cut, copy, or paste information using the Clipboard

■ **Scripting Of Java Applets**   Determines whether scripts within the zone can use objects that exist within Java applets. This capability allows a script on a Web page to interact with a Java applet. You can set this option to one of these settings:

❏ **Disable**   Prevents scripts from accessing applets

❏ **Enable**   Allows scripts to access applets without user intervention

❏ **Prompt**   Prompts users about whether to allow scripts to access applets

User Authentication Option

Only one User Authentication option exists: the Logon option. This option controls how HTTP user authentication is handled. Logon has the following settings:

■ **Anonymous Logon**   Disables HTTP authentication and uses the Guest account only for authentication by using the Common Internet File System (CIFS) protocol.

■ **Automatic Logon Only In Intranet Zone**   Prompts users for user IDs and passwords in security zones other than the Local Intranet zone. After users are prompted, these values can be used for the remainder of the session without user interaction.

■ **Automatic Logon With Current User Name And Password**   Attempts logon by using NT LAN Manager (NTLM) authentication. If NTLM is supported by the server, the logon uses the network user name and password for logon. If the server does not support NTLM, users are prompted to provide their user names and passwords. You should use this setting only for sites in the Intranet zone.

■ **Prompt For User Name And Password**   Always prompts users for user IDs and passwords. User names and passwords are cached for the remainder of the session.

Global Security Settings

In addition to the security settings in security zones, some global security settings apply to all security zones when using Internet Explorer. You can configure these global options in the Advanced tab of the Internet Options dialog box. Here are the security settings in the Advanced tab and their default values:

■ **Allow Active Content From CDs To Run On My Computer**   Allows active content to be run automatically from CDs without prompting the user as would normally happen for other active content being run from the LMZ. This setting is not enabled by default.

- **Allow Active Content To Run Files In My Computer**   Runs active content from the local computer without prompting the user. This setting is not enabled by default.

- **Allow Software To Run Or Install Even If Signature Is Invalid**   Runs or installs software even if the digital signature is invalid. This setting is not enabled by default. Active content with invalid signatures is prevented from running or being installed regardless of security zone settings.

- **Check For Publisher's Certificate Revocation**   Checks the certificate revocation list (CRL) for the status of a software publisher's certificate when downloading ActiveX controls. This option is enabled by default.

- **Check For Server Certificate Revocation**   Checks the CRL for Web sites that require SSL or TLS. Enabling this option might cause a slight delay in connecting to secure Web sites but adds to the security of browsing the Internet. This option is disabled by default.

- **Check For Signatures On Downloaded Programs**   Verifies the digital signatures on ActiveX controls. This option is enabled by default.

- **Do Not Save Encrypted Pages To Disk**   Ensures that no Web pages or parts of Web pages viewed in a secure session are saved in the Temporary Internet Files folder. This option should be enabled on all public computers or computers with high security requirements. This option is disabled by default.

- **Empty Temporary Internet Files Folder When Browser Is Closed**   Deletes the contents of the Temporary Internet Files folder each time the Web browser is closed. This option should be enabled on all public computers or computers with high security requirements. This option is disabled by default.

- **Enable Integrated Windows Authentication**   Ensures that only NTLM-based authentication methods are used to authenticate users if prompted by the Web server. This option is enabled by default.

- **Enable Profile Assistant**   Allows you to use the Profile Assistant to store and maintain personal information. This option is enabled by default.

- **Use SSL 2.0**   Allows the use of SSL 2.0 to create secure channels. This option is enabled by default.

- **Use SSL 3.0**   Allows the use of SSL 3.0 to create secure channels. This option is enabled by default.

- **Use TLS 1.0**   Allows the use of TLS 1.0 to create secure channels. This option is disabled by default.

- **Warn About Invalid Site Certificates**   Presents a message box to users, warning them that the secure Web site they are connecting to is using a certificate that is no longer valid. This option is enabled by default.

- **Warn If Changing Between Secure And Not Secure Methods**   Presents a message box to users, warning them that they are moving between Web sites that are either secure or not secure. This option is disabled by default.

- **Warn If Forms Submittal Is Being Redirected**   Presents a message box to users, warning them that Internet Explorer is being redirected to another Web site or location to retrieve content. This option is enabled by default.

Enhanced Security Configuration in Windows Server 2003

One of the most obvious changes in Windows Server 2003 is the addition of Enhanced Security Configuration (ESC), which locks down Internet Explorer to help prevent administrators from casually misusing Internet browsing capabilities on servers. ESC prompts users to add the URLs of sites they would like to open to the Trusted Sites list. Users are prompted to add to the Trusted Sites list each time they enter a URL in the Address bar that is not already on the Trusted Sites list. Additionally, the default security zone templates are preset to a higher level of security than in Windows 2000 or Windows XP. The security zones in ESC are configured to use the default zone templates listed in Table 12-2.

Table 12-2   Default Security Zone Templates in ESC

Security Zone	Default Security Zone Template
LMZ	LMZ Lockdown
Local Intranet	Medium-Low
Trusted Sites	Medium
Internet	High
Restricted Sites	High

Additionally the following settings from the Advanced tab of the Internet Options dialog box are configured to more secure defaults than Windows XP or Windows 2000:

- Browsing
  - Enable Third-Party Browser Extensions: Not enabled
  - Enable Install On Demand (Internet Explorer): Not enabled
  - Enable Install On Demand (Other): Not enabled

- Multimedia
  - Don't Display Online Content In The Media Bar: Enabled
  - Play Sounds In Web Pages: Not enabled
  - Play Animations In Web Pages: Not enabled
  - Play Videos In Web Pages: Not enabled

- Security

    ❑ Check For Server Certificate Revocation: Enabled

    ❑ Check For Signatures On Downloaded Programs: Enabled

    ❑ Do Not Save Encrypted Pages To Disk: Enabled

    ❑ Empty Temporary Internet Files Folder When Browser Is Closed: Enabled

> **More Info**   For more information on managing the ESC for servers running Windows Server 2003, see the "Managing Internet Explorer Enhanced Security Configuration" white paper at *http://www.microsoft.com/downloads/details.aspx? FamilyID=d41b036c-e2e1-4960-99bb-9757f7e9e31b&displaylang=en.*

Configuring Privacy and Security Settings in Internet Explorer

You can configure privacy and security settings in Internet Explorer manually in the Internet Options dialog box from the Tools menu during installation by using the Internet Explorer Administration Kit (IEAK), or by using Group Policy.

> **More Info**   The IEAK is beyond the scope of this book, but you can get more information about it from the IEAK Web site at *http://www.microsoft.com/windows /ieak/default.asp.*

Group Policy enables you to centrally configure and manage Internet Explorer security on a per-user basis. You can use Group Policy to manage the privacy and security settings in Internet Explorer on a per-user basis and control whether users can change settings on a per-user basis or a per-computer basis. To configure Internet Explorer privacy and security settings through Group Policy, open the Microsoft Management Console (MMC) on a computer running Windows XP or Windows Server 2003 and add the Group Policy snap-in. If you create a Group Policy object (GPO) in Windows 2000, you might not have the settings that were added in Windows XP SP2 or Windows Server 2003 SP1.

After importing the security zones and privacy settings from the computer on which you are editing the GPO, you can modify the settings and apply the GPO to a site, domain, or OU containing the user accounts that should be subject to the privacy and security settings. You can also export the settings into .ins and .cab files for use with the IEAK.

In addition to configuring the privacy and security zone settings and templates to be used for each zone, as a network administrator you can configure whether the user can modify Internet Explorer security settings in the user-related portion of Group Policy by selecting the Administrative Templates menu option, Windows Components, and then Internet Explorer.

Best Practices

- **Educate users.**   The best defense against e-mail viruses and Web viruses is to educate users about how to use the Internet safely. You should teach users how to answer common prompts relating to ActiveX controls and macros.

- **Install and maintain antivirus software.**   Keeping antivirus software up to date is especially critical on computers where users have the ability to download and run files from untrusted sources on the Internet.

- **Apply security updates.**   Always apply the latest security updates to any application that you use on your network, including Internet Explorer.

- **Do not browse the Internet from high-value computers or with high-value credentials.**   Browsing the Internet from high-value computers, such as servers, or with high-value accounts, such as a domain Administrator's account, can unnecessarily expose your network to risk. Use other computers and lower-value accounts to browse the Internet.

- **Implement secure default settings.**   Use the IEAK and Group Policy to install and maintain default security settings for Internet Explorer.

Additional Information

- "Changes to Functionality in Microsoft Windows XP Service Pack 2" white paper (*http://www.microsoft.com/technet/prodtechnol/winxppro/maintain/sp2brows.mspx*)

- "Application Compatibility Testing and Mitigation Guide for Windows XP Service Pack 2 (SP2)" white paper (*http://www.microsoft.com/technet/prodtechnol/winxppro/deploy/appcom/apcmitig.mspx*)

- "Managing Windows XP Service Pack 2 Features Using Group Policy" white paper (*http://www.microsoft.com/technet/prodtechnol/winxppro/maintain/mangxpsp2/mngieps.mspx*)

- "Enhanced Security Configuration for Internet Explorer" (*http://msdn.microsoft.com/workshop/security/szone/overview/esc_changes.asp*)

- Internet Explorer Administration Kit (IEAK) home page (*http://www.microsoft.com/windows/ieak/default.asp*)

- Knowledge Base article 182569: "Description of Internet Explorer Security Zones Registry Entries" (*http://support.microsoft.com/kb/182569*)

- Knowledge Base article 296287: "Port Numbers Are Missing from URL of Web Sites Assigned to Security Zones" (*http://support.microsoft.com/kb/296287*)

- Knowledge Base article 283185: "How to Manage Cookies in Internet Explorer 6" (*http://support.microsoft.com/kb/283185*)

- Knowledge Base article 300443: "A Description of the Changes to the Security Settings of the Web Content Zones in Internet Explorer 6" (*http://support.microsoft.com/kb/300443*)

Chapter 13

Managing Microsoft Office XP Security and Privacy

Microsoft Office XP provides several methods for managing application and document security. A basic understanding of how the Office XP security features work can help you create a secure environment for your users' applications and data. The primary areas for Office XP security are Microsoft ActiveX and macros security.

Configuring ActiveX and Macros Security

Office XP enables you to configure security for ActiveX controls and macros that are signed using Microsoft Authenticode. Office XP verifies that the control or macro code remains unchanged after being signed with a digital certificate. Signing controls and macros also provides assurance that they originated from the signer.

ActiveX controls are used to add dynamic or interactive content and functionality to Office XP documents. When the ActiveX security controls are active or when a user attempts to load an unregistered ActiveX control, the Office XP application checks to see whether the control has been digitally signed by a trusted provider.

Macros are used to complete a series of application commands and instructions that are grouped together as a single command to accomplish a task automatically. Many viruses attempt to exploit macro features in Microsoft Office applications. In many cases, a user need only open an infected file to launch the attack embedded in the malicious macro. Thus, you must consider the level of macro security configured on your network.

Signing macros enables you to exercise control over the macros users can run. You can specify that unsigned macros can or cannot run. You can also control which certificates are trusted by Office XP for signing macros. Because the digital certificates that you create yourself are not issued by a formal Certification Authority (CA), macro projects signed by using such a certificate are referred to as *self-signed projects*. Certificates you create yourself are considered unauthenticated and generate warning messages if the security level is set to High or Medium.

You can configure how Office XP applications handle ActiveX controls and macros by configuring the level of macro security in Office XP. Three levels of macro security exist:

- **High Security**   ActiveX controls not signed by a trusted authority will not run.

- **Medium Security**   Users are prompted to accept or reject the digital signature of the control. If the signature is verified, the control is loaded and run.

- **Low Security**   Digital signatures are ignored and the ActiveX controls are run without user intervention. You should configure this setting only if you have specific technical reasons for doing so.

> **Note**   After the control is registered on the user's system, the control no longer displays code-signing dialog boxes asking the user whether the control should be allowed to run. Once a control is installed, it is considered safe, even if it did not have a digital signature when it was installed.

The Office XP Trusted Sources feature enables you to specify that executables must be digitally signed to run on users' computers and that only executables from a list of trusted providers can be executed. Using the Trusted Sources feature requires that a digital certificate be used to sign each executable. The digital signature identifies the source, providing assurance to the user that the code is safe to run.

With Office XP, you can turn the Trusted Sources feature off or create a list of trusted sources as a default. When the use of trusted sources is enabled, any installable code (such as COM add-ins, applets, and executables) is automatically copied to, or run from, the user's computer on the condition that the signature on the code indicates that it came from a trusted source.

You can configure Office XP security settings on computers running Microsoft Windows Server 2003, Windows 2000, and Windows XP by using Group Policy. To add the Administrative Template for Office XP to Group Policy, follow the instructions in Microsoft Knowledge Base article 307732, "How to Add a Windows 2000 ADM Template to a Group Policy Snap-In in Office XP" (*http://support.microsoft.com/kb /307732*). Figure 13-1 shows the computer-related security settings in Group Policy for Office XP.

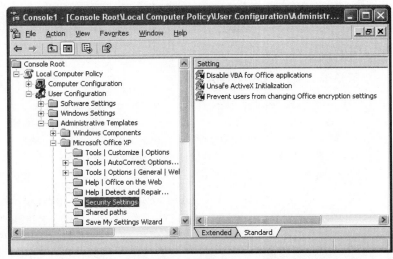

Figure 13-1   Computer-related security settings for Office XP in Group Policy

Protecting Documents in Office XP

Outside of viruses and other malware, preserving the confidentiality and integrity of the content of Office XP might be the most critical area of Office XP security. Office XP provides a number of features to enable varying degrees of protection to documents depending on the level of protection that users require. These features can be grouped into three primary areas:

- Preventing others from reading documents
- Protecting metadata in documents
- Preserving the content of documents

Preventing Others from Reading Documents

Office provides very basic protection of documents through password controls. This protection is not designed to be secure against attackers, but rather an easy-to-use protection scheme to keep nonmalicious coworkers or family from accessing data on shared computers. In reality, the password protection feature is more a deterrent than anything else. Microsoft Word, Excel, and PowerPoint all provide a file open protection feature. This control requires users to enter a password before opening the file. The document is encrypted with the password you set so that it can be opened by only those who know the password.

If you require protection against attackers, a file encryption protocol, such as the encrypting file system (EFS), is more appropriate. See Chapter 8, "Controlling Access to Data" for detailed information on using EFS.

Protecting Metadata in Documents

Along with the text of Word, Excel, or PowerPoint documents a certain amount of metadata is also stored. Some of this metadata is easy to see in the user interface, such as information stored in the document properties. Other information is hidden from plain sight, including hidden text, and still other types of data, such as previous versions, are accessible only through low-level binary analysis tools.

If you share documents with people, you might want to remove metadata, such as comments and previously changed or deleted text. You also might want to protect your privacy as the author of a document by removing the author information. In Word, Excel, PowerPoint, and Publisher, you can remove author information by choosing Options on the Tools menu, clicking the Security tab, and then enabling the Remove Personal Information From File Properties On Save option. Information in the Author, Manager, and Company document properties will be removed as will the author's name in comments and in tracked changes. Enabling this setting does not remove fields in headers and footers or recorded macros. It also does not remove text or areas that have been hidden, customized properties, or links to other data sources that might contain personal authentication information. Additionally, you might want to accept all changes and delete all comments from documents before sharing them outside your company or with anyone who should not have access to draft text or comments. In the Security tab of the Options dialog box of a document you can select the Warn Before Printing, Saving, Or Sending A File That Contains Tracked Changes Or Comments option to help alert users to the presence of previous revisions.

Microsoft also provides a more robust metadata removal tool on the Microsoft Web site. You can download the add-in to remove hidden data from Office documents from the Download Center at *http://www.microsoft.com/downloads/details.aspx?FamilyID=144e54ed-d43e-42ca-bc7b-5446d34e5360&displaylang=en*. Once installed, you can use the Remove Hidden Data add-in to remove metadata from documents by selecting Remove Hidden Data from the File menu in an open document, or you can run the tool from the command line.

Preserving the Content of Documents

Word, Excel, and PowerPoint documents are frequently shared among users who are collaborating on a project or within a company. Not all of a document's readers should have the capability of changing content within the document. Word, Excel, and PowerPoint each allow you to set a password for read-only access to a document. Once set, only users who know the password can make changes to the document.

Additionally, when protecting the document, you can opt to allow read-only users to make changes to the document with Track Changes automatically enabled. All changes are tracked so that the author can see the changes and choose whether to accept or reject them. When a document is protected in this way, users cannot turn off tracking and they cannot accept or reject tracked changes to the following items:

- **Comments**   When selected, this option allows a user to insert comments but does not allow the user to change the contents of the document.

- **Forms**   When selected, this option protects the document from changes except in form fields or unprotected sections.

- **Sections**   When selected, this option allows you to turn on protection for a specific section within the document. By enabling protection using both the Forms and Sections settings, you can create a multisection document that contains forms and instructions and that allows users to change content in some areas while protecting other areas. In Excel, you can protect any part of a spreadsheet.

If your organization distributes information in Office XP documents, you also might want to digitally sign the document. A digital signature provides the identity of the author, assuming she has protected her private key and the integrity of the file at the time it was signed. To add a digital signature to a document, click Digital Signatures in the Security tab of the Options dialog box in a document and select a certificate with which to sign the document. After a document is signed, a red ribbon appears in the status bar at the bottom of the document window.

Configuring Security for Outlook 2002

Arguably, the biggest security threats to most computers are e-mail viruses and Web viruses. Although user education and antivirus software are the best defenses against these viruses, you can also configure the security in Outlook 2002 to help prevent attacks from these threats. Default settings for security can be created during deployment by using the Custom Installation Wizard (CIW). After the deployment, the security settings can be maintained and updated by using the Custom Maintenance Wizard (CMW). However, the CIW and CMW do not provide any policy enforcement. For policy enforcement, you can use Group Policy.

Attachment Security

Code attached to e-mail messages can contain worms or viruses. After one machine is infected with a worm or virus, the nature of networked e-mail systems allows these rogue applications to propagate themselves rapidly. To protect against virus infection, Outlook checks the file type of each message attachment against an internally maintained list of attachment file types. Administrators can also specify a list in a Microsoft

Exchange public folder so that specific Outlook clients in an organization have a custom list. Each file type on the list is assigned one of these levels:

- **Level 1**   File types, such as .bat, .exe, .vbs, and .js, are blocked by Outlook, and users cannot view or execute the attachment. A message is displayed to the user, letting him know about the blocked attachments. In addition, when you send an attachment that has a Level 1 file type extension, a message displays to warn you that Outlook recipients might not be able to access this type of attachment. Outlook XP Server Pack 3 adds the file types .asp, .tmp, .vsmacros, .vss, .vst, .vsw, and .ws to the Level 1 file attachment handling.

- **Level 2**   This level applies to file types that you configure. You will be able to see the icon for the attachment. When you double-click this icon, you are prompted to save the attachment to your hard disk, but you cannot run the file directly from its location. After you have saved the attachment, you can decide how to handle it.

When you try to open an attachment other than those in the "unsafe" or the Level 2 lists, you are prompted to either open the file directly or to save it to a disk. When you are prompted, you have the option to turn off future prompts for that file name extension if you click to clear the Always Ask Before Opening This Type Of File check box.

Protecting HTML Messages

To protect against viruses that might be contained in HTML messages you receive, you can use the default security zone in Outlook 2002: Restricted Sites. When you use this security zone, scripts in HTML-formatted e-mail messages will not run and ActiveX controls will be deactivated. You also should consider turning off JavaScript to protect against malicious exploits that are based on JavaScript. However, note that doing so can reduce some mail functionality when you are reading mail sent by users or organizations that depend on embedded JavaScript. You can turn off JavaScript by customizing the security options in the Restricted Sites zone to disable JavaScript or by prompting users to choose Active Scripting.

Best Practices

- **Educate users.**   The best defense against e-mail viruses and Web viruses is to educate users about how to use the Internet safely. You should teach users how to answer common prompts relating to ActiveX controls and macros.

- **Install and maintain antivirus software.**   By keeping antivirus software up to date, you will be protected from nearly all known attacks on Office applications and documents.

- **Apply security updates.**   Always apply the latest security updates to any application that you use on your network, including Microsoft Internet Explorer and Office.

- **Implement secure default settings.**   Use the CIW to install security default settings for Office XP.

- **Use Group Policy to manage security settings.**   Import the Administrative Templates included with the *Microsoft Office XP Resource Kit* (Microsoft Press, 2001) into Group Policy and configure the security settings for Office applications that users work with on your network.

- **Do not install software that will not be used.**   Do not install applications on computers if they will not be used. For example, if a user will be using only Word and Outlook, do not install PowerPoint and Excel on his computer, which would increase the potential attack surface of the computer.

Additional Information

- *Microsoft Office XP Resource Kit/Toolbox*, including downloadable deployment and maintenance tools (*http://office.microsoft.com/en-us/assistance /HA011362751033.aspx*)

- The following Knowledge Base articles:

    - 308983: "How to Specify Trusted Sources for Digital Certificates in Excel 2002, PowerPoint 2002, and Word 2002" (*http://support.microsoft.com /kb/308983*)

    - 300443: "A Description of the Changes to the Security Settings of the Web Content Zones in Internet Explorer 6" (*http://support.microsoft.com/kb /300443*)

- ❑ 287567: "Considerations for Disabling VBA in Office XP" (*http://support.microsoft.com/kb/287567*)

- ❑ 822924: "Description of Office Features That Are Intended to Enable Collaboration and That Are Not Intended to Increase Security" (*http://support.microsoft.com/kb/822924*)

- ❑ 290945: "How to Minimize Metadata in Word 2002" (*http://support.microsoft.com/kb/290945*)

- ❑ 223789: "How to Minimize Metadata in Microsoft Excel Workbooks" (*http://support.microsoft.com/kb/223789*)

- ❑ 314800: "How to Minimize the Amount of Metadata in PowerPoint 2002 Presentations" (*http://support.microsoft.com/kb/314800*)

- ❑ 829982: "Cannot open attachments in Microsoft Outlook" (*http://support.microsoft.com/kb/829982*)

- ❑ 253396: "How to Reduce the Chances of Macro Virus Infection" (*http://support.microsoft.com/kb/253396*)

- ❑ 211607: "Frequently Asked Questions About Word Macro Viruses" (*http://support.microsoft.com/kb/211607*)

- ❑ 307732: "How to add a Windows 2000 ADM template to a Group Policy snap-in in Office XP" (*http://support.microsoft.com/kb/307732*)

- ■ "Help Protect Word 2002 and Excel 2002 Files with Passwords"

    (*http://office.microsoft.com/en-us/assistance/HA010429211033.aspx*)

- ■ Office 2003/XP add-in: Remove Hidden Data (*http://www.microsoft.com /downloads/details.aspx?familyid=144e54ed-d43e-42ca-bc7b-5446d34e5360 &displaylang=en*)

Chapter 14

Managing Microsoft Office System 2003 Security and Privacy

Microsoft Office System 2003 provides several methods for managing application and document security. A basic understanding of how the Office System 2003 security features work can help you create a secure environment for your users' applications and data. The primary areas for Office System 2003 security are Microsoft ActiveX and macros security.

Configuring ActiveX and Macros Security

Office System 2003 enables you to configure security for ActiveX controls and macros that are signed using Microsoft Authenticode. Office System 2003 verifies that the control or macro code remains unchanged after being signed with a digital certificate. Signing controls and macros also provides assurance that they originated from the signer.

ActiveX controls are used to add dynamic or interactive content and functionality to Office System 2003 documents. When the ActiveX security controls are active or when a user attempts to load an unregistered ActiveX control, the Office System 2003 application checks to see whether the control has been digitally signed by a trusted provider.

Macros are used to complete a series of application commands and instructions that are grouped together as a single command to accomplish a task automatically. Many viruses attempt to exploit macro features in Office applications. In many cases, a user need only open an infected file to launch the attack embedded in the malicious macro. Thus, you must consider the level of macro security configured on your network.

Signing macros enables you to exercise control over the macros users can run. You can specify that unsigned macros can or cannot run. You can also control which certificates are trusted by Office System 2003 for signing macros. Because the digital certificates that you create yourself are not issued by a formal Certification Authority (CA), macro projects signed by using such a certificate are referred to as *self-signed projects*. Certificates you create yourself are considered unauthenticated and generate warning messages if the security level is set to High or Medium.

You can configure how Office System 2003 applications handle ActiveX controls and macros by configuring the level of macro security. Office System 2003 has four levels of macro security, which are described in Table 14-1.

Table 14-1   Macro Security Levels in Office System 2003

Macro Security Level	Trust All Installed Add-Ins And Templates Option	Macro Digitally Signed?	Macro from Trusted Publisher?	Excel, PowerPoint, and Word Will:
Very High	Not selected	Yes or No	Yes or No	Disable all macros, COM add-ins, and smart tag .dlls. This might interfere with some processes in Office.
High	Not selected	Yes	Yes	Run the add-in or macro silently.
		Yes	No	Open the Security Warning dialog box so that you can choose to enable or disable macros.
		No	N/A	Disable add-ins or macros.
Medium	Not selected	Yes	Yes	Run the add-in or macro silently.
		Yes	No	Open the Security Warning dialog box so that you can choose to enable or disable macros.
		No	N/A	Open the Security Warning dialog box so that you can choose to enable or disable macros.
Low	Not selected	Yes or No	Yes or No	Run the add-in or macro silently.
Very High, High, Medium, or Low	Selected	Yes or No	Yes or No	Run all add-ins silently. Macros will be run silently if they are in the User Templates folder, Workgroup Templates folder, or Startup folder.
				Other macros will be picked up according to the security settings described in this table.

Note   After the control is registered on the user's system, the control no longer displays code-signing dialog boxes asking the user whether the control should be allowed to run. Once a control is installed, it is considered safe, even if it did not have a digital signature when it was installed.

The Office System 2003 Trusted Sources feature enables you to specify that executables must be digitally signed to run on users' computers and that only executables from a list of trusted providers can be executed. Using the Trusted Sources feature requires that a digital certificate be used to sign each executable. The digital signature identifies the source, providing assurance to the user that the code is safe to run.

With Office System 2003, you can turn the Trusted Sources feature off or create a list of trusted sources as a default. When the use of trusted sources is enabled, any installable code (such as COM add-ins, applets, and executables) is automatically copied to, or run from, the user's computer on the condition that the signature on the code indicates that it came from a trusted source.

You can configure Office System 2003 security settings on computers running Microsoft Windows Server 2003, Windows 2000, and Windows XP by using Group Policy. To add the Administrative Templates files for Office System 2003 to Group Policy, follow the instructions in "Office 2003 Policy Template Files and Deployment Planning Tools" (*http://office.microsoft.com/en-us/assistance/ha011513711033.aspx*).

Protecting Documents in Office System 2003

Outside of viruses and other malware, preserving the confidentiality and integrity of the content of Office System 2003 might be the most critical area of Office System 2003 security. Office System 2003 provides a number of features to enable varying degrees of protection to documents depending on the level of protection that users require. These features can be grouped into three primary areas:

- Preventing others from reading documents
- Protecting metadata in documents
- Preserving the content of documents

Preventing Others from Reading Documents

Office provides very basic protection of documents through password controls. This protection is not designed to be secure against attackers, but rather an easy-to-use protection scheme to keep nonmalicious coworkers or family from accessing data on shared computers. In reality, the password protection feature is more a deterrent than anything else. Microsoft Word, Excel, and PowerPoint all provide a file open protection feature. This control requires the user to enter a password before opening the file. The document is encrypted with the password you set so that it can be opened only by those who know the password.

If you require protection against attackers, a file encryption protocol, such as the encrypting file system (EFS), is more appropriate. See Chapter 8, "Controlling Access to Data," for detailed information on using EFS. You can also use Information Rights Management (IRM) in combination with the Windows Rights Management Service (RMS) to control access to documents. IRM enables users to control who can open documents; control how a user can print, copy, or programmatically alter a document; and set expiration time limits. Additionally, RMS administrators can create an audit trail for the document. IRM is an excellent vehicle for written corporate policy enforcement. A complete discussion of IRM and RMS is outside the scope of this book. You can find more information on IRM on the Microsoft Web site at *http:// office.microsoft.com/en-us/assistance/HA011401841033.aspx*.

Protecting Metadata in Documents

Along with the text of a Word, Excel, or PowerPoint document a certain amount of metadata is also stored. Some of this metadata is easy to see in the user interface, such as information stored in the document properties. Other information is hidden from plain sight, including hidden text, and still other types of data, such as previous versions, are accessible only through low-level binary analysis tools.

If you share documents with people, you might want to remove metadata, such as comments and previously changed or deleted text. You also might want to protect your privacy as the author of a document by removing the author information. In Word, Excel, PowerPoint, and Publisher, you can remove author information by choosing Options on the Tools menu, clicking the Security tab, and enabling the Remove Personal Information From File Properties On Save option. Information in the Author, Manager, and Company document properties will be removed as will the author's name in comments and in tracked changes. Enabling this setting does not remove fields in headers and footers. It also does not remove text or areas that have been hidden, customized properties, or links to other data sources that might contain personal authentication information. Additionally, you might want to accept all changes and delete all comments from documents before sharing them outside your company or with anyone who should not have access to draft text or comments. In the

Security tab of the Options dialog box in a document you can select the Warn Before Printing, Saving, Or Sending A File That Contains Tracked Changes Or Comments option to help alert users to the presence of previous revisions. By default, Word also displays all hidden markup text, such as revision marks, when opening and saving documents.

Microsoft also provides a more robust metadata removal tool on its Web site. You can download the add-in to remove hidden data from the Download Center at *http:// www.microsoft.com/downloads/details.aspx?FamilyID=144e54ed-d43e-42ca-bc7b- 5446d34e5360&displaylang=en*. Once installed, you can use the Remove Hidden Data add-in to remove metadata from documents by selecting Remove Hidden Data from the File menu in an open document, or you can run the tool from the command line.

Preserving the Content of Documents

Word, Excel, and PowerPoint documents are frequently shared among users who are collaborating on a project or within a company. Not all of a document's readers should have the capability of changing content within the document. Word, Excel, and PowerPoint each allow you to set a password for read-only access to a document. Once set, only users who know the password can make changes to the document. Additionally, when protecting the document, you can opt to allow read-only users to make changes to the document with Track Changes automatically enabled. All changes are tracked so that the author can see the changes and choose whether to accept or reject them. When a document is protected in this way, users cannot turn off tracking and they cannot accept or reject tracked changes to the following items:

- **Comments**   When selected, this option allows a user to insert comments but does not allow the user to change the contents of the document.

- **Forms**   When selected, this option protects the document from changes except in form fields or unprotected sections.

- **Sections**   When selected, this option allows you to turn on protection for specific sections in the document. By enabling protection using both the Forms and Sections settings, you can create a multisection document that contains forms and instructions and that allows users to change content in some areas while protecting other areas. In Excel, you can protect any part of a spreadsheet.

If your organization distributes information in Office System 2003 documents, you also might want to digitally sign the document. A digital signature provides the identity of the author, assuming she has protected her private key and the integrity of the file at the time it was signed. To add a digital signature to a document, click Digital Signatures in the Security tab of the Options dialog box in a document and select a certificate with which to sign the document. After a document is signed, a red ribbon appears in the status bar at the bottom of the document window.

Configuring Security for Outlook 2003

Arguably, the biggest security threats to most computers are e-mail viruses and Web viruses. Although user education and antivirus software are the best defenses against these viruses, you can also configure the security in Outlook 2003 to help prevent these threats. Default settings for security can be created during deployment by using the Custom Installation Wizard. After the deployment, the security settings can be maintained and updated by using the Custom Maintenance Wizard. However, these wizards do not provide any policy enforcement. For policy enforcement, you can use Group Policy.

Attachment Security

Code attached to e-mail messages can contain worms or viruses. After one machine is infected with a worm or virus, the nature of networked e-mail systems allows these rogue applications to propagate themselves rapidly. To protect against virus infection, Outlook 2003 checks the file type of each message attachment against an internally maintained list of attachment file types. Administrators can also specify a list in a Microsoft Exchange public folder so that specific Outlook clients in an organization have a custom list. Each file type on the list is assigned one of these levels:

- **Level 1**   File types, such as .bat, .exe, .vbs, and .js, are blocked by Outlook, and users cannot view or execute the attachment. A message is displayed to the user, letting him know about the blocked attachments. In addition, when you send an attachment that has a Level 1 file type extension, a message displays to warn you that Outlook recipients might not be able to access this type of attachment. Outlook System 2003 SP1 added the file types .asp, .tmp, .vsmacros, .vss, .vst, .vsw, and .ws to the Level 1 file attachment handling.

- **Level 2**   This level applies to file types that you configure. You will be able to see the icon for the attachment. When you double-click this icon, you are prompted to save the attachment to your hard disk, but you cannot run the file directly from its location. After you have saved the attachment, you can decide how to handle it.

When you try to open an attachment other than those in the "unsafe" or Level 2 lists, you are prompted to either open the file directly or to save it to a disk. When you are prompted, you can turn off future prompts for that file name extension if you clear the Always Ask Before Opening This Type Of File check box.

Protecting HTML Messages

To protect against viruses that might be contained in HTML messages you receive, you can use the default security zone in Outlook 2003: Restricted Sites. When you use this security zone, scripts in HTML-formatted e-mail messages will not run and ActiveX controls will be deactivated. In Outlook 2003, by default graphics in HTML e-mail are displayed only for senders that are in your Safe Senders list, which by default includes everyone in your Exchange organization, your address books, and senders that you have explicitly authorized. You can configure the handling of HTML e-mail by clicking Change Automatic Download Settings in the Security tab of your mailbox's Options dialog box. The Safe Senders list can be configured in the Junk E-mail options by clicking Junk E-mail in the Preferences tab of your mailbox's Options dialog box. In fact, Outlook 2003, through the Junk E-mail options, enables you to configure Outlook so that only e-mail from people on the Safe Senders list will be delivered to your Inbox. All other mail is routed to the Junk E-mail folder or is permanently deleted.

You also should consider turning off JavaScript to protect against malicious exploits that are based on JavaScript. However, note that doing so can reduce some mail functionality when you are reading mail sent by users or organizations that depend on embedded JavaScript. You can turn off JavaScript by customizing the security options in the Restricted Sites zone to disable JavaScript or by prompting users to choose Active Scripting.

Best Practices

- **Educate users.** The best defense against e-mail viruses and Web viruses is to educate users about how to use the Internet safely. You should teach users how to answer common prompts relating to ActiveX controls and macros.

- **Install and maintain antivirus software.** By keeping antivirus software up to date, you will be protected from nearly all known attacks on Office applications and documents.

- **Apply security updates.** Always apply the latest security updates to any application that you use on your network, including Microsoft Internet Explorer and Office.

- **Implement secure default settings.** Use the Custom Installation Wizard to install security default settings for Office System 2003.

- **Use Group Policy to manage security settings.** Import the Administrative Templates included with the *Microsoft Office System 2003 Resource Kit* (Microsoft Press, 2003) into Group Policy and configure the security settings for Office applications that users work with on your network. (*http://office.microsoft.com/en-us/assistance/ha011513711033*)

- **Do not install software that will not be used.** Do not install applications on computers if they will not be used. For example, if a user will be using only Word and Outlook, do not install PowerPoint and Excel on his computer, which would increase the potential attack surface of the computer.

Additional Information

- Microsoft Office System 2003 Resource Kit/Toolbox, including downloadable deployment and maintenance tools (*http://office.microsoft.com/en-us/assistance /HA011402981033.aspx*)

- "Disabling Visual Basic for Applications" (*http://office.microsoft.com/en-us /assistance/ha011403131033.aspx*)

- Office 2003/XP add-in: Remove Hidden Data (*http://www.microsoft.com /downloads/details.aspx?FamilyID=144e54ed-d43e-42ca-bc7b-5446d34e5360&displaylang=en*)

- The following Knowledge Base articles:

  - 308983: "How to Specify Trusted Sources for Digital Certificates in Excel 2002, PowerPoint 2002, and Word 2002" (*http://support.microsoft.com/kb /308983*)

  - 300443: "A Description of the Changes to the Security Settings of the Web Content Zones in Internet Explorer 6" (*http://support.microsoft.com/kb /300443*)

  - 822924: "Description of Office Features That Are Intended to Enable Collaboration and That Are Not Intended to Increase Security" (*http:// support.microsoft.com/kb/822924*)

  - 825576: "How to Minimize Metadata in Word 2003" (*http://support.microsoft.com/kb/825576*)

  - 223789: "How to Minimize Metadata in Microsoft Excel Workbooks" (*http://support.microsoft.com/kb/223789*)

  - 826825: "How to Minimize the Amount of Metadata in PowerPoint 2002 Presentations" (*http://support.microsoft.com/kb/826825*)

  - 831608: "How to Use the Automatic Picture Download Setting Feature to Determine How Outlook 2003 Blocks External HTML Content" (*http://support.microsoft.com/kb/831608*)

  - 829982: "Cannot open attachments in Microsoft Outlook" (*http:// support.microsoft.com/kb/829982*)

  - 233396: "How to Reduce the Chances of Macro Virus Infection" (*http:// support.microsoft.com/kb/233396*)

  - 211607: "Frequently Asked Questions About Word Macro Viruses" (*http://support.microsoft.com/kb/211607*)

Chapter 15
Auditing Microsoft Windows Security Events

No security strategy is complete without a comprehensive auditing strategy. More often than not, organizations learn this the hard way—only after they have experienced a security incident. Without an audit trail of actions made by the intruder, it is almost impossible to investigate a security incident successfully. As part of your overall security strategy, you must determine which events you need to audit, the level of auditing appropriate for your environment, how the audited events will be collected, and how they will be reviewed. Following are several reasons to enable auditing and monitor audit logs:

- To create a baseline for normal network and computer operations

- To detect attempts to break into the network or computer

- To determine which systems and data have been compromised during or after a security incident

In addition, by regularly monitoring audit logs, especially by using automatic event-monitoring software, you can help prevent further damage to networks or computers once an attacker has penetrated the network but has not yet inflicted widespread damage.

Your organization might be subject to industry or government regulations that not only dictate that certain events must be audited but also specify how audit logs are handled and how long they are archived. Check with your organization's legal representatives to ensure that your strategy for auditing is in compliance with these regulations, if applicable.

Determining Which Events to Audit

The first step in creating a strategy for auditing the operating system is to determine the type of actions or operations to record. Which operating system events should you audit? The easy answer to this question is *all of them*. Unfortunately, auditing all operating system events would require enormous system resources and could negatively affect system performance. Bear in mind that the more you audit, the more events you generate and the more difficult it can be to spot critical events.

If you plan to monitor the audited events manually or if you do not have a clear understanding of how to read audit logs, it can be extremely difficult to isolate potential malicious events from harmless ones. You will need to work with other security specialists—ideally those who specialize in forensics or computer crime investigations—and IT decision makers to determine the operating system events to audit. Audit only those events that you believe will be useful for later reference. Although this is certainly easier said than done, many of these events will be readily apparent. For example, you should audit account management and account logon events.

If your organization does not have a security policy for auditing, an effective way to begin determining which events to audit is to gather all the relevant people in your organization in a room and brainstorm. Determine the following:

- The actions or operations you want to track
- The systems on which you want these events tracked

For example:

- We want to track all domain and local logon events to all computers.
- We want to track the use of all files in the payroll folder on the HR server.

You can later match these audit statements to the audit policies and settings in the operating system.

In Microsoft Windows Server 2003, Windows 2000, and Windows XP, audit events can be split into two categories: *success events* and *failure events*. A success event indicates that the action or operation has been successfully completed by the operating system, whereas a failure event shows that the action or operation was attempted but did not succeed. Failure events are useful in tracking attempted attacks on your environment; success events are much more difficult to interpret. Although the vast majority of successful audit events are simply indications of normal activity, an attacker who manages to gain access to a system will also generate a success event. Often, a pattern of events is as important as the events themselves. For example, a series of failures followed by a success might indicate an attempted attack that was eventually successful. Similarly, the deviation from a pattern might also indicate suspicious activity. For example, suppose the audit logs show that a user at your company logs on every workday between 8 A.M. and 10 P.M., but suddenly you see that this user is logging on to the network at 3 A.M. Although this behavior might be harmless, it should be investigated.

Managing the Event Viewer

All operating system security events in Windows Server 2003, Windows 2000, and Windows XP are recorded in the Event Viewer Security log. In addition, security-related events might be recorded in the Application log and System log.

Before you enable audit policies, you must evaluate whether the default configuration of the log files in the Event Viewer are set properly for your organization. The default settings for the security Event log are shown in Figure 15-1.

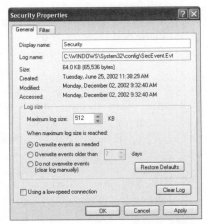

Figure 15-1   Security Event log default settings

For each Event log, you must determine the following:

- Storage location
- Maximum log file size
- Overwrite behavior

Determining the Storage Location

By default, the security Event log is stored in the %systemroot%\system32\config\ directory in a file named SecEvent.evt. In Windows Server 2003, Windows 2000, and Windows XP, you can edit the registry to change the storage location of each log file. The path and file name for the Security log are stored in the registry value HKEY_LOCAL_MACHINE\SYSTEM\CurrentControlSet\Services\Eventlog\Security.

By default, only the System account and the Administrators group have access to the security Event log to ensure that nonadministrators do not have access to read, write, or delete security events. If you move the log to a new location, ensure that the new file has the correct NTFS file system permissions. Because the Event Log service cannot be stopped, changes to this setting will not take place until after the server is rebooted.

> **Note**   Windows Server 2003 permits you to change the permissions on application and system Event log files, but not the Security log. Detailed information on changing the access control on the application and system log files can be found in Microsoft Knowledge Base article 323076: "How to Set Event Log Security Locally or by Using Group Policy in Windows Server 2003" (*http://support.microsoft.com/kb/323076*).

Determining the Maximum Log File Size

By default, the maximum size that the security Event log can reach before the overwrite behavior is initiated is 16 MB in Windows Server 2003, up from 512 KB in Windows XP and Windows 2000. Because hard disk space is more readily available now than in the past, you will likely want to increase this setting. How much you increase this setting depends on your overwrite behavior, but a general guideline is to set the maximum size to at least 50 MB. Because of the architecture of the Event Log service, the maximum cumulative size of all Event log files should not exceed 300 MB. Each security event is 350 to 500 bytes, so a 10-MB Event log will contain approximately 20,000 to 25,000 security events.

You can change the maximum size of the log file on individual computers on the security Event log Properties page or by editing the registry. You can also change the maximum log file size on many computers by using Group Policy security templates. The maximum size for the security Event log is stored in the registry value HKEY_LOCAL_MACHINE\SYSTEM\CurrentControlSet\Services\Eventlog \Security\MaxSize.

Configuring the Overwrite Behavior

When configuring the security Event log settings, you must define what will happen when the maximum log file size is reached—also known as the *overwrite behavior.* Windows Server 2003, Windows 2000, and Windows XP provide three overwrite behavior settings:

- **Overwrite Events As Needed**   New events will continue to be written when the log is full. Each new event replaces the oldest event in the log.

- **Overwrite Events Older Than [x] Days**   Events in the log are retained for the number of days you specify before events are overwritten. The default is 7 days.

- **Do Not Overwrite Events**   New events will not be recorded, and the Event log will need to be cleared manually.

In addition, you can configure the operating system to shut down if security events cannot be written to the security Event log file. When this setting is enabled and events cannot be written to the security Event log, the computer will initiate a stop error, commonly known as the *blue screen of death*, with the following error message:

```
STOP: C0000244 {Audit Failed}
An attempt to generate a security audit failed
```

After this stop error has occurred, only members of the local Administrators group will be allowed to log on to troubleshoot why the events cannot be written to the Event log. Until events can be written to the Event log, the computer will not operate normally. This is an important setting for high-security environments because it ensures that all security events are recorded. However, a large number of security events generated by an attacker or network problem could cause a denial-of-service condition. Similarly, shutting down the server might not necessarily be in accordance with availability service level agreements (SLAs). If your organization has high security needs and high availability needs, you should implement a method of removing auditing events from the system programmatically.

 Note   You can configure Windows 2000 and later versions to shut down if security events cannot be logged by setting the registry value HKEY_LOCAL_MACHINE \SYSTEM\CurrentControlSet\Control\Lsa\CrashOnAuditFail to 1.

If the computer shuts down because events cannot be written to the Security log file, this value is changed to 2. A local Administrator must log on to the system and reset this value from 2 to 1. Setting this value to 0 disables the CrashOnAuditFail functionality.

Unless you have a centralized auditing system, such as the Microsoft Operations Manager, you must carefully evaluate which overwrite behavior settings are best for your organization. In general, you will want to ensure that the security Event log size is large enough to record all events that occur between the archival of events.

Configuring Audit Policies

Windows Server 2003, Windows 2000, and Windows XP provide several categories of auditing for security events. When designing your enterprise audit strategy, you will need to decide whether to include success and failure events for the following categories of security audit events:

- Account logon events
- Account management events
- Directory service access
- Logon events
- Object access
- Policy change
- Privilege use
- Process tracking
- System events

You can see the current status of auditing for each area by looking in the Local Security Policy Microsoft Management Console (MMC) in Windows Server 2003, Windows 2000, or Windows XP. Figure 15-2 shows how the audit policy settings are displayed in Windows 2000.

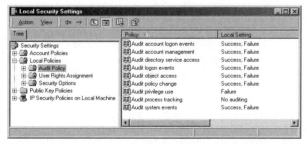

Figure 15-2   Viewing audit policy settings in the Local Security Policy MMC in Windows 2000

Auditing Account Logon Events

When a user logs on to a domain, the logon is processed at a domain controller. When you audit account logon events on all domain controllers, domain logon attempts will be recorded on the domain controller that validates the account. Account logon events are created when an authentication package validates—successfully or not—a user's or computer's credentials. When domain credentials are used, account logon events are generated only in domain controllers' Event logs. If the credentials presented are local computer credentials, the account logon events are created in the server's or workstation's local security Event log.

> **Tip**   Because an account logon event can be recorded at any valid domain controller in the domain, you must ensure that you consolidate the Security log across domain controllers to analyze all account logon events in the domain.

If you define this policy setting, you can specify whether to audit successes or audit failures. Success audits generate an audit entry when an account logon attempt succeeds. Failure audits generate an audit entry when an account logon attempt fails.

Auditing successful account logon events will provide you with a record of users' and computers' successful logons to a domain or local computer. By auditing failed account logon attempts, you might be able to detect attempts to attack the network by compromising an account. For example, you might notice hundreds or thousands of failed logon attempts for a given user account within the span of a few seconds. This can be a sign of a brute force attack on the user account's password.

By examining successful and failed logon attempts, you not only can determine the account—or the security identifier (SID) of the account—whose logon succeeded or failed, you also can detect the following information:

- Name of the computer on which the logon attempt originated. Attackers often use *unprintable characters*—those from the extended character set—in their computer names to mask their identity from the Event Viewer.

- Domain or computer name for the account being used from a workgroup computer attempting an attack.

■ Type of logon attempt, which can be one of those listed in Table 15-1.

Table 15-1   Types of Logon Attempts

Logon Type	Name	Description
2	Interactive	Includes both logons from Terminal Services users in Windows 2000 and users who are physically at the computer
3	Network	Generally for file and print access
4	Batch	Initiated by a process with batch logon rights
5	Service	Initiated by services using the Logon As A Service right
6	Proxy	Has never been implemented by any version of the Windows operating system
7	Unlock Workstation Logon	Recorded when the console of a computer is unlocked
8	NetworkCleartext	Reserved for cleartext logons over the network
9	NewCredentials	Initiated by using the RunAs command with the /netonly switch
10	RemoteInteractive	Recorded for Terminal Services logons in Windows Server 2003 and Windows XP
11	CachedInteractive	Recorded when cached credentials are used to log on locally to a computer
13	CachedUnlock	Recorded when the computer was unlocked and the user's credentials were verified against previously cached credentials

■ The process that originated the logon, which can be one of the following:

❑ **Advapi**   For API calls to LogonUser

❑ **Microsoft Internet Information Services (IIS)**   For logons using the Anonymous account or logon attempts using basic or digest authentication

❑ **LAN Manager Workstation Service**   For logon attempts using the LAN Manager (LM) protocol

❑ **Kerberos**   For calls from the Kerberos Security Support Provider (SSP)

❑ **KSecDD**   For network connections

❑ **MS.RADIU**   For logon attempts from the Microsoft Internet Authentication Service (IAS)

❑ **NT LAN Manager (NTLM) or NTLM Security Support Provider (NtLmSsp)**   For logon attempts using the NTLM protocol

❑ **Service Control Manager (SCMgr)**   For service logon attempts

❑ **Seclogon**   For logon attempts using the RunAs command

❑ **User32 or WinLogon\MSGina**   For interactive logon attempts

■ The authentication package used for the logon attempt, which can be one of the following:

❑ Kerberos

❑ Negotiate

❑ NTLM

❑ Microsoft_Authentication_Package_v10

■ The IP address and source port of the logon attempt in Windows Server 2003 only

Always audit both account logon success events and account logon failure events. Success events are critical in building a baseline of user behavior and can be important information in a security investigation. Failure events can be a sign of an attacker attempting to penetrate the network. By proactively monitoring failure events, you might prevent attacks in which the attacker does significant damage to the network. Table 15-2 describes common account logon events.

Table 15-2   Common Account Logon Events

Event ID	Description
672	An Authentication Service ticket was successfully issued and validated.
673	A Ticket Granting Service ticket was granted.
674	A security principal renewed an Authentication Service ticket or Ticket Granting Service ticket.
675	Kerberos preauthentication failed.
676	Authentication ticket request failed. This event is not implemented in Windows XP or Windows Server 2003.
677	A Ticket Granting Service ticket was not granted. This event is not implemented in Windows XP or Windows Server 2003.
678	An account was successfully mapped to a domain account.
679	An account failed to map to a domain account.
680	The account used for the successful logon attempt was identified. This event also indicates the authentication package used to authenticate the account.
681	A failed domain account logon was attempted. This event is not implemented in Windows XP or Windows Server 2003. Instead, event 672 is logged.
682	A user has reconnected to a disconnected Terminal Services session.
683	A user disconnected from a Terminal Services session without logging off. Terminal Services sessions can be left in a connected state that allows processes to continue running after the session ends. Event ID 683 indicates when a user does not log off from the Terminal Services session, and event ID 682 indicates when a connection to a previously disconnected session has occurred.

In addition, if the logon attempt should fail in Windows 2000, an event ID 681 will be recorded. This event will also contain code that gives the reason the authentication attempt failed. This reason code will appear in a decimal value. Table 15-3 contains a list of the failure codes in both decimal and hexadecimal format, along with a description of each code.

Table 15-3   Event 681 Failure Reason Codes

Decimal Value	Hexadecimal Value	Reason
3221225572	C0000064	User logged on with a misspelled or bad user account.
3221225578	C000006A	User logged on with a misspelled or bad password.
3221225583	C000006F	User logged on outside authorized hours.
3221225584	C0000070	User logged on from an unauthorized workstation.
3221225585	C0000071	User logged on with an expired password.
3221225586	C0000072	User logged on to an account disabled by the administrator.
3221225875	C0000193	User logged on with an expired account.
3221226020	C0000224	User logged on with Change Password At Next Logon flagged.
3221226036	C0000234	User logged on with the account locked.

Auditing Account Management Events

Because anyone with access to an administrative account has the authority to grant other accounts increased rights and permissions and create additional accounts, auditing account management events is an essential part of any network security design and implementation. Unless sophisticated biometrics or similar high-security measures are employed, it might be difficult or even impossible to guarantee that the person using the administrative account is the user to whom the account was issued. Similarly, auditing is one of the ways organizations can hold administrators accountable for their actions.

By enabling the auditing of account management events, you will be able to record events such as these:

- A user account or group is created, changed, or deleted.
- A user account is renamed, disabled, or enabled.
- A password is set or changed.
- A computer's security policy is changed.

Although changes to user rights appear as account management events on the surface, they are actually policy change events. If both audit policies are disabled, a rogue administrator might be able to subvert the security of a network without an audit trail. For example, if an administrator made the user account Sally a member of the Backup Operators group, an account management event would be recorded. However, if the same administrator directly granted Sally's account the Back Up Files And Folders advanced user right, an account management event would not be recorded. Changes to a computer's security policy are also recorded under account management auditing. Unexpected changes to security policy can be a prelude to the compromise or destruction of data. For example, an attacker might weaken the security policy on a computer to carry out a specific attack that requires a resource that has been disabled.

You should enable the auditing of both success and failure account management events. Success audits generate an audit entry when any account management event succeeds. Failure audits generate an audit entry when any account management event fails. Although successful account management events are more often than not completely harmless, they provide an invaluable record of activities when a network has been compromised. For example, you can see which accounts were modified and created by the attacker. Account management failure events often indicate that a lower-level administrator (or an attacker who has compromised a lower-level Administrator account) might be attempting to elevate his privilege. You might see an account used for the Backup service try to grant itself or another account domain administrator group membership. Hence, monitoring account management failures is critical. Table 15-4 contains descriptions of common account management events.

Table 15-4   Common Account Management Events

Event ID	Description
624	A user account was created.
627	A password change was attempted; this event records both successful and failed attempts.
632	A global group member was added.
633	A global group member was removed.
634	A global group was deleted.
635	A local group (distribution) was created.
636	A security local group member was added.
637	A local group member was removed.
638	A local group was deleted.
639	A local group was changed.
641	A global group was changed.
642	A user account was changed.

Table 15-4 **Common Account Management Events**

Event ID	Description
643	A domain policy was changed.
644	A user account was locked out; when an account is locked out, two events will be logged at the primary domain controller (PDC) emulator operations master. A 644 event will occur, indicating that the account name was locked out. Then a 642 event will be recorded, indicating that the user account is now locked out. This event is logged only at the PDC emulator.
645	A computer account was created.
646	A computer account was changed.
647	A computer account was deleted.
648	A local security group (distribution) was created.
649	A local security group (distribution) was changed.
650	A member was added to a local security group (distribution).
651	A member was removed from a local security group (distribution).
652	A local group was deleted (distribution).
653	A global group was created (distribution).
654	A global group was changed (distribution).
655	A member was added to a global group (distribution).
656	A member was removed from a global group (distribution).
657	A distribution global group was deleted.
658	A security universal group was created.
659	A security universal group was changed.
660	A member was added to a security universal group.
661	A member was removed from a security universal group.
662	A security universal group was deleted.
663	A distribution universal group was created.
664	A distribution universal group was changed.
665	A member was added to a distribution universal group.
666	A member was removed from a distribution universal group.
667	A distribution universal group was deleted.
668	A group type was changed.
684	The security descriptor of members of administrative groups was set. Every 60 minutes on domain controllers, a background thread searches all members of administrative groups, including domain, enterprise, and schema administrators, and reapplies the security descriptor on them. This event is logged each time the ACL is reset.
685	A name of an account was changed.

Auditing Directory Service Access

You can audit changes to the Active Directory directory service by enabling directory service auditing. Although enabling auditing of account management events records changes to user, computer, and group objects, you might need to track changes to other objects or attributes in Active Directory. For example, you might want to record changes to Active Directory infrastructure components, such as site objects, or changes to the Active Directory schema. Another common set of objects to audit in Active Directory is the enterprise Certification Authority (CA) objects stored in the configuration container when you install a Windows Server 2003 or Windows 2000 enterprise public-key infrastructure (PKI).

To audit successful or failed changes to Active Directory objects or attributes, you not only must enable directory services auditing on all domain controllers, but you must configure the system access control list (SACL) for each object or attribute you want to audit. In addition to recording changes to Active Directory objects and attributes, directory service auditing also records Active Directory events such as replication. Consequently, enabling directory service auditing for successful events will greatly increase the number of events recorded in the security Event log. Besides resulting in an increase in log file size, this will also make it more difficult to locate meaningful events without the assistance of sophisticated tools to parse the security Event log.

If you define this policy setting, you can specify whether to audit successes or failures. Success audits generate an audit entry when a user successfully accesses an Active Directory object that has a SACL specified. Failure audits generate an audit entry when a user unsuccessfully attempts to access an Active Directory object that has a SACL specified.

> **Tip**   Because Active Directory is a multiple master database, meaning that changes can be written on any domain controller, you must ensure that you enable directory service auditing on all domain controllers. The best way to ensure this is to create an audit policy Group Policy object (GPO) at the domain level.

All directory service events, both successful and failed, will have the event ID 565 or 566 in the security Event log. You will have to examine the details of each 565 or 566 event to see whether it was or was not successfully completed.

Auditing Logon Events

By enabling the auditing of logon events, you can track every time a user logs on or logs off a computer. The event is recorded in the security Event log of the computer where the logon attempt occurs. Similarly, when a user or computer connects to a remote computer, a logon event is generated in the security Event log of the remote computer for the network logon. Logon events are created when the logon session and token are created or destroyed.

> **Note**   In Windows 2000, because Terminal Services logons are treated as interactive logons, creating a terminal server session remotely causes a logon event to be recorded. If you enable logon events on a computer running Terminal Services, you must differentiate between console logons and Terminal Services logons. In Windows Server 2003 and Windows XP, Terminal Services has been separated from interactive logons.

Logon events audit logon attempts from users as well as those from computers. You will see separate security Event log entries for both the computer account and the user account if a network connection is attempted from a computer running Windows Server 2003, Windows 2000, or Windows XP.

> **Note**   Only the user account logon event is recorded when a user logs on to the domain from a computer running Microsoft Windows 95 or Windows 98. Computers that run Windows 95 and Windows 98 do not have computer accounts in the directory and consequently do not generate computer logon event entries for network logon events.

Logon events can be useful for tracking attempts to log on interactively at servers or to investigate attacks launched from a particular computer. Success audits generate an audit entry when a logon attempt succeeds. Failure audits generate an audit entry when a logon attempt fails.

A subtle but very important difference between auditing account logon events and logon events exists. Account logon events are recorded on the computer that authenticates the account, whereas logon events are created where the account is used. For example, if a user uses her domain account to log on to the network on a computer that is part of the domain, an account logon event will be recorded on the domain controller that performed the authentication of the account and a logon event will be recorded on the computer the user used to log on to the network.

On domain controllers that have logon events audited, only interactive and network logon attempts to the domain controller itself generate logon events—computer logon attempts are not audited. Success audits generate an audit entry when a logon attempt succeeds. Failure audits generate an audit entry when a logon attempt fails.

You should always enable both successful and failed logon attempts. Successful logon attempts provide a baseline record of a user's logon behavior that can be useful in identifying suspicious behavior. Similarly, a record of successful logon events is essential evidence in any computer investigation. By tracking failed logon events, your organization might be able to prevent network attacks or further damage to a network by proactively responding to suspicious behavior. For example, suppose that in a weekly review of a server's audit logs you notice many failed logon attempts with various user accounts. Upon further investigation, you notice that even though the server is located in a physically secure area, the logon attempts have been made at the console of the server. In this situation, you can respond proactively to the suspicious behavior, prevent damage to information, and start an investigation into the possible compromise of physical security. Table 15-5 contains descriptions of common logon events.

Table 15-5   Common Logon Events

Event ID	Description
528	A user successfully logged on to a computer.
529	The logon attempt was made with an unknown user name or a known user name with a bad password.
530	The user account tried to log on outside the allowed time.
531	A logon attempt was made by using a disabled account.
532	A logon attempt was made by using an expired account.
533	The user is not allowed to log on at this computer.
534	The user attempted to log on with a logon type that is not allowed, such as network, interactive, batch, service, or remote interactive.
535	The password for the specified account has expired.
536	The Netlogon service is not active.
537	The logon attempt failed for other reasons.
538	A user logged off.
539	The account was locked out at the time the logon attempt was made. This event is logged when a user or computer attempts to authenticate with an account that has been previously locked out.
540	Network logon succeeded.
682	A user has reconnected to a disconnected Terminal Services session.
683	A user disconnected a Terminal Services session without logging off.

Auditing Object Access

When you enable object auditing, you can track successful and failed attempts at accessing file, print, and registry resources. As with directory services auditing, when you enable object auditing, you will also need to configure the SACL for each resource you want to audit. Figure 15-3 displays where auditing is enabled on a file in Windows XP.

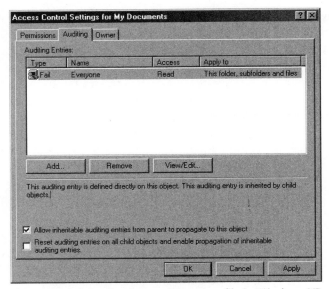

Figure 15-3 Configuring auditing on a file in Windows XP

A SACL is comprised of access control entries (ACEs). Each ACE contains three pieces of information:

- The security principal (user, computer, or group) to be audited
- The specific access type to be audited, called an *access mask*
- A flag to indicate whether to audit failed access events, successful access events, or both

If your organization has clear business reasons for recording access attempts on files, registry keys, or printers, you should enable object auditing and create the appropriate SACL on the resource. When configuring file auditing, you should decide in advance which types of actions on a file you want to track. For example, opening a text file, changing one line, and saving the file creates more than 30 events in the security Event log in Windows XP when all actions are logged. (This occurs when you select to audit Full Control on a file.)

> **Tip**   Exercise caution when auditing Read & Execute permissions on executable files because this type of auditing causes a large amount of events to be logged. Antivirus software causes thousands of object access events each time the system is scanned if Full Control auditing is enabled.

You should define only the actions you want enabled when configuring SACLs. For example, you might want to enable Write and Append Data auditing on executable files to track the replacement or changes to those files, which computer viruses, worms, and Trojan horses commonly do. Similarly, you might want to track changes or even the reading of sensitive documents.

> **Tip**   Before implementing the auditing of files, registry keys, and printers, you should ensure auditing the resource does not impact the performance of the server and the resource in such a way that it disrupts business processes.

By enabling the auditing of object access, you can record the successful and failed attempts at accessing files, folders, registry keys, and printers. Success audits generate an audit entry when a user successfully accesses an object that has a SACL specified. Failure audits generate an audit entry when a user unsuccessfully attempts to access an object that has a SACL specified. Table 15-6 contains descriptions of common object access events.

Table 15-6   Common Object Access Events

Event ID	Description
560	Access was granted to an already-existing object.
561	A handle to an object was allocated.
562	A handle to an object was closed.
563	An attempt was made to open an object with the intent to delete it.
564	A protected object was deleted.
565	Access was granted to an already-existing object type.
567	A permission associated with a handle was used. Note: A handle is created with certain granted permissions (Read, Write, and so on). When the handle is used, up to one audit event is generated for each of the permissions that were used.
568	An attempt was made to create a hard link to a file that is being audited.
569	The resource manager in Authorization Manager attempted to create a client context.
570	A client attempted to access an object. Note: An audit event is generated for every attempted operation on the object.

Table 15-6   **Common Object Access Events**

Event ID	Description
571	The client context was deleted by the Authorization Manager application.
572	The Administrator Manager initialized the application.
772	The Certificate Manager denied a pending certificate request.
773	Certificate Services received a resubmitted certificate request.
774	Certificate Services revoked a certificate.
775	Certificate Services received a request to publish the certificate revocation list (CRL).
776	Certificate Services published the CRL.
777	A certificate request extension was made.
778	One or more certificate request attributes changed.
779	Certificate Services received a request to shut down.
780	Certificate Services backup was started.
781	Certificate Services backup was completed.
782	Certificate Services restore was started.
783	Certificate Services restore was completed.
784	Certificate Services was started.
785	Certificate Services was stopped.
786	The security permissions for Certificate Services changed.
787	Certificate Services retrieved an archived key.
788	Certificate Services imported a certificate into its database.
789	The audit filter for Certificate Services changed.
790	Certificate Services received a certificate request.
791	Certificate Services approved a certificate request and issued a certificate.
792	Certificate Services denied a certificate request.
793	Certificate Services set the status of a certificate request to pending.
794	The Certificate Manager settings for Certificate Services changed.
795	A configuration entry changed in Certificate Services.
796	A property of Certificate Services changed.
797	Certificate Services archived a key.
798	Certificate Services imported and archived a key.
799	Certificate Services published the Certification Authority (CA) certificate to Active Directory.
800	One or more rows have been deleted from the certificate database.
801	Role separation was enabled.

Events 772 through 801 are generated only by computers that are running Windows Server 2003 and Certificate Services.

Auditing Policy Change

Auditing policy changes enables you to track changes in three areas:

- User rights assignment
- Audit policies
- Domain trust relationships

Although the name *audit policy change* implies that this event records the security policy of computers, this event is recorded when account management auditing is enabled with event ID 643. Changes to the assignment of user rights are recorded when policy changes are audited. An attacker can elevate her own privileges or those of another account—for example, by adding the Debug privilege or the Back Up Files And Folders privilege. Policy change auditing also includes making changes to the audit policy itself as well as changes to trust relationships.

You should enable the auditing of both successful and failed policy changes to track the granting and removal of user rights and changes to the audit policy. Successful and failed attempts generate an audit entry when an attempt to change security policies, user rights assignment policies, audit policies, or trust policies is successful. Table 15-7 contains descriptions of common policy change events.

Table 15-7   Common Policy Change Events

Event ID	Description
608	A user right was assigned.
609	A user right was removed.
610	A trust relationship with another domain was created.
611	A trust relationship with another domain was removed.
612	An audit policy was changed.
613	An Internet Protocol Security (IPSec) policy agent was started.
614	An IPSec policy agent was disabled.
615	An IPSec policy agent was changed.
616	An IPSec policy agent encountered a potentially serious failure.
617	A Kerberos version 5 policy was changed.
618	Encrypted Data Recovery policy was changed.
620	A trust relationship with another domain was modified.
621	System access was granted to an account.
622	System access was removed from an account.
623	Auditing policy was set on a per-user basis.
625	Auditing policy was refreshed on a per-user basis.

Table 15-7   **Common Policy Change Events**

Event ID	Description
671	Security policy was changed or refreshed. ("--" in the Changes Made field means that no changes were made during the refresh.)
768	A collision was detected between a namespace element in one forest and a namespace element in another forest.
769	Trusted forest information was added.
770	Trusted forest information was deleted.
771	Trusted forest information was modified.
805	The Event Log service read the Security log configuration for a session.

Auditing Privilege Use

By enabling privilege use auditing, you can record when user and service accounts use one of the user rights to carry out a procedure, with the exception of a few user rights that are not audited. These rights are the exceptions:

- Bypass Traverse Checking
- Debug Programs
- Create A Token Object
- Replace Process Level Token
- Generate Security Audits
- Back Up Files And Directories
- Restore Files And Directories

Windows Server 2003, Windows 2000, and Windows XP have a Group Policy setting under Security Options named Audit Use Of Backup And Restore Privilege, which enables you to audit the use of the Back Up And Restore Files And Folders privilege.

Privilege use auditing enables you to detect events associated with many common attacks. These types of events include the following:

- Shutting down a local or remote system
- Loading and unloading device drivers
- Viewing the security Event log
- Taking ownership of objects
- Acting as part of the operating system

You should enable the logging of failed privilege use events at a minimum. Failed use of a user right is an indicator of a general network problem and often can be a sign of an attempted security breach. You should enable auditing of the successful use of privileges if you have a specific business reason do so. Success audits generate an audit entry when exercising a user right succeeds. Failure audits generate an audit entry when exercising a user right fails. Table 15-8 describes common privilege use events.

Table 15-8 Common Privilege Use Events

Event ID	Description
576	Specified privileges were added to a user's access token. (This event is generated when the user logs on.)
577	A user attempted to perform a privileged system service operation.
578	Privileges were used on an already-open handle to a protected object.

Auditing Process Tracking

Process tracking auditing enables you to have a detailed record of the execution of processes, including program activation, process exit, handle duplication, and indirect object access. Process tracking, at a minimum, generates an event for the activation and exit of every process. Thus, by enabling the auditing of success events, a large number of events will be recorded in the security Event Viewer.

Enabling process tracking is excellent for troubleshooting applications and learning about how applications work; however, you should enable process tracking only if you have a clear business reason. You will also likely need an automated method of parsing Event logs to analyze log files successfully where process tracking has been enabled. Success audits generate an audit entry when the process being tracked succeeds. Failure audits generate an audit entry when the process being tracked fails. Table 15-9 contains descriptions of common process tracking events.

Table 15-9 Common Process Tracking Events

Event ID	Description
592	A new process was created.
593	A process exited.
594	A handle to an object was duplicated.
595	Indirect access to an object was obtained.

Auditing System Events

By enabling the auditing of system events, you can track when a user or process alters aspects of the computer environment. Common system events include clearing the security Event log of events, shutting down the local computer, and making changes to the authentication packages operating on the computer.

You should enable the successful auditing of system events to record system restarts. An unexpected system reboot might be an indicator that a security compromise has occurred and generally is a sign of some sort of problem, security related or not. Success audits generate an audit entry when a system event is executed successfully. Failure audits generate an audit entry when a system event is attempted unsuccessfully.

Successful attempts at clearing the security Event log are recorded regardless of whether system event auditing is enabled. Table 15-10 contains descriptions of common system events.

Table 15-10   Common System Events

Event ID	Description
512	The Windows operating system is starting up.
513	The Windows operating system is shutting down.
514	An authentication package was loaded by the Local Security Authority (LSA).
515	A trusted logon process has registered with the LSA.
516	Internal resources allocated for the queuing of security event messages have been exhausted, leading to the loss of some security event messages.
517	The Security log was cleared.
518	A notification package was loaded by the Security Accounts Manager (SAM).
520	The system time was changed.

How to Enable Audit Policies

You can enable audit policies locally in Windows Server 2003, Windows 2000, and Windows XP by using the Local Security Policy MMC or by applying security templates. You can also apply audit policies remotely to computers running Windows Server 2003, Windows 2000, and Windows XP by using Group Policy. The following steps explain how to enable an audit policy locally by using the Local Security Policy MMC, and Figure 15-4 shows what you will see on-screen when doing so. To enable an audit policy, follow these steps:

1. Open the Local Security Policy MMC.

2. Double-click Local Policies to expand it, and then double-click Audit Policy.

3. In the right pane, double-click the policy that you want to enable or disable.

4. Click the Success and Fail check boxes to designate which audit policies you want to enable.

5. Close the MMC.

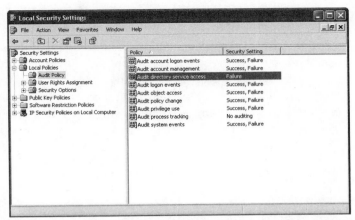

Figure 15-4 Configuring the audit policy by using the Local Security Policy MMC

Table 15-11 contains the audit policies that you should enable to track security events. For object access and directory service events, you also must configure the SACL on the objects or on the attributes of each object on which you want to track operations.

Table 15-11   Baseline Audit Policy

Audit Policy	Events to Audit
Audit Account Logon Events	Success, Failure
Audit Account Management	Success, Failure
Audit Directory Service Access	Success, Failure
Audit Logon Events	Success, Failure
Audit Object Access	Success, Failure
Audit Policy Change	Success
Audit Privilege Use	Failure
Audit Process Tracking	None
Audit System Events	Success

> **More Info**   For detailed information on configuring audit policies by using security templates and Group Policy, see Chapter 11, "Creating and Configuring Security Templates."

Monitoring Audited Events

A number of methods exist for monitoring events written to the security Event log. These methods range from reading the events manually by using the Event Viewer to using powerful automated event-consolidating and event-monitoring software such as Microsoft Operations Manager. Each method serves a specific purpose; you need to select a method that is most appropriate for your environment and particular situation. These are the four primary methods for monitoring events:

- Event Viewer
- Custom scripts
- Event Comb
- Fully automated tools, such as Microsoft Operations Manager

The discussion of fully automated event-monitoring tools is outside the scope of this book. This section covers the other three methods.

Using the Event Viewer

The simplest method for monitoring the operating system for security events is to use the Event Viewer. The Event Viewer enables you to perform the following:

- View event details
- Sort events by type, audit policy, and time
- Search for events by using common fields
- Filter events by common fields
- Export event logs to an .evt, .csv, or .txt format
- Connect to remote computers to view and manage the Event log

The Event Viewer does not allow for the consolidation of events. Thus, it might be difficult to monitor events that are recorded on many servers, such as account logon events, which are recorded on the authenticating domain controller for domain accounts. The Event Viewer also does not allow for the searching of event details. By exporting the events to a file, you can import them into a database or run custom scripts on the exported files from many computers.

Using Custom Scripts

Several scripts are available for managing events. A few of them are as follows:

■ **Dumpel.exe**   Also known as the Dump Event log, this script is a command-line tool that dumps an Event log for a local or remote system into a tab-separated text file. This file can then be imported into a spreadsheet or database for further investigation. Dumpel.exe can also be used to filter for or filter out certain event types. (Dumpel.exe is located in the Tools folder on the CD included with this book.)

■ **Eventlog.pl**   This Perl script clears and copies log files, and it displays and changes the properties of log files on local and remote computers that are running Windows 2000. You can use this script tool to perform the following Event log management tasks:

   ❑ Change the properties of Event logs

   ❑ Back up (save) Event logs

   ❑ Export event lists to text files

   ❑ Clear (delete) all events from Event logs

   ❑ Query the properties of Event logs

■ **Eventquery.vbs**   This Microsoft VBScript script displays events from the Event Viewer logs on local and remote computers running Windows Server 2003 and Windows XP. For Windows 2000, you can use the Perl equivalent to this tool that is included in the *Microsoft Windows 2000 Server Resource Kit*, Supplement One (Microsoft Press, 2000) along with Eventlog.pl.

■ **Logparser 2.2**   Logparser is a versatile tool that parses text files and other text-based data sources, such as audit log files, and creates reports by using T-SQL-like statements. It can also be used to import audit log files into more robust data storage applications, such as Microsoft SQL Server. You can download Logparser 2.2 from the Microsoft Web site at *http://www.microsoft.com/technet/scriptcenter/tools/logparser/default.mspx.*

Using Event Comb

Event Comb parses Event logs from many servers at the same time, spawning a separate thread of execution for each server that is included in the search criteria. With Event Comb, you can collect events from many computers running Windows Server 2003, Windows 2000, and Windows XP. You can also search for occurrences of events by any field in the event record in the collected log files. Event Comb can also search archived log files.

> **On the CD**   Event Comb (EventcombMT.exe) is located on the CD included with this book. You can also download it from the Microsoft Web site at *http://www.microsoft.com/downloads/details.aspx?displaylang=en&familyid=7af2e69c-91f3-4e63-8629-b999adde0b9e*.

Event Comb enables you to do the following:

- **Define either a single event ID or multiple event IDs to search for**   You can include a single event ID or multiple event IDs separated by spaces.

- **Define a range of event IDs to search for**   The endpoints are inclusive. For example, if you want to search for all events from event ID 528 through event ID 540, you would define the range as 528 < ID < 540. This feature is useful because most applications that write to the Event log use a sequential range of events.

- **Limit the search to specific Event logs**   You can choose to search the System, Application, and Security logs. If executed locally at a domain controller, you can also choose to search the file replication service (FRS), Domain Name System (DNS), and Active Directory Event logs in addition to the Application, Security, and System logs.

- **Limit the search to specific event message types**   You can choose to limit the search to error, informational, warning, success audit, failure audit, or success events.

- **Limit the search to specific event sources**   You can choose to limit the search to events from specific event sources to increase the speed of the search.

- **Search for specific text within an event description**   With each event, you can search for specific text. This is useful if you are trying to track specific users or groups.

- **Define specific time intervals to scan back from the current date and time**   This allows you to limit your search to events in the past day, week, or month.

The first thing you must do when using Event Comb is select the computers you want to search for events. To add computers to the search list in Event Comb, follow these steps:

1. In the Event Comb utility, ensure that the correct domain is autodetected in the Domain box. If you want to search Event logs in a different domain, manually type the new domain name in the Domain box.

2. To add computers to the search list, right-click the box below Select To Search/ Right Click To Add. The following options are available:

   ❑ **Get DCs In Domain**   Adds all domain controllers for the current domain to the listing.

   ❑ **Add Single Server**   Allows you to add a server or workstation by name to the listing.

   ❑ **Add All GCs In This Domain**   Allows you to add all domain controllers in the selected domain that are configured to be global catalog servers.

   ❑ **Get All Servers**   Adds all servers found in the domain using the Browser service. The servers exclude all domain controllers.

   ❑ **Get Servers From File**   Allows you to import a file that lists all servers to be included in the search scope. Each server should be entered on a separate line in the text file.

3. Once the servers are added to the list, you must select which servers to perform the search against. When selected, the server appears highlighted in the list. You can choose multiple servers by holding down the Ctrl key and clicking each server to select it.

Once you have selected the servers to be included in your Event log search, you can narrow the scope of the search by selecting the Event logs and event types to include. You can select the Event log, the type of event, and other important search criteria. Event Comb also enables you to save your searches and reload them later. This can be useful if you frequently use Event Comb to search for the same event. Search criteria are saved in the registry under HKLM\SOFTWARE\Microsoft\EventCombMT.

The results of the search are saved to the C:\Temp folder by default. Because the permissions on many computers allow users to read files from this folder to support legacy applications, you should consider changing this path. The results include a summary file named EventCombMT.txt. For each computer included in the Event log search, a separate text file named *ComputerName-EventLogName*_LOG.txt is generated. These individual text files contain all the events extracted from the Event logs that match your search criteria.

Best Practices

- **Determine which events should be recorded.**   Work with business and technical decision makers to ensure that all actions and operations that should be audited are audited. Because auditing does result in performance degradation, you should audit only for events to which you believe you might need to refer in the future.

- **Synchronize the time on all computers and network devices**   To correlate events that take place on different computers and network devices, you must ensure that the time is synchronized. Ideally, all computers and devices should be synchronized with the same time source.

- **Create a baseline of events**   Create a baseline of security events under normal conditions that can be used later for comparisons with possibly suspicious behavior. Without being able to refer to a baseline log file, it is often difficult to distinguish between events that are harmless and those that are malicious.

- **Monitor log files for suspicious behavior**   For auditing to be an effective security measure, you must monitor the audit log files for suspicious behavior. You might also want to use a test environment to stage common attacks and analyze the audit log files. This will enable you to better detect common attacks on the production environment. You should consider using automated software or writing custom scripts to parse event files for common events that indicate suspicious behavior.

Additional Information

- The following Knowledge Base articles:

    - 300549: "How to Enable and Apply Security Auditing in Windows 2000" (*http://support.microsoft.com/kb/300549*)

    - 814595: "How to Audit Active Directory Objects in Windows Server 2003" (*http://support.microsoft.com/kb/814595*)

    - 314955: "How to Audit Active Directory Objects in Windows 2000" (*http://support.microsoft.com/kb/314955*)

    - 246120: "How to Determine Audit Policies from the Registry" (*http://support.microsoft.com/kb/246120*)

    - 232714: "How to Enable Auditing of Directory Service Access" (*http://support.microsoft.com/kb/232714*)

- ❑ 299475: "Windows 2000 Security Event Descriptions (Part 1 of 2)" (*http://support.microsoft.com/kb/299475*)

- ❑ 301677: "Windows 2000 Security Event Descriptions (Part 2 of 2)" (*http://support.microsoft.com/kb/301677*)

- ❑ 824209: "How to Use the EventcombMT Utility to Search Event Logs for Account Lockouts" (*http://support.microsoft.com/kb/824209*)

- ❑ 323076: "How to set event log security locally or by using Group Policy in Windows Server 2003" (*http://support.microsoft.com/kb/323076*)

- ■ EventCombMT from the Microsoft Download Center (*http://www.microsoft.com/downloads/details.aspx?displaylang=en&familyid=7af2e69c-91f3-4e63-8629-b999adde0b9e*)

- ■ Logparser 2.2 download from the Microsoft Scripting Center Web site (*http://www.microsoft.com/technet/scriptcenter/tools/logparser/default.mspx*)

Chapter 16

Implementing Security for Mobile Computers

Mobile computers present a special security risk because of their portability and small size. They are at much greater risk of physical compromise and are much more difficult to manage. Often, when people hear the term *mobile computers*, they think it applies only to laptop computers. But mobile computers also include PDAs, Microsoft Pocket PCs, Microsoft Smartphones, Research In Motion (RIM) Limited BlackBerry devices, and wireless phones. Each of these devices can carry secret information, such as passwords, or information that could be used to break into their respective networks. Further complicating the issue is that a great many of these devices were designed and built without consideration as to their place in the IT landscape—rather, they were designed and built with single users in mind, and hence they have few security or manageability features.

Understanding Mobile Computers

Mobile computers face all the threats that desktop computers do, but they also face additional threats. These vulnerabilities include the following:

- Increase in the possibility of being lost or stolen
- Difficulty in applying security updates
- Exposure to untrusted networks
- Eavesdropping on wireless connectivity

Increase in the Possibility of Being Lost or Stolen

Laptops and other mobile devices have a much greater chance of being stolen because of their mobility and small size. A thief could easily hide a laptop in a briefcase or under a coat. Even organizations that have tight physical security are susceptible to this type of theft. For example, several high-profile, documented accounts exist of laptops and removable laptop hard drives containing top-secret information being stolen from a conference room and office from places such as the U.S. State Department and the U.S. Department of Energy's top-secret research facility at White Sands. Furthermore, although some laptops will always remain within the boundaries of company facilities, most users will work on their laptops away from the office. Consequently, the network security of such laptop computers is enforced by those organizations' corporate security and IT departments. But the users themselves are responsible for the physical security of their laptops. Users take their laptops home, on business and personal trips, and to school, and they sometimes leave their laptops in their cars—unattended and in plain view—during those stops. In July 2000, a commander in the British Royal Navy had his laptop stolen from his car, which was parked outside his house. His laptop was reported to hold top-secret information.

Thieves target laptops because they are small, high-value items that can easily be sold. If a thief is sufficiently computer-savvy or sells the laptop to an attacker, he or the attacker can potentially retrieve all the information from the laptop. This information includes cached passwords for network accounts; cached personal information from Microsoft Internet Explorer; personal information, such as names, addresses, and birthdates for people in address books; and the actual company data on the laptop. An attacker can use this information to attack the organization's network or steal the identity of the user or her friends and family. Furthermore, the stolen laptop might contain information that is confidential or secret. An information leak resulting from a stolen laptop could have a tremendous impact on your organization if that information falls into the wrong hands. This might sound alarmist, but several high-profile incidents of laptop theft have occurred in the past few years, including those government examples mentioned earlier.

The corporate world has not been immune to such incidents of laptop theft. A few years ago, the laptop belonging to the CEO of Qualcomm was stolen after he delivered a presentation at an industry conference. According to the media, the CEO was less than 30 feet away when his laptop was stolen from the podium from which he had been speaking. Because the CEO had been using his laptop to give the presentation, it is likely that he left it unlocked when he walked off the podium, rendering many types of data protection, such as encrypting file system (EFS), useless. Although the thieves in the cases we have mentioned so far might not have been targeting the organizations whose laptops they stole or the information on those laptops, no evidence to the contrary exists.

Some organizations face a greater threat of having their laptops stolen. For example, hardware and software companies might be targeted by attackers hoping to steal the companies' latest and greatest inventions. And law enforcement and government agencies might be targeted by attackers hoping to gain access to the secret information contained on their networks.

Mobile telephone devices also have a high incidence of theft and loss. At the very least, a thief can use a stolen phone to make long-distance and international phone calls, creating very expensive phone bills for the owner. A thief can also retrieve contact information from a phone's address book, potentially subjecting the phone owner's friends and family to identity theft. A more serious vulnerability, however, is that many mobile phones have Internet access, or even full computing power, as do the Pocket PC Phone Edition devices. These devices can have confidential information stored on them, including passwords and private e-mail messages. Other types of devices in this category include handheld e-mail devices such as the BlackBerry, PDA devices such as Palm Pilots, and handheld PCs such as the Compaq iPAQ. Because it is often difficult for users to input data into these devices, perhaps because they must use an on-screen keyboard or handwriting recognition software, users of these devices frequently store network credentials, such as passwords, persistently. An attacker could retrieve these credentials to later attack the network of the device user's organization. These mobile devices also have the capability to store files, which an attacker could retrieve from the device if stolen.

Laptop computers and mobile devices often have accessories and add-ons that might hold confidential information. Such accessories include conventional removable media, such as floppy disks and CDs. Another class of removable media includes high-capacity, solid-state devices, such as the myriad USB-enabled media, Compact-Flash cards, Secure Digital (SD) cards, smart cards, and Subscriber Identity Module (SIM) cards for cellular and wireless phones. If they fall into the wrong hands, smart cards and SIM cards, in particular, can contain data such as private keys and personal information that could be used to attack the network of the device user's organization.

Difficulty in Applying Security Updates

Unlike desktop computers, which have a somewhat static place in the network infrastructure, laptop computers often roam among many subnets and networks, not to mention leaving the local area network (LAN) altogether. These types of devices have historically been among the most difficult to secure and manage. The mobility of laptop computers makes them much more difficult to manage centrally, which greatly increases the difficulty in applying security updates, including hotfixes, service packs, and virus definition files. This mobility also increases the difficulty of assessing how current the security updates are. Traditional methods of applying security updates, including manual application and the use of network management software such as Microsoft Systems Management Server (SMS), are often ineffective with laptop computers because these methods depend on computers being in a static physical location as well as a logical one on the network.

This issue is especially problematic for laptop computers that rarely or never are connected to the LAN. When these computers do connect to the network, they often do so through low-bandwidth connections, such as modems. For all intents and purposes, these computers are self-managed by their users, making these users responsible for knowing how to locate and apply security updates themselves. If security updates are not installed, the laptop computer will be vulnerable to known exploits, which is particularly alarming because these computers are often directly connected to untrusted networks. Although better technology, such as Automatic Updates, helps solve this problem to some extent, the security management of remote laptops remains an issue.

Unfortunately, wireless telephone devices do not have such a clear patch management solution and almost no centralized security controls. The patching of wireless devices and the embedded or nonembedded operating systems is the responsibility of the carrier, rather than the software vendor. As these devices increasingly become persistently or near persistently connected to the Internet by IP, security threats to mobile devices and information stored on the devices could become a very difficult situation for wireless carriers and users.

Exposure to Untrusted Networks

Desktop computers are always connected to the LAN on which their security settings can be managed, and they are protected from the Internet and other untrusted networks by firewalls. On the other hand, network administrators cannot be sure to which networks laptop users will connect. When at home or in hotels, a laptop user will connect directly to the Internet without any protection—and the machine will be exposed to the legions of attackers scanning for vulnerable computers connected to the Internet. A user might also connect her laptop to the networks of her business partners and the semipublic networks at industry conventions, where confidential information can be exposed to anyone who succeeds in breaking into the laptop. Once the user connects her computer to such an untrusted network, a network administrator can do little to protect the machine from attacks that can be launched against it. For example, when configured properly, Windows Firewall in Microsoft Windows XP can provide excellent protection against attacks attempted against the computer when connected to untrusted networks. However, host firewalls such as Windows Firewall can cause problems, including preventing the deployment of Group Policy, client security checks, and the use of the network management software, when the user is connected to the corporate network if the computer cannot be detected and reconfigured for corporate network use. See Chapter 10, "Implementing TCP/IP Security," for detailed information on Windows Firewall.

Eavesdropping on Wireless Connectivity

Many laptops and mobile devices are now equipped with 802.11 or Bluetooth wireless network interfaces. Many users do not realize that connecting their laptop or mobile device to a wireless network that is not secure is similar to having a sensitive conversation in a crowded restaurant or subway—anyone who wants to listen in can. Public and private wireless networks are becoming more common in public areas, such as airport terminals and cafes. Users might be tempted to connect their laptop or mobile device to these networks for the convenience it affords, not realizing that the information they are sending and receiving might be traveling over an untrusted network.

Many home computer users and businesses are installing 802.11 wireless networks these days. Unfortunately, the built-in security measure of these networks—Wired Equivalent Privacy (WEP)—has an inherent security vulnerability because of a poor implementation of the RC4 encryption protocol. When exploited by an attacker, this vulnerability can enable the attacker to connect to the wireless network directly. In addition, many users and administrators are lulled into a false sense of security by the signal strength of their wireless access points. These users and administrators assume that their laptops can achieve this maximum signal strength, but in reality, attackers can build or purchase inexpensive wireless antennae to intercept wireless network transmissions from more than half a mile to a mile away.

Implementing Additional Security for Laptop Computers

Mobile computers are one of the most difficult IT assets to secure because network administrators must rely on users to be responsible for the security of their computers on a daily basis. To secure mobile computers, you not only must implement technology-based security, you must ensure that users understand the threats to their mobile computers and can make appropriate judgments about using their machines so that they do not jeopardize the security of information on their mobile computers or the network.

When implementing security for laptop computers beyond the baseline configuration, you should have two goals in mind: to secure the information on the laptop, and to prevent a compromise of the laptop from leading to the compromise of the network. To accomplish these goals you must address the following areas:

- Hardware protection
- Boot protection
- Data protection
- User education

Hardware Protection

The first area of additional security for laptop computers is protecting the laptop itself. To help prevent a laptop from being stolen when left unattended, you can use hardware locks. Several types of hardware locks exist, and they vary in cost and degree of protection. The most basic type of lock is a passive cable lock. Passive cable locks use a cable connected to the security slot on a laptop that wraps around an unmovable object. For example, a user storing a laptop in the trunk of a car could wrap the cable around the frame of the car. Typically, these locks use a key or combination lock and have cables that cannot be easily cut with handheld cable cutters. To circumvent a passive hardware lock, an attacker must pick the lock, cut the cable, or figure out a way to move the object the laptop is attached to. Some passive cable locks have alarms built into them. When the cable is looped around an object and reattached to the cable lock base, the lock creates a weak electric circuit that passes through the cable. If the circuit is broken because the cable is cut, the alarm sounds. These alarms are typically loud enough to be heard clearly from 100 yards or more. The alarm will continue to sound until the lock is unlocked or the internal battery runs out.

The effectiveness of a cable lock is dependent on the laptop user using the lock properly. Two common mistakes that users make with cable locks are leaving the key to the lock in an obvious location and attaching the cable to an object that is not secure. For example, users might leave the key to the lock in their laptop carrying case and place the case on the floor near the locked laptop, or they might loop the cable around the leg of a table, which could easily be picked up. Thus, if you implement hardware locks, you must train users in how to use them properly; otherwise, the locks can be ineffective. Hardware locks are by no means undefeatable, but if properly used, they can deter would-be thieves. The addition of an alarm to such a lock increases the likelihood of capturing the thief immediately after he steals the laptop.

Instead of (or in addition to) using passive cable locks, you can use active security systems. The most common types of active security systems use a hardware token that detects unusual motion of the laptop and sounds an alarm. If an unusual amount of motion is detected, the security system will activate. In the event of unusual motion—depending on the computer you are protecting—the security system might prevent the computer from being booted without the deactivation code, encrypt sensitive information (including data already encrypted by the operating system, such as passwords), and sound an alarm. Some active security systems use proximity switches instead of motion detectors. These hardware protection systems prevent computers from leaving a confined area, such as an office building or a particular floor in the building. Active security systems typically cost two to three times more than passive cable locks.

In addition to using locks, alarms, and countermeasures to protect laptops that have highly confidential information, you might consider using a hardware tracking system. Such a system enables you to locate the laptop after it has been stolen and thereby catch the thief (and have her arrested). Hardware tracking systems for laptops or desktops typically rely on one of two mechanisms: an Internet tracking system, or a Global Positioning System (GPS). The client-side tracking agent is installed in protected areas on the computer's hard drive or in hardware tokens installed inside the laptop's case. The agent contacts the tracking service periodically with information about where the computer is located, on the Internet or physically. If the computer is reported stolen, the tracking service can wait for the device to contact it. When contacted by the agent running on the device, the tracking service can retrieve the information about the location of the device. You can then give this information to law enforcement officials to attempt to track the stolen computer. Obviously, not all laptops need this degree of protection. This type of protection is very expensive. You might want to consider hardware tracking services on laptops that you know could hold information that, if compromised, might result in the loss of human life. For example, such hardware tracking services might be more appropriate for laptops that are used by government agencies, law enforcement agencies, or mission-critical assets, such as offline root Certification Authorities (CAs).

One other type of hardware protection for computers that you should consider is removing removable media drives from the laptop. One of the most common methods of breaking into computers that have been stolen or otherwise taken control of physically is to boot the computer by using a bootable floppy disk or CD. The Windows operating system is not immune to this type of attack. Although this is by no means a foolproof security measure, by removing these drives, you make compromising the laptop computer much more difficult and time-consuming. If you remove the floppy disk and CD-ROM drives from a computer, you should also disable the use of USB ports in the BIOS. Otherwise, the attacker might be able to attach a USB floppy or CD-ROM drive to the computer and use it as a boot device.

Boot Protection

One way that you can protect information contained on a laptop and protect account information stored on the laptop from being used to attack your organization's network if the computer is stolen is to prevent the operating system from loading. You can do this by using BIOS passwords or the Windows System Key feature (Syskey).

Although different BIOS versions have different names for passwords, most BIOS versions on laptop computers have two types of passwords that you can install: *boot passwords* and *setup passwords*. Both password types are configured in the BIOS. A boot password prevents the BIOS from transferring control to the operating system installed on the hard drive or any other type of media, including bootable floppy disks and CDs, without entering the password. A boot password does not prevent a user or attacker from entering the BIOS configuration; however, in newer BIOS versions, you must enter the existing password to change the boot password. BIOS setup passwords prevent a user or attacker from entering the BIOS configuration and changing information stored in the BIOS, such as the boot password or the order of precedence for boot devices.

There are only two ways to reset the BIOS setup password and boot password: by entering the existing password, or by clearing the CMOS. To clear the CMOS memory on a laptop, you must disassemble the laptop and remove the CMOS battery, which completely clears the BIOS settings. Although BIOS passwords will not completely prevent an attacker from booting the computer, under most conditions, these passwords will buy network administrators enough time to disable the user's user account and any other accounts that need to be disabled. The use of BIOS passwords also can give the user enough time to have accounts that protect important information disabled or have their password changed for persistently stored credentials on the laptop.

You can also use the Windows System Key utility to prevent the operating system from being loaded by unauthorized people. To do so, set System Key to use Mode 2 or Mode 3 (explained in the following list). You can configure System Key by typing **syskey** at the command prompt. Only members of the Administrators group can initialize or change the system key level. The system key is the *master key* used to protect the password database encryption key. System keys have three modes:

- **Mode 1**   Uses a machine-generated random key as the system key and stores the key on the local system. Because the key is stored on the operating system, it allows for unattended system restart. By default, System Key Mode 1 is enabled during installation on all computers running Microsoft Windows Server 2003, Windows 2000, and Windows XP.

- **Mode 2**   Uses a machine-generated random key and stores the key on a floppy disk. The floppy disk with the system key is required for the system to start before the system is available for users to log on. The operating system will not load unless the floppy disk is in the floppy drive. When System Key is enabled in Mode 2, the operating system will never be able to be loaded if the floppy disk is damaged or lost, unless you have previously created a copy of the disk.

- **Mode 3**   Uses a password chosen by the administrator to derive the system key. The operating system will prompt for the system key password when the system begins the initial startup sequence, before the system is available for users to log on. The system key password is not stored anywhere on the system; instead, an MD5 hash of the password is used as the master key to protect the password encryption key. If the password is forgotten, the operating system will be rendered unbootable.

Setting the System Key to Mode 2 or Mode 3 can greatly increase the security of the operating system and the password-based keys it contains, such as the contents of the Security Accounts Manager (SAM) database and Local Security Authority (LSA) secrets.

Caution   Because there is no way to recover from a damaged or lost floppy disk or a forgotten System Key password, you should implement System Key Mode 2 or Mode 3 with great caution. Develop a secure method of archiving system keys if you decide to implement System Key Mode 2 or Mode 3 on your network. Because there are no methods of centrally managing system keys, this task can be more difficult than it first appears.

Data Protection

Regardless of whether you use hardware alarms or boot protection mechanisms, you should implement protection for data that is stored on a laptop computer. On network servers, discretionary access control lists (DACLs) are the primary method of protecting files. Unfortunately, access control lists (ACLs) are of little use when a computer is in the possession of an attacker. Unlike network servers, whose physical security can be protected by network administrators, laptop computers can easily be stolen. An attacker can remove the hard drive from a laptop and install it in a computer on which the attacker has administrative privileges. The attacker can take ownership of the files and folders on the laptop computer's hard drive and read the files and folders.

> ## Truth in Advertising: Hardware Security Technology
>
> You might have seen the advertisements that promise, based on increased security technologies built into the laptop, that mobile computers will be much more resistant to information disclosure—even if critical components, such as hard drives, are removed from them. As security expert Bruce Schneier would note, a distinct smell of snake oil is in the air. Presumably, the information stored on the laptop would not be permanently rendered inaccessible or encrypted when a potential security compromise is detected—this would carry a major risk to the user if he, or his four-year-old daughter, should accidentally trip one of the theft sensors. So what is the truth of the matter? A skilled engineer with good knowledge of hard drive architecture and the Advanced Technology Attachment (ATA) specifications can likely retrieve the hard drive power-on password stored on the disk. Of course, there is an easier way: professional data recovery companies already retain the people with these skills and the necessary equipment, such as clean rooms. Retrieving the data might cost no more than a few hundred to a few thousand dollars. These security technologies certainly raise the bar, most likely too high for the petty criminal or 15-year-old kid down the street, but it is unlikely they will stop the determined, well-funded attacker.

To lessen this risk, you can use EFS to secure the information on a laptop. When you use EFS properly, the only way to retrieve the information contained in the files is by performing a brute force attack on the encryption algorithm. In Windows 2000 and Windows XP, EFS uses the 56-bit DESX algorithm. Although computationally feasible, this algorithm is difficult to break. Windows XP and Windows Server 2003 also allow you to use the 3DES algorithm, which is presumably computationally infeasible and thereby makes performing a brute force attack virtually impossible, given current hardware constraints.

> **More Info**   EFS is covered in detail in Chapter 8, "Controlling Access to Data."

The other data protection issue to address with laptop computers is their logical security. Unlike desktop computers, which are protected from untrusted networks by firewalls and routers, laptop computers might be connected to untrusted networks on a regular basis. For example, a user might use the high-speed connection in her hotel room to create a virtual private network (VPN) connection to the corporate network. By doing this, the user creates a relatively unprotected, authenticated route to the corporate network from the Internet, not to mention that she places the data stored locally on her laptop in danger. To prevent this situation, users can use personal firewall applications, such as Windows Firewall in Windows XP.

> **More Info**   Windows Firewall is covered in detail in Chapter 10, "Implementing TCP/IP Security."

You might have certain users in your organization who have especially high security requirements, such as those needed to safeguard information that, if disclosed, could lead to the loss of life. You should avoid storing any important information persistently on the laptops of these users. You should also require these users to create a VPN connection to the corporate network and then use Terminal Services to connect to a computer on the network to access information. Furthermore, you should disable the option of storing cached credentials by setting the number of cached credentials to 0 in the registry and restarting the computer. When you prevent credentials from being cached on the laptop, the user will not be able to log on to his laptop when a domain controller cannot be located to authenticate his credentials. You also should not install any applications locally on the laptop. This means the laptop will have little functionality other than acting as a remote access point to the network, but it will not place precious data or the network in danger.

> ### Securing Mobile Devices
>
> Securing mobile devices, such as devices running Windows Mobile 2003 (collectively known as SmartPhones), Pocket PCs, and Pocket PC Phone Edition devices, is similar to securing laptop computers. Mobile devices should have user passwords to prevent unauthorized users and attackers from accessing them. For example, Pocket PC 2002 supports both four-digit passwords and alphanumeric passwords for protecting access to the device. Each time an incorrect password is attempted, a time delay is activated before the logon screen will reappear. The delay increases exponentially upon each successive incorrect attempt.
>
> In addition, if the mobile device will be connecting to the Internet or untrusted networks, such as public 802.11b wireless networks, you should ensure that the device securely transmits authentication packets and data. For example, Pocket PC 2002 supports connecting to Web sites that have Secure Sockets Layer (SSL) connections enabled and wireless networks that use WEP.
>
> Although few viruses or Trojan horses resulting in significant damage that specifically attack the Pocket PC platform or other types of mobile devices have been reported, because these types of mobile devices are increasingly being connected to IP networks for long periods of time, as with laptop computers, you must install and maintain antivirus software on mobile devices and ensure that all security updates are applied as soon as they are released.

User Education

All the security measures discussed so far are completely dependent on the user properly protecting his laptop or other mobile device. Consequently, you must train users in the potential threats to their laptops and the measures they must take to secure their computers. Although most of the measures users must take to protect their laptops might seem obvious to you—such as not leaving a laptop in the car while buying groceries, or at least using a hardware lock to secure the laptop inside the trunk—they might not be obvious to your users. As with any type of training, it's best to be creative in how you get your message across to users in a way that they will understand. For example, when explaining to users the level of attention they should give to protecting their laptops, you can use this analogy: tell them to secure their laptops as though they were $2,000 bundles of cash. Few people would ever consider locking $2,000 in a car or leaving it on a table in a restaurant while they used the restroom. Posters, wallet cards, and e-mail reminders containing laptop security tips are also particularly effective in helping train users.

Securing Wireless Networking in Windows XP

Windows XP natively supports automatic configuration for the IEEE 802.11 standard for wireless networks, which minimizes the configuration that is required to access wireless networks. Users can roam between different wireless networks without the need to reconfigure the network connection settings on their computer for each location. When a user moves from one wireless network to another, Windows XP searches for available wireless networks and connects to them or prompts the user to select a wireless network to connect to. From a usability standpoint, the automatic—and even transparent—configuration of wireless networking in Windows XP is great. From a security standpoint, it can present some serious problems. Not all wireless networks are secure, and thus, a user could unwittingly endanger his laptop computer or even the corporate network.

Using Wireless Zero Configuration in Windows XP

The Wireless Zero Configuration service in Windows XP enables automatic connection to the following:

- **Infrastructure networks**   Computers and devices connect to wireless access points. Access points function as network bridges between the wireless clients and a wired network infrastructure. When a user enters the transmission area of an infrastructure network, where the access points broadcast their service set identifier (SSID), Windows XP automatically attempts to connect to the access point from which it gets the strongest signal. For example, your organization might have more than one building equipped with a wireless network. When a user moves between buildings, Windows XP will always connect to the wireless network without intervention from the user.

> **Tip**   Disabling SSID broadcasting does not provide any degree of protection for your wireless network and will prevent Wireless Zero Configuration from working properly the first time a client attempts to locate the wireless network. Because wireless networks simply rely on radio waves, you cannot prevent anyone from receiving the signal provided that person is close enough to the transmission point; given the strength of the receiving antennae, the mere presence of the wireless network is enough for detection.

- **Ad hoc networks**   Ad hoc networks are formed when computers and devices with wireless network connectivity connect directly to each other instead of connecting to access points. Unlike infrastructure networks, which operate as network bridges to other networks, ad hoc networks allow you to access resources only on the computer or devices that you connect to.

By default, Windows XP connects to both infrastructure networks and ad hoc networks, even those that the computer has not connected to before. For security purposes, you might not want the laptop computers in your organization to connect to untrusted networks automatically. You can define how Windows XP connects to wireless networks in the advanced wireless network connection properties. To increase the security of Windows XP laptops with wireless network cards, you should select to connect to only infrastructure networks and deselect the option to automatically connect to *nonpreferred networks,* which are networks that are not stored as preferred networks in the wireless network configuration utility (shown in Figure 16-1).

Figure 16-1   Advanced wireless network connection properties

Configuring Security for 802.11 Wireless Network Connectivity

The most basic type of security for 802.11 wireless networks is Wired Equivalent Privacy, or WEP. WEP provides for authentication and data transmission security for wireless clients to protect against unauthorized access and eavesdropping. Unlike Windows XP and Windows Server 2003, Windows 2000 does not have integrated wireless network management features. In Windows XP and Windows Server 2003, you can configure the network key that is used for WEP. The key is used for authentication to the wireless network. In addition, data encryption is enabled, which means a shared encryption key is generated to encrypt the data transmission between the computer and the wireless access point. In Windows 2000, 802.11 configuration must be done in the application provided by the wireless network interface vendor.

Configuring 802.11 Security with WEP

The 802.11 standard supports two subtypes of network authentication service: open system and shared key. When open system authentication is used, any computer or device can request authentication for the access point, and consequently, any computer or device can connect to the network. Using open system authentication does not prevent data transmission encryption. Unlike open system authentication, shared key authentication requires that the client computer or device have knowledge of a secret key that is shared by the wireless access point and all other wireless clients.

When using shared key authentication, the access point generates a random 64-bit or 128-bit number that is used as a challenge. The wireless client returns the challenge, which is encrypted with the WEP shared key. The encryption process involves using the RC4 stream cipher to perform an exclusive or (XOR) binary operation on the plaintext payload. The RC4 keystream is generated by using a random number generator (RNG). The seed of the RNG is the result of concatenating the 40-bit or 104-bit WEP key with a 24-bit initialization vector. The encrypted payload and the initialization vector are sent to the access point. The access point concatenates the WEP key with the initialization vector to seed the keystream for RC4 to perform an XOR binary operation on the encrypted payload to reveal the plaintext payload.

Unfortunately, an attacker who captures these frames possesses the plaintext challenge, the ciphertext challenge, and the initialization vector. Because of the way that XOR operations work, the attacker would then know the keystream that was used, which is the concatenated initialization vector and the WEP key. Although the attacker still does not know the WEP key, she can attempt to authenticate to the access point and use the keystream derived from the captured packets to encrypt the challenge and retransmit the captured initialization vector.

 Note   Several utilities available on the Internet automate this process of compromising shared key authentication.

Although shared key authentication is not completely secure, it does provide more protection than open system authentication. Thus, when combined with Media Access Control (MAC) address filtering, implementing shared key authentication provides a base level of security for wireless networks against novice attackers. If your organization issues laptops to users with wireless network cards, the users will likely install a home wireless network. To ensure that employees do not expose information contained on their laptops to potential attackers, you should create guidelines for installing home wireless networks, and these guidelines should include enabling shared key authentication.

WEP also provides data-encrypted services by using the same process as defined for shared key authentication. Because only 2^24 (roughly 16 million) initialization vectors exist, if you assume that each packet uses a new initialization vector, the probability is over 50 percent that one initialization vector will be repeated after about 4500 packets have been transmitted. This is an example of a birthday attack on a cryptography algorithm. Thus, if an attacker can get the access point to send known plaintext (such as ping packets) and then capture all encrypted packets, he will be able to compute the keystream by performing an XOR on the plaintext with the ciphertext. The attacker could then place the keystream in a database organized by the initialization vector. The next time the attacker intercepts a packet with that initialization vector, he can look up the keystream in the database and decrypt the packet.

In addition, a known vulnerability exists in the scheduling algorithm in RC4, meaning that a small subset of initialization vectors will be weak. Researchers at AT&T labs estimate that this vulnerability could be exploited by intercepting as few as 1,000,000 packets. By exploiting this vulnerability, an attacker could retrieve the static WEP key. If the attacker knows what the WEP key is, she can decrypt any packet she wants to view. Most newer, enterprise-oriented access points and wireless network cards are programmed not to use these weak initialization vectors. You can protect your wireless clients that use Windows Server 2003 and Windows XP by using 802.1x. See Chapter 25, "Designing an 802.1x Authentication Infrastructure," for more information on 802.1x.

How XOR Operations Work

To understand how an attacker can compromise WEP security, you must know how the binary XOR operation works. An XOR takes two binary numbers of equal lengths and performs a comparison of each bit, yielding a result of bits that is equal to the two numbers. The following list shows the result of XOR operations:

```
0 XOR 0 = 0
0 XOR 1 = 1
1 XOR 0 = 1
1 XOR 1 = 0
```

The XOR is frequently used by stream ciphers to encrypt data. For example, the name BEN can be represented in ASCII as 0x42 0x45 0x4E and converted to binary for transmission or storage. The RC4 algorithm might generate the keystream shown next. You then perform an XOR on the plaintext with the keystream. The result is the ciphertext.

```
Plaintext            01000010    01000101    01001110
Keystream    XOR     01101100    00010111    01101111
Ciphertext           00101110    01010010    00100001
```

If you convert the ciphertext back to ASCII characters, you get the following: þ - Ñ. The problem with using XOR for encryption is that if you know any two of the three elements, you can determine the one you do not know. For example, if you can intercept the plaintext and the ciphertext, you can determine the keystream by performing an XOR on the plaintext with the ciphertext:

```
Plaintext            01000010    01000101    01001110
Ciphertext   XOR     00101110    01010010    00100001
Keystream            01101100    00010111    01101111
```

Best Practices

- **Educate your users.** Ultimately, the security of information stored on laptop computers and mobile devices will rest with how seriously users take securing these assets and how well users follow guidelines and security polices for protecting their laptops. Although you can use technology to secure these devices to a certain extent, you must train users to do their part in securing laptop computers and mobile devices.

- **Use hardware locks for laptop computers.** If the risk to your organization from supplying users with laptop computers is high enough, consider using hardware locking devices.

- **Use BIOS or System Key passwords.** Passwords that prevent an attacker from booting a laptop computer, even temporarily, increase the security of your network and the information stored on a stolen computer.

- **Install personal firewall applications for mobile users.** For users that will be connecting to untrusted networks, use a host-based firewall application, such as Windows Firewall, to prevent an attacker from compromising the computer. Be sure to show the user how to use the application.

- **Implement 802.1x to secure corporate wireless networks.** The security provided by WEP is not strong enough to prevent knowledgeable and skilled attackers from compromising data sent on wireless networks. The 802.1x standard provides secure authentication, dynamic key exchanges, and data transmission security.

- **Create guidelines for home wireless network configuration.** To protect information on laptops issued to employees who will install wireless networks in their homes, create guidelines on which wireless access point to install and how to implement basic security measures, such as enabling WEP with shared key authentication and MAC address filtering.

Additional Information

- "5-Minute Security Advisor: The Road Warrior's Guide to Laptop Protection" (*http://www.microsoft.com/technet/columns/security/5min/5min-203.mspx*)

- Knowledge Base article 314647: "How to Increase Information Security on the Pocket PC" (*http://support.microsoft.com/kb/314647*)

- Knowledge Base article 310105: "How to Use the SysKey Utility to Secure the Windows Security Accounts Manager Database" (*http://support.microsoft.com/kb/310105*)

- "Enterprise Deployment of IEEE 802.11 Networks Using Microsoft Windows" white paper, which covers 802.1x (*http://www.microsoft.com/technet/prodtechnol/winxppro/deploy/ed80211.mspx*)

Part IV
Securing Common Services

Chapter 17
Implementing Security for Domain Controllers

Microsoft Windows 2000 and Windows Server 2003 domain controllers provide the Active Directory directory service to Windows forests. The domain controllers maintain the Active Directory database and must be secure to prevent the compromise of the Active Directory database and the objects stored within the database. This chapter looks at the security measures you must take to protect domain controllers and to ensure that the Active Directory database is secure.

Threats to Domain Controllers

Windows domain controllers are likely targets of attacks that attempt to compromise user and computer accounts, as well as other objects stored within Active Directory. Specifically, Windows 2000 and Windows Server 2003 domain controllers face the following threats:

- Modification or addition of Active Directory objects
- Password attacks
- Denial-of-service attacks
- Replication prevention attacks
- Exploitation of known vulnerabilities

Modification or Addition of Active Directory Objects

If attackers can compromise a domain controller, they can effectively make any changes or additions they want to Active Directory. This includes the deletion or modification of existing objects and the creation of new objects in Active Directory. For example, attackers who gain administrative access to a domain controller can create a user account for their purposes, as well as add that user account to any number of administrative groups in the domain.

Password Attacks

If attackers can gain access to a domain controller, they can back up the Active Directory database by performing a System State backup or by copying the Active Directory database and logs to another computer by booting the domain controller into another operating system. This backup of the domain controller can be restored to a remote computer and used to mount an offline password attack. The advantage to the attacker is that the password attack is not taking place against the production network, but on a computer that is removed from the network.

Denial-of-Service Attacks

Attackers can prevent users from performing authentication by performing denial-of-service attacks against domain controllers. Denial-of-service attacks typically take advantage of unpatched Windows security flaws. Denial-of-service attacks can also be launched against Domain Name System (DNS) servers, preventing clients from finding domain controllers. Clients find domain controllers by requesting a Service (SRV) resource record from a DNS server. If the DNS server is unable to respond, clients will not be able to find a domain controller for their domain.

Replication Prevention Attacks

If attackers are able to disrupt replication between domain controllers, they might be able to prevent the application of Group Policy objects (GPOs), which lock down domain controllers. For example, if you modify the GPO applied to all domain controllers and the GPO is not replicated to all domain controllers, some of the domain controllers will not have the new security settings applied.

Attackers can prevent replication between domain controllers by performing a number of attacks. If DNS resource records are modified or deleted, a domain controller might not be able to find its replication partners. Likewise, if wide area network (WAN) links are blocked, replication traffic might not be able to reach domain controllers at remote sites.

Exploitation of Known Vulnerabilities

Attackers might be able to compromise a domain controller that is not kept up to date with the latest service packs and security updates. For example, if the latest service packs are not applied to a domain controller, attackers might be able to disable the domain controller by performing a buffer overflow attack that prevents the operating system from responding to any network requests. In the worst-case scenario, a buffer overflow might allow attackers to modify configuration and take control of a domain controller.

Implementing Security on Domain Controllers

To prevent attacks against Windows 2000 and Windows Server 2003 domain controllers, you must implement security measures that lessen the vulnerabilities. These security measures range from physically securing domain controllers to prevent direct access by attackers to logically configuring domain controllers to reduce threats. Specifically, you must take the following security measures to secure Windows 2000 and Windows Server 2003 domain controllers:

- Provide physical security.
- Increase the security of stored passwords.
- Eliminate nonessential services.
- Apply security settings by using Group Policy.
- Protect against the failure of a domain controller.
- Implement Syskey.
- Secure built-in accounts and groups.
- Enable auditing.
- Secure Active Directory communications.
- Limit which users can authenticate at the domain controller console.

Providing Physical Security

A physical compromise of a domain controller can easily lead to the compromise of the Active Directory database copy stored at the domain controller. You must protect domain controllers by storing them in physically secure locations, such as a server room that requires card-key access.

For example, if attackers gain physical access to a domain controller, they can boot the computer with a boot disk. Once attackers have administrator access, they can back up Active Directory by performing a System State backup, restore Active Directory to another server, and run any number of offline password attacks against the Active Directory database.

Increasing the Security of Stored Passwords

To protect passwords stored in Active Directory, enable the following configuration options:

- Do not implement protocols that require passwords to be stored in a reversibly encrypted format, such as Challenge Handshake Authentication Protocol (CHAP) or digest authentication for Web applications. A password stored in this format is more susceptible to password attacks if attackers gain physical access to a domain controller. A password attack can easily decrypt passwords if they are stored in this format.

> **Note**   A password cracker can still crack passwords stored in Active Directory that are not reversibly encrypted. The difference is that cracking a normally stored password takes much longer.

- Disable LAN Manager (LM) hash values in the Active Directory database. A password stored in an LM hash value is more susceptible to password attacks. You can disable the storage of passwords in this format by enabling the Network Security: Do Not Store LAN Manager Hash Values On Next Password Change Group Policy setting in Security Options. This security option is available only when you modify the GPO from a computer running Microsoft Windows XP or Windows Server 2003. Group Policy is applicable to computers that run Windows 2000 with Service Pack 2 or later, Windows XP, and Windows Server 2003.

> **Caution**   Ensure that no client computers that require LM authentication exist on the network. For clients running Microsoft Windows 95, Windows 98, or Windows Millennium Edition (Me), install the Directory Services Client software from the Windows 2000 Server CD. This client software ensures that computers running Windows 95 and Windows 98 authenticate by using NT LAN Manager version 2 (NTLMv2) authentication.

- Enable password complexity at the domain. When the Password Must Meet Complexity Requirements group policy is enabled, passwords must be at least six characters in length and consist of at least three of the following four forms:

English uppercase letters	A, B, C, ... Z
English lowercase letters	a, b, c, ... z
Westernized Arabic numerals	1, 2, ... 9
Nonalphanumeric characters	!, @, #, spaces, characters that can be produced only by pressing the Alt key, and so on

Note Use characters created by pressing the ALT key and then pressing a three-digit numeric combination. For example, the following character, ≈ , is created by pressing ALT and then pressing 2-4-7.

Passwords or Pass Phrases

In the three-part series titled "The Great Debates: Pass Phrases vs. Passwords," Jesper Johansson of Microsoft Corporation compared and contrasted passwords versus pass phrases. Many people find the task of creating complex passwords to be very difficult. People will commonly do one of the following:

- Replace specific characters with numbers and symbols. For example, the word *password* can become P@ssw0rd.

- Use the first character of each word in a sentence, again replacing specific characters with numbers and symbols. For example, the phrase "I am working at the Grocery store until nine tonight" becomes I@w@tGsu9t.

Although both of these methods form complex passwords, the passwords are still crackable by the latest generation of password crackers because of their short length. In addition, users often find the passwords difficult to remember.

What Jesper recommends is to use pass phrases rather than passwords. So, considering the preceding examples, the phrase "I am working at the Grocery store until nine tonight" is an excellent pass phrase. If you need, or desire, more complexity, consider using "I @m working @t the Grocery store until 9:00pm tonite".

Eliminating Nonessential Services

A domain controller should not run nonrequired services. The Security Operations Guide for Microsoft Windows 2000 Server and the Windows Server 2003 Security Guide recommend that only specific services be enabled on Windows 2000 and Windows Server 2003 domain controllers. Table 17-1 shows the recommended startup configuration for services required by Windows 2000 and Windows Server 2003 domain controllers.

> **Note**   For detailed information on the services included in Table 17-1, see Chapter 9, "Managing Security for System Services."

Table 17-1   Domain Controller Services

Service	Windows 2000 State	Windows Server 2003 State
Alerter	Disabled	Disabled
Application Layer Gateway Service	Not Applicable	Manual
Application Management	Disabled	Disabled
ASP.NET State Services	Not Applicable	Disabled
Automatic Updates	Automatic	Automatic
Background Intelligent Transfer Service	Manual	Manual
Certificate Services	Disabled	Disabled
MS Software Shadow Copy Provider	Not Applicable	Manual
Client Service for NetWare	Disabled	Disabled
ClipBook	Disabled	Disabled
Cluster Service	Disabled	Disabled
COM+ Event System	Manual	Manual
COM+ System Application	Not Applicable	Disabled
Computer Browser	Automatic	Automatic
Cryptographic Services	Not Applicable	Automatic
DHCP Client	Automatic	Automatic
DHCP Server	Disabled, unless acting as a DHCP server	Disabled, unless acting as a DHCP server
Distributed File System	Automatic	Automatic
Distributed Link Tracking Client	Disabled	Disabled
Distributed Transaction Coordinator	Automatic	Disabled
DNS Client	Automatic	Automatic
DNS Server	Automatic	Automatic

Table 17-1   Domain Controller Services

Service	Windows 2000 State	Windows Server 2003 State
Error Reporting Service	Not Applicable	Disabled
Event Log	Automatic	Automatic
Fax Service	Disabled	Disabled
File Replication Service	Automatic	Automatic
File Server for Macintosh	Disabled	Disabled
FTP Publishing Service	Disabled	Disabled
Help and Support	Not Applicable	Disabled
HTTP SSL	Not Applicable	Disabled
Human Interface Device Access	Not Applicable	Disabled
IAS Jet Database Access	Not Applicable	Disabled
IIS Admin Service	Disabled	Disabled
IMAPI CD-Burning COM Service	Not Applicable	Disabled
Indexing Service	Disabled	Disabled
Internet Authentication Service	Disabled	Disabled
Windows Firewall/Internet Connection Sharing (ICS)	Disabled	Disabled
Intersite Messaging	Automatic, if using SMTP for intersite replication	Automatic, if using SMTP for intersite replication
IP Version 6 Helper Service	Not Applicable	Disabled
IPSec Policy Agent (IPSec Service)	Automatic	Automatic
Kerberos Key Distribution Center	Automatic	Automatic
License Logging Service	Disabled	Disabled
Logical Disk Manager	Manual	Manual
Logical Disk Manager Administrative Service	Manual	Manual
Message Queuing	Not Applicable	Disabled
Message Queuing Down Level Clients	Not Applicable	Disabled
Message Queuing Triggers	Not Applicable	Disabled
Messenger	Disabled, unless using an uninterruptible power supply (UPS)	Disabled, unless using a UPS
Microsoft POP3 Service	Not Applicable	Disabled
MSSQL$UDDI	Not Applicable	Disabled
MSSQLServerADHelper	Not Applicable	Disabled
.NET Framework Support Service	Not Applicable	Disabled

Table 17-1   **Domain Controller Services**

Service	Windows 2000 State	Windows Server 2003 State
Net Logon	Automatic	Automatic
NetMeeting Remote Desktop Sharing	Disabled	Disabled
Network Connections	Manual	Manual
Network DDE	Disabled	Disabled
Network DDE DSDM	Disabled	Disabled
Network Location Awareness (NLA)	Not Applicable	Manual
Network News Transfer Protocol (NNTP)	Disabled	Disabled
NTLM Security Support Provider	Automatic	Automatic
Performance Logs and Alerts	Manual	Manual
Plug and Play	Automatic	Automatic
Portable Media Serial Number	Not Applicable	Disabled
Print Server for Macintosh	Disabled	Disabled
Print Spooler	Disabled	Disabled
Protected Storage	Automatic	Automatic
QoS RSVP	Disabled	Not Applicable
Remote Access Auto Connection Manager	Disabled	Disabled
Remote Access Connection Manager	Disabled	Disabled
Remote Administration Service	Not Applicable	Manual
Remote Desktop Help Session Manager	Not Applicable	Disabled
Remote Installation	Disabled	Disabled
Remote Procedure Call (RPC)	Automatic	Automatic
Remote Procedure Call (RPC) Locator	Disabled	Disabled
Remote Registry	Automatic	Automatic
Remote Server Manager	Not Applicable	Disabled
Remote Server Monitor	Not Applicable	Disabled
Remote Storage Notification	Disabled	Disabled
Remote Storage Server	Disabled	Disabled
Removable Storage	Disable	Disable
Resultant Set of Policy Provider	Not Applicable	Automatic
Routing and Remote Access	Disabled	Disabled
SAP	Not Applicable	Disabled
Secondary Logon/RunAs Service	Disabled	Disabled
Security Accounts Manager	Automatic	Automatic
Server	Automatic	Automatic
Shell Hardware Detection	Not Applicable	Disabled

Table 17-1   Domain Controller Services

Service	Windows 2000 State	Windows Server 2003 State
Simple Mail Transfer Protocol (SMTP)	Automatic, if using SMTP for replication	Automatic, if using SMTP for replication
Simple TCP/IP Services	Disabled	Disabled
Single Instance Storage Groveler	Not Applicable	Disabled
Smart Card	Automatic, if using smart cards	Automatic, if using smart cards
SNMP Service	Disabled unless required in your network	Disabled unless required in your network
SNMP Trap Service	Disabled	Disabled
Special Administration Console Helper	Not Applicable	Disabled
SQLAgent$* (*UDDI or WebDB)	Not Applicable	Disabled
System Event Notification	Automatic	Automatic
Task Scheduler	Manual	Manual
TCP/IP Net BIOS Helper Service	Automatic	Automatic
TCP/IP Print Server	Disabled	Disabled
Telephony	Disabled	Disabled
Telnet	Disabled	Disabled
Terminal Services	Automatic, if using remote administration mode	Automatic
Terminal Services Licensing	Disabled	Disabled
Terminal Services Session Directory	Not Applicable	Disabled
Themes	Not Applicable	Disabled
Trivial FTP Daemon	Not Applicable	Disabled
Uninterruptible Power Supply	Automatic, if using a UPS; otherwise, Disabled	Automatic, if using a UPS; otherwise, Disabled
Upload Manager	Not Applicable	Disabled
Virtual Disk Service	Not Applicable	Disabled
Volume Shadow Copy	Not Applicable	Manual
WebClient	Not Applicable	Disabled
Web Element Manager	Not Applicable	Disabled
Windows Audio	Not Applicable	Disabled
Windows Image Acquisition (WIA)	Not Applicable	Disabled

Table 17-1   **Domain Controller Services**

Service	Windows 2000 State	Windows Server 2003 State
Windows Installer	Manual	Manual
Windows Internet Name Service (WINS)	Disabled, unless the domain controllers is hosting a WINS server	Disabled, unless the domain controllers is hosting a WINS server
Windows Management Instrumentation	Automatic	Automatic
Windows Management Instrumentation Driver Extensions	Manual	Manual
Windows Media Services	Not Applicable	Disabled
Windows System Resource Manager	Not Applicable	Disabled
Windows Time	Automatic	Automatic
WinHTTP Web Proxy Auto-Discovery Service	Disabled	Disabled
Wireless Configuration	Disabled	Disabled
WMI Performance Adapter	Not Applicable	Manual
Workstation	Automatic	Automatic
World Wide Web Publishing Service	Disabled	Disabled

Applying Security Settings by Using Group Policy

The simplest way to ensure consistent security settings across all domain controllers is to create a security template that defines the required settings and to apply the template by using Group Policy. When defining Group Policy settings, remember the following guidelines:

■ Define account policy settings in the default domain policy. The account policy settings include the domain's password policy, account lockout policy, and Kerberos policy. These settings must be defined at the domain because the domain is the only Group Policy container that ensures that every domain controller has a uniform account policy defined if domain controller computer accounts are moved from the Domain Controllers OU.

■ Review the recommended security settings for domain controllers:

❑ For Windows 2000, consider reviewing the BaselineDC.inf security template included in the "Security Operations Guide for Windows 2000 Server," the W2KHG-DomainController.inf security template included in the "Windows 2000 Hardening Guide," and the U.S. National Security Agency (NSA) W2kdc.inf security template.

❑ For Windows Server 2003, review the settings included in the Enterprise Client - Domain Controller.inf and High Security - Domain Controller.inf security templates included in the Windows Server 2003 Security Guide. Also review the settings recommended by the Security Configuration Wizard included in Windows Server 2003 Service Pack 1.

Note   Use these recommendations as the starting point for your company's domain controller security configuration. You should modify these security templates to enforce your company's security policy.

Protecting Against the Failure of a Domain Controller

You can protect against the failure of a domain controller in two ways: by performing regular backups of your domain controller and by implementing at least two domain controllers for each domain.

By performing regular backups of your company's domain controllers, you ensure that the domain controllers can be quickly recovered in the event of hardware failure or data corruption on the hard disk. To back up Active Directory, you must include the System State, which comprises the Active Directory database and log files, in your backup set. The backup strategy should make certain that backups are performed at regular intervals and are periodically tested by performing test restores, which ensure that disaster recovery will work in the event of a domain controller failure.

In addition to performing regular backups, you should make sure that at least two domain controllers exist in each domain in your forest. Doing so ensures that if a single domain controller fails, an additional domain controller can service authentication requests and maintain the Active Directory database.

Implementing Syskey

Windows 2000 and Windows Server 2003, by default, implement strong encryption of the account information stored in Active Directory. This information is protected by the System Key. The level of protection offered by the System Key is configured by using the Syskey.exe utility. When you run the Syskey.exe utility, you can choose to protect the System Key by using one of three methods:

■ **A machine-generated random key stored on the local system by using a complex encryption algorithm**   Syskey level 1 is the default configuration of Syskey.exe, and it provides strong encryption of password information in the registry. Because the System Key is stored on the local system, this method allows for unattended system restarts.

- **An administrator-chosen password to derive the System Key**   Syskey level 2 prompts a user to input the System Key password when the system is in the initial startup sequence, but before the system is available for users to log on. An MD5 digest of the password is used as the System Key to protect the password encryption key.

- **A machine-generated random key stored on a floppy disk**   Syskey level 3 requires that the floppy disk with the System Key be in the floppy drive to start the domain controller. This disk must be inserted when the Windows 2000 or Windows Server 2003 domain controller prompts you for it after beginning the startup sequence, but before the system is available for users to log on.

The method you use to protect the System Key will depend on your company's security policy. Although storing the System Key on a floppy disk or requiring a password to start the computer increases the security of the Active Directory database, both of these methods remove the possibility of an unattended domain controller startup.

Securing Built-In Accounts and Groups

Several built-in groups and user accounts must be protected in an Active Directory environment. These users and groups are assigned specific permissions and user rights that allow them to manage Active Directory. Specifically, you should manage the membership of the following user and group accounts:

- **Administrator**   The Administrator account in each domain is a built-in user account that is a member of the Domain Admins and Administrators groups in each domain. In the forest root domain, this account is also a member of the Schema Admins and Enterprise Admins groups. To secure this group, consider renaming the Administrator account and changing the description of the user account because it is a well-known description.

> **Tip**   Consider creating another account named Administrator with the description "Built-in account for administering the computer/domain." This user account should be tracked to determine whether anyone is attempting to connect to the account with the user's credentials. Verify that this account is only a member of the Domain Guests global group to ensure that the group is assigned minimum network privileges.

- **Administrators**   The Administrators built-in local group is assigned administrative permissions and user rights for a domain. Members of this group can manage all aspects of the Active Directory domain in which the Administrators group exists.

- **Domain Admins** In each domain, the Domain Admins global group is a member of the Administrators built-in local group. Through this membership, the group can modify the membership of the Administrators group and has full administrative privileges for the domain. In the forest root domain, members of this group can modify the membership of the Enterprise Admins and Schema Admins groups.

- **Enterprise Admins** The Enterprise Admins group can administer all domains in the forest and is assigned permissions to manage several objects stored in the configuration-naming context. For example, members of the Enterprise Admins group can add enterprise Certification Authorities (CAs) to the forest.

- **Schema Admins** The members of the Schema Admins group can modify the schema by defining new attributes and classes in the Active Directory Schema.

- **Account Operators** The members of the Account Operators group can modify all user accounts and groups in a domain except for the membership of the administrative and operators groups.

- **Server Operators** The members of the Server Operators group can manage all computer accounts in the domain, including server accounts.

- **Backup Operators** The members of the Backup Operators group can back up and restore all data on computers that are members of the same domain.

- **Print Operators** The members of the Print Operators group can manage all print shares and queues on computers that are members of the same domain.

You can manage the membership of these groups by using the Restricted Groups group policy. The Restricted Groups group policy prevents the addition and deletion of user accounts and groups from a group defined in this policy.

 More Info For more information on implementing Restricted Groups, please see Microsoft Knowledge Base article 320045: "How to Restrict Group Membership by Using Group Policy in Windows 2000."

Enabling Auditing

To ensure that attacks against domain controllers are detected, enable auditing in the Default Domain Controllers Policy. Auditing will record events to the Security log that can aid in detecting intrusion attempts and attacks against the domain controller. Table 17-2 outlines the recommended auditing settings for a domain controller.

Table 17-2   Recommended Domain Controller Audit Settings

Audit Policy	Prescribed Setting
Audit account logon events	Success, Failure
Audit account management	Success, Failure
Audit directory service access	Failure
Audit logon events	Success, Failure
Audit object access	Success, Failure
Audit policy change	Success, Failure
Audit privilege use	Failure
Audit process tracking	No auditing
Audit system events	Success, Failure

> **More Info**   For more details on configuring auditing in Windows 2000 and Windows Server 2003 network environments, see Chapter 15, "Auditing Microsoft Windows Security Events."

Securing Active Directory Communications

You can increase the security of data transmitted to and from domain controllers by implementing different strategies. These strategies include restricting which users and computers can connect to the domain controller and protecting the data as it is transmitted to and from domain controllers.

Implementing SMB Signing

You can protect data from modification in transit by implementing Server Message Block (SMB) signing or IP Security (IPSec) by using Authentication Header (AH). In addition, IPSec with AH can restrict which computers can connect to a domain controller.

To implement SMB signing, you must implement the Digitally Sign Server Communications (Always) security option in a GPO applied to the domain controller's OU. To ensure that client computers also implement SMB signing, you must implement the Digitally Sign Client Communications (Always) security option in a GPO linked to the domain. This GPO will affect only computers running Windows Server 2003, Windows XP, and Windows 2000.

> **More Info**   If you need to enable SMB signing for computers that run Windows 98 or Microsoft Windows NT, see Knowledge Base article 230545: "How to Enable SMB Signing in Windows 98," and article 161372: "How to Enable SMB Signing in Windows NT."

Disabling Anonymous Connections

In most cases, you might want to prevent anonymous access to resources on a domain controller. You can do this by configuring the RestrictAnonymous registry key at each domain controller. You can implement this in a GPO by configuring the Network Access: Do Not Allow Anonymous Enumeration Of Sam Accounts And Shares policy under Security Options.

Enable the RestrictAnonymous registry entry only if your domain does not include downlevel member workstations, servers, or Windows NT 4.0 backup domain controllers. When you enable this option, the following conditions will be in effect:

- Windows 95, Windows 98, and Windows NT 4.0 member workstations or servers cannot set up a Netlogon secure channel.

- Windows NT 4.0 domain controllers in trusting domains cannot set up a Netlogon secure channel.

- Macintosh users cannot change their passwords at all.

- The Browser service cannot retrieve domain lists or server lists from backup browsers, master browsers, or domain master browsers that have the RestrictAnonymous registry key set to a value of 2.

Implementing IPSec

To protect from inspection of data transmitted to and from domain controllers, you can implement IPSec. Because communications with domain controllers might also require communications with other services, such as DNS, you typically implement IPSec encryption for all network traffic.

 Warning To implement IPSec for all network traffic, all network clients must be running Windows Server 2003, Windows 2000, or Windows XP as the operating system. IPSec encryption is not available for previous versions of the Windows operating system.

If you want to implement IPSec to protect all data transmitted to and from a domain controller, you must first ensure that all other computers in the domain are configured to implement IPSec if required to do so. You can accomplish this by assigning the default Client (Respond Only) IPSec policy at the domain level. This policy allows any client computer to use IPSec to protect data if requested to do so by a server running Windows 2000 or Windows Server 2003.

> **Note**   The Client (Respond Only) IPSec policy assumes that a server protected by IPSec has the Accept Unsecured Communications, But Always Respond Using IPSec option enabled. If this option is not enabled, the Client (Respond Only) IPSec policy will not work because IPSec is implemented only if the server requests IPSec. Because the client always initiates communications with the server, all communications will fail if this option is not enabled.

To ensure that IPSec is used to protect data transmitted to and from domain controllers, assign the Secure Server (Require Security) IPSec policy in a GPO linked to the domain controller's OU. This IPSec policy ensures that all network traffic is encrypted by using Encapsulating Security Payload (ESP). The actual encryption and integrity algorithms are negotiated between the client and the server during the Internet Key Exchange (IKE) negotiations.

> **Note**   If your security policy does not require the actual encryption of data, but requires that only authorized computers be allowed to connect to domain controllers, either create a new IPSec policy or modify the Secure Server (Require Security) IPSec policy to implement ESP with NULL encryption. This policy ensures that only clients that can negotiate a security association with the domain controllers are allowed to connect to the domain controllers. The implementation of NULL encryption ensures that no encryption is applied. Finally, the implementation of ESP ensures that the traffic can pass through network address translation (NAT) devices if NAT is implemented between network segments. Previously, AH was recommended for signing all traffic on the network, but AH, by its very definition, cannot pass through NAT devices because the NAT process would have to modify fields within the AH packet that are signed to detect modification of the packets.

Limiting Which Users Can Authenticate at the Domain Controller Console

The default configuration for Windows 2000 and Windows Server 2003 assigns multiple groups the Allow Log On Locally user right. Both the default assignments and recommended assignment are provided in Table 17-3.

Table 17-3   Default and Recommended Assignments for the Allow Log On Locally User Right

Operating System	Default Assignments	Recommended Assignment
Windows 2000 and Windows Server 2003	Account Operators Administrators Backup Operators Print Operators Server Operators TSInternetUser	Administrators

The recommended assignment limits the ability to log on locally at a domain controller console to members of the Administrators domain local group. This includes any global groups or universal groups added to the membership of the Administrators group.

> **Note**   Restricting which groups can log on locally at the console removes the need to use the Secondary Logon or RunAs service at a domain controller. It does not make sense to allow lower-privileged accounts the ability to log on locally at a domain controller console and then use the Secondary Logon service to log on with an administrative account.

Best Practices

- **Physically secure domain controllers.**   All domain controllers should be stored in network server rooms secure from unauthorized personnel. A domain controller should not be used as a desktop computer. The domain controllers ideally should be stored in a card-key-access room where access is restricted to network administrators.

- **Leave domain controller computer accounts in the Domain Controllers OU.**   Domain controllers should have consistent application of security settings. You can ensure that the same security settings are applied to all domain controllers by keeping domain controllers in a common OU. The Domain Controllers OU is defined by default as the Active Directory storage location for domain controller computer accounts. Ensure that the domain controller computer accounts remain in this default OU.

- **Develop the baseline domain controller settings in a security template.**   Defining the security settings in a security template ensures that the security settings are reproducible. You can import the security template into a GPO linked to the Domain Controllers OU to ensure consistent application. In addition, the security template provides documentation of the security settings defined by your company for domain controllers.

- **Apply the security template in a separate GPO linked to the Domain Controllers OU.**   By applying the security template in a GPO other than the Default Domain Controllers Policy, you allow users to disable the security template settings by either unlinking the GPO from the Domain Controllers OU or disabling the GPO entirely. If the security template is imported into the Domain Controllers OU, it is more difficult to modify changes and reverse the settings of the security template.

■ **Enable auditing and increase log size settings.**   Auditing should be defined in a GPO applied at the domain controller's OU to ensure that the Security Log contains relevant information about potential attacks against your company's domain controllers.

■ **Store baseline security templates in a central, secure location.**   To ensure that version control is maintained, maintain a single store for all security templates or use version control software such as Microsoft Visual SourceSafe. Version control ensures that a single master version of the security template is maintained and applied to computers.

■ **Restrict who can manage and link GPOs.**   You can protect domain controllers from incorrect security settings by restricting who is delegated permissions to modify the GPO that applies the security settings. In addition, you can restrict which users and groups can link GPOs to the Domain Controllers OU.

■ **Restrict who can log on locally at a domain controller console.**   Do not use the default settings for the Allow Log On Locally user right, which allow lower-security groups to log on locally. Limit which user accounts can log on locally at a domain controller. After doing so, these groups can still perform management functions by using Microsoft Management Consoles (MMCs) from remote workstations.

■ **Install more than one domain controller in each domain.**   By installing two or more domain controllers in each domain, you ensure that at least one domain controller exists for the domain in case a domain controller fails. The second domain controller ensures that a domain controller is available to handle authentication requests and modifications to Active Directory objects in the event of a single domain controller failure.

■ **Consider implementing IPSec filters to limit traffic accepted by domain controllers.**   The IPSec filters listed in Table 17-4 limit the traffic accepted by a domain controller to only domain controller– and DNS-related traffic.

Table 17-4   Recommended IPSec Filters for Domain Controllers

Service	Protocol	Source Port	Destination Port	Source Address	Destination Address	Action	Mirror
CIFS Server	TCP	ANY	445	ANY	ME	Allow	Yes
	UDP	ANY	445	ANY	ME	Allow	Yes
RPC Server	TCP	ANY	135	ANY	ME	Allow	Yes
	UDP	ANY	135	ANY	ME	Allow	Yes
Predefined RPC Range	TCP	ANY	57901–57950	ANY	ME	Allow	Yes
NetBIOS Server	TCP	ANY	137	ANY	ME	Allow	Yes
	UDP	ANY	137	ANY	ME	Allow	Yes
	UDP	ANY	138	ANY	ME	Allow	Yes
	TCP	ANY	139	ANY	ME	Allow	Yes
Monitoring Client	ANY	ANY	ANY	ME	MOM Server	Allow	Yes
Terminal Services	TCP	ANY	3389	ANY	ME	Allow	Yes
Global Catalog Server	TCP	ANY	3268	ANY	ME	Allow	Yes
	UDP	ANY	3268	ANY	ME	Allow	Yes
	TCP	ANY	3269	ANY	ME	Allow	Yes
	UDP	ANY	3269	ANY	ME	Allow	Yes
DNS Server	TCP	ANY	53	ANY	ME	Allow	Yes
	UDP	ANY	53	ANY	ME	Allow	Yes
Kerberos Server	TCP	ANY	88	ANY	ME	Allow	Yes
	UDP	ANY	88	ANY	ME	Allow	Yes
LDAP Server	TCP	ANY	389	ANY	ME	Allow	Yes
	UDP	ANY	389	ANY	ME	Allow	Yes
	TCP	ANY	636	ANY	ME	Allow	Yes
	UDP	ANY	636	ANY	ME	Allow	Yes
NTP Server	TCP	ANY	123	ANY	ME	Allow	Yes
	UDP	ANY	123	ANY	ME	Allow	Yes
DC Communications	ANY	ANY	ANY	ME	Domain controller number	Allow	Yes
ICMP	ICMP	ANY	ANY	ME	ANY	Allow	Yes
All inbound traffic	ANY	ANY	ANY	ANY	ME	Block	Yes

Note   These IPSec filters assume that the domain controller also functions as a DNS server. If the server holds additional roles, additional IPSec filters are required to allow the traffic associated with the additional roles.

On the CD   A script file called PacketFilters-DC.CMD.txt that implements the IPSec filters listed in Table 17-4 is included on the CD-ROM that accompanies this book. The script must be modified with the IP addresses of all domain controllers and Microsoft Operations Manager (MOM) servers before being executed.

Additional Information

- RFC 3022: "Traditional IP Network Address Translator (Traditional NAT)" (*http://www.ietf.org/rfc/rfc3022.txt*)

- RFC 3715: "IPsec–Network Address Translation (NAT) Compatibility Requirements" (*http://www.ietf.org/rfc/rfc3715.txt*)

- "Security Operations Guide for Windows 2000 Server" (*http://www.microsoft.com/downloads/release.asp?releaseid=37123*)

- "Security Operations Guide for Windows 2000 Server–Tools and Scripts" (*http://www.microsoft.com/downloads/release.asp?releaseid=36834*)

- "Windows 2000 Security Hardening Guide" (*http://www.microsoft.com /downloads/details.aspx?FamilyID=15E83186-A2C8-4C8F-A9D0-A0201F639A56&DisplayLang=en*)

- U.S. National Security Agency, "Guide to Securing Microsoft Windows 2000 Active Directory" (*http://www.nsa.gov/snac/os/win2k/w2k_active_dir.pdf*)

- U.S. National Security Agency baseline domain controller security template (*http://www.nsa.gov/snac/os/win2k/w2kdc.inf*)

- "Best Practice Guide for Securing Active Directory Installations" (*http://www.microsoft.com/downloads/details.aspx?FamilyID=4e734065-3f18-488a-be1e-f03390ec5f91&DisplayLang=en*)

- "Windows Server 2003 Security Guide" (*http://www.microsoft.com/downloads /details.aspx?familyid=8A2643C1-0685-4D89-B655-521EA6C7B4DB&display-lang=en*)

- "The Great Debates: Pass Phrases vs. Passwords. Part 1 of 3" (*http:// www.microsoft.com/technet/community/columns/secmgmt/sm1004.mspx*)

- "The Great Debates: Pass Phrases vs. Passwords. Part 2 of 3" (*http:// www.microsoft.com/technet/community/columns/secmgmt/sm1104.mspx*)

- "The Great Debates: Pass Phrases vs. Passwords. Part 3 of 3" (*http:// www.microsoft.com/technet/community/columns/secmgmt/sm1204.mspx*)

- "Active Directory in Networks Segmented by Firewalls" (*http:// www.microsoft.com/downloads/details.aspx?FamilyID=c2ef3846-43f0-4caf-9767- a9166368434e&DisplayLang=en*)

- The following Knowledge Base articles:

  - 259576: "Group Policy Application Rules for Domain Controllers" (*http://support.microsoft.com/kb/259576*)

  - 143475: "Windows NT System Key Permits Strong Encryption of the SAM" (*http://support.microsoft.com/kb/143475*)

  - 320045: "How to Restrict Group Membership by Using Group Policy in Windows 2000" (*http://support.microsoft.com/kb/320045*)

  - 230545: "How to Enable SMB Signing in Windows 98" (*http://support.microsoft.com/kb/230545*)

  - 161372: "How to Enable SMB Signing in Windows NT" (*http://support.microsoft.com/kb/161372*)

  - 246261: "How to Use the RestrictAnonymous Registry Value in Windows 2000" (*http://support.microsoft.com/kb/246261*)

  - 254949: "Client-to-Domain Controller and Domain Controller-to-Domain Controller IPSec Support" (*http://support.microsoft.com/kb/254949*)

  - 299656: "New Registry Key to Remove LM Hashes from Active Directory and Security Accounts Manager" (*http://support.microsoft.com/kb /299656*)

Chapter 18
Implementing Security for DNS Servers

A Domain Name System (DNS) server provides resolution of DNS names to IP addresses and resolution of IP addresses to DNS names. The Active Directory directory service is dependent on DNS and uses DNS as its default name resolution service. The Microsoft Windows 2000 and Windows Server 2003 DNS services provide new features to ease administration and configuration of DNS. The new features introduced since the DNS service of Microsoft Windows NT 4.0 include the following:

- **Dynamic DNS updates** A Windows 2000 or Windows Server 2003 DNS server can accept dynamic updates from DNS clients that support the dynamic update protocols described in RFC 2136, "Dynamic Updates in the Domain Name System (DNS UPDATE)."

- **Secure DNS updates** To protect the DNS server against unauthorized updates, Windows 2000 or Windows Server 2003 can enforce DNS client authentication for updates. DNS clients must authenticate with the Windows 2000 or Windows Server 2003 DNS server by using the Generic Security Service Application Program Interface (GSS-API), as described in the RFC draft "GSS Algorithm for TSIG (GSS-TSIG)."

- **Active Directory–integrated zones** The security of DNS zone data is ensured by storing each DNS resource record as an individual Active Directory object. Each DNS resource record has its own discretionary access control list (DACL) that determines which security principals can modify the resource records.

■ **Service (SRV) resource records**   Windows 2000 and Windows Server 2003 advertise their Active Directory services in DNS by using SRV resource records. SRV resource records identify the host name of the servers that host Active Directory services so that a DNS client can connect to the required Active Directory service. This is the format of the SRV resource record:

```
_ldap._tcp.example.com. 600 SRV 0 100 389 dc1.example.com
```

The following components are defined in an SRV resource record:

❑ **_ldap._tcp.example.com**   Refers to the advertised service (_ldap), the transport protocol (_tcp), and the domain (example.com). In this case, the Lightweight Directory Access Protocol (LDAP) service resolves LDAP queries for the example.com domain.

❑ **600**   Refers to the Time to Live (TTL), which is the amount of time, in seconds, that the SRV resource record will be cached at a DNS server or DNS client in the resolver cache.

❑ **SRV**   Indicates that the resource record is a service resource record that specifies the location of a network service.

❑ **0 100**   Refers to the priority and weight, which allow you to configure preferences for one SRV resource record over another SRV resource record for the same service.

❑ **389**   References the port upon which the service is listening. In this case, the LDAP service listens on Transmission Control Protocol (TCP) port 389.

❑ **dc1.example.com**   Refers to the network host where the LDAP service resides.

■ **Application partitions**   Windows Server 2003 introduces the ability to store DNS-related data in application partitions rather than in the domain naming context. An application partition can be shared between domain controllers running the DNS service in the same Active Directory domain, between domain controllers in any domain in the Active Directory forest, or between any domain controllers based on a user-defined topology. When replicated between any Active Directory domain, the net result is a reduction in the amount of DNS configuration, such as secondary zones, when requiring DNS servers in different domains to host data for the same DNS zone.

Threats to DNS Servers

Because Windows 2000 and Windows Server 2003 depend on the DNS name service, DNS servers are targets for attacks. Attackers can pose the following threats to the DNS service:

- Overwriting of existing DNS resource records and hijacking sessions
- Acquisition of DNS zone data by performing unauthorized zone transfers
- Exposure of the internal IP addressing scheme to the public network
- Denial-of-service attacks that disable all DNS services
- Preventing access to the forest root domain's DNS resource records

Modification of DNS Records

By supporting dynamic DNS updates, a Windows 2000 or Windows Server 2003 DNS server is susceptible to modification of DNS resource records if the security of the DNS server is not configured correctly. If an attacker can modify a DNS resource record at a DNS server, the attacker can redirect clients to a server impersonating the original server. Once the resource record is modified at the DNS server, all DNS clients receive the fraudulent information from the DNS service.

Alternatively, attackers might attempt to pollute the cache of the DNS server with false DNS information. When a DNS server responds to a DNS query, it first verifies that the requested DNS name exists in the DNS server's DNS cache. If the requested DNS resource record exists in the cache, the response is based upon the cached information. If attackers can modify or inject information into the DNS server's cache, the DNS server will send the modified response to the DNS clients, rather than contacting the authoritative DNS server for the zone.

Zone Transfer of DNS Data by an Unauthorized Server

The DNS zone contains SRV resource records and IP address information that can provide an attacker with the layout of the network and location of key Active Directory services. If attackers can obtain the DNS zone data, they can easily generate a diagram of the network.

The simplest way for attackers to gain the DNS zone data is to request a *zone transfer* of the zone data from an existing DNS server. The zone transfer moves all DNS zone data to the target server.

Exposure of Internal IP Addressing Schemes

When DNS is poorly designed, Active Directory information is published to DNS zones accessible from the Internet. The Active Directory information is required only on the private network, where network clients must authenticate with and connect to Active Directory resources.

> **Tip**   If an external client must connect to Active Directory resources, Microsoft rec-ommends you provide external clients access to the private network by deploying the Routing and Remote Access Service (RRAS) on a computer hosting virtual private network (VPN) connections. By connecting to the private network using a VPN, the client will have an IP address on the private network and can securely access an internal DNS server.

Denial-of-Service Attacks Against DNS Services

An attacker can prevent access to DNS services on the network by launching a denial-of-service attack against the DNS server. A denial-of-service attack will prevent the DNS server from responding to normal queries. Because of Active Directory's dependence on DNS for name resolution, the removal of the DNS service from the network by a denial-of-service attack prevents network authentication and the resolution of host names on the network.

Preventing Access to the Forest Root Domain's DNS Resource Records

The forest root domain's DNS zone contains forestwide DNS resource records, including globally unique identifier (GUID) SRV resource records for every domain controller in the forest, GUID resource records for every domain in the forest, and global catalog SRV resource records for all global catalog servers in the forest. Preventing access to the forest root domain's DNS resource records can result in replication failures when a domain controller cannot find its replication partners' GUID SRV resource record, or it can result in a user logging on with cached credentials when a global catalog server SRV resource record cannot be found.

Securing DNS Servers

When planning the security of DNS servers, you should prepare for attacks against both DNS clients and DNS servers. Either type of attack can lead to clients being directed to unauthorized DNS servers or referenced to incorrect servers by fraudulent DNS resource records. By implementing the following security measures, you can reduce the probability of a successful attack against your DNS servers. These measures increase the security of your DNS servers and lessen the chances of a successful attack:

- Implementing Active Directory–integrated zones
- Implementing separate internal and external DNS name servers
- Restricting zone transfers
- Implementing IP Security (IPSec) between DNS clients and DNS servers
- Restricting DNS traffic at the firewall
- Limiting management of DNS
- Protecting the DNS cache

Implementing Active Directory–Integrated Zones

Active Directory–integrated zones store zone information in the domain naming context, rather than in plaintext files on the local file system. An Active Directory–integrated zone implements each resource record as a separate *dnsNode* object in the following Active Directory location:

```
DC=DNSZoneName, CN=MicrosoftDNS, CN=System, DC=DomainDN
```

DNSZoneName is the DNS fully qualified domain name (FQDN) of the DNS zone, and *DomainDN* is the LDAP distinguished name of the Active Directory domain where the DNS zone is stored. For example, the zone named example.com stored in an Active Directory domain named south.example.com would be stored in the following location:

```
DC=example.com, CN=MicrosoftDNS, CN=System, DC=south,DC=example,DC=com
```

The zone information is replicated to all other domain controllers in the domain. This information is accessible to DNS clients if the DNS service is installed at a specific domain controller and if the DNS clients are configured to use that domain controller as a DNS server.

If the zone must be hosted on DNS servers in other domains, the DNS servers in those domains must be configured with secondary zones, with the domain controllers in the initial domain acting as master DNS servers for the zone. Active Directory replication does not provide replication of Active Directory–integrated zones to other domains in the forest.

> **Note** If you are using Windows Server 2003 for your DNS service, you can alternatively store the data in an application partition that is replicated to a domain controller in the forest or to a defined subset of domain controllers. The use of application partitions is discussed in the sidebar that follows titled "Application Partitions."

Because each DNS resource record is stored as a separate *dnsNode* object, each resource record has its own individual DACL. By default, the only security principals with the permission to modify a DNS resource record are members of the local Administrators group, the Domain Admins group, the Enterprise Admins group, the DNSAdmins group, and the Enterprise Domain Controllers group, as well as the computer account that registered the DNS resource record with the DNS zone if you have enabled Secure Dynamic Updates for the zone.

Application Partitions

One of the most common misconfigurations in a multidomain Windows 2000 Active Directory forest is to not provide other domains in the forest full access to the forest root domain's DNS resource records. The forest root domain contains forest-specific records, such as global catalog and domain controller GUID records, that are not replicated to other domains.

In a Windows 2000 network, you must configure secondary zones to the forest root domain or more specifically to the _msdcs.*ForestRootDomain* zone to allow access to the forest root domain's DNS resource records in the event that an authenticating domain controller cannot contact a DNS server from the forest root domain.

Windows Server 2003 introduces a new type of partition to Active Directory, the application partition, which directly affects DNS configuration. DNS data stored in an application partition can be replicated to domain controllers in *different* domains in an Active Directory forest.

Rather than storing the DNS-related resource records in DC=*DNSZoneName*, CN=MicrosoftDNS, CN=System, DC=*DomainDN*, an application partition stores its data in ForestDnsZones.*DnsForestName* (if the application partition is forest-wide) or in DomainDnsZones.*DnsDomainName* (if the application partition is only domainwide). Alternatively, you can store the DNS-related zone records in a custom application partition.

You can modify an existing Active Directory–integrated zone to use an application partition by modifying the properties of the zone in the DNS console, as shown in Figure 18-1.

Figure 18-1   Changing a DNS zone to use an application partition

In the Change Zone Replication Scope dialog box, you can choose from the following options:

- **To All DNS Servers In The Active Directory Forest** *ForestName*   Stores the DNS zone information in a forestwide application partition.

- **To All DNS Servers In The Active Directory Domain** *DomainName*   Stores the DNS zone information in a domain-specific application partition.

- **To All Domain Controllers In The Active Directory Domain** *Domain-Name*   Stores the DNS zone information in the domain partition for the designated *DomainName*.

- **To All Domain Controllers In The Scope Of The Following Application Directory Partition**   If you implement a custom application partition to store the DNS resource records, you can limit the replication of the zone data to only those DNS servers that are enlisted in the custom application partition.

> **Note**   To implement a custom DNS application partition, use the procedures described in Microsoft Knowledge Base article 884116: "How to Create and Apply a Custom Application Directory Partition on an Active Directory Integrated DNS Zone in Windows Server 2003" (*http://support.microsoft.com/kb /884116*).

Implementing Separate Internal and External DNS Name Servers

Even if you implement the same DNS namespace on both the private and public networks, you should create separate zones for the internal and external DNS servers. The external DNS servers must contain only externally accessible DNS resource records. The internal DNS servers must contain internally accessible DNS resource records and can contain externally accessible DNS resource records, depending on the namespace implemented for Active Directory and the addressing scheme implemented in the perimeter network (also known as the DMZ, demilitarized zone, or screened subnet) of the network. See Figure 18-2 for an example of this DNS configuration.

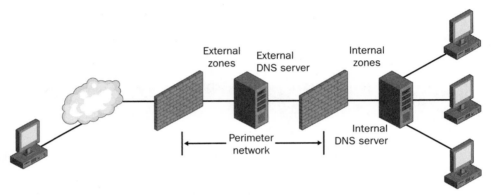

Figure 18-2   A namespace protected by implementing separate external and internal DNS servers

> **Note**   Implementing separate internal and external DNS servers might require you to include external resource records in the internal DNS zone. You need to do this when the Active Directory forest root uses the same DNS domain name as the external network or when you want to reference the externally accessible resources by their true IP addresses in the perimeter network, rather than using the addresses published to the Internet by the firewall protecting the perimeter network.
>
> If the same namespace is used both internally and externally, you cannot use forwarders to resolve the DNS resource records hosted at the external DNS server because the internal DNS server is authoritative for the DNS zone. If the resource record is not found in an authoritative zone, DNS reports that the resource record does not exist and the DNS request will not be forwarded to the configured forwarder.

Restricting Zone Transfers

Another method that attackers can use to obtain DNS zone data is to perform a zone transfer, transferring all DNS resource records from the target DNS zone. Attackers can accomplish this by typing the following command within the Nslookup console:

`ls -d` *DNSDomain*

This command attempts to acquire all DNS resource records for the *DNSDomain* by requesting a zone transfer from the DNS server you connect to using the Nslookup console. You can block this type of attack by restricting zone transfers in the properties of the DNS zone as shown in Figure 18-3.

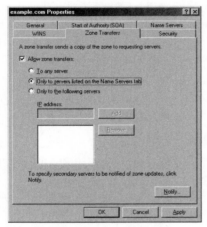

Figure 18-3   Restricting DNS zone transfers for the example.com zone

In the Zone Transfers tab, you can restrict DNS zone transfers to the following:

- **Servers listed in the Name Servers tab**   A zone transfer is possible only from DNS servers listed in the Name Servers tab of the DNS zone Properties page. If a DNS server requests a zone transfer and a DNS Name Server (NS) resource record does not exist in the DNS zone for the requesting IP address, the zone transfer is blocked. We recommend you use this option when you have numerous DNS servers that might request zone transfers.

- **Specific IP addresses**   A zone transfer is possible only if the requesting DNS server's IP address is included in the list of approved DNS servers. If the requesting IP address is not included in the list, the zone transfer is blocked. We recommend you use this option only when a small number of secondary DNS servers exist for a zone.

Tip   Implementing application partitions for the DNS zones also eliminates the need to implement zone transfers in a pure Windows Server 2003 DNS environment. Rather than implementing a conventional DNS configuration comprising primary and secondary DNS zones, application partitions enable DNS servers in multiple domains to be authoritative for a DNS zone and accept modifications to DNS resource records in the zones. This allows you to clear the Allow Zone Transfers check box, shown in Figure 18-3, preventing the risk of any zone transfer to any host on the network.

Implementing IPSec Between DNS Clients and DNS Servers

You can prevent unauthorized DNS clients from requesting DNS information from the internal DNS server by implementing IPSec to authorize connections to the DNS servers. By using IPSec, a DNS client must successfully negotiate an IPSec security association (SA) with the DNS server before the DNS client can perform any DNS queries. If the DNS client is unable to establish an IPSec SA, the DNS client is blocked from all communications with the DNS server.

When configuring the IPSec filters for the DNS clients, you can choose from one of two IPSec protocols:

- **Authentication Header (AH)**   Protects the DNS packets by requiring the DNS client to authenticate with DNS servers before communications can be established. AH also protects the DNS queries against modification and proves the source of the DNS queries. AH does not provide any encryption for the transmitted data, making DNS queries and responses subject to network inspection.

- **Encapsulating Security Payload (ESP)**   Protects the DNS packets by encrypting them during the transmission between a DNS server and the DNS clients. In addition to encrypting the data, the ESP protocol signs the data payload, protecting it from modification.

Warning   Be careful when applying IPSec filters to protect network traffic. Ensure that the IPSec filters describe all forms of network traffic in which the client or server participates. If you omit any forms of traffic from the listing of IPSec filters, the client will not be able to transmit data using those forms. Be sure to include communications with DNS servers, domain controllers, and other essential network services in the IPSec filter listing. Do not include all traffic to the domain controllers in the filter because Microsoft does not support the encryption of all traffic transmitted between clients and domain controllers.

Restricting DNS Traffic at the Firewall

A firewall can be used to restrict and protect the DNS traffic allowed to enter and exit the network. Depending on the network's DNS configuration, consider implementing the following packet filters at your firewall:

- **Prevent external DNS clients from querying the internal DNS server.**   Ensure that the firewall does not allow connections from the Internet to the DNS server hosting the internal DNS zone data. You must prevent connections from the Internet to the internal DNS server's TCP port 53 (for zone transfers) and User Datagram Protocol (UDP) port 53 (for DNS queries).

- **Prevent internal DNS clients from directly querying DNS servers on the Internet.**   You can configure the firewall to allow only approved hosts, such as the internal DNS servers, to query DNS servers on the Internet. The actual packet filter configuration will depend on whether you use forwarders or root hints when resolving DNS queries.

  If you use forwarders, configure the firewall to allow DNS communications only to TCP port 53 and UDP port 53 of the DNS servers included in the Forwarders tab of the internal DNS servers. This ensures that internal DNS servers can forward DNS requests only to the approved DNS servers. If you use root hints, an internal DNS server can send a DNS query to any DNS server on the Internet, not just the root hint DNS servers. You must configure the firewall to allow all outbound queries sent from the IP addresses of the internal DNS servers sent to TCP port 53 or UDP port 53.

Limiting Management of DNS

Windows 2000 and Windows Server 2003 include a custom domain local group, named DNSAdmins, in each domain in an Active Directory forest. The DNSAdmins group is delegated permission to fully manage DNS, without providing excess permissions to manage other services or objects in Active Directory.

You must ensure that membership in each DNSAdmins group is monitored to verify that unauthorized users or groups are not added. In addition, you should monitor membership in the local Administrators group, the Domain Admins group in each domain, the Enterprise Admins group, and the Enterprise Domain Controllers group. This is because members of these groups also have permissions to modify DNS configuration or Active Directory resource records.

Protecting the DNS Cache

If a DNS server receives a DNS query for a DNS resource record for which the DNS server is not authoritative, the DNS server will check its DNS cache for a queried entry before it queries other DNS servers to resolve the DNS query. If an attacker is able to add unauthorized entries directly into the cache of the DNS server, he can redirect DNS clients to unauthorized hosts. This process is known as *cache pollution*.

To prevent corruption of the cache on a Windows 2000 or Windows Server 2003 DNS server, you can enable the Secure Cache Against Pollution option. This option is enabled in the Advanced tab of a DNS server's Properties page in the DNS console.

When enabled, the Secure Cache Against Pollution option inspects the response from another DNS server to determine whether any referenced names are attempts to pollute the DNS cache. For example, if a query is made for a Mail Exchange (MX) record for south.example.com and the response includes a referral record for host.contoso.com, the host.contoso.com response would not be cached because it is from a different namespace than was queried. This can result in a valid response not being cached. For example, contoso.com might be hosting the Internet e-mail services for south.example.com.

Best Practices

- **Use Active Directory–integrated zones with secure dynamic updates.**   Active Directory–integrated zones implement all DNS resource records as *dnsNode* objects in Active Directory. The *dnsNode* objects are protected against modification by security principals—not assigned permissions—in the object's DACL. To host Active Directory–integrated zones, the DNS service must be running on a Windows 2000 or Windows Server 2003 domain controller. DNS servers installed on member servers or workgroup members cannot host Active Directory–integrated zones.

- **Implement DNS zones in forestwide application partitions for the forest root domain and other domains that are accessed frequently from all other domains in the forest.**   Application partitions can be replicated to any domain controller in the forest running the DNS service, removing the need to configure a mesh of primary and secondary DNS zones. Application partitions remove the need to allow zone transfers for replication of the zone data.

- **Implement DNS cache protection at the DNS servers.**   Enable the Secure Cache Against Pollution option in the properties of all DNS servers implemented on the network to prevent attackers from adding fraudulent DNS responses to the cache of a DNS server.

- **Restrict membership in the DNSAdmins group.**   Members of the DNSAdmins group can modify any DNS resource record hosted at the DNS server and are assigned permission to modify the DNS server's configuration. You should also restrict the membership in all other groups with the necessary permissions to manage DNS. This includes the local Administrators, Enterprise Admins, and Enterprise Domain Controllers groups, as well as the Domain Admins group in the domain where the DNS server's computer account resides.

- **Restrict zone transfers only to authorized DNS servers.**   Prevent unauthorized DNS servers or external clients from obtaining all content of the DNS zone by restricting DNS zone transfers either to servers listed in the Name Servers tab of the DNS zone or to IP addresses specified in the DNS zone's properties. Alternatively, store the DNS data in application partitions in a Windows Server 2003 Active Directory environment to eliminate the need for zone transfers altogether.

- **Do not expose any Active Directory–related DNS resource records to the Internet.**   Ensure that you implement separate zones for internal and external resources. The DNS server hosting the external zone must contain only DNS resource records for externally accessible resources. The IP addressing in this zone must reference the IP addresses exposed to the Internet. Active Directory–related DNS resource records should not be included in this externally accessible DNS zone.

- **Increase the size of the DNS Service log.**   Increasing the size of the DNS Service log at all domain controllers ensures that no events are missed related to the DNS service. Implement a minimum log size of 16 MB and enable the option Overwrite Events As Needed to ensure that the maximum number of log entries is maintained.

Additional Information

- Microsoft Windows 2000 Server Resource Kit: TCP/IP Core Networking Guide, "Introduction to DNS" (*http://www.microsoft.com/resources/documentation /Windows/2000/server/reskit/en-us/cnet/cncc_dns_wgga.asp*)

- *Windows Server 2003 Deployment Kit,* "Deploying DNS" (*http://www.microsoft.com/resources/documentation/WindowsServ/2003/all /deployguide/en-us/DNSBD_DNS_OVERVIEW.asp*)

- RFC 3645: "Generic Security Service Algorithm for Secret Key Transaction Authentication for DNS" (*http://www.ietf.org/rfc/rfc3645.txt*)

- RFC 3007: "Secure Domain Name System (DNS) Dynamic Update" (*http://www.ietf.org/rfc/rfc3007.txt*)

- RFC 2782: "A DNS RR for Specifying the Location of Services (DNS SRV)" (*http://www.ietf.org/rfc/rfc2782.txt*)

- "IP Security for Local Communication Systems" white paper (*http://www.microsoft.com/technet/security/bestprac/bpent/sec3/ipsecloc.mspx*)

- U.S. National Security Agency, "Guide to Securing Microsoft Windows 2000 DNS" (*http://www.nsa.gov/notices/notic00004.cfm?Address=/snac/os/win2k /w2k_dns.pdf*)

- *Windows Server 2003 Security Guide*, "Hardening Domain Controllers: Additional Security Settings" (*http://www.microsoft.com/downloads/details.aspx?familyid= 8A2643C1-0685-4D89-B655-521EA6C7B4DB&displaylang=en*)

- "Checklist: Securing Your DNS Infrastructure" (*http://www.microsoft.com /resources/documentation/WindowsServ/2003/standard/proddocs/en-us /Default.asp?url=/resources/documentation/WindowsServ/2003/standard /proddocs/en-us/sag_dns_chk_security.asp*

- Knowledge Base article 884116: "How to Create and Apply a Custom Application Directory Partitions on an Active Directory Integrated DNS Zone in Windows Server 2003" (*http://support.microsoft.com/kb/884116*)

- Microsoft Official Curriculum course 1561, *Designing Microsoft Windows 2000 Directory Services Infrastructure*, Module 2: "Designing an Active Directory Naming Strategy" (*http://www.microsoft.com/learning/syllabi/en-us/1561Bfinal.mspx*)

- Microsoft Official Curriculum course 2279, *Planning, Implementing, and Maintaining a Microsoft Windows Server 2003 Active Directory Infrastructure*, Module 2: "Implementing an Active Directory Forest and Domain Structure" (*http://www.microsoft.com/learning/syllabi/en-us/2279Bfinal.mspx*)

- Microsoft Official Curriculum course 2282, *Designing a Microsoft Windows Server 2003 Active Directory and Network Infrastructure*, Module 2: "Designing a Forest and Domain Infrastructure" (*http://www.microsoft.com/learning/syllabi/en-us /2282Afinal.mspx*)

- Microsoft Official Curriculum course 2823, *Implementing and Administering Security in a Microsoft Windows Server 2003 Network*, Module 7: "Planning, Configuring, and Implementing Secure Baselines for Server Roles" (*http:// www.microsoft.com/learning/syllabi/en-us/2823afinal.mspx*)

Chapter 19

Implementing Security for Terminal Services

Terminal Services in Microsoft Windows 2000 and Windows Server 2003 permits remote clients to execute programs on a remote server by using the Windows desktop. When a user connects to a terminal server using a Remote Desktop client, keyboard and mouse actions are transmitted from the Remote Desktop client to the terminal server. The responses of the terminal server, which appear as changes in the display, are sent back to the Remote Desktop client.

All applications execute on the terminal server, and performance is dependent upon the hardware at the terminal server. The Remote Desktop client requires only sufficient hardware to run the Terminal Services client.

Terminal Services can be installed on a computer running Microsoft Windows 2000 Server, Windows 2000 Advanced Server, Windows 2000 Datacenter Server, Windows XP, or Windows Server 2003. When installing Terminal Services on servers running Windows 2000 Server family products or Windows Server 2003, you can choose between two modes—application mode or remote administration mode—which are discussed in detail later in this chapter.

For servers running Windows 2000 Server, you install Terminal Services by using Add/Remove Windows Components in Control Panel. For Windows XP, you must enable the Remote Desktop option in the Remote tab of the computer's System Control Panel.

> **Note**   A client that runs Windows XP with the Remote Desktop option enabled can support only a single client connection, regardless of whether the connection is made by the locally logged-on user or by using a Remote Desktop client. If a user is logged on at a client computer running Windows XP, he is logged off when a Remote Desktop client connects. The same is true if a local user logs on while a Remote Desktop client is connected.

How you implement Terminal Services in Windows Server 2003 depends on the mode you implement. Remote administration mode requires enabling the Remote Desktop option only as in Windows XP. For application mode, you must add the service through Add/Remove Programs in Control Panel.

Threats to Terminal Services

When Terminal Services is installed on a server running Windows 2000 or Windows Server 2003, it allows remote computers to connect to the terminal server and launch a remote Windows desktop. When Terminal Services is installed, nonauthorized users can attempt to connect to the terminal server. If not configured for security, Terminal Services on a server running Windows 2000 or Windows Server 2003 is a security vulnerability. For example, when Terminal Services is installed on a server that runs Windows 2000 or Windows Server 2003, the following vulnerabilities exist:

- Terminal Services users might be connecting with excess permissions.
- Firewall security might be bypassed by Internet clients.
- Users require excess privileges to connect to a Windows 2000 Terminal Server.

Grants Excess Permissions for Users

If Terminal Services is installed with Permissions Compatible With Terminal Server 4.0 Users on Windows 2000 or with Relaxed Security on Windows Server 2003, all users will connect with excess permissions. The excess permissions provide all terminal server clients with full access to critical registry locations and file locations on the disk. When users connect to a terminal server in this relaxed permission state, they are automatically made members of the Terminal Server User group and will receive all permissions assigned to the Terminal Server User group. Rather than being assigned individual permissions, Terminal Services users are all assigned the same permissions based upon their membership in the Terminal Server User group.

Allows Bypass of Firewall Security

If a firewall allows remote clients to connect to a terminal server, the firewall cannot apply additional filters to the protocols and applications running within the Terminal Services session. Even if the firewall applies specific filters—for example, by preventing the use of FTP through the firewall—the Remote Desktop client can run an FTP client and transfer data on the network by using FTP.

The firewall will allow only connections to the terminal server's Transmission Control Protocol (TCP) port 3389. All data streams within a Remote Desktop client session are initiated at the terminal server, not at the terminal server client. The only information transmitted between the terminal server client and the terminal server is mouse input, keyboard input, and display information. Depending on the level of encryption employed, this information is encrypted as it passes through the firewall.

Requires the Log On Locally User Right

To connect to a Windows 2000 terminal server, the user or group that contains the user's account must be assigned the Log On Locally user right. This user right applies to Terminal Services connections and physical connections at the computer hosting Terminal Services. The user right does not differentiate between a Terminal Services connection and a local logon at the terminal server.

 Note   On a Windows Server 2003 terminal server, the user does not require the Log On Locally user right. A Windows Server 2003 terminal server requires that the user be assigned the Allow Log On Through Terminal Services user right and have membership in the Remote Desktop Users group if the user is not a member of the terminal server's local Administrators group. You can either add the membership explicitly to the Remote Desktop Users group or designate the users in the Remote tab of the System Control Panel.

Provides an Attacker with a Full Windows Desktop

Terminal Services is the most functional remote connectivity solution. By default, when you connect to a terminal server, you gain total access to the remote terminal server's desktop. This includes all text-based and graphical applications installed on the terminal server, subject to the permissions assigned to the applications.

Securing Terminal Services

Once you have identified the vulnerabilities facing your Terminal Services deployment, you can take action. The measures you can take include the following:

- Choose the correct Terminal Services mode.
- Restrict which users and groups are assigned rights to connect to a Terminal Server.
- Restrict which applications can be executed.
- Implement strong encryption to data transmitted between the client and server.
- Strengthen the security configuration of the terminal server.
- Implement strong authentication of the Windows Server 2003 terminal server.

> **Tip**   Additional security measures for Terminal Services in Windows Server 2003 are discussed in the "Locking Down Windows Server 2003 Terminal Server Sessions" white paper available at *http://www.microsoft.com/windowsserver2003/techinfo/overview /lockdown.mspx*.

Choosing the Correct Terminal Services Mode

When you install Terminal Services on a server running Windows 2000, you must select between two modes: remote administration mode and application server mode.

> **Note**   This is a major difference between Windows 2000 and Windows Server 2003. In Windows Server 2003, remote administration mode is included in the base operating system. You have to install Terminal Services only when you want to enable application server mode.

Remote Administration Mode

Remote administration mode, by default, allows only members of the local Administrators group to connect by using Terminal Services. Nonmembers cannot connect to the terminal server, and the maximum number of simultaneous connections is two Remote Desktop connections plus one console session, which can be to the local console or to a Remote Desktop console session.

Remote administration mode should be implemented when administrators require the ability to manage servers such as domain controllers remotely. Microsoft recommends you implement Terminal Services only in remote administration mode on domain controllers so that nonadministrators are not assigned the Log On Locally user right.

> ### Enabling Remote Administration Mode in Windows XP and Windows Server 2003
>
> In Windows XP and Windows Server 2003, remote administration mode is not enabled by default. You must enable remote administration mode in the System Control Panel. This is accomplished by using the following procedure:
>
> 1. In Control Panel, select the System icon.
>
> 2. In the System Properties page, click the Remote tab.
>
> 3. In the Remote tab, in the Remote Desktop section, enable the Allow Users To Connect Remotely To This Computer, and then click OK.

Application Server Mode

Application server mode allows Remote Desktop clients to connect to the terminal server and run any installed applications. The only limiting factors to the number of simultaneous connections that can be made are the physical hardware implemented for the terminal server and the number of licenses you have purchased. For example, if the users implement applications that are processor dependent, such as Microsoft Excel, you should allocate 10 MB of RAM for each Remote Desktop client session.

Microsoft recommends you implement application server mode on member servers when you want users to run an application remotely. For example, you might consider using Terminal Services to deploy an application with a corporate security policy that does not allow it to be run locally on multiple client computers. Terminal Services allows the application to be run from a single location (at the terminal server), rather than at each of the remote client computers.

You also can use Terminal Services when client computers on your network do not have sufficient hardware to run Windows 2000 Professional or Windows XP Professional. In these cases, clients can connect to a server by using application server mode to gain access to a full Windows 2000 desktop without upgrading the client operating system to Windows 2000 Professional or Windows XP Professional.

> **Caution**   Installing applications once Terminal Services is installed in application server mode has its issues. Applications must be installed to allow execution by multiple users. We recommend you either run the command Change User/Install in a command prompt before installing applications or install all applications by using the Add New Programs option in Control Panel.

Restricting Which Users and Groups Are Assigned Rights to Connect to a Terminal Server

The Log On Locally user right is required to connect to a Windows 2000 terminal server. You can restrict which users or groups can connect by using Group Policy to define the users or groups assigned the Log On Locally user right.

To ensure consistent application of the user rights, consider placing all terminal servers in the same OU and defining the user rights in a Group Policy object (GPO) linked to the OU. Ensure that terminal servers are dedicated terminal servers or that they do not host other network services or data that would restrict the assignment of the Log On Locally user right. For example, it is not a good idea to install Terminal Services in application server mode on a domain controller because nonadministrators would require the Log On Locally user right.

Windows Server 2003 Terminal Servers require that all authorized users are assigned the Allow Log On Through Terminal Services user right and that the users are members of the Remote Desktop Users group. If the user is not assigned this user right or is not a member of the Remote Desktop Users group, that person will be unable to connect to the terminal server.

> **Note**   All members of the local Administrators group are allowed to connect through Terminal Services and do not require membership in the Remote Desktop Users group.

Restricting Which Applications Can Be Executed

Rather than allowing Terminal Services users to connect to any application running on the Windows 2000 terminal server, you can restrict which applications they can execute. You can choose to either restrict users to a single application or create a list of approved applications that can be executed in a Terminal Services session.

Restricting Terminal Services Sessions to a Single Application

In the Terminal Services Configuration console at the terminal server, you can configure Terminal Services to execute a single application rather than launch the Windows desktop. This setting is defined in the Environment tab of the RDP-TCP Properties page. When you enable the option to override settings from the user profile and Client Connection Manager Wizard, you must define which application executable is launched and which folder is the default folder.

When Terminal Services is configured to launch a single application, the application is immediately launched when a user connects to a terminal server. When the user exits the application, the Terminal Services session terminates.

> **Note**   Configuring Terminal Services to launch a single application does not preclude the user from launching another application from within that single application. For example, if you restrict a Terminal Services user to running Microsoft Word, nothing will prevent that user from launching Explorer.exe from a Word macro.

Restricting Terminal Services Sessions to Specified Applications

In most cases, you will want to restrict which applications are available to Terminal Services users. By using the Microsoft Application Security tool (Appsec.exe) from the *Microsoft Windows 2000 Server Resource Kit* (Microsoft Press, 2000), you can control which applications can be executed in a Windows 2000 Terminal Services environment.

The Appsec.exe tool enables you to designate which executables are available to Terminal Services users when they connect to a terminal server running in application server mode. Each application is referenced by its full path. For example, C:\Program Files\Microsoft Office\Office11\Winword.exe is the default path for Microsoft Word 2003. If you copy the Winword executable to another folder, the Appsec.exe tool blocks its execution.

> **Caution**   The Appsec.exe tool does not perform any hashing functions on the executable. The tool only looks at the full path of the executable to determine whether the application is allowed to run. If attackers are able to overwrite the allowed application, they can run that application in place of the approved application. For example, if attackers overwrite Winword.exe in the path detailed previously with Cmd.exe, they can gain access to a command prompt.

Once the Application Security tool is enabled, nonadministrators are limited to the applications included in the listing. Default applications are included in the Appsec.exe tool. You should review the default applications listed and determine whether you need them in your environment. Administrators of a computer are not affected by the Appsec.exe restrictions and can run any application loaded at the terminal server.

> **More Info**   If you implement the Appsec.exe tool, ensure that you also apply the patch discussed in Microsoft Knowledge Base article 320181, "How to Use the Application Security Tool to Restrict Access to Programs in Windows 2000 Terminal Services."

In a Windows Server 2003 Terminal Services environment, rather than using the Appsec.exe tool, it is recommended you implement software restriction policies through Group Policy. Software restriction policies enable an administrator to identify and specify which software is allowed to run on a terminal server to protect the terminal server from untrusted code.

A software restriction policy enables one of two default security levels:

- **Disallowed**   No programs are allowed to be executed on a host where the software restriction policy is applied.

- **Unrestricted**   All programs are allowed to be executed on a host where the software restriction policy is applied.

In both cases, exceptions can be included either to allow or disallow specific applications from being executed. These exceptions are defined in one of four ways:

- **Hash rules**   An application file is passed through a hashing algorithm to create a thumbprint or hash value. The resulting thumbprint will identify the application file, even if the file name is changed or the location of the file is changed.

- **Certificate rules**   An application file is signed with a trusted code-signing software publisher certificate issued either by an internally trusted Certification Authority (CA) or by a commercial CA. As with a hash rule, a certificate rule will recognize the application file if the file name is changed or the location of the file is changed.

- **Path rules**   An application file is identified by its storage in the specified local or network path. The designated path applies to the designated folder and all subfolders.

- **Internet zone rules**   For Microsoft Windows Installer packages, an Internet zone rule can designate which Internet Security zones allow the execution of installer packages. Although they prevent software installation by installer packages, Internet zone rules do not prevent the execution of programs downloaded by using Microsoft Internet Explorer.

Note   The advantage of using software restriction policy is that the policies apply to both console sessions, whether logon is at the console or using the Remote Desktop client with the /console option, and Terminal Services sessions. They are not limited to Terminal Services sessions, as is security defined by using the Appsec.exe tool.

Implementing the Strongest Form of Encryption

Terminal Services can implement different levels of encryption to protect data transmitted between the Remote Desktop client and the terminal server. The level you select should be based on your company's security policy.

The Terminal Services encryption level is defined in the Terminal Services Configuration console in the General tab of the RDP-TCP Properties page of the terminal server. You can choose from the following encryption levels in Windows 2000:

- **Low encryption** Network traffic is encrypted only when sent from the client to the server. Data is encrypted by using the RC4 encryption algorithm with either a 40-bit key or a 56-bit key. The 40-bit key is required for RDP 4.0 clients. RDP 5.0 clients implement a 56-bit key by default. This encryption format protects passwords input by users, but does not protect the screen data returned from the server to the client.

- **Medium encryption** Network traffic is encrypted in both directions as it transmits between the client and server. Data is encrypted by using the RC4 encryption algorithm with either a 40-bit key or a 56-bit key.

- **High encryption** Network traffic is encrypted in both directions as it transmits between the client and server. Data is encrypted by using the RC4 encryption algorithm with a 128-bit key and requires the installation of the Windows 2000 High Encryption Pack at both the client and server. If the High Encryption Pack is not installed, encryption will fall back to the 40-bit or 56-bit key used for medium encryption.

> **Note** The High Encryption Pack is included in Windows 2000 Service Pack 2 and later. If you have maintained your service packs, there should be no need to apply the High Encryption Pack.

The encryption levels differ for Windows Server 2003. The following levels are available in Windows Server 2003:

- **Low** Network traffic sent from the client to the server is encrypted using 56-bit RC4 encryption.

- **Client Compatible** Network traffic is encrypted between the client and the server at the maximum key strength supported by the client. Use this level when the terminal server is running in an environment containing mixed or legacy clients.

- **High** Network traffic is encrypted in both directions as it transmits between the client and server. Data is encrypted by using the RC4 encryption algorithm with a 128-bit key. Clients that do not support the 128-bit RC4 encryption key will not be able to connect.

■ **FIPS Compliant** Network traffic is encrypted in both directions as it transmits between the client and the server. Data is encrypted with the Federal Information Processing Standard (FIPS) encryption algorithms using the Microsoft cryptographic modules.

> **Note** If the System Cryptography: Use FIPS Compliant Algorithms For Encryption, Hashing, And Signing Group Policy is enabled, the Terminal Services encryption level will be set to FIPS Compliant and cannot be changed.

> **Note** If you want to further increase the encryption level used for Terminal Services communications, you can implement Internet Protocol Security (IPSec) for all communications between the Remote Desktop clients. For details on how to implement IPSec for this configuration, see the two documents cited in the "Additional Information" section of this chapter that reference IPSec.

Strengthening the Security Configuration of the Terminal Server

You can increase the default security configuration of a Windows 2000 terminal server by installing Terminal Services with the Permissions Compatible With Windows 2000 Users option enabled. The default setting, Permissions Compatible With Terminal Server 4.0 Users, allows users connecting with Remote Desktop clients to modify critical registry and file system locations. Access is granted by using the Terminal Server User account in discretionary access control lists (DACLs).

If you install Terminal Services with Permissions Compatible With Terminal Server 4.0 Users, you can strengthen the security by implementing the Notssid.inf security template. This template reverses weakened security settings and ensures that registry and file system permissions do not refer to the Terminal Server User account. To implement the Notssid.inf security template, have a local administrator run the following command at the terminal server:

```
secedit /configure /db notssid.sdb /cfg notssid.inf /log notssid.log /verbose
```

This command applies the Notssid.inf security template and records a log file in a file named Notssid.log.

> **Note** For a Windows Server 2003 Terminal Server environment, you can switch between the two security modes by using the Terminal Services Configuration console to change the Permission Compatibility setting.

Increasing Authentication Security in Windows Server 2003 SP1

Windows Server 2003 Service Pack 1 includes the ability to implement Secure Sockets Layer (SSL) authentication and encryption for connections between a Remote Desktop client and a Windows Server 2003 terminal server.

To use SSL protection in a Windows Server 2003 Terminal Services connection, the following conditions must be met:

- A Web server certificate (or other SSL-enabling certificate) must be installed on the terminal server.

- The Web server certificate must chain to a root CA that is trusted by both the terminal server and the Terminal Services clients.

- The Web server certificate subject name must match the Domain Name System (DNS) name used by the Remote Desktop clients to connect to the terminal server.

- The client computer running Windows 2000, Windows XP, or Windows Server 2003 must install the updated version of the Remote Desktop client software.

Tip   You can install the updated Remote Desktop Connection software from the %windir%\system32\clients\tsclient\win32\msrdpcli.msi folder on a computer running Windows Server 2003 family products with Windows Server 2003 Service Pack 1 installed.

Enabling SSL at the Terminal Server

To enable SSL at a terminal server that has Windows Server 2003 Service Pack 1 installed, you must first select a certificate for server authentication. Use the following procedure:

1. From Administrative Tools, open Terminal Services Configuration.

2. In the console tree, click Connections.

3. In the details pane, right-click the connection you want to modify, and then click Properties.

4. In the General tab, in the Security section, click Edit, click an available certificate, and then click View Certificate.

5. Verify that the certificate's private key is installed locally and that the subject name matches the DNS name of the terminal server.

> **Tip** If the private key is installed locally, the bottom of the General tab will show the message text "You have a private key that corresponds to this certificate."

6. After you have verified that the certificate has a private key, click OK.

7. In the Select Certificate window, click OK.

> **Tip** If you do not have a certificate installed for use by Terminal Services, you must request a SSL-enabling certificate from either a commercial CA or from an internal CA that contains the correct DNS name in the subject of the certificate.

Once you have selected a certificate, you must enable SSL server authentication at the terminal server:

1. From Administrative Tools, open Terminal Services Configuration.

2. In the console tree, click Connections.

3. In the details pane, right-click the connection you want to modify, and then click Properties.

4. In the General tab, in the Security section, in the Security Layer drop-down list, choose one of the following options:

   ❑ **RDP Security Layer** Do not enable SSL authentication. Only use RDP encryption levels discussed earlier in this chapter: Low, Client Compatible, High, or FIPS Compliant.

   ❑ **Negotiate** Attempt to implement an SSL connection between the Remote Desktop client and the terminal server. If unable to implement an SSL connection, implement RDP security.

   ❑ **SSL** Only allow SSL connections to the terminal server. In addition, the encryption level must be set to Client Compatible, High, or FIPS Compliant.

5. After you have finished making your selection, click OK.

Configuring the Terminal Server Client to Use SSL

As mentioned earlier, the client computer must have the latest version of the Remote Desktop Connection software installed from a computer running Windows Server 2003 with Service Pack 1 applied. Once the Remote Desktop software is installed, the following procedure enables SSL for a Remote Desktop Connection attempt:

1. From the Start menu, point to All Programs, Accessories, Communications, and then click Remote Desktop Connection.

2. In the Remote Desktop Connection application, click Options.

3. In the Security tab, under Authentication Setting, enable one of the following options:

   ❏ **No Authentication**   Do not implement SSL for server authentication. This is the default behavior setting.

   ❏ **Attempt Authentication**   Attempt to implement SSL for server authentication. If the Remote Desktop Connection is presented with an expired certificate, a certificate for which the subject name of the certificate does not contain the DNS name specified in the Remote Desktop Connection application, or a certificate that does not chain to a trusted root, the user will be allowed to choose whether to continue with the connection attempt. If any other authentication errors occur, the connection will fail.

   ❏ **Require Authentication**   The client must implement SSL for server authentication. If the connection attempt fails for any reason, including presentation of an expired certificate, a certificate for which the subject name of the certificate does not contain the DNS name specified in the Remote Desktop Connection application, or a certificate that does not chain to a trusted root, the connection will fail.

Implementing Two Factor Authentication

In addition to using SSL, you can also increase the authentication strength by implementing two factor authentication when connecting to a Windows Server 2003 terminal server. A user connecting from a Windows XP or Windows Server 2003 computer can use a smart card or other two factor device to authenticate with a Windows Server 2003 terminal server.

Note   Smart card authentication is not available when connecting to a Windows 2000 terminal server. Smart card authentication is only possible when the terminal server is running the Windows Server 2003 operating system.

Best Practices

■ **Install the latest service pack and security updates.**   Ensure that your terminal server is protected by installing the latest service packs and security updates to protect against any known Terminal Services vulnerabilities.

■ **Implement the strongest available form of encryption between the Remote Desktop client and server.**   Ensure that you enable the implementation of high encryption for Terminal Services to protect data sent both to the terminal server and from the terminal server.

■ **Use the Appsec tool or software restriction policies to limit which applications can be executed.**   Appsec.exe enables you to designate which applications are available to nonadministrators in a Terminal Services session. Users are limited to executing the programs listed within the Appsec.exe console. Likewise, software restriction policies can define which applications can be executed for both Terminal Services and console sessions.

■ **Choose the correct mode for your Terminal Services deployment.**   If remote administration is your only requirement, configure Terminal Services to implement remote administration mode rather than application server mode. Remote administration mode allows only two simultaneous connections by members of the Administrators group to a Windows 2000 terminal server. A Windows Server 2003 terminal server also allows an additional console session. By default, nonadministrators are blocked from connecting to the terminal server.

■ **Do not implement application server mode on domain controllers.**   To connect to a Windows 2000 terminal server from the network, users must have the Log On Locally user right assigned. If you implement application server mode on a domain controller, nonadministrators must be assigned the Log On Locally user right at the domain controller. Because this user right is typically assigned in Group Policy, it enables users to log on at the console of any domain controller in the domain, greatly reducing security. Windows Server 2003 increases security by eliminating the need to assign the Log On Locally user right. Instead, the user must be assigned the Allow Log On Through Terminal Services user right and must have membership in the Remote Desktop Users group.

■ **Apply the Notssid.inf security template to Windows 2000 terminal servers running Permissions Compatible With Terminal Server 4.0 Users.**   This security template ensures that excess permissions are not granted to Remote Desktop clients. This option might not allow some older applications to execute, so we recommend you upgrade to newer applications that follow the Windows 2000 security model.

■ **Monitor the membership of the Remote Desktop Users group in Windows Server 2003.**   Members of the Remote Desktop Users group can connect to a Windows Server 2003 terminal server running in remote administration mode if they are also assigned the Allow Log On Through Terminal Services user right.

Additional Information

- U.S. National Security Agency, "Guide to Securing Microsoft Windows 2000 Terminal Services" (*http://www.nsa.gov/snac/os/win2k/w2k_terminal_serv.pdf*)

- *Microsoft Windows 2000 Server Deployment Planning Guide*, Chapter 16, "Deploying Terminal Services" (*http://www.microsoft.com/resources /documentation/windows/2000/server/reskit/en-us/deploy/dgbm_win_vrci.asp*)

- "Windows 2000 Terminal Services Capacity and Scaling" (*http:// www.microsoft.com/technet/prodtechnol/win2kts/maintain/optimize /w2ktsscl.mspx*)

- "Securing Windows 2000 Terminal Services" (*http://www.microsoft.com /technet/prodtechnol/win2kts/maintain/optimize/secw2kts.mspx*)

- "Locking Down Windows Server 2003 Terminal Server Sessions" (*http:// www.microsoft.com/windowsserver2003/techinfo/overview/lockdown.mspx*)

- *Windows Server 2003 Security Guide* (*http://www.microsoft.com/downloads /details.aspx?familyid=8A2643C1-0685-4D89-B655-521EA6C7B4DB&display-lang=en*)

- Windows Server 2003 Service Pack 1 Readme file

- The following Knowledge Base articles:

    - 187623: "How to Change Terminal Server's Listening Port" (*http://support.microsoft.com/kb/187623*)

    - 238965: "Removing Additional Permissions Granted to Terminal Services Users" (*http://support.microsoft.com/kb/238965*)

    - 247989: "Domain Controllers Require the 'Log on Locally' Group Policy Object for Terminal Services Client Connections" (*http://support.microsoft.com/kb/247989*)

    - 257980: "Appsec Tool in the Windows 2000 Resource Kit Is Missing Critical Files" (*http://support.microsoft.com/kb/257980*)

    - 260370: "How to Apply Group Policy Objects to Terminal Services Servers" (*http://support.microsoft.com/kb/260370*)

    - 315055: "How to Use IPSec Policy to Secure Terminal Services Communications in Windows 2000" (*http://support.microsoft.com/kb/315055*)

    - 816521: "How to Use IPSec Policy to Secure Terminal Services Communications in Windows Server 2003" (*http://support.microsoft.com/kb /816521*)

❑ 324036: "How to Use Software Restriction Policies in Windows Server 2003" (*http://support.microsoft.com/kb/324036*)

❑ 320181: "How to Use the Application Security Tool to Restrict Access to Programs in Windows 2000 Terminal Services" (*http://support.microsoft.com/kb/320181*)

Chapter 20
Implementing Security for DHCP Servers

Dynamic Host Configuration Protocol (DHCP) eases the deployment of IP addresses to TCP/IP-based network hosts, including client computers and network devices such as TCP/IP-based print servers. A DHCP client acquires an IP address and related TCP/IP configuration information from a DHCP server.

When you implement DHCP on your network, DHCP clients send out broadcast information to User Datagram Protocol (UDP) port 67, requesting TCP/IP configuration information. DHCP servers listen for the DHCP requests and respond with DHCP configuration information. Technically, four packets are exchanged between the DHCP server and the DHCP client during the DHCP lease process:

1. The DHCP client sends a DHCPDISCOVER message that contains the requesting host's Media Access Control (MAC) address and, if the client is a computer, the client computer's name.

2. All DHCP servers that receive the DHCPDISCOVER message and have available addresses for the subnet where the DHCP request was initiated respond with a DHCPOFFER message. The message contains the client's MAC address, an offered IP address and subnet mask, the length of the DHCP lease, and the IP address of the offering DHCP server.

3. The DHCP client responds to the first offer it receives by broadcasting a DHCPREQUEST message. This message includes the IP address of the DHCP server whose offer is accepted so that other DHCP servers will withdraw their offers and return the IP addresses to the available pool of DHCP IP addresses.

4. The DHCP server issues the address information to the requesting client in a DHCPACK message. The message contains the final lease period for the address, along with other TCP/IP configuration information.

A typical attack against DHCP involves an attempt to prevent an authorized DHCP server from responding to a DHCPDISCOVER message, or it involves modifying a DHCP server to assign incorrect TCP/IP configuration information. This chapter looks at the configuration measures you can take to prevent attacks against DHCP servers.

Threats to DHCP Servers

If attackers are able to compromise a DHCP server on the network, they might disrupt network services, preventing DHCP clients from connecting to network resources. By gaining control of a DHCP server, attackers can configure DHCP clients with fraudulent TCP/IP configuration information, including an invalid default gateway or Domain Name System (DNS) server configuration.

The following threats exist when you implement DHCP on your network:

- Unauthorized DHCP servers can issue incorrect TCP/IP configuration information to DHCP clients.
- DHCP servers can overwrite valid DNS resource records with incorrect information.
- DHCP can create DNS resource records without ownership defined.
- Unauthorized DHCP clients can obtain IP addresses on the network.

Unauthorized DHCP Servers

If attackers can connect a computer to your company's network, they can launch an unauthorized DHCP server. This DHCP server can provide incorrect IP addressing information to DHCP clients. Microsoft Windows 2000 and Windows Server 2003 reduce the possibility of unauthorized Windows 2000–based and Windows Server 2003–based DHCP servers by requiring that Windows 2000–based and Windows Server 2003–based DHCP servers be authorized in the Active Directory directory service.

> **Note**   Only members of the Enterprise Admins group can authorize a Windows 2000–based or Windows Server 2003–based DHCP server to issue IP addresses to DHCP clients.

A Windows 2000 or Windows Server 2003 DHCP server uses DHCPINFORM messages to determine whether it is authorized. When a DHCP server starts, the DHCP server queries any domain controller to ensure it is listed as an authorized DHCP server in the Configuration naming context. If the DHCP server is authorized, the

DHCP service initializes and provides IP address information to DHCP clients. If the server is not authorized, DHCP services do not initialize. The DHCP service will also start if it determines that Active Directory does not exist on the network, indicating that DHCP servers do not require authorization.

> **Warning**   The DHCPINFORM process does not prevent DHCP servers that do not support DHCPINFORM messages, such as a Microsoft Windows NT 4.0 DHCP server, from issuing addresses on the network.

DHCP Servers Overwriting Valid DNS Resource Records

By default, the DHCP server and the DHCP client split the process of registering DNS resource records with the DNS server. By default, the DHCP server registers and owns the Pointer (PTR) resource records written to the reverse lookup zone at the DNS server. The DHCP client registers its Host (or A) resource record in the forward lookup zone.

If attackers modify the DHCP server's configuration, it is possible for the DHCP server to register and own both resource records. If the DHCP server overwrites the client information, the client can be blocked from updating its IP address information in DNS. The client is blocked because the DNS resource record's discretionary access control list (DACL) allows only the owner of the resource record to modify the resource record when secure dynamic updates are implemented at the DNS server.

> **Note**   Modifying DHCP to register both the PTR and A resource records is required for clients running versions earlier than Windows 2000 that do not support dynamic DNS updates but is not recommended for Windows 2000, Microsoft Windows XP, Windows Server 2003, or other operating systems that support dynamic DNS updates.

DHCP Not Taking Ownership of DNS Resource Records

If a DHCP server is configured as a member of the DnsUpdateProxy group, the DHCP server does not take ownership of the DNS resource records it registers. Although this behavior is desired when a DHCP server registers Host (A) resource records for client computers running versions earlier than Windows 2000, allowing these client computers to take ownership of the A resource record when upgraded to Windows 2000, Windows XP, or Windows Server 2003 requires additional configuration if the DHCP server is also a domain controller.

It also is not desirable for a DHCP server to take ownership of DNS resource records when multiple DHCP servers provide IP addresses for the network. If the DHCP server took ownership of A resource records registered on behalf of a downlevel client, another DHCP server would not be able to overwrite the record if the client acquired its IP address from a different DHCP server.

Unauthorized DHCP Clients

By default, a DHCP server will issue an IP address to any DHCP client that requests one, as long as addresses are available in the *DHCP scope*, which is a pool of IP addresses leased by the DHCP server. This means that any DHCP client can obtain an IP address and TCP/IP configuration information from a DHCP server, even if the DHCP client is not an authorized computer. Once a DHCP client has obtained TCP/IP configuration information, the DHCP client can communicate with any TCP/IP services on the network, including file servers and other Active Directory services.

Securing DHCP Servers

You can take several measures to prevent attacks against DHCP servers and DHCP clients. These measures range from monitoring membership in the DHCP Administrators group to performing specific DHCP service configuration. Specifically, consider the following measures:

- Keep default name registration behavior.
- Determine which account to include in the membership of the DnsUpdateProxy group.
- Review the DHCP database frequently for BAD_ADDRESS entries.
- Monitor membership in the DHCP Administrators group.
- Enable DHCP auditing.

Keeping Default Name Registration Behavior

By default, when a DHCP client obtains IP configuration information from a DHCP server, the DHCP server registers the PTR resource record for the client and the client registers its own A resource record. We recommend you maintain this default behavior so that the DHCP server maintains ownership of PTR resource records and the clients maintain ownership of the A resource records. When you implement secure updates, only the owner of the resource record can update the resource record. You can change this default behavior, but doing so can lead to incorrect DNS information if the client changes subnets and the TCP/IP address configuration information is supplied by a different DHCP server that cannot modify the DNS resource records.

Tip   If a computer running Windows 2000, Windows XP, or Windows Server 2003 is assigned a static IP address, that computer will use the DHCP Client service to register both its A and PTR resource records. You must not disable the DHCP Client service on computers that are assigned a static TCP/IP configuration.

Determining Which Account to Include in the DnsUpdateProxy Group Membership

Some Microsoft documentation recommends adding a DHCP server's computer account to the membership of the DnsUpdateProxy group. Membership in this group prevents the DHCP computer from taking ownership of resource records it registers in DNS. In upgrade scenarios, it is common to configure the DHCP server to register DNS information on behalf of Windows clients that do not support dynamic DNS updates. Including the DHCP server's computer account in the DnsUpdateProxy group ensures that the DHCP server does not take ownership of DNS resource records it updates. This enables the Windows client to take ownership of the A resource record when the operating system is upgraded to Windows 2000, Windows XP, or Windows Server 2003. If the computer account is included in the DnsUpdateProxy group's membership, the DHCP server computer will not take ownership of *any* DNS resource records it registers with DNS. This includes all Service (SRV) resource records if the DHCP server is installed on a domain controller.

Windows 2000 with Service Pack 1 or higher applied and Windows Server 2003 allow you to configure the DHCP service to impersonate another user account when registering DHCP-related DNS resource records. When implemented, all DNS registrations performed by the DHCP service are performed in the security context of this designated user account, rather than using the DHCP server's computer account.

To designate the user account in Windows 2000, you must use the Netsh.exe command. The process for designating the user account is as follows:

1. Create a user account in the Active Directory Users and Computers console. This user account will be used by the DHCP Server service for all DNS registrations.

2. Add the user account to the membership of the DnsUpdateProxy group.

3. In a command prompt, use the Netsh.exe tool to designate the user account:

    ```
    Netsh dhcp server set dnscredentials UserName DomainName Password
    ```

> **Tip** Alternatively, you can replace the *Password* option with an asterisk (*) to have the command prompt you for the password assigned to the user account. Once you have typed this command, you must restart the DHCP Server service.

For Windows Server 2003, you can now designate the user account in the DHCP console by using the following procedure:

1. Create a user account in the Active Directory Users and Computers console. This user account will be used by the DHCP Server service for all DNS registrations.

2. Add the user account to the membership of the DnsUpdateProxy group.

3. In the DHCP console, click the *DNS name* of the DHCP server, right-click the server name, and then click Properties.

4. In the Advanced tab, click Credentials.

5. In the DNS Dynamic Update Credentials dialog box (see Figure 20-1), provide the user name, domain, and password for the user account created in step 1, and then click OK.

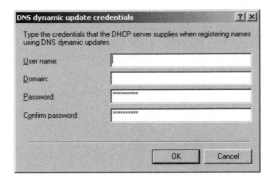

Figure 20-1   Designating the user account to use for DHCP dynamic update registrations

Reviewing the DHCP Database for BAD_ADDRESS Entries

The existence of BAD_ADDRESS entries in the DHCP database can indicate an attempt to prevent a DHCP server from assigning DHCP addresses or could indicate a poorly configured DHCP environment.

A BAD_ADDRESS lease can take place under different circumstances. If you overlap DHCP scopes between DHCP servers, it is possible for two DHCP servers to issue the same IP address. When a second DHCP server attempts to issue a duplicate IP address, the second DHCP server will register the IP address as a BAD_ADDRESS.

Alternatively, an attacker could assign multiple static IP addresses to her computer. If those addresses are assigned by a DHCP server, DHCP clients determine that the IP addresses are in use and reject the offered DHCP-assigned IP address.

Monitoring Membership in the DHCP Administrators Group

Members of the DHCP Administrators group are delegated permissions to configure a DHCP server. DHCP Administrators can create DHCP scopes, define DHCP configuration options, and create DHCP reservations.

Closely monitor membership in the DHCP Administrators group—as well as membership in the local Administrators group, the Domain Admins group, and the Enterprise Admins group—to determine who has the necessary permissions to manage DHCP services. Membership in these groups allows management of all DHCP servers in the domain.

> **Note**   A member of the DHCP Administrators group cannot authorize a DHCP server in Active Directory. Only members of the Enterprise Admins group can perform this task. You can delegate the right to authorize DHCP servers by following the solution proposed in Microsoft Knowledge Base article 239004, "How to Allow Non-Root or Enterprise Administrators to Authorize RIS Servers in Active Directory."

Enabling DHCP Auditing

To determine exactly which DHCP clients are connecting to the DHCP server and where BAD_ADDRESS entries originate, enable DHCP auditing at the DHCP server. You can permit DHCP server auditing by enabling the Enable DHCP Auditing Logging option in the properties of the DHCP server in the DHCP console. This option provides daily log files for the DHCP service in the %windir%\system32\dhcp folder. In addition to enabling DHCP auditing in the DHCP console, you can further adjust DHCP auditing by modifying the HKLM\SYSTEM\CurrentControlSet\Services\DhcpServer\Parameters\DhcpLogFilesMaxSize registry entry, which defines the maximum size of DHCP log files.

Best Practices

■ **Designate a user account for DHCP registrations rather than using the computer account.**   When you configure a DHCP server, ensure that you designate a specific user account for the DHCP service to use when updating DNS resource records for DHCP clients. The user account's membership in the DnsUpdateProxy group prevents the DHCP server from taking ownership of the DHCP-related DNS records, but still allows the computer account to register and take ownership of all SRV resource records registered by the DHCP's Netlogon service when DHCP is installed on a domain controller or other application server that registers SRV resource records.

- **Do not use DHCP-assigned addresses for servers.** It is preferable to assign static IP addresses to servers and critical workstations to ensure they cannot receive incorrect TCP/IP configuration information from a rogue DHCP server.

- **Monitor membership in the DnsUpdateProxy group.** Unless you are performing computer upgrades on the network, the DnsUpdateProxy group should not have any members. If you do include members in the DnsUpdateProxy group, ensure that designated user accounts, rather than the DHCP server's computer account, is included in the DnsUpdateProxy group.

- **Monitor membership in the DHCP Administrators group.** Members of the DHCP Administrators group can modify DHCP configuration. Also watch membership in the local Administrators group, the Domain Admins group, and the Enterprise Admins group because these groups have permissions to allow management of the DHCP server.

- **Enable DHCP auditing.** DHCP auditing enables you to track which devices are assigned DHCP addresses and to troubleshoot address conflicts when BAD_ADDRESS entries appear in the DHCP database.

- **Do not change the default behavior for DNS registration.** The default behavior for DHCP is that the DHCP server owns the PTR resource records and the DHCP client owns the A resource records. Do not change this behavior unless you require the DHCP server to own all DNS resource records.

- **Consider implementing IPSec filters to limit traffic accepted by DHCP servers.** The Internet Protocol Security (IPSec) filters listed in Table 20-1 limit the traffic accepted by a DHCP server to only DHCP-related traffic.

Table 20-1   Recommended IPSec Filters for DHCP Servers

Service	Protocol	Source Port	Destination Port	Source Address	Destination Address	Action	Mirror
One Point Client	ANY	ANY	ANY	ME	MOM server	Allow	Yes
Terminal Services	TCP	ANY	3389	ANY	ME	Allow	Yes
Domain Member	ANY	ANY	ANY	ME	Each domain controller's IP address	Allow	Yes
DHCP Server	UDP	68	67	ANY	ME	Allow	Yes
All inbound traffic	ANY	ANY	ANY	ANY	ME	Block	Yes

Note   These IPSec filters assume that the DHCP server functions only as a DHCP server and a domain member. If the server holds additional roles, additional IPSec filters are required to allow the traffic associated with the additional roles.

On the CD   A script file, PacketFilters-DHCP.CMD.txt, that implements the IPSec filters listed in the preceding table is included on the CD-ROM that accompanies this book. The script must be modified with the IP addresses of domain controllers and Microsoft Operations Manager (MOM) servers before being executed.

Additional Information

- U.S. National Security Agency, "Guide to Securing Microsoft Windows 2000 DHCP" (*http://www.nsa.gov/snac/os/win2k/w2k_dhcp.pdf*)

- *Microsoft Windows 2000 Server Resource Kit,* "TCP/IP Core Networking Guide— Dynamic Host Configuration Protocol" (*http://www.microsoft.com/resources /documentation/Windows/2000/server/reskit/en-us/cnet/cncb_dhc_klom.asp*)

- *Windows Server 2003 Security Guide* (*http://www.microsoft.com/downloads /details.aspx?familyid=8A2643C1-0685-4D89-B655-521EA6C7B4DB&display-lang=en*)

- "Security Information for DHCP" (*http://www.microsoft.com/resources /documentation/windowsserv/2003/standard/proddocs/en-us /sag_dhcp_ovr_security.asp*)

- "Enterprise Design for DHCP" (*http://www.microsoft.com/technet/itsolutions /wssra/raguide/Network_Services_SB_2.mspx*)

- RFC 2131: "Dynamic Host Configuration Protocol" (*http://www.ietf.org/rfc /rfc2131.txt*)

- Knowledge Base article 239004: "How to Allow Non-Root or Enterprise Administrators to Authorize RIS Servers in Active Directory" (*http://support.microsoft.com /kb/239004*)

- Knowledge Base article 255134: "Installing Dynamic Host Configuration Protocol (DHCP) and Domain Name System (DNS) on a Domain Controller" (*http://support.microsoft.com/kb/255134*)

- Knowledge Base article 317590: "How to Configure DNS Dynamic Update in Windows 2000" (*http://support.microsoft.com/kb/317590*)

- Knowledge Base article 816592: "How to Configure DNS Dynamic Update in Windows 2003" (*http://support.microsoft.com/kb/816592*)

Chapter 21
Implementing Security for WINS Servers

Windows Internet Name Service (WINS) servers provide resolution of computer and group NetBIOS names, such as a workgroup name, to IP addresses. For example, when you log on to the network from a computer running a version earlier than Microsoft Windows 2000, the computer, by default, will query the WINS server configured in the TCP/IP properties to find a domain controller for network authentication.

NetBIOS names can be broken into two general categories: *unique registrations* and *group registrations*. A unique registration is registered by a single user or computer. By default, if a record exists, that record is not modified. The only time a record is modified is when the current owner cannot be contacted by the WINS server. A group registration is registered by mapping a NetBIOS name to multiple IP addresses. For example, the first 25 domain controllers in a domain will register their IP address in the *Domain*[1C] group NetBIOS name.

The following records are unique registration NetBIOS records you generally will see. Attackers can attempt to hijack these registrations by registering the NetBIOS names with the WINS server, preventing the correct host or user from registering the names, or performing a denial-of-service attack against the registered user or computer, thereby preventing that user or computer from responding to the WINS server verification.

- *Computer*[00]   The Workstation service registration for a computer. Enabled when the Workstation service is enabled.
- *Computer*[20]   The Server service registration for a computer.
- *Computer*[03]   The Messenger service registration for a computer account. This service allows NET SEND messages to reach the computer.

- *User*[03]   The Messenger service registration for a user account. This service allows NET SEND messages to reach the user.

- *Domain*[1B]   The domain master browser registration.

> **Note**   Typically, this NetBIOS name is registered by the domain controller holding the Primary Domain Controller (PDC) Emulator role in a Windows 2000 or Windows Server 2003 domain. If the PDC is unavailable, another domain controller in the domain will register the *Domain*[1B] registration.

For group registrations, the behavior depends on the specific group record. For example, the *Domain*[1C] record contains a maximum of 25 IP addresses of domain controllers in a domain. If any additional domain controllers attempt to add their IP addresses to the current list, the WINS server will first try to remove any replicated entries, those not owned by the current WINS server, and failing that, will remove the oldest entry in the listing. Other group registrations might indicate only the domain or workgroup of which a computer is a member (for example, *Domain*[20]).

The Death of NetBIOS

With Windows 2000 and Microsoft Windows Server 2003, NetBIOS is not necessarily required. In fact, you can remove NetBIOS support in the TCP/IP properties of computers that run Windows 2000, Microsoft Windows XP, and Windows Server 2003. Rather than connecting to a computer on the NetBIOS port (Transmission Control Protocol port 139), computers running Windows Server 2003, Windows 2000, and Windows XP can implement file shares by using Common Internet File System (CIFS), an evolution of NetBIOS that does not require NetBIOS implementation. CIFS-compliant applications will connect to TCP port 445 rather than TCP port 139.

You can remove NetBIOS support from the TCP/IP stack, thereby eliminating the need for WINS servers Before you perform this task, make sure that no applications or computers running versions earlier than Windows 2000 that require NetBIOS remain.

Threats to WINS Servers

A WINS server faces several threats that can result in compromised or unauthorized modifications of records in the WINS server database. These threats include the following:

- Preventing replication between WINS servers
- Registration of false NetBIOS records
- Incorrect registration of WINS records
- Modification of WINS configuration
- Denial-of-service attacks against WINS servers

Preventing Replication Between WINS Servers

The WINS database is a distributed database. Clients register their NetBIOS names with the first WINS servers listed in the client's TCP/IP properties. The WINS servers then replicate their portion of the WINS database with the other WINS servers on the network. If replication is prevented, a WINS client will not be able to reach any NetBIOS clients whose NetBIOS records are missing from their WINS server database. Replication can be prevented by denial-of-service attacks against the WINS server or by compromising the WINS servers, resulting in the modification of the WINS replication settings.

Registration of False NetBIOS Records

A WINS client will register its NetBIOS host and group records with its configured WINS server. If the record already exists in the WINS database, the WINS server will attempt to detect whether the current owner of the record exists on the network. If the previous client cannot be reached, a new client replaces the current record. An attacker can hijack the WINS database record by performing a denial-of-service attack against the current record holder. The denial-of-service attack prevents the previous client from responding to the WINS server's validation request.

Incorrect Registration of WINS Records

An attacker can register a computer record with the same name as a group record. For example, to block authentication with a domain named NWTRADERS, an attacker might attempt to register a host record with the name NWTRADERS. Although the names are technically different (one is a host name and the other is a group name), the existence of the host record will prevent registration of the domain record. This results in authentication failure for clients attempting to connect to the domain record.

Modification of WINS Configuration

If an attacker gains access to the WINS console with the appropriate permissions, she can modify the configuration of the WINS server. The attacker can modify the settings for WINS replication, add static WINS records, or remove valid WINS records and replace them with false WINS records.

Denial-of-Service Attacks Against WINS Servers

If an attacker gains access to a network implementing a WINS server, the attacker could perform a denial-of-service attack in one of two ways: sending numerous name registration messages or sending numerous name resolution requests. The overloading of the WINS server with fraudulent registrations or requests ties up WINS so that required name resolutions or registrations are queued or dropped by the WINS server, resulting in WINS clients being unable to resolve NetBIOS names on remote subnets.

Securing WINS Servers

To protect a WINS server against these threats, you must take measures that limit the probability of a successful attack. The following measures can be taken:

- Monitor membership in administrative groups.
- Validate WINS replication configuration.
- Implement static WINS entries for critical NetBIOS applications.
- Eliminate NetBIOS applications and decommission them.
- Implement detailed WINS logging in the Event log.

Monitor Membership in Administrative Groups

Members of the Server Operators and local Administrators groups at a WINS server can modify the WINS server's configuration, including replication and the capability to add static WINS records to the WINS database. By restricting membership, you restrict who can make these modifications. Periodically review the membership of these administrative groups to ensure that members are authorized.

Note In Windows Server 2003, the WINS administration console improves management by enabling a WINS administrator to choose multiple WINS records for deletion and providing improved search and filtering capabilities, which are essential for large WINS deployments.

Validate WINS Replication Configuration

Periodically review the WINS replication configuration to make certain that sufficient connectivity exists between the deployed WINS servers. Sufficient connectivity enables full replication of the WINS database between all WINS servers. If a WINS server is removed from the network, it is possible for duplicate WINS records—including false records—to be created in the WINS database.

> **Note**   In Windows Server 2003, you can protect against rogue WINS servers by defining a list of *approved* WINS servers for the incoming NetBIOS name records and designating the IP address of WINS servers from which the WINS servers will not accept replicated data. For a trusted WINS server, an administrator can define a persistent connection to a WINS replication partner, resulting in more timely replication of updated WINS records.

Implement Static WINS Entries for Critical NetBIOS Applications

An administrator can prevent the fraudulent update of critical WINS name registrations by defining static WINS entries. A static WINS entry can prevent a rogue server from hijacking WINS records.

> **Note**   If you're using Windows Server 2003, you can prevent the overwriting of static WINS entries by *disabling* the Overwrite Unique Static Mappings At This Server option. For a Windows 2000 WINS server, you can prevent the overwriting of static records by disabling the Migrate On option.

Eliminate NetBIOS Applications and Decommission Them

Ultimately, attacks against a WINS server can be prevented by eliminating NetBIOS applications. Upgrade all applications that require NetBIOS to versions that do not.

You can disable NetBIOS on clients that run Windows 2000, Windows XP, and Windows Server 2003 by clicking Disable NetBIOS Over TCP/IP in the WINS tab of Advanced TCP/IP Settings for a network adapter. Alternatively, you can disable NetBIOS under Advanced Scope Options For A DHCP Scope by clicking the Microsoft Disable NetBIOS option under Microsoft Windows 2000 or Windows Server 2003 Options For DHCP Clients.

Ensure that NetBIOS is not used on the network before disabling NetBIOS at each computer running Windows 2000. You can determine whether NetBIOS is required by monitoring the following Performance Monitor counters at each WINS server:

- WINS Server: Total Number Of Registrations/Sec
- WINS Server: Queries/Sec
- WINS Server: Successful Queries/Sec

Remember that if a client computer is configured with a WINS server's IP address, it will send queries to the WINS server.

Implement Detailed WINS Logging in the Event Log

By implementing detailed WINS logging, you can detect a denial-of-service attack earlier by monitoring the WINS server's Event log. The System log will include the following events that help detect large volumes of activity against the WINS server:

- **WINS 4338**   Identifies that the WINS server has started the burst handling of incoming requests. Although this can imply an attack against the WINS server, there is the possibility that you must improve the hardware implemented for the WINS server.

- **WINS 4339**   Identifies that the WINS server has ceased to use burst handling of incoming requests. The event is triggered when the queue length reaches a size of one-quarter the size attained when burst handling was implemented.

To implement detailed WINS logging, use the following procedure:

1. From Administrative Tools, open the WINS console.
2. In the console tree, click the applicable WINS server.
3. Right-click the applicable WINS server, and then click Properties.
4. In the Advanced tab, enable the Log Detailed Events To Windows Event Log option.

Best Practices

- **Minimize the number of WINS servers on the network.**   By minimizing the number of WINS servers, you reduce the number of server configurations that must be verified. In addition, minimizing the number of WINS servers lessens the complexity of configuring WINS replication.

- **Manually define WINS replication.**   If you minimize the number of WINS servers, you can manually configure WINS replication partners to ensure that all WINS servers receive all updates to the WINS database, including all updates registered at the other WINS servers.

- **Define the sources for incoming replication.**   If deploying a Windows Server 2003 WINS environment, limit the source of incoming name registration records to only known WINS servers to prevent the registration of resource records from a fraudulent WINS server.

- **Monitor the membership of all administrative groups.**   The Administrators and Server Operators groups have the necessary permissions to modify a WINS server's configuration. Validate the membership of these groups at regular intervals.

- **Apply the latest hotfixes and security patches.**   Application of the latest hotfixes and security patches ensures that your WINS servers are protected against any known WINS attacks.

- **Eliminate NetBIOS applications.**   By eliminating NetBIOS-dependent applications, you remove the need for NetBIOS name resolution. Take measures—such as upgrading applications and installing the Microsoft Directory Services client on clients that run Microsoft Windows 95, Windows 98, Windows Millennium Edition (Me), and Windows NT 4.0—to remove their dependency on NetBIOS for network authentication.

- **Consider implementing IPSec filters to limit traffic accepted by WINS servers.**   The Internet Protocol Security (IPSec) filters listed in Table 21-1 limit the traffic accepted by a WINS server to only WINS-related traffic.

Table 21-1   Recommended IPSec Filters for WINS Servers

Service	Protocol	Source Port	Destination Port	Source Address	Destination Address	Action	Mirror
One Point Client	ANY	ANY	ANY	ME	MOM Server	Allow	Yes
Terminal Services	TCP	ANY	3389	ANY	ME	Allow	Yes
Domain Member	ANY	ANY	ANY	ME	Each domain controller's IP address	Allow	Yes
WINS Resolution Server	TCP	ANY	1512	ANY	ME	Allow	Yes
WINS Resolution Server	UDP	ANY	1512	ANY	ME	Allow	Yes
WINS Replication Client	TCP	ANY	42	ME	WINS replication partner	Allow	Yes

Table 21-1   Recommended IPSec Filters for WINS Servers

Service	Protocol	Source Port	Destination Port	Source Address	Destination Address	Action	Mirror
WINS Replication Client	UDP	ANY	42	ME	WINS replication partner	Allow	Yes
WINS Replication Server	TCP	ANY	42	WINS replication partner	ME	Allow	Yes
WINS Replication Server	UDP	ANY	42	WINS replication partner	ME	Allow	Yes
All inbound traffic	ANY	ANY	ANY	ANY	ME	Block	Yes

Note   These IPSec filters assume that the WINS server functions only as a WINS server and domain member. If the server holds additional roles, additional IPSec filters are required to allow the traffic associated with the additional roles.

On the CD   A script file, PacketFilters-WINS.CMD.txt, that implements the IPSec filters listed in Table 21-1 is included on the CD-ROM that accompanies this book. The script must be modified with the IP addresses of each domain controller and Microsoft Operations Manager (MOM) server before being executed.

Additional Information

- "New Features for WINS" (*http://www.microsoft.com/resources/documentation /windowsserv/2003/standard/proddocs/en-us/sag_WINS_ovr_NewFeatures.asp*)

- "Security Information for WINS" (*http://www.microsoft.com/resources /documentation/WindowsServ/2003/standard/proddocs/en-us /sag_WINS_ovr_Security.asp*)

- "Securing a Windows 2003 Server—Hardening Windows Server 2003 Infrastructure Servers" (*http://www.microsoft.com/technet/security/guidance /secmod121.mspx*)

- *Windows Server 2003 Security Guide* (*http://www.microsoft.com/downloads /details.aspx?familyid=8A2643C1-0685-4D89-B655-521EA6C7B4DB&display-lang=en*)

- The following Knowledge Base articles:

  - Knowledge Base article 185786: "Recommended Practices for WINS" (*http://support.microsoft.com/kb/185786*)

  - Knowledge Base article 225130: "Verifying Name Records in WINS in Windows 2000" (*http://support.microsoft.com/kb/225130*)

  - Knowledge Base article 316835: "Windows Server WINS Event Log Messages, Part 1: Event ID 4096 to 4209" (*http://support.microsoft.com /kb/316835*)

  - Knowledge Base article 316836: "Windows Server WINS Event Log Messages, Part 2: Event ID 4210 to 5300" (*http://support.microsoft.com /kb/316836*)

Chapter 22
Implementing Security for Routing and Remote Access

The Routing and Remote Access Service (RRAS) enables remote computers to connect to corporate networks by using either dial-up connections or virtual private network (VPN) connections. The extension of the corporate network to these remote access clients requires a review on your part to ensure that the security of your network is not weakened when you allow remote access connectivity. Specifically, you must look at how the available components for a remote access solution work together to provide security. In addition, with Microsoft Windows Server 2003 or Microsoft Internet Security and Acceleration (ISA) Server 2004, you can deploy the Remote Access Quarantine Service to ensure that all remote clients meet the minimum security requirements defined by your organization before those clients can connect to corporate resources remotely.

Remote Access Solution Components

Remote access to the corporate network is provided through the interaction of different network services and client software to enable remote clients to connect securely to the corporate network. Remote access solution components include the following:

- Authentication protocols
- VPN protocols
- Client software
- Server services and software
- Quarantine services

Authentication Protocols

When a remote access client connects to the network, the user authenticates with the remote access server by providing credentials. These credentials can include the user's name, password, and the domain in which the user account exists. When a user connects to a remote access server, authentication is performed by using Point-to-Point Protocol (PPP) authentication methods. The authentication methods supported by RRAS include the following:

- **Password Authentication Protocol (PAP)**   Although supported by almost all dial-up network services, PAP transmits user credentials to the remote access server as plaintext, offering no protection against password determination and replay attacks.

- **Shiva Password Authentication Protocol (SPAP)**   Provides support for Shiva remote access clients. SPAP uses a reversible encryption method called *base64 encoding*, which is minimally stronger than the protection offered by PAP. However, SPAP is still susceptible to replay attacks.

- **Challenge Handshake Authentication Protocol (CHAP)**   Provides a stronger form of authentication by sending a hash of the password and a challenge string to the server. The remote access server identifies the user, obtains the password from the directory, and performs the same hashing algorithm against the password and challenge string. If the results match, the user is authenticated. This form of authentication provides protection against replay attacks.

> **Warning**   CHAP authentication requires that the user's password be stored in a reversibly encrypted format at the domain controller for comparison purposes. This weakens password security at the domain controller and requires stronger physical security of the domain controller. In addition, the password is not stored in a reversibly encrypted format until the next time the user changes the password after this attribute is enabled.

- **Microsoft Challenge Handshake Authentication Protocol (MS-CHAP)**   Differs from CHAP in that the remote access client creates the challenge/response by encrypting the challenge string and MD4 hash version of the user's password. User passwords, by default, are stored in the directory in an MD4 hashed form. Encryption keys for Microsoft Point-to-Point Encryption (MPPE) are derived from the MS-CHAP authentication process. MPPE is used as the encryption algorithm for PPP payloads for dial-up and remote access connections based on Point-to-Point Tunneling Protocol (PPTP). In addition, MS-CHAP does not require storage of passwords in reversibly encrypted format at the domain controller, as is required by CHAP.

- **Microsoft Challenge Handshake Authentication Protocol version 2 (MS-CHAPv2)**
  When a remote access client authenticates by using Differs from CHAP in that
  the MS-CHAPv2, the remote access client sends a challenge/response based on
  a challenge from the remote access server, and the remote access server sends a
  challenge/response based on a challenge from the remote access client. This is
  known as *mutual authentication*. For MS-CHAPv2, the remote access client and
  remote access server prove to each other that they have knowledge of the user's
  password. In addition, MS-CHAPv2 derives stronger MPPE encryption keys and
  uses two different encryption keys: one for sending data and one for receiving
  data.

- **Extensible Authentication Protocol (EAP)**   Provides an extensible Differs from
  CHAP in that the architecture for advanced PPP authentication methods, such
  as two-factor authentication. EAP-MD5 CHAP is the CHAP authentication
  method using EAP. EAP-TLS (Extensible Authentication Protocol-Transport
  Layer Security) is used for public-key certificate–based authentication and provides mutual authentication and secured MPPE key exchange between the
  remote access server and the remote access client.

VPN Protocols

If remote access clients connect to the corporate network by using VPN connections,
two protocols are supported:

- **Point-to-Point Tunneling Protocol (PPTP)**   A tunneling protocol supported by all
  Microsoft operating systems since Microsoft Windows NT 4.0. PPTP uses MPPE
  to encrypt transmitted data by using a 40-bit, 56-bit, or 128-bit encryption key.
  PPTP is often used because it supports legacy clients and can cross most network address translation (NAT) devices.

- **Layer Two Tunneling Protocol (L2TP)**   A tunneling protocol natively supported
  by Microsoft Windows 2000 and Microsoft Windows XP and supported by
  Microsoft Windows 98, Windows Millennium Edition (Me), and Windows NT 4.0
  Workstation clients running Microsoft L2TP/IPSec VPN client. L2TP does not
  provide native encryption but uses IP Security (IPSec) with Encapsulating Security Payload (ESP) in transport mode, which implements either Data Encryption
  Standard (DES) with a 56-bit key or 3DES encryption using three 56-bit keys.

> **Note**   RRAS in Windows 2000 does not support NAT traversal (NAT-T) with L2TP/IPSec. Only the updated version of RRAS in Windows Server 2003 supports NAT traversal with L2TP/IPSec. NAT traversal is supported by the Microsoft L2TP/IPSec VPN client for Windows 98, Windows Me, and Windows NT 4.0 Workstation. To implement NAT traversal for Windows 2000 and Windows XP, you must apply the L2TP/IPSec NAT-T update for Windows XP and Windows 2000 available at *http://support.microsoft.com/kb/818043*.

Client Software

Microsoft operating systems since Windows 95 have supported PPP-based remote access connectivity software, either in the base operating system or in software freely distributed from the Microsoft Web site, such as the Microsoft Dial-Up Networking client software. Windows 2000 includes the Connection Manager Administration Kit (CMAK) and Connection Point Services (CPS) to ease client remote access configuration and deployment.

The CMAK provides the ability to define remote access connectivity software packages that are preconfigured with your company's remote access settings. The version of CMAK in Windows Server 2003 enables you to define a postconnection script that tests the security configuration of a remote client. While the client is being tested, it remains in a quarantined state, limited by filters defined either at the Remote Authentication Dial-In User Service (RADIUS) server or at an ISA Server 2004 server, until it proves that it can pass all tests. For example, if your company requires that a client implement the corporate virus detection software for remote connectivity, the CMAK package can run a postconnection script that ensures that the latest virus signatures are installed.

CPS provides the capability to download an updated list of ISP dial-in numbers, referred to as the *phone book*, to remote access clients. The phone book provides the latest local access phone numbers for Internet connectivity so that clients always have updated phone book information and do not have to input phone numbers manually for Internet connectivity.

Server Services and Software

Remote access solutions require that services and software be configured at the server to accept remote access connections and, possibly, at servers that reside between the remote access clients and the remote access server if deploying VPN solutions. When deploying remote access solutions, you might need the following services:

- **Routing and Remote Access Service (RRAS)** As mentioned earlier, this service enables you to provide both dial-up and VPN connectivity to the corporate network. RRAS can use the Active Directory directory service, the local Security Accounts Manager (SAM) database of the server, or a centralized account database provided by a RADIUS server. To provide additional security to remote access connections, you can define remote access policies that outline constraints and configuration settings that must be implemented before remote client connectivity is allowed.

- **Internet Authentication Service (IAS)** This service provides RADIUS authentication for remote access connections. Rather than each server running RRAS to authenticate remote access clients, remote access servers can forward authentication requests to the IAS server by using the RADIUS protocol. In addition to authentication, the IAS server provides centralized accounting and authorization through remote access policies to the remote access servers.

In addition to these services, you can implement Internet Security and Acceleration (ISA) Server 2004 as a firewall between the remote clients and the remote access server, or you can actually deploy it on the computer running RRAS. ISA Server provides the capability to filter connections so that authorized VPN protocols are allowed to connect to the remote access server.

Quarantine Services

As mentioned earlier, Windows Server 2003 RRAS enables you to place remote access clients in a quarantined state until the client passes a series of scripted tests, defined by the VPN administrator, that proves that the remote access client meets all corporate security guidelines. While the remote access client is in a quarantined state, it is limited to network resources that pass a filter defined either at the IAS server or an ISA Server 2004 server.

A VPN quarantine solution can be provided either by using Windows Server 2003 RRAS, ISA Server 2004, or a combination of both software solutions. An organization can choose the method based on that organization's centralization strategy:

- If the organization chooses to centralize all remote access configuration at the RADIUS server, it is best to define the VPN quarantine filters and maximum duration of the VPN quarantine state at the RADIUS server.

> **Note** To support defining the quarantine filters and maximum duration of a quarantine, the RADIUS server must support the MS-Quarantine-IPFilter and MS-Quarantine-Session-Timeout attributes. These conditions are supported in IAS for Windows Server 2003. The advanced conditions are not supported in IAS for Microsoft Windows 2000 Server products.

- If the organization chooses to centralize all filter definitions at a firewall, it is best to define the VPN quarantine rules and maximum duration of the VPN quarantine state in ISA Server 2004. ISA enables you to define both regular firewall and application rules alongside the VPN quarantine rules.

> **Note**   Windows Server 2003 supports quarantine solutions only for VPN clients. In the future, Network Access Protection (NAP) will allow quarantine solutions for networked clients, such as wireless or wired clients. NAP will not be introduced until the next version of the Windows operating system code-named "Longhorn."

Threats to Remote Access Solutions

When you extend network connectivity to remote access clients, several threats exist that can compromise your network's security. These threats exist because the remote clients are no longer directly connected to the corporate network, but they are connected to public networks (phone or Internet) and are connecting to the corporate network over public networks. The threats caused by this extension of the corporate network to remote clients are as follows:

- Authentication interception
- Data interception
- Bypass of the firewall to the private network
- Nonstandardized policy application
- Network perimeter extended to location of dial-in user
- Denial of service caused by password attempts
- Stolen laptops with saved credentials
- Connections by remote clients that do not meet corporate security requirements

Authentication Interception

Remote access solutions require users to send authentication credentials to your private network across public networks. Some early remote access authentication protocols do not provide security mechanisms, or they provide weak security for these credentials.

If you use authentication protocols such as PAP, SPAP, or CHAP, be aware that some tools can intercept these authentication streams and determine the password of the authenticating user through inspection or brute force techniques. Likewise, the implementation of CHAP weakens security of a user's password at domain controllers because CHAP requires that the password be stored in a reversibly encrypted format.

The interception of the user's password compromises the user's remote access password. Also, in a Windows 2000 or Windows Server 2003 Active Directory environment, the remote access password is the user's domain password.

 Note Although the risk of password interception is more likely in a VPN scenario, it is still possible for a dial-in client's password information to be intercepted if the required tapping equipment is attached to the phone system.

Data Interception

When connecting remotely to a corporate network, the protocols you use for authentication and VPNs determine the level of protection against interception. For dial-up connections, encryption of transmitted data is performed only if you use EAP-TLS, MS-CHAP, or MS-CHAPv2 as the authentication protocol. Only these authentication protocols determine encryption keys for MPPE.

For VPN connections, varying strengths of encryption are provided. If you implement PPTP, the highest level of encryption possible is MPPE with 128-bit encryption. PPTP can also implement 40-bit and 56-bit encryption. If you implement L2TP/IPSec as your VPN protocol, IPSec encryption strengths range from 56 bits for DES encryption to three 56-bit keys for 3DES encryption. The stronger the encryption, the less chance you have of data being deciphered.

 Warning The MPPE encryption implemented by dial-up and PPTP connections is based on the user's password. If the user implements a poor password, the MPPE encryption strength is weakened. L2TP's use of IPSec for encryption ensures that the encryption strength is not affected by the user's password strength.

Bypass of the Firewall to the Private Network

If a user's account is provided local administrative access to computers, it is possible for him to install and configure RRAS to accept dial-up connections, thereby bypassing perimeter network security devices such as firewalls.

Establishing unauthorized remote access servers weakens your network's security because doing so enables unauthorized users or attackers to bypass existing perimeter security. In addition, these unauthorized remote access servers do not have the required remote access policy applied and might allow less-secure connections.

Nonstandardized Policy Application

If more than one remote access server exists on your network, it is possible that remote access security is being applied in a nonstandard fashion. If the different sets of constraints and policies are applied, connection attempts might yield varied results.

The nonstandardized application of remote access policy can lead to unauthorized connections to the network or, in some cases, connections that do not meet your company's security policy. For example, your company might require that all remote access connections use MS-CHAPv2 or EAP-TLS for authentication. If you do not uniformly mandate that the remote access policy requires this authentication for a successful connection attempt, a user might be able to connect by using PAP authentication, which transmits the authentication credentials in clear text.

Network Perimeter Extended to Location of Dial-In User

When you implement remote access solutions, the perimeter of your company's network is extended to the location of the remote access client. The security of your network is then lowered to the level of security implemented at the remote client. For example, if clients are connected to a remote network that is infected with a new virus, they might become infected and in turn infect your network through their remote access connection. Ensure that all computers that participate on your network—whether attached locally or connecting by remote access solutions—are protected with the latest antivirus software.

Likewise, if clients modify their routing table so that they have routing entries to both the Internet and the company's network through the VPN or dial-up connection, it might be possible for attackers to route information through the remote access client to the corporate network. This modification of the routing table by clients to access both the Internet and the intranet simultaneously is referred to as *split tunneling*.

Denial of Service Caused by Password Attempts

Sometimes taking good security measures can lead to security threats. For example, your company might implement an account policy that locks out a user account after a specified number of incorrect password attempts.

Although this security setting is intended to prevent online dictionary attacks against the user account, it is possible for attackers to use this setting to launch a denial-of-service attack. Rather than attempt to guess a user's password, attackers can use this setting to intentionally lock out the user's account by inputting the required number of incorrect passwords, which results in the user's account being locked out from all network activities. The user can participate in the network only after her account is unlocked by a user account administrator. There is no way to prevent future attacks of this nature because the attacker is not attempting to guess the user's password. The attacker is only trying to lock out the user's account by inputting incorrect passwords.

Stolen Laptops with Saved Credentials

Remote users typically use notebook or laptop computers to connect to the corporate office. Because these computers are removed from the corporate offices and are taken to public locations, they are more susceptible to theft. If a laptop is stolen, it is subject to attacks against the local account database if local SAM accounts are used. Likewise, if a user saves his credentials for dial-up or VPN connections, an attacker can simply launch the connection, rather than attempt to guess the user's domain credentials.

Another threat to your remote access security exists if you implement shared secrets, rather than certificates, for IPSec authentication of L2TP/IPSec VPN connections. When you implement a shared secret—as described in Microsoft Knowledge Base article 240262, "How to Configure a L2TP/IPSec Connection Using Pre-shared Key Authentication"—all remote access clients use the same shared secret to authenticate with the remote access server for the IPSec security association (SA). If one laptop is compromised, all laptops effectively are compromised because the shared secret is stored in clear text in the registry of the laptop, and a new shared secret must be deployed.

Connections by Remote Clients That Do Not Meet Corporate Security Requirements

As mentioned earlier, when a remote client connects to an organization's network using a VPN, the network's perimeter is extended to the remote client. If the remote client computer is infected with a virus, the client effectively bypasses the firewall and any other security mechanisms implemented by the organization.

When quarantine services are implemented, the client computer is placed in quarantine until it passes a series of tests that validates its security configuration. These tests can include the following:

- Verifying that the client computer has the latest hotfixes and security updates installed
- Verifying that the client computer does not have Internet Connection Sharing (ICS) enabled allowing other computers at the remote location to route traffic to the organization's network
- Verifying that the client computer has the latest antivirus signatures loaded
- Verifying that the client computer's antivirus software is in a running state

- Verifying that the client computer's screen saver is enabled with a password protecting the system

- Verifying that the client computer's Windows Firewall is enabled

This is just a sample of the tests that can be performed. Through custom scripting, just about any configuration attribute of the remote client can be tested against the organization's prescribed security settings.

Securing Remote Access Servers

To implement security for remote access servers, you must consider the configuration of servers running RRAS, IAS, and ISA Server. The combination of these servers and services provides the required security for remote access dial-up and VPN connections. Specifically, when designing security for remote access servers, consider taking the following measures:

- Implement RADIUS authentication and accounting.

- Secure RADIUS authentication traffic between the remote access server and the RADIUS server.

- Configure a remote access policy.

- If using L2TP/IPSec, deploy required certificates.

- Restrict which servers can start or stop RRAS.

- Implement remote access account lockout.

- Implement a quarantine solution.

Implementing RADIUS Authentication and Accounting

RADIUS authentication and accounting allow for centralized authentication, authorization, and accounting for remote access connectivity. Rather than authentication and authorization being performed at individual remote access servers, connection request messages are sent to the RADIUS server, which is a server running IAS in a Windows 2000 or Windows Server 2003 network.

The RADIUS packets are sent to specific ports on the IAS server. Authentication packets are sent to User Datagram Protocol (UDP) port 1812, and the accounting packets are sent to UDP port 1813. The format of the RADIUS packets allows for NAT traversal. This permits you to place the IAS server on the private network behind firewalls, rather than in your network's perimeter network (also known as the DMZ, demilitarized zone, or screened subnet). Therefore, the IAS server can connect directly to a domain controller to validate a user's provided credentials and access the user's account properties.

The IAS server then validates the authentication attempt against Active Directory. If the credentials sent to the RADIUS server match the credentials in Active Directory, the authentication succeeds and the RADIUS server directs the remote access server to authenticate the user.

In addition to providing centralized authentication and accounting, IAS provides centralized remote access policy for remote access connection authorization. Rather than having to configure a remote access policy at each remote access server, the remote access policy is configured at the IAS server. The RADIUS clients implicitly trust the answer they receive from the IAS server when a RADIUS connection request response is received. By implementing the remote access policy at a single location, you ensure that the same conditions and policy configuration are applied to each remote access client, no matter which remote access server sends the connection request.

Securing RADIUS Authentication Traffic Between the Remote Access Server and the RADIUS Server

Security experts have raised concerns that RADIUS traffic between the remote access server and the RADIUS server is susceptible to inspection and brute force attacks. To protect against these attacks, you can implement an IPSec policy that requires ESP encryption of RADIUS traffic. This ensures that RADIUS traffic is protected against inspection and brute force attacks. If you are using Windows 2000, you must ensure that the remote access server and the IAS server are not separated by a NAT device to ensure that IPSec traffic can be transmitted between the two servers.

 Note You can separate the remote access server and the IAS server with a NAT device if you're using Windows Server 2003.

Configuring a Remote Access Policy

To authorize remote access connections, you must define remote access policy. The remote access policy must be defined at each remote access server (when using Windows authentication) or at the configured IAS server (when using RADIUS authentication). The remote access policy must enforce the company's security policy for remote access connections. Remote connections are secured by configuring conditions and profiles for each remote access policy.

Remote Access Policy Conditions

All remote access connections are evaluated against conditions defined for each remote access policy. If a remote access connection matches these conditions, the connection attempt is either allowed or denied based on the first matching remote access policy (its remote access permissions and profile settings) and the dial-in properties of the user's account.

You can use the following condition attributes to identify a remote access connection attempt:

- **Called-Station-ID** The phone number dialed by the remote access client. This condition enables you to apply different remote access policies depending on the phone number the remote client uses.

- **Calling-Station-ID** The phone number from which the call originates. This condition enables you to apply remote access policies depending on from which phone number the connection originates.

- **Client-Friendly-Name** The name of the RADIUS client that forwards the authentication request. This condition enables you to apply differing remote access policies based on the RADIUS client that forwards the request. This condition can be implemented only in a remote access policy defined at an IAS server.

- **Client-IP-Address** The IP address of the RADIUS client that sent the authentication request. This condition is used to identify RADIUS clients for VPN authentication requests. This condition can be implemented only in a remote access policy defined at an IAS server.

- **Client-Vendor** Identifies the manufacturer of the RADIUS client that forwards the authentication request. This condition enables you to apply manufacturer-specific remote access policies. This condition can be implemented only in a remote access policy defined at an IAS server.

- **Day And Time Restrictions** Enables you to restrict connections to specific days of the week or times of day. For example, you can prevent remote connections from being made outside office hours.

- **Framed Protocol** Enables you to define which remote access protocols are allowed for connections. For example, you can restrict connections to only Point-to-Point Protocol (PPP) connections, while preventing Serial Line Internet Protocol (SLIP) connections that transmit all data in plaintext.

> **Note** Although a Windows Server 2003 or Windows 2000 server running RRAS cannot accept SLIP connections, an IAS server can authenticate dial-in requests to a non-Microsoft remote access server.

- **NAS-Identifier** Enables you to identify the RADIUS client that forwards the request by comparing the string sent by the RADIUS client to a string defined in the remote access policy.

- **NAS-IP-Address**   Enables you to identify the RADIUS client by its IP address. This is useful if you want to apply different remote access policies to a specific VPN server based on its IP address.

- **NAS-Port-Type**   Enables you to identify the medium used by the remote access client. You can indicate dial-up, Integrated Services Digital Network (ISDN), or VPN connections. For wireless communications, you can choose 802.11 connections.

- **Service-Type**   Enables you to identify the service requested by the client. For remote access clients, the type of service typically is Framed.

- **Tunnel-Type**   Enables you to restrict which protocol a client uses for a VPN connection. You can specify PPTP or L2TP, subject to the existing network infrastructure.

- **Windows-Groups**   Enables you to restrict access by Windows group membership. You can select only Windows universal groups or global groups.

Remote Access Policy Profiles

Remote access policy enables you to apply additional security that extends beyond condition matching. Once a remote connection attempt matches the conditions of a defined remote access policy, the remote access policy profile is applied to the connection. The remote access policy profile defines which security settings must be implemented by the remote access connections. These profile settings include the following:

- **Dial-In Constraints**   Includes how long a connection can remain idle before it is disconnected, the maximum time for session lengths, the day and time limitations, the dial-in number constraints, and the dial-in media constraints. Typically, the dial-in constraints ensure that remote access sessions are terminated if left idle for long periods of time and that they take place only during specific times of the day or week.

- **IP Constraints**   Enables you to define packet filters that restrict access to the network for the remote access client. These packet filters can limit which protocols can be used by remote access clients.

- **Multilink**   Defines whether multilink sessions are allowed and where a client can make multiple remote access connections to the remote access server, thus effectively increasing available bandwidth.

- **Authentication**   Enables you to define which protocols are allowed for a remote access connection. If the remote client is not configured to use the required authentication protocol(s), the connection attempt is terminated.

- **Encryption**   Enables you to define which type of encryption must be applied to the remote access session. You can choose to require no encryption, basic encryption (56-bit keys for DES and 40-bit keys for MPPE), strong encryption (56-bit keys for DES or MPPE), or the strongest encryption (3DES or 128-bit MPPE).

- **Advanced**   Enables you to define advanced RADIUS attributes that are used when remote access connections are using RADIUS authentication.

Deploying Required Certificates for L2TP/IPSec

If you are implementing L2TP/IPSec for VPN connections to the corporate network, you must deploy the necessary certificates to your network's computers and users. Computer certificates are required for IPSec authentication, and user certificates are required for EAP-TLS authentication.

IPSec Certificate Deployment

Computer certificates are required for the authentication of the remote client computer with the remote access server. Computer certificates authenticate the IPSec main mode SA established between the VPN client and the VPN server. The certificate used by the VPN client must chain to a Certification Authority (CA) located in the trusted root store of the VPN server. The certificate used by the VPN server must chain to a CA located in the trusted root store of the VPN client. Although it is possible for the VPN client and server to use certificates from different chains, it is easiest to issue certificates to both the client and the server from CAs in the same chain.

To deploy certificates automatically, you can implement a Windows 2000 or Windows Server 2003 enterprise CA that publishes the IPSec or Computer certificate template (for client computers or domain controllers). If an enterprise CA is deployed, you can automatically send the computer certificates to the remote access client computers by using the Automatic Certificate Request Settings Group Policy setting. This setting automatically deploys the defined computer-based certificates to the computer accounts against which the Group Policy object (GPO) is applied.

Note   If you must deploy certificates to nondomain members, you must publish the IPSec (Offline Request) certificate template at the enterprise CA. This template allows nondomain members to enroll the certificate template by using Web-based certificate enrollment. The nondomain members must provide credentials that are assigned the Read and Enroll permissions for the IPSec (Offline Request) certificate template.

Alternatively, if the user is a local administrator, the IPSec certificate can be deployed by using the Certificates Microsoft Management Console (MMC) focused on the local machine.

> **Caution**   Although it is possible to use shared secrets for L2TP/IPSec computer authentication, it is not recommended because doing so weakens remote access computer security. Always use certificate-based authentication for L2TP/IPSec computer authentication. Kerberos authentication for L2TP/IPSec computer authentication is not possible.

User Authentication Certificates

If your remote access solution uses EAP-TLS authentication, regardless of whether you are using dial-up connections, PPTP connections, or L2TP/IPSec connections, you must deploy user authentication certificates to the remote access user and server authentication certificates to either the remote access server or the IAS server. If you are using Windows authentication, the server authentication certificate (either a Computer certificate or a Domain Controller certificate) must be installed on the remote access server. If you are using RADIUS authentication, the server authentication certificate must be installed on the IAS server. These two certificate deployment scenarios are shown in Figure 22-1.

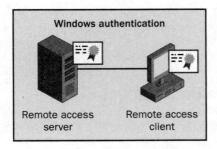

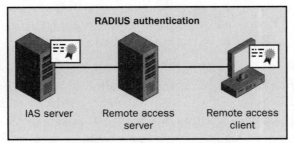

Figure 22-1   The deployment of user authentication certificates, which varies depending on whether you implement RADIUS authentication

The remote access client will require either a Smart Card Logon certificate, which is recommended, or a User certificate that is stored in the user's certificate store. This proves the user's identify for the remote access connection.

Restricting Which Servers Can Start or Stop RRAS

To prevent unauthorized remote access connections to the network, not only must you implement remote access policy to define the allowed remote access connections, you also must prevent users from running unauthorized remote access servers. You can accomplish this by implementing a security policy that requires all servers and computers be members of the local domain or forest of your company. If the computers are members of the domain, you can utilize Group Policy to ensure that only authorized remote access servers can start RRAS. The start state of any system service is defined in the following Group Policy location: Computer Configuration\Windows Settings\Security Settings\System Services. For each service listed in the details pane, you can define the default start state of the service as well as permissions defining which users or security groups can start, pause, or stop the service.

To ensure that only approved remote access servers can start RRAS, verify that all approved remote access servers are placed in a common OU or OU structure in which a GPO is linked. The GPO should set RRAS as an automatic startup mode and allow only administrators or the System account to change the startup mode for the service.

For all other computers, configure the Default Domain Policy to disable RRAS. To prevent RRAS from ever being started, do not assign any security groups other than the System account and local Administrators group the permission to start, stop, or pause the service.

Implementing Remote Access Account Lockout

To prevent online dictionary attacks against a user's password, you can enable remote access account lockout, which denies remote access to user accounts but does not lock out user accounts for local network activities. If attackers attempt an online dictionary attack, the account is blocked from further remote access attempts when the remote access account lockout threshold is reached.

You activate remote access account lockout by enabling two registry entries at the server that performs remote access authentication. If using Windows authentication, the registry settings are defined at each remote access server. If using RADIUS authentication, the registry settings must be defined at the IAS server.

These are the registry settings that enable remote access account lockout:

- **HKEY_LOCAL_MACHINE\SYSTEM\CurrentControlSet\Services \RemoteAccess\Parameters\AccountLockout\MaxDenials**   Must be set to the required maximum attempts before remote access is prevented. If the counter exceeds the configured value, remote access is prevented for the account until the reset time. A successful authentication resets a failed attempt's counter for each account. If the value is set to 0, account lockout is disabled.

- **HKEY_LOCAL_MACHINE\SYSTEM\CurrentControlSet\Services \RemoteAccess\Parameters\AccountLockout\ResetTime (mins)**   Defines the interval, in minutes, when the failed attempts counter is reset to 0. The default for this value is 2880 minutes (48 hours).

Implementing a Quarantine Solution

When configuring quarantine, a process must be followed that implements the required quarantine testing. The process is similar whether you are deploying the quarantine solution using filters applied by IAS or implementing filters applied by using ISA Server 2004. The following steps enable you to configure Network Access Quarantine Control:

1. Create quarantine resources.
2. Implement the client notification component.
3. Create client-side quarantine testing scripts.
4. Implement a listener component at the VPN gateway.
5. Create a Connection Manager profile for quarantine access.
6. Deploy the Connection Manager profile.
7. Create a remote access policy.
8. Implement quarantine filters.

Step 1.   Create Quarantine Resources

When the remote client is in a quarantined state, you must provide it access to some basic services on the network. Two strategies are commonly used by organizations:

- Provide access to a dedicated quarantine subnet.
- Provide access only to specific resources.

> **Tip**   In either scenario, you should create Web pages that will display which actions a remote client must take if it does *not* pass the quarantine inspection. The Web pages should indicate required actions and, if possible, provide access to resources for meeting compliance. The resources can, in fact, link to external Web sites such as Windows Update or an extranet-accessible Web server.

Provide Access to a Dedicated Quarantine Subnet   One of the simplest VPN quarantine solutions is to deploy all quarantine resources in a dedicated subnet as shown in Figure 22-2.

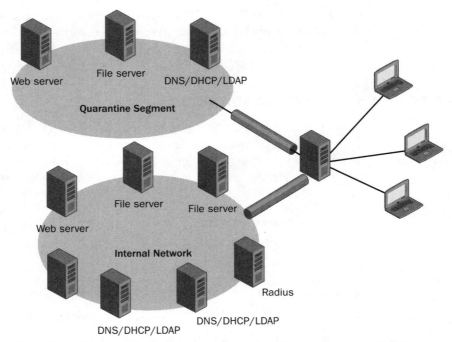

Figure 22-2   A dedicated quarantine subnet simplifies input or firewall filters

In this scenario, a dedicated subnet provides access to all services required by the quarantined client. The benefit of this configuration is that the filters required to access the segment are simplified. The only negative aspect is that all forms of traffic are enabled between the remote access client and the quarantine segment. For example, a remote access client can attempt to connect to a shared folder on the Web server.

Provide Access Only to Specific Resources   A second strategy is to limit to which resources a remote access client can connect when it is in a quarantine state. As shown in Figure 22-3, the remote access clients are allowed to connect only to the indicated Web server, file server, and domain controller.

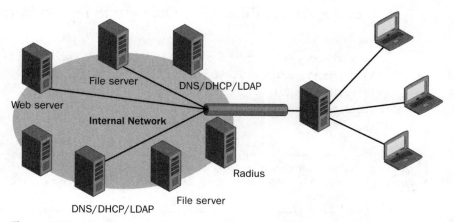

Figure 22-3 Limiting to which servers and services a VPN quarantine client can connect on the internal network

In addition to limiting computers, the input filters can also limit which protocols are used. For example, connections to the Web server can be limited to destination filters for Transmission Control Protocol (TCP) port 80 and TCP port 443.

> **Note** Your input filters must provide access to some basic network services, including Domain Name System (DNS), Dynamic Host Configuration Protocol (DHCP), Lightweight Directory Access Protocol (LDAP), Web servers (using cleartext or Secure Sockets Layer [SSL]), and file servers. In addition, the input filters must allow access to the notification service on the RRAS server.

Step 2. Implement the Client Notification Component

The Windows Server 2003 Resource Kit tools include a default client notification component, Rqc.exe. The notification component is responsible for sending a message to a listener on the remote access server that indicates whether the client has passed the quarantine tests. The listener component must pass the expected parameters and a version string to indicate that the quarantine scripts have found no discrepancies with the required security configuration.

> **Note** You can create your own custom notification component rather than using Rqc.exe from the Windows Server 2003 Resource Kit tools.
>
> With the release of Windows Server 2003 SP1, Rqc.exe and Rqs.exe are now part of the base operating system.

Step 3.   Create Client-Side Quarantine Testing Scripts

You must create and test the client-side scripts that will validate whether the remote client meets your organization's security policies. The script can be a batch file, a Visual Basic script, or a compiled executable that is run at the client as a postconnection action. If the remote client passes the tests performed in the client-side script, the client-side script must execute the deployed notification component to indicate that the quarantine condition must be lifted.

> **Note**   Samples of quarantine scripts are available at *http://www.microsoft.com /downloads/details.aspx?FamilyID=a290f2ee-0b55-491e-bc4c-8161671b2462& displaylang=en*.

Step 4.   Implement a Listener Component at the VPN Gateway

At the RRAS or ISA Server 2004 computer, you must implement the listener component Rqs.exe from the Windows Server 2003 Resource Kit tools. The listener component installs as the Remote Access Quarantine Agent (RQS.exe) service that listens on TCP port 7250 for successful quarantine test notification messages from remote clients. The method that you use to install the listener depends on whether the listener is installed on an RRAS server or an ISA Server 2004 server:

- **RRAS in Windows Server 2003**   To install Rqs.exe, you must modify and execute the rqs_setup.cmd file included with the Windows Server 2003 Resource Kit tools. The batch file must be modified to include an organization-specific version string. This version string must match the version string submitted by the client's notification component. Once the version string is updated, you must execute rqs_setup /install to install the Remote Access Quarantine Agent service.

- **ISA Server 2004**   An updated version of Rqs.exe that also includes an updated installation script must be installed on an ISA Server 2004 computer. The updated installation script, ConfigureRQSForISA.vbs, not only installs the Remote Access Quarantine Agent service, it performs the following tasks:

  - ❑ Adds an RQS protocol definition to the ISA Server 2004 protocol definition listing

  - ❑ Installs RQS as the Network Quarantine Service and starts the service

  - ❑ Creates an access rule that allows the Quarantine VPN Clients and VPN Clients networks to connect to the local host network using the RQS protocol

  - ❑ Applies the designated version string to the HKLM\SYSTEM \CurrentControlSet\Services\Rqs registry key.

To install the RQS service, you must copy rqc.exe and rqsmsg.dll from the Windows Server 2003 Resource Kit tools to a folder on the ISA Server 2004 server and then install the updated version of Rqs.exe in the same folder.

Once the prerequisites are met, you can install RQS by running cscript Configure RQSForISA.vbs /install <*AllowedSet*> <*RqsToolsPath*>, where <*AllowedSet*> is the version string required by RQS and <*RqsToolsPath*> is the location where the updated Rqs.exe file is located.

Step 5.   Create a Connection Manager Profile for Quarantine Access

You must use the Connection Manager Administration Kit (CMAK) from Windows Server 2003 to create a Connection Manager profile. The profile must implement the following measures:

- Call the quarantine client-side script as a postconnection action. The postconnection action must implement the parameters required by Rqc.exe to indicate that the client has passed all quarantine tests.

- All custom scripts and the notification component (Rqc.exe) as part of the profile's package.

- Any other security requirements for your organization, such as enforcing required authentication protocols and encryption levels.

Step 6.   Deploy the Connection Manager Profile

Deploy the Connection Manager profile to all remote access clients that require access to the organization's network. The profile can be distributed by e-mail, over an extranet Web site, or through a share on the organization's network.

Note   Many e-mail antivirus programs prevent the installation of the Connection Manager profile through e-mail because the profile installation file is an executable file that is often stripped by e-mail gateways.

Step 7.   Create a Remote Access Policy

The remote access policy is best deployed at an IAS server, allowing RADIUS authentication to be used by the RRAS or ISA Server server for all VPN connections. The remote access policy should identify the VPN quarantine clients and enforce the required authentication levels and encryption levels required by the organization.

Step 8.   Implement Quarantine Filters

The implementation of the quarantine filters depends on whether your organization centralizes the management of VPN quarantine:

■ If your company centralizes all management of VPN quarantine at the IAS server, favor managing the VPN quarantine filters in the remote access policy. The remote access policy must implement the following attributes:

❑ **MS-Quarantine-Session-Timeout**   Defines the maximum connection time allowed for a quarantined remote client.

❑ **MS-Quarantine-IPFilter**   Defines which traffic is allowed to pass to and from the remote client during the quarantine. The filter listing must include a filter allowing the remote client to connect to TCP port 7250, the listener component on the RRAS server. If this filter is omitted, the RRAS server cannot receive messages from the notification component (Rqc.exe) indicating that the quarantine tests have passed.

> **Note**   If you are deploying VPN quarantine and do not use ISA Server 2004, implementing the preceding attributes is the only method of deploying the VPN quarantine filters.

■ If your company centralizes all access filters at an ISA Server 2004 server, you must implement the VPN quarantine filters in the access filters at the ISA Server 2004 server. The access filters are easy to implement by using the built-in network definition of Quarantined VPN Clients and defining which resources the Quarantined VPN Clients can access. If you implement the quarantine filters at the ISA Server 2004 server, you must modify the properties of the Quarantined VPN Clients network definition to enable quarantine control as shown in Figure 22-4. In addition, you must configure whether the quarantine filters are defined at the RADIUS server or the ISA Server 2004 server, define the quarantine timeout, and indicate whether any specific security groups are exempt from the quarantine controls.

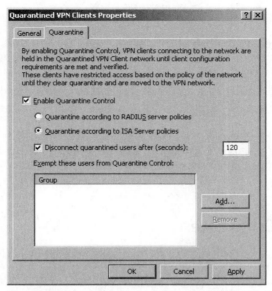

Figure 22-4   Enabling quarantine control in ISA Server 2004

Securing Remote Access Clients

In addition to securing the remote access server, you must implement security measures at client computers. These security measures ensure that the client is configured with the required security settings for remotely accessing your corporate network. The measures that you can implement at the remote access client include the following:

- Configuring the CMAK packages
- Deploying quarantine-related files
- Implementing strong authentication
- Deploying required certificates

Configuring the CMAK Packages

The CMAK enables you to create Connection Manager profiles that are preconfigured with your company's required security settings. In addition to choosing the type of authentication and encryption strength used by remote clients, the CMAK enables you to define other options, such as preventing a user's password from being saved or removing specific tabs from the Properties dialog box of the dial-up or VPN connection. If you implement a VPN quarantine solution, the profile includes all of the scripts required to validate whether the client passes quarantine tests and defines the quarantine script as a postconnection script for execution.

Implementing Strong Authentication

To ensure that user credentials cannot be determined from intercepted traffic, you should implement the strongest form of authentication available. Microsoft recommends using MS-CHAPv2 only for password-based authentication and using EAP-TLS only for certificate-based authentication because these forms of authentication mutually authenticate both the remote client and the remote access server.

> **Note**   If you use the CMAK to create the remote client connection packages, you can specify within the packages that only MS-CHAPv2 and EAP-TLS authentication are supported.

Deploying Required Certificates

The remote client will require certificates if either of the following conditions exist:

- The remote client connects by using an L2TP/IPSec connection. L2TP/IPSec requires that an IPSec or Computer certificate be installed at the remote access client.

- The remote client authenticates with the remote access server by using EAP-TLS authentication. In this case, the user must have a certificate that includes the Client Authentication object ID (OID) in the Enhanced Key Usage attribute of the certificate. This OID indicates that the certificate can be used for client authentication. The certificate can be stored in either the user's profile or on a physical device, such as a smart card.

> **Note**   It is always recommended you use a smart card rather than a certificate stored in the user's profile because a smart card is a form of two-factor authentication. To compromise a smart card, attackers must obtain both the smart card and the personal identification number (PIN) that protects the private key stored on the smart card. For a certificate stored in the user's profile, the attacker can access the private key material if she can compromise the user's password.

Best Practices

- **Allow only MS-CHAPv2 or EAP-TLS for remote client authentication.**   Only these forms of authentication provide maximum protection of user credentials as well as mutual authentication of the remote client and the remote access server.

- **Implement RADIUS authentication for all remote access authentication.**   By implementing RADIUS authentication, you ensure that remote access policy is applied centrally from the IAS server, rather than by each remote access server.

- **If implementing L2TP/IPSec as your VPN protocol, use certificates to authenticate the remote access client computer and the remote access server.**   Using pre-shared keys for IPSec authentication of L2TP/IPSec connections is considered a security weakness and should be avoided.

- **Create remote access client packages by using the CMAK.**   The CMAK packages ensure that the correct configuration is implemented and enforced at remote client computers.

- **Create separate remote access policies for each remote access solution.**   Ensure that remote access policies are ordered correctly at the remote access server or the IAS server so that the correct remote access policy is applied for each type of connection attempt.

- **Implement remote access account lockout.**   This prevents online dictionary attacks against a user's password.

- **Prevent RRAS from starting on nonauthorized computers in the domain.**   You can do so by defining System Services policies. Allow only the local Administrators and the System account on approved remote access servers to start, stop, or pause the service.

- **Implement quarantine control.**   Quarantine control ensures that all remote access clients meet your organization's security policies. The quarantine scripts that you implement ensure that the remote clients have all required security patches applied, that the latest virus signatures are implemented, and that any other security requirements are implemented before allowing the remote clients to access internal resources.

Additional Information

- *MCSE Training Kit: Designing Microsoft Windows 2000 Network Security*, Chapter 13, "Securing Access for Remote Users and Networks" (Microsoft Press, 2001)

- *Microsoft Windows Server 2003 PKI and Certificate Security*, Chapter 19, "Virtual Private Networking" (Microsoft Press, 2004)

- "Deploying Remote Access Clients Using Connection Manager" (*http://www.microsoft.com/resources/documentation/WindowsServ/2003/all/deployguide/en-us/DNSBG_RAC_OVERVIEW.asp*)

- "Administrator's Guide to Microsoft L2TP/IPSec VPN Client" white paper (*http://www.microsoft.com/technet/itsolutions/network/maintain/security/VPNClntA.asp*)

- "Virtual Private Networking with Windows 2000: Deploying Remote Access VPNs" white paper (*http://www.microsoft.com/windows2000/techinfo/planning/incremental/vpndeploy.asp*)

- "Internet Authentication Service for Windows 2000" white paper (*http://www.microsoft.com/technet/prodtechnol/windows2000serv/evaluate/featfunc/ias.mspx*)

- Internet Authentication Service Technology Center (*http://www.microsoft.com/windowsserver2003/technologies/ias/default.mspx*)

- "Configuring Network Access Quarantine Control" (*http://www.microsoft.com/resources/documentation/WindowsServ/2003/all/deployguide/en-us/dnsbf_vpn_myfb.asp*)

- "IAS Network Access Quarantine Control" (*http://www.microsoft.com/resources/documentation/WindowsServ/2003/standard/proddocs/en-us/sag_rap_quarantine_network.asp*)

- "Network Access Quarantine Control in Windows Server 2003" (*http://www.microsoft.com/windowsserver2003/techinfo/overview/quarantine.mspx*)

- "Network Access Quarantine Control" (*http://www.microsoft.com/technet/community/columns/cableguy/cg0203.mspx*)

- "VPN Quarantine Sample Scripts for Verifying Client Health Configurations" (*http://www.microsoft.com/downloads/details.aspx?FamilyID=a290f2ee-0b55-491e-bc4c-8161671b2462&displaylang=en*)

- "VPN Roaming Clients and Quarantine Control in ISA Server 2004" (*http://www.microsoft.com/technet/prodtechnol/isa/2004/plan/vpnroamingquarantine.mspx*)

- Windows Server 2003 Resource Kit Tools (*http://www.microsoft.com/downloads/details.aspx?familyid=9d467a69-57ff-4ae7-96ee-b18c4790cffd&displaylang=en*)

- Remote Access Quarantine Tool for ISA Server 2004 (*http://www.microsoft.com/downloads/details.aspx?FamilyId=3396C852-717F-4B2E-AB4D-1C44356CE37A&displaylang=en*)

- RFC 2637: "Point-to-Point Tunneling Protocol (PPTP)" (*http://www.ietf.org/rfc/rfc2637.txt*)

- RFC 2661: "Layer Two Tunneling Protocol 'L2TP' " (*http://www.ietf.org/rfc/rfc2661.txt*)

- RFC 2809: "Implementation of L2TP Compulsory Tunneling via RADIUS" (*http://www.ietf.org/rfc/rfc2809.txt*)

- RFC 2865: "Remote Authentication Dial In User Service (RADIUS)" (*http: //www.ietf.org/rfc/rfc2865.txt*)

- RFC 2866: "RADIUS Accounting" (*http://www.ietf.org/rfc/rfc2866.txt*)

- RFC 3715: "IPSec–Network Address Translation (NAT) Compatibility Requirements" (*http://www.ietf.org/rfc/rfc3715.txt*)

- The following Knowledge Base articles:

    ❑ 240262: "How to Configure a L2TP/IPSec Connection Using Pre-shared Key Authentication" (*http://support.microsoft.com/kb/240262*)

    ❑ 325034: "How to Troubleshoot a Microsoft L2TP/IPSec Virtual Private Network Client Connection" (*http://support.microsoft.com/kb/325034*)

    ❑ 818043: "L2TP/IPSec NAT-T Update for Windows XP and Windows 2000" (*http://support.microsoft.com/kb/818043*)

    ❑ 885407: "The Default Behavior of IPSec NAT Traversal (NAT-T) Is Changed in Windows XP Service Pack 2" (*http://support.microsoft.com /kb/885407*)

Chapter 23
Implementing Security for Certificate Services

The installation of Certificate Services enables you to configure a Certification Authority (CA) in a Microsoft network that issues digital certificates to users and computers. Certificate Services is the core component of the Microsoft Windows 2000 and Windows Server 2003 Public Key Infrastructure (PKI).

Certificate Services allows for the installation of two types of CAs: *standalone CAs* and *enterprise CAs*. A standalone CA is typically used for offline CAs (CAs that are removed from the network to increase security). An enterprise CA is typically used to issue certificates to users, computers, and network devices.

Threats to Certificate Services

When you deploy Certificate Services, threats exist to CAs on the network. These include the following:

- Compromise of a CA's key pair
- Attacks against servers hosting certificate revocation lists (CRLs) and CA certificates
- Attempts to modify the CA configuration
- Attempts to modify certificate templates
- Attacks that disable CRL checking
- Addition of nontrusted CAs to the trusted root CA store

- Issuance of fraudulent certificates
- Publication of false certificates to the Active Directory directory service
- Compromise of a CA by a single administrator
- Unauthorized recovery of a user's private key from the CA database

Compromise of a CA's Key Pair

If attackers can gain access to a CA's private key, they can build a replica of the CA and issue network-valid certificates. You must protect all the CA's private and public key pairs so that attackers cannot gain access. The keys can be protected by monitoring and controlling membership in the local Administrators group because all members of the local Administrators group can export the CA's private key and certificate if a software-based cryptographic service provider (CSP) is implemented. To combat this threat, many organizations implement a hardware-based CSP so that the private key material is moved from the physical computer hosting Certificate Services to a hardware device known as a hardware security module, or HSM.

Attacks Against Servers Hosting CRLs and CA Certificates

If an application or service performs CRL checking, the application or service must validate the certificate to ensure that the certificate is not revoked. If an attacker can prevent access to the servers hosting the CRLs or CA certificates, or prevent the publication of CRLs to the CRL publication point before the previous CRL expires, a client will not be able to validate presented certificates. If an application cannot determine the revocation status of a presented certificate, the application might prevent access to the user or computer presenting the certificate.

Attempts to Modify the CA Configuration

If an attacker can gain local Administrator access to the computer running Certificate Services, the attacker can modify the CA configuration. This modification can include altering URLs for CRL publication, revoking legitimate certificates, and issuing certificates to nonvalid computers or users.

Attempts to Modify Certificate Templates

If attackers gain Enterprise Admins– or forest root domain Domain Admins–level access, they can modify certificate template properties in the CN=Certificate Templates, CN=Public Key Services, CN=Services, CN=Configuration, *ForestName* container (where *ForestName* is the Lightweight Directory Access Protocol distinguished name of the forest root domain).

When a Windows 2000 CA is deployed, the only change an attacker can make is to modify permissions for the individual certificate templates. Modifying permissions might enable the attacker to enroll a certificate that provides excess permissions (such as an Enrollment Agent certificate), thereby permitting the attacker to request certificates on behalf of other users.

Windows Server 2003 CAs running Windows Server 2003, Enterprise Edition, or Windows Server 2003, Datacenter Edition, can issue certificates based on version 2 certificate templates. If version 2 certificate templates are available on the network, an attacker can modify the certificate template to affect all certificates that are based on the affected certificate template. Modifications can include changing the purpose of the certificate template to enabling key archival if the certificate template is an encryption-enabled certificate template.

 Note For more information on the role of certificate templates in a Microsoft Windows network, see the white paper titled "Implementing and Administering Certificate Templates in Windows Server 2003" available at *http://www.microsoft.com/technet /prodtechnol/windowsserver2003/deploy/confeat/ws03crtm.asp*.

Attacks That Disable CRL Checking

Attackers might attempt to turn off revocation checking for an application. If CRL checking is turned off, the application does not determine whether a presented certificate is revoked. A certificate revocation invalidates the certificate before its validity period has expired. Common reasons for revoking a certificate include revoking all certificates issued to a terminated user or to a user whose computer was stolen.

Addition of Nontrusted CAs to the Trusted Root CA Store

If attackers can publish a nontrusted CA certificate to the trusted root store, all certificates that chain to that trusted root CA certificate are considered trusted. A certificate that chains to a trusted root CA certificate is trusted for any and all purposes, thereby allowing attackers to create their own trusted certificates. Alternatively, if attackers can create a certificate trust list (CTL), a list of CA certificates that are not issued by your company's CA hierarchy but are trusted for specific purposes and periods of time, or implement a Cross Certification Authority certificate, a CA certificate that extends trust to a foreign CA hierarchy based on restrictions defined in the Cross Certification Authority certificate, they can use a certificate issued by a foreign, nontrusted CA on your network.

> **Note**   Microsoft Security Bulletin MS02-048, described in Knowledge Base article
> 323172 (*http://support.microsoft.com/kb/323172*), changed the behavior of Microsoft
> Internet Explorer to prevent a rogue Web site from installing a certificate in the trusted
> root store. When a user clicks a link that attempts to install a certificate in any store on
> the user's computer, the user is notified that the link is attempting to install a certifi-
> cate, and the user is asked whether she wishes to proceed with the installation.

Issuance of Fraudulent Certificates

Before the creation of the security update 329115, "Certificate Validation Flaw Might
Permit Identity Spoofing," it was technically possible for attackers to sign certificates
with their own user certificates. This created a false certificate chain that included a
certificate that was not issued by a CA in the CA hierarchy but that was still trusted.
This type of attack worked because Windows 2000 Certificate Services did not
enforce basic constraints. Basic constraints ensure that only CAs can issue certificates
and prevent a user or computer certificate from signing another user or computer certificate.

> **Note**   This security update is not required for Windows Server 2003 because Certif-
> icate Services in Windows Server 2003 does enforce basic constraints.

Publication of False Certificates to Active Directory

If an attacker gains administrative access to a user account in Active Directory, the
attacker can add a certificate to the properties of the user's account. The attacker can
use this certificate to authenticate as that user without providing a password. If an
attacker holds the private key associated with the certificate, he can perform any
action permitted for that user.

Compromise of a CA by a Single Administrator

By default, both Windows 2000 Server and Windows Server 2003 enable default
administrative groups the permissions and user rights to perform all administrative
tasks. If the computer hosting Certificate Services is a standalone computer, the permissions are assigned to the local Administrators group. If the computer is a member
of a domain, the permissions are also assigned to the Enterprise Admins and forest
root domain Domain Admins groups.

Assigning all management permissions to a single account enables any member of the
administrative groups to perform *any* management function, without oversight by
other administrators. There exists the potential that a rogue administrator could make

any change to the CA configuration, revoke a mass quantity of certificates, delete the Audit log to cover up her tracks, or perform a backup of the CA's private key and database to build a duplicate of the CA.

Unauthorized Recovery of a User's Private Key from the CA Database

Windows Server 2003 provides the capability to archive the private key associated with a user's encryption certificates if the CA is running on Windows Server 2003, Enterprise Edition, or Windows Server 2003, Datacenter Edition. An attacker could acquire any user's certificate and private key from the CA database if the attacker is both a local Administrator and a Key Recovery Agent at the CA computer where the user's private key is archived.

If the attacker gains access to the user's private key, the attacker can then decrypt any information protected with the related certificate's public key. In addition, if the certificate enables signing, the attacker can impersonate the user by signing information as the user.

Securing Certificate Services

To prevent the likelihood of these threats, you can take the following measures:

- Implement physical security measures.
- Implement logical security measures.
- Modify CRL and CA certificate publication points.
- Enable CRL checking in all applications.
- Manage permissions of certificate templates.
- Implement role separation.

Implementing Physical Security Measures

Physical security measures prevent attackers from gaining physical access to the computer running Certificate Services. When an attacker gains physical access to a computer, any number of attacks can take place. Physical security measures can include the following:

- Creating a three-tier hierarchy that deploys the root CA and the second-level CAs (also referred to as *policy CAs*) or a two-tier hierarchy that deploys only the root CA as an offline CA. An offline CA is removed from the network and is turned on only to issue new CA certificates and to publish updated CRLs.

- Deploying hardware-based key modules, such as hardware security modules (HSMs), for the generation and protection of the CA key pair and for the signing of all issued certificates. HSMs enable you to implement split key management where a quorum of key holders must be present to access an offline CA's private key. For example, you can designate that any attempts to access a root CA's private key require the presentation of 4 tokens from a total pool of 11 tokens.

- Removing offline CAs from the network and storing them in physically secure locations, such as vaults, safes, or secured server rooms, based on your company's security policy.

- Disabling hardware in the CA computer BIOS. If you wish to prevent the attachment of the CA computer to the network, you can disable the network cards in the server's BIOS and protect the BIOS with a password. In addition, you can consider disabling USB ports and other devices to prevent data from being copied from the CA computer hard disk.

- Implementing BIOS startup passwords for offline computers to further restrict access to the computer. To start the offline CA computer, you must enter the BIOS startup password. This prevents a user that does not know the startup password from booting the offline CA.

> **Warning**   BIOS startup passwords can be reset to a blank password in some systems by shorting out the battery on the motherboard of the computer. If you physically store the computer in a safe or limited-access server room, you protect against an unauthorized user physically accessing the server to reset the BIOS password.

- Implementing Syskey level 2 or level 3 security to restrict the booting of an offline CA. Syskey level 2 requires that a password be entered before the local accounts database is accessed, allowing the offline CA computer to start. The Syskey level 3 setting increases security by requiring that a floppy disk containing the Syskey password be inserted to boot the computer.

> **Warning**   If you implement Syskey level 2 or level 3 security and either forget the password or lose access to the password on the Syskey disk, you lose all access to the offline CA computer. Ensure that the password is recorded in a secure location or that a copy of the Syskey disk is maintained to protect against this type of failure.

Implementing Logical Security Measures

In addition to physical security measures, modifying the configuration of Certificate Services can increase the security of a CA. Logical security measures can include these:

- Restricting membership in the local Administrators group at the CA. Only local Administrators can modify CA configuration by default.

- Modifying permissions of the %systemroot%\system32\Certsrv folder so that Administrators and System have Full Control permissions and Authenticated Users have Read & Execute, List Folder Contents, and Read permissions.

- Modifying the permissions to the %systemroot%\system32\Certlog folder so that only Administrators, System, and Enterprise Admins have Full Control permissions.

- Assigning Administrators, System, and Enterprise Admins Full Control permissions if a shared folder location is specified in the configuration of the CA for the CertEnroll share.

- Monitoring and controlling the membership of the Cert Publishers group in each domain. Membership in the Cert Publishers group allows member CA computer accounts to publish certificates in user objects. Only members of the Cert Publishers group have this permission.

> **Tip**   The Cert Publishers group is a global group in Windows 2000 forests and in forests upgraded from Windows 2000. If multiple domains exist in your forest, a CA in one domain cannot publish certificates to user account objects in other domains. You can change this behavior by modifying permissions in Active Directory, as described in Knowledge Base article 281271: "Windows 2000 Certification Authority Configuration to Publish Certificates in Active Directory of Trusted Domain." This Knowledge Base article recommends creating a custom universal group that contains the Cert Publishers group from each domain in the forest, as well as assigning required permissions to the universal group. If the forest is a newly installed Windows Server 2003 forest, the scope of the Cert Publishers group is a domain local group. In the case of a domain local group, you can simply add the computer accounts from another domain's CA to the membership of the Cert Publishers group rather than modifying permissions.

For Windows Server 2003, additional security configuration options are available that are not available in Windows 2000. These configuration options include the following:

- **Implementing role separation** "Certificate Issuing and Management Components (CIMC) Family of Protection Profiles" is a standards document that defines requirements for the issuance, revocation, and management of X.509 certificates. The Windows Server 2003 PKI follows the recommendations in the standards document, allowing an organization to deploy a PKI that meets the Security Level 4 protection profile.

> **Note** The specific PKI management roles and implementation are discussed in the "Implementing Role Separation" section in this chapter.

- **Implementing all auditing options in Certificate Services** Windows Server 2003 enables you to define which management actions are included in the CA's Security log. To ensure that all events related to Certificate Services auditing are logged to the Security log, enable both success and failure events for Object Access at the CA. The settings can be applied directly in the Local Security Settings console or by applying a Group Policy object (GPO) with the required auditing settings. The available auditing settings for a CA include the following:

  - ❑ **Back Up And Restore The CA Database** Logs any attempts to back up or restore the CA database to the Windows Security log.

  - ❑ **Change CA Configurations** Logs any attempts to modify CA configuration, including defining Authority Information Access (AIA) and CRL distribution point (CDP) URLs or a Key Recovery Agent.

  - ❑ **Change CA Security Settings** Logs any attempts to modify CA permissions, including adding CA administrators or certificate managers.

  - ❑ **Issue And Manage Certificate Requests** Logs any attempts by a certificate manager to approve or deny certificate requests that are pending subject approval.

  - ❑ **Revoke Certificates And Publish CRLs** Logs any attempts by a certificate manager to revoke an issued certificate or by a CA administrator to publish an updated CRL.

  - ❑ **Store And Retrieve Archived Keys** Logs any attempts during the enrollment process to archive private keys in the CA database or attempts by certificate managers to extract archived private keys from the CA database.

  - ❑ **Start And Stop Certificate Services** Logs any attempts by the CA administrator to start or stop Certificate Services.

> **Note**   Windows Server 2003 Service Pack 1 allows the CA administrator role to modify which actions are audited at the CA. Prior to Service Pack 1, only users assigned the Manage Auditing and Security Log user right could modify the CA's audit settings.

- **Separating the Key Recovery Agent and certificate manager roles**   Windows Server 2003, Enterprise Edition, and Windows Server 2003, Datacenter Edition, enable you to recover private keys associated with encryption certificates. The process is split between two roles:

    ❑ The certificate manager role holder determines who the Key Recovery Agent is for the archived private key and extracts an encrypted PKCS#7 blob file from the CA database. Only the certificate manager role holder can perform this extraction of the blob file.

    ❑ The Key Recovery Agent role holder can decrypt the encrypted blob file with the Key Recovery Agent certificate's private key. Only the Key Recovery Agent has access to the private key that can decrypt the encrypted blob file.

Using Certificate Services with Windows Server 2003 Service Pack 1

Windows Server 2003 Service Pack 1 locks down remote access, remote activation, and remote launch on Distributed Component Object Model (DCOM) interfaces by limiting remote access to local administrators. Windows Server 2003 Certificate Services was built based on a less restrictive model that assumes that remote activation and remote access are allowed for all users.

To allow remote access to and activation of Certificate Services, the following permission modifications are required after the application of Service Pack 1:

1. The CertSrv Request DCOM interface access control list (ACL) must be modified as follows:

    ❑ Local and Remote Access are allowed for the Everyone group.

    ❑ Local and Remote Activation are allowed for the Everyone group.

    ❑ Local and Remote Launch settings are reset to an empty ACL.

> **Warning**   If you have assigned any custom permissions to the CertSrv Request DCOM interface, beware that the upgrade to Service Pack 1 will remove the custom settings and apply the preceding settings described here.

2. The global DCOM security configuration is modified as follows:

   ❑ A new group is created named CERTSVC_DCOM_ACCESS. If the CA is installed on a member server, the group scope will be a local group. If the CA is installed on a domain controller, the group scope will be a domain local group.

   ❑ The CERTSVC_DCOM_ACCESS group is populated. If the CA is installed on a member server, the Everyone group is added to the CERTSVC_DCOM_ACCESS membership. If the CA is installed on a domain controller, the Domain Users and Domain Computers global groups are added to the CERTSVC_DCOM_ACCESS membership.

3. If the CERTSVC_DCOM_ACCESS group is created and populated successfully, a registry flag (DCOM_SECURITY_UPDATED_FLAG) is set, indicating that the DCOM security update is complete.

Note   If Service Pack 1 is applied to a slipstreamed setup image, the discussed modification is performed during setup. If Service Pack 1 is applied to an existing Certificate Services installation, the DCOM_SECURITY_UPDATED_FLAG will not be set, causing the updates to be applied when Certificate Services attempts to start.

Modifying CRL and CA Certificate Publication Points

Publish CRLs and AIA to locations accessible by all users. The certificate-chaining engine must have access to the CRL and CA certificate for each CA in the certificate chain. If any CA in the certificate chain's CRL or CA certificate is not available, the chaining engine will prevent that certificate from being used if certificate revocation is enabled.

When you define the CDP and AIA URLs, ensure that the following conditions are met:

■ The URLs are ordered so that the majority of applications performing revocation checking can access them. For example, if you have several non-Windows computers that perform revocation checking, do not implement an Active Directory LDAP URL as the first URL. Change the order of the URLs so that an HTTP URL that is accessible to all applications is implemented as the first URL.

■ The publication intervals are possible in your network. If you implement both base CRLs (all certificates that have been revoked by the CA) and delta CRLs (CRLs containing only the certificates revoked since the publication of the last base CRL), you must ensure that the publication interval is not more frequent than the time it takes to replicate the updated CRL to the CDPs.

Enabling CRL Checking in All Applications

When you enable CRL checking in all applications, you ensure that every presented certificate is validated. Doing so confirms that the certificate has not been revoked, is time valid, and meets any constraints defined for the application. If an application does not perform CRL checking, it is possible for an attacker to use a certificate that was revoked for authentication or encryption purposes.

Note The security update MS04-011 includes a major modification to the Windows 2000 certificate-chaining engine. Prior to MS04-011, Windows 2000 clients supported only base CRLs for revocation checking. With the application of MS04-011, Windows 2000 clients can support both base CRLs and delta CRLs, which enables them to obtain the more current revocation information contained in delta CRLs. Microsoft Windows XP and Windows Server 2003 also support the use of base and delta CRLs for revocation status information.

Managing Permissions of Certificate Templates

You can modify the default permissions for any certificate template to identify which security groups can acquire certificates based on a certificate template and to define which security groups can modify the configuration of specific certificate templates. If the permissions of a certificate template are modified, attackers could acquire a certificate with special privileges, such as an Enrollment Agent certificate that allows the subject to request certificates on behalf of other users, or modify an existing certificate template to issue certificates that do not meet the original intended purpose. For example, an attacker could modify a secure e-mail certificate to request certificates on behalf of another user.

Implementing Role Separation

Windows Server 2003 Certificate Services allows you to implement Security Level 4 profiles as defined in the standard document "Certificate Issuing and Management Components (CIMC) Family of Protection Profiles."

Note The CIMC protection profiles are often referred to as Common Criteria guidelines.

The Security Level 4 profile defines four PKI management roles:

- **CA Administrator**   This role is responsible for account administration and key generation of the CA certificate's key pair.

- **Certificate Manager**   This role is responsible for certificate management. Management functions include issuing and revoking certificates.

- **Auditor**   This role is responsible for maintaining and configuring CA Audit logs.

- **Backup Operator**   This role is responsible for performing backups of PKI information.

Windows Server 2003, Enterprise Edition, and Windows Server 2003, Datacenter Edition, enable you to enforce Common Criteria role separation so that a single person cannot hold multiple Common Criteria roles. A user can hold only one of the CA Administrator, Certificate Manager, Auditor, or Backup Operator roles. Assignment of two or more of these roles results in the user being blocked from *all* certificate management actions.

> **Note**   Common Criteria role separation is enforced by a local Administrator running **certutil –setreg CA\RoleSeparationEnabled 1** at the command prompt and then restarting Certificate Services. Remember that any user who is assigned two or more administrative roles will be blocked from all CA management activities from that point forward, unless you disable the enforcement of Common Criteria role separation by running **certutil –delreg CA\RoleSeparationEnabled** and then restarting Certificate Services.

Best Practices

- **Increase the security of root CA computers.**   You can do this by deploying offline CAs and, if possible, by deploying offline policy CAs, depending on your company's security policy.

- **Implement a hardware security module.**   You should do this only if your company's security policy requires strong protection of CA key pairs.

- **Ensure that CRLs and CA certificates are published to accessible locations.**   The certificate-chaining engine must have access to all CRLs and CA certificates in the certificate chain to validate a presented certificate. If any certificate or CRL is unavailable, its status cannot be determined.

- **Enable CRL checking in all applications.**   CRL checking ensures that a presented certificate passes validation tests for approval. If the certificate fails any tests, it is considered invalid.

- **Apply the latest service packs and security updates to CAs.**   This way, you ensure that the CA is protected against known vulnerabilities.

- **Separate the certificate manager and Key Recovery Agent roles.**   If a person holds both roles, it is possible for that single user to extract an encrypted private key from a Windows Server 2003 CA and decrypt the private key for his own use. Separating the roles ensures that two people must be involved in the recovery process.

- **Implement role separation.**   By following Common Criteria guidelines, your organization can ensure that one person does not hold all PKI management roles. Implementing role separation enables oversight of the PKI management process to ensure that one person cannot perform all management functions. In some cases, you might want to enforce role separation to block any person from PKI management tasks if that person holds two or more Common Criteria roles.

- **Enable all audit options in a Windows Server 2003 CA.**   Enabling all auditing options ensures that all modifications to the PKI are captured in each CA's Security Event log.

Additional Information

- Microsoft Official Curriculum course 2821: Designing and Managing a Windows Public Key Infrastructure (*http://www.microsoft.com/traincert/syllabi /2821afinal.asp*)

- *Microsoft Windows Server 2003 PKI and Certificate Security* by Brian Komar with the Microsoft PKI Team (Microsoft Press, 2004) (*http://www.microsoft.com /learning/books/6745.asp*)

- *Windows Server 2003 Security Guide* (*http://www.microsoft.com/downloads /details.aspx?familyid=8A2643C1-0685-4D89-B655-521EA6C7B4DB&display-lang=en*)

- "An Introduction to the Windows 2000 Public Key Infrastructure" white paper (*http://www.microsoft.com/windows2000/techinfo/howitworks/security /pkiintro.asp*)

- "Microsoft Windows 2000 Public Key Infrastructure" white paper (*http: //www.microsoft.com/windows2000/techinfo/planning/security/pki.asp*)

- *Microsoft Windows 2000 Security Technical Reference*, Chapter 6, "Cryptography and Microsoft Public Key Infrastructure" (Microsoft Press, 2000) (*http: //www.microsoft.com/mspress/books/3873.asp*)

- "Best Practices for Implementing a Microsoft Windows Server 2003 Public Key Infrastructure" white paper (*http://www.microsoft.com/technet/prodtechnol /windowsserver2003/maintain/operate/ws3pkibp.asp*)

- "Key Archival and Management in Windows Server 2003" white paper (*http: //www.microsoft.com/technet/prodtechnol/windowsserver2003/maintain /operate/kyacws03.asp*)

- "Troubleshooting Certificate Status and Revocation" white paper (*http: //www.microsoft.com/technet/prodtechnol/windowsserver2003/maintain /operate/kyacws03.asp*)

- "Windows Server 2003 PKI Operations Guide" white paper (*http: //www.microsoft.com/technet/prodtechnol/windowsserver2003/technologies /security/ws03pkog.mspx*)

- "Certificate Authority Root Key Protection: Recommended Practices" security assurance white paper from Deloitte & Touche (*http://www.chrysalis-its.com /news/library/industry_white_papers/dt-wp.pdf*)

- "Certificate Issuing and Management Components Family of Protection Profiles" (*http://csrc.nist.gov/pki/documents/CIMC_PP_20011031.pdf*)

- "Windows 2000 Server and PKI: Using the nCipher Hardware Security Module" white paper (*http://www.microsoft.com/windows2000/techinfo/administration /security/win2kpki.asp*)

- nCipher nShield HSM (*http://www.ncipher.com/nshield/index.html*)

- nCipher netHSM (*http://www.ncipher.com/nethsm/index.html*)

- Knowledge Base article 329115: "Certificate Validation Flaw Might Permit Identity Spoofing" (*http://support.microsoft.com/kb/329115*)

- Knowledge Base article 281271: "Windows 2000 Certification Authority Configuration to Publish Certificates in Active Directory of Trusted Domain" (*http: //support.microsoft.com/kb/281271*)

Chapter 24

Implementing Security for Microsoft IIS

Microsoft Internet Information Services (IIS) version 5.0 is included with the Microsoft Windows 2000 operating system and version 6.0 is included with the Windows Server 2003 operating system. IIS provides you with the ability to host Web and FTP sites on a Windows server. When implementing a Web server or an FTP server, you must install the latest service packs and security patches to ensure your server is protected. In addition, you must implement measures to increase baseline security of the Web server. The measures you can take to secure IIS include the following:

- **Implement Windows security.** The Web or FTP server you deploy must run on a computer running Windows 2000 or Windows Server 2003 that is properly configured for security. You must configure user accounts, the file system, and the registry to implement baseline security required for Internet services.

- **Configure IIS security.** The Internet Services Manager console in Windows 2000 or Internet Information Services (IIS) Manager console in Windows Server 2003 enables you to implement an IIS-specific security configuration to ensure that the maximum level of security is implemented for your Web server. This includes defining authentication and Web site permissions and securing communication channels.

- **Implement additional IIS 5.0 security measures.**   For IIS 5.0, Microsoft provides two tools that you can use to configure the security of an IIS 5.0 server. The IIS Lockdown tool and the URLScan filter increase IIS 5.0 server security by removing or disabling unnecessary services, restricting which scripts are allowed to execute, and removing unnecessary IIS 5.0 server components.

- **Implement additional IIS 6.0 security measures.**   With IIS 6.0, Microsoft has redesigned IIS to remove several of the security design issues found in IIS 5.0. The additional security measures in IIS 6.0 can prevent one Web application from affecting other Web applications running on the same IIS 6.0 server.

- **Configure the FTP service.**   If you implement an FTP server, you must configure IIS to increase FTP service security. This includes limiting authentication to anonymous access and configuring an FTP folder structure to reduce attacks against the disk system.

Implementing Windows Security

When implementing an IIS server, you must first ensure that the Windows server hosting the IIS service is secure. Measures you can take include the following:

- Minimize services.

- Define the user account for anonymous access.

- Secure the file system.

- Apply specific registry settings.

> **Note**   These Windows security setting recommendations are the same whether you are hosting IIS on Windows 2000 Server or Windows Server 2003 hosts.

Minimizing Services

At a minimum, IIS server requires that you configure the following services to start automatically:

- **IISAdmin**   Enables administration of the Web server

- **World Wide Web Publishing Service**   Enables the World Wide Web (WWW) Publishing service on the IIS server

You might have to enable additional Internet-based services if they are required on your IIS server. Enable these services in Add/Remove Programs in Control Panel by adjusting the properties of IIS. These services include the following:

- **FTP Publishing Service**   Enables the IIS server to function as an FTP server
- **Network News Transport Protocol (NNTP)**   Enables the IIS server to host NNTP newsgroups
- **Simple Mail Transfer Protocol (SMTP)**   Enables the IIS server to send and receive e-mail as an SMTP server

In addition to these services, you should configure baseline security services as recommended in the Chapter 9, "Managing Security for System Services."

Defining User Accounts for Anonymous Access

For anonymous access to the Web server, IIS provides a user account, IUSR_*ComputerName*, where *ComputerName* is the NetBIOS name of the member server. By default, all anonymous Web access is performed in the security context of the IUSR_*ComputerName* account. When created, the IUSR_*ComputerName* account is configured as a member of the local Guests group on the member server.

> **Warning**   If you install IIS on a domain controller, the IUSR_*ComputerName* user account is assigned excess privileges. Any user account created in the Active Directory directory service is automatically assigned membership in the Domain Users global group. Membership in this group results in the IUSR_*ComputerName* user account having the same permissions as the Users domain local group. To rectify this security issue, add the IUSR_*ComputerName* user account to the membership of the Domain Guests global group, change the primary group for the user account to the Domain Guests global group, and delete the membership in the Domain Users global group. You must designate a new primary group before you can delete the Domain Users group's membership.

You should implement a custom account for anonymous access to the Web server. Rather than maintain default memberships, create a custom local group or domain local group. By creating a custom group, you can assign all anonymous permissions to that group, rather than assigning permissions to the Everyone group or to the Guests group.

> **Tip**   If you implement a custom IIS anonymous account, disable the IUSR_*ComputerName* account to prevent attackers from using this account to attempt network connections.

You must assign specific account options and user rights to the anonymous Web access account. These custom settings include the following:

- **Account options**   The custom user account must have the User Cannot Change Password and Password Never Expires options enabled.

- **User rights**   You must assign the custom user account the Log On Locally user right.

In addition to these custom settings, you must configure IIS to manage the user account's password. This is accomplished by enabling the Allow IIS To Control Password check box on the properties page of the IIS anonymous user account.

Securing the File System

To allow configuration of local file system security, all volumes that host Web content should be formatted by using the NTFS file system. In addition to using NTFS, you should consider hosting all Web content on a volume separate from the operating system to prevent attackers from performing *directory traversal attacks* to gain access to operating system files.

In a directory traversal attack, an attacker attempts to navigate to a location on the file system not published by the Web server. For example, the default path for the Web server root is %systemdrive%\Inetpub\WWWroot. An attacker might attempt to gain access to the command shell by using the URL *http://../../windows/system32/cmd.exe.*

In addition to storing all Web content on a separate drive from the operating system, you should create a folder structure that separates available content by type to allow specific permissions for the assignment of file types. For example, you can create the folder structure shown in Figure 24-1 to separate content into the categories of executables, scripts, include files, images, and static Web pages.

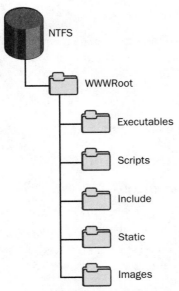

Figure 24-1 Dividing Web content into separate folders

Once you create the required folder structure, you can apply NTFS permissions specific to the Web content type, as shown in Table 24-1. The AnonWebAccess group is a custom local group created at the Web server that contains only the custom anonymous IIS user account.

Table 24-1 Securing Web Content by Content Type

Content Type	Recommended NTFS Permissions
Executables (.exe, .dll, .cmd, and .pl)	AnonWebAccess (Execute)
	Administrators (Full Control)
	System (Full Control)
Scripts (.asp)	AnonWebAccess (Execute)
	Administrators (Full Control)
	System (Full Control)
Server-side includes (.inc, .shtm, and .shtml)	AnonWebAccess (Execute)
	Administrators (Full Control)
	System (Full Control)
Images (.jpg, .gif)	AnonWebAccess (Read)
	Administrators (Full Control)
	System (Full Control)
Static content (.htm, .html)	AnonWebAccess (Read)
	Administrators (Full Control)
	System (Full Control)

Applying Specific Registry Settings

Web servers are frequently targets of denial-of-service attacks. You can help protect a Web server against a synchronization (SYN) attack by enabling the SynAttackProtect registry value:

```
HKLM\System\CurrentControlSet\Services\Tcpip\Parameters\SynAttackProtect
```

This REG_DWORD registry value protects against SYN attacks by adjusting the retransmission of SYN acknowledgment packets. These are the allowed values for the registry value:

- **0**   Provides typical protection against SYN attacks.

- **1**   Adjusts the retransmission of SYN acknowledgments. This setting causes responses to time out faster if a SYN attack is detected.

- **2**   Adds delays to connection indications and times out Transmission Control Protocol (TCP) connection requests at a faster rate if a SYN attack is detected.

A computer detects a SYN attack by inspecting three other registry values in the Tcpip\Parameters registry key:

- **TCPMaxPortsExhausted**   Determines how many connection requests the system refuses before initiating SYN attack protection. This should be set to a value of 2 or greater.

- **TCPMaxHalfOpen**   Determines how many connections the server maintains in the half-open state before TCP/IP initiates SYN attack protection. A half-open state occurs when a client starts a TCP/IP three-way handshake but does not respond to the server's synchronization request. This should be set to a value of 2 or greater.

- **TCPMaxHalfOpenRetried**   Determines how many connections the server maintains in the half-open state even after a connection request is retransmitted. This should be set to a value of 2 or greater.

Configuring IIS Security Settings Common to Windows 2000 and Windows Server 2003

Within the Internet Services Manager console (called the Internet Information Services (IIS) Manager console in Windows Server 2003) you can configure additional security for IIS by modifying the Web server's Master Properties and properties of individual Web sites, virtual directories, and Web content. The properties that affect security include the following:

- Authentication
- Web site permissions
- Communication channels

Authentication

IIS provides different methods for authenticating users when they connect to a Web site hosted by the Web server. The method you choose depends on the type of data stored on the Web site, as well as your network environment. The network environment includes the domain membership of the Web server and the Web browser implemented by Web clients.

Configuring Authentication Methods

IIS authentication methods can be configured in two locations. The first location is on the properties page of the Master Properties for the WWW Service. Master Properties affect default settings for all future Web sites installed at the Web server. The following steps explain how to configure IIS authentication methods by using Master Properties in Windows 2000:

1. From Administrative Tools, open the Internet Services Manager.

2. In the console tree, right-click *ComputerName*, where *ComputerName* is the NetBIOS name of the Web server, and then click Properties.

3. In the Master Properties section of the *ComputerName* properties page, select WWW Service from the Master Properties drop-down list. Then click Edit.

4. In the Anonymous Access And Authentication Control section of the Directory Security tab in the WWW Service Master Properties For *ComputerName* dialog box, click Edit.

5. In the Authentication Methods dialog box (shown in Figure 24-2), enable all required authentication methods and click OK.

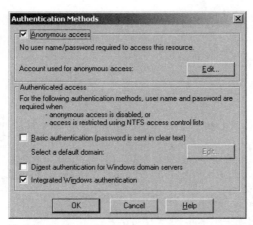

Figure 24-2 Defining authentication methods allowed for an IIS 5.0 Web site

In Windows Server 2003, the steps vary slightly with the introduction of the new Internet Information Services (IIS) Manager console:

1. From Administrative Tools, open the Internet Services Manager.

2. In the console tree, expand *ComputerName*, where *ComputerName* is the NetBIOS name of the Web server, and then click Web Sites.

3. Right-click Web Sites and then click Properties.

4. On the Web Site properties page, in the Directory Security tab, in the Authentication And Access Control section, click Edit.

5. In the Authentication Methods dialog box (shown in Figure 24-3), enable all required authentication methods and click OK.

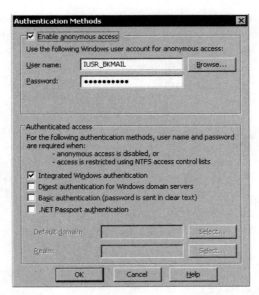

Figure 24-3   Defining authentication methods allowed for an IIS 6.0 Web site

In both IIS 5.0 and IIS 6.0, you can also configure authentication methods for each Web site or virtual directory hosted on the Web server. Individual Web site properties take precedence over those of the Master Properties. To modify authentication methods for a specific Web site or a virtual directory within a Web site, you must edit authentication methods in the Directory Security tab of the properties page for the Web site or the virtual directory.

Choosing Authentication Methods

The following methods are available for authenticating users as they connect to a Web site or virtual directory:

- Anonymous authentication
- Basic authentication
- Digest authentication
- Integrated Windows authentication
- Microsoft .NET Passport authentication
- Certificate-based authentication

Note   .NET Passport authentication is available only in IIS 6.0. You cannot enable .NET Passport authentication for Web servers hosted on IIS 5.0.

Anonymous Authentication   Anonymous authentication allows users to access a Web site without providing a user name and password for credentials. The Web site implements a predefined user account and password for the connection. By default, a local user account is created when IIS is installed. The name of this default account is IUSR_*ComputerName* and is a member of the local Guests group account.

You can increase anonymous user account security by creating a custom user account and custom group for all security assignments. The user account's password must be controlled by IIS to ensure the password is changed when required. By using a custom group, you assign all anonymous permissions for the Web site directly to the custom group, while prohibiting the application of other permissions to the Web site's anonymous user account. If you implement a custom IIS anonymous user account, you must assign the account the Log On Locally user right either in the local security policy of the Web server or at the OU where the computer account for the Web server exists.

Basic Authentication   Basic authentication is supported by most Web browsers. Basic authentication allows a user to provide credentials when requested by a Web site. The security issue with basic authentication is that the user's account and password are sent to the Web server in an unencrypted format that uses base64 encoding, meaning that the user's credentials are susceptible to inspection.

Note   You can increase the security of basic authentication by implementing Secure Sockets Layer (SSL) to encrypt all data sent to the Web site. The user's credentials are then encrypted as they are transmitted from the Web client to the Web server.

Digest Authentication   Digest authentication increases the security of the user's credentials by not sending the user's password over the network. Instead, the user's password and other information about the account are used to create a hash value that is sent to the Web server. The Web server compares this hash value with the Active Directory version of the hash. If the two hash values match, the user is considered authenticated.

Digest authentication requires that the Store Password Using Reversible Encryption option is enabled at the user account in a Windows 2000 network. This option effectively stores the user's password as plaintext in Active Directory, but the setting does not take effect until the next time the user changes her password. The password's reversibly encrypted format is stored when the user's password is set. In an IIS 6.0 environment, you can disable the use of reversible encryption by enabling Advanced Digest Authentication by changing the UseDigestSSP metabase value to True from the default value of false. When Advanced Digest Authentication is enabled, the need to store the user's password using reversible encryption is removed.

Integrated Windows Authentication   Integrated Windows authentication uses NT LAN Manager (NTLM) or Kerberos version 5 to authenticate a Web client with a Web server. The user name and password are not sent across the network, protecting against credential interception. Integrated Windows authentication requires that the Web client use the Microsoft Internet Explorer Web browser because other browsers do not support this form of authentication.

Deploying N-Tiered Applications

If you are implementing an n-tiered application at an IIS 5.0 or IIS 6.0 server, the authentication must use Kerberos v5. Kerberos authentication allows the IIS server to impersonate the user when submitting requests to a back-end application server, such as a Microsoft SQL Server.

To ensure that Kerberos v5 is used for authentication when using Integrated Windows Authentication, the computer account of the Web server must be trusted for delegation in Active Directory. In addition, the computer's Service Principal Name (SPN) must be resolvable through the Domain Name System (DNS), allowing the computer account to impersonate the authenticated user when the Web site performs a request to a back-end application server.

On the CD accompanying this book, the AuthenticationMethod.asp Web page is provided. By connecting to the AuthenticationMethod.asp Web page, you can determine whether a Web site is using Kerberos or NTLM authentication when Integrated Web Authentication is implemented. The Web page determines which authentication method is used by examining the size and contents of the HTTP_Authorization header.

.NET Passport Authentication   An IIS 6.0 Web server can implement .NET Passport authentication to allow users to use a single sign-in name and password that provides them access to any Web site that implements .NET Passport authentication.

A Web site that implements .NET Passport authentication depends on the .NET Passport central server to authenticate users. This removes all requirements to host and manage an authentication system for the Web site. The user is still responsible for defining permissions for the domain and providing a default domain for all authenticated users.

Certificate-Based Authentication   Windows 2000 and Windows Server 2003 allow certificates with the Client Authentication Enhanced Key Usage (EKU) to be used for user account authentication when connecting to a Web server with a Web Server certificate installed.

When a user connects to a Web server, he is prompted to select an authentication certificate. The user's certificate is sent to the Web server, which associates the presented certificate to a user account either in the local Security Accounts Manager (SAM) database of the Web server or in Active Directory. The certificate is implicitly mapped to a user account in Active Directory if the Enable The Windows Directory Service Mapper option is enabled in the Web site's Master Properties page. The user's User Principal Name (UPN) must be included in the certificate's Subject Alternative Name (SAN) to enable this implicit mapping. If implicit mapping is used, the public key from the presented certificate is used to encrypt the authentication data. If an explicit mapping is used, the public key associated with the certificate is retrieved from Active Directory and then is used to encrypt authentication data. Only the holder of the certificate's private key can decrypt the authentication data.

> **Note**   The certificate of the certification authority (CA) that issued the user's client authentication certificate must be included in the NTAuth store (CN=NTAuthCertificates,CN=Public Key Services,CN=Services,CN=Configuration,*ForestRootDomain*, where *ForestRootDomain* is the Lightweight Directory Access Protocol (LDAP) distinguished name of the forest root domain.

Alternatively, a specific certificate can be explicitly mapped to a user account in either the local SAM database of the IIS server or in Active Directory. When an explicit mapping is defined, the Web server queries the local SAM database or Active Directory when a certificate is presented to determine which account is associated with the certificate.

You enforce certificate-based authentication by performing two steps:

1. Enforce client-based certificates on the Web site's properties page. In the Secure Communications dialog box, you can require client certificates by enabling SSL for the Web site and clicking the Require Client Certificates button, as shown in Figure 24-4.

2. Remove all other forms of authentication from the properties page of the Web site. If you clear all the authentication method check boxes shown in Figure 24-2 or Figure 24-3, you prevent all forms of authentication other than certificate-based authentication. This prevents IIS from presenting alternate authentication forms if the certificate-based authentication fails.

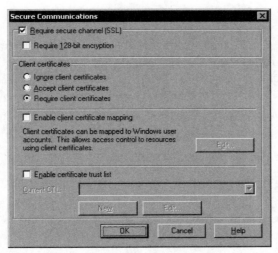

Figure 24-4   Configuring the Web site to require client certificate-based authentication

Web Site Permissions

The Internet Services Manager console allows you to define permissions for a Web site or virtual directory. These permissions are separate from NTFS permissions applied to the actual Web content folder.

If NTFS permissions and Web site permissions are in conflict, the more restrictive permissions are applied. For example, if NTFS permissions allow a user to modify the contents of a folder but the Web permissions grant only Read permissions, the user is assigned Read permissions.

You define the permissions for a Web site in the Home Directory tab of a Web site's properties page, as shown in Figure 24-5. When defining a Web site's permissions, you can apply any combination of the following permissions:

- **Script Source Access**   Allows users of the Web site or virtual directory to access the source code for a Web site, including Microsoft Active Server Pages (ASP) applications, if the Read or Write permissions are also defined for the Web site or virtual directory. This permission is available for Web sites, virtual directories, and individual files.

- **Read**   Allows users of the Web site to read Web content posted at the Web site and to navigate between pages on the Web site. This permission is available for Web sites, virtual directories, and individual files.

- **Write**   Allows users to upload files to the Web site or the Web site's specific upload folder. This permission also allows a user to modify the contents of a Write-enabled file at the Web server. This permission is available for Web sites, virtual directories, and individual files. Write permissions are available only to Web browsers that support the HTTP 1.1 protocol standard PUT feature.

- **Directory Browsing**   Allows users to view hypertext listings of all files and sub-directories within a Web site folder or a virtual directory, if a default document is not located in the folder or virtual directory. Virtual directories will not appear in the hypertext listing. The user must know the virtual directory's alias or must click a link that refers her to the virtual directory. This permission is available only for Web sites and virtual directories.

- **Execute Permissions**   Defines the level of script execution allowed for users of the Web site or virtual directory. Options include the following:

  - ❑ **None**   Script executables are not allowed to run on the Web server.

  - ❑ **Scripts Only**   Only scripts are allowed to run on the Web server, executables are not allowed to execute.

  - ❑ **Scripts And Executables**   Both scripts and executables are allowed to run on the Web server.

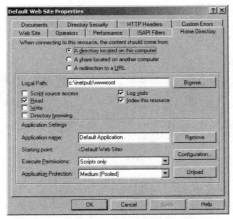

Figure 24-5   Defining permissions for a Web site

Communication Channels

Additional security can be provided for connections to the Web server by implementing SSL encryption between the Web server and Web clients. SSL is enabled by installing a Web Server certificate at the Web server. Specifically, the Web Server certificate must have the following attributes:

- The certificate must chain to a trusted root authority. The root Certification Authority (CA) in the certificate chain must be included in the trusted root store of all clients that connect to the SSL-protected Web server.

- The installed certificate must have a Server Authentication object ID (OID) in the EKU attribute of the certificate. The Server Authentication OID (1.3.6.1.5.5.7.3.1) indicates that the Web Server certificate can be used to authenticate the Web server's identity and can also be used to encrypt session data between the Web server and Web clients.

- The subject of the certificate must match the DNS name used to access the Web site. For example, if the Web site is accessed by connecting to *http://www.example.com*, the subject of the Web Server certificate must be *www.example.com*.

> **Caution**   A common mistake administrators make when requesting a Web Server certificate is to request the certificate with the Web server's NetBIOS name as the subject, rather than the Web site's DNS name as the subject. If you do not use the Web site's DNS name as the subject, a user connecting to the Web site will receive a warning that the Web site's certificate name does not match the name of the Web site.

Enabling SSL

To enable SSL, you must install a Web Server certificate at the Web server. You can install a Web Server certificate by running the Web Server Certificate Wizard:

1. From Administrative Tools, open the Internet Service Manager or Internet Information Services (IIS) Management console.

2. In the console tree, right-click Default Web Site, and click Properties.

3. On the Default Web Site properties page, in the Directory Security tab, click Server Certificate.

4. On the Welcome To The Web Server Certificate Wizard page, click Next.

5. On the Server Certificate page, click Create A New Certificate, and then click Next.

6. On the Delayed Or Immediate Request page, perform one of the following and then click Next:

   - If submitting the request to an enterprise CA on the local network, click Send The Request Immediately To An Online Certification Authority.

   - If submitting the request to a commercial CA such as VeriSign, click Prepare The Request Now, But Send It Later. This will create a PKCS#10 certificate request format file.

7. On the Name And Security Settings page, type a name for the Web site, define the bit length for the certificate encryption key, and click Next.

8. On the Organization Information page, type the organization and OU names, and click Next.

9.   On the Your Site's Common Name page, type the DNS fully qualified domain name (FQDN) of your Web server, and click Next.

10. On the Geographical Information page, identify the country/region, state/province, and city/locality for your Web server, and click Next.

11. If you use IIS 6.0, on the SSL Port page, type the TCP port number that the SSL-protected Web site will use (the default value is 443), and then click Next.

12. If you select Send The Request Immediately To An Online Certification Authority, the Choose A Certification Authority page appears. You must select an enterprise CA from the drop-down list and click Next. If you select Prepare The Request Now, But Send It Later, the Certificate Request File Name page appears. You must type the file name for the certificate request and click Next.

13. A summary page will appear that displays the naming information provided to the Web Server Certificate Request Wizard. Verify the information and click Next.

14. On the Completing The Web Server Certificate Request Wizard page, click Finish.

If you request the Web Server certificate from a commercial CA, you must submit the certificate request file to the commercial CA. Once you receive the certificate from the commercial CA, you must install it at the Web server. The Web Server certificate is installed by using the following process:

1.   From Administrative Tools, open the Internet Service Manager or Internet Information Services (IIS) Management console.

2.   In the console tree, right-click Default Web Site, and click Properties.

3.   In the Default Web Site properties page, in the Directory Security tab, click Server Certificate.

4.   On the Welcome To The Web Server Certificate Wizard page, click Next.

5.   On the Pending Certificate Request page, click Process The Pending Request And Install The Certificate, and then click Next.

6.   On the Process A Pending Request page, provide the full path to the certificate file returned to you from the commercial CA, and click Next.

7.   On the Certificate Summary page, ensure that the information provided in the certificate is correct, and click Next.

8.   On the Completing The Web Server Certificate Request Wizard page, click Finish.

Configuring SSL

Once you have completed the installation of the Web Server certificate, you are ready to configure SSL options for the Web server. SSL configuration options are defined by clicking the Edit button in the Secure Communications section in the Directory Security tab of a Web site or virtual directory. The options that can be defined for SSL include the following:

- **Choose where to implement SSL encryption.** You can choose to enable SSL encryption for a Web site, virtual directory, or specific file at a Web site. You enable SSL by enabling the Require Secure Channel (SSL) option. We recommend that you provide encryption either for the entire Web site or for a specific virtual directory to ensure the security of all data sent to and from a specific Web application.

- **Enforce 128-bit encryption.** This encryption level increases the encryption strength for data transmitted to and from an SSL-protected Web site. If you enable this option, all Web browsers must support 128-bit encryption. If a Web browser does not have the High Encryption Pack installed or a service pack that enables strong encryption, connection attempts to the SSL-protected Web site will fail.

- **Define client certificate requirements.** Once a Web Server certificate is installed at the Web server, you can enable certificate-based authentication. The user authenticates with the Web site by presenting a certificate from his certificate store. The Web server will associate (or map) the certificate to a user account. The possession of the private key associated with the certificate proves the user's identity. When enabled, you can choose to either accept or require client certificates for authentication.

- **Enable client certificate mapping.** If you enable the mapping of certificates to user accounts, you must enable client certificate mapping. This option enables mappings defined in Active Directory or IIS.

- **Enable certificate trust lists.** A certificate trust list defines trust for external CAs. You can limit which external certificates are trusted by determining the accepted enhanced key usages and validity periods for external certificates, as well as identifying trusted CAs.

In addition to these settings, you can define the SSL listening port for the Web site or virtual directory. By default, the Web SSL listening port is TCP port 443, but you can configure a custom SSL listening port. This is required when a Web server hosts multiple SSL-protected Web sites.

Implementing Additional Security Measures for IIS 5.0

Two tools are available to secure an IIS 5.0 server: the IIS Lockdown tool and the URLScan filter. These tools remove known weaknesses in the IIS configuration and provide filters to prevent known attacks against the IIS server.

IIS Lockdown Tool

By default, Windows 2000 includes the installation of IIS. The IIS Lockdown tool enables you to secure IIS configuration without removing and reinstalling the service. The IIS Lockdown tool can be run by an administrator or can be scripted to allow the unattended application of IIS Lockdown settings to an IIS server. The installation of the tool is broken down into security configuration sections:

- Selecting a server template
- Configuring Internet services
- Enabling script maps
- Applying additional security

Selecting a Server Template

The Select Server Template page provides a list of predefined IIS configuration templates. Each template contains IIS settings designed for the software in the IIS Server template name. By selecting a server template from the list, the IIS Lockdown tool will apply the necessary settings to secure IIS in that environment.

When you select a server template, you can view the specific settings by enabling the View Template Settings check box. This option enables you to review the configured settings and apply any modifications necessary for your IIS environment.

Creating a Custom Server Template

You can create custom server templates in the IISlockd.ini file for use with the IIS Lockdown tool. All custom server templates appear in the IIS Lockdown tool as available templates. You can create a custom server template by editing the IISlockd.ini file to include your custom settings.

The first step is to include pointers to your custom server template section. You must declare your custom template in either the *ServerTypesNT4*, the *ServerTypes*, or *UnattendedServerType* lines in the *[Info]* section, as shown next. In this case, *CustomTemplate* is available for both manual and unattended installations.

```
[Info]
ServerTypesNT4=sbs4.5,exchange5.5,frontpage,proxy,staticweb,dynamicweb,
    other,iis_uninstalled
ServerTypes=CustomTemplate,sbs2000,exchange5.5,exchange2k,
    sharepoint_portal,frontpage,biztalk,commerce,proxy,staticweb,
    dynamicweb,other,iis_uninstalled
UnattendedServerType=CustomTemplate
Unattended=TRUE
Undo=FALSE
```

Once you define the pointers, you must create a section based on the referral in the *[Info]* section that details the settings for the custom server template. The following example ensures that the following settings are made:

- Only the Web service is installed. All other services are disabled, rather than uninstalled.

- Only ASPs are enabled.

- Anonymous rights for running system utilities and viewing content are enabled.

- IIS Samples, IIS scripts, the Microsoft Advanced Data Connector (MSADC) virtual directory, the IIS Administration virtual directory, and the IIS Help virtual directory are removed from the IIS server.

- URLScan is enabled and the URLScan.ini file is stored in the %windir%\system32\Inetsrv\URLscan folder.

These settings are all defined in the *[CustomTemplate]* section, which enforces the previous settings and is shown next. The section name is based on the tag assigned to the section in the *[Info]* section shown earlier.

```
[CustomTemplate]
label="A Custom Server Template"
Enable_iis_http=TRUE
Enable_iis_ftp= FALSE
Enable_iis_smtp= FALSE
Enable_iis_nntp= FALSE
Enable_asp= TRUE
Enable_index_server_web_interface= FALSE
Enable_server_side_includes= FALSE
Enable_internet_data_connector= FALSE
Enable_internet_printing= FALSE
Enable_HTR_scripting= FALSE
Enable_webDAV= FALSE
Disable_Anonymous_user_system_utility_execute_rights= TRUE
Disable_Anonymous_user_content_directory_write_rights= TRUE
```

```
Remove_iissamples_virtual_directory=TRUE
Remove_scripts_directory=TRUE
Remove_MSADC_virtual_directory=TRUE
Remove_iisadmin_virtual_directory=TRUE
Remove_iishelp_virtual_directory=TRUE
UrlScan_Install=ENABLED
UrlScan_IniFileLocation=%windir%\System32\Inetsrv\Urlscan
AdvancedSetup =
UninstallServices=FALSE
```

Configuring Internet Services

If you enable the View Template Settings option or choose to configure the other
server template, you can configure which Internet services are available at the IIS
server. You can select whether each service is enabled or disabled, as shown in
Figure 24-6.

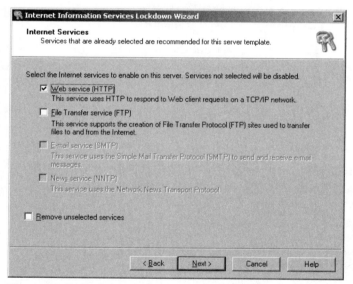

Figure 24-6   Defining the startup state for IIS

An enabled service is indicated by a selected check box. A disabled service is indicated
by an unselected check box. If a service is dimmed, it is not installed on the IIS server.
You can remove unselected services, rather than leaving the services disabled, by
enabling the Remove Unselected Services option.

Caution You should leave services disabled. Many applications depend on dynamic-link libraries (DLLs) enabled by IIS. If a service is disabled, the DLLs remain available for other applications. If the service is removed, some applications will reinstall and enable IIS to gain access to the required DLLs.

Enabling Script Maps

IIS can limit which scripts can be executed on an IIS server by defining script maps. Script maps associate script files, such as ASP pages, with a specific scripting engine for processing. Script maps are implemented by using Internet Server Application Programming Interface (ISAPI).

On the Script Maps page, you can enable and disable predefined script maps. If a script map is disabled, the default script map is replaced with a script that causes the server to respond with a "HTTP 404–File not found" error. The following script maps can be enabled or disabled:

- **Active Server Pages (.asp)** This technology enables the creation of dynamic Web pages. When a user connects to an ASP page, the server executes the ASP script at the server and generates an HTML page. The resultant HTML page is returned to the user who connected to the ASP page.

- **Index Server Web Interface (.idq)** These scripts enable an administrator to manage Index Server services remotely from the Web. The scripts also enable a user to create custom Web-based queries against an Index Server. If you do not require these features, you can disable this script map.

Note Disabling .idq script mapping does not prevent your Web site from allowing standard Web-based searches that utilize Index Server.

- **Server-Side Includes (.shtml, .shtm, .stm)** These scripts enable a Web server to add text, graphics, or application information to a Web page before it is sent to a user.

- **Internet Data Connector (.idc)** These scripts enable queries to be sent to back-end databases and then display the results in an HTML-formatted page.

- **HTR Scripting (.htr)** These scripts are similar to ASP scripts. HTR scripts are commonly used for allowing logon passwords to be changed by using a Web server. For example, Microsoft Outlook Web Access (OWA) in Microsoft Exchange Server 2000 uses HTR scripts to enable users to change their passwords from the OWA Web site.

- **Internet Printing (.printer)** These scripts enable you to send and manage print jobs sent from the Internet to your network's TCP/IP-based printers.

You must determine whether each script map is required for your IIS environment. Some script maps (such as server-side includes and Internet data connector scripts) can be updated to use ASP pages.

Applying Additional Security

The Additional Security page enables you to implement extra measures for your IIS server, as shown in Figure 24-7.

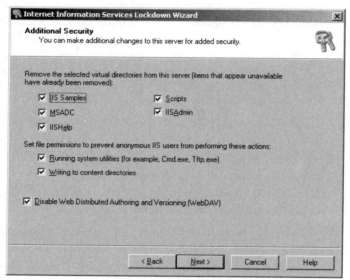

Figure 24-7   Defining additional security settings in the IIS Lockdown tool

The extra measures that you can take include the following:

- **Remove Selected Virtual Directories**   IIS automatically installs with several virtual directories that provide access to IIS Samples, MSADC, IIS Help files, sample scripts, and the Web-based IIS Administration pages. You can choose to remove each of these from the IIS server.

- **Define Permissions For Anonymous Users**   You can configure IIS to prevent anonymous Web users from executing system utilities such as the command prompt or Trivial File Transfer Protocol (TFTP). Also, you can prevent anonymous users from uploading data to content directories.

- **Disable Web-Based Distributed Authoring And Versioning (WebDAV)**   This option enables you to prevent the creation of Web folders on the IIS server. Web folders allow a share to be published as a virtual directory with directory browsing enabled. In addition, a drive letter can be mapped to the WebDAV folder. This option must not be enabled at an Exchange 2000 server because WebDAV is used for the mail store drive.

URLScan

URLScan is an ISAPI filter that screens and analyzes HTTP requests as IIS receives them. The URLScan filter applies settings based on the IIS Server template selected in the IIS Lockdown tool.

URLScan Filter

As mentioned in the description of the IIS Lockdown tool, URLScan is an ISAPI filter that screens and analyzes inbound HTTP requests as IIS receives them. The URLScan filter applies settings based on the IIS Server template selected in the IIS Lockdown tool. This ISAPI filter can be installed on IIS. If you install the Microsoft Internet Security and Acceleration (ISA) Server Feature Pack, the ISAPI filter can be installed on an ISA server that protects multiple IIS servers.

URLScan analyzes all incoming HTTP requests against a URLScan filter configuration file to determine whether the request should be allowed. If the request is allowed, the Web server responds with the requested resource. If the request is denied, the Web server sends an "Object not found" response to the client, rather than sending details about why the request is denied.

Installing URLScan

URLScan can be automatically installed when you run the IIS Lockdown tool or manually installed by modifying the properties of the IIS server. When you install the IIS Lockdown tool, you have the option to install URLScan. In this case, the URLScan filter is configured to match the server environment selected in the IIS Lockdown tool. After you complete installation, you can manually modify the configuration of the URLScan.ini file to customize Web server security.

Configuring URLScan

The URLScan ISAPI filter screens incoming HTTP requests and blocks requests based on the configuration of the URLScan.ini file. By default, this file is stored in the %windir%\system32\Inetsrv\URLScan folder and must reside in the same folder as URLScan.dll if you modify the default storage location.

 Note   You must restart the WWW Publishing Service to enable any configuration changes in the URLScan.ini file.

The URLScan.ini file consists of seven sections:

- **Options**   Allows the definition of default security options for the URLScan ISAPI filter.

- **AllowVerbs**   Defines which HTTP verbs or methods are allowed in HTTP requests.

- **DenyVerbs**   Defines which HTTP verbs or methods are explicitly not allowed in HTTP requests.

- **DenyHeaders**   Defines which HTTP request headers are explicitly not allowed in HTTP requests.

- **AllowExtensions**   Defines a list of file extensions that are allowed in HTTP URL requests.

- **DenyExtensions**   Defines a list of file extensions that are explicitly not allowed in HTTP URL requests.

- **RequestLimits**   Defines and enforces limits on the size for each part of an HTTP request that reaches the Web server. All sizes are defined in bytes. The Request-Limits section is recognized only when running URLScan version 2.5 or later.

Options Section   The Options section defines the main options for the URLScan filter. It also designates which additional sections are used while processing incoming HTTP requests. You can define the following options:

- **UseAllowVerbs**   If set to a value of 1, URLScan reads the AllowVerbs section of URLScan.ini and rejects any request that does not contain an HTTP verb included in the AllowVerbs section. If set to 0, URLScan reads the DenyVerbs section of URLScan.ini and rejects any request that contains a listed HTTP verb. The default value is 1.

- **UseAllowExtensions**   If set to a value of 1, URLScan allows only HTTP requests for files whose extensions are included in the AllowExtensions section of URLScan.ini. If set to 0, URLScan reads the DenyExtensions section of URLScan.ini and rejects any HTTP requests for files with an extension included in the DenyExtensions list. The default value is 0.

- **NormalizeURLBeforeScan**   If set to a value of 1, URLScan analyzes the requested URL after IIS decodes and normalizes the URL. If set to 0, URLScan analyzes the raw URL sent by the Web client. The default value is 1.

> **Tip**   Do not set the *NormalizeURLBeforeScan* option to a value of 0. Doing so exposes the IIS 5.0 server to canonicalization attacks that bypass proper analysis of the URL extensions and gain permissions to certain types of files hosted on a Web server that are file types implemented through ISAPI extensions.

- **VerifyNormalization**   If set to a value of 1, URLScan verifies normalization of the URL. This action defends against canonicalization attacks that attempt to conceal the true URL requested. For instance, the string %252e is an example of a double-encoded string for the dot (.) character. The %25 decodes to a percent sign (%) character, and the resulting %2e decodes to the dot (.) character. If set to 0, this test is not performed by URLScan. The default value is 1.

- **AllowHighBitCharacters**   If set to a value of 1, URLScan allows any characters outside the ASCII character set to exist in the URL. If set to 0, URLScan rejects any request in which the URL contains a character outside the ASCII character set. Although this feature can protect against Unicode attacks, it can lead to the rejection of valid URLs if you implement URLs with Unicode characters. The default value is 0.

- **AllowDotInPath**   If set to a value of 0, URLScan rejects any requests containing multiple instances of the dot (.) character in a URL. If set to 1, URLScan does not perform this test. URLScan assumes that an extension is the part of the URL beginning after the last dot in the string and ending at the first question mark, the first slash character after the dot, or the end of the string. The default value is 0.

- **RemoveServerHeader**   If set to a value of 1, URLScan removes the server header on all responses. If set to 0, URLScan does not perform this action. The default value is 0.

> **Note**   This option prevents only one method of determining that the Web server is an IIS server. Many other ways of determining whether the Web server is running IIS exist.

- **EnableLogging**   If set to a value of 1, URLScan logs its actions in the URLScan.log file that is in the same directory as the URLScan.dll file. If set to 0, logging is disabled. The default value is 1.

- **LoggingDirectory**   Allows you to specify a custom folder in which to store the URLScan log file. The folder must be a local folder, such as C:\Logfiles. If this option is not specified, URLScan creates the log file in the same folder as the URLScan.dll file. This option is available only in URLScan version 2.5 and later.

- **LogLongURLs**   If set to a value of 1, URLScan will log up to 128 KB per request. If set to 0, URLScan will log the first 1024 bytes of the request. The default value is 0. This option is available only in URLScan version 2.5 and later.

- **PerProcessLogging**   If set to a value of 1, URLScan appends the process ID of the IIS process hosting URLScan.dll to the log file name. If set to 0, all processes are logged in the same log file, which is named URLScan.log. The default value is 0.

- **AlternateServerName**   Allows you to create a different string that is presented in the server header. This setting is ignored if the RemoveServerHeader option is set to a value of 1. By default, the AlternateServerName is a null value.

- **AllowLateScanning**   If set to a value of 1, URLScan registers as a low-priority filter. This allows other ISAPI filters to modify the URL before it is analyzed by URLScan. If set to 0, URLScan registers as a high-priority filter. The default value is 0.

> **Note**   If you implement both Microsoft FrontPage Server Extensions and URLScan, you must set the AllowLateScanning option to a value of 1. In addition, URLScan must be placed after FrontPage Server Extensions on the filter load list.

- **PerDayLogging**   If set to a value of 1, URLScan creates a new log file each day and adds a date to the log file name. If a day passes with no URLScan activity, no log is created for that day. If set to 0, URLScan opens a single file called URLScan.log. The default value is 1.

- **RejectResponseURL**   Enables you to define a response URL string that is returned to a Web client when URLScan rejects an HTTP request. In the RejectResponseURL string, you can use the following variables to tailor a response:

  - HTTP_URLSCAN_STATUS_HEADER provides the reason why the HTTP request is rejected.

  - HTTP_URLSCAN_ORIGINAL_VERB provides the verb given in the original HTTP request.

  - HTTP_URLSCAN_ORIGINAL_URL provides the rejected URL requested in the original HTTP request.

> **Note**   You can place URLScan into a logging-only mode by setting RejectResponseURL to a value of /~*. With this setting, URLScan performs all configured scanning and logs the results but still allows IIS to serve the rejected page. This mode enables you to test URLScan.ini settings without actually rejecting any requests.

- **UseFastPathReject**   If set to a value of 1, URLScan ignores the RejectResponseURL and returns a short "HTTP 404—File not found" response to the client when an HTTP request is rejected. If set to 0, the RejectResponseURL option is used to create the rejection response. The default value is 0.

AllowVerbs Section   The AllowVerbs section contains a list of HTTP verbs that are allowed in HTTP requests. If the UseAllowVerbs option is set to 1, URLScan rejects any HTTP requests containing a verb not explicitly listed. The entries in this section are case sensitive.

DenyVerbs Section   The DenyVerbs section contains a list of HTTP verbs that are explicitly not allowed in HTTP requests. If the UseAllowVerbs option is set to 0, URLScan rejects any HTTP requests that contain a listed verb. The entries in this section are case insensitive.

DenyHeaders Section   The DenyHeaders section contains a list of request headers. Any HTTP requests that contain a request header listed in this section are rejected. The entries in this section are case insensitive.

AllowExtensions Section   The AllowExtensions section contains a list of allowed file extensions. If the UseAllowExtensions option is set to a value of 1, any request containing a URL with an extension not listed is rejected. You can specify URLs that do not have an extension by adding an extension represented by a dot and no trailing characters.

DenyExtensions Section   The DenyExtensions section contains a list of disallowed file extensions. If the UseAllowExtensions option is set to 0, any request containing a URL with an extension in the listing is rejected. The entries in this section are case insensitive.

RequestLimits Section   This section enables you to enforce limits on the size of an HTTP request. The size definitions can be defined for each section of an HTTP request. The size restrictions are defined in the following three entries:

- **MaxAllowedContentLength**   Enforces a maximum value for the content length. If the action is performed by using a chunk transfer, in which the data is broken into separate chunks, transferred, and then reassembled, MaxAllowedContentLength does not actually prevent the server from accepting more data than the amount to which this value is set. The default value is roughly 2 GB.

- **MaxURL**   Restricts the length of the requested URL, not the length of the query string. The value of this registry setting will vary depending on how you install URLScan. If you manually extract URLScan.dll, the default setting is 260 bytes. If you install URLScan by installing the IIS Lockdown tool, the default setting is 16 KB.

- **MaxQueryString**   Restricts the length of the query string. The value is defined in bytes, with a default value of 4 KB.

In addition to these settings, you can create custom limitations by request header type by creating an entry based on the header name with the prefix "Max-". For example, to limit the length of the "Content-Type" header to 200 bytes, you can add the entry "Max-Content-Type=200" in the RequestLimits section.

URLScan Logging

If URLScan denies a Web request, it will log the action in the %windir%\system32\inetsrv\urlscan\URLScan.log file. The log file will include the reason for the denial and additional information about the request as follows:

- **The complete URL requested**   Details whether a false URL was requested or whether an attacker attempted to gain access to a nonpublished folder by using a directory traversal attack.

- **IP address of the source of the request**   Helps determine the origin of the attack. Remember that the IP address can also be the IP address of a network address translation (NAT) device, a proxy server address, or a spoofed IP address.

Note   If the IP address is a spoofed IP address, you will not be able to determine the true IP address that initiated the request. The IP address recorded in the URLScan log file is the spoofed IP address, not the true IP address of the remote client.

Configuring Additional Security Measures for IIS 6.0

In IIS 6.0, Microsoft increased the default security measures for IIS. IIS is no longer installed by default when you install Windows Server 2003, and the default installation locks down the service to limit the server to hosting static HTML initially. Table 24-2 compares the default installation states for IIS 5.0 and IIS 6.0.

Table 24-2   Default Installation States for IIS 5.0 and IIS 6.0

IIS Component	IIS 5.0 Default Installation	IIS 6.0 Default Installation
Static file support	Enabled	Enabled
Active Server Pages	Enabled	Disabled
Server-side includes	Enabled	Disabled
Internet Data Connector	Enabled	Disabled
WebDAV	Enabled	Disabled
Index Server ISAPI	Enabled	Disabled
Internet Printing ISAPI	Enabled	Disabled
CGI	Enabled	Disabled
Microsoft FrontPage Server extensions	Enabled	Disabled

Table 24-2   **Default Installation States for IIS 5.0 and IIS 6.0**

IIS Component	IIS 5.0 Default Installation	IIS 6.0 Default Installation
Password change interface	Enabled	Disabled
SMTP	Enabled	Disabled
FTP	Enabled	Disabled
ASP.NET	Not applicable	Disabled
Background Intelligence Transfer Services (BITS)	Not applicable	Disabled

Note   If you upgrade a Web server from Windows 2000 to Windows Server 2003, IIS 6.0 services will be installed on the upgraded Web server. If the IIS Lockdown tool was executed on the Web server before the upgrade, the current security configuration is maintained. If the IIS Lockdown Wizard was not executed, the IIS 6.0 services are disabled.

In addition to locking down the default installation state of IIS 6.0, additional security measures are implemented in IIS 6.0, including the following:

- Reducing privilege requirements
- Automatic health monitoring
- Implementing application isolation
- Improved Http.sys security
- Supporting ASP.NET security
- Securing the default settings
- Protection against common attacks

Reducing Privilege Requirements

With the redesign of IIS 6.0, the need to run code as the LocalSystem user account has been reduced. All code that is required to run as LocalSystem is now included in Http.sys. Instead of using the LocalSystem account, worker processes can launch using the built-in account Network Service. The network service account is limited to the following user rights:

- **Adjust Memory Quotas For A Process**   A worker process must be able to control its memory usage during execution.
- **Generate Security Audits**   A worker process must be able to log security events to the Windows Security Event log.
- **Logon As A Service**   The worker process is implemented as a service. The Network Service account must have this user right to authenticate as a service.

- **Replace Process Level Token**   In an n-tiered application model, the worker process must be able to impersonate the user when performing a request in the security context of the user. To impersonate the user, the worker process must replace its process-level token.

- **Impersonate A Client After Authentication**   As with the Replace Process Level Token user right, the worker process must be allowed to impersonate a client to perform requests in the security context of the user.

- **Allow Logon Locally**   The Network Service account must be allowed to log on at the local computer to act as a service.

- **Access This Computer From The Network**   In an n-tiered application, the Network Service account might have to authenticate with a remote computer, connecting to that remote computer over the network.

In addition to implementing all worker processes in the security context of the Network Service account, IIS 6.0 also reduces the privilege requirements in other operations:

- All built-in ASP functions require no special privileges for execution.

- To execute a command-line tool, the authenticated user must be a member of the local Administrators group. This prevents a non-Administrator from using these tools to exploit the Web site.

- Anonymous users are no longer assigned write access to the home directory of the Web site. This prevents an anonymous user from modifying or defacing a Web site.

Automatic Health Monitoring

IIS 6.0 actively monitors all worker processes to detect failed processes. The monitoring options available in IIS 6.0 include these:

- **Active Monitor Of Each Worker Process**   By pinging each active worker process, IIS 6.0 is able to detect a failed worker process and automatically restart a failed worker process. If any requests are received during the time that the worker process is either failed or restarting, the requests are queued until the worker process is available. Likewise, if an application fails to respond to a ping request, the worker process can be flagged as orphaned. When flagged as orphaned, the worker process remains running but is replaced with a new worker process. An administrator can still perform diagnostics on the failed worker process, but the application continues to operate.

- **Periodically Restarting Worker Processes**   If an administrator suspects that a memory leak exists for an application, the worker process can be configured to restart at intervals designated ahead of time. An automated restart releases all resources used by the worker process and then reallocates the resources.

■ **Identifying Unstable Applications** If an application pool repeatedly fails over a predefined time interval, IIS 6.0 can automatically take the application pool offline and disable all associated worker processes. This action prevents an attack against one application from affecting all other applications hosted by the Web server.

Implementing Application Isolation

IIS 6.0 improves fault tolerance by isolating Web applications. In IIS 5.0 and earlier, all applications run in a single process instance. IIS 6.0 changes this model by enabling you to isolate each Web application from the others running on the server. As shown in Figure 24-8, related applications and Web sites are groups together in application pools.

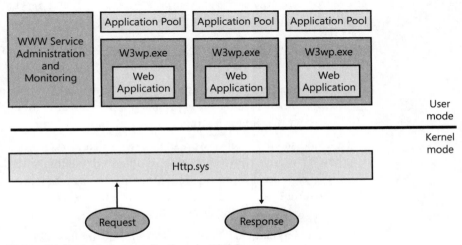

Figure 24-8   Isolating applications in IIS 6.0

Each application pool is served by one or more worker processes (W3wp.exe). The worker processes operate independently, ensuring that the failure of one worker process does not affect the other worker processes executing on the Web server.

In IIS 6.0, any Web directory or virtual directory can be assigned to an application pool. For each application pool, you must assigned an application pool identity. Although you can assign the LocalSystem account as the identity used by the application pool, it is not recommended because this grants excessive privilege to the worker processes associated with the application pool. If the application were breached, users running the application could end up with higher privileges than those assigned to their user accounts. Use the principle of least privilege and use the Network Service account as the identity associated with each application pool.

> **Note**   This is a major change from IIS 5.0, where the identity used for processes was the IWAM_*ComputerName* account. In IIS 5.0, you define the account used by a Web application in Component Services, whereas in IIS 6.0, the identity is configured in the properties of the Web site or virtual directory in the Internet Information Services (IIS) Manager console.

Improved Http.sys Security

In IIS 6.0, Http.sys is moved to kernel mode from user mode (as shown in Figure 24-8). The move of HTTP.sys to kernel mode results in performance gains but also increases security of Web-based applications. The worker process described earlier resides in user mode and cannot directly access privileged resources. Instead, the worker processes send all requests for privileged resources to Http.sys, which performs the requests on behalf of the worker processes.

In addition to operating in kernel mode, the following other enhancements have been included in Http.sys:

- **Screening incoming requests**   Http.sys scans all incoming requests to identify any abnormally large requests that might be an attempt to exploit a buffer or memory overflow vulnerability.

- **Taking action for failed worker processes**   If a worker process fails because of an overflow attack, Http.sys can be configured to either shut down or restart the worker process. Shutting down the process prevents the worker process from consuming all resources on the CA, whereas restarting the process clears all resources previously used by the process.

- **Improving logging**   Http.sys writes to the log file before a request is processed by a worker process thereby enabling an administrator to identify a request that causes a worker process to fail.

Supporting ASP.NET Security

IIS 6.0 includes support for the Microsoft .NET Framework. The framework provides tools to develop Web applications and XML-based Web services that use Active Server Pages. ASP.NET integrates with IIS 5.0 to provide a framework enabling authentication, or identifying the user that is connecting to the application on the Web server, and authorization, or controlling which resources a specific user can access on the Web server or back-end application servers.

Figure 24-9 shows how the two services interoperate to provide secure resource access in an ASP.NET Web application environment. This interoperation can be described as follows:

1. The user submits an HTTP or HTTPS request to a Web site on the Web server that requires user authentication. The user is authenticated using one of the authentication protocols configured for the Web site: anonymous, basic, digest, integrated, or certificate-based authentication.

2. IIS 6.0 determines whether the user is authorized to access the requested resources. The access control can be based on the requested URL, NTFS file permissions on the files and folders being accessed, or IP address filters.

3. A process token is generated that is passed on to the ASP.NET subsystem. The process token indicates who the user is and whether the user is authorized to access the requested ASP.NET resources. The ASP.NET subsystem can perform additional authentication of the user by using Windows Forms tied to a back-end credentials database such as a Microsoft SQL Server or Microsoft Passport.

> **Note** If anonymous authentication is used, the process token uses the identity of the Network Services account. The Network Services account is a new default account for running applications as a low-privileged user account.

4. ASP.NET can authorize the user's access to the ASP.NET application by using NTFS file permissions, URL restrictions, or the user's designated security role in ASP.NET.

5. The process results in the IIS 6.0 and ASP.NET application identity that is used for all future resource access.

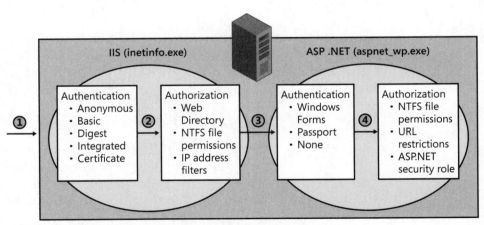

Figure 24-9 IIS 6.0 and ASP.NET security working together

> **Note** Any combination of IIS 6.0 and ASP.NET authentication and authorization mechanisms can be used when you develop an ASP.NET framework application. The capability of mixing and matching the authentication and authorization mechanisms provides the most flexibility to the developer of the application.

Securing the Default Settings

IIS 6.0 uses more restrictive default settings than IIS 5.0. Rather than installing all options by default and then having to use the IIS Lockdown Wizard, IIS 6.0 provides a simple-to-use interface to manage which applications are supported by the Web server as shown in Figure 24-10.

> **Note** You should never run the IIS Lockdown tool on an IIS 6.0 Web server. The changes in default settings replace the functionality of the IIS Lockdown Wizard.

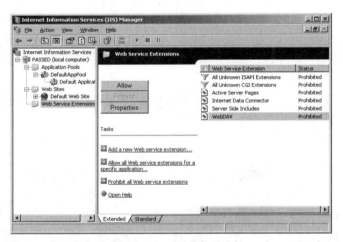

Figure 24-10   Configuring security for Web service extensions

In the Internet Information Services (IIS) Manager console, in the Web Service Extension container, you can define which Web service extensions are allowed and which are prohibited from executing at the Web server. If new Web service extensions are implemented at a later date, they can be added and managed through the Internet Information Services (IIS) Manager console.

> **Note** If a client asks for a dynamic file that is either explicitly prohibited or not listed as an allowed Web service extension, IIS 6.0 returns a "HTTP 404—File not found" error rather than indicating that the content is of a restricted data type. This prevents an attacker from determining whether the content is restricted or the file does not exist on the Web server.

Protection Against Common Attacks

IIS 6.0 was redesigned to take specific measures against attacks commonly launched against Web servers. The redesign took place during a security review performed against all Windows Server 2003 components during the development of Windows Server 2003. The redesign resulted in improved protection in IS 6.0 against the following common attacks:

- **Buffer overflow attacks**   A buffer overflow attack attempts to get a Web server to execute code by overflowing the memory buffers used to accept incoming requests. To help prevent buffer overflow attacks, Microsoft examined all code during the noted security review of IIS 6.0 and added testing for buffer overflow issues to development products such as Microsoft Visual Studio .NET 2003. In addition, using the Network Service user account for an application's associated user account restricts what can happen if a buffer overflow attack succeeds. The attacker can access only those resources assigned to the Network Service account rather than the LocalSystem account.

- **Canonical form attacks**   A canonical form attack attempts to access operating system files on the Web server that are not made available through the Web services. For example, the attacker might attempt to gain access to ../../windows/system32/cmd.exe. To protect against canonical attacks, IIS strips relative path information from URL requests. In addition, IIS 6.0 serves only files with extensions approved by the Web server's administrator. If an attacker attempts to access a *.exe file, the Web server's administrator must allow the serving of *.exe files.

- **Cross-site scripting attacks**   A cross-site scripting attack takes place when a user provides or calls a malicious script in a user request. For example, a SQL injection attack occurs when a user provides a SQL scripting command in a form's input field. IIS 6.0 protects against these attacks by enabling you to implement the ASP.NET data validation engine to strip any scripts from user input before the data is processed by a back-end application server.

- **Denial-of-service attacks**   A denial-of-service attack attempts to flood a Web server with so many requests that it cannot respond to valid requests for Web resources. By using isolation of application pools and configuring the worker processes to restart if the worker processes stop responding, you can protect the Web server from denial-of-service attacks.

- **Web site modification attacks**   A Web site modification attack replaces the original content of a Web site with content designed by the attacker, typically defacing the original Web site. The modification of default permissions by not assigning write permissions to anonymous users reduces the likelihood of this attack.

Configuring the FTP Service

In addition to providing Web server functionality to Windows 2000 and Windows Server 2003, IIS 5.0 and IIS 6.0 provide an FTP service. This service, if implemented, must be secured to ensure that the server hosting the FTP service is not compromised.

FTP enables users to transfer files to and from an FTP server. If you must implement FTP on your network, consider the following security guidelines:

- **Implement only anonymous access.**   Like most Internet-based protocols, the FTP protocol does not provide any security mechanisms for user credentials. User credentials are passed in clear text, which can lead to the compromise of a user's domain credentials. You can configure the FTP service to allow only anonymous connections to prevent credential interception.

> **Warning**   Configuring FTP to allow only anonymous connections does not prevent a user from inputting his user name and password in an FTP session. It only prevents those credentials from being accepted by the FTP server.

- **Prevent Write access to the FTP server.**   Disabling Write access prevents users from uploading information to the FTP server. If you require the ability to upload files to the FTP server, consider creating a separate folder in the FTP site that allows only uploads. This is configured by assigning only Write permissions to the folder.

- **Implement a custom anonymous user account.**   The account defined for the Web service can be implemented as the anonymous user account for the FTP service. NTFS permissions can be assigned to a custom local group at the FTP server that contains only the custom anonymous user account.

- **Implement the FTP home folder on a different volume from the operating system.**   As with the Web service, it is recommended you create a folder structure for the FTP service that resides on a different volume from the operating system. This involves changing the default folder from the default of %systemdrive%\Inetpub\Ftproot.

- **Enable logging.**   Enable logging of the FTP service so that all connections to the FTP server are recorded to FTP Audit logs. This allows you to review all connections to the FTP server.

In IIS 6.0, FTP has been further secured by isolating FTP users in their home directory. This prevents an FTP user from attempting to modify files or executables in other locations.

Best Practices

- **Ensure that the base operating system is secure.**   The operating system must be secure on a server hosting the IIS service. If the operating system—including its services, user accounts, files system, or registry—is not secure, IIS is susceptible to vulnerabilities caused by the poor operating system security configuration.

- **Implement the strongest form of user authentication supported by users connecting to an IIS server.**   Weak authentication configuration can lead to the compromise of a user's domain account and password. By enforcing strong authentication methods—be they integrated Windows or certificate-based methods—you provide the strongest protection of user credentials.

- **Assign the minimum required permissions for Web sites.**   Implement a combination of NTFS and Web site permissions that provide the minimum permissions required to access a Web site. Do not assign excess permissions because this reduces the overall security of the Web site

- **Implement SSL for Web sites or virtual directories that provide access to nonpublic data.**   SSL ensures that all data transmitted between the Web browser and the IIS server is encrypted. SSL also protects weaker forms of authentication, such as basic authentication, by encrypting the weaker credential information as it is sent to the Web server.

- **Implement Microsoft security tools to lock down the IIS 5.0 server.**   Implement the IIS Lockdown tool and the URLScan filter to configure IIS services, enable script maps, and apply additional security to an IIS server.

- **Implement IIS 6.0 application isolation.**   Isolation prevents one application hosted on a Web server from causing failures of other applications on the Web server. Each application pool is assigned one or more worker processes that are independent of the worker processes used by other application pools.

- **Consider implementing IPSec filters to limit traffic accepted by IIS servers.**   Table 24-3 lists the Internet Protocol Security (IPSec) filters that limit an IIS server to accept only IIS-related traffic.

Table 24-3   Recommended IPSec Filters for IIS Servers

Service	Protocol	Source Port	Destination Port	Source Address	Destination Address	Action	Mirror
Monitoring Client	ANY	ANY	ANY	ME	MOM Server	Allow	Yes
Terminal Services	TCP	ANY	3389	ANY	ME	Allow	Yes
Domain Member	ANY	ANY	ANY	ME	Each domain controller's IP address	Allow	Yes
HTTP Server	TCP	ANY	80	ANY	ME	Allow	Yes
HTTPS Server	TCP	ANY	443	ANY	ME	Allow	Yes
All inbound traffic	ANY	ANY	ANY	ANY	ME	Block	Yes

Note   These IPSec filters assume that the computer functions only as an IIS server. If the server holds additional roles, additional IPSec filters are required to allow the traffic associated with the additional roles.

On the CD   You can find on the CD that accompanies this book a script file, PacketFilters-IIS.CMD.txt, that implements the IPSec filters listed in the preceding table. The script must be modified with the IP addresses of each domain controller and Microsoft Operations Manager (MOM) server before being executed.

Additional Information

- Microsoft Official Curriculum course 2821, *Designing and Managing a Windows Public Key Infrastructure*, Module 10: "Securing Web Traffic by Using SSL" (*http://www.microsoft.com/learning/syllabi/en-us/2821afinal.mspx*)

- *Security Operations Guide for Windows 2000 Server*, Chapter 4, "Securing Servers Based on Role" (*http://www.microsoft.com/downloads/details.aspx? FamilyID=f0b7b4ee-201a-4b40-a0d2-cdd9775aeff8&displaylang=en*)

- *MCSE Training Kit: Designing Microsoft Windows 2000 Network Security*, Chapter 14, "Securing an Extranet" (Microsoft Press, 2001)

- IIS Security Planning tool (*http://www.microsoft.com/downloads /details.aspx?displaylang=en&FamilyID=166D3102-F5A8-49A2-B779- 153B7F59BCD3*)

- IIS Lockdown tool (*http://www.microsoft.com/technet/security/tools /locktool.mspx*)

- "How to Use IISLockdown" (*http://msdn.microsoft.com/library/en-us/secmod /html/secmod113.asp*)

- URLScan security tool (*http://microsoft.com/downloads/details.aspx? familyid=23d18937-dd7e-4613-9928-7f94ef1c902a&displaylang=en*)

- "How to Use URLScan" (*http://msdn.microsoft.com/library/en-us/secmod/html /secmod113.asp*)

- "Secure Internet Information Services 5 Checklist" (*http://www.microsoft.com /technet/prodtechnol/windows2000serv/technologies/iis/tips/iis5chk.mspx*)

- "IIS 5.0 Baseline Security Checklist" (*http://www.microsoft.com/technet /Security/chklist/iis5cl.mspx*)

- Microsoft Windows 2000 Advanced Documentation: "Mapping Certificates to User Accounts" (*http://www.microsoft.com/windows2000/en/advanced/help /sag_CS_CertMapAccounts.htm*)

- U.S. National Security Agency, "Guide to the Secure Configuration and Administration of Microsoft Internet Information Services 5.0" (*http://www.nsa.gov /notices/notic00004.cfm?Address=/snac/os/win2k/iis_5_v1_4.pdf*)

- "Security Enhancements in Internet Information Services 6.0" (*http:// www.microsoft.com/windowsserver2003/techinfo/overview/iisenhance.mspx*)

- *Windows Server 2003 Security Guide* (*http://www.microsoft.com/downloads /details.aspx?familyid=8A2643C1-0685-4D89-B655-521EA6C7B4DB&display-lang=en*)

- "Hardening Windows Server 2003 IIS Servers" (*http://www.microsoft.com /technet/security/guidance/secmod124.mspx*)

- Internet Information Services (IIS) Security Center (*http://www.microsoft.com /technet/security/prodtech/iis/default.mspx*)

- "Checklist: Securing Web Service" (*http://msdn.microsoft.com/library/en-us /secmod/html/secmod99.asp*)

- "Improving Web Application Security: Threats and Countermeasures" (*http: //microsoft.com/downloads/details.aspx?FamilyId=E9C4BFAA-AF88-4AA5-88D4-0DEA898C31B9&displaylang=en*)

- The following Knowledge Base articles:

  ❑ 309508: "IIS Lockdown and URLscan Configurations in an Exchange Environment" (*http://support.microsoft.com/kb/309508*)

  ❑ 307608: "Using URLScan on IIS" (*http://support.microsoft.com/kb/307608*)

  ❑ 309675: "IIS Lockdown Tool Affects SharePoint Portal Server" (*http://support.microsoft.com/kb/309675*)

  ❑ 309677: "Known Issues and Fine Tuning When You Use the IIS Lockdown Wizard in an Exchange 2000 Environment" (*http://support.microsoft.com/kb/309677*)

  ❑ 311350: "How to Create a Custom Server Type for Use with the IIS Lockdown Wizard" (*http://support.microsoft.com/kb/311350*)

  ❑ 315669: "How to Harden the TCP/IP Stack Against Denial of Service Attacks in Windows 2000" (*http://support.microsoft.com/kb/315669*)

  ❑ 325864: "How to Install and Use the IIS Lockdown Wizard" (*http://support.microsoft.com/kb/325864*)

  ❑ 326444: "How to Configure the URLScan Tool" (*http://support.microsoft.com/kb/326444*)

  ❑ 817807: "Support WebCast: Internet Information Services: Configuring IIS Using the IIS Lockdown Tool and the URLScan Tool" (*http://support.microsoft.com/kb/817807*)

Chapter 25
Designing an 802.1x Authentication Infrastructure

Many organizations are investigating the implementation of port-based authentication for both wireless and wired networking. Implementing 802.1x port-based authentication ensures that only computers and users that can authenticate with the network are allowed to connect to the network.

This chapter looks at how to increase your wired and wireless networks' security by requiring certificate-based authentication for network access.

How 802.1x Authentication Works

By implementing 802.1x authentication, an organization can require users and computers to authenticate with the network before they are allowed full network access. The process includes enforcing mutual authentication of the client computer or user account with a Remote Authentication Dial-In User Service (RADIUS) server. The process shown in Figure 25-1 takes place when a wireless client attempts to connect to a wireless network requiring 802.1x authentication.

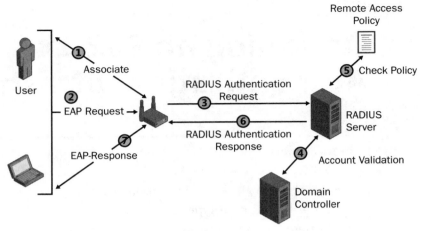

Figure 25-1 The 802.1x authentication process

Note The only difference in the 802.1x authentication process when connecting to a wired network is that the wireless access point (WAP) component is replaced with an 802.1x-compliant switch.

The following steps correspond to the process shown in Figure 25-1:

1. The computer attempts to associate with the WAP, which responds that the user or computer must provide Extensible Authentication Protocol (EAP) authentication.

2. The computer or user passes its credentials to the WAP.

   ❑ If using Extensible Authentication Protocol–Transport Layer Security (EAP-TLS) authentication, a signed request is submitted to the WAP, proving that the user or computer has access to the private key associated with the Client Authentication certificate.

   ❑ If using Protected Extensible Authentication Protocol (PEAP) authentication, users must type their user account and password combination in an authentication dialog box.

3. The WAP translates EAP authentication packets into RADIUS authentication packets and forwards the authentication packets to the RADIUS server.

Note The WAP is simply an intermediary for the authentication process, translating EAP request messages into RADIUS request messages and translating RADIUS response messages into EAP response messages.

4. The RADIUS server contacts a domain controller either to validate the user account and the password combination or to use the user principal name (UPN) in the certificate's Subject Alternative Name to map the certificate to a user account in the Active Directory directory service.

5. The RADIUS server determines whether the identified user or computer is granted access to the network based on the RADIUS server's configured remote access policies.

6. The RADIUS server sends a RADIUS authentication success or failure message to the WAP.

7. The WAP sends an EAP success or failure message to the wireless client.

After the completion of the 802.1x authentication process, the process will differ, depending on whether you are connecting to a wired or a wireless network:

- If you are connecting to a wired network, a successful authentication will result in the switch opening the port allowing the client full access to the network.

- If you are connecting to a wireless network, if the client is authorized, the user or computer exchanges encryption keys with the WAP. The encryption keys are used by the client and the WAP, allowing the client internal network connectivity.

In both wired and wireless networks, if the client is not authorized, no network connectivity is allowed.

Threats Faced in Networked Environments

When you implement wireless and wired networking in your organization, different threats are introduced to the environment. When an organization implements a wireless network, several threats are introduced, including the following:

- **Accidental connections to the wireless network**   People might not realize that their computers automatically connect to the organization's wireless network. This can lead to the computer being connected to the network without appropriate security measures, such as the Windows Firewall or a host-based intrusion detection system, making the computer a target for attackers. These visiting computers can then be used as launch points to attack the network.

> **Note**   If a wireless network is detected, Microsoft Windows XP's default behavior prior to the installation of Service Pack 2 is to connect automatically to any available wireless network. Service Pack 2 changes the default behavior to require users to affirm that they wish to connect to unprotected networks.

- **Inspection of data**   As data is sent from the computer over the wireless network, it might be possible for user credentials or other confidential data to be viewed by an unauthorized person connected to the wireless network.

- **Data modification**   If attackers can gain access to the wireless network, it might be possible for them to implement a man-in-the-middle attack, where legitimate packets are intercepted and modified as they are transmitted from source to destination. Likewise, false packets can be transmitted from attackers who are impersonating valid users.

- **Rogue WAPs**   Prior to Windows XP Service Pack 2, the default behavior of Windows XP was to connect automatically to any detectable wireless networks. An attacker or malicious user can easily connect a WAP to the network and start using the WAP to connect to the corporate network, and the rogue WAP can prevent users from connecting to an authorized WAP.

- **Unauthorized network connections**   An attacker can gain access to a wireless network without entering the physical premises. You cannot stop the transmission of packets beyond the walls of your building. The distance the transmissions reach is dependent upon the strength of the WAPs you deploy and the materials used in the construction of your company's building.

Although wireless networks face more threats of unauthorized users connecting, wired networks face threats as well:

- **Unauthorized network connections**   In most organizations, network jacks exist in board rooms, meeting rooms, and at each employee's desk. Visitors to the organization can often plug their laptops into the network, obtain an IP address, and attempt to connect to the organization's resources.

- **Inspection of data**   As data is sent from the computer over the wired network, it might be possible for user credentials or other confidential data to be viewed by an unauthorized person connected to the wired network.

- **Data modification**   If attackers can gain access to the wired network, it might be possible for them to implement a man-in-the-middle attack, where legitimate packets are intercepted and modified as they are transmitted from source to destination. Likewise, false packets can be transmitted from attackers who are impersonating valid users.

A Threat Introduced by Implementing 802.1x Authentication on a Wired Network

Although 802.1x authentication ensures that only authenticated clients can connect to the network, 802.1x performs the authentication only at the establishment of a connection. Once the client is authenticated and the switch port is opened, no further authentication is performed. Unless you configure the switch to re-authenticate the client at regular intervals, there exists the possibility of an attacker hijacking the connection.

> **Note**   This attack is possible only if the attacker has physical access to your building. The attack cannot take place in a wireless environment or when the attacker cannot touch the target computer.

To hijack the connection, the attacker performs the following actions:

1.   The attacker disconnects the authenticated computer from the 802.1x-protected network switch port.

2.   The attacker connects a hub to the network switch port.

3.   The attacker plugs the authenticated computer into the hub.

4.   The attacker then plugs the attack computer into the same network hub.

Once connected, the attacker can then determine the authenticated computer's IP address and Media Access Control (MAC) address and implement the same addresses on his computer. The attacker's computer also has a firewall configured to drop all inbound traffic that isn't a reply to communications that it initiates.

In this state, the attacker's computer can connect to the network using stateless protocols such as Internet Control Message Protocol (ICMP) or User Datagram Protocol (UDP). The attacker might or might not be able to connect to the network using a stateful protocol, such as Transmission Control Protocol (TCP). The success of a TCP connection depends on whether the client has Windows Firewall enabled.

If Windows Firewall is not enabled, the attacker cannot communicate by using TCP. The authenticated client will reset any connection that is initiated by the attacker's computer as shown in the following process:

1.   The attacker's computer sends a TCP Synchronize (SYN) packet to a server on the protected network.

2. The server returns a Synchronization Acknowledgment (SYN-ACK), which both the attacker and the authenticated computer receive.

3. The authenticated computer isn't expecting this SYN-ACK, so it returns a Reset (RST) to the server.

4. The server returns a Reset Acknowledgment (RST-ACK), acknowledging the received RST and sending its own, which both the attacker and the authenticated computer receive.

5. The attacker isn't expecting this RST-ACK, but it will abide and terminate the connection.

If Windows Firewall is enabled at the authenticated computer, which is the default behavior after the application of Windows XP Service Pack 2, the authenticated computer cannot accept any unsolicited TCP traffic. When the firewall is enabled, the following process takes place:

1. The attacker's computer sends a TCP Synchronize (SYN) packet to a server on the protected network.

2. The server returns a Synchronization Acknowledgment (SYN-ACK), which both the attacker and the authenticated computer receive.

3. Because Windows Firewall is enabled on the authenticated computer, the SYN-ACK packet is dropped because it is not a response to a data stream initiated by the authenticated computer.

4. At the attacking computer, the SYN-ACK is received, and the attacking computer sends its own SYN-ACK to the target server, establishing a TCP connection to the target server.

Although the probability of this attack is minute, if your organization feels that the threat is relevant, it is recommended not to implement 802.1x authentication for wired networks. Instead, consider implementing Internet Protocol Security (IPSec) using Encapsulating Security Payload (ESP) with NULL encryption. In some cases, you can also configure the switches to force reauthentication at defined intervals, forcing the clients to reauthenticate with RADIUS at those intervals.

Wireless networks do not have this problem. When 802.1x is implemented in a wireless network, mutually authenticated sessions are established with per-supplicant encryption keys. The attacker's computer is unable to connect to the access point where the authenticated computer is already connected. In addition, the attacker's computer is unable to acquire the encryption key that the authenticated computer is using.

802.1x Authentication Types

A Microsoft Windows Server 2003 Public Key Infrastructure (PKI) provides the necessary certificates for 802.1x authentication for wireless and wired networks. When a user or computer performs 802.1x authentication, the following two authentication types are available:

- Extensible Authentication Protocol using Transport Layer Security (EAP-TLS)
- Protected Extensible Authentication Protocol (PEAP)

Note Several WLAN security solutions similar to PEAP and EAP-TLS are based on EAP solutions. For example, Cisco's Light EAP (LEAP) and Funk Software's Tunneled Transport Layer Security (EAP-TTLS) provide security comparable to PEAP or EAP-TLS, but they are vendor-specific, locking your organization into specific vendor solutions. EAP-TLS and PEAP are supported by the majority of WAP and switch manufacturers.

EAP-TLS Authentication

EAP-TLS is a certificate-based authentication method that provides mutual authentication between the user or computer and the RADIUS server when implemented for an 802.1x authentication networking solution. To implement EAP-TLS authentication, the following certificates are required:

- **Client Computer or User** The client end of the 802.1x connection must have a certificate with the Client Authentication Enhanced Key Usage (EKU) object identifier (OID). This certificate proves the identity of the client computer or the user account.
- **Server** The server end of the 802.1x connection must have a certificate with the Server Authentication EKU OID. This certificate proves the RADIUS server's identity to all connecting 802.1x clients.

Note No certificate is required for the WAP or switch when implementing 802.1x authentication. The role of the WAP or switch is to translate EAP messages sent from the client to the WAP or switch into RADIUS messages sent from the WAP or switch to the RADIUS server, and vice versa.

PEAP Authentication

PEAP authentication allows the transmission of other EAP types within a TLS-secured channel. When PEAP is used, the user must type in a user account and a password that is sent to the RADIUS server. The user's identity is proved through knowledge of a user account and password, which are protected by using Microsoft Challenge Authentication Protocol version 2 (MS-CHAPv2). The RADIUS server still requires a certificate with the Server Authentication EKU OID to prove its identity, but no certificate is required for the user.

Note It is possible to implement PEAP authentication with certificates on the user side. This configuration is equivalent to implementing EAP-TLS authentication.

Protecting Communications

When data is transmitted between the 802.1x client and the WAP or switch, the data is subject to inspection attacks. The methods used to protect this transmitted data differ between wireless and wired networks.

Protecting Wireless Communications

When you implement a wireless network, you must develop a plan for securing the network to reduce the likelihood of the threats mentioned in the previous section. Some of the more common methods of protecting a wireless network are mentioned in the sections that follow.

MAC Filtering

One of the most basic ways of protecting a wireless network is to implement MAC filtering. At the WAP, you can configure which MAC addresses (the low-level firmware address of a wireless card) are allowed to connect to the WAP. Although this sounds like an ideal, easy way to secure a wireless network, consider the following issues:

- **It is easy to spoof an approved MAC address.** Software, such as SMAC, enables you to modify your wireless card's MAC to an approved MAC address manually.

Note You can read more information on the SMAC at *http://www.klcconsulting.net/smac/default.htm?v=readme11.*

- **MAC filtering is hard to manage.**   If you have several wireless computers, each MAC address must be managed manually at the WAP.

- **MAC filtering authenticates only the computer, not the user.**   If attackers steal a laptop or use a laptop included in the approved MAC listing, they can access the network.

- **The size of the approved MAC list is limited**.   In large environments, you might not be able to input all approved MAC addresses.

Wired Equivalent Privacy

Wired Equivalent Privacy (WEP) is one method of providing encryption services to wired and wireless networks. When a connection enables WEP, the network interface card (NIC) encrypts each data packet transmitted on the network using the RC4 stream cipher algorithm. The WAP or switch then decrypts the data packets upon receipt.

Warning   Wireless encryption encrypts data only between the wireless client and the WAP or switch. Once the data is on the wired network, no encryption is applied, unless the wireless client applies other encryption technologies, such as virtual private networking or IPSec.

WEP requires that both the wireless client and WAP share a 40-bit or a 104-bit symmetric encryption key. When WEP is implemented alone, the wireless client and WAP must configure the encryption key manually. If 802.1x authentication (as described later in this chapter) is implemented, the encryption key is configured only at the WAP and is securely transmitted to the wireless client.

Note   Most hardware vendors provide support for a 128-bit WEP key.

The symmetric encryption key is concatenated to a randomly generated 24-bit initialization vector (IV). The IV lengthens the lifetime of the symmetric key because of its random generation. A new IV is used for each frame transmitted between the wireless client and the WAP.

The problem with WEP is that a brute force attack can be executed successfully in a very short period of time. The weakness in WEP's implementation is twofold:

- **The symmetric encryption key is rarely changed.**   Once an organization inputs a WEP key, it typically does not change the key. This is especially true if both the wireless client and the WAP must input the key manually.

- **The IV is only 24 bits and is reused over time.**   When WEP is deployed on a large network, an IV is reused about every hour. An application such as AirSnort can capture frames over a period of time and determine what the WEP key is, based on identifying frames that use the same IV.

> **Note**   For a detailed analysis of the weaknesses in WEP, see the article "Security of the WEP Algorithm," referenced in the "Additional Information" section of this chapter.

Wi-Fi Protected Access

Wi-Fi Protected Access (WPA) is an encryption method produced by the Wi-Fi Alliance to address the security issues found in WEP. The following major enhancements are included in WPA:

- **Increased data encryption**   WPA implements Temporal Key Integrity Protocol (TKIP), which uses a per-packet key mixing function; a message integrity check (MIC), known as *Michael*; and an extended IV with rules on sequencing. In addition, WPA implements a rekeying mechanism so that the same key is not used for long periods of time.

- **Dependency on 802.1x authentication**   The use of 802.1x authentication is optional for WEP encryption only. WPA requires 802.1x authentication to ensure that only authorized users or computers are allowed connectivity to the wireless network. 802.1x authentication also ensures mutual authentication so that a wireless client does not connect to a rogue network rather than the corporate network.

Wi-Fi Protected Access Version 2

Wi-Fi Protected Access version 2 (WPA2) is an update to WPA. The update is to increase the security of WPA to meet the recently passed IEEE 802.11i security specification. The update was not released to address any flaws in WPA.

The major difference between WPA and WPA2 is the change in the encryption algorithm. WPA2 uses Advanced Encryption Standard (AES) rather than TKIP. The change reflects the recommendations in the IEEE 802.11i security specification and meets the requirements of organizations to implement FIPS 140-2–compliant algorithms.

The other major change in WPA2 is that there will no longer be backward compatibility support for WEP. A WPA2-compliant WAP will not be able to service both WEP and WPA2 connections at the same time.

> **Note**   A WPA2 device will be able to interoperate with products that are certified for WPA. The WPA devices might have to use TKIP rather than AES, but will be able to connect to the WPA2-compliant WAP.

Protecting Wired Communications

Once a wired client authenticates with an 802.1x-enabled switch, all communications between the client and the network are sent unencrypted, unless using specific protocols such as Hypertext Transfer Protocol Secure (HTTPS) that implement encryption.

If you want to encrypt all traffic transmitted between the wired client and the network after authentication, you must consider implementing IPSec.

> **Note**   For information on how Microsoft implements IPSec to protect network communications, see "Improving Security with Domain Isolation: Microsoft IT Implements IP Security (IPSec)" available at *http://www.microsoft.com/downloads /details.aspx?FamilyId=A97DDC48-A364-4756-BB3C-91DA274118FE&displaylang=en*.

Planning Certificates for 802.1x Authentication

To use 802.1x authentication, you must deploy to the RADIUS server, at minimum, a certificate with the Server Authentication EKU OID. If you are implementing EAP-TLS authentication, you must also deploy a computer certificate or a user certificate, or both.

Computer Certificates for RADIUS Servers

For RADIUS servers, it is recommended you deploy the default RAS and IAS Server certificate template. This certificate template implements the required Server Authentication EKU OID and is intended for deployment at remote access and RADIUS servers.

The only modification required for the RAS and IAS Server certificate template is to assign the RAS and IAS Servers domain local group Read, Enroll, and Autoenroll permissions. If multiple domains exist in the forest, you must create a custom global group in each domain and assign each domain's custom global group Read, Enroll, and Autoenroll permissions.

> **Note**   You must also ensure that all RADIUS server computer accounts are added to the custom global group.

User Certificates for Clients

If EAP-TLS authentication is implemented, a user must provide a certificate for authentication. To enhance the network's security, you should implement a custom version 2 certificate template based on the Authenticated Session certificate template.

Only two modifications are recommended for the custom certificate template:

- **Add a custom application policy to the certificate template named** *Organization* **802.1x User.**   When you define the application policy, ensure that you assign the application policy an OID from your organization's assigned OID arc.

> **Note**   You can increase the connection's security by requiring that the user certificate include the *Organization* 802.1x User application policy OID, in addition to the required Client Authentication OID. This prevents users from using other certificates that have the Client Authentication application policy OID and restricts access to the custom certificate.

- **Assign Read, Enroll, and Autoenroll permissions to a custom universal or global group that contains all user accounts that can connect to the wireless or wired network.**   This enables autoenrollment to automate distribution of certificates to users. If users have computers running Microsoft Windows 2000, they can still manually enroll the certificate by using the Certificates Microsoft Management Console (MMC) or the Certificate Services Web Enrollment pages.

If you are implementing PEAP, no certificates are required for the user account. Instead of providing a certificate, the user is prompted to provide her domain credentials and password to authenticate with the RADIUS server.

Computer Certificates for Clients

If a computer account is a member of the forest, installing a computer certificate allows the computer to connect to the network before a user logs on to the computer. This enables the application of the following:

- Computer Group Policy objects (GPOs)
- User GPOs

If the computer is not issued a certificate and you are implementing EAP-TLS, users log on to the computer with cached credentials. Only after the logon process is complete do users gain access to their Client Authentication certificates, permitting them to connect to the corporate network.

The Workstation Authentication or Computer certificate template can be used to provide the client computer a certificate with the Client Authentication application policy OID. A universal or global group containing the computer account must be assigned Read, Enroll, and Autoenroll permissions for the Workstation Authentication certificate or Read and Enroll permissions for the Computer certificate.

If you are implementing PEAP, no certificates are required for the computer account. Instead of providing a certificate, the computer account uses its computer account and password to authenticate with the RADIUS server.

Deploying Certificates to Users and Computers

The following sections provide recommendations for deploying the necessary certificates for 802.1x authentication for wireless and wired networks.

RADIUS Server

When implementing 802.1x authentication, it is recommended you use Microsoft Windows Server 2003 Internet Authentication Service (IAS) as the RADIUS server. The implementation of a computer running Windows Server 2003 enables you to restrict certificate-based authentication to certificates with a designated OID, such as a custom application policy OID.

Note   The Windows 2000 version of IAS allows 802.1x authentication for wired and wireless networks, but cannot implement restrictions based on OIDs in the client authentication certificates.

To enable autoenrollment of the RAS and IAS Server certificates, complete the following:

- Ensure that the forest, if running Windows 2000 domain controllers, has the Windows Server 2003 schema extensions applied, upgrading the schema from version 13 to version 30.

- Ensure that the RADIUS server's computer account has membership in a group assigned Read, Enroll, and Autoenroll permissions for the RAS and IAS Server certificate template.

- Ensure that the RAS and IAS Server certificate template does not require user input for autoenrollment.

- Ensure that the RAS and IAS Server certificate template is available for enrollment on one or more Windows Server 2003, Enterprise Edition, enterprise Certification Authorities (CAs).

- Ensure that the RADIUS server's computer account is in an OU where the Autoenrollment Settings Group Policy setting for computers is applied.

> **Note**   Alternatively, a user assigned Read and Enroll permissions who is a member of the local Administrators group at the RADIUS server can manually enroll a RAS and IAS Server certificate.

Client Computers

Client computers require a certificate for 802.1x authentication only if the computer is a member of the forest. If not, a computer certificate does not associate with any computer account in Active Directory.

The method used to deploy the computer certificate depends upon whether you are deploying the Computer version 1 certificate template or the Workstation Authentication version 2 certificate template.

If you are deploying to computers that run Windows 2000, you can deploy the Computer version 1 certificate template by adding the Computer certificate template to the Automatic Certificate Request Settings Group Policy setting. The GPO with the Automatic Certificate Request Settings defined must be linked to the OU where the computer account exists.

If you are deploying to computers running Windows XP or Windows Server 2003, you can deploy the Workstation Authentication version 2 certificate template by using Autoenrollment Settings. As with the RADIUS certificate template, the computer account must belong to a group assigned Read, Enroll, and Autoenroll permissions; the Workstation Authentication certificate template must allow autoenrollment without user input; and the computer account must be in an OU where the GPO is applied.

Users

To connect to an 802.1x authenticated network that implements user authentication, a user must acquire a certificate based on the custom version 2 certificate template discussed earlier in this chapter. To minimize the risks involved with deploying certificates, it is recommended you use autoenrollment for computers running Windows XP and scripted enrollment for computers running Windows 2000.

To enable certificate autoenrollment for the User certificate template for computers running Windows XP and Windows Server 2003, you must do the following:

1. Modify the permissions of the custom certificate template to assign Read, Enroll, and Autoenroll permissions to each domain's Domain Users group.

2. Modify the custom certificate template to not require user input during the enrollment process. By not requiring user input, certificates are issued to the user invisibly.

3. Ensure that the custom version 2 certificate template is available at one or more enterprise CAs for enrollment.

4. Enable the Autoenrollment Settings Group Policy setting at each domain in the forest.

To enable scripted enrollment, you can use the enroll.vbs script (provided on the CD that accompanies this text). The enroll.vbs script automates certificate enrollment for users with Windows 2000 client computers. The enroll.vbs script can be used in a logon script to allow automated certificate enrollment for users with computers that run Windows 2000.

 Note The enroll.vbs script requires that CAPICOM be installed on the client computer.

Assuming that you have implemented an *Organization* 802.1x User application policy OID in the 802.1x User certificate template and that the OID assigned is 1.3.6.1.4.1.311.509.4.2.1, you can use the following code in your logon script to enroll the 802.1x User certificate:

```
cscript enroll.vbs /certtype 8021xuser /key1 1024 /csp enhanced /
app_policy 1.3.6.1.5.5.7.3.2 /app_policy 1.3.6.1.4.1.311.509.4.2.1 /fn
"802.1x User"
```

This command enrolls the certificate template named *8021xuser* with a key length of 1024 bits using the Microsoft Enhanced Cryptographic Service Provider v1.0. In addition, the certificate is requested only if the user does not have an existing certificate with the Client Authentication (1.3.6.1.5.5.7.3.2) and *Organization* 802.1x User (1.3.6.1.4.1.311.509.4.2.1) application policy OIDs. Finally, the certificate is assigned the friendly name of 802.1x User when placed in the user's certificate store.

> **Note**   Alternatively, you can use manual enrollment for the Wireless User certificate template. A user with a computer running Windows XP or Windows Server 2003 can use the Certificates MMC or the Certificate Services Web Enrollment pages. A user with a computer running Windows 2000 can use only the Certificate Services Web Enrollment pages.

Implementing 802.1x Authentication

To implement 802.1x authentication, you must configure the RADIUS server and the WAP or switch to implement RADIUS.

Configuring the RADIUS Server

In a Microsoft network, IAS provides RADIUS capabilities on the network. To deploy IAS for wireless networking, you must do the following:

- Install IAS.
- Add the IAS server to the RAS and IAS Servers group.
- Define the RADIUS clients.
- Create a 802.1x Wireless Computer remote access policy.
- Create a 802.1x Wired Computer remote access policy.
- Create a 802.1x Wireless User remote access policy.
- Create a 802.1x Wired User remote access policy.

Install IAS

IAS is the Microsoft implementation of a RADIUS server. To install IAS on the server that runs Windows Server 2003, use the following procedure:

1. Log on as a member of the local Administrators group.
2. On the Start menu, point to Control Panel, and click Add Or Remove Programs.

3. In the Add Or Remove Programs dialog box, click Add/Remove Windows Components.

4. On the Windows Components page, select the words Networking Services, and click Details.

5. In the Networking Services dialog box, enable Internet Authentication Services, and click OK.

6. On the Windows Components page, click Next.

7. If prompted, insert the Windows Server 2003, Standard Edition or Enterprise Edition, compact disc into the CD-ROM drive and choose the i386 folder.

8. On the Completing The Windows Components Wizard page, click Finish.

9. Close the Add Or Remove Programs dialog box.

> **Note**   It is recommended you install IAS on at least two computers in the domain to ensure that the failure of a single computer does not prevent 802.1x authentication for wired and wireless networks.

Add the IAS Server to the RAS and IAS Servers Group

Once you have installed IAS, you must add the IAS server's computer account to the RAS and IAS Servers group in the computer account's domain. Follow these steps:

1. Ensure you are logged on as a member of the Domain Admins group.

2. From Administrative Tools, open Active Directory Users And Computers.

3. Ensure that you are connected to the domain where the IAS server's computer account exists.

4. In the console tree, expand the domain, and click Users.

5. In the details pane, double-click the RAS And IAS Servers group.

6. In the RAS And IAS Servers Properties dialog box, in the Members tab, click Add.

7. In the Select Users, Contacts, Computers, Or Groups dialog box, click Object Types.

8. In the Object Types dialog box, ensure that the Computers option is enabled, and click OK.

9. In the Select Users, Contacts, Computers, Or Groups dialog box, in the Enter The Object Names To Select box, type ComputerName (where *ComputerName* is the NetBIOS name of the computer hosting IAS), and then click Check Names.

10. Ensure that the correct computer name appears, and click OK.

11. In the RAS And IAS Servers Properties dialog box, click OK.

12. Close Active Directory Users and Computers.

13. Reboot the computer hosting the IAS service to use the new group membership.

Define RADIUS Clients

Each WAP or switch that forwards authentication requests to the RADIUS server must be added to the IAS server's known clients list. The WAP's IP address, as well as a RADIUS secret or password, must be defined.

To define a RADIUS client at the IAS server, do the following:

1. From Administrative Tools, open Internet Authentication Service.

2. In the console tree, right-click RADIUS Clients, and click New RADIUS Client.

3. On the Name And Address page, in the Friendly Name box, type a descriptor for the WAP. In the Client Address box, type the IP address of the WAP, and click Next.

4. On the Additional Information page, enter the following information:

    ❑ Client-Vendor drop-down list: Select the WAP or switch vendor.

> **Tip**   If the hardware vendor is not available in the listing, choose the standard RADIUS option.

    ❑ Shared Secret: Enter a password that identifies the valid WAP.

    ❑ Confirm Shared Secret: Retype the password for verification.

> **Warning**   Do *not* enable the Request Must Contain The Message Authenticator attribute.

5. Click Finish.

6. Repeat this process for every WAP that uses the IAS server for 802.1x authentication.

> **Note**   TheMicrosoft IAS server does not support the use of the "Any" designation. Each WAP or switch must be manually defined as a RADIUS client at the IAS server.

Define an 802.1x Wireless Computer Remote Access Policy

Once you designate all RADIUS clients at the IAS server, you must define a remote access policy for computer accounts. This remote access policy allows wireless computers to connect initially for logon and GPO download.

Use the following process to create and configure a remote access policy for computer authentication:

1. From Administrative Tools, open Internet Authentication Service.

2. In the console tree, select Remote Access Policies.

3. In the details pane, delete any default remote access policies.

> **Warning**   If the IAS server is used for virtual private network (VPN) authentication or other applications that support RADIUS authentication, do not delete any existing remote access policies.

4. In the console tree, select Remote Access Policies, and click New Remote Access Policy.

5. In the New Remote Access Policy Wizard, click Next.

6. On the Policy Configuration Method page, click Use The Wizard To Set Up A Typical Policy For A Common Scenario, name the policy 802.1x Wireless Computers, and click Next.

7. On the Access Method page, click Wireless, and then click Next.

8. On the User Or Group Access page, click Group, and then click Add.

9. In the Select Groups dialog box, type Domain**Domain Computers** if you wish to allow all computers to connect to the network or Domain\\Custom Group if you wish to restrict which computers can connect, and click OK.

10. Repeat steps 8 and 9 for each domain in your forest allowed to connect to the wireless network.

11. On the User Or Group Access page, click Next.

12. On the Authentication Methods page, select Smart Card Or Other Certificate, and click Configure.

13. On the Smart Card Or Other Certificate properties page, select the Certificate Issued To *DNSName* (where *DNSName* is the Domain Name System (DNS) name of the IAS server), and click OK.

14. On the Authentication Methods page, click Next.

15. On the Completing The New Remote Access Policy Wizard page, click Finish.

16. In the details pane, double-click 802.1x Wireless Computers.

17. In the Settings tab, select the NAS-Port-Type policy condition, and click Edit.

18. In the NAS-Port-Type dialog box, in the Selected Types list, select Wireless – Other, click Remove, and click OK.

19. In the Settings tab, click Edit Profile.

20. In the Edit Dial-In Profile dialog box, in the Encryption tab, clear all encryption types except Strongest Encryption (MPPE 128 Bit).

21. In the Edit Dial-In Profile dialog box, click OK.

22. In the 802.1x Computer Properties dialog box, click OK.

23. Close the Internet Authentication Service dialog box.

Define an 802.1x Wired Computer Remote Access Policy

A separate wired remote access policy is often desired because typically all domain computers are allowed to connect to the wired network, whereas only a subset might be allowed to connect to the wireless network.

The only differences between the wireless and the wired remote access policy are the following:

■ In the Select Groups dialog box, you must select Domain**Domain Computers** and Domain**Domain Controllers** to allow all computers and domain controllers in each domain to authenticate.

■ Define the NAS-Port-Type dialog box to be Ethernet.

The combination of these two conditions uniquely identifies the difference between wireless and wired connection attempts.

Define the 802.1x Wireless User Remote Access Policy

When enabling 802.1x authentication, you must configure a separate remote access policy for wireless users. Although similar to the 802.1x wireless computer remote access policy, the main difference in the two policies is that the user remote access policy requires the custom *Organization* 802.1x User OID in the user's certificate.

The following process creates and configures the user remote access policy:

1. From Administrative Tools, open Internet Authentication Service.

2. In the console tree, select Remote Access Policies.

3. In the console tree, right-click Remote Access Policies, and click New Remote Access Policy.

4. In the New Remote Access Policy Wizard, click Next.

5. On the Policy Configuration Method page, click Use The Wizard To Set Up A Typical Policy For A Common Scenario, name the policy 802.1x Wireless Users, and click Next.

6. On the Access Method page, click Wireless, and click Next.

7. On the User Or Group Access page, click Group, and click Add.

8. In the Select Groups dialog box, type **Domain\Domain Users**, and click OK.

> **Note**   Alternatively, you can create a custom group and allow only wireless access to members of the custom group.

9. On the User Or Group Access page, click Next.

10. On the Authentication Methods page, select Smart Card Or Other Certificate, and click Configure.

11. On the Smart Card Or Other Certificate properties page, select the Certificate Issued To *DNSName* (where *DNSName* is the DNS name of the IAS server), and click OK.

12. On the Authentication Methods page, click Next.

13. On the Completing The New Remote Access Policy Wizard page, click Finish.

14. In the details pane, double-click 802.1x Wireless Users.

15. In the Settings tab, select the NAS-Port-Type policy condition, and click Edit.

16. In the NAS-Port-Type dialog box, in the Selected Types list, select Wireless – Other, click Remove, and click OK.

> **Note**   Removing Wireless – Other ensures that only wireless connections based on IEEE 802.11 are allowed. This includes 802.11a, 802.11b, 802.11g, and 802.11i in the future.

17. In the Settings tab, click Edit Profile.

18. In the Edit Dial-In Profile dialog box, in the Encryption tab, clear *all* encryption types except Strongest Encryption (MPPE 128 Bit).

19. In the Edit Dial-In Profile dialog box, in the Advanced tab, click Add.

20. In the Add Attribute dialog box, in the Attribute list, select Allowed-Certificate–OID, and click Add.

21. In the Multivalued Attribute Information dialog box, click Add.

22. In the Attribute Information dialog box, in the Attribute value box, type OID (where *OID* is the OID assigned to the *Organization* 802.1x User application policy), and click OK.

> **Tip** You can also copy this OID by viewing the OIDs in the Certificate Templates console (Certtmpl.msc).

23. In the Multivalued Attribute Information dialog box, click OK.

24. In the Add Attribute dialog box, click Close.

25. In the Edit Dial-In Profile dialog box, click OK.

26. On the 802.1x Wireless Users properties page, click OK.

Define an 802.1x Wired User Remote Access Policy

A separate wired remote access policy for users is often desired because typically all domain users are allowed to connect to the wired network, whereas only a subset might be allowed to connect to the wireless network.

The only differences between the wireless and the wired remote access policies are the following:

- In the Select Groups dialog box, you must select each domain's Domain Users group to allow all users to authenticate.

- Define the NAS-Port-Type dialog box to be Ethernet.

The combination of these two conditions uniquely identifies the difference between wireless and wired connection attempts. The remote access policy must still test for the existence of the Allowed-Certificate–OID to ensure that only the correct authentication certificates are used

Configuring a Wireless Access Point or Switch

WAP configuration is dependent upon the installed Internetwork Operating System (IOS). Rather than provide the details for a single vendor, ensure that you define the following settings at your WAP:

1. Configure the WAP or switch to implement RADIUS authentication.

   ❑ Add the IP addresses of both a primary and secondary IAS server for RADIUS authentication.

❑   Input the RADIUS secret for each IAS server.

❑   Define the RADIUS listening port used by each IAS server (UDP port 1812).

2.   Configure the WAP or switch to implement RADIUS accounting.

❑   Add the IP addresses of both a primary and secondary IAS server for RADIUS accounting.

❑   Input the RADIUS secret for each IAS server.

❑   Define the RADIUS listening port used by each IAS server (UDP port 1813).

> **Important**   The WAP must support RADIUS authentication. If the WAP or switch does not support RADIUS authentication, you cannot implement 802.1x authentication for your network when using that WAP or switch.

3.   Configure which form of encryption is used by the WAP.

❑   Define whether the WAP uses WEP, WPA, a combination of WEP and WPA, WPA2, or a combination of WPA and WPA2.

❑   For WEP, enable dynamic key provision, and if possible, support key roll-over.

❑   For WPA, enable the TKIP cipher suite and define rekeying intervals.

❑   For WPA2, enable the AES cipher suite and define rekeying intervals.

Configuring a Switch

Switch configuration is also dependent upon the installed Internetwork Operating System (IOS). Rather than provide the details for a single vendor, ensure that you define the following settings at your switch:

1.   Configure the switch to implement RADIUS authentication.

❑   Add the IP addresses of both a primary and secondary IAS server for RADIUS authentication.

❑   Input the RADIUS secret for each IAS server.

❑   Define the RADIUS listening port used by each IAS server (UDP port 1812).

2. Configure the switch to implement RADIUS accounting.

    ❑ Add the IP addresses of both a primary and secondary IAS server for RADIUS accounting.

    ❑ Input the RADIUS secret for each IAS server.

    ❑ Define the RADIUS listening port used by each IAS server (UDP port 1813).

3. Enable periodic reauthentication on the switch. Periodic reauthentication protects against attackers attempting to hijack a session as discussed earlier in this chapter. Ensure that you set the reauthentication period to an interval that does not cause large amounts of network traffic, but ensures that the client is reauthenticated at required intervals.

Connecting to a Wireless Network

Once the infrastructure installation is complete, the wireless clients can connect to the wireless network by using 802.1x authentication. To connect, the following procedure is required:

1. Open the Network Connections window.

2. Right-click your wireless adapter and click Properties.

3. On the properties page of the wireless adapter, in the Wireless Networks tab, in the Preferred Networks section, choose the Service Set Identifier (SSID) of the wireless network, and click Properties.

4. On the *SSID* properties page, in the Association tab, define the following settings.

Option	WEP	WPA	WPA2
Network Authentication	Open	WPA or WPA-PSK (preshared key)	WPA or WPA-PSK
Data Encryption	WEP	TKIP or AES	AES
The Key Is Provided For Me Automatically	Enabled	Enabled	Enabled

5. On the SSID properties page, in the Authentication tab, define the following settings.

Option	WEP	WPA	WPA2
Enable 802.1x Authentication For The Network	Enabled	Enabled	Enabled
EAP Type	Smart Card Or Other Certificate	Smart Card Or Other Certificate	Smart Card Or Other Certificate
Authenticate As Computer When Computer Information Is Available	Enabled if computer is a member of the forest	Enabled if computer is a member of the forest	Enabled if computer is a member of the forest

6. On the SSID properties page, in the Authentication tab, click Properties.

7. On the Smart Card Or Other Certificate properties page (shown in Figure 25-2), enable the following options:

   ❑ **Use A Smart Card** Enable if using a smart card certificate.

   ❑ **Use A Certificate On This Computer** Enable if using a certificate stored in the user's certificate store.

   ❑ **Use Simple Certificate Selection (Recommended)** Enable if the certificate's subject is the same as the user's logon name.

> **Warning** Do not enable simple certificate selection if the computer is from a different forest or workgroup. By not enabling simple certificate selection, the user can choose the certificate for authentication manually.

   ❑ **Validate Server Certificate** Enable this option to require mutual authentication. The client validates the RADIUS server's certificate and ensures that it chains to the root CA certificate designated in the Trusted Root Certification Authorities store on the local client machines.

   ❑ **Use A Different User Name For The Connection** Only enable this option if the computer is not a member of the forest. This allows users to choose a certificate that does not contain their current user name.

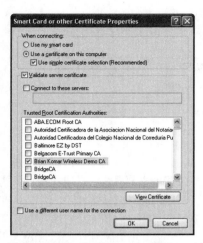

Figure 25-2   Defining certificate settings for EAP-TLS authentication

Using Group Policy to Enforce Wireless Client Configuration

Group Policy can be used to ensure that wireless networking settings are configured correctly for EAP-TLS authentication (for 802.1x authentication).

The GPO is applied to computer accounts and should be linked to either the domain or to the OU where wireless computer accounts are located. A wireless network policy enables an organization to do the following:

■ Enforce 802.1x authentication.

■ Restrict wireless connectivity to WAPs, not allowing ad hoc connections.

> **Note**   An *ad hoc wireless network* is configured directly between two wireless clients, rather than clients connecting to a WAP connected to the corporate network.

■ Enable the Windows operating system to configure wireless network settings automatically.

■ Provide preferred network SSIDs and prevent connections to nonpreferred networks.

■ Enforce the use of WEP or WPA encryption.

■ Define which form of EAP authentication is required: PEAP or EAP-TLS.

■ Define whether computer authentication, user authentication, or a combination of both is required for connectivity to the wireless network.

■ Enforce mutual authentication by validating the RADIUS server's certificate.

Connecting to a Wired Network

To implement 802.1x authentication when connecting to a wired network, the network connection must be configured to implement 802.1x authentication.

> **Note**   There is no Group Policy setting that defines wired 802.1x configuration settings. The Group Policy settings described for wireless networking affect only wireless network connections and are not applicable to wired network connections.

To configure EAP-TLS authentication manually on a wired network connection, use the following procedure:

1. Open the Network Connections window.

2. Right-click your wired network connection, and click Properties.

3. On the properties page of the network connection, in the Authentication tab (see Figure 25-3), do the following:

   ❑ Enable the Enable Network Access Control Using IEEE 802.1X And The Smart Card Or Other Certificate EAP Type check box. This enables 802.1x authentication for the network connection and is enabled by default.

   ❑ Enable the Authenticate As A Computer When Computer Information Is Available check box. This enables both computer and user authentication for the network connection.

   ❑ Disable the Authenticate As A Guest When User Or Computer Information Is Unavailable check box. This ensures that only authenticated users can connect to the network and prevents a nondomain user from attempting to authenticate as the Guest account.

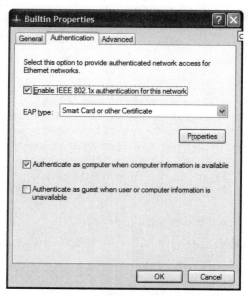

Figure 25-3 Enabling EAP-TLS authentication for a wired network connection

4. In the Authentication tab, click Properties.

5. On the Smart Card Or Other Certificate properties page (as shown previously in Figure 25-2), enable the same options recommended for a wireless client:

   ❑ **Use A Smart Card** Enable if using a smart card certificate.

   ❑ **Use A Certificate On This Computer** Enable if using a certificate stored in the user's certificate store.

   ❑ **Use Simple Certificate Selection (Recommended)** Enable if the certificate's subject is the same as the user's logon name.

   ❑ **Validate Server Certificate** Enable this option to require mutual authentication. The client validates the RADIUS server's certificate and ensures that it chains to the root CA certificate designated in the Trusted Root Certification Authorities store on the local client machines.

   ❑ **Use A Different User Name For The Connection** Only enable this option if the computer is not a member of the forest. This allows users to choose a certificate that does not contain their current user name.

6. Click OK to save changes to the Smart Card Or Other Certificate EAP type.

After your wired clients are configured, they will use only 802.1x authentication if prompted to by the switch. This is a difference in behavior when compared to wireless clients. Wired clients implement a passive mode, where they wait for an EAPOL-Start message from the authenticating switch. Wireless clients use an active mode, where they send an EAPOL-Start message to the WAP when they associate with the WAP.

> **Tip**   If you want to change the behavior so that a wired client will send an EAPOL-Start message, you must set the HKLM\SOFTWARE\Microsoft\EAPOL\Parameters \General\Global\SupplicantMode registry setting to 3 (REG_DWORD data type) from the default value of 2.

Best Practices

- **Implement the strongest form of wireless encryption available on your WAPs.**   Any form of encryption is better than no encryption. Even though WEP has known weaknesses, it is still better to enable WEP than to have no encryption at all if your WAP does not support WPA or WPA2. If you do implement WEP, ensure that you regularly modify the WEP key to protect against attacks against the WEP key.

- **Implement only WAPs that support 802.1x authentication.**   802.1x authentication decreases some of the weaknesses associated with WEP encryption. 802.1x ensures that only authenticated clients (computers and users) can connect to the wireless network and provides automated distribution of the encryption keys.

- **Implement PEAP or EAP-TLS for authenticating all wireless clients.**   Both authentication methods provide strong protection of the user's credentials. In addition, EAP-TLS and PEAP ensure that the computer or user performs mutual authentication with a RADIUS server when connecting to the wireless network.

- **Deploy certificates using autoenrollment or scripted enrollment for domain members.**   Automating the deployment of certificates ensures that all users and computers obtain the necessary certificates for wireless networking. Automated deployment reduces the chance of user error during the enrollment process.

- **Use Group Policy to define wireless networking settings.**   Group Policy can ensure that computers running Windows XP or Windows Server 2003 are correctly configured when connecting to a wireless network. Group Policy eliminates user error when configuring the wireless networking connection.

- **Implement forced reauthentication for wired networks.**   Forced re-authentication protects against hijacking attempts, when an attacker attaches a hub to the switch and assumes the MAC address and IP address of the attacked computer.

- **Implement primary and secondary RADIUS servers.**   Providing a secondary RADIUS server for 802.1x authentication ensures that the failure of a single RADIUS server does not prevent client and user authentication to the network.

Additional Information

- "Deploying Secure 802.11 Wireless Networks with Microsoft Windows" (*http://www.microsoft.com/mspress/books/6749.asp*)

- "802.11 WEP: Concepts and Vulnerability" (*http://www.wi-fiplanet.com/tutorials/article.php/1368661*)

- "Security of the WEP Algorithm" (*http://www.isaac.cs.berkeley.edu/isaac/wep-faq.html*)

- "Configuring Wireless Settings Using Windows Server 2003 Group Policy" (*http://www.microsoft.com/technet/community/columns/cableguy/cg0703.mspx*)

- "Designing and Deploying Wireless LAN Connectivity for the Microsoft Corporate Network" (*http://www.microsoft.com/technet/prodtechnol/winxppro/deploy/wlandply.mspx*)

- "Enterprise Deployment of Secure 802.11 Networks Using Microsoft Windows" (*http://www.microsoft.com/technet/prodtechnol/winxppro/deploy/ed80211.mspx*)

- "Enterprise Deployment of Secure Wired Networks Using Microsoft Windows" (*http://www.microsoft.com/downloads/details.aspx?FamilyID=05951071-6b20-4cef-9939-47c397ffd3dd&displaylang=en*)

- "Configuring 802.1x Port-Base Authentication for Cisco Switches" (*http://www.cisco.com/univercd/cc/td/doc/product/lan/cat4000/12_1_12/config/dot1x.pdf*)

- "Configuring Port-Based Access Control (802.1x) for HP ProCurve Switches" (*ftp://ftp.hp.com/pub/networking/software/59906024-1004-Security-ch08-PortAccess-8021x.pdf*)

- "Enterprise Solutions for Wireless LAN Security" (*http://www.wi-fi.org/OpenSection/pdf/Whitepaper_Wi-Fi_Enterprise2-6-03.pdf*)

- "Microsoft 802.1x Authentication Client for Windows 2000" (*http://www.microsoft.com/windows2000/server/evaluation/news/bulletins/8021xclient.asp*)

- "Securing Wireless LANs—A Windows Server 2003 Certificate Services Solution" (*http://www.microsoft.com/technet/security/prodtech/win2003/pkiwire/swlan.mspx*)

- "Step-by-Step Guide for Setting Up Secure Wireless Access in a Test Lab" (*http://www.microsoft.com/downloads/details.aspx?FamilyID=0f7fa9a2-e113-415b-b2a9-b6a3d64c48f5&DisplayLang=en*)

- "Troubleshooting Windows XP IEEE 802.11 Wireless Access" (*http://www.microsoft.com/technet/prodtechnol/winxppro/maintain /wifitrbl.mspx*)

- Wi-Fi Alliance (*http://www.weca.net/OpenSection/index.asp*)

- "Wi-Fi Protected Access" (*http://www.weca.net/OpenSection /protected_access.asp*)

- "Wi-Fi Protected Access (WPA) Overview" (*http://www.microsoft.com/technet /community/columns/cableguy/cg0303.mspx*)

- "Windows Server 2003 Deployment Kit: Deploying a Wireless LAN" (*http://www.microsoft.com/technet/prodtechnol/windowsserver2003/proddocs /deployguide/dnsbm_wir_overview.asp?frame=true*)

- "Windows XP Wireless Deployment Technology and Component Overview" (*http://www.microsoft.com/technet/prodtechnol/winxppro/maintain /wificomp.mspx*)

- "Windows XP Support Patch for Wi-Fi Protected Access" (*http://microsoft.com /downloads/details.aspx?FamilyId=009D8425-CE2B-47A4-ABEC- 274845DC9E91&displaylang=en*)

- "Improving Security with Domain Isolation: Microsoft IT implements IP Security (IPSec)" (*http://www.microsoft.com/downloads/details.aspx?FamilyId= A97DDC48-A364-4756-BB3C-91DA274118FE&displaylang=en*)

- SMAC tool (*http://www.klcconsulting.net/smac/default.htm?v=readme11*)

- The following Knowledge Base articles:

  - 313664: "Using 802.1x Authentication on Computers Running Windows 2000" (*http://support.microsoft.com/kb/313664*)

  - 318710: "How to Support Wireless Connections in Windows 2000" (*http://support.microsoft.com/kb/318710*)

  - 815485: "Overview of the WPA Wireless Security Update in Windows XP" (*http://support.microsoft.com/kb/815485*)

  - 837911: "Windows for Wireless and Wired Networks" (*http://support.microsoft.com/kb/837911*)

Part V
Managing Security Updates

Chapter 26
Patch Management

Patch management is required in a Microsoft network because software is not bug free. Security update and software updates must be periodically applied to the Microsoft Windows Server 2003, Windows 2000, and Windows XP operating systems to address security and functionality issues. Typically, updates are developed to resolve one of the following issues:

- **Testing for all the design possibilities is difficult.** As network designs become more complex, it is increasingly problematic to test every use of a Windows operating system component during initial testing and development of the operating system by Microsoft.

- **More legacy versions must be supported.** Although Windows XP is Microsoft's latest client operating system, not all customers will deploy it immediately. Customers will continue to use their common base operating systems, and these versions must be patched to protect against newer vulnerabilities.

- **Customers demand higher quality.** The quality bar rises as customers' network infrastructures change. More companies are connected to the Internet and are vulnerable to Internet attacks. This awareness drives higher the quality requirements for Internet-related components of Windows Server 2003.

- **Critical security issues must be fixed before the next product release.** Many issues cannot wait for a new version of the product to ship. Security issues, memory leaks, and other problems must be addressed immediately, especially if the vulnerabilities can lead to the compromise of a Windows 2000– or Windows Server 2003–based computer.

This chapter examines the following topics:

- **Types of patches**   Not all patches are the same. This section looks at update formats and how Microsoft rates security patches.

- **Development of a security update**   The development cycle of a security update illustrates what happens after a security vulnerability or bug is reported to Microsoft, before the security update is released to the public.

- **Patch management in six steps**   The last section of this chapter proposes a methodology for patch management that will enable you to deploy patches successfully.

Types of Patches

Microsoft releases patches to provide updates to the Windows operating system and Microsoft applications. These patches fix known problems, or bugs, in an operating system or application and are shipped in the following formats:

- **Hotfixes**   These updates address a single problem or bug encountered by a customer. They are developed in a short period of time and are released with less testing than other update types. Some hotfixes are referred to as *security fixes*. Security fixes differ from hotfixes in that the issues related to hotfixes are identified by the Microsoft Security Response Center (MSRC), rather than by Microsoft Product Support Services (PSS). Hotfixes are sometimes referred to as *Quick Fix Engineering (QFE) fixes*.

- **Emergency releases**   These updates are designed to address issues that demand immediate attention, which include fast-moving virus attacks spreading throughout the Internet. An emergency release is tested to ensure it is suitable for broad distribution. These updates are placed on the Microsoft Windows Update site, which pushes updates quickly and automatically to millions of machines.

- **Monthly security updates**   These updates provide fixes for recently discovered security vulnerabilities. Monthly security updates are released on the first Tuesday of every month. A notification of the upcoming updates is released a few days before the release of the update so that customers are aware of the upcoming month's updates. This process ensures that there is the smallest possible time between announcements of vulnerabilities and fixes being available, but also limits the amount of testing that can be performed by customers and partners because of the risk of information leaking to hackers.

- **Roll-ups** As the name suggests, a roll-up fix combines the updates of several security updates and software updates into a single update file. Roll-up fixes are run through more testing than single security updates or software updates, but are released more frequently than service packs (discussed next).

- **Software updates** These are any update, update roll-up, service pack, feature pack, critical update, security update, or hotfix that is used to improve or to fix a software product that is released by Microsoft Corporation.

- **Service packs** At fairly regular intervals, Microsoft produces a collection of all software updates released since the operating system's or application's release, including software updates released in previous service pack versions. These collections include fixes not previously released and can introduce new functionality. Service packs undergo extensive testing before their release to ensure no deployment issues exist. Microsoft might issue several beta releases of a service pack before the service pack is ready for the public.

When a security fix is released, MSRC issues a security bulletin that identifies the addressed vulnerability. In addition, a severity rating is applied to the security bulletin. If a security fix is a roll-up fix, the highest security rating of the individual security updates in the roll-up is applied.

Following is the ratings system implemented by the MSRC in November 2002:

- **Critical** A vulnerability that might enable an attacker to gain control of your computer through elevation of privilege or by allowing access to sensitive data. You should always apply critical-rating updates after testing. It is recommended that you apply a critical update within 24 hours of the update's release. If your organization is testing the update before deploying it on your network, it is recommended you deploy the tested update within two weeks of release.

- **Important** A vulnerability that might compromise the confidentiality, integrity, or availability of user data, as well as the integrity or availability of processing resources. You should always apply important-rating updates after testing. It is recommended that you apply an important update within one month of the update's release. If your organization is testing the update before deploying it on your network, it is recommended you take no longer than two months to apply the important update.

- **Moderate**   A vulnerability that might be mitigated by good security measures, such as implementing a security baseline configuration or performing regular network auditing. This rating can also be applied to vulnerabilities that are difficult to exploit. You should evaluate a moderate update to determine whether the vulnerability addressed is relevant to your company before testing and deployment. It is recommended that you apply a moderate update within four months of the update's release or wait until the next service pack or roll-up that includes the patch. If your organization is performing extensive testing of the update before deploying it on your network, it is recommended you deploy the tested update within six months of release.

- **Low**   A vulnerability that is extremely difficult to exploit or whose impact is minimal. You should determine whether a low-rating update is necessary before testing and deployment. It is recommended that you wait for the next service pack or roll-up that includes the low update. In some cases, you might decide not to deploy the update at all because it is not relevant to your organization.

Development of a Security Update

Once product support or the MSRC identifies the need for a security update, the development process begins. This process differs for operating systems and applications, but the same general method is used:

1. The vulnerability identified by MSRC or the bug identified by product support is escalated to the Microsoft sustained engineering team.

2. The sustained engineering team investigates the bug and assigns it to a developer. The developer might be on the sustained engineering team or might be the core team developer responsible for the operating system or application component.

3. The developer creates an initial security update. This security update addresses the vulnerability or bug but does not undergo testing other than that performed by the developer. This version of the security update is referred to as a *private*.

4. The private is sent to the customer who reported the problem to MSRC or to product support. The customer deploys the private to determine whether it corrects the problem.

5. If the customer reports that the bug is fixed, the sustained engineering team registers the bug against the next version of the operating system or application. This ensures that the next release does not include the same bug.

6. The private is provided to the core team developer responsible for the operating system or application component affected by the vulnerability. The developer reviews the security update to ensure no other issues exist.

7. When the developer completes her analysis, the security update is submitted to the build lab, which creates the security update and runs it through several build verification tests.

8. The security update is then passed through testers. The testers ensure that the security update works as expected. Because of time constraints, testing is not as extensive as the testing performed on service packs.

9. Localization teams review the security update to determine whether localized versions are required for different language versions of the operating system or application. If required, localized versions are developed.

10. The completed security update is released to customers. In addition, Microsoft releases a related security bulletin that applies a vulnerability rating and provides further descriptions of the vulnerability.

Once the security update is released to customers, the race begins between the organizations applying the patch and attackers attempting to create an attack that takes advantage of the vulnerability. An attacker will typically reverse engineer the patch to figure out what changes it made to the operating system or application to determine what is being fixed. Once determined, the attacker creates worm or virus code that takes advantage of the vulnerability. The attacker then releases the worm or virus—no testing is necessary because he has the entire Internet to test the worm or virus. Table 26-1 shows the time between when a security and an associated exploit were released for some of the more recognizable attacks in recent years.

Table 26-1   Time Between Security Update Release and Exploit Release

Attack	Patch Release Date	Attack Date	Number of days patch was available before the attack
Trojan.Kaht	March 17, 2003	May 5, 2003	49
SQL Slammer	July 24, 2002	January 24, 2003	184
Klez-E	March 29, 2001	January 17, 2002	294
Nimda	October 17, 2000	September 18, 2001	336
Code Red	June 18, 2001	July 16, 2001	28

Patch Management in Six Steps

It is recommended you use a six-step process for patch management. This process ensures that you apply the patches in an organized manner that prevents other applications on the network from failing. This is the recommended six-step process for patch management:

1. **Notification**   You must be aware of new security updates or service packs to ensure that the updates or service packs are installed in a timely manner.

2. **Assessment**   You must identify which computers on the network require the security update or service pack.

3. **Obtainment**   You must acquire the security update or service pack installation files from Microsoft.

4. **Testing**   You must test the security update or service pack before you apply it to all affected computers on your network to ensure that undesired effects do not occur.

5. **Deployment**   You must deploy the security update or service pack to the affected computers in a timely manner, taking advantage of tools to assist in the deployment.

6. **Validation**   You must ensure that the security update or service pack is successfully installed on all affected computers.

> **Note**   Other methodologies will work for patch management as long as they follow a systematic, repeatable process.

Step 1. Notification

The first step in patch management is being aware of when Microsoft releases security patches. When a security patch is released, Microsoft issues a security bulletin that details the vulnerability fixed by the security patch as well as a vulnerability rating so that you can assess whether to deploy the security patch immediately after testing.

One way to stay on top of releases is to subscribe to the Microsoft Security Notification Service, which you access at *http://register.microsoft.com/subscription /subscribeme.asp?ID=135*. The notification service sends you an e-mail message when a new security bulletin is released. If you desire even more timely information, consider subscribing to the Microsoft Security Bulletin Advance Notification announcement, available at *http://www.microsoft.com/technet/security/news/bulletinadvance.mspx*. The advance notification provides e-mail notification of upcoming security bulletins and timely notification of any minor changes to previously released Microsoft security bulletins.

> **Note**   All e-mail messages from the Microsoft Security Notification Service are signed with a Pretty Good Privacy (PGP) key. The Microsoft PGP key is available at *http://www.microsoft.com/technet/security/bulletin/pgp.mspx*. You can verify the Microsoft PGP key by inspecting its fingerprint, which is 9502 BE22 B497 5112 FBE0 BFC9 8ADE 1206 AA55 BC66.

In addition to the Microsoft Security Notification Service, several other notification services can inform you when new security issues arise for Microsoft Windows NT 4.0, Windows Server 2003, Windows 2000, and Windows XP:

- **NTBugtraq**   The *http://www.ntbugtraq.com* Web site, hosted by Russ Cooper, maintains a mailing list that discusses security bugs and exploits in Windows NT 4.0, Windows 2000, Windows XP, and Windows Server 2003.

- **United States Computer Emergency Readiness Team (US-CERT) Cyber Security Alerts and Bulletins**   The National Cyber Alert System maintains its own mailing list that notifies participants when computer-related security problems arise. You can subscribe to the US-CERT Security Alerts (sent whenever a security alert is released) at *http://www.us-cert.gov/cas/signup.html#ta* or to the US-CERT Security Bulletins (weekly summaries of security issues) at *http://www.us-cert.gov/cas/signup.html#tb*.

Step 2. Assessment

Once you identify the release of a security patch, you must determine whether the vulnerability affects your company and whether your computers require the patch. As mentioned earlier, you can utilize the Microsoft security bulletin rating system to assist in this decision. If a security bulletin is rated as critical or important, you should consider immediately applying the patch once you have tested it.

After testing, you must identify which computers require patch application. In many ways, this is the most difficult part of patch management. Keeping manual records of which patches and service packs are applied to every network computer is not possible if you have a large number of computers. Sometimes just determining which operating system a computer is running is a challenge, never mind which service packs and security patches are applied.

Keeping an inventory of your systems assists you in planning patch deployment. By categorizing your computer systems, you can quickly identify how many computers are affected by a reported vulnerability. For example, if Microsoft releases a new security bulletin relating to a bug in Microsoft Exchange Server 2003, it will be useful to know how many instances of Exchange Server 2003 are on the network, as well as their physical location and which service packs and software updates are current.

By utilizing software, such as Microsoft Systems Management Server (SMS), you can create a detailed inventory of network computers. The inventory information should help you determine which service packs and software updates are applied to each computer.

Based on the inventory, you can categorize computers into common collections for deploying service packs and software updates. For example, creating a collection of all Windows 2000–based computers will assist in the deployment of the latest Windows 2000 service pack.

Step 3. Obtainment

Once you identify the computers you must patch, you must obtain the patches or service pack files. The online location you choose to download from will depend on several factors, including which application or operating system is affected by the patch, whether all network computers are connected to the Internet, and whether you have a service pack or software update deployment solution in operation.

The following locations are available for downloading service packs and software updates:

- Microsoft Windows Update (*http://windowsupdate.microsoft.com*)
- Microsoft Office Product Updates (*http://officeupdate.microsoft.com/*)
- Microsoft Download Center (*http://www.microsoft.com/downloads/*)

Microsoft Windows Update

The Microsoft Windows Update site is available for the download and application of Windows security updates, software updates, and service packs. In addition to downloading and installing patches, you can also use the Windows Update Catalog to download patches for future application. The Windows Update Catalog provides a searchable collection of updates that can be installed on Windows-based computers across your home network or corporate network. The Windows Update Catalog enables you to download service packs, security updates, and driver updates without installing them on the local computer. Instead, the files are downloaded into a folder containing instructions for future application to one or more computers on your network.

Enabling the Windows Update Catalog   By default, the Windows Update Catalog is not enabled when you connect to the Microsoft Windows Update Web site. To enable the Windows Update Catalog in Windows 2000 or Windows Server 2003, you must use the following procedure:

1. Open Microsoft Internet Explorer.

2. Open *http://windowsupdate.microsoft.com*.

3. In the leftmost pane of the Microsoft Windows Update site, click Personalize Windows Update.

4. In the details pane, enable the Display The Link To The Windows Update Catalog Under See Also option.

5. In the details pane, click the Save Settings button.

This procedure adds a link to the Windows Update Catalog in the left-hand pane of the Microsoft Windows Update site under the heading See Also.

For Windows XP, the process is slightly different:

1. Open Internet Explorer.

2. Open *http://windowsupdate.microsoft.com*.

3. In the leftmost pane of the Microsoft Windows Update site, click Administrator Options.

4. In the Update Multiple Operating Systems section of the Web page, click the Windows Update Catalog link.

Using the Windows Update Catalog   The Windows Update Catalog enables you to find patches for Windows operating systems and hardware device drivers. You can download updates for specific operating systems, including the following:

- The 64-bit version of the Windows Server 2003 family

- Windows Server 2003 family

- The 64-bit version of Windows XP

- Windows XP family

- Windows 2000 family

- Microsoft Windows Millennium Edition (Me)

- Microsoft Windows 98

In addition to selecting the operating system version, you can choose to download localized versions of the updates by indicating the preferred language for the updates. You can search for updates based on the date they were posted to the Microsoft Windows Update Web site, the keywords in the update descriptions, and the type of update (such as critical updates, service packs, and recommended updates).

As mentioned, you can also use the Windows Update Catalog to download updated device drivers. You can select these device drivers based upon the type of hardware. For example, you can select network drivers by manufacturer, operating system, language, date posted, and specific keywords.

Once you select the operating system and device driver updates, you can download updates to your download basket. The Windows Update Catalog allows you to designate a local folder for downloads. The files are stored in the folder structure shown in Figure 26-1.

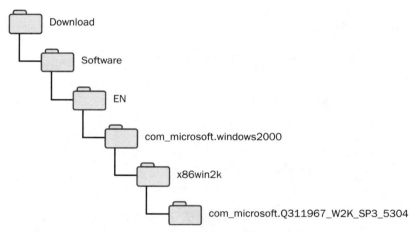

Figure 26-1   The folder structure created for the Windows Update Catalog

The folder structure created by the Windows Update Catalog depends upon whether you download a Windows operating system or device driver update. Below the folder you select as the download location—in this example, \Download—the Windows Update Catalog creates one of two folders. For operating system updates, a folder named Software is created, as shown in Figure 26-1. For device driver updates, a folder named Drivers is created.

Below this top-level folder, the next level of folders is based on the language selected. As Figure 26-1 shows, the English (EN) version of the update was downloaded. The next two levels of folders designate the update's operating system version. The example shown in Figure 26-1 is a Windows 2000 update designated by two folders: com_microsoft.windows2000 and x86win2k.

The final folder designates the actual downloaded update. The update's name indicates the related Microsoft Knowledge Base article, the update's intended operating system, the update's service pack version, and a unique identifier number. As shown in Figure 26-1, the update relates to Knowledge Base article 311967, "Unchecked Buffer in the Multiple UNC Provider." The update is intended for computers running Windows 2000 and is included in Windows 2000 Service Pack 3. If the update is an updated device driver, the final folder's name is assigned by the updated device driver's manufacturer.

Microsoft Office Product Updates

The Microsoft Office Product Updates site provides updates, add-ins, extras, converters, viewers, and downloads for Microsoft Office 97/98, Office 2000, Office 2002, and Office 2003. The updates can be selected by individual Office software components or for all Office applications.

To download Office updates to your computer, use the following procedure:

1. Open Internet Explorer.

2. Open *http://officeupdate.microsoft.com*.

3. Select the Office product and version updates you want to download.

4. Select whether to download updates, add-ins, and extras or converters and viewers for the selected Office component.

5. Select the individual updates from the list of available downloads.

> **Note**   You also have the option to view downloads from other providers. The Microsoft Office Product Updates site also displays a list of third-party updates for the Office suite components.

The Microsoft Office Product Updates site does not download the update files into any specific folder structure. You must designate a custom location for the download.

Microsoft Download Center

The Microsoft Download Center enables you to search for other software and updates from Microsoft. As with Microsoft Office Product Updates, you must manually designate a download location.

The following update categories are available from the Microsoft Download Center:

- **Games**   Includes trial versions and updates for games from Microsoft.
- **DirectX**   Includes updates and the latest versions of DirectX. DirectX provides innovations in graphics, sound, music, and 3-D animation for gaming and graphics.
- **Internet**   Includes updates for all Internet-based applications, such as Windows Messenger and Internet Explorer.
- **Windows (Security & Updates)**   Includes security updates for any components of the Windows operating system. This includes service packs, Internet Explorer updates, and security updates.
- **Windows Media**   Includes updates and codecs for Windows Media Player for various operating systems.
- **Drivers**   Includes updated drivers for Microsoft hardware, as well as updates for common operating system components, such as Microsoft Data Access Components (MDAC).
- **Office and Home Applications**   Includes updates for Office and other home applications, such as Microsoft MapPoint.
- **Mobile Devices**   Includes updates for the Palm PC, Microsoft ActiveSync, and Microsoft Windows CE.
- **Macintosh & Other Platforms**   Includes updates of software for Macintosh, Solaris, and Unix computers.
- **Server Applications**   Includes updates for Microsoft BackOffice components, such as Microsoft SQL Server, Exchange Server, Microsoft Systems Management Server (SMS), and Microsoft SharePoint Portal Server.
- **System Management Tools**   Includes updates for Windows management, including Windows Installer, the Microsoft Internet Information Services (IIS) Lockdown Tool, and Sysprep.
- **Development Resources**   Includes updates for Microsoft Visual Basic, the Microsoft .NET Framework, and Microsoft Visual Studio.

Each download category presents a list of the 10 most popular downloads. You can also search for a download by specific products, technologies, and keywords.

Step 4. Testing

In an enterprise network, you cannot take the risk of deploying service packs or software updates without testing them in your environment. Testing ensures that the application of a service pack or software update does not create any undesired side effects.

To ensure that the testing is valid, consider implementing the following measures:

- **Deploy a test network.**   A test network contains computers with the standard configuration used on your network. This allows you to determine if a security update or service pack causes issues with other applications installed on a standard desktop computer.

- **Implement a pilot project.**   Service packs should be tested by a subset of your network computers. The subset will determine whether the service pack causes any issues on the corporate network for the affected computers.

> **Note**   Typically, you would perform pilot projects only for service packs, not for security updates or security roll-ups. But the decision is typically based on the security policies and previous experience of the organization applying the updates.

Once this initial testing is completed, you can start the deployment of the service pack or software update to all affected computers.

Step 5. Deployment

Once you download and test the necessary software update or service pack, you must install it on the affected computers. As mentioned earlier, you can determine the affected computers on your network by reviewing your computer inventory. The method you use to deploy a software update or service pack will depend on whether your company uses manual or automated distribution.

> **More Info**   This chapter discusses only the manual deployment of service packs or software updates. For detailed information on automating service pack or software update distribution, see Chapter 27, "Using Patch Management Tools."

Installing Service Packs

The easiest way to obtain the latest service packs for Windows Server 2003, Windows 2000, and Windows XP is to use the Microsoft Windows Update site at *http://windowsupdate.microsoft.com/* to download them. The available updates will include the latest service pack for your operating system.

If you are deploying a service pack to a large segment of your network, it might be better to download the Network Installation version of the service pack to reduce the amount of bandwidth consumed while downloading.

> **Note**   If you implement a patch management system, you might be able to download the network version of the service pack and deploy the service pack using only internal network bandwidth after the initial download.

The Network Installation download of a service pack includes all updated files for the selected operating system. You can extract the service pack files from the downloaded executable by running **ServicePackName.exe -x** (where *ServicePackName* is the name of the service pack file). Once you extract the service pack files, you can run **\download folder\i386\Update\Update.exe** to install. If you have not extracted the service pack files, run **\download folder\ServicePackName.exe**.

Alternatively, you can use the packaged *download folder*\i386\Update\Update.msi file to deploy the service pack to computer accounts in a software installation Group Policy object (GPO). By assigning the Update.msi package to a GPO applied to an OU with computer accounts running the targeted operating system, you can deploy the service pack through Group Policy.

Installing Software Updates

All Windows Server 2003, Windows 2000, or Windows XP software updates—whether released prior to or since Windows 2000 Service Pack 3—are packaged in a format that automatically installs the service pack when you run the downloaded software update executable. The executable automatically extracts all files related to the software update and installs them. The following two subsections discuss the manual installation of software updates on computers.

Installing Software Updates Released Prior to Windows 2000 Service Pack 3

Software Updates released prior to Windows 2000 Service Pack 3 are installed by using Hotfix.exe. When you install a software update, you can use several command-line switches to customize installation. The available command-line switches for hot-fixes released prior to Windows 2000 Service Pack 3 include the following:

- **/f**   Causes all other programs to quit when the computer is shut down.
- **/l**   Displays a list of all hotfixes currently installed on the computer.
- **/m**   Performs an unattended software update installation.
- **/n**   Prevents the computer from archiving previous versions of files replaced by the software update. (This switch prevents the uninstallation of the software update.)
- **/q**   Performs the installation in quiet mode. (Quiet mode does not require user interaction.)
- **/y**   Uninstalls the software update. (This option must be used with /m or /q.)
- **/z**   Prevents the computer from restarting after installation.

When performing an unattended software update installation, you typically use the following command line:

```
Hotfix.exe /m /q /z
```

This command line allows the installation of multiple software updates in a single batch file.

> **Warning**   Hotfix.exe does not perform version control when you install multiple software updates. If you create a batch process that installs multiple software updates, you must ensure that the last line of the batch file is QChain.exe. QChain.exe ensures that if a file is modified by multiple software updates, the most recent version is maintained when the computer restarts. For more information on QChain.exe, see Knowledge Base article 296861: "Use QChain.exe to Install Multiple Hotfixes with Only One Reboot" (*http://support.microsoft.com/kb/296861*).

Installing Software Updates Released Since Windows 2000 Service Pack 3

Software updates released after Windows 2000 Service Pack 3, including those for Windows XP and Windows Server 2003, are installed by using the Update.exe program. The Update.exe program includes the QChain.exe functionality, eliminating the need to run QChain.exe if multiple software updates are installed by a batch-file method. Update.exe is also used as the software update installation method for Windows XP software updates.

The following command-line switches are available when you install a software update released since Windows 2000 Service Pack 3:

- **-u**   Performs the installation in unattended mode.
- **-f**   Forces all other programs to quit when the computer shuts down.
- **-n**   Prevents the archiving of previous versions of files replaced by the software update. (This switch prevents the uninstallation of the software update.)
- **-o**   Overwrites original equipment manufacturer (OEM) files without prompting.
- **-z**   Prevents the computer from restarting after the software update installation. (This option allows the application of multiple software updates without rebooting.)
- **-q**   Performs an unattended installation but does not show the user interface during the installation process.
- **-l**   Lists all software updates currently installed on the computer.

Step 6. Validation

Once you complete the software update installation, verify that it was installed successfully. Numerous methods to determine whether a software update is correctly applied to a computer exist, including the following:

- **Inspect the file system**   When a software update is installed so that the previous versions of replaced files are archived, the archived files are stored in the %windir%\$NTUninstallQ######$ folder, where ###### is the related Knowledge Base article number. If the folder exists, you can assume the software update was applied correctly. Be aware that this does not prevent the updated version from being replaced by an incorrect version at a later time, especially with software updates released prior to Service Pack 3 that do not have QChain.exe functionality.

- **Inspect the registry**   When a software update is successfully installed, the installation program registers the software update in the HKLM\SOFTWARE\Microsoft\Windows NT\CurrentVersion\Hotfix\Q###### or \KB###### registry key, where ###### is the related Knowledge Base article. As with inspecting the file system, examining the registry does not detect whether updated files are later replaced.

- **Use software update diagnosis tools**   To inspect the system for currently applied software updates and determine which software updates are required for your computer, you can use software update diagnosis tools, such as the Microsoft Baseline Security Analyzer command-line version executable Mbsacli.exe, Shavlik's hotfix network checker HfNetChk.exe (found at *http://www.shavlik.com*), and those found on the Microsoft Windows Update Web site (*http://windows update.microsoft.com*). By inspecting the checksums on the updated files, these tools can determine whether the hotfix needs reapplication.

> **More Info**   For more information on using these patch management tools, see Chapter 27, "Using Patch Management Tools."

Best Practices

- **Subscribe to security update and service pack notification services.**   Notification services assist you in identifying recently released security updates and service packs, enabling you to deploy the updates or service packs in a timely manner.

- **Assess your network to determine which computers require the security update or service pack.**   A security update or service pack might not be applicable to all computers on your network. You must identify which computers will require the update or service pack.

- **Obtain security update or service pack installation files from download locations.**   Depending on which operating system or application is affected by the security update or service pack, you must connect to the appropriate Web site to download the installation files.

- **Test the security update or service pack on test computers before performing a full deployment.**   By performing a pilot deployment, you identify any issues that might arise with the security update or service pack installation. This prevents the security update or service pack installation from causing undesired side effects on the target computers or network.

- **Use the appropriate tools to deploy the security update or service pack.**   The tools that you choose for deploying the security update or service pack will determine the administrative effort required for the deployment.

- **Validate the installation of the security update or service pack.**   Once you complete the installation of the security update or service pack, you must ensure that the security update or service pack is installed correctly on the target computers.

- **Always have a rollback plan.**   In some cases, a security update might not interact as expected with your organization's computers. Have a plan on how to roll back the changes and return the machine to the expected operating status.

Additional Information

- Microsoft Security Notification Service (*http://www.microsoft.com/technet /security/bulletin/notify.asp*)

- Microsoft Security Bulletin Advance Notification (*http://www.microsoft.com /technet/security/bulletin/advance.mspx*)

- Microsoft Security Response Policy and Practices (*http://www.microsoft.com /technet/security/topics/policy/msrpracs.mspx*)

- Microsoft Security Guidance Center: Patch Management Index (*http://www.microsoft.com/security/guidance/topics/PatchManagement.mspx*)

- Microsoft Security Bulletin Advance Notification Announcement (*http://www.microsoft.com/technet/security/news/bulletinadvance.mspx*)

- Microsoft Windows 2000 Hotfix Installation and Deployment Guide (HFDeploy.htm) (*http://www.microsoft.com/windows2000/downloads /servicepacks/sp4/HFDeploy.htm*)

- Microsoft Windows XP Hotfix Installation and Deployment Guide (*http:// www.microsoft.com/WindowsXP/pro/downloads/servicepacks/sp1/hfdeploy.asp*)

- Guide for Installing and Deploying Updates for Microsoft Windows XP Service Pack 2 (*http://www.microsoft.com/technet/prodtechnol/winxppro/deploy /hfdeploy.mspx*)

- Guide for Installing and Deploying Updates for Microsoft Windows Server 2003 and Windows XP 64-Bit Edition Version 2003 (HFDeploy.htm) (*http://www.microsoft.com/technet/security/topics/patch/HFDeploy.mspx*)

- Microsoft TechNet Security Web site (*http://www.microsoft.com/technet /security/default.asp*)

- "Managing Security Hotfixes," by Paul Niser, *Windows & .NET Magazine* (July 2002) (*http://www.microsoft.com/technet/security/tips/sechotfx.asp*)

- *Security Operations Guide for Windows 2000 Server*, Chapter 5, "Patch Management" (*http://www.microsoft.com/downloads/details.aspx?FamilyID=f0b7b4ee-201a-4b40-a0d2-cdd9775aeff8&displaylang=en*)

- NTBugtraq Web site (*http://www.ntbugtraq.com*)

- United States Computer Emergency Readiness Team—Nation Cyber Alert System Web site (*http://www.us-cert.gov/cas/index.html*)

- "Patch Management Process" (*http://www.microsoft.com/technet/security /guidance/secmod193.mspx*)

- The following Knowledge Base articles:
    - 262841: "Windows 2000 Hotfix.exe Program Description and Command-Line Switches" (*http://support.microsoft.com/kb/262841*)
    - 296861: "Use QChain.exe to Install Multiple Hotfixes with Only One Reboot" (*http://support.microsoft.com/kb/296861*)
    - 810232: "Summary of Command-Line Syntax for Software Updates" (*http://support.microsoft.com/kb/810232*)
    - *824684: "Description of the Standard Terminology That Is Used to Describe Microsoft Software Updates" (http://support.microsoft.com/kb/824684)*
    - 824687: "Command-Line Switches for Microsoft Software Update Packages" (*http://support.microsoft.com/kb/824687*)

Chapter 27

Using Patch Management Tools

Several tools enable you to apply Microsoft Windows patches and determine patch deployment status. This chapter looks at available patch management tools, describes how they operate, and provides recommendations on when to use each of them.

Currently, many organizations manually distribute service packs and security updates. Although you can script update deployments, you often end up falling behind in security update distribution, leaving your computers vulnerable. In addition, when using versions of Microsoft Windows 2000 that do not have the latest services packs installed, it is possible to overwrite an updated executable or dynamic-link library (DLL) file with an older version if the security updates are not applied in the correct order.

Using the QChain Tool

The QChain tool (QChain.exe) enables you to install multiple security updates without having to reboot between installations. The QChain tool evaluates the drivers, DLLs, and executable files updated by each security update and ensures that only the most recent versions of the files are maintained after reboot.

To use the QChain tool, you must create a batch file for the security update installation. The batch file looks something like the following sample:

```
@echo off
setlocal
set PATHTOFIXES=c:\patches
%PATHTOFIXES%\Q123456_w2k_sp2_x86.exe -z -m
%PATHTOFIXES%\Q123321_w2k_sp2_x86.exe -z -m
%PATHTOFIXES%\Q123789_w2k_sp2_x86.exe -z -m
%PATHTOFIXES%\qchain.exe
```

The batch file installs each security update with the -z switch to prevent reboots after each security update installation and uses the -m switch to enable unattended installs. Once all updates are installed, the QChain tool is executed to ensure that only the most current versions of updated files are maintained.

QChain is not required if you are deploying security updates to computers running Microsoft Windows XP, Windows 2000 with Service Pack 3 or later, or Windows Server 2003 because QChain functionality is built into these versions.

To reduce the cost of deploying security updates and patches, many companies use tools to automatically deploy security updates. Microsoft's current roster of security patch management tools includes the following:

- Windows Update
- Automatic Updates
- Microsoft Software Update Services (SUS)
- Office Update
- Windows Update Services (WUS)
- Microsoft Baseline Security Analyzer (MBSA)
- Microsoft Systems Management Server (SMS) Software Update Services Feature Pack
- Microsoft Systems Management Server 2003

You must understand that the catalog used by these tools determines which security patches are installed on target computers and, more important, which security patches are required by the target computer.

The Security Patch Bulletin Catalog

MBSA and SMS use the Security Patch Bulletin Catalog (MSSecure.xml) to determine which security updates are installed and which are required on target computers. Every time a patch management tool is executed, it automatically downloads the latest version of MSSecure.xml to ensure that you check for the application of the latest security bulletins.

> **Note** The MSSecure.xml file is now distributed in a cabinet format that is digitally signed by Microsoft to identify when it is modified, and it provides proof that you have the legitimate version of the latest Security Patch Bulletin Catalog. You can obtain the latest version of the English cabinet file from *http://go.microsoft.com /fwlink/?LinkId=18922*.

The following code sample shows the entry for MS04-009, a security patch that protects against a buffer overflow attack against Microsoft Outlook 2002. The MSSecure.xml file contains a section named <Bulletins> that provides all available bulletins included in the file:

```
- <Bulletin BulletinID="MS04-009" BulletinLocationID="1" FAQLocationID="1"
FAQPageName="FQ04-009" Title="Vulnerability in Microsoft Outlook Could Allow Code
Execution (828040)" DatePosted="2004/03/09" DateRevised="2004/03/09" Supported="Yes"
Summary="A security vulnerability exists within Outlook 2002 that could allow Internet
Explorer to execute script code in the Local Machine zone on an affected system. The
vulnerability results from the incorrect parsing of specially crafted mailto URLs by
Outlook 2002. To exploit this vulnerability, an attacker would have to host a malicious
Web site that contained a Web page designed to exploit the vulnerability and then
persuade a user to view the Web page. The attacker could also create an HTML e-mail
message designed to exploit the vulnerability and persuade the user to view the HTML
e-mail message. After the user has visited the malicious Web site or viewed the
malicious HTML e-mail message an attacker who successfully exploited this
vulnerability could access files on a user's system, and run arbitrary code on a user's
system. This code would run in the security context of the currently logged on user.
Outlook 2002 is available as a separate product and is also included as part of Office
XP." Issue="" ImpactSeverityID="0" PreReqSeverityID="0" MitigationSeverityID="0"
PopularitySeverityID="0">
  <BulletinComments />
- <QNumbers>
  <QNumber QNumber="828040" />
  </QNumbers>
- <Patches>
- <Patch PatchName="OXP828040" PatchLocationID="1" SBID="0" SQNumber="828040"
```

```
NoReboot="0" SeverityID="0">
  <PatchComments />
- <AffectedProduct ProductID="95" FixedInSP="0">
  <AffectedServicePack ServicePackID="140" />
  </AffectedProduct>
- <AffectedProduct ProductID="93" FixedInSP="0">
  <AffectedServicePack ServicePackID="140" />
  </AffectedProduct>
  </Patch>
  </Patches>
  </Bulletin>
```

> **Note**   We do not expect you to memorize the syntax of the MSSecure.xml file. This example is provided to enable you to see what information is provided in the file for patch tools to determine whether a security update is applied on a target computer.

The <Bulletin BulletinID="MS04-009"> line provides detailed information on the security bulletin related to the MS04-009 security patch. The line includes a summary of the security vulnerability as well as the ratings of the security bulletin. The line also includes the BulletinLocationID and FAQLocationID references, which indicate where the security bulletin can be acquired. These two location IDs reference location ID "1", which is detailed in a later section of the MSSecure.xml file:

```
<Locations>
   <Location LocationID="1"
         Path="http://www.microsoft.com/technet/security/bulletin"
         AbsolutePath="False" />
</Locations>
```

The <QNumbers> section details the Microsoft Knowledge Base article or articles detailing the security vulnerability. In this case, the security vulnerability is detailed in Knowledge Base article 828040, "Vulnerability in Microsoft Outlook Could Allow Code Execution (828040)."

The <Patches> section details specific patches required to protect against a security vulnerability. The <Patches> section includes information on the affected products (in this case, ProductID="95") and the affected service pack level (ServicePackID="140"). These two numbers also reference sections appearing later in the MSSecure.xml file:

```
- <Product ProductID="95" Name="Outlook 2002" MinimumSupportedServicePackID="139"
CurrentServicePackID="140" CurrentVersion="10.0">
- <ProductFamilies>
  <ProductFamily ProductFamilyID="27" />
  </ProductFamilies>
- <AvailableSPs>
  <AvailableSP ServicePackID="139" />
  <AvailableSP ServicePackID="140" />
  </AvailableSPs>
  </Product>
```

As with most security patches, the MS04-009 security patch is dependent upon the service pack level at the target computer. In the <Bulletins> section, the MS04-009 security update entry indicates that the affected ServicePackID is "140". In the <Products> section, the entry for Outlook 2002 indicates that two ServicePackIDs are available: "139" and "140". The actual names of these service pack levels are detailed in the <ServicePacks> section of the MSSecure.xml file:

```
<ServicePacks>
    <ServicePack ServicePackID="139" Name="Office XP SP1" URL="" ReleaseDate="" />
    ServicePack ServicePackID="140" Name="Office XP SP2" URL="" ReleaseDate="" />
</ServicePacks>
```

Based on this information, you can see that the MS04-009 security update requires the application of Microsoft Office XP Service Pack 2.

Note   Once a security patch is released, it can be updated later. The <Bulletin> line includes information on the date the security patch was released as well as the date it was revised, if revision was required. Typically, the summary of the bulletin is updated to reflect which modifications were performed to the security patch.

Windows Update

Microsoft Windows Update is a Web-based application that enables you to determine whether new updates are required for your computer. You can use Windows Update by connecting to the Microsoft Windows Update Web site at *http://windowsupdate.microsoft.com.*

Windows Update can determine necessary security updates and service packs for the following Windows operating systems:

- Microsoft Windows 98
- Microsoft Windows 98 Second Edition
- Microsoft Windows 2000 Professional
- Microsoft Windows 2000 Server
- Microsoft Windows 2000 Advanced Server
- Microsoft Windows Millennium Edition (Me)
- Microsoft Windows XP
- Microsoft Windows Server 2003 family

To use the Microsoft Windows Update site, the following requirements must be met:

- **Microsoft Internet Explorer must enable cookies.**   The Microsoft Windows Update site uses cookies to track and record security patch installation data. Windows Update identifies your computer by generating a globally unique identifier (GUID), which is stored in a cookie. The cookie contains the following information to identify your computer:

  - ❏   The operating system version for determining security patches related to your operating system and service pack level

  - ❏   The Internet Explorer version for determining Internet Explorer version-specific updates

  - ❏   The version number for other software that can be updated by Windows Update, including Windows Media Player and Microsoft SQL Server

  - ❏   The Plug and Play identification numbers of hardware devices to identify required hardware device driver updates

  - ❏   The region and language settings to determine whether a localized version of a security patch must be installed

- **Internet Explorer must allow Microsoft ActiveX controls.**   The Microsoft Windows Update site downloads an ActiveX control to determine which security patches are required by your computer. To enable the download of the ActiveX control, the security settings for the Internet zone in Internet Explorer must be set to Medium or lower.

- **The person running the ActiveX control must be a member of the local Administrators group.**   Only members of the local Administrators group have the necessary permissions to scan the file system and registry to determine whether a security update is installed. In addition, only members of the local Administrators group have the necessary permissions to install security updates.

To use Windows Update to scan for required security updates and other patches for your operating system and applications, following these steps:

1.   Ensure that you are logged on as a local administrator. As mentioned, only members of the local Administrators group have permissions to download and install updates from the Microsoft Windows Update site.

2.   Open Internet Explorer and on the Tools menu, click Windows Update. You must use Internet Explorer because the Microsoft Windows Update site uses an ActiveX control to determine which updates your computer requires. If prompted, click Yes to download the latest version of the Windows Update ActiveX control.

3. On the Welcome To Windows Update page, click Scan For Updates. Based on your operating system and current updates, the Microsoft Windows Update site will determine which updates are required.

4. On the Pick Updates To Install page, click Review And Install Updates. This option enables you to pick exactly which updates to apply during this connection to the Microsoft Windows Update site.

5. On the Total Selected Updates page, critical updates are automatically populated in the selected updates list. Some updates might require separate installation, so be sure to scan the list of proposed updates. You can remove individual updates by clicking the Remove button. You can add operating system–specific updates or driver updates to the list by clicking the link for your operating system (Windows 2000, Windows XP, or Windows Server 2003 family) or the Driver Updates link in the left-hand pane and then clicking the Add button for individual updates in the details pane (as shown in Figure 27-1).

6. Once you have selected all updates to apply to your computer, click Review And Install Updates.

7. On the Total Selected Updates page, click Install Now.

8. The Microsoft Windows Update–Web Page dialog box appears showing you the status of the download and installation of the selected updates.

9. When all updates are installed, a listing will appear indicating which updates were successfully installed and which, if any, were not. After you review the list, you typically must restart the computer by clicking OK in the Microsoft Internet Explorer dialog box.

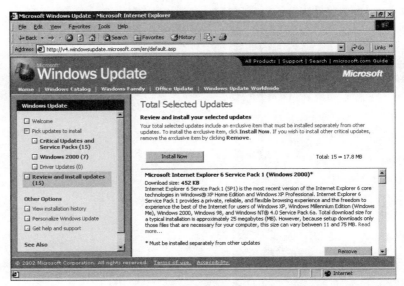

Figure 27-1 Choosing which critical updates, Windows operating system updates, or driver updates are applied to a computer

A newer version of Windows Update was introduced with the release of Windows XP Service Pack 2. The updates include the following:

- **Offers two installation methods**   The updated version of Windows Update enables you to choose between an Express Install, where critical and security updates are found, downloaded, and installed on the host computer, and a Custom Install, where optional updates are added to the list of available updates and the user is allowed to choose which updates to apply to the target computer.

- **Enabling Automatic Updates**   The updated version of Windows Update allows you to enable Automatic Updates (discussed in the next section) and choose a time for the installation of critical and security updates.

- **Offers different categories of updates**   Updates are now broken into three different categories: high-priority updates (those installed when an express installation is selected), optional software updates, and optional hardware updates.

Automatic Updates

On computers running Windows Server 2003, Windows 2000 Service Pack 3 or later, or Windows XP Service Pack 1 or later you can take advantage of Automatic Updates to apply security updates. In Windows XP with Service Pack 1 or later and Windows Server 2003, Automatic Updates is configured in the property pages of System Control Panel. On Windows 2000–based computers, the application of Service Pack 3 adds Automatic Updates to Control Panel as shown in Figure 27-2.

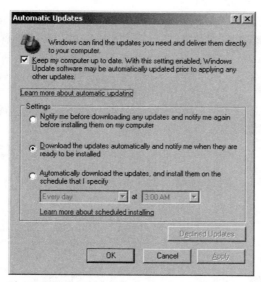

Figure 27-2   Scheduling the download and application of Windows updates by using Automatic Updates

The Automatic Updates application simplifies the maintenance of Windows Server 2003, Windows 2000, and Windows XP updates by periodically connecting to the Microsoft Windows Update site and determining whether your computer requires any updates. Specifically, you can configure the following options:

- **Enable or disable Automatic Updates**   You can choose whether to keep your computer's updates current by using Automatic Updates.

- **Define how Automatic Updates are applied**   You can choose from three options:

    - **Notify Me Before Downloading Any Updates And Notify Me Again Before Installing Them On My Computer**   Notifies you before update applications are downloaded. This option enables you to choose when to download updates as well as which updates to apply once the downloads are complete.

    - **Download The Updates Automatically And Notify Me When They Are Ready To Be Installed**   Automatically downloads required updates as background tasks. When updates are downloaded, you are notified that they are ready to be installed. This provides you with the opportunity to review updates and choose which ones to apply.

    - **Automatically Download The Updates And Install Them On The Schedule That I Specify**   Automates the download and application of updates. Updates are installed based on the schedule configured in Automatic Updates.

As with all Windows updates, the computer might require a restart to finish the update application. If you are currently logged on to the computer, you will be notified of the pending restart and provided with the option of delaying the restart.

Microsoft Software Update Services

Microsoft Software Update Services (SUS) leverages the Windows Update and Automatic Updates technology to enable a company to choose which updates to apply. Rather than connecting to the Microsoft Windows Update site for the download of security patches and Windows updates, clients connect to an internal SUS server that issues only approved updates.

How SUS Works

SUS depends on the interaction of the SUS server and Automatic Updates on the SUS clients. The following process is used to deploy security updates through SUS:

1. The SUS server is configured to synchronize its available updates with either the Microsoft Windows Update site or with another SUS server on the corporate network. The synchronization can be scheduled or initiated manually by the SUS administrator.

2. The SUS administrator reviews the list of available updates at the SUS server and approves the updates for distribution. Updates should be approved only after being tested on network computers.

3. SUS clients connect to the SUS server and download any approved updates but do not download already installed updates. Depending on the SUS client configuration, updates either are installed automatically or require a member of the local Administrators group to initiate installation.

4. SUS clients send information to a configured SUS statistics server. This information details whether the updates were successfully applied to the client computer.

> **Note**   SUS can be used only for the application of updates and services packs to the Windows operating system and supported applications.

Configuring the SUS Server

To configure the computer designated as the SUS server, you must first install the SUS server software. The SUS server software is a free download available at *http://www.microsoft.com/downloads/details.aspx?FamilyId=A7AA96E4-6E41-4F54-972C-AE66A4E4BF6C&displaylang=en*.

Installing the SUS Server Software

Once you download the SUSSetup.msi file, you must ensure that the SUS server meets the minimum software requirements. The SUS server application is a Web-based application and requires for installation Internet Explorer 5.5 or later in addition to the following Microsoft Internet Information Services (IIS) components:

- Common Files
- Internet Information Services snap-in
- World Wide Web Service

> **Warning**   The SUS server with Service Pack 1 can be installed on a domain controller or a computer running Microsoft Small Business Server (SBS) with Service Pack 1. This functionality was not available in the initial SUS 1.0 release.

Once the SUS server has the required IIS components as well as the latest service packs and updates, you can install the software by using the following process:

1.   At the SUS server, double-click the SUSSetup.msi file.

2.   On the Welcome screen, click Next.

3.   Read and accept the End User License Agreement (EULA) and click Next.

4.   On the Installation Type page, click Typical.

5.   Record the URL that SUS clients must connect to when interacting with the SUS server and click Install.

6.   If you are installing on a computer running Windows 2000, the SUS server setup then executes the IIS Lockdown tool. The IIS Lockdown tool removes the IIS Administration Web site and templates from the SUS server, disables all scripting mappings except for Microsoft Active Server Pages (ASP), disables Web-Based Distributed Authoring and Versioning (WebDAV), and prevents the anonymous Web user account from executing system utilities and writing Web content. The scripting mappings are enforced by the URLScan Internet Server Application Programming Interface (ISAPI) filter.

> **Note**   If you are installing on a computer running Windows Server 2003, IIS 6.0 is installed in a locked-down state, removing the need to run a lockdown tool.

7.   The installation completes and opens the SUS Administration Web site.

Defining SUS Server Options

Once you install the SUS server, best practice is to configure its options. You can define the server's options by connecting to the SUS Administration Web page at *http://SUSServerFQDN/susadmin* (where *SUSServerFQDN* is the fully qualified domain name of the SUS server) and then clicking the Set Options link. The Set Options Web page enables you to define the following options for the SUS server:

- **Proxy server configuration**   If the SUS server is on a network protected by a Microsoft Internet Security and Acceleration (ISA) Server or another vendor's proxy server, you must designate the proxy server configuration information. This can include the name, the listening port, and any required credential information for the proxy server.

■ **SUS server name**   This is the name that SUS clients use when connecting to the SUS server. Use a Domain Name System (DNS) name rather than a NetBIOS name so that DNS is used to resolve the SUS server name instead of Windows Internet Name Service (WINS).

■ **Master server**   You can designate whether the SUS server synchronizes its content with the Microsoft Windows Update server or connects to another SUS server on your network.

■ **Approval settings for new versions of previously approved updates**   You can choose to approve all updates to previously approved updates automatically or manually.

■ **Storage and locale information**   You can choose to store updates on the SUS server's local file system or to connect to the Windows Update server for the download of all updates. In addition, you can choose for which locales to download updates, such as English, Arabic, or Japanese.

Synchronizing the SUS Server

Installing SUS server software adds the Software Update Services Synchronization Service. This service enables the SUS server to synchronize update content with either the Microsoft Windows Update Web site or with another SUS server in your company.

To modify synchronization settings for an SUS server, you must perform the following procedure:

1. Connect to the SUS Administration Web page at *http://SUSServerFQDN /susadmin* (where *SUSServerFQDN* is the fully qualified domain name of the SUS server).

2. Click the Synchronize Server link.

3. If you want to perform a manual synchronization of the SUS server, click Synchronize Now. If you want to schedule standard synchronization times for the SUS server, click Synchronization Schedule.

4. In the Schedule Synchronization dialog box (see Figure 27-3), specify the time for the scheduled update, whether you want to synchronize daily or weekly, and how many times to retry a synchronization in the event of a failure. Once you configure your required settings, click OK.

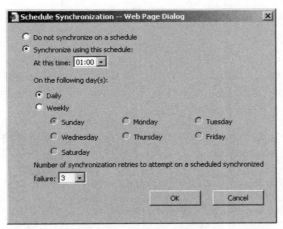

Figure 27-3   Defining the synchronization schedule for the SUS server

Approving Updates

Once you synchronize the SUS server, you must define which updates are approved for distribution to SUS clients. When you click the Approve Updates link in the SUS Administration Web site, you are presented with all the available updates.

After testing the updates on your network—either by testing the update distribution on a pilot network or performing a test on your computer—you must select all updates you want to distribute to SUS clients in the listing and then click the Approve button.

> **Warning**   You cannot select which SUS clients will receive a security update. All SUS clients that connect to your SUS server will receive the security update if they are running software that requires it. If you want to apply a security update to a subset of clients, you must use an alternate solution such as Systems Management Server (SMS), as described later in this chapter, deploy multiple SUS servers for each subset of clients, or move to Windows Update Services when it is released.

Configuring the SUS Clients

SUS requires that client computers have the Automatic Updates client loaded. As mentioned earlier in this chapter, the Automatic Updates client is automatically installed on Windows 2000–based computers with Service Pack 3 or late, on Windows XP–based computers with Service Pack 1 or later, and on Windows Server 2003–based computers. If you are running Windows 2000–based computers that do not have Service Pack 3 or a later version or Windows XP–based computers that do not have Service Pack 1 installed, you can download the Automatic Updates client software from *http://www.microsoft.com/windows2000/downloads/recommended/susclient/*.

Configuration in an Active Directory Environment

Once you deploy the Automatic Updates client, you can configure it by using Group Policy. The Automatic Updates client settings are included in the Wuau.adm policy template, which is installed in the %systemroot%\inf folder. The inclusion of the policy template adds Administrative Templates settings for Windows Update, as shown in Figure 27-4.

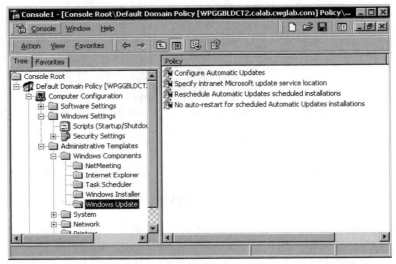

Figure 27-4 Configuring Windows Update settings in Group Policy

Once you have added the Wuau.adm policy template, you can configure the following settings to assist with your SUS deployment:

- **Configure Automatic Updates** Enables you to specify the Automatic Updates client settings. As mentioned earlier, Microsoft recommends you automatically download updates from the SUS server and schedule the install.

- **Specify Intranet Microsoft Update Service Location** Enables you to designate an SUS server as the update service for detecting updates, rather than using the default Microsoft Windows Update servers. In addition, you can designate an internal server to which statistics for Windows Update are sent. The statistics server must be running IIS. The statistics sent to the server will be stored in the IIS logs.

- **Reschedule Automatic Updates Scheduled Installations** Enables you to specify the amount of time for Automatic Updates to wait after system startup to proceed with a scheduled update installation that was missed previously.

- **No Auto-Restart For Scheduled Automatic Updates Installation**   Enables you to specify that Automatic Updates will wait for the computer to be restarted by any user that is logged on rather than automatically restarting the computer. If this setting is enabled, the computer will not restart, nor will it detect new updates until a user manually restarts the computer. If disabled, the currently logged on user will be notified that the computer will automatically restart in five minutes.

Configuration in a Non–Active Directory Environment

In a non–Active Directory environment, you can designate SUS client settings by editing the registry. Registry updates can be applied by manually editing the registry or deploying registry keys.

To define Automatic Updates settings, you must add the following registry values to the HKLM\Software\Policies\Microsoft\Windows\WindowsUpdate\AU registry key:

- **RescheduleWaitTime (Reg_DWORD)**   Defines how long Automatic Updates waits after system startup to install a previously scheduled update that was not installed. Values can range from 1 to 60 minutes.

- **NoAutoRebootWithLoggedOnUsers (Reg_DWORD)**   Allows users to choose whether to reboot their computers after application of Automatic Updates. This option is enabled if the registry entry is set to a value of 1.

- **NoAutoUpdate (Reg_DWORD)**   Allows you to enable (0) or disable (1) Automatic Updates. If not specified, the default value is Enable (0).

- **AUOptions (Reg_DWORD)**   Defines how updates are downloaded and installed. You can choose to be notified for both downloads and installations (2), to automatically perform downloads and be notified for installations (3), or to automatically perform downloads and installations using a predefined schedule (4).

- **ScheduledInstallDay (Reg_DWORD)**   Defines the days on which the scheduled installation of Automatic Updates takes place. You can specify that the installation occur every day (0) or on a specific day from Sunday (1) to Saturday (7).

- **ScheduledInstallTime (Reg_DWORD)**   Defines the hour the scheduled installation of Automatic Updates takes place. Values ranging from 0 to 23 are based on the 24-hour clock.

- **UseWUServer (Reg_DWORD)**   Indicates whether the Automatic Updates client will contact an SUS server rather than contact the Microsoft Windows Update site. A value of 1 indicates that updates will be determined by connecting to an SUS server.

If you enable the SUS client to contact an SUS server, you must designate a server to act as the SUS server, and you must designate where statistics information will be sent. These statistics are stored in the HKLM\Software\Policies\Microsoft\Windows \WindowsUpdate registry key:

- **WUServer (Reg_SZ)**   This defines the URL of the SUS server. To designate the SUS server in the example.com domain as the SUS server, you would enter a value of **http://sus.example.com**, for example.

- **WUStatusServer (Reg_SZ)**   This defines the URL for the SUS statistics server. As with WUServer, you must enter the value in a URL format.

Office Update

In addition to updating the operating system, Windows computers running the Microsoft Office suite might have to apply updates to their software. The Microsoft Office Update Web site provides updates for the following versions:

- Microsoft Office 2000
- Microsoft Office XP
- Microsoft Office 2003

The Office Update Web site will search for relevant security updates, service packs, and other critical Office updates that are not related to security issues. A local administrator can update Microsoft Office files by connecting to the Web site and applying any updates recommended by the Web site.

Warning   To apply the updates from the Microsoft Office Update site, you require access to the original software distribution files. Be prepared to insert your Microsoft Office installation CD or to connect to the network installation distribution point.

To apply Microsoft Office security updates, use the following procedure:

1. Ensure that you are logged on as a local administrator.

2. Open Internet Explorer and open the Office Update site at *http://officeupdate.microsoft.com*.

3. On the Office Update page, click the Check For Updates link.

4. If prompted, click Yes to download the latest version of the Office Update Installation Engine.

5. The progress of the Office Update Inspection Engine is shown on the screen. Once complete, the required updates for your Microsoft Office installation are displayed. Select the updates you want to apply, and then click Agree And Start Installation.

6. On the Please Confirm Your Selection page, review your selections, and then click Next.

7. On the Please Have Your Office Product CD Ready page, ensure that you have access to the Office installation files, and then click Next.

Note If you have Office 2003 installed on your computer, you should *not* require the original installation files, unless you have chosen to delete the installation files during setup.

The download progress is displayed. When the download is complete, the installation of the selected Office updates proceeds. When the installation is complete, the Installation Result page should indicate that the installation was successful.

Note You might have to repeat the Office Update process a few times. Some Office updates have dependencies and cannot be installed until the depending updates are installed first. Repeat the process until no further updates are recommended.

Windows Update Services

Windows Update Services (WUS) is the evolution of Software Update Services. WUS automates the update management process in a Windows network, but increases the scope of available applications for update. WUS not only updates the Windows operating system, it can also provide updates for other Microsoft software.

Note WUS was in beta testing at the time this book was written. Some changes in the product might occur before the product is released to production.

WUS will initially support updates for the Windows operating system, Office, Microsoft Exchange Server, SQL Server, and SQL Server 2000 Desktop Engine (MSDE). WUS is built to allow expansion of the software products it supports and that can be updated without having to upgrade or redeploy the existing WUS infrastructure.

New Features in Windows Update Services

In addition to supporting updates for more than just the Windows operating system, WUS introduces several new features based on the input of the user community.

Target Groups

Updates can be deployed to target groups. Before WUS, if you wished to deploy updates to a focus group, you had to deploy SMS with the Update Services Feature Pack or a separate SUS server for the target group. WUS allows you to define target groups and to approve specific updates for each target group. The use of target groups enables you to pilot updates on a smaller focus group.

Two default target groups exist in WUS: *All Computers* and *Unassigned Computers*. Each client computer is added to both of the default groups. You can move computers from the Unassigned Computers group to any custom target groups that you define. A client computer can be assigned to a specific target group within the registry of the client or by using Group Policy applied to the OU where the computer's account exists.

SQL Database Backend

The WUS database is moved to a SQL Server–based backend storage. The WUS database stores the following WUS information:

- WUS server configuration
- Metadata descriptions for each update stored on the WUS server
- Client information, including target groups created on the WUS server
- Updates for the Windows operating system and other applications
- Information on how clients interact with the available, approved updates

> **Note**   WUS must be managed from the WUS Web console or by using WUS APIs. You cannot manage WUS by directly manipulating the WUS database.

Each WUS server must have its own SQL Server–compatible database. Multiple WUS servers cannot connect to the same SQL Server server, but a WUS server can connect to an existing, remote SQL Server computer. The SQL Server database server must support Windows authentication because WUS does not support SQL Server authentication.

The following three SQL Server database options have been tested for use with WUS:

- **SQL Server 2000 Desktop Engine (MSDE)**   MSDE is available from Microsoft as a free download. It is based on SQL Server 2000, but is restricted for performance and restricts the maximum database size to 2 GB.

- **Windows SQL Server 2000 Desktop Engine (WMSDE)**   WMSDE is a lightweight SQL Server included with the WUS distribution files. WMSDE can be installed only on a computer running Windows Server 2003. WMSDE must be managed from the WUS interface because no user interface or tools are provided for WMSDE. WMSDE does not limit the database size or the maximum number of connections allowed to connect to the database.

- **SQL Server 2000**   WUS supports the full-featured SQL Server 2000 database software. SQL Server 2000 must have Service Pack 3a or later applied to work with WUS.

> **Note**   If you implement SQL Server 2000, you must enable the *nested triggers* server global option. The installation of WUS enables the *recursive triggers* option for the WUS database, but cannot enable a global option automatically.

Bandwidth Improvements

WUS improves the use of bandwidth for the update process. The improvements are gained through the following changes in the WUS architecture:

- **Deferral of updates**   WUS allows an administrator to download an update's metadata separately from the update itself. This separation enables the administrator to review the purpose of the update and to approve the update without actually downloading the update to the local WUS server.

- **Download of approved updates only**   Once an update is approved by a WUS administrator, it is then downloaded to the WUS server. Nonapproved updates are not downloaded until they are approved, saving on both bandwidth and disk space.

- **Filtering of updates**   A WUS administrator can filter the updates that are downloaded to the WUS server. A WUS administrator can filter on products and classification of updates as shown in Figure 27-5.

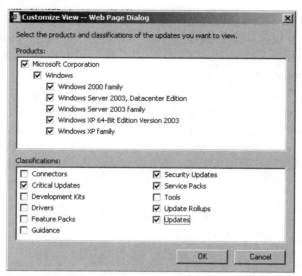

Figure 27-5   Choosing what products and classification of updates are applied by WUS

■ **Use of the Background Intelligent Transfer Service (BITS) 2.0**   BITS 2.0 provides file transfer capability to all WUS transfer actions. BITS enables asynchronous transfer of updates files, takes advantage of spare bandwidth to transfer the files in the background, and enables a file transfer to be resumed in the event that the client computer is disconnected from the network during the transfer.

■ **Use of express installation files**   WUS can implement express installation files to limit the bandwidth used to deploy updates to clients on the internal network. The tradeoff of reducing the bandwidth usage on the internal network is that the initial download from the Microsoft Windows Update site is larger. Express installation files identify the actual bytes that change between the existing version of the file and the updated version included in the security update. An express installation downloads only the changes necessary to the existing files rather than the entire updated version of the file. The net result is the same, but the amount of data transferred to the client is much smaller.

Warning   Express installation files are always larger on the initial download than standard update files because they must have knowledge about all existing versions of the updated files so that the correct updated bits are sent to each version client.

Migrating from Software Update Services

If you have an existing SUS deployment, you cannot migrate directly to WUS. You can, however, migrate the existing approvals and updates that are already downloaded. The migration of the approvals and updates is performed by using the Wusutil.exe command-line tool.

Note The Wusutil.exe command-line tool must be run at the WUS target server by a member of the local Administrators group. The WUS server must be running on a 32-bit version of the Windows operating system.

The Wusutil.exe commandline tool, found in the WUS install drive:\Program Files\Microsoft Windows Update Services\Tools folder, uses the following syntax:

```
WUSUTIL.EXE migratesus /content SUSContentLocation /approvals SUSServerName
TargetGroup /log LogFileName
```

Where:

- **/content *SUSContentLocation*** Indicates the source location for the SUS content. The SUSContentLocation can be a local folder designation or a remote Universal Naming Convention (UNC) path to the SUS update location.

- **/approvals *SUSServerName*** Indicates the DNS or NetBIOS name of the SUS server that will provide the source of approval information.

- ***TargetGroupName*** Indicates the target group to which the approvals and updates are applied. Delimit the target group name with quotes if the name contains spaces. If no name is provided, the installation assumes that the approvals and contents are intended for the All Computers target group.

- **/log *LogFileName*** Indicates that the process is logged and that the log results are stored in the provided file name.

Note The Wsutil.exe commandline tool can migrate the approvals, the content, or the content and approvals.

Microsoft Baseline Security Analyzer

The Microsoft Baseline Security Analyzer (MBSA) is a tool that can determine which critical updates are installed on a target computer, as well as which security updates are required. MBSA enables you to analyze the current computer, a remote computer, a specified list of computers, a range of IP addresses, or all computers in a designated domain. The tool scans computers for an update status based on a downloaded XML catalog file and reports the status in output files or to the screen.

MBSA allows scanning for common security misconfiguration errors on target computers. MBSA reports only on the current status of the computer and does not provide you with any distribution functionality. After a computer is analyzed, other tools must be used to deploy the missing service packs and updates. Otherwise, the missing service packs and updates must be manually downloaded and installed.

Note To run MBSA, a user must be a local administrator on the target computer. This prevents attackers from using MBSA to scan a remote computer to determine potential weaknesses.

MBSA version 1.2.1 scans for the latest service packs and security updates for the following products:

- Microsoft Windows NT 4.0 (remote scans only)
- Windows Server 2003, Windows 2000, and Windows XP (local and remote scans)
- IIS 4.0, IIS 5.0, IIS 5.1, and IIS 6.0
- SQL Server 7 and SQL Server 2000 (including Microsoft Data Engine)
- Internet Explorer 5.01 or later
- Windows Media Player 6.4 or later
- Exchange Server 5.5 and Exchange 2000 Server (including Exchange Admin Tools)
- Exchange Server 2003
- Office 2000, Office XP, and Office 2003 (local scans only)
- Microsoft Data Access Components (MDAC) 2.5, 2.6, 2.7, and 2.8
- Microsoft Virtual Machine
- MSXML 2.5, 2.6, 3.0, and 4.0

- BizTalk® Server 2000, BizTalk Server 2002, and BizTalk Server 2004

- Commerce Server 2000 and Commerce Server 2002

- Content Management Server (CMS) 2001 and CMS 2002

- Host Integration Server (HIS) 2000 and HIS 2004

- SNA Server 4.0

Note   In addition to scanning for service pack and security updates, MBSA scans for common security-related configuration issues for the operating system and stores the results of the scans in XML format files.

What About HfNetChk?

MBSA version 1.2.1 includes the same functionality provided by Shavlik's hotfix network checker (HfNetChk) tool, meaning that Microsoft no longer provides updates to the HfNetChk tool. You can still download and use the HfNetChk tool from the Shavlik Web site to scan for security updates. The functionality is the same as the MBSA command-line version. Because Microsoft no longer provides updates to the HfNetChk tool, we recommend you visit the Shavlik Web site for updates.

In addition, Shavlik produces a full-feature version of the tool, known as HfNetChkPro, which provides a GUI interface and allows the distribution and installation of missing security updates after the initial scan. For more information on Shavlik tools for security updates, see *http://www.shavlik.com*.

Scanning for Updates in the GUI Mode

By default, MBSA runs in a GUI mode that enables you to define scanning options and view the results of the security scan in the MBSA window. The security update scan performed by MBSA scans and reports only on updates designated as critical security updates by the Microsoft Windows Update site.

Note   If you enable the option to use an SUS server, MBSA does not download the updates from the SUS server. Instead, MBSA reports only updates approved at the SUS server in its XML report for the target computer.

When scanning for security updates, perform the following procedure:

1. Open MBSA.

2. Choose whether to scan a single computer or multiple computers.

3. To scan for security updates only, designate your target computer or computers as shown in Figure 27-6, enable the Check For Security Updates option, and click Start Scan.

4. When the scan is complete, you can view an XML file for each computer. For each computer, the output will report any missing security updates for the Windows operating system, IIS, Windows Media Player, Exchange Server, and SQL Server, as well as give a security assessment rating for the target computer.

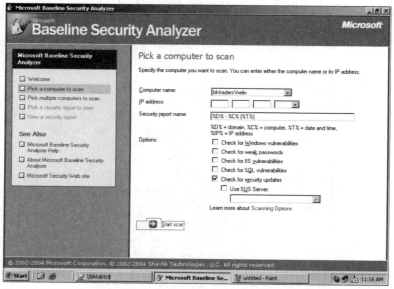

Figure 27-6 Scanning for security updates with MBSA

Security scan reports are stored in the %userprofile%\SecurityScans folder at the computer where MBSA is executed. The reports are in an XML format and are best viewed in the MBSA interface.

More Info For more information on using MBSA for performing security audits, see Chapter 29, "Using Security Assessment Tools."

Scanning for Updates with the Command-Line Version of MBSA

MBSA includes a command-line version executable, Mbsacli.exe, which can perform scans for security updates and service packs. Version 1.2.1 of the Mbsacli.exe utility can perform the same tests performed by Shavlik's HfNetChk.exe utility.

When you execute Mbsacli.exe with the /hf switch, indicating an HfNetChk-style scan, all security-related updates are included in the scan and the resulting reports. The results of the Mbsacli.exe scan are displayed in the command window rather than in XML files.

When scanning for security updates with the Mbsacli.exe /hf command, you can use the following parameters:

- **-h** *hostname* Scans the computer designated by the NetBIOS computer name. If not included, the local host is scanned. Multiple computers can be scanned by separating each host name with a comma.

- **-fh** *filename* Scans the computer names specified in the named text file. The text file must contain one computer name per line, with a maximum of 256 names.

- **-i** *xxx.xxx.xxx.xxx* Scans the designated IP address. You can designate multiple IP addresses by separating each entry with a comma.

- **-fip** *filename* Scans the IP addresses designated in the named text file. The text file must contain one IP address per line, with a maximum of 256 IP addresses.

- **-fq** *ignorefile* Identifies a file that includes Microsoft Knowledge Base articles to ignore during the security updates scan. The file must contain one Knowledge Base article number per line.

- **-r** *xxx.xxx.xxx.xxx–xxx.xxx.xxx.xxx* Specifies a range of IP addresses to be scanned.

- **-d** *domainname* Specifies that all computer accounts in the designated domain name are to be scanned.

- **-n** Scans all computers on the local network. The computers scanned include all computers listed in Network Neighborhood or My Network Places, no matter what domain membership is held by the computer accounts.

- **-history** *level* Filters the display of software updates so that only software updates are displayed that meet the designated level: (1) explicitly installed, (2) explicitly not installed, or (3) effectively installed.

- **-sus** *SUSServer*   Uses the indicated SUS server to determine which updates to scan for during a security updates scan.

- **-t** *threads*   Designates how many threads to use when executing a scan. The default value is 64, but can be set to a value between 1 and 128 inclusive.

- **-o** *output*   Specifies the format of the output produced by the scan. You can choose from (tab), which outputs the data in a tab-delimited format, or (wrap), which produces output in a Word wrapped format.

- **-s 1**   Suppresses NOTE messages. NOTE messages do not include an installable executable but provide a detailed procedure that must be performed to prevent the security vulnerability associated with the update.

- **-s 2**   Suppresses WARNING messages. WARNING messages do not prescribe remedies to prevent vulnerabilities. They simply state that the usage of the specific service is considered a security weakness.

- **-nvc**   Suppresses searching for an updated version of MBSA during the scan process.

- **-nosum**   Specifies that the computer should not perform checksum validation for the security update files.

- **-z**   Specifies that the computer should not perform registry checks.

- **-v**   Displays verbose details when a security update is determined to be missing. This is useful when you receive NOTE or WARNING messages.

- **-f** *filename*   Specifies the name of a file in which to store the results.

- **-u** *username*   Specifies the user name to use when scanning a local or remote computer or groups of computers.

- **-p** *password*   Specifies the password to use when scanning a local or remote computer or groups of computers. You must use this switch with the user name switch. Note that this password is not sent over the network in cleartext. Instead, Mbsacli.exe implements NT LAN Manager (NTLM) authentication.

- **-unicode**   Produces Unicode output during the scan.

- **-x** *XMLfile*   Specifies an XML data source for the security scan. If not specified, the latest version of MSSecure.xml is downloaded from the Microsoft Web site.

- **-sum**   Performs file checksum tests. It is recommended you use this option if you are using a custom XML file that includes language-specific checksums.

More Info   For a complete listing of the parameters available when running Mbsacli.exe /hf, see Knowledge Base article 303215: "Microsoft Network Security Hotfix Checker (HfNetChk.exe) Tool Is Available" (*http://support.microsoft.com/kb /303215*).

SMS 2.0 Software Update Services Feature Pack

The SMS 2.0 Software Update Services Feature Pack provides the capability of determining the security update status for SMS clients and distributing and installing the necessary updates to them. In addition, the feature pack provides reporting tools that allow the creation of detailed reports outlining your company's security update distribution.

The SMS 2.0 Software Update Services Feature Pack provides stronger management capabilities than any of the other Microsoft patch management solutions because it enables you to target specific computers within the company for security updates. Likewise, by leveraging the capabilities of SMS 2.0, you can perform the following tasks:

- **Identify all computers on the network.**   SMS inventory capabilities enable you to identify all computers connected to the corporate network, identify installed applications, and determine current security updates.

- **Schedule the deployment of security updates.**   SMS software can distribute identified security updates to SMS clients during nonpeak hours.

- **Enable status reporting.**   SMS queries can determine the progress of security update distribution to identify computers that have not yet received and installed critical updates.

- **Enable local distribution of updates.**   SMS allows security updates to be replicated to multiple software distribution servers. This enables clients to connect to local or nearby software distribution servers for security update installations.

- **Enable support for more operating systems.**   All SMS clients—not just Windows 2000–based, Windows XP, and Windows Server 2003–based computers—can receive security updates by using the SMS 2.0 Software Update Services Feature Pack.

The SMS 2.0 Software Update Services Feature Pack is composed of four tools for the distribution of security and Microsoft Office software updates:

- **Security Update Inventory tool**   Creates an inventory of security updates for each SMS client computer. The inventory identifies current and missing security updates for each computer and stores the results in the SMS inventory. The Security Update Inventory tool is composed of three components:

    - **Security Update Inventory Installer**   Runs on the SMS site server and builds the packages, collections, and advertisements to deploy other SMS tool components to SMS clients.

❑ **Security Update Inventory tool**   Uses MSSecure.xml and MBSA to carry out security scans of SMS client computers for installed or required security updates. The resulting data is converted into SMS inventory data.

❑ **Security Update Sync tool**   Runs on a single computer with Internet access. This computer checks with the Microsoft Windows Update Web site to download the latest MSSecure.xml file.

■ **Microsoft Office Inventory tool**   Creates an inventory of installed and required Microsoft Office updates for SMS client computers. The Microsoft Office Inventory tool consists of three components:

❑ **Office Update Inventory Installer**   Runs on the SMS site server and builds the necessary packages, collections, and advertisements to deploy the other components required for Microsoft Office updates.

❑ **Office Update Inventory tool**   Performs scans of SMS client computers for installed or required Office updates. The collected information is stored as SMS inventory data.

❑ **Office Update Sync tool**   Runs on a single, Internet-accessible computer. This tool downloads the latest Office Update Inventory tool and Office Update inventory database and uses SMS distribution points to deploy the latest versions to SMS client computers.

■ **Distribute Software Updates Wizard**   Performs the software and security update distribution tasks in the SMS environment. The wizard consists of three components:

❑ **Distribute Software Updates Wizard Installer**   Runs on the SMS site server and installs the Distribute Software Updates Wizard component.

❑ **Distribute Software Updates Wizard**   Analyzes the update status for all SMS client computers based on the SMS inventory information. Once the status is determined, the wizard allows you to review and authorize updates for distribution, download updates, create packages and advertisements for each update, distribute advertisements to SMS clients, and deploy the Software Updates Installation Wizard (discussed next).

❑ **Software Updates Installation Wizard**   Evaluates advertised software updates against current updates on the client computer to ensure that only required updates are installed at the SMS client computer.

■ **SMS Web Reporting tool**   Provides the ability to create and view reports based on the inventory information collected by the software inventory tools. You can track the deployment of individual updates as well as the update status of a specific computer or group of computers. When this tool is used with the Web Report add-in for Software Updates, the software update inventory information can be viewed with a Web browser.

Microsoft Systems Management Server 2003

SMS Server 2003 improves the patch management process in both the administration and end-user experiences. The following sections outline the major changes included in the SMS 2003 patch management solution.

> **Note**   The updates to SMS 2003 are mainly operational updates. The actual process of checking for update requirements and installation of the updates has not changed greatly between SMS 2000 and SMS 2003.

Administrative Experience

SMS 2003 improves the experience for administrators deploying software updates. Some of the improvements include the following:

- **Enforcing deployment time windows**   Software updates can be restricted to specific time windows, preventing updates from being applied between company-enforced restricted hours.

- **Separating update deadlines from the advertisement schedule**   Update deadlines are enforced independently of the advertisement schedule. If an update advertisement is received just one hour before the deadline for installation, the deadline is enforced.

- **Improving source location management**   Source locations for MSI-based applications can be maintained dynamically, removing the need to display prompts for the installation CD-ROM during updating or repair of an MSI package.

- **Allowing multiple program items in a package**   You no longer must create separate packages for separate programs. Multiple programs can now be bundled in a single package and assigned a custom program name.

- **Allowing different deployment settings for the same package**   You can deploy package subset and superset content using different end-user settings, such as enforcing that some users have 5 days in which to apply the update, whereas others have 21 days.

- **Identifying shutdowns caused by patch management**   The Windows Server 2003 Shutdown Event Tracker (SET) can identify shutdowns caused by known updating operations, identifying that the shutdown operations were expected.

- **Improving deployment methods**   You can now target updates to Active Directory containers and OUs and even delegate the ability to target updates. The deployment wizard also supports designation of Distribution Point Groups *within* the wizard.

- **Extending Support for all forms of updates**   You can now deploy MSI-based updates (*.msp) directly, not just *.exe updates.

- **Improving upgrade options**   The scanning tools used by SMS 2003 can be upgraded in place rather than having to uninstall the previous version and reinstall the update as in SMS 2.0.

- **Improving testing of updates**   You can now test the deployment on a pilot group while updates are safely replicated to full production staging locations. Once the pilot is complete, you can move the update to production at a faster pace.

- **Improving reporting**   You can now produce reports on infrastructure health, deployment status, and compliance of target computers. In addition, compliance data is automatically summarized in SQL views. You can also determine whether updates are uninstalled by users of the computer.

- **Improving status messages**   Status messages are clearer and include localized, detailed text with remediation procedures for failures and warnings.

End-User Experience

In addition to improving the administrative experience, SMS 2003 also provides improvements for the end users of the SMS 2003 patch management system. These improvements include the following:

- **Improving reboot scenarios**   Reboot scenarios are improved in SMS 2003 in many ways, including the following:

    - ❏ **Separating installation and reboot tasks**   Separate schedules can be maintained for installation of updates and reboots following the updates.

    - ❏ **Protecting open application data**   The reboot process will use a graceful shutdown, saving any data before shutting down the computer.

    - ❏ **Minimizing the number of reboots**   Fewer reboots are needed because of the optimization of reboot detection for temp files versus required file replacement and previous update attempts.

- **Improving the installation experience**   Users can now apply an update at their convenience without having to follow the SMS 2003 advertisement schedule. In addition, each advertised update can provide custom context information that will inform users why they are applying the update to their computers. SMS 2003 also uses less resources and scans faster than SMS 2000, providing a better experience for the end user.

- **Improving notification**   SMS 2003 can implement periodic reminders on a three-hour interval. The notifications allow users to click an icon in the notification area to view reminders for upcoming patch update deadlines.

Best Practices

■ **If you manually install multiple security updates on target computers, use the QChain tool.**   sousing QChain.exe ensures that the most current version of any DLL or executable is retained. If the operating system is Windows XP, Windows 2000 with Service Pack 3 or later, or Windows Server 2003, QChain is not required because the QChain functionality is built in.

■ **Maintain a copy of the Office installation files.**   The application of software updates for Microsoft Office 2000 and Office XP requires access to the original installation source files. Office 2003 might not require access if the original installation files are maintained on the client and were not deleted during the installation process.

■ **Configure the Automatic Updates client to implement the desired installation method.**   By configuring the installation method for Automatic Updates, you ensure that your organization's updates are downloaded and installed regularly.

■ **Use Windows Update only for scanning a single computer or a small group of computers.**   Windows Update scans can be performed only against the current computer.

■ **Use MBSA to diagnose security update status.**   MBSA allows you to scan multiple computers to determine if security updates are current.

■ **Use the command-line version of MBSA to script security update reporting.**   The Mbsacli.exe tool enables you to create scripts that scan a single computer, an IP address range, or an entire domain for security update status.

■ **Use the SMS 2.0 Software Update Services Feature Pack or SMS 2003 to deploy software patches to a subset of computers on your network.**   The SMS 2.0 Software Update Services Feature Pack and SMS 2003 allow you to define specific targets for software patch deployment, enabling you to pick and choose targets for patch deployment.

■ **Use SUS and the SMS 2.0 Software Update Services Feature Pack to enable reporting on the status of software patch deployment.**   Because of the data stored in SMS inventory, the SMS 2.0 Software Update Services Feature Pack can produce more detailed reports.

■ **Use SUS to support up to 5,000 client computers.**   If you must support more than 5,000 computers, consider using the SMS 2.0 Software Update Services Feature Pack or other third-party security update deployment software.

Additional Information

- "Understanding Patch and Update Management: Microsoft's Software Update Strategy" (*http://www.microsoft.com/technet/security/topics/patch/patchmanagement.mspx*)

- Microsoft Software Update Services Web site (*http://www.microsoft.com/windowsserversystem/sus/default.mspx*)

- Software Update Services Interactive Simulation (*http://www.microsoft.com/windowsserver2003/evaluation/demos/sims/sus/viewer.htm*)

- "Software Update Services Overview" white paper (*http://www.microsoft.com/windowsserversystem/sus/susoverview.mspx*)

- "Software Update Services Deployment" white paper (*http://www.microsoft.com/windowsserversystem/sus/susdeployment.mspx*)

- "Deploying Windows XP SP2 Using Software Update Services (SUS)" (*http://www.microsoft.com/technet/prodtechnol/winxppro/deploy/xpsp2sus.mspx*)

- SMS 2.0 Software Update Services Feature Pack (*http://www.microsoft.com/SMServer/downloads/20/featurepacks/suspack/default.asp*)

- *Systems Management Server 2003 Concepts, Planning, and Deployment Guide* (*http://www.microsoft.com/downloads/details.aspx?familyid=784838b3-34e0-4122-b3e2-17c5b4eef8f4&displaylang=en*)

- Microsoft Windows Update Services Web site (*http://www.microsoft.com/windowsserversystem/wus/default.mspx*)

- *Microsoft Windows Update Services Deployment Guide* (*http://www.microsoft.com/windowsserversystem/wus/deployment.mspx*)

- "Step-by-Step Guide to Getting Started with Microsoft Windows Update Services" (*http://www.microsoft.com/windowsserversystem/wus/stepbystep.mspx*)

- Background Intelligent Transfer Service 2.0 (*http://go.microsoft.com/fwlink/?LinkId=15106*)

- Microsoft Baseline Security Analyzer home page (*http://www.microsoft.com/technet/security/tools/Tools/MBSAhome.asp*)

- Shavlik Technologies (*http://www.shavlik.com*)

- Microsoft Windows Update Web site (*http://windowsupdate.microsoft.com*)

- Microsoft Office Update Web site (*http://officeupdate.microsoft.com*)

- The following Knowledge Base articles:

  ❑ 296861: "Use QChain.exe to Install Multiple Hotfixes with Only One Reboot" (*http://support.microsoft.com/kb/296861*)

  ❑ 303215: "Microsoft Network Security Hotfix Checker (HfNetChk.exe) Tool Is Available" (*http://support.microsoft.com/kb/303215*)

  ❑ 320454: "Microsoft Baseline Security Analyzer (MBSA) Version 1.2.1 Is Available" (*http://support.microsoft.com/kb/320454*)

  ❑ 322365: "Server requirements and recommendations for installing Microsoft Software Update Services" (*http://support.microsoft.com/kb/322365*)

  ❑ 843183: "Versions of Microsoft Baseline Security Analyzer that are earlier than MBSA version 1.2 are no longer supported" (*http://support.microsoft.com/kb/843183*)

Part VI
Planning and Performing Security Assessments and Incident Responses

Chapter 28

Assessing the Security of a Network

By now, you have vigilantly implemented security measures and deployed security updates. But how do you know if your network is really secure? If you have not yet asked yourself this question, now is a good time to do so. Security trickles down through organizations, from executives to IT managers, and eventually to you, the network administrator. Unlike many IT implementations, where clear, tangible indicators of success exist and direct proof of this question can be delivered, no network is 100 percent secure.

For example, if you deploy a Dynamic Host Configuration Protocol (DHCP) infrastructure, you can see when it is functioning properly. If the DHCP infrastructure is not functioning properly, users will be quick to recognize the symptoms and notify the help desk. Similarly, over time, you can prove the success of the DHCP infrastructure through the number of support incidents received by the help desk and the uptime of the DHCP services. The same cannot be said of security. It is much more difficult to provably secure a resource. Also, security compromises can go undetected for extended periods of time.

Often the first indicator of a security malfunction is the compromise of the network. Even good security can become susceptible to compromise when a new vulnerability is exposed or a tool is published to exploit a previously little-known, difficult-to-execute vulnerability. In truth, at any point in time, your organization is secure only to the best of your knowledge. By conducting security assessments, you can provide executives and managers with some evidence of how secure the network is, as well as give yourself some peace of mind.

More Info   This chapter provides only an introduction to performing security assessments; for in-depth information on how to plan and perform security assessments, see *Assessing Network Security* (Microsoft Press, 2004).

Types of Security Assessments

Your organization can use different types of security assessments to verify its level of security on network resources. You must choose the method that best suits the requirements of your situation. Each type of security assessment requires that the people conducting the assessment have different skills. Consequently, you must be sure that the people—whether they are employees or external security experts—have extensive experience with the type of assessment you are interested in.

Vulnerability Scanning

Vulnerability scanning is the most basic type of security assessment. Vulnerability scanning assesses a network for potential security weaknesses that are well known and well understood. Vulnerability scanning is generally carried out by a software package but can also be accomplished through custom scripts. Vulnerability scanning software frequently requires administrative rights on a network because of technical reasons or controls built into the scanning software, but some scanning does not require this level of access. In general, vulnerability scanning assessments assume that the person carrying out the scan is an administrator. Most commercial vulnerability scanning software packages do the following:

- **Enumerate computers, operating systems, and applications**   Vulnerability scanning software searches network segments for IP-enabled devices, including computers and network devices. It also identifies the configuration of the devices, including the operating system version running on computers or devices, IP protocols and Transmission Control Protocol/User Datagram Protocol (TCP/UDP) ports that are listening, and applications installed on computers.

- **Identify common security misconfigurations**   Such software scans for common security mistakes, such as accounts that have weak passwords, files and folders with weak permissions, default services and applications that might need to be uninstalled, and mistakes in the security configuration of common applications.

- **Search for computers with known vulnerabilities**   Vulnerability scanning software scans computers for publicly reported vulnerabilities in operating systems and applications. Most vulnerability scanning software packages scan computers against the Common Vulnerabilities and Exposures (CVE) index and security bulletins from software vendors. The CVE is a vendor-neutral listing of reported security vulnerabilities in major operating systems and applications and is maintained at *http://cve.mitre.org*.

■ **Test for exposure to common attacks**   Such software tests computer and network devices to see whether they are vulnerable to common attacks, such as the enumeration of security-related information and denial-of-service attacks.

Vulnerability scanning is effective in assessing a common weakness discovered on a network that has not been previously scanned and when verifying that security policy is being implemented on software configuration. Because vulnerability scanning reports can expose weaknesses in arcane areas of applications and frequently include many false positives, network administrators who analyze vulnerability scan results must have sufficient knowledge and experience with the operating systems, network devices, and applications being scanned and their role in the network.

For example, a vulnerability scan of a server running Microsoft Windows 2000 might reveal that global system objects and process tracking are not audited. An inexperienced administrator who has no knowledge of the functionality of global system objects and process tracking might see this report and decide to enable auditing on these two things, reasoning that auditing is a recommended security measure. In reality, enabling auditing on global system objects and process tracking does little to augment an organization's security and will almost certainly result in filling up the Event log quickly with no real benefit.

> **Caution**   Vulnerability scanning software is limited to what it can detect at any one point in time. As with antivirus software, which requires that the signature file be updated when new viruses are discovered, vulnerability scanning software must be updated when new vulnerabilities are discovered and improvements are made to the software being scanned. Thus, the vulnerability scanning software is only as effective as the maintenance performed on it by the software vendor and by the administrator who uses it. Vulnerability scanning software is not immune to software engineering flaws that might lead it to miss or misreport serious vulnerabilities.

The Microsoft Baseline Security Analyzer (MBSA) is an example of a primitive vulnerability scanning application. The MBSA can scan computers that are running Microsoft Windows NT 4.0, Windows 2000, Windows XP, and Windows Server 2003, as well as applications such as Microsoft Internet Explorer, Microsoft Internet Information Services (IIS), and Microsoft SQL Server. The MBSA scans for the installation of security updates and service packs, common vulnerabilities such as weak passwords, and security best practices such as checking to see whether auditing is enabled.

> **More Info**   For detailed information on MBSA, see Chapter 29, "Using Security Assessment Tools," in this book.

Penetration Testing

Penetration testing, often called pen testing, is a much more sophisticated type of security assessment than vulnerability scanning is. Unlike vulnerability scanning, which generally examines the security of only individual computers, network devices, or applications, penetration testing assesses the security of the network as a whole. Also, penetration testing, by definition, assumes that the pen tester does not yet have administrator rights in contrast to vulnerability scanning. (In fact, the goal of many pen tests is to obtain administrator credentials.) Penetration testing can help educate network administrators, IT managers, and executives about the potential consequences of a real attacker breaking into the network. Penetration testing also reveals security weaknesses missed by vulnerability scanning, including how vulnerabilities are exploited and weaknesses in people and processes:

- **How vulnerabilities are exploited**   A penetration test not only will point out vulnerabilities, it also will document how the weaknesses can be exploited and how several minor vulnerabilities can link those exploited vulnerabilities and, in combination with them, compromise a computer or network. Most networks inevitably will have vulnerabilities you will not be able to resolve because of business or technical reasons. By knowing how these vulnerabilities can be exploited, you might be able to take other types of security measures to prevent them from compromising the network—without disrupting business continuity.

- **Weaknesses in people and processes**   Because vulnerability scanning is based on software, it cannot assess security that is not related to technology. Both people and processes can be the source of security vulnerabilities just as easily as technology can. A penetration test might reveal that employees routinely allow people without identification to enter company facilities where they have physical access to computers. Similarly, a penetration test might reveal process problems, such as not applying security updates until a month or two after they are released, which would give attackers a seven-day window to strike known vulnerabilities on servers.

Because a penetration tester is differentiated from an attacker only by intent and permission, you must use caution when allowing employees or external experts to conduct penetration tests. Penetration testing that is not completed professionally can result in the loss of services and disruption of business continuity.

Caution   Before conducting any type of penetration testing, you must get the appropriate approval from management. If you are not an employee of the company and specifically employed to perform pen tests, you should ensure that you have the appropriate contract in place for performing any type of security assessment. The contract should include a clear description of what will be tested and when the testing will take place. Because of the nature of penetration testing, failure to obtain this approval might result in committing computer crime, despite your best intentions. Because national and local laws on computer crime and contracts vary greatly, you are best advised to consult a lawyer before accepting consulting engagements that include pen testing.

IT Security Audit

IT security auditing differs greatly from vulnerability scanning and penetration testing. IT security auditing generally focuses on the people and processes used to design, implement, and manage security on a network. In an IT security audit, the auditor and your organization's security policies and procedures use a baseline. A proper IT security audit helps determine whether your organization has the necessary components to build and operate a risk-appropriate, secure computing environment.

Unlike vulnerability scanning and penetration testing, IT security audits can be conducted by people without significant technical skills; conversely, the skills needed to perform a good audit are not necessarily those possessed by technical employees. IT security audits are essential elements of regulatory compliance. For example, if you work in the health care industry in the United States, your organization might be subject to Heath Insurance Portability and Accountability Act (HIPAA) security and privacy regulation. There is a reasonable chance that your organization's insurance company will ask for some type of proof of compliance, and this is where the IT security audit comes in. However, discussing how to conduct IT security audits is beyond the scope of this book.

More Info   The National Institute of Standards and Technology (NIST) has created an IT security audit manual and associated tool set to conduct the audit. You can download the manual and tool set from the NIST Automated Security Self-Evaluated Tool (ASSET) Web site at *http://csrc.nist.gov/asset/*.

How to Conduct Security Assessments

Conducting a security audit might help you answer the question, "How do I know if my network is really secure?" However, it will not improve the security of your network. Regardless of the type of security assessment that your organization undertakes, you can help increase the security of your network by implementing your security assessment in these three phases:

- Planning a security assessment
- Conducting a security assessment
- Resolving issues discovered during the security assessment

Planning a Security Assessment

The success of a security assessment is largely determined before the actual assessment begins: in the planning phase. Like most IT projects, the major cause of failure for security assessments is poor planning. To avoid this common pitfall, you can create project vision and scope documents.

Creating a Project Vision

The project vision for your security assessment should precisely describe the reason you are conducting the security assessment, the type of security assessment that will be done, the milestones for completing the project, and the project goals. Other items that the project vision commonly contains include the proposed budget for the project, explanations of project team roles and responsibilities, and metrics that can be used to determine the success of the security assessment.

The project vision document will help ensure that everyone working on the project understands the project goals and how the project will accomplish them. It is essential that you obtain executive sponsorship on the vision for the security assessment. Without executive sponsorship, the project will suffer from a lack of prioritization on the part of middle management and consequently might not receive the necessary budget.

Creating a Project Scope

The project scope for your security assessment details what you will be assessing the security of, which tools will be used, which methodology will be employed, and the time constraints of the project. The scope also defines which tasks are beyond the parameters of the project. For example, you might create a project scope for a two-week penetration test on a Web server, specifying that only publicly available tools will be used to attack a given Web server but prohibiting testers from using denial-of-service attacks or disrupting the services that the Web server provides.

Conducting a Security Assessment

Although it is obvious that you must document the results of a security assessment, the fact that you must document the procedures used in a security assessment might not be obvious. Unfortunately, well-organized and detailed documentation often is not created during IT projects, including security assessments, because it is somewhat time-consuming and often falls outside the skill set of administrators. Regardless of the type of security assessment that your organization plans to undertake, you must diligently document the procedures used during the security assessment to ensure that the result of the assessment can be used to augment the security of the network.

Documenting the methodology used during the security assessment will ensure that the results can be independently reviewed and reproduced if necessary. This documentation includes the tools used during the assessment and operating conditions and the assumptions made by the people conducting the assessment.

With vulnerability scanning, the methodology used might impact the result of the test. For example, vulnerability scanning software that runs under the security context of the domain administrator will yield different results than if it were run under the security context of an authenticated user or a nonauthenticated user. Similarly, different vulnerability scanning software packages assess security differently and have unique features, which both can influence the result of the assessment.

For penetration tests, detailed documentation of the methodology that was used during the test—regardless of whether it was successful in compromising the network—can be reviewed to find areas where your organization must make changes to secure the network. For example, knowing that a penetration tester compromised a domain controller does little to help you secure your network. However, knowing that a penetration tester was able to break into a file server by enumerating account information on local accounts through a null connection to the IPC$ share and discovering that the password for a local service account was contained in the description of the account can help you make the necessary changes to secure your network.

For IT security audits, documenting the methodology and tools used to perform the audit is essential. After the items found deficient in the audit have been resolved, or at some scheduled point in the future, the audit can be repeated in the same manner to assess the progress made since the previous audit. Because organizations frequently use progress made since prior audit findings as metrics to judge their relative success, maintaining such documentation is crucial.

Resolving Issues Discovered During the Security Assessment

After the security assessment is complete, the work of securing the network begins. You will need to analyze the results of the security assessment and determine which methods you can use to address the deficiencies discovered. The first step is to prioritize the deficiencies according to their impact on your organization. The following list details how you should prioritize such impacts:

1. **Danger to human safety**   Although not all organizations will have security vulnerabilities that, if exploited, could lead to the loss of life or otherwise jeopardize human safety, such vulnerabilities should always be given the highest priority.

2. **Destruction of data**   The next priority should be given to the destruction of data, especially when it results in total data loss. At any given point in time, data exists that has not been backed up to remote storage; if an attacker can gain access to this data and delete it, there is a good chance that it will not be able to be restored. For some organizations, losing even a day's worth of data would be devastating.

3. **Disclosure of confidential information**   Confidential data includes customer information, employee information, business plans, financial information, and trade secrets. The disclosure of this information can cause loss of customer confidence, litigation against the organization, loss of competitive advantage, and loss of intellectual property.

4. **Loss of services**   A denial-of-service attack causes organizations or their customers to lose the use of IT services. The impact of a denial-of-service attack depends on the nature of your organization's business. For example, the loss of IT services impacts a business-to-consumer (B2C) Web site or an ISP much more that it does a software vendor.

5. **Annoyances**   The least critical category of impact is that of attack vulnerabilities, which, if exploited, result in the minor disruption of business continuity, leading to nothing more than mere annoyances. For example, attacks that require a user to reboot her computer—such as attacks that flood a user's computer with NetBIOS messages sent to the console—will cause a minor disruption of business services and be a general annoyance to the user but will have no lasting consequences.

After you have prioritized the security issues discovered in the security assessment, you should incorporate them into your organization's risk management plan or at least apply them to the process your organization normally uses to mitigate security risks.

> **More Info**   See Chapter 1, "Key Principles of Security," for more information about managing risk.

Conducting Penetration Tests

Not all network administrators think like attackers or have the skill set required to break into networks. Conducting penetration tests requires you to think like an attacker. Additionally, you will need to have experience identifying weaknesses in network security, experience with tools that are used to compromise networks, and at least a basic level of expertise with one or more programming languages. If you are not confident in your abilities to think like an attacker, you should consider enlisting the help of another administrator or a consultant who is.

For a penetration test to be useful to your organization for more than just proving that weaknesses in security exist, you must carefully document your actions. The first step in conducting a penetration test is to create a methodology that you will follow when attempting to break into the network. This methodology will help ensure that you complete all the attacks that you have outlined, budget your time appropriately, and establish a foundation for creating documentation on the results of the penetration test.

The objective of the penetration test is to compromise the intended target or application. To accomplish this goal, a patient attacker will stick to a well-defined methodology. For example, if you are conducting a penetration test, you might want to follow these steps:

1. Gather information.

2. Research vulnerabilities.

3. Compromise the target application or network.

> **Note**   Within each of these steps, you should diligently document your actions and their results for reporting purposes. Many pen tests are unsuccessful at driving changes to increase the security of networks because this critical documentation is not compiled.

Step 1.   Gathering Information

Like an attacker, at first you might have little to no knowledge about your target network. But by the end of this step, you will have constructed a detailed road map of the network that you can use to break into the network in an organized manner. The goal of performing this step is to gather as much information as possible about the target network through publicly available sources. This will give you an indication of how large the target might be, how many potential entry points exist, and which security mechanisms exist to thwart the attack.

Gathering information, often called footprinting, requires you to be patient, detail oriented, and resourceful. During this step, you should gather the following types of information:

- Basic information about the target
- Domain Name System (DNS) domain name and IP address information
- Information about hosts on publicly available networks

Obtaining Basic Information About the Target

All information about the target and subsidiaries of the target is useful, including Web sites and other IT services offered by the target, contact information for the target, organizational structure, and names of employees. You can get most of this information on the Internet simply by searching the target organization's Web site and querying search engines by using the name of the target.

Basic information about the company will reveal details that might be used to generate passwords, points of entry into the target's network—including physical buildings and logical entry points such as phone numbers and names of key employees—that can be used in social engineering attacks, and a general understanding of the technical sophistication of the target. (For more on social engineering, see the "Social Engineering" sidebar.) For example, you can query Internet search engines on the name of the target and the strings "password for" and "ftp." Surprisingly, with a little fine-tuning, this tactic will unearth the logins to FTP servers used by many large organizations.

Social Engineering

Sometimes the easiest way to get information about a network or break into that network is to ask. As strange as it sounds, employees have been known to wittingly or unwittingly reveal important information about their company. For the attacker, it is about asking the right questions to the right person with the right tone. This exploitation of trust is called social engineering.

For example, an attacker might find the telephone number for the company switchboard operator and ask to be transferred to the help desk. Because the call is transferred rather than directly dialed, the call identification will appear to the help desk as though it originated internally. The attacker might then explain that he is a new employee and is very afraid of computers. The attacker might continue by saying he is not sure what his account name is and how long his password needs to be. After the help desk administrator patiently explains how account names are generated and the organization's password policy, the attacker might explain—while complimenting the help desk administrator on how smart she is and how well she explained the account and password problem—that his boss told him his account was enabled for remote access but that he lost the information about which server to connect to.

By the end of the conversation, the attacker will have a good idea of how hard breaking into the network by logging on with a valid user's credentials might be. The attacker can use the names of employees he has gathered from the Web site and information learned from the help desk about the password policy to attempt to log on to the remote access server by using passwords that users are likely to pick. Meanwhile, the help desk administrator will end the conversation feeling as though she did a great job in assisting a user who really needed help.

An attacker might even gain access directly to the network simply by asking. In July 2002, a student at the University of Delaware was caught changing her grades in the school's database system by calling the university's help desk and pretending to be her professors. In all cases, she reportedly stated that she had forgotten her password and asked to have it reset, and in all cases, the help desk obliged.

Social engineering is difficult for organizations to defend against, especially if network administrators and other employees in key positions (such as administrative assistants) do not know that they might be the target of such attacks. Consequently, security awareness training is essential for everyone in the company.

Using DNS Domain Name and IP Address Information

By using information about the target network stored on DNS servers, you can begin to create a diagram of the target organization's network. You can analyze DNS zones for the target organization to obtain information, including the server host names, services offered by certain servers, IP addresses of servers, and contact information for members of the IT staff.

By analyzing DNS records, you also can get a pretty good idea about the location of the servers and the operating system or applications that are being run on the server. For example, you might be able to deduce that a computer with the host name SFO04E2K that is registered with a Mail Exchange (MX) record is a server running Windows 2000 and Microsoft Exchange 2000 Server and is located in San Francisco, or that a network device named cis2500dt2 is a Cisco Systems 2500 series router directly connected to the target's ISP. One of the first things that attackers do is create a network diagram with information gained from analyzing DNS zones.

The IP address information about the target—gained from the DNS zone, American Registry of Internet Numbers (ARIN), and other sources—can be scanned with port-scanning software to further develop your network diagram. Attackers have been known to use publicly available sources to create better network diagrams on the target network than the target network's administrators have.

Enumerating Information About Hosts on Publicly Available Networks

After gathering the IP addresses used by the target network, an attacker can begin the process of profiling the network to find possible points of entry. You can mimic common approaches taken by attackers by enumerating information about hosts that are exposed to the Internet by the target organization. To accomplish this, you can use port-scanning software to scan hosts for listening TCP/UDP ports and IP protocols. Port scans will reveal information about hosts such as the operating system running on the host and the services running on the host.

You can use port scanning to determine how router and firewall IP filters are configured. An effective attacker will be able to produce a network diagram for all publicly accessible screened subnets and a reasonably complete listing of the types of traffic allowed in and out of the network.

An attacker also can use software to crawl the target organization's public Web sites and FTP sites. Often, organizations have information that is not intended for public use posted on their public Web sites or FTP sites but not listed in these sites' directory structures. Similarly, information that would be useful for breaking into the network might be embedded in the code that the Web pages are written in. For example, a developer might have placed a note to himself about a test login ID and password in the comments of an HTML page or might have used static login information for connections to a server running SQL Server. After downloading the Web pages or FTP files to a local computer, an attacker can run a program such as Grep to search for text strings in the files.

Step 2.   Researching Vulnerabilities

After the attacker has completed gathering information about the target network and has created a list of operating systems, network devices, and applications running on the network (including information about how they are configured), her next step is to research their vulnerabilities. Aside from weak passwords and servers with no access control, the easiest way to break into a network is to exploit known vulnerabilities to the hardware and software used by the target organization.

Simple methods of compromising the security of computers, network devices, and applications might already exist. So before you spend any time attempting to break into your networks—using elaborate techniques that might reveal your existence—do your homework. Researching vulnerabilities when acting as an attacker is not any different from the research that you must do as a network administrator. Use the following resources for your sleuthing:

- **Hardware and software vendor Web sites**   The most obvious place to look for vulnerabilities in hardware or software is the vendor's Web site. In general, you can find product documentation that describes the default security of the hardware or software, knowledge base articles that describe how security works on the hardware or software, and security bulletins that describe known vulnerabilities in the vendor's products.

- **Security-related Web sites and newsgroups**   Numerous Web sites for security professionals discuss security and security weaknesses. You can often use this information to break into networks, too. For example, the Web site *http://www.netstumbler.com* has extensive information about wireless network security. Another good Web site is *http://www.securityfocus.com*, from which a mailing list called Bugtraq is operated. Bugtraq contains discussions about the latest security vulnerabilities in hardware and software.

■ **Web sites run by attackers and security researchers** Web sites run by attackers and security researchers often contain detailed information and tools that can be used to break into networks. If you are not familiar with how networks are compromised, you can learn a lot about how attackers compromise networks by browsing these Web sites. As with all information, the content of these sites can be used for good purposes and malicious ones. Because in some countries possessing tools that are used to break into computer networks is against the law, you should be careful about downloading tools from these Web sites. Check your local computer crime laws first. Furthermore, many of the applications that can be downloaded from these Web sites have to be modified and are Trojan horse applications themselves.

Step 3. Compromising the Target Application or Network

After you have gathered information about the target network and fully researched potential avenues of attack, you can begin the process of attempting to compromise the network. In general, the compromise of a network starts with the compromise of a single host. Many ways to compromise a network exist, and without knowing the details of a specific scenario, it is difficult to prescribe a precise set of actions. However, when compromising a network, attackers will attempt to accomplish several tasks, including these:

1. **Get passwords** The first thing that an attacker will do is copy the passwords or password databases from the compromised host to a computer controlled by the attacker. If the compromised host is a member server running Windows 2000, the attacker will retrieve the password hashes from the Security Accounts Manager (SAM) database, the local security authority (LSA) secrets, and the passwords stored by Internet Explorer autocomplete. Immediately after obtaining the password hashes, the attacker will begin an offline attack on them.

2. **Gather information** After the attacker gains access to a host inside the target's network—whether in a screened subnet or in the internal network—the attacker gains a new source of information about the network. Consequently, the attacker returns to step 1 in this methodology and begins gathering basic information about the network from the inside.

3. **Elevate privileges** After an attacker has initially penetrated the network, one of her first goals is to gain access to or create elevated security credentials. Once an attacker has Administrator or System privileges on a computer or network device, little can be done to prevent her from doing whatever she wants to that computer or device. Similarly, if an attacker can obtain control over a domain administrator account, the attacker functionally controls the entire network.

4. **Leverage the compromised host**   Once under the control of the attacker, a compromised host becomes a platform for attacking other computers on the network from the inside. The attacker might also use the host as a zombie system to attack another network.

5. **Replace files**   An attacker might want to either ensure that she can continue to access the compromised computer or gather information from users of the computer. To accomplish this, the attacker can install a backdoor application or keystroke logging software to record the keystrokes of locally logged on users, including their passwords.

> **Important**   During a penetration test, you should compromise the network only in ways agreed to by the target organization ahead of time. You should not disrupt business continuity when performing a penetration test.

Best Practices

- **Use security assessments to evaluate the security of your network.**   Security assessments will help answer the question, "How do I know that my network is really secure?" You can also track progress toward improving the security of your network by repeating a security assessment after you have addressed the weaknesses discovered in the initial security assessment.

- **Choose the appropriate type of security assessment for your business or technical requirements.**   The security assessments discussed in this chapter are very different: each attempts to assess different areas of security, requires special areas of expertise, and calls for different levels of investment from your organization. To ensure that the security audit you perform meets the needs of your organization, choose the appropriate security assessment. For example, conducting a vulnerability scan probably will not reveal issues with IT security policies and procedures, just as an IT security audit probably will not reveal that weak passwords are used on servers.

- **Take time to carefully plan your security assessment project.**   As with most IT projects, the major reason that security assessments fail is poor planning. To avoid this pitfall, take time during the planning stage to create a project vision and a scope to guide the security assessment. Do not conduct a security assessment without executive sponsorship.

- **Document in detail the methodology used to conduct the security assessment.**   To ensure that the security assessment results can be independently reviewed and reproduced if necessary, carefully document the methodology used to conduct the security assessment.

Additional Information

- *Assessing Network Security* (Microsoft Press, 2004)

- The MBSA Web site (*http://www.microsoft.com/technet/security/tools /mbsahome.mspx*)

- Automated Security Self-Evaluation Tool (ASSET) on the National Institute of Standards and Technology (NIST) Web site (*http://csrc.nist.gov/asset/*)

- *Hacking Exposed: Windows 2000* (McGraw-Hill Osborne, 2001), and *Hacking Exposed: Windows Server 2003* (McGraw-Hill Osborne, 2003)

Chapter 29

Using Security Assessment Tools

Once you have implemented a security baseline configuration on your computers that run Microsoft Windows Server 2003, Windows 2000, and Windows XP, you should periodically review the security configuration by using security assessment tools. These tools enable an administrator to perform three separate yet related tasks:

- **Define security baselines by role**   Security tools can define the required security configuration for a specific server role. For computers running Windows 2000 and Windows XP, you can define the required baseline security settings in a security template. Windows Server 2003 Service Pack 1 introduces the Security Configuration Wizard. The Security Configuration Wizard uses a predefined and extensible knowledge base to help you create baseline security configurations for servers based on their role in the network.

- **Identify when computers deviate from the established security baseline**   Security assessment tools can identify when a computer's configuration has been modified, which would result in weaker overall security of the host.

- **Identify new risks to computers**   Assessment software can scan for newly discovered vulnerabilities by detecting whether recent hotfixes have been applied or by determining whether recommended security configurations have been implemented on scanned hosts.

This chapter discusses how to implement security assessment tools to perform these tasks.

Defining Baseline Security

The Security Configuration Wizard is a tool that enables administrators to reduce the attack surface of Windows servers. This wizard is included with Windows Server 2003 Service Pack 1 and is available only for the Windows Server 2003 operating system at the time of this book being published.

> **Note**   For computers running Windows 2000, Windows XP, and Windows Server 2003 pre–Service Pack 1, it is recommended you continue designing and implementing security templates to enforce a security baseline. The process of creating and implementing security templates is covered in Chapter 11, "Creating and Configuring Security Templates."

The user running the Security Configuration Wizard is asked a series of questions designed to determine the functional requirements of a server. Based on both the current configuration of the server and the answers provided to the wizard, the Security Configuration Wizard uses its security configuration database to configure a security policy to lock down the target computer.

The primary goal of the Security Configuration Wizard is to define security based on the role played by the target computer. The wizard contains predefined security configuration definitions for over 50 roles, including those for servers running Microsoft SQL Server, Microsoft Exchange Server, and Certificate Services and domain controllers. Not only does the Security Configuration Wizard provide configuration settings for computers configured for a single role, but also determines dependencies if a computer holds several roles.

The Security Configuration Wizard determines the security configuration from information stored in its XML-based security configuration database. The database contains role-specific security configuration information that is derived from best practice documents, white papers, prescriptive architecture guides, and other Microsoft security documentation and literature. Rather than having to read all of the documentation and determine the best way to secure a specific role, you can use the Security Configuration Wizard, which enables you to apply the recommended guidelines by selecting roles and answering a few questions posed by the wizard.

> **Tip**   Rather than using the local copy of the security configuration database, you can implement a network share that maintains a centralized copy of the security configuration database. To use a centralized copy, the person running the Security Configuration Wizard must specify the location of the central database by running **scw /kb \\server\scwkbshare**.

Installing the Security Configuration Wizard

The Security Configuration Wizard is available only as an installation option once you upgrade a computer running Windows Server 2003 to Service Pack 1. Once upgraded, the Security Configuration Wizard is available as an installable option in Add/Remove Programs. To install the Security Configuration Wizard, use the following procedure:

1. Log on as a user that is a member of the local Administrators group on the target computer.

2. In Control Panel, open Add Or Remove Programs.

3. In the Add Or Remove Programs dialog box, click Add/Remove Windows Components.

4. On the Windows Components dialog box (see Figure 29-1), in the Components listing, select Security Configuration Wizard, and then click Next.

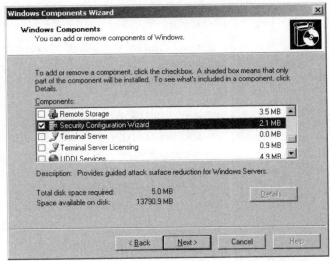

Figure 29-1   Installing the Security Configuration Wizard

5. When the installation is complete, click Finish.

6. Close the Add Or Remote Programs dialog box.

The installation installs both a graphical and command-line version of the Security Configuration Wizard. The graphical version is added to the Administrative Tools folder and the command-line version (Scwcmd.exe) is added to the %Windir%\System32 folder.

Security Configuration Wizard Actions

When authoring the security policy, the Security Configuration Wizard performs the following actions:

- **Disables unnecessary services**   Only the services required by the roles implemented at the target computer are enabled. All other services are disabled by the wizard. If a service is unknown to the wizard, you have the choice of disabling the service or leaving the service with its current startup state.

- **Blocks unused ports**   Once all services are defined, only the ports required by those services are enabled on the target computer. If the target computer is multihomed, the wizard can limit services to specific interfaces. Port blocking is accomplished using a combination of the Windows Firewall and Internet Protocol Security (IPSec).

- **Configures audit settings**   The Security Configuration Wizard enables you to define your auditing objectives, allowing you to range your audit collection from auditing for intrusion detection to enabling forensic investigation. You can choose to enable auditing for successes or for both successes and failures.

- **Disables unnecessary IIS Web extensions**   If Microsoft Internet Information Services (IIS) is installed on the target computer, unnecessary IIS Web extensions are disabled. For example, if the role does not require Active Server Pages, the Active Server Pages are disabled by the wizard if they are currently enabled on the target computer.

- **Reduces protocol exposure for LDAP, NTLM, and SMB**   The Security Configuration Wizard poses a series of questions to identify which clients will connect to the target computer, and then secures Lightweight Directory Access Protocol (LDAP), NTLM, and Server Message Blocks (SMBs) based on the answers you provide. Specifically, the wizard implements the following security measures:

  - **LDAP**   Implements LDAP signing, which ensures that the data received by domain controllers comes from a known source and that the data has not been tampered with by an attacker.

  - **SMB**   Enables SMB signing and removes support for file sharing using Transmission Control Protocol (TCP) port 139 if older clients do not exist on the network.

Note   Client computers that run Windows Server 2003, Windows 2000, and Windows XP can connect to file shares using the Common Internet File System (CIFS), which establishes a connection to TCP port 445 on the server.

❑ **NTLM** Removes support for LAN Manager authentication if the user indicates that no clients running earlier versions of the Windows operating system, including Windows 95 and Windows 98, exist on the network. Also enforces use of NTLMv2 if the clients on the network support this measure. The inputs provided to the wizard determine the LmCompatibilityLevel registry setting enforced on the target computer.

■ **Uses IPSec and Windows Firewall to secures ports that are left open** If a port is enabled at the target computer, IPSec and Windows Firewall can be implemented to restrict which computers are allowed to connect to the port. Windows Firewall can be implemented to allow access only to the enabled ports.

■ **Imports existing Windows security templates** The Security Configuration Wizard also enables users to import existing Windows security templates. The existing security templates can include existing role definitions and settings that are not configured by the wizard.

Security Configuration Wizard Capabilities

In addition to authoring security policies, the Security Configuration Wizard includes the following additional capabilities to configure and analyze target computers:

■ **Active Directory integration** Security policies, transformed into group policies using the Scwcmd.exe command-line utility, can be linked to sites, domains, or OUs in the Active Directory directory service to apply the required security settings to computer accounts using the Group Policy engine.

■ **Analysis** A target computer's security configuration can be compared to a defined security policy to indicate whether the target computer is compliant or deficient when compared to the designated security policy.

■ **Command-line support** The Scwcmd.exe command-line utility can be used to perform configuration and analysis on multiple target computers. The command-line utility can also be used to transform a security policy into a Group Policy object (GPO).

■ **Editing** Security policies created using the Security Configuration Wizard can be modified based on changes in the network or in an organization's security policies.

■ **Remotability** You do not have to perform all operations and analysis on the local computer. A remote computer can be selected as a target for configuring a security policy or performing analysis for compliancy with a designated security policy.

> **Note**   To perform remote configuration and configuration and analysis operations, the user performing the operation must be a member of the local Administrators group on the target computer.

- **Rollback**   If an applied security policy does not work as expected, you can completely undo the effects of the security policy, returning the computer to its pre-policy state.

- **Extensibility**   The Security Configuration Wizard can be extended to include custom server role definitions. The XML-based security database can be extended to apply the security configuration your organization defines for custom or third-party applications.

- **XSL views**   Extensible Stylesheet Language (XSL) can be used to transform the XML definitions of the Security Configuration Wizard knowledge base, security policies, and analysis results into HTML documents for viewing.

Assessing Security Configuration

Windows Server 2003, Windows 2000, and Windows XP enable you to define security configuration settings in security templates. Security templates contain security configuration settings for computer accounts, and the templates can be applied to the local computer directly or can be imported into a GPO. Importing a security template into a GPO linked to the OU where a computer account is located ensures consistent application of security template settings to all computers affected by the GPO.

Security templates applied by using a GPO can be affected by other GPOs and the local security policy applied to the computer account. Local policies and GPOs are processed in the following order:

1.   The local security policy defined for the local computer.

2.   Any GPOs defined for the site where the computer is located.

3.   Any GPOs defined for the domain in which the computer account exists.

4.   Any GPOs defined in the OU in which the computer account exists. GPOs are applied based on where they exist in the OU structure, with the GPOs applied at the OU where the computer account resides last.

> **Note**   If multiple GPOs are defined at a Group Policy container, GPOs are applied based on their order in the container's Group Policy tab. The GPO at the top of the list is applied last, ensuring that if conflicts exist, the GPO at the top takes precedence.

In addition to the default Group Policy inheritance model, the Resultant Set of Policies (RSoP)—the effective policies applied to the computer or user after the local policy and all group policies are applied—can be affected by the No Override and Block Policy Inheritance settings at the Group Policy container.

To determine whether security policy matches the security template, you can use one of two tools to analyze the computer's security configuration:

- The Security Configuration and Analysis console
- The Secedit command-line utility

The Security Configuration and Analysis Console

You can use the Security Configuration and Analysis console to determine whether the RSoPs applied to a computer differ from those defined in a security template.

When performing a security analysis, you import the security settings defined in one or more security templates into an analysis database. When you import the security templates, you can merge the template settings and create a composite security template. The order in which you import the security templates is important. As with GPOs, the settings of the security template imported last take precedence if settings in different security templates conflict.

 More Info   For more information on creating custom security templates to enforce security settings, see Chapter 11, "Creating and Configuring Security Templates."

To analyze current security settings of a local computer by using the Security Configuration and Analysis console, follow these steps:

- Open a blank Microsoft Management Console (MMC) and add the Security Configuration and Analysis console.
- In the console tree, right-click Security Configuration And Analysis and click Open Database.
- In the Open Database dialog box, create a new database by entering a name in the File Name box. Then click Open.
- In the Import Template window, select the security template that defines the required settings for the computer and click Open.
- In the details pane, right-click Security Configuration And Analysis and click Analyze Computer Now.
- In the Error log file path, click OK to create a log file in the default location.

When the analysis is complete, the Security Configuration and Analysis console displays the results, as shown in Figure 29-2.

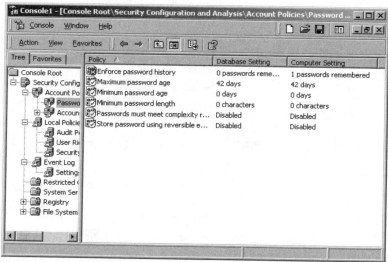

Figure 29-2   Analysis results of the Security Configuration and Analysis console

The console uses the icons shown in Table 29-1 to describe how well the security template settings are enforced at the analyzed computer.

Table 29-1   Output of the Security Configuration and Analysis Console

Icon	Description
Red X	The entry is defined in the analysis database and on the system, but the security setting values do not match.
Green check	The entry is defined in the analysis database and on the system, and the setting values match.
Question mark	The entry is not defined in the analysis database and therefore is not analyzed. This occurs when a setting is not defined in the analysis database or when the user running the analysis does not have sufficient permissions.
Exclamation point	This item is defined in the analysis database but does not exist on the actual system.
No highlight	The item is not defined in the analysis database or on the system.

> **Warning** A red *X* does not necessarily indicate a security configuration weakness. The actual system can be configured more securely than the security level indicated by settings of the security template. For example, in Figure 29-2, the Enforce Password History setting indicates a mismatch between the security template and the actual computer configuration. In the security template, no passwords are kept in the password history, whereas the computer's current configuration does not allow a password to be reused when a user must change his password.

The Secedit.exe Command-Line Utility

The Secedit.exe utility includes all the analysis functionality of the Security Configuration and Analysis console. To use the Secedit utility to analyze whether a computer implements the security settings defined in a security template, use the following syntax:

```
secedit /analyze /db DBFileName /CFG SecurityTemplate /log LogPath /verbose
```

This command is composed of the following parts:

- **/analyze** Indicates that Secedit will compare the current security settings of the local computer against the security settings defined in *SecurityTemplate*.

- **/db *DBFileName*** Determines the analysis database file into which the *SecurityTemplate* settings are imported. You must indicate the full path to the security analysis database.

- **/cfg *SecurityTemplate*** Indicates one or more security template files to import into the security analysis database. You must indicate the full path to the security template file or files. This option is not required if the security analysis database exists and the desired security template is already imported.

- **/log *LogPath*** Provides the path to the folder where the log file is generated for security analysis.

- **/verbose** Enables verbose output during the security analysis.

Once the Secedit command process is complete, you can view the results in the Security Configuration and Analysis console by opening the database file referenced in the Secedit command in the Security Configuration and Analysis console.

Performing Security Assessments

In addition to comparing the security configuration of your computers running the Windows operating system with the baseline security settings defined in security templates, you should assess your computers for common security misconfigurations. You can use different tools for security assessments, including the following:

- **Microsoft Baseline Security Analyzer (MBSA)**   Analyzes common security misconfigurations
- **Port scanners**   Determine which available server ports are exposed to the Internet

Microsoft Baseline Security Analyzer

The MBSA tool enables you to assess the security configuration of one or more Windows-based computers. MBSA performs two major tasks:

- Scans for missing service packs and security updates. MBSA determines which hotfixes and service packs are not applied to a target computer. The MBSA tool can also filter the list of missing updates and service packs based on approved updates configured at a Microsoft Software Update Services (SUS) server.

> **More Info**   For more information about using the Mbsacli.exe command-line tool to determine which service packs and security updates are applied, see Chapter 27, "Using Patch Management Tools."

- Scans the Windows operating system, IIS, SQL Server, desktop applications, Windows Media Player, Exchange Server, and other Microsoft BackOffice applications for common security misconfigurations.

Tests Performed

The MBSA tool can be run from both a GUI and the command line. Both versions of MBSA perform the tests outlined in this section.

Security Update Checks   MBSA performs checks for security updates and service packs released for the following Windows operating systems, Windows components, and applications:

- Microsoft Windows NT 4.0 (remote scans only)
- Windows Server 2003, and Windows 2000, Windows XP (local and remote scans)

- IIS 4.0, IIS 5.0, IIS 5.1, and IIS 6.0

- SQL Server 7 and SQL Server 2000 (including Microsoft Data Engine)

- Internet Explorer 5.01 or later

- Windows Media Player 6.4 or later

- Exchange Server 5.5 and Exchange 2000 Server (including Exchange Admin Tools)

- Exchange Server 2003

- Microsoft Office 2003, Office 2000, and Office XP (local scans only)

- Microsoft Data Access Components (MDAC) 2.5, 2.6, 2.7, and 2.8

- Microsoft Virtual Machine

- MSXML 2.5, 2.6, 3.0, and 4.0

- BizTalk® Server 2000, BizTalk Server 2002, and BizTalk 2004

- Commerce Server 2000 and Commerce Server 2002

- Content Management Server (CMS) 2001 and CMS 2002

- Host Integration Server (HIS) 2000 and HIS 2004

- SNA Server 4.0

Windows Scan Results   MBSA will perform various operating system security checks for target computers running Windows NT 4.0, Windows Server 2003, Windows 2000, and Windows XP. The report shows whether the following vulnerabilities are found:

- **Administrators group membership**   MBSA identifies and lists all members of the local Administrators group. If more than two accounts are detected, MBSA reports a potential vulnerability.

- **Auto Logon feature**   MBSA reports whether Auto Logon is enabled at a target computer. If Auto Logon is enabled, MBSA determines how user credentials are stored. If user credentials are stored in an encrypted format in the registry, the tool reports the enabling of Auto Logon as a potential vulnerability. If user credentials are stored in plaintext, the tool reports a high-level vulnerability.

- **Automatic Updates**   MBSA reports whether the Automatic Updates feature is enabled and whether the updates are automatically installed on the target computer.

- **File system**   MBSA identifies whether all the target computer's volumes use the NTFS file system. Only the NTFS file system allows for local file security by implementing discretionary access control lists (DACLs) for each file and folder on the disk volume and auditing of all access attempts to files or folders.

> **Note**   To determine whether a remote computer implements the NTFS file system, the default administrative shares must be enabled on the target computer. For example, the C drive must be shared as C$.

- **Guest account**   MBSA identifies whether the Guest account is enabled on the target computer. An enabled Guest account can allow remote users to access the computer without providing credentials and will be reported as a vulnerability.

- **Local account passwords**   All passwords in the local account database are scanned to determine whether they are weak. MBSA will scan for blank passwords, passwords that match the user's account name, passwords that match the computer name, and commonly used passwords such as *password*, *admin*, or *administrator*.

- **Password expiration**   MBSA determines whether local accounts are configured with nonexpiring passwords.

- **RestrictAnonymous registry key**   MBSA determines whether the target computer restricts anonymous connections. You can allow all anonymous connections (which has an associated value of 0), prevent anonymous connections from enumerating Security Accounts Manager (SAM) accounts and names (which has an associated value of 1), or prevent all access without explicit anonymous permissions (which has an associated value of 2).

> **Warning**   If you configure the RestrictAnonymous registry key to prevent all access without explicit anonymous permissions at a Windows 2000 or Windows Server 2003 domain controller, you can prevent computers running earlier versions of Windows from connecting to the domain controller. Computers running earlier versions of Windows that are members of the domain cannot set up a Netlogon secure channel for authentication, domain controllers running previous versions of Windows in trusting domains cannot set up a Netlogon secure channel to allow interdomain authentication, the Browser service cannot retrieve domain and server lists from computers, Windows NT users cannot change an expired password, and Macintosh users can never change their passwords.

- **Windows Firewall**   If the scan is run on the local computer, the scan identifies whether the Internet Connection Firewall or the Windows Firewall is enabled on the scanned computer and whether the firewall is enabled for all network connections. The scan also identifies whether any exceptions or static inbound ports are enabled on the firewall.

In addition to reporting any Windows operating system vulnerabilities that are unpatched, MBSA will also report additional information about the target computer that could be relevant to a security assessment. These tests include the following:

- **Auditing**   MBSA determines whether auditing is enabled at the target computer. The tool does not look for specific audit settings—it only ensures that some form of auditing is enabled.

- **Services**   You can configure MBSA to scan for specific unnecessary services by editing the %Systemdrive%\Program Files\Microsoft Baseline Security Analyzer\Services.txt file. MBSA will scan the target computer to determine whether any of the listed services are enabled on the target computer.

> **Note**   When adding service names to the Services.txt file, you must use the registry-based name of the service. You can find the registry-based name for each service in the properties of the specific service in the Services console. For example, the registry-based name for the World Wide Web Publishing service is W3SVC.

- **Shares**   MBSA reports all shares on the target computer. This includes both manually created shares and administrative shares. For each share, the detected share and NTFS permissions are reported.

- **Operating system version**   MBSA identifies whether the operating system of the scanned computer is Windows Server 2003, Windows 2000, or Windows XP. Any older operating systems are flagged as insecure because of the lack of updates and patching for older operating systems.

IIS Tests   If any IIS components are installed on the target computer, MBSA performs a series of tests to detect common IIS security misconfigurations. These tests include the following:

- **Domain controller identification**   MBSA identifies whether a target computer is functioning as a domain controller. This allows the scanner to identify whether IIS is running on a domain controller. This is not reported as a high-level vulnerability if the target computer is running Microsoft Windows Small Business Server.

- **IIS Lockdown tool**   MBSA determines whether the IIS Lockdown tool is used to secure the target computer. If the target computer is running Windows Server 2003, MBSA identifies that IIS Lockdown is not required for computers running IIS 6.0.

- **IIS logging**   MBSA determines whether IIS logging is enabled on the target computer. IIS logging provides detailed information about each connection attempt to Web sites hosted on the IIS computer. The test also ensures that the World Wide Web Consortium (W3C) extended log file format is implemented.

- **IIS parent paths**   MBSA determines whether the ASPEnableParentPaths setting is enabled on the target computer. If enabled, this setting allows attackers to use the ".."syntax in URLs, permitting them to access files not available, by default, from the Web service. (The ".." syntax attempts to access files and folders in the parent folder of the current folder.)

- **Virtual directories**   MBSA scans for Microsoft Advanced Data Connector (MSADC) and Scripts virtual directories. These directories contain sample scripts that attackers can use to compromise IIS. The tool also looks for the IISadmpwd virtual directory on IIS 4.0 target servers. This virtual directory allows users to change their Windows passwords from a Web site.

> **More Info**   Virtual directories can be removed by running the IIS Lockdown tool. For more information on the IIS Lockdown tool, please see Chapter 24, "Implementing Security for Microsoft IIS."

- **IIS sample applications**   MBSA determines whether the default IIS sample applications are installed on the target server. The sample applications provide script samples that attackers can use to compromise the target server. These sample applications can be removed by running the IIS Lockdown tool against the IIS server.

SQL Server Checks   If SQL Server is detected on a target computer, MBSA scans for SQL Server security configuration issues. SQL Server tests are run against each SQL Server instance found on the computer. The specific tests include the following:

- **CmdExec rights**   MBSA ensures that only members of the Sysadmin role are assigned the CmdExec right.

- **Domain controller identification**   MBSA identifies whether a target computer is functioning as a domain controller. This allows the scanner to identify whether SQL Server or SQL Server 2000 Desktop Engine (MSDE) is running on the domain controller. This is not reported as a high-level vulnerability if the target computer is running Small Business Server.

- **SA password protection** MBSA determines whether the sa password or SQL Server service account and password are stored in plaintext in the Setup.iss, Sqlsp.log, or Sqlstp.log file found in the %Windir%\Temp and %Temp% folders.

- **SQL Server and MSDE local account password checks** MBSA determines whether the SA account's password is written in plaintext to the Setup.iss, Sqlstp.log, or Sqlspx.log file in a Microsoft SQL Server 7.0 environment. The Sqlstp.log and Sqlspx.log files are also checked for SQL Server 2000 if domain credentials are used to start SQL Server services.

- **SQL Server folder permissions** MBSA verifies that only the SQL Server service account and members of the target computer's local Administrators group have access to the following folders within the %Systemdrive%\Program Files folder:

  - ❑ Microsoft SQL Server\MSSQL$InstanceName\Binn
  - ❑ Microsoft SQL Server\MSSQL$InstanceName\Data
  - ❑ Microsoft SQL Server\MSSQL\Binn
  - ❑ Microsoft SQL Server\MSSQL\Data

- **SQL Server Guest account** MBSA determines whether the Guest account is assigned access to any databases other than Master, Tempdb, and Msdb. All databases that enable Guest access are included in the security report.

- **SQL Server registry permissions** MBSA ensures that the Everyone group is assigned only Read permissions for the HKLM\Software\Microsoft\Microsoft SQL Server and HKLM\Software\Microsoft\MSSQLServer registry keys.

- **Service account check** MBSA determines whether the SQL Server service account is a member of the local Administrators group or is assigned membership in the domain's Administrators or Domain Admins groups.

- **SQL Server account password strength** MBSA scans for blank or simple passwords used by the local Microsoft SQL Server accounts. The password checks include inspections for the following:

  - ❑ Blank passwords
  - ❑ Passwords that are the same as the user account name
  - ❑ Passwords that are the same as the computer account name
  - ❑ Passwords that are set to *password*, *sa*, *admin*, or *administrator*

- **SQL Server security mode**   MBSA reports whether the server running SQL Server is configured to implement Windows authentication mode or mixed mode. When Windows authentication mode is implemented, the instance of SQL Server depends on Windows authentication for all user authentication. In mixed mode, users might be authenticated by using Windows authentication or by the server running SQL Server. If authenticated by the server running SQL Server, the users' account and password pairs are maintained within the SQL Server system tables.

- **Sysadmin membership**   MBSA scans the target server to identify all members of the Sysadmin role on the server running SQL Server.

- **Sysadmin role membership**   MBSA determines whether the local Administrators group is assigned the local Sysadmin role on the SQL Server server, which gives the administrators full access to all databases hosted by the SQL Server server.

Note   If you receive a "No permission to access database" error message when scanning a server running SQL Server, the account used to execute MBSA does not have sufficient permissions for the Master database on the target SQL Server computer.

Desktop Application Checks   MBSA also checks for security issues with commonly used desktop applications. Specifically, MBSA scans for the following:

- **Internet Explorer Enhanced Security configuration for administrators and nonadministrators**   Internet Explorer Enhanced Security reduces a server's vulnerability by applying more restrictive Microsoft Internet Explorer security settings to reduce the exposure to attacks from Web content. Separate reporting indicates whether the Internet Explorer Enhanced Security is enabled for both administrators and nonadministrators of the target computer.

- **Internet Explorer security zones**   MBSA scans all defined Internet Explorer security zones and identifies zones not defined at the recommended level. Microsoft recommends that you implement Medium security for the Local Intranet, Trusted Sites, and Internet zones and High security for the Restricted Sites zone.

Note   A custom level might be reported as a false positive by MBSA. MBSA does not evaluate individual settings within a custom security level to determine whether security meets or exceeds recommended settings.

- **Macro security**   MBSA issues a warning if macro security is not at the recommended level for Microsoft Office applications. You should implement High macro security for Microsoft Word, Outlook, and PowerPoint and Medium macro security for Microsoft Excel.

Requirements for Running MBSA

The requirements for running MBSA vary, depending on the type of scan you are performing and whether you are scanning the local computer or performing a scan against remote computers. To perform a security assessment of the local computer, the following requirements must be met:

- The user must be a local Administrator of the target computer.

- The computer must be running Windows Server 2003, Windows 2000, or Windows XP.

- The computer must have Internet Explorer 5.01 or later installed.

Additional requirements exist when you perform a scan of a remote computer:

- The user must be a member of the local Administrators group on all target computers.

- To allow remote IIS scanning, IIS Common Files must be installed on the computer running MBSA.

- The Workstation service and the Client for Microsoft Networks must be installed.

Requirements also exist for the remote computers that is the target of the MBSA scan. The remote computer must meet the following requirements:

- The remote computer must be running Windows NT 4.0 Service Pack 4 or later, Windows Server 2003, Windows 2000, or Windows XP.

- The remote computer must have the Workstation, Server, and Remote Registry services running. In addition, File And Print Sharing must be enabled.

- The remote computer must be running Internet Explorer 5.01 or later.

- To inspect for IIS vulnerabilities, the target computer must be running IIS 4.0 or IIS 5.0.

- To inspect for SQL Server vulnerabilities, the target computer must be running SQL Server 7.0 or SQL Server 2000.

- To inspect for desktop application vulnerabilities, the target computer must be running applications from Office 2003, Office 2000, or Office XP.

- If inspecting a remote computer, the scanning computer must be allowed to connect to TCP port 139, TCP port 445, User Datagram Prot (UDP) port 137, and UDP port 138 in the configuration of the Windows Firewall or Internet Connection Firewall.

Performing Graphical MBSA Assessments

The primary reason for using MBSA is to run security assessments from the GUI. To perform a scan against a single computer, you can use the following procedure:

1. On the desktop, double-click the Microsoft Baseline Security Analyzer shortcut. By default, the MBSA icon is automatically placed on the desktop upon installation.

2. On the Welcome To The Microsoft Baseline Security Analyzer screen, click Scan A Computer.

3. On the Pick A Computer To Scan page, you must indicate the computer name or the IP address of the computer, a name for the resulting XML report, and the specific security tests to perform, as shown in Figure 29-3.

4. Once the options are defined, click the Start Scan link. When the scan is complete, the results of the current scan are shown in the details pane and will include an overall security assessment.

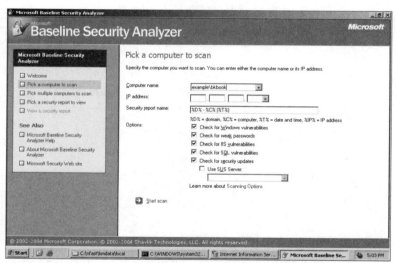

Figure 29-3   Defining scanning options for a single computer

You can choose to scan all computers in a specific domain or all computers within a specific IP subnet. The following procedure is used to scan multiple computers:

1. On the desktop, double-click the Microsoft Baseline Security Analyzer shortcut.

2. On the Welcome To The Microsoft Baseline Security Analyzer screen, click Scan More Than One Computer.

3. On the Pick Multiple Computers To Scan page, you must indicate either the domain or the IP address range to scan, a name format for the resulting XML reports, and the specific tests to perform, as shown in Figure 29-4.

4. When all options are defined, click the Start Scan link.

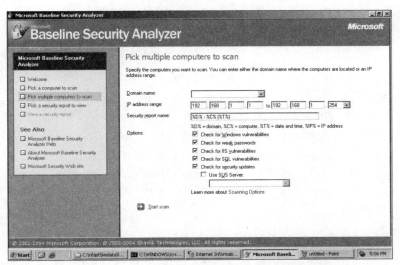

Figure 29-4   Defining scanning options for a multiple-computer scan

Once you complete either a single-computer or multiple-computer scan, the resulting reports are stored in XML format in the %UserProfile%\SecurityScans folder, where %UserProfile% is the full path of the user's profile folder. These reports are best viewed in the MBSA console by clicking the View Existing Security Reports link on the Welcome page.

Note   If a scan is performed against an entire domain or IP subnet, an individual report is produced for each detected computer.

Performing Text-Based MBSA Assessments

To perform a text-based MBSA assessment, you must use the text-based version of MBSA, Mbsacli.exe. This version of MBSA performs security assessments of either a single computer or multiple computers from a command prompt. The results are stored in XML format output files that can be viewed in the graphical version of the MBSA.

The command-line options for Mbsacli.exe include the following:

- **/c** *domain\computer*   Performs a security assessment of the designated computer.

- **/i** *xx.xx.xx.xx*   Performs a security assessment of the computer at the designated IP address.

- **/r** *xx.xx.xx.xx–yy.yy.yy.yy*   Performs security assessments of all computers with IP addresses in the designated range.

- **/d** *domain*   Performs security assessments of all computers in the designated domain.

- **/n** *options*   Bypasses the designated scanning options. Options include IIS, OS, Password, SQL, or Updates.

> **Note**   To bypass multiple tests, you can identify the test names in a single option. Valid values include OS, SQL, IIS, Updates, and Password. For example, to bypass IIS and SQL tests, you would type **/n IIS+SQL**.

- **/o** *Format*   Defines the format of the output XML file name. You can use a combination of %D% (domain), %C% (computer name), and %T% (date/time) when designating the format. The default format name is %D% -%C% (%T%).

- **/f** *Filename*   Redirects the output of the Mbsacli.exe command-line tool to the designated file name.

- **/qp**   Suppresses output of the scan progress.

- **/qe**   Suppresses output of any error listing.

- **/qr**   Suppresses output of any report listing.

- **/q**   Suppresses output of any scan progress, error, and report listing.

- **/s #**   Suppresses output for scan options. If you designate /s 1, all security update check notes are suppressed. If you designate /s 2, both security update check notes and warnings are suppressed. If you designate /s 3, all warnings except service pack warnings are suppressed.

- **/nvc**   Prevents Mbsacli.exe from checking for an updated version of MBSA.

- **/nosum**   Bypasses testing of file checksums when determining whether a security update is installed on the target computer or computers.

- **/sus** *SusServer*   Filters security updates so that only security updates approved at the designated Software Update Services (SUS) server are displayed.

Note   If no options are provided when running Mbsacli.exe, a security assessment of the local computer is performed, using all default options.

For a complete listing of all Mbsacli.exe command-line switches, see the MBSA Help file, available from the Welcome screen of the MBSA graphical tool.

More Info   For details on using the Mbsacli.exe text-based tool to scan for security updates by using a HfNetChk-style scan, see the "Scanning for Updates with the Command-Line Version of MBSA" section in Chapter 27, "Using Patch Management Tools."

Port Scanning

Another common security assessment task is to determine which ports are open to the Internet. Attackers can use port information to determine which services are accessible from the Internet. A port scanner inspects a target computer on the network and probes each port to determine whether the target computer is listening for connections on the scanner ports. A port scanner also identifies which ports are available to the scanner.

As part of your network security assessment, you should periodically perform external scans of your network to ensure that only authorized ports are exposed to the Internet. For example, if you perform a scan against the IP address of your company's Web server, the only ports open should be the ports for HTTP on TCP port 80 and for Secure Sockets Layer–protected HTTP on TCP port 443. Assuming you are not running any other services on the Web server, no other ports should be visible.

Tip   A common misconception is that you can "hide" a service by changing its listening port. This is not security, but more of a form of obfuscation. A port scanner can still show that the port is open, and a query to the port typically reveals the application that is listening on that port.

Common Windows Ports

When you perform a port scan, the main goal is to identify all open ports on the target computer. Ideally, if the computer is exposed to the Internet, the only exposed ports will be those the firewall publishes to the Internet.

When performing port scans, it is useful to identify common ports used by Windows and Windows services. Some of the more common ports on computers running Windows Server 2003, Windows 2000, and Windows XP are listed in Table 29-2.

The ports listed in Table 29-2 are the listening ports at a server. Typically, a client computer will use a random TCP or UDP source port above port 1023 when connecting to the server's listening port.

Table 29-2   Common Windows Ports

Port	Application
TCP port 20	FTP data
TCP port 21	FTP control
TCP port 23	Telnet
TCP port 25	Simple Mail Transfer Protocol (SMTP)
TCP port 53	Domain Name System (DNS) zone transfer
UDP port 53	DNS name resolution
UDP port 67	Dynamic Host Configuration Protocol (DHCP) server
UDP port 68	DHCP client
TCP port 80	Hypertext Transfer Protocol (HTTP)
TCP port 88/UDP port 88	Kerberos authentication
TCP port 110	Post Office Protocol version 3 (POP3)
TCP port 119	Network News Transfer Protocol (NNTP)
UDP port 123	Network Time Protocol (NTP)
TCP port 135/UDP port 135	Microsoft remote procedure calls (RPCs)
UDP port 137	NetBIOS Name Service
UDP port 138	NetBIOS Datagram Service
TCP port 139	NetBIOS Session Service
TCP port 143	Internet Message Access Protocol (IMAP) version 4
UDP port 161	Simple Network Management Protocol (SNMP)
UDP port 162	SNMP traps
TCP port 389/UDP port 389	Lightweight Directory Access Protocol (LDAP)
TCP port 443	Hypertext Transfer Protocol Secure (HTTPS)
TCP port 445/UDP port 445	Microsoft Common Internet File System (CIFS)
TCP port 464/UDP port 464	Kerberos password
UDP port 500	Internet Key Exchange (IKE) for IPSec
TCP port 563	NNTP with Secure Sockets Layer (SSL)
TCP port 636	LDAP with SSL (LDAPS)
TCP port 993	IMAP4 SSL
TCP port 995	POP3 SSL
TCP port 1433	SQL Server
UDP port 1701	Layer Two Tunneling Protocol (L2TP)

Table 29-2 **Common Windows Ports**

Port	Application
TCP port 1723	Point-to-Point Tunneling Protocol (PPTP)
UDP port 1812	Remote Authentication Dial-In User Service (RADIUS) authentication
UDP port 1813	RADIUS accounting
UDP port 2504	Microsoft Network Load Balancing (NLB) service remote control
TCP port 3268	LDAP Global Catalog
TCP port 3269	LDAP Global Catalog with SSL
TCP port 3389	Remote Desktop Protocol (RDP)
TCP port 5900	Virtual Network Computer (VNC) used by the Microsoft Virtual Server Remote Client listener
TCP port 8080	Microsoft Internet Security and Acceleration (ISA) Server proxy port

More Info   For a complete listing of assigned port numbers, see the Internet Assigned Numbers Authority (IANA) Web site at *http://www.iana.org/assignments /port-numbers*.

Determining Open Ports on the Local Computer

On the local computer, you can use the Netstat.exe command-line tool to show all open TCP and UDP ports. To show all open ports on the current computer, you can use the following Netstat command syntax:

```
Netstat -a -n
```

The -a indicates that all TCP and UDP listening ports are enumerated. The -n forces the output to show the actual open port numbers, rather than translating the port numbers to protocol names from the %windir%\system32\drivers\etc\services file.

Note   If you are running Netstat on a Windows XP–based or Windows Server 2003–based computer, you can also use the -o switch, which shows the process that is listening on each open port. This can help identify rogue applications on the local computer.

Alternatively, you can download the Port Reporter. The Port Reporter runs as a service on computers running Windows Server 2003, Windows 2000, and Windows XP. The benefit of the Port Reporter over the Netstat command is that the Port Reporter can provide service information over a specific time period, whereas Netstat shows only the currently open ports. For example, Port Reporter can detect a service that periodically opens a port, and then shuts down the port. Netstat would have to be executed at the same time that the port was open to detect and identify the port.

The reporting of the services differs between platforms. On computers running Windows XP, the service can log the following information:

- The ports that are used
- The processes that use the port
- Whether a process is a service
- The modules that a process loaded
- The user accounts that run a process

On Windows 2000–based computers, the service logs only the ports that are used and the times that the ports were used. In both cases, the Port Reporter service writes information to the %systemroot%\System32\LogFiles\PortReporter folder. By default, a log file can grow to 5 MB in size. Once the 5-MB limit is reached, new log files are generated.

Tip   You can download the Port Report Parser tool to view the log files in a Windows GUI interface. The Port Report Parser enables you to apply a filter against the logged data to better analyze the data. The tool is available at *http://www.microsoft.com /downloads/details.aspx?FamilyID=69ba779b-bae9-4243-b9d6-63e62b4bcd2e& displaylang=en*.

Install the Port Reporter service by running Pr-setup.exe from the extracted download file. Once it is installed, you must start the service to start the logging process.

Note   To stop recording data to the Port Reporter log files, you must stop the Port Reporter service. If you choose to remove the Port Reporter service, you must uninstall the service by running **Pr-setup.exe -u**.

Determining Open Ports on a Remote Computer

When performing security assessments, you can use a port scanner from the Internet to ensure that only required ports are open on an externally accessible server, such as a Web server.

To perform the port scan, you can use the Portqry.exe tool from the Windows 2000 or Windows Server 2003 Support Tools. The Portqry.exe tool enables you to scan specific port ranges on a remote computer to determine which ports are open.

> **Note**   The Portqry.exe tool uses the %systemroot%\system32\drivers\etc\services file to translate the port numbers to logical names when displaying its output.

The Portqry.exe tool uses the following syntax:

```
portqry -n server -p protocol [-e endpoint] [-r startpoint:endpoint]
[-o endpointList ]-l logfile -s -i -q
```

where:

- **-n** *server*   Performs the port scan against the IP address or DNS name provided for *server*.

- **-p** *protocol*   Performs the port scan for the TCP, UDP, or both protocols. If the option is not specified, the port scan will scan only TCP ports.

- **-e** *endpoint*   Performs the port scan against the single *endpoint port between 1 and 65535*.

- **-r** *startpoint:endpoint*   Performs the port scan over the range of ports designated. For example, to scan all ports between 1 and 80 inclusive, you would use **−r 1:80**.

- **-o** *endpointList*   Performs the port scan against the ports specified in the *endpointList* in the order specfied.

- **-l** *logfile*   Records the results of the port scan to the designated log file.

- **-s**   Implements a slow link delay to allow a longer time for UDP replies from remote systems.

- **-i**   Disables an IP address–to-name lookup if an IP address is specified for the remote host.

- **-q**   Performs the port scan with no output. The command will still return a 0 if the remote computer is listening on the designated port, a 1 if the target computer is not listening on the designated port, and a 2 if the target computer is listening on the port, but the response is filtered.

Best Practices

- **Define baseline security settings in security templates for Windows XP, Windows 2000, and Windows Server 2003 pre–Service Pack 1.**   By defining baseline security settings in security templates, you ensure that the required security settings can be reproduced on additional computers. Security templates also document the required security settings.

- **Define baseline security settings for Windows Server 2003 Service Pack 1 servers with the Security Configuration Wizard.**   The Security Configuration Wizard uses its knowledge base to provide prescriptive security settings based on server roles.

- **Use GPOs to ensure consistent application of security templates.**   By importing the security template settings into a GPO, you ensure that the security settings are consistently applied to the target computers and you prevent modification of the settings in the local security policy of a target computer. If you are using the Security Configuration Wizard, you can transform the results of the Security Configuration Wizard directly into a GPO, rather than import a security template.

- **Review security configuration of computers.**   Periodically, you should use tools such as the Security Configuration and Analysis console or the Secedit.exe utility to ensure that the security settings defined at a target computer do not differ from the security template defined for that computer configuration.

- **Test the proposed security configurations for servers.**   Ensure that the desired settings still allow the servers to function on your network. Once defined, a working baseline is available for other servers of the same role.

- **Perform regular security assessments of the computers on your network.**   Security assessments identify common security misconfigurations and security patches or updates that must be applied to the target computer.

- **Identify all open ports on computers exposed to the Internet.**   An attacker will typically scan an Internet-exposed computer to identify which ports are open and exposed to the Internet. By performing port scans from both the Internet and the local computer, you can ensure that only desired ports are exposed to the Internet. For example, a Web server should expose only TCP port 80 and TCP port 443 to the Internet. All other ports should not be accessible to the Internet.

Additional Information

- *Microsoft Windows 2000 Server Resource Kit*, Supplement 1, "Internet Information Services Resource Guide" (*http://www.microsoft.com/resources/documentation /Windows/2000/server/reskit/en-us/Default.asp?url=/resources/documentation /Windows/2000/server/reskit/en-us/w2rkbook/iis.asp*)

- Microsoft Baseline Security Analyzer (*http://www.microsoft.com/technet /security/tools/mbsahome.mspx*)

- Shavlik Technologies (*http://www.shavlik.com*)

- Microsoft Portqry.exe command-line port scanner (*http://www.microsoft.com /downloads/release.asp?ReleaseID=37344*)

- Port Reporter (PortRptr.exe) (*http://www.microsoft.com/downloads/ details.aspx?FamilyID=69ba779b-bae9-4243-b9d6-63e62b4bcd2e&displaylang=en*)

- Security Configuration Tool Set (*http://www.microsoft.com/windows2000 /techinfo/howitworks/security/sctoolset.asp*)

- Security Configuration Wizard for Windows Server 2003 (*http:// www.microsoft.com/windowsserver2003/technologies/security/configwiz /default.mspx*)

- "Step-by-Step Guide to Using the Security Configuration Tool Set" (*http:// www.microsoft.com/technet/prodtechnol/windows2000serv/howto/seconfig.mspx*)

- LmCompatibilityLevel (*http://www.microsoft.com/resources/documentation /Windows/2000/server/reskit/en-us/Default.asp?url=/resources/documentation /Windows/2000/server/reskit/en-us/regentry/76052.asp*)

- IANA port number assignments (*http://www.iana.org/assignments /port-numbers*)

- The following Knowledge Base articles:

  - 246261: "How to Use the RestrictAnonymous Registry Value in Windows 2000" (*http://support.microsoft.com/kb/246261*)

  - 310099: "Description of the Portqry.exe Command-Line Utility" (*http:// support.microsoft.com/kb/310099*)

  - 320454: "Microsoft Baseline Security Analyzer (MBSA) version 1.2.1 Is Available" (*http://support.microsoft.com/kb/320454*)

❑ 325494: "Support WebCast: Port Scanning Using PortQry" (*http://support.microsoft.com/kb/325494*)

❑ 832017: "Port Requirements for the Microsoft Windows Server System" (*http://support.microsoft.com/kb/832017*)

❑ 837243: "Availability and description of the Port Reporter Tool" (*http://support.microsoft.com/kb/837243*)

❑ 840832: "Support WebCast: Port Reporter" (*http://support.microsoft.com/kb/840832*)

❑ 839267: "Support WebCast: Vulnerability Assessment and the Microsoft Baseline Security Analyzer" (*http://support.microsoft.com/kb/839267*)

❑ 884289: "Description of the Port Reporter Parser (PR-Parser) Tool" (*http://support.microsoft.com/kb/884289*)

Chapter 30
Planning for Incident Response

Even if your network has solid protections in place, a determined attacker will almost certainly be able to penetrate your defenses at some point in time. Without a solid knowledge of what is normal, it can be very difficult to detect attackers. In addition to understanding the baseline of your network and its "normal" behavior, monitoring audits and other logs to detect anomalous behavior, and maintaining an inquisitive skepticism, you must have a framework to respond to security incidents. In this chapter, we look at the planning that your organization must do to be prepared to respond to security incidents.

Creating an Incident Response Team

The first step in creating a successful incident response process is to identify and enlist the necessary staffing resources. Although it is not essential that these staff members devote all of their time to incident response, defining an incident response team and the capacity in which they will act prevents any uncertainty from occurring during an incident response. Even if you have personnel who devote all of their time to incident response, taking the time now to define the employees who will assist that core group (to provide either specialized skills or additional manpower) will save time during a large-scale response. Furthermore, the members of the incident response team will be in the best position to create, maintain, and update the processes and guidelines associated with incident response. The three primary goals of this phase are the following:

- Obtaining an executive sponsor
- Identifying the stakeholders
- Choosing a team leader

Obtaining an Executive Sponsor

Before selecting a team, you must obtain an executive sponsor for your incident response efforts. The sponsor should likely be the CEO or one of her direct reports, though this can differ based on the structure and size of your organization. You need the executive sponsor to help remove obstacles associated with implementing the policies that support your incident response work and make the difficult decisions that sometimes must be made when responding to security incidents, such as turning off incoming traffic from the Internet. You will also need the sponsor any time a policy must be enforced by a member of your organization who is reluctant to do so for fear of retribution.

Your sponsor will need to be kept aware of the activities of the incident response team. She will likely want some form of tangible reporting on the successes and challenges of the incident response team, as well as the details of any incident, so that she can educate other members of senior management on the importance of security to your organization. Coupling such reporting with an accurate assessment of risk and exposure can be a powerful tool during budget discussions and one that affects the incident response team's long-term potential for success.

Identifying the Stakeholders

After a sponsor is in place, you must identify all stakeholders so that they can be included in policy discussions. Although senior IT staff will likely perform most core activities during an incident response, other individuals will need to be involved to ensure that the response is optimally successful from an overall business perspective.

As just implied, the members of the incident response team will not be limited to technical staff. Although senior members representing each technical specialty (operating systems, networks, databases, development, and so on) will certainly rank among the team's core members, the team also needs to include key representatives from all the company's major lines of business. These business leaders will ensure that an incident response protects the most essential assets of their work, intrudes minimally on specific initiatives they might have under way, and hopefully protects their ability to be successful as a business unit and contribute to the company's overall success.

The team will also need supporting members from various administration groups such as helpdesk, internal communications, and the legal department to ensure that the company minimizes liability during any incident response activities. The internal communications and helpdesk representatives will help facilitate communications with end users when such communications are required. Regardless of whether the legal representative is internal or external to your organization, he must be familiar with the concepts of expectation of privacy, evidentiary procedure, and downstream liability as well as the laws used in prosecuting computer crime—not only in your company's local jurisdiction but also worldwide to a certain extent. Rounding out the team will be members of your public relations department, who will be responsible for the communications described later in this chapter in the section "Creating a Communications Plan."

When not responding to incidents, team members can still conduct a wide variety of security-related activities. Some of these activities require additional planning and executive sponsorship, and all of them will benefit from a prescribed format that stems from process discussions about forming the incident response team. These activities include the following:

- Staying up-to-date on patches issued by vendors
- Staying up-to-date on industry trends by reading various online lists and IT trade periodicals
- Conducting security awareness activities to inform all staff how they contribute to the security of the organization
- Reviewing and testing new security products
- Analyzing publicly available information about the organization
- Baselining systems and reviewing related logs
- Performing an architectural review of the company's networks from a security perspective
- Testing restoration of systems from backup media
- Auditing systems to ensure compliance to policy
- Performing approved penetration testing of key systems

All these activities contribute in some manner to the incident response capability of your organization.

Choosing a Team Leader

Once the members of the team are in place, the team needs a leader. The team leader will be responsible for the actions of the entire incident response team and will coordinate those actions as well as sessions on the lessons learned during the response process. These sessions should follow each incident response. In addition, such sessions should be conducted periodically throughout the year (for example, every six months). The team leader will use the lessons learned to make policy update recommendations.

The role of the team leader differs from that of the incident response leader. Each incident will require a leader who will direct the response activities. All communications regarding the incident's progress should flow through this incident response leader to ensure that no duplication of efforts occurs and that the response team is optimally effective in its activities. The incident response leader is similar to a project manager in this respect.

Table 30-1 outlines the activities and roles of a typical incident response team.

Table 30-1   Incident Response Team Activities and Roles

| Activities | Basic Roles | | | | |
	Incident Leader	IT Contact	Legal Representative	Public Relations Representative	Line of Business Management
Performs initial assessment	Owner	Advises	None	None	None
Provides initial response	Owner	Implements	Informed	Informed	Informed
Collects forensic evidence	Owner	Implements	Advises	None	None
Implements temporary fix	Owner	Implements	Informed	Informed	Advises
Sends communication	Advises	Advises	Advises	Implements	Owner
Checks with local law enforcement	Updater	Informed	Implements	Informed	Owner
Implements permanent fix	Owner	Implements	Informed	Informed	Informed
Determines financial impact on business	Updater	Informed	Advises	Informed	Owner
Determines impact on brand or goodwill	Informed	Informed	Advises	Advises	Owner

Defining Incident Response Policy

Once the members of the incident response team have been identified, they should convene to build an incident response process and a supporting policy. Some of the related policies might already be in place in your organization, but the team will need to review how each of these policies relates to incident response and recommend changes that support incident response activities. The team must also formalize the approach to take should responding to an incident become necessary.

Categorizing Types of Incidents

Up to this point, we have been using the term *incident* in a generic manner. An incident is an occurrence that creates some level of crisis and requires action to reduce or eliminate the risk caused. Possible incidents, or threats, range from computer intrusion, denial of service, virus infestation, and inappropriate access to events that normally call for disaster recovery measures, such as power outages and other forms of force majeure.

Because of the wide range of incident types, it is helpful to define policies and procedures for each type of incident. Steps appropriate to foiling an attacker might not work as well when dealing with a citywide blackout or an insider viewing the salary details of the rest of the company's employees. By categorizing each type of threat and defining both proactive and reactive responses, your team can eliminate much of the ambiguity that occurs when executing a response.

Whether the occurrences to which your incident response team responds are accidental, malicious, or happenstance, the team members will require guidance on the response techniques expected of them. Such techniques must be defined in advance so that valuable response time is not wasted to define them during the crisis. As part of the overall incident response policy and process, a number of difficult decisions must be made and documented in advance of any incident. Doing so ensures that the roles and responsibilities of any given team member are not called into question during an incident response and that the boundaries of the activities that can be conducted without seeking additional approval are clear.

For example, when a federal agency in the United States reports a security incident, it is asked to give a severity rating based on the potential or confirmed damages. This listing is shown for example purposes in Table 30-2. Complete U.S. federal incident response information can be found on the U.S. Computer Emergency Response Team (CERT) Web site at *http://www.us-cert.gov/federal*.

Table 30-2   Incident Severity Guidelines for U.S. Federal Agencies

Priority Level	Priority Definition	Examples of Incidents	Time Frame to Report
1	Possible life-threatening activity, or affects classified or critical systems or information.	Root compromise User compromise Denial-of-service attacks Web site defacements Detection of malicious logic	Immediately
2	Incident could become public and provides unauthorized access to network and/or unclassified, noncritical information; affects systems resources; or shows active targeting of classified/critical systems.	User compromise Successful virus/worm infection Successful introduction of a virus/worm into a network Scanning of classified or critical systems	Within 2 hours of discovery/detection
3	Incident shows active targeting of unclassified, noncritical systems or potential threat to network.	Scanning of unclassified, noncritical systems Detection and elimination of malicious logic before infestation	Weekly
4	Incident shows possible malicious intent or unintentional violation of security policy.	Misuse of resources Spam e-mail Fraudulent e-mail Social engineering	Monthly

Although these severity levels might not be indicative of the threats that your organization faces, they do serve as good examples.

Tip   Ensure that the incident response team's escalation path, priorities, process, and constraints are clearly defined and documented before an incident occurs. Failing to do so will likely result in wasted time during critical periods of the incident response as team members try to define their roles and responsibilities on the spot or locate members of the management team for additional approval or instruction.

Outlining Proactive and Reactive Responses

Once you have detailed the different types of threats, you should examine the methods needed to exploit each of them. Once you have developed a list of methods, you should go through the list methodically to define the proactive and reactive approaches your team will take for each incident type.

From a proactive standpoint, you should predict the following:

- The possible damage your organization can incur
- Any potential vulnerabilities in your network
- The security measures and controls needed to minimize those vulnerabilities
- The contingency plans needed should your protective measures fail

From a reactive standpoint, you will need to determine the following:

- The amount of damage inflicted and its cause
- How to prevent additional damage from occurring
- How to repair the damage that has been done
- How you will document and learn from the experience
- How to implement any contingency plans necessitated by the event

Determining Whether to Prosecute the Attacker

When defining procedures for a reactive response, you need to make a number of difficult decisions. Though primarily business decisions, these decisions will have a dramatic effect on the tasks your team members perform. One example of how business requirements can impact an investigation is the decision to prosecute an attacker. If your organization intends to prosecute the offender, the proper collection of evidence will often take precedence over the restoration of service. For instance, if a system will be used as evidence in a court of law, that system must not be modified at all, from the moment the incident occurs until the court date—which makes securing the system and restoring service problematic.

We discuss specific investigative techniques in more detail in Chapter 31, "Responding to Security Incidents," but this example illustrates some of the challenging decisions the incident response team must make. By making such difficult decisions proactively during your incident response planning stage—rather than reactively during an incident response—you buy yourself a great deal of time to discuss the relative merits of each approach. Of course, this also allows for the possibility of "analysis paralysis," where an extended discussion is the only thing that gets accomplished. Be wary of that outcome in your response planning meetings.

A corollary issue to deciding whether to pursue a law enforcement solution (rather than simply restoring service) is the likelihood that such prosecution will bring media attention to your organization. Weigh carefully the impact that this could have on your company's reputation and brand image. Although a positive outcome is possible when pursuing law enforcement, your team's handling and communication of the incident will play a significant role in shaping the outcome. We discuss this in greater detail later in the "Creating a Communications Plan" section of this chapter. The bottom line is that to balance preserving the chain of custody on evidence, getting business systems back online, and preserving secrecy of the incident, during a security incident your organization must decide in advance the circumstance in which it will wish to pursue law enforcement channels.

Tip   Simply preserving the evidence when investigating a security incident is not enough to meet legal standards of evidence. You must also be able to prove how the integrity of the evidence was ensured when it was obtained and handled. In legal terms, this is called preserving the chain of evidence.

Deciding Whether to Stop the Attack

Another frequent challenge faced by incident response teams is whether to stop the attack or collect additional information about its root cause. Although preventing the spread of an attack or virus might seem like the obvious choice, tipping off an attacker that you are onto him could have devastating results—for example, if the attacker decides to wipe out the entire system in an effort to reduce his risk of being caught. By disconnecting a computer from the network to preserve its state for further examination, you could be alerting the attacker that you have discovered his presence. This could result in the attacker attempting to compromise other computers on your network that have not yet been compromised or immediately initiating destructive methods on other computers he has already compromised to prevent collection of evidence that could be used to track him. In a similar vein, deciding to watch the attacker and gain more information about the extent of control he has over systems in your network and the techniques being employed to expand influence could open your firm to downstream liability if your network becomes a launching point for an attack against another network.

Constructing Policies to Support Incident Response

The incident response team cannot be successful if the rest of the organization is not prepared to support the team's activities properly. The most effective way to drive behavior that will support the team is to codify these behaviors into policies and guidelines and use them to direct the organization as a whole. When crafting these policies, be sure to consider how staff will receive them. If the policies are written in a dictatorial manner, they might lack effectiveness because of people's inherent resistance to authority. Similarly, employees might not take the policies seriously if they are too restive or unreasonably strict. If, however, they are written as thoughtful explanations—outlining not only the "what" but also the "why," they will be better received and more diligently followed.

That latter point is critical: the best policies are useless if they are not observed. Again, owing to people's resistance to change, the best policies will be those that stand the test of time rather than those continuously rewritten and distributed. A policy should be written in a manner that will not require frequent revision. Lasting policies describe the needs of the business and the direction that must be taken to support those needs—not the specific steps to be taken. Lasting policies are the "what" and the "why," but they are not the "how."

Acceptable Use Policy

A primary policy supporting incident response for end users is generally contained in an acceptable use policy (AUP). This policy reduces overall risk by providing guidance to staff about the appropriate use of the company's network (and by extension, the types of activities that are higher risk and therefore not appropriate). In addition, this policy provides a method for paring down the potential traffic types to allow for easier baselining of network traffic.

The AUP should also contain language that covers the employees' rights and privacy, in addition to their responsibilities. Although your legal counsel should be involved in crafting this policy, you should consider a couple of key points. First, clarify the company's stance on personal privacy. Is personal use of company resources allowed and, if so, to what extent? Many companies recognize that their staff can make reasonable judgments about when their use of company resources is excessive and use a self-managed approach; others are stricter in their guidelines. Second, note that this portion of the policy should indicate that e-mail is considered a corporate resource that should not be misused and—under the course of normal security operations—can be monitored.

Clarifying that the possibility of monitoring exists can eliminate the expectation of privacy on the part of employees. Privacy laws and expectations can dramatically impede an investigation. If an expectation of privacy or privacy laws exist, it might not be possible to review e-mail records or, in some cases, to utilize network monitoring software. Furthermore, if your organization uses encryption, a user's unwillingness to share her encryption keys because of privacy concerns could further complicate the investigation. Again, consult your legal counsel if you have questions on this topic, and note that privacy laws vary by jurisdiction.

Access Policy

Another important policy involves access. This policy will define the conditions under which connections to other networks (such as the Internet, your business partners' networks, and so on) can be implemented. The policy should also clarify which groups in your organization can provide the best security practices for ensuring that such connections are deployed and managed appropriately. Access policy should do the following:

- Discuss guest or vendor access to the company network
- Detail the circumstances under which such access is and is not allowed
- List the appropriate contacts for any questions or comments

Availability Requirements

Requirements for availability are another area to address in incident response policy. Specifically, you need to clarify how availability might be affected during an incident response and during security-related maintenance. Availability requirements can usually be found in various service level agreements (SLAs) for business IT services. By clearly stating that security is a priority for your organization, you support the needs of your team in the inevitable situation of being forced to take a system or network connection offline to defend your environment. This can help to ensure that incident response needs are not immediately subordinated by uptime requirements. In addition, you send a message on the importance of security to the firm—which can be a component of a larger security awareness campaign.

Classification Policies

Defining who should be granted access to which type of information and how broadly that information can be shared is another critical component of ensuring the protection of your company's assets. Classifying data into different sensitivity layers provides guidance to staff on the circulation restrictions of any given document and helps to protect against inappropriate leaks. Examples of classification schemes include "unlabeled, secret, top secret, eyes only" and "public, internal only, internal-restricted viewing, highly sensitive." You must choose labeling that is appropriate to your business rather than blindly copying from another organization's classification policy. Too often military classification schemes that are ill-suited for private organizations because of their lack of sophistication and emphasis on mandatory system controls are used for data classification in private organizations to the detriment of security and privacy. You need to do a business analysis of the types of information your company creates and work with your business managers to identify the minimum appropriate levels of confidentiality.

Password Policy

Because one goal of the incident response process is the elimination of incidents throughout the organization, you should consider providing further guidance to all staff on how they contribute to the overall security of the company. Because every employee is a link in your firm's security chain, ensuring that steps are taken to eliminate weak links can be just as important as the work that is done after a breach occurs.

One common place where weak links exist is in an organization's password policy. The password policy will indicate choices the organization has made about authentication. This policy is not limited to text-based passwords—it includes other forms of authentication, such as smart cards, biometrics, and tokens. Beyond simply covering the requirements of each authentication type, your organization's password policy should differentiate specific access types that require specific authentication factors. Policy might be different for service accounts, user accounts, administrator accounts, remote access accounts, and so on.

When addressing each access scenario—local area network, virtual private network (VPN), wireless, and so forth—take into account the specific business requirements and the security threats that type of access involves. The password policy should also discuss the following:

- Whether it is appropriate for individuals to share credential information and under which circumstances
- The process for granting and receiving assistance on password resets that protect against social engineering
- Standard considerations for the duration of password life
- Complexity requirements for passwords
- Number of failed logons allowed before lockout

> **More Info**   See Chapter 3, "Configuring Security for User Accounts and Passwords," for more information on configuring password policies.

Security Reporting Policy

Policy relating to security reporting is often overlooked, but it plays a critical role in the speed of your incident response. You will need to describe the types of potential threats clearly enough so that all staff can understand those risks and identify when one of those risks is being realized. Security reporting policy will also clarify who should be contacted if a potential compromise to your organization's security is occurring, what information needs to be provided, whether the contact is anonymous, and how information about the incident is collected.

Putting It All Together

Finally, you need to craft an incident response policy that describes how each of these pieces fits together to support your incident response efforts. The overall incident response policy will also detail issues that must be addressed during an incident response that might differ from normal, day-to-day operations. Items such as monitoring, availability, chain of command, and other components of the investigation are essential here. In addition, this blanket policy must include a discussion of the consequences associated with impeding the investigation or performing a policy violation that leads to a security incident.

Creating a Communications Plan

A communications plan is the framework for how information about your organization is shared among those who need it. This plan will be different during an incident than during normal day-to-day operations. Communications techniques and content will also differ depending on whether the audience is internal or external. Determining communications policies that deal with incident response likely will represent some of the most difficult decisions a company must make. Err on the side of disseminating too much or the wrong pieces of information and you run the risk of negatively impacting the perception of your organization or—worse—clouding key information, thereby causing the intended recipient to miss it. And providing too little information can cause unfounded speculation or prevent an active participant from taking a specific appropriate action.

Pre-incident Internal Communications

Internal communications begin the first time a potential employee contacts your firm and continue until the end of that employee's affiliation with your organization. It is critical that all communications are positioned appropriately to support business requirements—especially those involving security. Coordination with your HR, public relations, and legal teams will be essential for successfully creating a proper framework for communications.

New Employee Orientation

Some of the most important communications within your organization will be with new hires. Orientation sessions need to acquaint new employees with all the policies described earlier in the "Defining Incident Response Policy" section of this chapter—as well as why these policies are important. Each employee must understand his role in the security of the organization, know the steps required to protect company assets, know where to seek additional information or report a circumstance that warrants investigation, and anticipate the result—both to the organization and himself—should he fail to observe policies. These orientation discussions afford you the greatest opportunity to gain a new employee's acceptance of these security concepts. Information imparted during these initial meetings can shape every workplace decision an employee makes from that point on.

Security Refresher Courses

As a supplement to the new-hire training, an organization should consider security refresher courses. Ideally, these courses should do the following:

- Occur regularly throughout an employee's career
- Recertify that employees understand what is expected of them
- Update employees on changes to important policies
- Provide employees with a forum to obtain clarification on any security topic
- Reinforce the importance of security to the firm

Holding short trainings annually (or more frequently) or in conjunction with major events such as a reorganization or proposed merger is a good approach.

Additional Training

Certain groups in your organization might require additional training on concepts specific to their job function. For example, you might want to provide ongoing training for security incident management teams on legal issues, new software or hardware being used on the network, or internal policy compliance. You can separate additional training into two dimensions: breadth training, which is designed to expand the knowledge and skills of the student; or depth training, which is designed to increase the knowledge and improve the skills in a specific topic the student is already familiar with. Both dimensions are important and should be balanced with the size of your security incident management team. Because larger teams generally contain more specialists, depth training is usually a higher priority, whereas smaller teams give higher priority to breadth training so that the team can survive the absence of single team member.

Awareness Campaigns

Rounding out pre-incident internal communications is the concept of awareness campaigns. An awareness campaign can take many forms. Regardless of the methods employed, the goals of such a campaign are to change specific, undesirable behavior centered around security and to reinforce the importance of security to all staff. Awareness campaigns are most successful when they are least intrusive. For example, you should not send out daily, multiple-page memos on security because, over time, people will stop reading them. Awareness activities should be simple, should be easy to consume, and should contain the minimum verbiage required to make their point.

Examples of awareness activities include the following:

- Posters of the *Loose lips sink ships* variety
- Targeted e-mails reminding employees of a specific policy
- A one-line sidebar in a company newsletter
- Wallet cards with a short list of tips telling individuals how they can improve the overall security of the organization
- Distribution of critical phone numbers and e-mail addresses

The key is to impart a message that employees can quickly absorb before making a conscious decision about whether the information is important to them (especially because you have already determined that the information is important to them). Behaviors to target with these awareness campaigns are those most likely to lead to a security incident but that cannot be easily mitigated by technology. For example, you no doubt want your employees to create passwords that are hard to crack and to not allow tailgaters to follow them into company buildings secured by a card key or similar system.

Communication During an Incident

Communication is not limited to disclosure and reinforcement of policy. During an incident, communication is a crucial component of response activity—one that can cause the overall success or failure of the incident response team.

Communication Among Response Team Members

During the course of an incident, a number of types of communication must be executed effectively for the team to succeed. The first of these is communication among team members. Although it seems obvious, this is an area often overlooked during an investigation. This is because everyone is operating in a time-sensitive, reactive mode. In other words, providing status reports and sharing intelligence gathered might not be the primary concerns.

However, during a crisis, communication needs to be a primary concern of response team members. The incident response leader needs to have a complete understanding of all aspects of the investigation at all times to ensure that the direction she provides to the team represents the best possible course of action. If the incident response leader does not have complete information, she likely will make less-than-optimal decisions and provide inappropriate guidance, both of which can have a negative impact on the speed or capability of team members. All information must flow through the incident response leader. The leader, in turn, will provide summaries to the team, along with any necessary analysis and instruction.

Communication among team members can be made more difficult by the nature of a specific incident. For example, if the incident is a denial-of-service attack against your e-mail servers or a worm that forces you to close down your routers or key systems to prevent its spread, communicating by e-mail might not be possible. Or, if a natural disaster occurs at night, other communications media might be impacted. Identifying all possible occurrences ahead of time and crafting a clear, easy-to-follow communications plan can mean the difference between a successful and failed incident response.

The communications plan should include both a primary and secondary form of communication as well as details on what to do when communication using either of those methods is not possible. The plan should also outline the chain of command in the event of an incident so that team members know what to do—and who to contact—should a key member of the team be unreachable.

Another team communication concern is that an intruder could be monitoring specific communications channels. If the e-mail system has been compromised, the attacker could be reading the e-mail of administrators involved in the investigation. If the voice mail system has been compromised, the intruder could be eavesdropping on those communications as well. Furthermore, Trojan horse applications can enable the microphone or Web cam of an infected computer system, thereby capturing information and activity conducted nearby. An attacker who can leverage your communications channels can easily gain the upper hand.

Frequently, investigation communications will extend beyond the technical members of the incident response team. In such cases, the incident response leader will also act as the liaison to the business managers likely to be impacted the most. Business managers whose workflow is impacted, who are at risk of sensitive information being leaked, or who might be at risk of missing internal or external deadlines as a result of the incident and its investigation become ad-hoc members of the incident response team. These managers will provide guidance to the incident leader on how to choose the best course of action—in other words, how to choose the "least bad" outcome, or the outcome that is least detrimental to the organization as a whole. Such choices are about mapping business need to technical implementation.

Communications with Law Enforcement Agencies

Communications with law enforcement agencies are also important in the early stages of an incident investigation. Before an incident occurs, you will have determined the circumstances under which you need to involve specific law enforcement agencies, and you will have established appropriate contact processes for each agency. By communicating with those channels early in an incident investigation, you bring additional resources to the response and ensure that evidentiary procedure is adhered to. You also ensure that any steps taken do not interfere with later prosecution. Only engage in conversations with law enforcement about security incidents with explicit permission from executive management. There might be circumstances outside your knowledge in place, such as a penetration test.

Companywide Communication

At various points during an investigation, it might be prudent to engage in companywide communication on the status of the investigation or remediative work. Such communication can minimize speculation and drive specific supporting behaviors. In the latter capacity, companywide communication is similar to an awareness campaign.

Companywide communication is very sensitive when conducted during an investigation. Whether an attack is internal or external, broad communications can tip off the attacker on the success or lack of success of the investigative process. The most appropriate communications in this scenario are brief, concise, and easily assimilated, without providing any specifics on the incident. For example,

> *We are experiencing intermittent outages of various network resources. IT personnel are working on correcting the problem, and we hope to have service restored quickly. If you have an immediate concern, please contact the service desk.*

would likely be more effective than

> *We are collecting evidence on an attacker who has compromised at least seven systems in our e-business unit, and the FBI will be shutting down systems intermittently to collect forensic images before the attacker has a chance to cover his tracks.*

Basically, you are keeping your cards close to your vest.

Companywide communication can also include a wrap-up message at the close of the investigation on lessons learned and next steps to be taken. For example,

> *Our security team, during a routine analysis of our network, has identified and removed several unapproved network services. Specific policy requires that all network services be approved by the Director of IT and implemented through our normal change control process. Because of the security implications, we will be forcing a password reset for all users over the next three days.*

Contacting the Attacker

One particularly sensitive area is communicating with the attacker. Depending on the specifics of the case, contacting the attacker might be a valuable component of the investigation. For example, if the attacker is trying to extort money or other gains from your firm, contact with the attacker could buy you valuable investigation time (by stalling the attacker) and stave off further intrusion. Of course, the opposite is also possible. Contacting the attacker could cause her to take additional action, such as formatting all your network systems to cover her tracks because she knows she has been discovered.

If law enforcement agencies are involved, they likely will have more experience dealing with these issues than your response team—so you should defer to their judgment. Of course, prudence dictates a careful evaluation of the capability of these agencies before deferring to them. You will find a wide range of capabilities and technical sophistication, depending on whether you are dealing with local or federal investigators and on the frequency with which an agency handles computer crime investigations. You might also want to involve your legal counsel because contact with an attacker could have an impact on any prosecution attempt.

Finally, you will want to evaluate the risk created by making contact with an attacker before deciding to do so. Profiling the attacker's behavior is a critical element in deciding this. Each of these questions can help you develop a fair amount of insight about the attacker's probable next moves:

- Does the attacker seem to be after something specific, or simply snooping around?

- Has the intrusion gone on for months, or did it begin recently?

- Was the attack method exceptionally crafty, or did your firm get caught with its defenses down by not being up-to-date with vendor-released patches?

- If the attacker has made contact with you, what can your response team infer about his education or locale based on the phrasing used in that contact?

- Is it possible to use this contact with the attacker to collect additional information that law enforcement authorities can use to locate him?

Once you have determined that the risk of contacting the attacker is appropriate, consider your goals for the communication and the method by which you will make contact. If the attacker's intrusions typically occur during certain hours of the day or night, it might be prudent to time your contact at the beginning of that window. If the attacker has not contacted your organization directly, you should determine the best way of contacting her. It is unlikely that the attacker will have left her home telephone number on any given compromised system.

Finally, make certain that the goal of your contact is clear: Are you trying to slow the intruder's attacks? Gain additional evidence against the attacker? Find out the extent of her intrusions? Ask her nicely to go away? Something else? Each answer might point toward a specific method of communication and the framework for the conversation, including whether you use a medium you can log and trace.

Dealing with the Press

When wider knowledge of a security breach exists, it is possible that the event will garner the attention of the press. In such cases, you must brief your public relations staff on the incident and prepare them to respond to inquiries. Contact with the press should be reserved for duly appointed individuals within your organization that you trust to represent the information in an appropriate manner. All other staff members should be trained to direct press inquiries to the appropriate resources.

When speaking to the press, your public relations representatives should adhere to several core principles:

- Be precise in your use of language. Say exactly what you intend to say in short, complete sentences that cannot be misinterpreted or taken out of context.

- Stick to the facts, and do not let emotion play into the discussion. Similarly, avoid speculation about the root cause or parties involved or their motives unless you have sufficient evidence to that effect.

- When being interviewed, ensure that with every answer you bring the conversation back to a point that you want to make.

- Keep the technical detail low enough that you do not inadvertently invite additional attacks and that you do not exceed the understanding of the interviewer.

- If you are working with law enforcement officials, ensure that any information, documents, photos, or other materials provided to the press do not impair the investigation or decrease the likelihood of successful prosecution.

- Ensure you are prepared with answers to the most likely questions. Do not go into any interview situation before you are ready.

- Recognize that, in many cases, your tone and manner say as much as your words.

- Do not allow media attention to interfere with the investigation.

In some cases, it might be appropriate to provide a press release about the incident. This might seem contrary to conventional wisdom about how best to protect your company's image and brand, but in some cases, it can be a valuable step. Specifically, releasing your own press announcement allows you to provide an appropriate context for the event and highlight important points you feel need to be made clear in light of how media organizations are characterizing the incident. For example, you might want to stress that even though a security breach occurred, no customer information was exposed if that should be the case. Be reassuring and honest.

Best Practices

- **Employ diligent planning to alleviate uncertainty when responding to incidents.**   Because time is of the essence when handling incidents, it is critical to do as much work up front as possible. This work includes the following:

    - ❑ Implementing preventative measures described throughout this book

    - ❑ Implementing policies that support incident response

    - ❑ Training all staff in their role in security

❑ Selecting the people who will be involved in incident response and designating the roles each will play

❑ Collecting and maintaining incident handling guidelines

❑ Assembling a comprehensive and accurate contact sheet

In addition, difficult scenarios should be discussed by the incident response team and management to establish boundaries and predefine response goals. Team members and management should also discuss and agree upon aspects of involving the media and law enforcement agencies in an incident investigation. The more decisions you make up front, the easier incident response will be.

■ **Remember that executive sponsorship is essential.**   Your sponsor will be able to make changes required to create the policies needed to support incident response. He also will be able to provide budget for training, staffing levels, and tools. For the most effective relationship with your sponsor, your team leader must be able to understand and communicate the core business issues to the sponsor and to present complex issues in a logical, concise manner.

■ **Formalize your incident response team.**   By formalizing the team—even in cases where incident response is not the team's core activity—you will dramatically improve response times and capability while minimizing uncertainty and power struggles.

■ **Use the best resources.**   Make certain that the leader for each incident response is the most technically appropriate person for that type of incident. It does not make sense to use a senior Microsoft Windows technician for a mainframe issue. Neither does it make sense to use an infrastructure engineer whose focus is routers and switches as leader on an intrusion in a database system.

Additional Information

■ RFC 2196: "Site Security Handbook" (*http://www.ietf.org/rfc/rfc2196.txt*)

■ RFC 2350: "Expectations for Computer Security Incident Response" (*http://www.ietf.org/rfc/rfc2350.txt*)

■ *The Cuckoo's Egg: Tracking a Spy Through the Maze of Computer Espionage* (Pocket Books, 2000)

■ *Incident Response: Investigating Computer Crime* (Osborne/McGraw-Hill, 2001)

■ *Incident Response: A Strategic Guide to Handling System and Network Security Breaches* (New Riders, 2002)

Chapter 31

Responding to Security Incidents

As a network administrator, you must be able to recognize when a security incident is under way. Unfortunately, not all attacks are obvious. Recognizing that the network is under attack early is essential to protecting information or computers that have not yet been compromised. The detection of security incidents centers on investigating events that fall outside of the normal behavior of the network or computers on the network. Consequently, the key to detecting security events is to have a clear understanding of the baseline network operation. Creating a baseline for the computers and network components includes cataloging applications and services that should be running, documenting appropriate user rights and group membership, and supporting these lists with solid change control processes that update them when an approved alteration occurs.

 More Info For more information on creating a performance baseline, see Chapter 27, "Overview of Performance Monitoring," of the *Microsoft Windows 2000 Professional Resource Kit* (Microsoft Press, 2000). For detailed information about performance monitoring, see the *Microsoft Windows Server 2003 Resource Kit Performance Guide* (Microsoft Press, 2005).

For example, suppose an organization has implemented a host-based and network-based intrusion detection system (IDS) and analyzes the log files from the IDS software regularly. The regular analysis shows a normal spike occurring in reported connection attempts every night at 1:00 A.M.; the rest of the time, the attempted attacks are recorded at a consistent level. If the organization encounters a dramatic spike in the number of attempted attacks at 4:00 A.M., the network administrator could conclude that the organization is under a coordinated attack. Without the baseline log files for comparison, the attempted attacks might easily be dismissed as unremarkable port-scanning activity. Similarly, without the baseline, the normal spike in attacks at 1:00 A.M. might appear as a coordinated attack against the organization. Both cases illustrate the importance of having a baseline record of normal behavior.

Once you have established a baseline of behavior, you can monitor the network for sudden variations from the baseline, including short-term spikes and longer-term, more gradual increases. You should investigate all these variations. In most cases, you will find no attack in progress. In some cases, you will find an incident in progress and will be able to take action before the attacker can steal or destroy information or otherwise damage the network. The earlier you detect an anomaly and investigate it, the greater your likelihood of minimizing damage to the network.

Common Indicators of Security Incidents

Several types of events are common indicators of security incidents. You should pay particular attention to these types of events. Although after investigation, most of these events will prove harmless, some will warrant closer investigation and possibly trigger your organization's incident response plan. Common indicators of security incidents include the following:

- Unusual Transmission Control Protocol/Internet Protocol (TCP/IP) or User Datagram Protocol (UDP) traffic
- Presence of certain events in the System log file
- Inability to access network resources
- Excessive CPU utilization
- Irregular service operations
- Irregular file system activity
- Permissions changes

Unusual TCP/IP or UDP Traffic

One of the earliest warnings of a security incident is unusual TCP and UDP port communication. Frequently, this will be nothing more than port scanning, but because port scanning can be a prelude to more serious penetration attempts, you should keep track of the amount and type of port scans your network receives. Variations in the number of scans or the sophistication of the scans used against your network can be an early indicator of a possible attack. More important, events such as dramatic increases in traffic to ports in normal use are strong signs that an attack might be in progress. For example, the earliest detectors of the SQL Slammer worm in January 2003 identified the worm as a result of the tremendous increase in traffic across the Internet destined for UDP port 1434, a little-used port for locating database instances on systems running Microsoft SQL Server.

> **More Info**   For more information on the mechanics of the SQL Slammer worm, see "Slammer Worm Dissection" on the *IEEE Security and Privacy* journal's Web site at *http://www.computer.org/security/v1n4/j4wea.htm*.

To create a baseline of normal network traffic you should analyze the log files from your routers, firewalls, and intrusion detection system (IDS) devices. Additionally, if you would like to monitor the traffic on a computer running Microsoft Windows Server 2003, Windows 2000, or Windows XP, you can use Port Reporter, which can be downloaded from the Microsoft Web site. Port Reporter is discussed in Chapter 10, "Implementing TCP/IP Security." Given the frequency of port scans, you should closely monitor log files, either manually or through a log collection and correlation system. You can use a variety of tools to monitor Event log files, including products such as Microsoft Operations Manager or tools that come at no cost, such as Event Comb and Dumpel.exe. (EventcombMT.exe and Dumpel.exe are located on the CD that accompanies this book.)

> **More Info**   See Chapter 15, "Auditing Microsoft Windows Security Events," in this book for detailed information on configuring auditing in Windows Server 2003, Windows 2000, and Windows XP.

Presence of Certain Events in the System Log File

If an attacker succeeds in penetrating your defenses, one common approach she might take is to attempt to cover her tracks by erasing or modifying the Event logs. Because of this, you must stay current with your logs either by exporting them to a well-secured network location (or to write-once media) or by analyzing them in real time.

The act of clearing the Security Event log creates an event 517. The presence of that event and the lack of events in a log that should be populated can indicate that a successful attack has occurred and evidence has been manipulated. Because attack tools that enable the manipulation of the event log now exist, optimally, you want to have logs written to a read-only, protected data store on a remote system in real time. These principles also apply to logs other than the Event logs.

You should also monitor the log files listed in Table 31-1, as well as any other log files that seem applicable based on the details of the specific incident. Consider implementing a process to collect these log files on a daily basis and place them in a secure, central location.

Table 31-1   Log Files of Interest to an Incident Response Team

Log File	Default Location	Description
URLScan log	%windir%\system 32\inetsrv \urlscan	The URLScan log file details why rejected requests were rejected (which specific rule in the URLScan.ini triggered the rejection) as well as the time and date, the URL in question, and the IP address of the requestor. The logging functionality for URLScan enables you to toggle logging on or off (the default is on) and allows for separate logs on a per-process or per-day basis.
Domain Name System (DNS) log	%windir%\system 32 \DNS\DnsEvent.Evt	The DNS Event log file can be used to identify any inappropriate DNS activity, such as unauthorized zone transfers, which can be a precursor to an attack on the network.

Table 31-1   Log Files of Interest to an Incident Response Team

Log File	Default Location	Description
Microsoft Internet Information Services (IIS) log	By default, when you install IIS the IIS logs are created in C:\%windir% \system32\LogFiles\W3SVC# (where # is the Web site number). To find the log file location, examine the properties of the Web site in the Internet Services Manager (ISM).	IIS extends beyond the scope of the event-logging or performance-monitoring features of the Windows operating system. The logs can include information such as who has visited your Web site, what the visitor viewed, and when the information was viewed last. You can monitor attempts, either successful or unsuccessful, to access your Web sites, virtual folders, or files. This includes events such as reading the file or writing to the file. You can choose which events you want to audit for any site, virtual folder, or file. By regularly reviewing these files, you can detect areas of your server or your sites that might be subject to attacks or other security problems. You can enable logging for individual Web sites and choose the log format. When logging is enabled, it is enabled for all the site's folders, but you can disable it for specific directories. Inspect the IIS logs for suspicious Web server activities, including (but not limited to) the following: ■ Multiple unsuccessful commands trying to run executable files or scripts. (Closely monitor the Scripts folder.) ■ Excessive unsuccessful attempts from a single IP address, with the possible intention of increasing network traffic and denying access to other users. ■ Unsuccessful attempts to access and modify .bat or .cmd files. ■ Unauthorized attempts to upload files and executable files to a folder that contains Execute permissions by using HTTP PUT or POST methods.
Internet Authentication Service (IAS) log	%windir%\system 32\LogFiles \iaslog.log	The IAS log contains listings of both successful and rejected authentication requests. This can help you determine baseline patterns for Remote Access Service (RAS) users, as well as identify anomalous activity and rejected authentication attempts, which might indicate an attack in progress.
Windows Firewall log	Windows XP or Windows Server 2003: %windir%\pfirewall.log	On network connections protected by Windows Firewall, the Windows Firewall logs can be configured to show successful and unsuccessful connections to that network interface, including the date and time, IP address, and ports utilized.

Table 31-1   Log Files of Interest to an Incident Response Team

Log File	Default Location	Description
Dr. Watson log	Windows 2000 and Windows XP: %AllUsersProfile%\Documents \Dr Watson\Drwtsn32.log Windows Server 2003: %userprofile%\local settings \application data\microsoft \dr watson\	The Dr. Watson log records process information for the processes that are running when an application crashes. If an application crashes, it might be possible to see information about the processes running at the time of the crash to help determine whether the cause was related to an attack.
IDS log	Varies based on the IDS in use	IDS systems create log files that can provide a great deal of information about what is happening at the network layer of the computer. Some IDS systems incorporate a GUI and search capability to correlate large volumes of detailed information quickly.

Inability to Access Network Resources

Another indication that an incident has occurred is the sudden inability to access a network resource or receiving a degraded response from that resource under otherwise normal conditions. If a system suddenly reboots, an application hangs unexpectedly, a system undergoes a routing change, or a modification to DNS occurs, clients might not be able to access network resources. Some or all of these events might occur in the event of an intrusion, depending on the attacker's approach. Investigate such outages to determine whether they were caused by an intruder. Be careful not to jump to conclusions.

Excessive CPU Utilization

Similarly, higher-than-normal CPU or network utilization can indicate rogue processes that might be indicators of an attack. It is normal for a system's processor to jump to 100 percent utilization periodically, or for high network traffic to be seen during a large file transfer to or from a file server. However, when a system that normally averages 40 percent CPU utilization operates at an average of 70 percent CPU utilization, or when large quantities of data travel to or from a server that normally does not generate such traffic, some form of attack might be in progress.

Although most processes being executed on a computer running the Windows operating system are displayed in the Task Manager, if an attacker has compromised the computer, some processes that are hidden from the Task Manager can be executed. Consequently, concluding that a system is in a trusted state based on the process list as reported by the operating system is not advisable. You should be careful about how you use computers that might have been compromised. For example, an attacker might have installed keystroke logging software that is responsible for the excess CPU utilization. When you log on to the computer to investigate this issue, the attacker could intercept your account logon name and password. Except in special cases where you do not want to disrupt services for investigative proposes, you should always disconnect potentially compromised systems from the network before logging on.

Irregular Service Operations

Other variances from baseline behavior that might require investigation relate to system services. Services that should be running but are paused or stopped, services that are new to the system, and services that should be running but are missing can all indicate that an attacker has made modifications to your system to suit his needs. Tools such as SvcMon.exe—which first shipped with *Microsoft Windows 2000 Server Resource Kit* (Microsoft Press, 2000) and is included in the *Microsoft Windows Server 2003 Resource Kit* (Microsoft Press, 2005)—can monitor local or remote systems to detect changes in state of the various services on a system that you select by using the SMConfig.exe tool. Should a service stop or start, the tool will notify the administrator by e-mail and log the event. Similarly, enterprise monitoring software such as Microsoft Operations Manager (MOM) or third-party products provide comprehensive service monitoring.

Tip   On computers running Windows XP and Windows Server 2003, you can list services, their state, and configuration using Windows Management Instrumentation (WMI). From the command line, you can access WMI through the WMI command-line shell by typing **WMIC** at the WMIC prompt, typing **service**, and then pressing Enter.

Irregular File System Activity

Indicators of an attack at the file system level can include missing files or folders or a noticeable decrease in the available space on a system. Missing files can result from the attacker modifying your system because she wants more space or to cover her tracks. A decrease in disk space can occur because the attacker is using your system for Internet Relay Chat (IRC) or file storage or because she has copied tools to that system to extend her attack to other systems in your environment. Other file system changes, such as changes to the datestamp on system files or to the SHA1 hash of system files, can be an indicator of an intrusion. Attackers will often replace executables with Trojan horse versions of the same program that can either help hide their presence or provide them with additional levels of access.

On the CD   You can use the file integrity verification tool Fciv.exe, which is located on the CD that accompanies this book, to create and verify hash signatures of files.

The presence of new drivers also can point to an attack. You can monitor the drivers on a system by using the Drivers.exe tool, which is included on the CD that ships with this book. This tool displays all installed device drivers on the computer on which the tool is executed. The output of the tool includes the driver's file name, the size of the driver on disk, and the date that the driver was linked. The link date can be used to identify any newly installed drivers. If an updated driver was not recently installed, this can indicate a replaced driver on the part of an attacker.

Permissions Changes

Changes to user permissions, group membership, or other security policy elements are also common attack indicators. If a user is granted permissions outside your change control process or if an account is added to a more privileged group, an attacker might be trying to access resources he currently cannot access. An example of this is the Nimda worm, which adds the Guest account to the Administrators group. Other changes along this vein include changes to Group Policy objects (GPOs) and auditing changes. If any of these events occur outside planned operations, we recommend you conduct an investigation. Event IDs 608–612 and 624–643 can denote such improper changes.

Analyzing a Security Incident

Once an incident has been identified—regardless of who identifies it—the information must be communicated to the incident response team. Following that communication, a number of steps must be taken by the response team. The individual steps taken will differ depending on the specifics of the incident. Possible steps include these:

- Determine the cause.
- Prevent further exploitation of the attack vector.
- Avoid attack escalation and further incidents.
- Restore the computers' services.
- Assess the impact and damage of the incident.
- Update policies and procedures as needed, based on the lessons learned from the security incident.

Find out who launched the attack (if appropriate and possible) and take business-appropriate action.

> **More Info** For more information on incident response teams and plans, see Chapter 30, "Planning for Incident Response."

Determining the Cause

At the outset of the investigation, the incident response team must determine the cause of the behavior, which software might be involved, how the software has been compromised, and the scope of the compromise. If hostile code is involved, the team should assess the capability and propagation methods of that code. Frequently, such analysis assistance can be obtained on the Web site of your antivirus software vendor.

> **Tip** Microsoft provides a free support hotline for viruses, worms, and similar attacks. The U.S. telephone number for this hotline is 1-866-PC SAFETY. Customers with a Premier Support agreement have additional support options and should contact their technical account manager. For international support, see *http://support.microsoft.com /common/international.aspx?*.

Preventing Further Exploitation

Following the initial analysis, the team should take steps to prevent further exploitation of this type of attack. See the section "Conducting Security Investigations" later in this chapter for important considerations for this stage of your response. This stage can involve many different approaches, including applying an already-existing patch for a particular vulnerability to all at-risk systems, modifying the network topology, temporarily suspending a service or application, and performing user awareness activities. The specific response will vary based on the details of the incident.

Avoiding Attack Escalation and Further Incidents

The next step in an incident response is to avoid escalation of the existing incident and prevent further incidents. This is a large concern when an attacker has interactive access to one or more of your systems. Shutting down the attacker's session might result in new and potentially more destructive attacks. This can also be an issue with automated attacks, such as the Nimda and Code Red worms. In those cases, the escalation is the spread of the worm or an attacker taking advantage of your vulnerable state to launch new attacks on your network.

Restoring Service

Restoration of service occurs next, once the scope and damage of the incident are fully understood. Service must be restored in a secure manner or workarounds must be put in place to enable the business activities requiring those services. Systems not being used as evidence in an attack investigation can be brought back online without reintroducing a security threat to the network after it is confirmed they are trustworthy.

One of the most difficult decisions a response team can face is determining the appropriate course of action to restore a system to service after it has been compromised. Although immediate restoration of service is laudable and appears to be in the best interest of the firm, it often is a poor choice. For example, if an attacker compromises one of your servers and you decide to secure the system as it stands and bring it back online, several events can happen:

The process of securing the system could overwrite evidence, making it difficult or impossible to determine the source of the attack.

More important, short of comparing known good file hashes for every file on the system, you cannot know whether the compromise extends beyond the elements you have identified. Too often an attacker will enter your system by exploiting one avenue and then expand her influence by installing additional software tools or Trojan horse applications. In such cases, the system might seem to be behaving normally when, instead, it is camouflaging its own improper behavior.

Although you have identified one intrusion, others of which you are unaware might exist. The system fell to one attacker, and it is folly to think that such a system could not be hosting others with ill will.

The process of taking a system offline; verifying the checksum of every file on the system against a known good baseline (using trusted executables from your forensics workstation or tools CD); reviewing and understanding every .ini file, registry entry, setting, and service; and correcting anything found to be out of line takes considerably more time than simply rebuilding the system from known clean media, securing the system before it is brought online, and restoring service on the rebuilt system. Having spare hardware can enable you to preserve evidence by restoring affected services to different equipment, thereby leaving the impacted systems untouched. Also, if your organization has automated a process for installing the operating system, you can create a single installation medium that incorporates the latest service packs and hotfixes. By incorporating security updates into the media used to install the operating system, a process often called *slipstreaming* or *integrated installation*, you can decrease the time it takes to recover the computer's services.

Once you have the situation under control, you should assess the impact and damage the event has caused. To better allocate resources for securing the network, you should determine the costs associated with the loss of productivity because of the security incident and the costs of recovering the disrupted services.

Incorporating Lessons Learned into Policy

Every incident is a learning experience. Your incident response team will learn about new techniques and tools as a result of the security breach, and your organization will learn where its policies and procedures might not sufficiently address risks to your environment. At this stage, it is essential to hold an incident debriefing and examine the lessons learned from the experience. Look at the cause of the event and how it could have been prevented. If your policy does not address the behavior or processes that allowed the incident to occur, look at what revisions might be necessary. If your policy does support such preventative behavior or processes, look to where the policy broke down and see what you can learn from that.

Tracking the Attacker

After you have incorporated the lessons learned into your operations, determine whether it is appropriate to track the intruder. Using the information collected from your investigation (logs, packet traces, timestamps, process lists, methods, and so on), you can trace the attacker's steps to determine his origin. This information can be useful in determining intent or for law enforcement. To do so, use the data shown in your logs to determine the owner of the IP address or domain. You can trace the IP address or domain used by the attacker by performing a whois search at *http://www.arin.net*, *http://www.samspade.org*, or another site that provides the whois search capability.

Although possible, more extensive tracing of attackers might be illegal in some countries. You should discuss this issue with your organization's IT management and legal representatives before taking any action. Based on your detective work, you might find an individual working alone, a corporation, or a government at the other end of the attack. Or you might hit a dead end and find that intervening network providers are unable or unwilling to cooperate without a subpoena. Knowing this type of information can help you determine whether your team is capable of undertaking this aspect of the incident response or whether additional assistance is required.

Conducting Security Investigations

Another challenging aspect of incident response is conducting the investigation. Although other stages of incident response have their own issues, the process used in the investigation can expand or inhibit the capabilities of the response team. Unskilled investigators often damage critical evidence that could lead to discovery of the attacker, or they otherwise hinder the team. Similarly, approaches that could yield additional information might be overlooked. For these reasons, the team should practice their response techniques before they are needed so that these techniques are already fine-tuned when an actual incident occurs.

Involving Law Enforcement

Many times, incident response involves making the least bad choice rather than making optimal choices. At no point is this truer than when you must decide whether to involve law enforcement authorities. Your organization should decide whether to involve law enforcement officials before a security incident occurs to ensure that the proper evidence collection techniques are used.

One consideration about involving law enforcement is that it will likely slow the restoration of network services. Also, if your organization does choose to work with law enforcement officials, there is a strong chance that the security incident will become public record and damage the reputation of your organization. If your organization does decide that it might want to prosecute attackers if an incident occurs, you should work with local or regional law enforcement agencies in advance to determine how to engage law enforcement and receive training in forensic investigation methods.

Conducting the Investigation

In cases where an incident response might ultimately include taking the attacker to court, it is imperative that you perform all your operations with the knowledge that they will contribute—positively or negatively—to the proceedings. The rule of thumb is always to follow the principle of best evidence while conducting the investigation. Criminal investigations involve something known as chain of custody, where specific processes for collecting evidence are required. Such processes vary by jurisdiction. If these processes are not followed, the chain is considered "broken" and the evidence might not be admitted into court or could be picked apart by opposing counsel. (We will discuss chain of custody and collecting evidence in more detail momentarily.)

Although your legal counsel can provide more details on the topic of evidence handling, some general principles exist. First, ensure that your handling and collection of information can stand up to legal and technical scrutiny. If you collect such incontrovertible evidence to prove, beyond the shadow of a doubt, a particular detail, be assured that the opposing counsel may attempt to undermine the credibility of the collectors and your incident response process instead of refuting the evidence itself. If discredited, usually the net effect is the same as invalid or no evidence.

With this in mind, ensuring precision in your investigative work is key, as is validating sources and details. Ensure that no possible questions can be raised about any of the investigative activities your team performs. Document in as much detail as possible all the actions of every member of the investigative team throughout the course of the investigation. If not documented, even the seemingly mundane details, such as a time difference between the computer BIOS and the operating system, can cause a great deal of heartache in court. Your documentation should include the time and date on the system—including the time zone, the name of the person conducting the action, details of the steps taken and their results, the timestamp following the steps taken, the signature of the investigator, and a signature of a skilled witness.

> **Note**   In addition to helping prove the quality of evidence in your own legal juris-
> diction, if you find yourself working with law enforcement authorities in another
> region or country, such documentation can clarify the steps taken to protect evidence
> from tampering and damage should that jurisdiction's rules of evidence differ from
> those of your own jurisdiction.

Limiting Investigative Work to Backup Media

Because the act of inspecting files on a live system can modify last-modified times and access times of individual files, thus eliminating potential evidence, you should conduct investigative work only on copies of the original media. These must be byte-level copies because slack space—the space between files—on drives can contain significant quantities of evidence that should be retained.

A number of tools can be used to make a forensic image of the drive, including Safe-Back from NTI (*http://www.forensics-intl.com/safeback.html*). Ensure that the receiving media has not been previously used because previous data on the target drive can lead to incorrect assumptions during the investigation. Furthermore, the target media must have the same or similar hardware geometry. If a receiving drive has a dramatically different number of cylinders or sectors, evidence can be lost during the transfer. If time permits, you might want to make additional, second-generation copies from the first set of copies. This guarantees that you have an unmodified first-generation copy at all times should one be needed for additional avenues of investigation. An illustration of this method is shown in Figure 31-1.

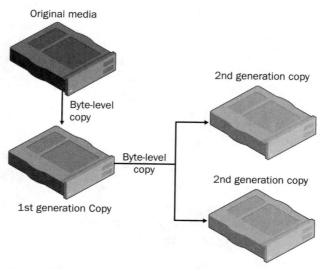

Figure 31-1   Preserving evidence by making forensically sound backups of the original media and working copies from the first-generation backup

Treatment of the original media, which is now your evidence copy, must also be handled properly throughout the investigation. You must be able to account for the whereabouts of the original media at all times, identify who has access to it at any given point, and pinpoint when possession of the evidence changed—along with the reason for any change. This is the chain of custody process we referred to earlier. To protect the chain of custody, place the media in a secure location that a minimal number of people have access to and require that all access be logged. Store the logs in such a way that no question about whether they have been altered can arise. These logs should contain the time, date, and circumstance under which the evidence changes hands, and they should document each person who takes possession of this evidence.

Collecting Evidence

If you decide to pursue a law enforcement solution, the agency you work with will have additional recommendations about the steps to take to preserve evidence and conduct the investigation. This is because the methods you use to collect one type of evidence can obscure or destroy the collection of another type. You should not begin collecting information about an attack until you have a good understanding of the type of attack that is occurring—without this understanding, you risk tipping off an intruder or destroying evidence.

When you begin collecting information about an attack, you might not know exactly what you are looking for. Even if you think you know, you might be wrong: as mentioned earlier, the attack might have occurred on more levels than you are aware of. With this in mind, a keen-eyed investigator—with journal in hand—will look at every potential clue to determine what occurred and the extent of any damages.

Two primary types of data exist on a computer system: volatile data and nonvolatile data. Simply put, volatile data is data that will disappear if the system loses power, and nonvolatile data is the data that persists after power is restored. Because many attacks leave only remnants in the form of volatile data, it is essential that you collect as much of this data as possible (without causing additional damage) before shutting down the system.

Volatile Data

Volatile data includes information about the following:

- The processes that are running, suspended, or disabled
- The network connections that are open
- The ports that are open and the applications listening on those open ports
- All recently executed programs
- The dynamic contents within the registry
- The contents of the system memory
- The pagefile (if it has been set to wipe itself clean upon shutdown)
- Any backup media inserted into the local system (because running processes might cause a backup to initiate and overwrite the contents of the media)
- The accounts that have sessions logged on (either locally or remotely)
- How long the system has been running since the last reboot

When capturing this information, keep in mind that it might not be possible to trust the executables on the machine you are cataloging because an attacker might have modified them with one or more Trojan horses. Because it is easy to overwrite or otherwise destroy forensic information, you should conduct this type of investigation only if you have received training or are working with more experienced administrators. To evaluate the forensic evidence properly, you must know what the state of the computer would be under normal conditions. For example, it is very difficult to look at a list of processes running on a computer and determine which normally execute on the computer and which are malicious. As mentioned previously, understanding the baseline operation of the computers on your network is essential during an investigation.

Tip   As you collect information, you also must ensure that you are capturing the time at which the collection occurs. Looking at your watch and noting it in your journal does not suffice because the system time might differ. A good rule of thumb is to note both the clock time and the system time in your journal before and after each command.

Nonvolatile Data

Nonvolatile data is also important to the investigation. The primary difference between volatile and nonvolatile data is when and how they can be collected. As mentioned, nonvolatile information persists after a system shutdown. Therefore, assuming no processes are running that will eliminate the evidence when the system is stopped, you can collect this information after the system is taken offline—ideally from a forensically sound backup of the media (described in the previous section).

Nonvolatile information includes the following:

- The contents of the registry
- Event logs and other log files
- The access and modification times of files
- Recently deleted files
- The slack space between the end of a file and the end of the cluster

Tip   Because normal activity that occurs when starting up a system can change the access and modification times of a large number of files—as well as cause processes set to run at startup to overwrite slack space or change other elements of the operating system configuration—we suggest you conduct analysis of these aspects offline.

Data Collection Tools

Incident response teams should be familiar with the wide variety of tools that are available for collecting data, along with their capabilities, strengths, and weaknesses. Practicing working with these tools before they are needed in an incident response will help investigators hone their skills. This can help reduce the number of steps required to collect the necessary information and prevent other evidence from being destroyed in the process—which, as we mentioned, is a large factor in determining the success of the investigation. Table 31-2 shows some of the tools available for gathering data in an incident investigation and where you obtain them.

Table 31-2   Tools for Gathering Information

Data Type	Command or Tool
Processes running	Task Manager or the command-line tools TList (Windows 2000) and Tasklist (Windows XP and Windows Server 2003)
	PsTools from Sysinternals at *http://www.systeminternals.com*
	Fport from Foundstone at *http://www.foundstone.com*
Current system activity	Filemon and Regmon from Sysinternals at *http://www.systeminternals.com*
Services and drivers	SC.exe, Sclist.exe, and Drivers.exe, found on the CD included with this book
	Net Start, which is available in default installations of Windows Server 2003,Windows 2000, and Windows XP, and WMIC, which is available in default installations of Windows Server 2003 and Windows XP
New files	Dir /q /-c /o:d /t:a /s > *filename*.txt, which is available in default installations of Windows Server 2003,Windows 2000, and Windows XP
	Forensic Toolkit from Foundstone at *http://www.foundstone.com*
Memory contents	CheckSym.exe, found on the CD included with this book
Registry	Reg.exe, which is available in default installations of Windows Server 2003, Windows 2000, and Windows XP
	Regdmp.exe, found in the Tools folder on the CD included with this book
Permissions	Xcacls.exe, Xcacls.vbs, and Subinacl.exe, which are found on the CD included with this book
Current network connections	Netstat.exe -ano and Nbtstat.exe, which are available in default installations of Windows Server 2003, Windows 2000, and Windows XP (the -o switch for Netstat.exe is not available in Windows 2000)
	Fport from Foundstone at *http://www.foundstone.com*
Network IP routes	Netstat.exe -r and Route Print, which are available in default installations of Windows Server 2003, Windows 2000, and Windows XP
Shares information	Net Share, which is available in default installations of Windows Server 2003, Windows 2000, and Windows XP
	Srvcheck.exe, found on the CD included with this book
	DumpSec from SomarSoft at *http://www.somarsoft.com*
	Vadump.exe, found on the CD included with this book
Scheduled tasks	At and Run registry keys, which are available in default installations of Windows Server 2003, Windows 2000, and Windows XP
Slack space	Tools such as EnCase (*http://www.guidancesoftware.com/*), NTI (*http://www.forensics-intl.com/tools.html*), WinHex (*http://www.sf-soft.de*), Norton Utilities Disk Editor (*http://www.sf-soft.de*)

The capabilities of tools listed in Table 31-2 vary widely. Not every tool will be valuable in every instance. In some cases, combining the output of multiple tools is necessary to gain information that is useful to the investigation—for example, when collecting information on running processes. Although it is useful to collect a list of the processes running, it is even more useful to combine that information with information on open network sessions. This combination can help you, as the investigator, ferret out abnormal system behavior.

You can extend the usefulness of this combination of data when comparing the results with a known good baseline. For example, if you are concerned about changes to the files that are listed in your services list, you can use a tool such as Tripwire (*http://www.tripwire.com*) to compare hashes of all system files to see whether any have changed. Alternately, you can use a command such as the following to output a complete, recursive file listing of all files on the system sorted in date order to the Filename.txt file:

```
dir /q /-c /o:d /t:a /s > filename.txt
```

To perform the same type of activity with the registry, you can leverage the Reg.exe tool and its /query and /compare switches. To review permissions, you can utilize Xcacls.exe, Xcacls.vbs, or Subinacl.exe.

Note   As many of the examples discussed in this section illustrate, if you want to be effective, you must collect a fair amount of data long before an incident occurs. In cases where you have not performed this preparatory activity, you might be able to obtain enough information from similarly configured systems for comparison. Keep in mind that if those other systems have also been compromised, the information you collect might be useless at best, or it might lead you to believe that no compromise has occurred.

Once volatile data has been collected, you must preserve the state of the original media either for evidence or for additional investigation by making one or more backup copies, as mentioned earlier. When making copies of the drives, it is not enough to simply copy files. Additional evidence can be found in the space between files—the slack space—in the form of previously deleted (but not yet overwritten) files. Additional evidence can also be found in the space between the end of a file and the end of the sector where the tail end of that file resides. Because of this, the backup needs to be a byte-level backup of the entire drive. Best results will be obtained by matching the original drive as closely as possible in terms of its geometry. The drive must not have been previously used because remnants of that earlier use could contaminate evidence and impede the investigation. A number of tools exist for performing a sector-by-sector copy of a hard drive, including SafeBack from NTI (*http://www.forensics-intl.com/safeback.html*), Norton Ghost from Symantec (only when using

the -IR switch, and found at *http://www.symantec.com/sabu/ghost/ghost_personal/*),
EnCase (*http://www.guidancesoftware.com/*), and dd, a tool for forensically sound
backups.

> **Note**   Redundant array of independent disks (RAID) arrays pose a challenge to the
> forensic recovery process because data often spans multiple drives and slack space is
> quickly overwritten by other data as the RAID array is optimized. It can be difficult, if
> not impossible, to extract data from the slack space on a RAID volume.

Performing Network Monitoring

If the information described throughout this section does not provide you with sufficient guidance, you might want to perform full network monitoring and inspect
traffic on the network. By analyzing which systems are talking to each other as well as
the contents of those communications, you can gain a great deal of information
about an attack in progress. However, the analysis of masses of raw data can be very
time-consuming.

Besides taking into account the tedium of network monitoring, you must consider the
issue of privacy. If an investigator reads all data passing on the wire, she likely will
review user data and thereby violate the privacy of those users. This is a larger issue
for some law enforcement personnel who might be legally barred from this type of
monitoring to prevent the possibility of inadvertent privacy violation.

Because privacy violation is a complex legal issue that varies among jurisdictions, we
recommend you discuss this topic with your organization's legal counsel. Even in
cases where full packet details cannot be reviewed because of privacy concerns, it is
possible to gain useful information by analyzing transactional data contained in
packet headers. Knowing which systems are talking to each other, which protocols are
being used, whether the traffic is encrypted, and the volume of the traffic flow can
allow an investigator to make inferences that can help with future investigative tasks.

Implementing Countermeasures to a Security Incident

Once the cause of the incident has been identified, you should close off any entry vector the attacker has utilized. In essence, you have identified a specific threat through
risk analysis and you should now mitigate that risk. This simple description applies
regardless of whether the threat is a denial-of-service condition, a malicious attacker
who has installed Trojan horse applications on a server, a curious employee viewing
files to which he should not have access, or any of the other myriad security risks networks face today. Although the response will differ depending on the threat, the goal
is to eliminate the risk and continue with normal operations.

When implementing countermeasures to an attack, you must consider the benefit produced by the countermeasure and the effects on business continuity. For example, the decision to disconnect an organization's connection to the Internet or its network connection to a business partner might cause the company loss of productivity, but if the alternative promises to cost more than this disruption, the alternative is not preferable. Such decisions should be made only by senior-level management. Other types of countermeasures have less drastic business consequences and can be more easily implemented.

For example, if upon reflection, you realize that a firewall was configured in a manner that is too permissive, the application of stricter settings is needed. If the method of attack exploits a known vulnerability for which a security update exists, you should test and apply the security update to all computers that have not yet had the update applied. If a user's password was compromised, that password should be changed immediately and all of that user's sessions should be terminated. If an account with administrative credentials has been compromised, all passwords throughout the organization might need to be reset.

Assessing the Scope of an Attack

The risk assessment for the particular attack will dictate the specific countermeasures required. If you cannot discern the full scope of an intrusion, more drastic measures might need to be taken than if you had noticed the attack early and are aware of its full scope. Given the nature of computer security, it is much more likely that the former will be the case. That said, a more conservative response is typically preferable to one that is permissive. This is because implementing a solution that lacks the necessary protections is no better than performing no countermeasures at all.

This is most clearly illustrated by a system-level compromise—one in which an attacker has gained high levels of privilege on one or more systems and might have utilized those privileges. Because an administrative user can do anything on the systems over which she has authority, an attacker who raises his privileges to that level can do the same. The attacker could add accounts to the system or domain, add privileges to existing accounts, add accounts to privileged groups, replace system files with Trojan horse applications, modify the core of the operating system to mask his continued presence, or perform any other task that an administrator can.

The industry consensus on the best practice for recovering from such a situation is to rebuild any system that has endured a system-level compromise, unless you are 100 percent certain that no additional damage has been done. Even restoring the system from backup might not resolve the issues created by the attacker because you might not have detected the attack until after the backup in question took place. The only way to be certain that the system has been restored is to rebuild it by using trusted media that employs secure build processes that protect the system from compromise until it has been secured.

> **Tip**   Building a system on an isolated network can protect the computer from being compromised by viruses or attackers that have penetrated the network before the system is secured.

Weighing Tradeoffs

As you implement countermeasures, be cognizant of the tradeoffs that might be involved. For example, by disconnecting a computer from the network to preserve its state for further examination, you could alert the attacker to the fact that you have discovered his presence. This could result in the attacker attempting to compromise other computers on your network that have not yet been compromised, or it could result in the attacker immediately initiating destructive methods on other computers he has already compromised to prevent you from collecting evidence that might be used to track him. However, allowing the attacker to continue unimpeded can cause further damage to your organization's network or computers. Consider the possible reactions an attacker might have to the countermeasures you put in place before you deploy them.

The implementation of countermeasures is more complex when the intruder is internal. In such situations, the incident response team must be careful not to alert the intruder that the team is aware of his activities so that further damage can be prevented. This situation is made even worse if the attacker is a trusted member of the response team. As a response team member, he will be aware of many or all details of the investigation and could change his attack posture to defeat the efforts of the response team. Or to protect himself from being discovered, the attacker could go dormant to make it appear that attacks have ceased.

> **Caution**   If you believe that the intruder is an employee of your organization, you should involve the HR department as soon as possible to avoid violating the employee rights of the suspect.

Recovering Services After a Security Incident

Once the incident has been controlled and countermeasures are in place against that type of attack, you should begin looking at the restoration of normal operations. Services that have been closed down will be reopened, network connections that have been rerouted will be restored, and systems that have been compromised will be rebuilt and brought online. Of course, it might not be prudent to return to normal operations all at once. For example, if you have terminated all external access to your network as a countermeasure to an attack in progress, turning on every service at once might not be the best course of action.

If all services that have been shut down are brought online at once, it might not be possible to monitor them adequately and ensure that no additional compromise is attempted. The result can be as bad as or even worse than the original incident if your countermeasures fail and the attacker regains her foothold on your network. In such a case, the stakes will be higher for the attacker: she might have concerns about covering her tracks to escape retribution for her actions, or her pride might be wounded, or both things might be case. In other words, you should consider an attacker in this position much more dangerous.

You should also be concerned with existing client sessions on any backup servers. If a secondary server is brought back online, either because it was taken offline for evidence or because it had been compromised and was later rebuilt, you need to be aware of the user experience of those accessing such a secondary system. Building a duplicate system with the same name can cause numerous network problems that can result in poor user experience (or worse) for that system's users. Instead, plan and implement a graceful transition that follows operational best practices, such as those described in Microsoft Operations Framework (MOF) under Release Management (*http://www.microsoft.com/technet/itsolutions/msm/smf/SMFRELMG.asp*). By applying a project management mind-set to service restoration, you can avoid many potentially devastating problems.

Conducting a Security Incident Postmortem

Because of the iterative nature of security, you need to ensure that your response team and organization learn from any incident that occurs, and you must incorporate those lessons into future protective measures and their supporting processes. Following each security issue, you should hold a debriefing session. In that session, all the participants and key stakeholders should discuss the specifics of the incident, including the following:

■ What went right

■ What could have gone more smoothly

■ Measures that could have prevented the incident

■ What the organization needs to do to ensure that this type of incident is not repeated

■ How much the security incident has cost the organization

During the postmortem review, you should determine changes that will need to be made to your organization's security policies and procedures, and you might need to implement new security measures to prevent such an incident from recurring or similar incidents from happening. You should assign a single person responsibility for recording this information and ensuring its follow-up. If these changes will impact business continuity, you should conduct a risk analysis to determine the appropriate solution.

The results of the debriefing should be fully documented and distributed on a need-to-know basis. Often, it makes sense to have two versions of the write-up—one that is couched in business terms and is appropriate for business managers, and another that delves into technical detail and is appropriate for the IT teams that will be implementing changes to the environment.

Best Practices

■ **Clearly establish and enforce all policies and procedures.**   Many security incidents are accidentally created by IT personnel who have not followed or understood change management procedures or have improperly configured security devices, such as firewalls and authentication systems. Your policies and procedures should be thoroughly tested to ensure that they are practical, clear, and provide the appropriate level of security.

■ **Provide comprehensive training on tools to your incident response team.**   Ensure that you provide training to your Computer Security and Incident Response Team (CSIRT) on the use and location of tools that will be used during an incident response. Consider providing portable computers preconfigured with these tools to ensure that no time is wasted installing and configuring tools when responding to an incident. These systems and the associated tools must be properly protected when not in use.

- **Verify your backup and restore procedures.**   Be aware of where backups are maintained, who can access them, and your procedures for data restoration and system recovery. Make sure that you regularly verify backups and media by selectively restoring data. Ensure that your backup retention policy supports incident response by including trusted copies of incident response tools and process documents in any offsite backup.

- **Assemble all relevant communication information.**   Ensure that you have contact names and phone numbers for people within your organization that need to be notified (including members of the CSIRT, those responsible for supporting all your systems, and those in charge of media relations). You will also need details for contacting your ISP and local and national law enforcement agencies. Consider contacting local law enforcement agencies before an incident happens to ensure you understand proper procedures for communicating incidents and collecting evidence.

- **Always conduct postmortem reviews of security incidents.**   Make sure to hold a session to discuss what can be learned from each incident and incorporate those lessons into your organization's policies, procedures, build process, and network design. Given the amount of effort typically associated with responding to an incident, missing out on this potential benefit would be a shame.

Additional Information

- RFC 2196: "Site Security Handbook" (*http://www.ietf.org/rfc/rfc2196.txt*)
- RFC 2350: "Expectations for Computer Security Incident Response" (*http://www.ietf.org/rfc/rfc2350.txt*)
- ISO 17799: "Code of Practice for Information Security Management" (*http://www.iso-17799.com/*)
- Microsoft Operations Framework (MOF) Resource Library (*http://www.microsoft.com/technet/itsolutions/tandp/opex/mofrl/default.asp*)
- Forum of Incident Response Security Teams Web site (*http://www.first.org*)
- "Steps for Recovering from a UNIX or NT System Compromise" white paper from the CERT Coordination Center at Carnegie Mellon University (*http://www.cert.org/tech_tips/root_compromise.html*)
- *The Cuckoo's Egg: Tracking a Spy Through the Maze of Computer Espionage* (Pocket Books, 2000)
- *Incident Response: Investigating Computer Crime* (Osborne/McGraw-Hill, 2001)

- *Incident Response: A Strategic Guide to Handling System and Network Security Breaches* (New Riders, 2002)

- *Network Intrusion Detection, Third Edition* (New Riders, 2002)

- The following Knowledge Base articles:

   - 296085" "How to Use SQL Server to Analyze Web Logs" (*http://support.microsoft.com/kb/296085*)

   - 313064: "Monitor Web Server Performance by Using Counter Logs in System Monitor in IIS" (*http://support.microsoft.com/kb/313064*)

   - 326444: "How to Configure the URLScan Tool" (*http://support.microsoft.com/kb/326444*)

   - 300390: "How to Enable IIS Logging Site Activity in Windows 2000" (*http://support.microsoft.com/kb/300390*)

Index

Numerics

802.11 networks. *See* wireless connectivity
802.1x authentication, 515–543. *See also* wireless
    connectivity
  communications protections, 522–525
  deploying certificates, 527–530
  Group Policy with, 540
  how it works, 515–517
  implementing, 530–542
    connecting to networks, 538–542
  planning certificates, 525–527
  threats, 517–520
  types of, 521
  on wired networks, 519, 525
    connecting to, 541
    remote access policies, 534, 536

A

abstract classes (Active Directory), 91
Accept All Cookies setting, 277
Accept Unsecured Communication options (IPSec), 226
acceptable use policies (AUPs), 657
acceptance, as motivation for attack, 22–23
access
  inability to access network resources, 674
  physical, 21. *See also* physical security
  remote. *See* RRAS (Routing and Remote Access
    Service)
  wireless. *See* wireless connectivity
access control entries. *See* ACEs (access control entries)
Access Data Sources Across Domains setting, 287
access policies, 658
Access This Computer From A Network right, 59, 240
access to data, 139–164
  EFS. *See* EFS (Encrypting File System)
  file and folder permissions, 139–152
    command-line tools for, 147–151
    DACLs. *See* DACLs (discretionary access control
      lists)
    share permissions, 151–152
    registry permissions, 162–164
access tokens, 41–42
accessories of mobile computers, 345. *See also* mobile
    computers
accidental connections to wireless networks, 517
Account Expiration option, 44
Account Is Disabled option, 43
Account Is Trusted For Delegation option, 44
account lockouts, 128, 238, 448

Account Operators group, 373
account policies, 236–238
account security, 31–54. *See also* passwords
  access tokens, 41–42
  administrative accounts, 45–46
  groups. *See* groups
  lockout settings, 53–54
  options for, 42–45
  SIDs (security identifiers), 32–40
accounting, RADIUS, 442
accounts
  auditing logon events, 319–322, 326
  domain controllers, 372
  management events, logging, 322–324
ACEs (access control entries), 93–95, 144
ACK message (TCP), 202
Act As Part Of The Operating System privilege, 55, 240
Active Directory, 89–101
  auditing, 325
  autonomy and isolation, 119–120
  DACLs for, 92–100
    command-line configuration, 99–100
    default, configuring, 96
    securing objects after creation, 97
  delegating authority, 131–133
  DNS design, 128–130
  domain design, 127–128
  false certificate publication, 464
  forests. *See* forests
  integrated zones, 131
  integration with, 387–388, 625
  namespace definitions, 129
  object modification or addition, 362
  permissions. *See* permissions
  publishing information to DNS zones, 386
  schema, 89–92, 122
  securing communications, 374–376
  SUS client configuration, 582
Active Directory Schema snap-in, 91
Active Scripting setting, 291
active security systems for mobile computers, 348
Active Server Pages scripts, 495
ActiveX controls, 283–285
  security controls, 297–298, 305–307
activism, as motivation for attack, 24
Add Workstations To Domain privilege, 55, 240
Address Resolution Protocol, 200
Adjust Memory Quotas For A Process (Increase Quotas
    in Windows 2000) setting, 240

About the Authors

Ben Smith is a senior security strategist at Microsoft, where he works on developing long-term security strategy. Ben's driving interest is in researching methods for improving security management and measurement techniques. In addition to being a featured speaker at IT industry conferences worldwide, Ben regularly consults with the National Science Foundation on improving cyber security at community colleges and universities. Ben was the inaugural chair of the vendor-neutral security certification CompTIA Security+ and currently is an adviser to the United States delegation to the International Organization for Standardization (ISO), working on information security standards. Ben is co-author of the *Microsoft® Windows® Security Resource Kit* and *Assessing Network Security,* both from Microsoft Press. Ben's regular column, "Business End," debuted in the September 2004 issue of *Windows IT Pro* magazine. He is certified as an MCSE, CISSP, and CCNA.

Brian Komar is the president and co-founder of IdentIT Inc., a consulting firm specializing in identity integration and network security solutions. Together with Paul Adare, Brian's business partner, IdentIT partners with Microsoft on several ventures, which include developing security-related courseware for Microsoft Learning and providing Public Key Infrastructure (PKI), Rights Management Server (RMS), Microsoft Identity Integration Server (MIIS), and network security consulting services. Brian has written several white papers for the Microsoft Security Team. He has also written books related to computer security, including the *Microsoft Windows Server™ 2003 PKI and Certificate Security*, the *Microsoft Windows Security Resource Kit*, and *Firewalls for Dummies*. Brian is a frequent speaker at IT industry conferences. If you wish to contact Brian, you can reach him at bkomar@identit.ca.

Security resources and guidance —direct from Microsoft

Microsoft® Windows® Security Resource Kit, Second Edition
ISBN: 0-7356-2174-8   Suggested Retail Price: $49.99 U.S., $72.99 Canada

Get the in-depth information and tools you need to help protect your Windows-based clients, servers, networks, and Internet services—with definitive technical guidance from the Microsoft Security team and two industry veterans. You'll learn how to plan and implement a comprehensive security strategy, assess security threats and vulnerabilities, configure system security settings, and more. You'll also find new coverage of service packs, Microsoft Office 2003 Editions, and Internet Information Services (IIS) 6.0. The CD provides must-have tools, scripts, templates, and other key resources.

Assessing Network Security
ISBN: 0-7356-2033-4   Suggested Retail Price: $49.99 U.S., $72.99 Canada

Don't wait for an attacker to find and exploit your security vulnerabilities—take the lead by assessing the state of your network's security. This book delivers advanced network testing strategies, including vulnerability scanning and penetration testing, from members of the Microsoft security teams. You'll find detailed information on how to perform security assessments, uncover security vulnerabilities, and apply appropriate countermeasures. The CD includes time-saving tools and scripts to reveal and help correct security vulnerabilities in your own network, plus a complete eBook.

Microsoft Windows Server™ 2003 PKI and Certificate Security
ISBN: 0-7356-2021-0   Suggested Retail Price: $59.99 U.S., $86.99 Canada

Capitalize on the built-in security services in Windows Server 2003—and deliver your own robust, public key infrastructure (PKI)-based solutions at a fraction of the cost and time. This in-depth reference cuts straight to the details of designing and implementing certificate-based security solutions for PKI-enabled applications. Get the inside information, real-world solutions, and best practices you need to avoid common design and implementation mistakes, help minimize risk, and optimize security administration. You'll find timesaving tools and scripts, plus an eBook, on the CD.

To see more Microsoft Press® products for IT professionals, please visit:

microsoft.com/mspress

For Windows Server 2003 administrators

Microsoft® Windows® Server 2003 Administrator's Companion
ISBN 0-7356-1367-2

The comprehensive, daily operations guide to planning, deployment, and maintenance.
Here's the ideal one-volume guide for anyone who administers Windows Server 2003. It offers up-to-date information on core system-administration topics for Windows, including Active Directory® services, security, disaster planning and recovery, interoperability with NetWare and UNIX, plus all-new sections about Microsoft Internet Security and Acceleration (ISA) Server and scripting. Featuring easy-to-use procedures and handy workarounds, it provides ready answers for on-the-job results.

Microsoft Windows Server 2003 Administrator's Pocket Consultant
ISBN 0-7356-1354-0

The practical, portable guide to Windows Server 2003. Here's the practical, pocket-sized reference for IT professionals who support Windows Server 2003. Designed for quick referencing, it covers all the essentials for performing everyday system-administration tasks. Topics covered include managing workstations and servers, using Active Directory services, creating and administering user and group accounts, managing files and directories, data security and auditing, data back-up and recovery, administration with TCP/IP, WINS, and DNS, and more.

Microsoft IIS 6.0 Administrator's Pocket Consultant
ISBN 0-7356-1560-8

The practical, portable guide to IIS 6.0. Here's the eminently practical, pocket-sized reference for IT and Web professionals who work with Internet Information Services (IIS) 6.0. Designed for quick referencing and compulsively readable, this portable guide covers all the basics needed for everyday tasks. Topics include Web administration fundamentals, Web server administration, essential services administration, and performance, optimization, and maintenance. It's the fast-answers guide that helps users consistently save time and energy as they administer IIS 6.0.

To learn more about the full line of Microsoft Press® products for IT professionals, please visit:

microsoft.com/mspress/IT

What do you think of this book? We want to hear from you!

Do you have a few minutes to participate in a brief online survey? Microsoft is interested in hearing your feedback about this publication so that we can continually improve our books and learning resources for you.

To participate in our survey, please visit:

www.microsoft.com/learning/booksurvey

And enter this book's ISBN, 0-7356-2174-8. As a thank-you to survey participants in the United States and Canada, each month we'll randomly select five respondents to win one of five $100 gift certificates from a leading online merchant.* At the conclusion of the survey, you can enter the drawing by providing your e-mail address, which will be used for prize notification *only*.

Thanks in advance for your input. Your opinion counts!

Sincerely,

Microsoft Learning

Microsoft | Learning

Learn More. Go Further.

To see special offers on Microsoft Learning products for developers, IT professionals, and home and office users, visit: *www.microsoft.com/learning/booksurvey*